The Death Penalty in Focus

A Special Topics Anthology

Edited by Vincent R. Jones, J.D. and
James R. "Chip" Coldren, Jr., Ph.D.

cognella
San Diego, CA

First published in the United States of America in 2012 by Cognella, a division of University Readers, Inc.

16 15 14 13 12 1 2 3 4 5

Printed in the United States of America

ISBN: 978-1-60927-890-8

cognella™

www.cognella.com 800.200.3908

CONTENTS

INTRODUCTION

The death penalty is one of the most debated issues in America. Should we abolish the sanction? Is the sanction utilized often enough? Does the existence of the death penalty deter crime? Have innocent people been executed? Does it cost more to execute or incarcerate for life? These are but a few of the questions that continuously fuel a controversial debate. Students, graduate and undergraduate alike, relish the opportunity to learn more about this compelling topic. They demonstrate as much interest in the legal case details as in the research findings. They enjoy testing their personal convictions against those of their classmates, general public opinion, and the opinions of experts. In addition, we can think of no better way to illustrate, in stark detail, the workings of the American criminal justice system with all of its flaws and facets, than to guide students through a series of important readings on the death penalty.

This anthology serves as a companion to general texts on capital punishment that exist for use in the college classroom (see, for example, Paternoster, Brame, and Bacon, 2007; Streib, 2009; Boehm, 2007). As an adjunct to general death penalty textbooks, this volume highlights a number of current and important issues in the death penalty debate. It touches on such matters as deterrence theory, cost of the death penalty, police line-up procedures, and disparities in death sentencing. We employ a reasoned approach, presenting the relevant facts and prevailing opinions regarding the topics in an unbiased manner. This is not to suggest however, that all of the information presented is unbiased. Stephen Bright's article, for example, clearly suggests that the death penalty should be abolished, and others present distinct positions on the topic at hand.

One fascinating aspect of the death penalty is that it touches on nearly every aspect of the administration of criminal justice—crime investigation, forensics, evidence, interrogations, prosecutorial decision making, public defender systems, judicial education, post-conviction appeal processes, and more. No system is perfect, and whether an individual supports the continued use of the sanction or is in favor of abolition, certain problems in the administration of justice highlighted by the death penalty debate should concern us all. To that end, we present articles concerning disproportionality, the costs associated with the administration of capital punishment, forensic science, and problems with eyewitness identification.

Finally, we present readings that approach the topic from a religious perspective, beginning with the question: do religious beliefs provide an indication of one's predisposition for or against capital punishment?

Each chapter in this volume presents studies or commentaries that take distinctly different positions, or that present different perspectives, or different data, on the same issue. We selected the articles with the distinct goal of challenging the student reader regarding their understanding of the facts, the variety of opinions, the volume of information available, and the sophistication of the research methodologies. We believe a fair and effective democracy rests on the active participation of an informed citizenry, so please read on. …

James R. "Chip" Coldren Jr., Ph.D. Vincent R. Jones, J.D.

September 2010

Boehm, Robert H. 2007. Deathquest III: An Introduction to the Theory and Practice of Capital Punishment in the United States/Edition 3. Anderson Publishing Company.

Paternoster, R., R. Brame, and S. Bacon. 2007. The Death Penalty: America's Experience with Capital Punishment. Oxford University Press.

Streib, Victor. 2009. Death Penalty in a Nutshell, 3d. Thomson/West.

HISTORY OF THE DEATH PENALTY

Introduction

Will the Death Penalty Remain Alive in the Twenty First Century?: International Norms, Discrimination, Arbitrariness, and the Risk of Executing the Innocent.
By Stephen B. Bright

Working Against the Past: The Function of American History of Race Relations and Capital Punishment in Supreme Court Opinions.
By Rita K. Lomio

Stephen Bright directly addresses problems with the death penalty as a sanction and as a policy. In his article, Bright notes that the long-term trend throughout the world has been to abolish the death penalty. He poignantly points out that if you were to name which of the following three countries still administer the death penalty—Russia, South Africa, or the United States—most outsiders would be shocked to find the answer is the United States. This is more troubling, he posits, since we have positioned ourselves as the champion of human rights throughout the world.

More directly however, Bright approaches the subject with a reasoned argument for why the sanction should be abolished. First, he notes the growing recognition that there is a lack of fundamental fairness inherent with capital cases. He, like so many others, is appalled that innocent people are sentenced to die and that executions of these innocent people are undoubtedly carried out. He points out that certain states, particularly Texas, Virginia and Florida, essentially threw "caution to the wind" and continued to execute the young, the old, the developmentally disabled, the mentally ill, and, most strikingly, those with unexplored claims of actual innocence.

Next, he points out that being sentenced to die depends largely upon the race of the defendant, the geographic location of the alleged crime occurrence, and the quality (or lack thereof) of the lawyer representing the defendant. According to Bright, these inequities represent blots on our criminal justice system.

Finally, he discussed the corrupting effect the existence of capital punishment has on the American system of justice. It is a relic, a sanction whose time is long passed and should be abolished, he argues. He points out that we have strayed from the principle that it is better that ten guilty men go free than to place one innocent man behind bars. The opposite appears to be true and the sacrifice of a few innocent people seems to be the price we are willing to pay to wage war on crime.

Lomio's article takes a closer look at the issue of race and its impact on capital punishment. She specifically examines pivotal Supreme Court cases such as Furman, Gregg, and McClesky in an effort to determine if the history of American race relations and injustices of the past form the basis for abandonment of, or continuation of the sanction. Lomio posits that whether one is pro or con, participants in the debate over capital punishment may use race as a cornerstone of support. In this manner, it is suggested that either view may be equally supported. Lomio's article eloquently states that, whatever form it takes, the history of American race relations and its appearance in Supreme Court opinions forces the past to be remembered and, as a result, the past becomes a puzzle, a tool, or a statement, that we must grapple with, "expressly or not, consciously or not" (Lomio, 2008, p. 15).

Will the Death Penalty Remain Alive in the Twenty-First Century?

International Norms, Discrimination, Arbitrariness, and the Risk of Executing the Innocent

Stephen B. Bright*

SUMMARY:

... Although most developed nations in the world have abandoned the death penalty, the United States, which purports to be a leader in the protection of human rights, retains capital punishment. ... The ABA does not oppose the death penalty, but year after year, it has called upon the states to improve the quality of counsel assigned the poor, to respond to racial discrimination in the criminal justice system, and to stop executing the mentally ill, the mentally retarded, and children. ... Houston, Texas, is the capital of capital punishment. ... The death penalty is imposed for some crimes in Houston that are not punished with death if they are committed in Dallas, Fort Worth, San Antonio or almost anywhere else in Texas. ... Houston's trial judges appointed Cannon to represent Burdine and nine others who ended up on Texas' death row. ... (Texas had only one death row at that time, which was located near Huntsville. ... The Corrupting Effect of the Death Penalty on the Criminal Justice System ... In Texas, Stephen W. Mansfield challenged a conservative judge who had written the opinion reversing the conviction in a particularly notorious capital case, campaigning on promises of greater use of the death penalty, greater use of the harmless-error doctrine, and sanctions for attorneys who file "frivolous appeals especially in death penalty cases. ...

* Director, Southern Center for Human Rights, Atlanta, Georgia; Senior Lecturer, Emory Law School; Visiting Lecturer, Yale and Harvard Law Schools; B.A. 1971, J.D. 1974, University of Kentucky.

Supreme Court Justice Arthur Goldberg once said that the deliberate institutionalized taking of human life by the state is the greatest degradation of the human personality imaginable. Although most developed nations in the world have abandoned the death penalty, the United States, which purports to be a leader in the protection of human rights, retains capital punishment. Thirty-eight states, the federal government and the military provide for death as a punishment for certain crimes. Over 3,600 people are on death rows across the country. Executions have become "routine" in Texas and the pace of executions is increasing throughout the country.

The death penalty is a relic of another era, before the federal government and the states developed the vast prison industrial complex that exists today. In a frontier society, when many communities did not have prisons or jails, the methods of punishment were limited to such things as whipping, branding, cutting off fingers, placing people in stocks, and hanging or shooting them. But today those punishments are no longer necessary because communities can be protected and offenders punished by prison sentences—even, in some cases, sentences of life imprisonment without any possibility of parole—in institutions such as the "super maximum" prisons where inmates never come in contact with another human being.

Of all the primitive punishments of a frontier society, the only one that has survived is the death penalty. It seems out of character for a society as generally conservative as ours, which is wary of too much government power and skeptical of the ability of government to do anything well, to trust the courts to decide whether a person lives or dies.[1] It seems equally out of character for a decent society, which places some practices off limits because a civilized society simply does not engage in them. For example, most people in the United States would oppose running an electric shock through a person to extract information, even if that information was urgently needed. They would be equally opposed to the notion of punishing people by giving them doses of electricity which hurt, but did not kill them. And yet the same society accepts running a sufficient amount of electricity or lethal drugs through people to extinguish their lives.

If people were asked thirty years ago which one of the following three countries—Russia, South Africa, and the United States—would be most likely to have the death penalty at the turn of the century, few people would have answered the United States. And yet, South Africa's Constitutional Court declared the death penalty unconstitutional in 1995 and Russia abolished the death penalty in 1999 in hope of eventually joining the Council of Europe.[2]

However, an increasing number of voices are expressing concern about the use of the death penalty in this country. Many people—including many supporters of capital punishment—have become alarmed about the danger of executing the innocent, and appalled by the way in which people are processed in assembly-line fashion to the death chambers in states like Texas and Virginia. Upon closer examination of the criminal justice system, many have been shocked by the poor quality of legal representation provided for poor people facing the death penalty, the extent to which race influences who is sentenced to death, and improper police and prosecution practices, such as obtaining favorable testimony from criminals against those facing death by giving them lenient treatment. Some are troubled by the execution of people who are mentally retarded, mentally ill or children at the times of their crimes. In short, people are concerned about how capital punishment works in practice.

I would like to discuss these concerns and practices in addressing whether the United States will continue to use this extreme, enormous, and irrevocable form of punishment throughout the twenty-first century or join the trend in the rest of the world in abandoning it.

I. The Trend Toward Abolition in the Rest of the World

The federal government and many states have expanded the use of the death penalty in the last twenty-five years, while the rest of the world has been abandoning it. In this country, the federal government adopted the death penalty in 1988,[3] expanded it to over forty crimes in 1994,[4] and restricted federal review of capital cases in 1996.[5] Many states expanded the crimes punishable by death and curtailed and expedited the review process.

In the rest of the world, thirty-five countries have abandoned capital punishment since 1985.[6] During that time, only four countries that did not have capital punishment adopted it.[7] One of those, Nepal, has since abolished it.[8] Only one other member of NATO, Turkey, has the death penalty. However, Turkey has not executed anyone since 1984, and is expected to follow Russia, Poland and other former Soviet-bloc countries and abolish capital punishment in order to join the Council of Europe.

Four countries accounted for eighty percent of all the executions that took place in the world last year.[9] They were China, Iran, the Congo, and the United States.[10] Since 1990, only six countries have executed people who were under eighteen at the time of the crime: Iran, Nigeria, Pakistan, Saudi Arabia, Yemen, and the United States.[11] In that rather undistinguished company, the United States leads by far in the number executed.[12] The United States is one of only two countries that have not ratified the International Covenant on the Rights of the Child, which among other things, would prohibit the execution of people who were children at the time of their crimes. The other country is Somalia.

Our neighbors to the north and south as well as other counties have repeatedly protested when their nationals are executed in this country. Neither Canada nor Mexico has the death penalty. Those protests have been even louder—and have raised serious international issues—when states have executed foreign nationals who were sentenced to death in violation of the Vienna Convention on Inter Consular Affairs.[13] Under the Vienna Convention, foreign nationals—whether it be someone from Mexico arrested in the United States or someone from the United States arrested in Mexico—are to be advised of their right to call their country's consul and given the opportunity to do so.

But this obligation is repeatedly violated in the United States. For example, none of the seventeen Mexican nationals on death row in Texas were advised of their rights under the Convention.

As the United States Ambassador to France, Felix Rohatyn, has observed, capital punishment is hurting the image of the United States in Europe.[14] It is compromising our ability to be a leader on human rights issues. It is difficult for the United States to lecture China on human rights when we lead the world in the execution of children. And one question that we will increasingly be asked to answer is whether the scorn of the rest of the world is a price we are willing to pay to continue this outdated form of punishment.

II. The Growing Recognition of the Lack of Fairness in Capital Cases

As the number of executions has increased in the United States, there has been growing realization that it is not being imposed fairly. In 1977, the American Bar Association called for a moratorium on capital punishment. The ABA does not oppose the death penalty, but year after year, it has called upon the states to improve the quality of counsel assigned the poor, to respond to racial discrimination in the criminal justice system, and to stop executing the mentally ill, the mentally retarded, and children. It has urged Congress and the courts to preserve full habeas corpus review.[15]

Not only were most of its recommendations ignored, but things worsened considerably in several areas. Many states still do not provide capable lawyers to defend those facing death at trial and some do not provide counsel at all for the later stages of review.[16] Congress eliminated funding for programs which had provided lawyers at the later stages of review.[17] For the first time since the reinstatement of the death penalty in 1976, some people stood in court without lawyers.[18] The Supreme Court held that states could carry out executions despite severe racial disparities[19] and Congress refused to adopt a Racial Justice Act to provide a remedy for racial discrimination in capital sentencing.[20] While some states prohibit executions of the mentally retarded[21] and children,[22] many others do not and no state prohibits execution of the mentally ill. Congress drastically curtailed federal habeas corpus review, adopting a statute of limitations, severely limiting the ability of federal courts to conduct evidentiary hearings, and requiring deference to legal conclusions by state courts.[23] Concerned about all of these problems and the resulting lack of fairness of the system by which people were being sentenced to death, the ABA called for a moratorium.

A. Innocent People Sentenced to Death

Another reality, closely related to the problems long identified by the ABA, soon emerged—innocent people were being sentenced to death. Over ninety people have been released from death rows since 1976 because they were innocent. Others had their death sentences commuted to life in prison without possibility of parole because of questions about their innocence. For example, in 1994, the governor of Virginia, Douglas Wilder, commuted the sentence of a mentally retarded man, Earl Washington, to life imprisonment without parole because of questions regarding his guilt.[24] Six years later, DNA evidence—not available at the time of Washington's trial or the commutation—established that Earl Washington was innocent.[25] And some people have been executed despite questions of innocence.

In early 2000, George Ryan, the Republican Governor of Illinois, declared a moratorium on capital punishment. Governor Ryan had supported the death penalty and other "tough on crime" measures as a member of the Illinois legislature. But when, as governor, he had to make decisions about whether to grant clemency to those being executed, he saw that the system did not work as well as he assumed it did.

One of those almost executed during Ryan's tenure was Anthony Porter. Porter had been convicted by a jury. He had been sentenced to death. His case had been reviewed and affirmed on appeal by the Illinois Supreme Court. He had gone through the state and federal post-conviction processes and every court had upheld his conviction and sentence. He was scheduled to be executed.

However, a question arose as to whether Porter was mentally competent to be executed; that is, whether he understood that he was being put to death as punishment for the crime of which he had been convicted. A person who lacks the mental ability to understand this relationship cannot be executed, but is instead treated until he is "restored to competency." When he has improved to the point that he can understand why he is being executed, he is put to death. Anthony Porter was a person of limited intellectual functioning and mental impairments. Because there was a question about whether he could understand why he was being executed, a court stayed his execution in order to determine his competency to be executed.[26]

After the stay was granted, the journalism class at Northwestern University and a private investigator examined the case and proved that Anthony Porter was innocent.[27] They obtained a confession from the person who committed the crime.[28] Anthony Porter was released from death row.[29] He was the third person released from Illinois's death row after being proven innocent by the journalism class at Northwestern.[30] Since Illinois adopted its present death penalty statute in 1977, thirteen people sentenced to death have been exonerated and twelve have been executed.[31]

Some have said that the fact that Porter and others have been released shows that the system works. However, someone spending sixteen years on death row for a crime he did not commit is not an example of the system working. When journalism students prove that police, prosecutors, judges, defense lawyers, and the entire legal system did not discover a man's innocence and instead condemned him to die, the system is not working. Recognizing this—that the system was not working—Governor Ryan called a halt to executions in Illinois until he is convinced that the system will not send innocent people to death row.[32] As he later explained:

I called a moratorium because I have grave concerns about our state's shameful record of convicting innocent people and putting them on Death Row. How do you prevent another Anthony Porter, another innocent man or woman from paying the ultimate penalty for a crime he or she did not commit? As I said when I announced the moratorium and many times since, I cannot support a system which in its administration has proven to be so fraught with error and has come so close to the ultimate nightmare, the taking of an innocent life.[33]

Looking at this record, Justice Moses Harrison of the Illinois Supreme Court observed:

When there have been so many mistakes in such a short span of time ... the only conclusion I can draw is that the system does not work as the Constitution requires it to.

If these men dodged the executioner, it was only because of luck and the dedication of the attorneys, reporters, family members and volunteers who labored to win their release. They survived despite the criminal justice system, not because of it. The truth is that left to the devices of the court system, they would probably have all ended up dead at the hands of the state for crimes they did not commit. One must wonder how many others have not been so fortunate.[34]

While there has been considerable attention paid to the moratorium in Illinois, what has gone unnoticed is that Illinois has a much better system of providing representation to the poor than Alabama, Arkansas, Georgia, Mississippi, Texas and other states that send many people to their death rows. Illinois has a public defender office in Chicago with an excellent homicide unit. None of the innocent people condemned to die were represented by that office. But Illinois also relies upon court-appointed lawyers, as do most states. The Chicago Tribune found that one-third of the lawyers who had represented people sentenced to death in Illinois, had been disbarred or suspended.[35] One lawyer who had been suspended from practice was assigned to defend a capital case only ten days after his law license was reinstated.[36]

The Tribune found other causes of innocent people being convicted that exist in any criminal justice system in the country: the use of informants, police and prosecutorial misconduct, and unreliable forensic evidence.[37] At least forty-six people were convicted and sentenced to death on the basis of the testimony of jailhouse snitches—people who testify in order to win their freedom or lenient treatment from prosecutors.[38]

Governor Ryan is one of a growing number of people who, upon viewing the death penalty up close, have concluded that the system is not working. Supreme Court Justices Lewis Powell and Harry Blackmun voted to uphold death sentences in numerous cases, but eventually came to the conclusion that capital punishment should be abandoned. Justice Blackmun, reviewing his efforts to assure the fairness of the death penalty during his career as a circuit and Supreme Court judges, found "the death penalty experiment has failed" and announced that he no longer would "tinker with the machinery of death."[39] Justice Powell said after his retirement from the Court that the death penalty "reflect discredit on the law."[40]

Gerald Kogan, formerly the head of the homicide unit of the prosecutor's office in Miami, Dade County, Florida, asked for the death penalty as a prosecutor, and supervised other prosecutors asking for and obtaining the death penalty. He presided over capital cases as a trial judge, later became a justice of the Florida Supreme Court and, finally, became the Chief Justice of Florida. Upon retiring, he stated that capital punishment "does not work at this time and has not worked in the State of Florida for many, many, many years."[41] Judge Gerald W. Heaney of the United States Court of Appeals for the Eighth Circuit announced:

My thirty years' experience on this court have compelled me to conclude that the imposition of the death penalty is arbitrary and capricious. At every stage, I believe the decision of who shall live and who shall die for his crime turns less on the nature of the offense and the incorrigibility of the offender and more on inappropriate and indefensible considerations: the political and personal inclinations of prosecutors; the defendant's wealth, race, and intellect; the race and economic status of the victim; the quality of the defendant's counsel; and the resources allocated to defense lawyers.[42]

Some officials have responded to these problems. The New Hampshire legislature repealed its death penalty law in 2000, but the repeal was vetoed by the governor. On the federal level, Senator Russell Feingold of Wisconsin has introduced legislation providing for a moratorium on executions nationwide[43] and repeal of the death penalty for federal crimes.[44] Senator Patrick Leahy and Representatives William Delahunt and Ray LeHood have introduced the Innocence Protection Act that would provide for DNA testing and, more importantly, improve the legal representation for people facing the death penalty.[45]

B. Caution Thrown to the Wind—The Accelerating Pace of Executions in Some States

Despite the recognition that innocent people are being sentenced to death in a system that is seriously flawed, and the irrevocablity of a death sentence once carried out, the calls for caution and study have gone totally unheeded in many parts of the country. As Justice Moses Harrison of the Illinois Supreme Court observed:

The prognosis for wrongly accused defendants facing capital charges is not improving. To the contrary, legislatures and the courts appear to have abandoned any genuine concern with insuring the fairness and reliability of the system. Achieving "finality" in death cases, and doing so as expeditiously as possible, have become the dominant goals in death penalty jurisprudence.[46]

Texas is the indisputable leader in abandoning fairness for expedition. The Texas courts dispatch people to its busy execution chamber with no regard for circumstances that might call for a less severe sentence.[47] Children are executed. The mentally retarded are executed. The mentally ill are executed. A grandmother was executed. A born-again Christian, Carla Faye Tucker, was executed.

Even questions of innocence do not slow the machinery of death in Texas.[48] Gary Graham was sentenced to death based upon the identification of a witness who said she saw the perpetrator for a second from forty feet away.[49] Graham was assigned a notoriously bad court-appointed lawyer, Ron Mock, who has had so many clients sentenced to death that some refer to the "Mock Wing" of death row.[50] Mock failed to investigate the case and interview six other witnesses at the scene who later said that Graham was not the person who committed the crime, that the perpetrator was much shorter than Graham.[51] Even if this evidence does not prove Graham is innocent, it certainly proves he did not receive a fair trial. It is not possible to say that Graham is guilty beyond reasonable doubt. Yet, he was executed anyway.

In just six years, then-Governor Bush presided over 152 executions. While no other state executed more than 80 people between the resumption of capital punishment in 1976 and the end of 2000, the Lone Star State executed 236 during that period.[52]

The Florida legislature, in a frantic three-day special session in early January 2000, brushed aside concerns about the dangers of execution of the innocent and the mentally retarded, racial discrimination, and legal representation for poor people condemned to die, and passed laws imposing deadlines and timetables for the speedy processing of capital cases.[53] (The Florida Supreme Court later unanimously declared some provisions of the law unconstitutional.)[54] Brad Thomas, Florida Governor Jeb Bush's top policy advisor on the issue, expressed his enthusiasm for the new laws by saying "bring in the witnesses, put [the defendants] on a gurney, and let's rock and roll."[55] Because Florida had botched numerous electrocutions, the legislature changed the method of execution to lethal injection. By the end of February, Florida had its new execution machinery up and running and was lethally injecting people.

The number of executions is rising not only in Texas but throughout the United States. Ninety-eight people were executed in 1999, the most since 1951.[56] In 2000, eighty-five were executed.[57] Over 3,700 men, women and children are waiting to be injected, electrocuted, shot or gassed in the United States.[58] And yet, the reasons for caution grow stronger with the accelerating pace of executions. For the infliction of the death penalty remains, as it has been throughout our history, a matter of race and place, a matter of inequity and iniquity.

C. Race

The legal system is the institution in our society that has been least affected by the civil rights movement. In many communities that once would not let black people drink out of the same water fountains as whites, African-Americans now have representation on school boards, on county commissions, state legislatures and even the Congress of the United States—often as a result of federal court orders. People of color are superintendents, principals and teachers in the schools. They run businesses. But in many courthouses in those same communities, everything looks the same as it did during the period of Jim Crow justice.[59] The judges are white, the prosecutors are white, the lawyers are white and, even in communities with substantial African-American populations, the jury may be all-white. In many cases, the only person of color who sits in front of the bar in the courtroom is the person on trial.

From arrest to sentencing, the criminal justice system treats people differently based on their race. A person of color is more likely than a white person to be stopped by the police, to be abused by the police during that stop,[60] to be arrested,[61] to be denied bail,[62] to be charged with a serious crime, to be convicted, and to receive a harsher sentence.[63] For example, in Georgia, a white person is three to six times more likely to be put on probation than a person of color.[64] Why? One answer is overt racism—which, unfortunately, despite bald assertions that it is a thing of the past, is still alive and an invidious factor in our society. But another answer is the unconscious racism of those who make every effort to be fair. Without knowing it, conscientious judges who have had no experience with people of other races may be influenced in their decision making by racial stereotypes and attitudes they have developed over their lives. Without realizing it, a white judge may see a young white man who is before the court for sentencing as a youth with potential in need of help, but see a young black man as a thug who is to be feared.

The same biases, whether conscious or unconscious, influence the decisions of prosecutors, jurors and other actors in the system. The two most important decisions in every death penalty case are made not by the judge, but by the prosecutor. First, the prosecutor decides whether to seek the death penalty. The prosecutor always has discretion to seek or not to seek the death penalty. She is never required to seek death. Second, the prosecutor has complete discretion in deciding whether to offer a sentence less than death in exchange for the defendant's guilty plea. The overwhelming majority of all criminal cases, including capital cases, are resolved not by trials, but by plea bargains. In the thirty-eight states that have the death penalty, 97.5 percent of the chief prosecutors are white.[65] In eighteen of the states, all of the prosecutors are white.[66]

Study after study has confirmed that race plays a role in capital sentencing.[67] Most recently, the U.S. Department of Justice examined its own record on the use of the death penalty and found that over three-fourths of the people given the death penalty were members of racial minorities.[68] Over half were African-Americans.[69]

Although African Americans constitute only twelve percent of the national population, they are victims of half the murders that are committed in this country. Yet eighty percent of those on death row are there for crimes against white people. The discrepancy is even greater in the death belt states of the South. In Georgia and Alabama, for example, African-Americans are the victims of sixty-five percent of the homicides, yet eighty percent of those sentenced to death are there for crimes against white persons. In Georgia, twenty-one of the twenty-three people executed since 1976, when the death penalty was reinstated, have been executed for crimes against white victims.

For those practicing in the South, the reason for these disparities soon becomes apparent. For example, an investigation of all murder cases prosecuted in Georgia's Chattahoochee Judicial Circuit from 1973 to 1990 revealed that in cases involving the murder of a white person, prosecutors often met with the victim's family and discussed whether to seek the death penalty.[70] In a case involving the murder of the daughter of a prominent white contractor, the prosecutor contacted the contractor and asked him if he wanted to seek the death penalty.[71] When the contractor replied in the affirmative, the prosecutor said that was all he needed to know.[72] The prosecutor obtained the death penalty at trial.[73] He was rewarded with a contribution of $5,000 from the contractor when he successfully ran for judge in the next election.[74] The contribution was the largest received by the District Attorney.[75] There were other cases in which the District Attorney issued press releases announcing that he was seeking the death penalty after meeting with the family of a white victim.[76]

But the story was very different with regard to the thirty percent of the community that was African-American. The prosecutors did not meet with African-Americans whose family members had been murdered and ask what sentence they wanted. Most families were not even notified that the case in which their loved one had been a victim had been resolved.[77] As a result of these practices, although African-Americans were the victims of sixty-five percent of the homicides in the Chattahoochee Judicial Circuit, eighty-five percent of the capital cases in that circuit were white victim cases.[78]

The racial discrimination in this circuit is stark and undeniable. In other places it is more subtle and less apparent. But the death penalty remains, as it always has throughout our history, a matter of race.

D. Place

As a result of the enormous discretion given prosecutors, the death penalty is also a matter of place. Within the same state, there are places where the death penalty is imposed frequently; other places where it is imposed infrequently, and still other places where it is not imposed at all.

Houston, Texas, is the capital of capital punishment. Houston sends more people to death row than most states. It has had more people executed in the last twenty-five years than any state except for Texas itself and Virginia. Harris County, which includes Houston, accounts for nearly one-third of the people on Texas' death row, while Dallas, which has a higher murder rate, has only about one-quarter of Houston's total.[79] The death penalty is imposed for some crimes in Houston that are not punished with death if they are committed in Dallas, Fort Worth, San Antonio or almost anywhere else in Texas. The reason is Johnny Holmes, who just ended a twenty-year tenure as district attorney in Houston.[80]

Similarly, the death penalty is imposed for some crimes in Philadelphia that would not be punished with death if they were committed in Pittsburgh or other parts of Pennsylvania because the district attorney in Philadelphia, Lynn Abraham, seeks the death penalty whenever she can.[81] Baldwin County, Georgia, which averages only two murders a year, has five people on Georgia's death row, while Fulton County, which includes Atlanta and averages 230 murders per year, has only four people under a death sentence.[82] The death penalty is imposed in the white-flight suburban communities around Atlanta, Baltimore, St. Louis and other cities much more often than it is imposed in those cities. The death penalty is sought in some parts of New York, but not in the Bronx or Manhattan.

Even though every federal capital prosecution must be approved by the Attorney General, there have also been remarkable geographical disparities in the federal death penalty cases. The Justice Department's study found that forty-two percent of the cases submitted to the attorney general for review came from five districts.[83]

The Supreme Court has said, and most fair-minded people would agree, that the death penalty should be imposed "with reasonable consistency, or not at all."[84] But the death penalty is imposed arbitrarily and capriciously in some places but not in others.

E. Inequity

The inequity in capital punishment is not just racial. Poverty increases the likelihood of being sentenced to death. Throughout history, the death penalty has been reserved almost exclusively for those who are poor. The major consequence of poverty is being represented by a court-appointed lawyer who may lack the skill, resources, and, in some cases, even the inclination to provide a competent defense.

At one time, the Supreme Court recognized the relation between poverty and justice. Justice Hugo Black—who once described the courts as "havens of refuge for those who might otherwise suffer because they are helpless, weak, outnumbered, or because they are ... victims of prejudice and public excitement,"[85]—wrote for the Court in Griffin v. Illinois,[86] that "there can be no equal justice where the kind of trial a [person] gets depends on the amount of money he [or she] has."[87] In that case, decided in 1956, the Court, in a five-to-four decision, held that poor people have a constitutional right to a transcript of their trial for purposes of appeal. Seven years later, in Gideon v. Wainwright,[88] the Supreme Court, recognizing that lawyers are "necessities, not luxuries," and that a poor person "cannot be assured a fair trial unless counsel is provided for him,"[89] held that the Constitution requires the states to provide lawyers to the accused in felony cases.[90]

Nevertheless, almost forty years after Gideon, the criminal justice system falls far short of the goals of fairness, equal protection, and due process for all, regardless of income status. The kind of trial, and the kind of justice, a person receives depends very much upon the amount of money he or she has. Judge Alvin B. Rubin of the United States Court of Appeals for Fifth Circuit put it bluntly in one capital case:

The Constitution, as interpreted by the courts, does not require that the accused, even in a capital case, be represented by able or effective counsel. ... Consequently, accused persons who are represented by "not-legally-ineffective" lawyers may be condemned to die when the same accused, if represented by effective counsel, would receive at least the clemency of a life sentence.[91]

That is a remarkable statement: "The Constitution, as interpreted by the courts, does not require that the accused, even in a capital case, be represented by able or effective counsel." It is a much different sentiment than Justice Black's declaration that there can be no justice when the kind of trial a people get depends upon the amount of money they have.

And yet, Judge Rubin's statement is undeniably true. The courts have held that the lawyer assigned to defend a poor person, even in a capital case, need not be aware of the governing law,[92] sober,[93] or even awake.[94] The trial of a woman facing the death penalty in Alabama had to be suspended for a day because the lawyer appointed to defend her was too drunk to go forward.[95] The judge sent him to jail for a day to dry out and then produced both the client and lawyer from jail and resumed the trial. She was sentenced to death. The woman, Judy Haney, and her children had testified that the victim, her husband, had abused her and her children for fifteen years, but the prosecutor pointed out to the jury that her testimony was not corroborated by any medical evidence. However, the reason was not because such evidence did not exist, but because the drunk lawyer never obtained hospital records that confirmed the abuse.

Juries receive only the evidence presented by the lawyers. And, as the Supreme Court pointed out in 1932, lawyers can present evidence and conduct meaningful cross-examination of the prosecution's witnesses only if they have conducted "thoroughgoing investigation and preparation."[96]

The jurors who condemned Horace Dunkins to die were never presented evidence that he was mentally retarded. Before Dunkins was executed by Alabama in 1989, a juror, upon learning that Dunkins was mentally retarded, said she would not have voted for the death sentence if she had known of his condition.[97] She and other members of the jury had not been informed of this compelling mitigating circumstance because the lawyer assigned to defend Dunkins did not present school records and other evidence of his retardation. Dunkins was executed.

John Young met his attorney at the yard at the county jail just a few weeks after he had been sentenced to death. The lawyer was not there for a legal visit. He had been sent there after pleading guilty to state and federal drug charges. The lawyer later admitted that during Young's trial he had been dependent on amphetamines and other drugs, was physically exhausted, suffering severe emotional strain, and distracted from his law practice because of marital problems, child custody arrangements, difficulties in a relationship with a lover, and the pressures of a family business.[98] As a result, the lawyer made little preparation for Young's trial, where his performance was inept. Young was executed.

Another reason that so many people have been sentenced to death in Houston, besides the prosecutor's practice of frequently asking for the death penalty, is that many people have been poorly defended. The Houston Chronicle described one case as follows:

Seated beside his client—a convicted capital murderer—defense attorney John Benn spent much of Thursday afternoon's trial in apparent deep sleep.

His mouth kept falling open and his head lolled back on his shoulders, and then he awakened just long enough to catch himself and sit upright. Then it happened again. And again. And again.

Every time he opened his eyes, a different prosecution witness was on the stand describing another aspect of the Nov. 19, 1991, arrest of George McFarland in the robbery-killing of grocer Kenneth Kwan.

When state District Judge Doug Shaver finally called a recess, Benn was asked if he truly had fallen asleep during a capital murder trial.

"It's boring," the 72-year-old longtime Houston lawyer explained …

Court observers said Benn seems to have slept his way through virtually the entire trial.[99]

This sleeping did not offend the Sixth Amendment, the trial judge explained, because, "the Constitution doesn't say the lawyer has to be awake."[100] On appeal, the Texas Court of Criminal Appeals rejected McFarland's claim that he was denied his right to counsel over the dissent of two judges who pointed out that "[a] sleeping counsel is unprepared to present evidence, to cross-examine witnesses, and to present any coordinated effort to evaluate evidence and present a defense."[101]

George McFarland is only one of three people sentenced to death in Houston at a trial where his lawyer slept. The Texas Court of Criminal Appeals upheld the conviction and death sentence imposed upon Calvin Burdine, even though the one lawyer appointed to defend him slept through substantial portions of the trial.[102] A United States District Court, making the unremarkable observation that "sleeping counsel is the equivalent of no counsel at all," granted Burdine habeas corpus relief,[103] but Texas appealed.

The Texas Attorney General's office argued to the appellate court that a sleeping lawyer is no different from a lawyer who is intoxicated, under the influence of drugs, suffering from Alzheimer's disease or mental illness. While this would seem to be an argument for upholding the district court's decision, it was not. Death sentences have been upheld in cases in which lawyers were drunk, drug impaired, and suffering from Alzheimer's and severe from mental illness. The judges even engaged counsel for Texas on the point, asking if there was not some difference between a lawyer who was under the influence of alcohol and one who was completely unconscious. The lawyer for Texas argued that while Burdine had received "shoddy" representation, it was not so bad that he was entitled to a new trial.

A panel of the Fifth Circuit reversed the grant of habeas corpus relief over a dissent that said the representation in Burdine's case "shocks the conscience."[104] Judges Rhesa Barksdale and Edith Jones agreed that sleeping was just as acceptable as being drunk at a capital trial.[105] Creating a cruel Catch-22, the two judges denied relief because the trial record did not show during which portions of the trial Cannon was sleeping. Of course the person responsible for making the record was Cannon himself, who was asleep. The full Court has voted to rehear the case en banc.[106] But regardless of how the case is ultimately decided, the spectacle of fourteen judges of a United States Court of Appeals seriously entertaining an argument that a lawyer sleeping through trial does not violate the right to counsel is a disgrace to the legal profession.

Calvin Burdine did not choose to be represented by a lawyer who could not stay awake during his trial. Houston's trial judges appointed Cannon to represent Burdine and nine others who ended up on Texas' death row.[107] Most people caught sleeping on the job in any line of work are fired. But Houston judges continued to appoint Cannon to capital and other criminal cases. Cannon also slept during the capital trial of Carl Johnson. But there will be no relief for Johnson. He was put to death by Texas in 1996.[108]

During the critical post-conviction review of capital cases, those condemned to die are not even entitled to a sleeping lawyer. Exzavious Gibson, whose I.Q. was found on different tests to be between 76 and 82, stood, totally bewildered, in front of a judge at his first state post-conviction hearing in Georgia without a lawyer. The case proceeded as follows:

> The Court: OK, Mr. Gibson are you ready to proceed?
> Mr. Gibson: I don't have an attorney.
> The Court: I understand that.
> Mr. Gibson: I am not waiving my rights.
> The Court: I understand that. Do you have any evidence to put up?
> Mr. Gibson: I don't know what to plead.
> The Court: Huh?
> Mr. Gibson: I don't know what to plead.[109]

The state of Georgia, which sought to bring about Gibson's execution, was represented by a lawyer who specializes in capital habeas corpus cases. After the state's lawyer presented testimony, the judge turned again to Mr. Gibson:

> The Court: Mr. Gibson, would you like to ask Mr. Mullis any questions?
> Mr. Gibson: I don't have counsel.

The Court: I understand that, but I am asking, can you tell me yes or no whether you want to ask him any questions or not?
Mr. Gibson: I'm not my own counsel.
The Court: I'm sorry, sir, I didn't understand you.
Mr. Gibson: I'm not my own counsel.
The Court: I understand, but do you want … to ask him anything?
Mr. Gibson: I don't know.
The Court: Okay, sir. Okay, thank you, Mr. Mullis, you can go down.[110]

This was a hearing which determined whether Exzavious Gibson would be put to death.

In Texas, Andrew Cantu resorted to representing himself after the first two lawyers assigned by the court withdrew and a third failed even to show up to interview him.[111] The first lawyer assigned to represent him had represented his co-defendant. The second had represented the state as an assistant attorney general in capital habeas corpus cases. At a hearing held five months after the third lawyer was assigned to represent Cantu, the lawyer admitted he had not visited Cantu, claiming that he did not know Cantu's location.[112] (Texas had only one death row at that time, which was located near Huntsville.)[113] The lawyer also admitted that he had made no effort to contact an investigator or an expert and was not familiar with the Antiterrorism and Effective Death Penalty Act of 1996,[114] which established a one-year statute of limitations for filing a federal habeas corpus petition.[115] Cantu was executed on February 16, 1999, without any state or federal review of the issues in his case.[116]

In Alabama there are thirty people currently condemned to die that have the right to ask the courts to review their cases, but do not have lawyers. Like Cantu, they face a one-year statute of limitations, but have no lawyer to enable them to comply with it.

At a time of unprecedented prosperity in the nation and the legal profession, there is no excuse for the poor quality of lawyers and the complete absence of lawyers in the most serious cases.

F. Iniquity

The death penalty is a matter of iniquity. It does not spare the mentally ill, the mentally retarded, or children. States put to death the delusional, the paranoid, the brain-damaged, the chemically imbalanced, the abused and the neglected. They execute people who were sent to Viet Nam and subjected to the most awful trauma imaginable, who came back with post-traumatic stress syndrome, addicted to drugs, with various mental and emotional problems.

Every expert who evaluated Varnall Weeks, who was sentenced to death in Alabama, concluded that he was a paranoid schizophrenic who suffered delusions and hallucinations. Weeks believed he was God in various manifestations, such as God the Father, Jesus

Christ, and Allah. In court proceedings shortly before he was executed, Weeks appeared with a domino tied by a string to his head. In response to the judge's questions, he gave a rambling discourse on serpents, "cybernetics," albinos, Egyptians, the Bible, and reproduction. Weeks believed that his execution was part of a millennial religious scheme to destroy a sinful mankind, and that he would not die but would be transformed into a tortoise to reign in heaven. Prison records revealed that, on occasion, he would stand in his cell naked smeared with feces while mouthing sounds which appeared to have no meaning. Nevertheless, the judge held the execution could proceed because Weeks could answer questions about the date and purpose of his execution. Weeks was executed by Alabama in 1995.[117]

Charles Rumbaugh, who was only seventeen at the time of his crime, suffered from schizophrenia and depression to the point that he mutilated himself and provoked a marshal to shoot him in open court.[118] He was allowed to withdraw his appeals and be executed by Texas.[119]

Pernell Ford was allowed to discharge his lawyers and represent himself at his capital trial in Alabama in 1984. During the guilt portion of the trial, Ford made no opening statement, made no objections or motions, and presented no witnesses. Ford wore only a sheet to the penalty phase of the trial. Ford's lawyers appealed his conviction in federal court, but Ford wrote to the court and asked that the petition be dismissed. The court held a hearing to determine whether Ford was competent to waive his right to appeals. During this hearing, Ford said that he wanted to die because he was a member of the Holy Trinity. He said that when he died, his 400 thousand wives would receive the millions of dollars he had put in Swiss bank accounts. He said that he had supernatural powers that would be enhanced when he died, and he would be able to transfer his soul to people outside the prison. One psychiatrist who evaluated Ford said that these statements were Ford's wishes, or reflective of his religious beliefs—not evidence of mental illness. Another psychiatrist found that Ford suffered from depression and personality disorder, but was still capable of making rational choices. A third psychiatrist found that Ford was incompetent. The court concluded that Ford was competent to waive his appeals because he understood the "bottom line" of his legal situation. Like Charles Rumbaugh, he was allowed to withdraw his appeals and be executed. The execution of these and other profoundly limited and impaired individuals demonstrates that existing law is wholly inadequate to prevent execution of the mentally retarded and the mentally ill.

III. The Corrupting Effect of the Death Penalty on the Criminal Justice System

Capital punishment is corrupting our courts and impeding the quest for an independent judiciary. The Governor of California announced in 1986 that he would campaign against justices of that state's supreme court unless they changed their votes on the death penalty.[120]

They did not, and he made good on his promise. He was successful in his campaign to have Chief Justice Rose Bird and two of her colleagues voted off the court.[121]

In Texas, Stephen W. Mansfield challenged a conservative judge who had written the opinion reversing the conviction in a particularly notorious capital case, campaigning on promises of greater use of the death penalty, greater use of the harmless-error doctrine, and sanctions for attorneys who file "frivolous appeals especially in death penalty cases."[122] Before the election, it came to light that Mansfield had misrepresented his prior background, experience, and record.[123] Mansfield admitted lying about his birthplace (he claimed to have been born in Texas, but was born in Massachusetts), his prior political experience (he portrayed himself as a political novice despite having twice unsuccessfully run for Congress), and the amount of time he had spent in Texas.[124] It was also disclosed that he had been fined for practicing law without a license in Florida,[125] and contrary to his assertions that he had experience in criminal cases and had "written extensively on criminal and civil justice issues," he had virtually no such experience.[126]

Nevertheless, Mansfield received fifty-four percent of the votes in the general election.[127] Texas Lawyer declared him an "unqualified success."[128] It was later discovered that Mansfield had failed to report ten thousand dollars in past-due child support when he applied for his Texas law license in 1992.[129] One indication of Judge Mansfield's fitness for the bench was his arrest on the University of Texas campus on Thanksgiving Day, 1998, on charges that he was scalping the complimentary football tickets that judges receive.[130] He was reprimanded by the state's judicial conduct commission.[131]

Justice Penny White was voted off the Tennessee Supreme Court after five members of that court voted to order a resentencing in a death penalty case.[132] Justice White's opponents told the voters that she had overturned the conviction and set free the condemned man.[133] Actually, the conviction was affirmed. The defendant was not released, but held for resentencing, where he was again subject to the death penalty. Justice White did not write the opinion. All five members of the Court agreed that there was at least one error requiring a new sentencing.

The courts in California, Texas, Tennessee and other states are paying an enormous price to carry out death sentences. The rule of law and the independence of the judiciary have been sacrificed to bring about executions.

Some are willing to sacrifice even more—the lives of innocent people. They argue that we are fighting a "war on crime," and, as in any war, there are going to be some innocent casualties. Once our notion of justice was that it was better for ten guilty people to go free than for an innocent person to be convicted. Now, it is acceptable to some to sacrifice a few innocent people to wage a war on crime.

We must reexamine this "war" and what we are willing to spend to wage it. Our commitment to fairness, our commitment to racial equality, our commitment to the rule of law and our commitment to decency are being spent to wage this "war on crime"—a war that we are fighting against our own people, against our own children, against the mentally ill and the mentally retarded. The death penalty has become the ultimate weapon in class warfare that is being fought top down against the poorest and the most powerless people in our society.

IV. Conclusion

For now, despite all its problems, the death penalty remains part of the legal system. What can you do about the injustices we have discussed?

You can refrain—particularly those of you who go into politics—from engaging in demagoguery on the issue of crime. You can refrain from denigrating the Bill of Rights as nothing more than a collection of technicalities and instead help educate lay people about the importance of constitutional and legal protections and the rule of law. You can refrain from taking cheap shots at judges who abide by the law and uphold the Constitution even in controversial cases. You can remind each other and your fellow citizens that the Bill of Rights does not request, but mandates that judges protect the rights of the poor, the unpopular, and the despised.

You can remind each other and your fellow members of the bar that the right to counsel should mean much more than a warm body with a bar card. You can help build indigent defense programs in places that do not have them, like Alabama, Georgia, Mississippi and Texas. You can staff them. You can respond individually by representing people who most desperately need your services.

You can also ask questions that build upon the momentum created by Governor Ryan and others who are questioning the death penalty. Do we have the humility to recognize the fallibility of our court system? Do we have the honesty to admit that our society is unwilling to pay the price of providing every poor person with competent legal representation, even in capital cases? Do we have the courage to acknowledge the role that race plays in the criminal justice system? Do we have the commitment to do something about it besides pretend that racial prejudice no longer exists?

We must remember that every human being is more than the worst thing he or she ever did—that there is such a thing as redemption. In 1988, I had the privilege of arguing the case of Tony Amadeo before the Supreme Court of the United States. He was not innocent. At age eighteen, he and two other people left the Marines, traveled across the country, stopped in a small town in Georgia and robbed and killed a man for his wallet. He was tried exactly two months after the day of the crime and was sentenced to death. Much later, we learned that the prosecutor had rigged the jury pools by directing the jury commissioners to underrepresent African-Americans. On that basis, the Supreme Court ordered a new trial,[134] and, ultimately, after a lot of hard work, Tony was sentenced to life imprisonment. Tony called me a few of years ago and asked me to come to the Hancock Correctional Facility to attend his graduation from Mercer University. He had taken courses in prison and earned a college degree.

In 1977, when he was just eighteen years of age, Georgia's rickety legal machinery had found Tony Amadeo to be so beyond redemption that he should be eliminated from the human community. In 1995, he graduated summa cum laude from Mercer University.

You can also address some of the larger questions presented by the death penalty: What kind of people do we want to be? What kind of society do we want to have? Are we willing to recognize the dignity of every person, even those who have offended us most grievously? Do we want a hateful, vengeful society, one that turns its back on its children and then executes them, that denies its mentally ill the treatment and the medicine they need and then puts them to death when demons are no longer kept at bay, that gives nothing to the survivors of the victims of the crime except a chance to ask for the maximum sentence and watch an execution?

The Constitutional Court of South Africa addressed many of these questions in deciding whether the death penalty violated that country's constitution. Despite a staggering crime rate and a long history of racial violence and oppression, the Court unanimously concluded that in a society in transition from hatred to understanding, from vengeance to reconciliation, there was no place for the death penalty.[135]

If we here in the United States examine our own system, face its flaws, and think about what kind of society we want to have, we will ultimately conclude that, like slavery and segregation, the death penalty is a relic of another era, that it represents the dark side of the human spirit, and that we are capable of more constructive approaches to the problem of crime in our society. And we will then join the rest of the civilized world in making permanent, absolute and unequivocal the injunction "Thou Shall Not Kill."

Legal Topics:

For related research and practice materials, see the following legal topics:
Criminal Law & Procedure Sentencing
Appeals
Capital Punishment
Mental Retardation
Stays of Execution

NOTES:

1. See George F. Will, Innocent on Death Row, Wash. Post, Apr. 6, 2000, at A23 (observing that "Capital punishment ... is a government program, so skepticism is in order.").
2. Amnesty Int'l, The Death Penalty Worldwide: Developments in 1999, at 11 (May 12, 2000), available at http://web.amnesty.org.
3. Anti-Drug Abuse Act of 1988, 21 U.S.C. 848 (1994).

4. The Violent Crime Control and Law Enforcement Act of 1994, Pub. L. No. 103–322, 108 Stat. 1796.
5. Antiterrorism and Effective Death Penalty Act of 1996, Pub. L. No. 104–132, 104(3), 110 Stat. 1214, 1219 (codified at 28 U.S.C. 2254 (West Supp. 1996)).
6. Amnesty International, Facts and Figures on the Death Penalty (Apr. 1999), http://www.amnestyusa.org/abolish/act500299.html.
7. Id.
8. Id.
9. Id.
10. Id.
11. Id.
12. Id.
13. Vienna Convention on Consular Relations and Optimal Protocol on Disputes, Apr. 24, 1963, 21 U.S.T. 77, 596 U. n.T.S. 262 [hereinafter Vienna Convention].
14. Felix Rohatyn, The Shadow Over America: How Our Use of the Death Penalty Hurts Our Image Abroad, *Newsweek*, May 29, 2000, at 27.
15. Randall Coyne & Lyn Entzeroth, Report Regarding Implementation of the American Bar Association's Recommendations and Resolutions Concerning the Death Penalty and Calling for a Moratorium on Executions, 4 Geo. J. on Fighting Pov. 3, 5–6 (1996) (describing the failure to address these problems and the ABA's call for a moratorium); Ira P. Robbins, Toward a More Just and Effective System of Review in State Death Penalty Cases, 40 Am. U. L. Rev. 1, 16 (1990) (reporting conclusions of an ABA task force that "the inadequacy and inadequate compensation of counsel at trial" was one of the "principal failings of the capital punishment review process today" and recommending measures to improve counsel and to maintain habeas corpus review by federal courts).
16. Stephen B. Bright, Neither Equal Nor Just: The Rationing and Denial of Legal Services to the Poor When Life and Liberty Are at Stake, 1997 N.Y.U. Annual Survey of American Law 783 (1997) (describing quality of counsel at trial and on post-conviction review and the failure of some states to provide counsel in post-conviction review); Sara Rimer, Questions of Death Row Justice For Poor People in Alabama, N.Y. Times, Mar. 1, 2000, at A1 (describing the poor quality of counsel in capital cases in Alabama); Max B. Baker & Linda P. Campbell, Unequal Justice, Ft. Worth Star-Telegram, Oct. 15, 2000, at 1 (describing the poor representation of indigent defendants in Texas); Paul Duggan, George W. Bush: The Record in Texas; Attorneys' Ineptitude Doesn't Halt Executions, Wash. Post, May 12, 2000, at A1 (describing the poor quality of representation in Texas); Ken Armstrong & Steve Mills, Inept Defenses Cloud Verdicts, Chi. Trib., Nov. 15, 1999, at 1 (describing the poor quality of counsel in capital cases in Illinois).

17. Roscoe C. Howard, Jr., The Defunding of the Post Conviction Defense Organizations as a Denial of the Right to Counsel, 98 W. Va. L. Rev. 863, 912–15 (1996).
18. See infra notes 108–15 and accompanying text.
19. See McCleskey v. Kemp, 481 U.S. 279 (1987).
20. The Racial Justice Act was adopted in a version of a crime bill that passed the House of Representatives in April, 1994. David Cole, A Fear of Too Much Justice, Legal Times, May 9, 1994, at 41. However, due to opposition in the Senate, it was not included in the final bill reported by the conference committee and adopted by both the Senate and the House later in the summer. See Violent Crime Control and Law Enforcement Act of 1994, Pub. L. No. 103–322, 108 Stat. 1796.
21. Thirteen of the thirty-eight states that have the death penalty and the federal government prohibit execution of the mentally retarded. Death Penalty Info. Ctr., Mentally Retarded and the Death Penalty, at http://www.deathpenaltyinfo.org/dpicmr.html (last visited Jan. 26, 2001).
22. Fifteen states and the federal government prohibit the execution of those under 18 at the time of their crimes. Death Penalty Info. Ctr., Juveniles and the Death Penalty, at http://www.deathpenaltyinfo.org/juvchar.html (last visited Jan. 26, 2001).
23. Antiterrorism and Effective Death Penalty Act of 1996, Pub. L. No. 104–132, 104(3), 110 Stat. 1214, 1219 (codified at 28 U.S.C. 2254 (West Supp. 1996)).
24. Brooke A. Masters, Missteps On Road To Injustice: In Va., Innocent Man Was Nearly Executed, Wash. Post, Dec. 1, 2000, at A1.
25. Id.
26. Pam Belluck, Class of Sleuths to Rescue on Death Row, N.Y. Times, Feb. 5, 1999, at A14.
27. Id.
28. Id.
29. Jon Jeter, A New Ending to an Old Story, Wash. Post, Feb. 17, 1999, at C1.
30. Don Terry, DNA Tests and a Confession Set Three on a Path to Freedom in 1978 Murders, N.Y. Times, June 15, 1996, at A6.
31. Steve Mills & Ken Armstrong, Governor to Halt Executions, Chi. Trib., Jan. 30, 2000, at 1.
32. Ken Armstrong & Steve Mills, Ryan Suspends Death Penalty: Illinois First State to Impose Moratorium on Executions, Chi. Trib., Jan. 31, 2000, at 1.
33. Hearing on the Innocence Protection Act Before the Crime Subcommittee of the House Judiciary Committee, 106th Cong. 76, 80 (2000) (statement of Governor George Ryan).
34. People v. Bull, 705 N.E.2d 824, 847 (Ill. 1998) (Harrison, J., dissenting).
35. Ken Armstrong & Steve Mills, Inept Defense Cloud Verdicts, Chi. Trib., Nov. 15, 1999, at 1.
36. Id.

37. Ken Armstrong & Steve Mills, Death Row Justice Derailed: Bias, Errors and Incompetence in Capital Cases Have Turned Illinois' Harshest Punishment Into its Least Credible, Chi. Trib, Nov, 14, 1999, at 1; Steve Mills & Ken Armstrong, The Inside Informant, Chi. Trib., Nov. 16, 1999, at 1; Steve Mills & Ken Armstrong, A Tortured Path to Death Row, Chi. Trib., Nov. 17, 1999, at 1; Steve Mills & Ken Armstrong, Convicted by a Hair, Chi. Trib., Nov. 18, 1999, at 1.
38. Steve Mills & Ken Armstrong, The Inside Informant, Chi. Trib., Nov. 16, 1999, at 1.
39. Callins v. Collins, 510 U.S. 1141, 1145 (1994) (Blackmun, J., dissenting), denying cert. to 998 F.2d 269 (5th Cir. 1993).
40. John C. Jeffries, Jr., Justice Lewis F. Powell, Jr. 451 (1994).
41. Mark D. Killian, Chief Justice Shares Parting Thoughts with Judges, Fla. Bar News, July 15, 1996, at 6.
42. Singleton v. Norris, 108 F.3d 872, 874–75 (8th Cir. 1997) (Heaney, J., concurring).
43. National Death Penalty Moratorium Act of 2001, S. 233, 107th Cong. (2001); National Death Penalty Moratorium Act of 2000, H.R. 5237, S. 2463, 106th Cong. (2000); Federal Death Penalty Moratorium Act of 2000, H.R. 5236, S. 3048, 106th Cong. (2000).
44. Federal Death Penalty Abolition Act of 1999, S. 1917, 106th Cong. (1999).
45. Innocence Protection Act of 2000, S. 2073, H.R. 4167, 107th Cong. (2000).
46. People v. Bull, 705 N.E.2d 834, 847 (Ill. 1998) (Harrison, J., dissenting).
47. Stephen B. Bright, Elected Judges and the Death Penalty in Texas: Why Full Habeas Corpus Review by Independent Federal Judges Is Indispensable to Protecting Constitutional Rights, 78 Tex. L. Rev. 1805, 1808–10 (2000).
48. Sara Rimer & Raymond Bonner, Bush Presidency Puts Focus on Executions, N.Y. Times, May 14, 2000, at 1 (describing several cases in which executions were carried out despite questions of innocence).
49. Susan Blaustein, The Executioner's Wrong, Wash. Post, Aug, 1, 1993, at C1.
50. Sara Rimer & Raymond Bonner, Texas Lawyer's Death Row Record a Concern, N.Y. Times, June 11, 2000, at A1.
51. Blaustein, supra note 49, at C1.
52. Death Penalty Info. Ctr., Texas, at http://www.deathpenaltyinfo.org/texas.html.
53. Steve Bousquet et al., Fla. Speeds up Death Row Appeals, Pittsburgh Post-Gazette, Jan. 8, 2000, at A4, available at 2000 WL 10872386 (reporting that Republican legislators at the special session criticized judges who "discover 'technicalities' to delay death sentences and deny justice to victims"); Marcia Gelbart, Limits Set on Appeals to Speed Executions, Palm Beach Post, Jan. 8, 2000, at 1A (reporting that Gov. Jeb Bush's bill requires inmates to meet strict deadlines for filing claims and limits the number of appeals they can file "with the goal of putting [inmates] to death within five years of conviction"); Sara Rimer, Florida Lawmakers Reject Electric Chair, N.Y. Times, Jan. 7, 2000, at A13 (describing defeat of a proposed amendment to Gov. Jeb Bush's bill that

would have allowed inmates to show that racial bias played a role in their sentencing); Larry P. Spalding, The High Price of Killing Killers, Palm Beach Post, Jan. 4, 2000, at A1, available at 2000 WL 7592885 (quoting the bill's primary sponsor, Republican Victor Crist, as saying that Florida "should be executing more people a year than [it] sends to Death Row, in order to catch up"); Jim Yardley, A Role Model for Executions, N.Y. Times, Jan. 9, 2000, 4, at 5 (reporting widespread criticism of Gov. Jeb Bush's bill as a "hurried proposal" that is "possibly unconstitutional" and "might result in executing wrongly convicted inmates").

54. Allen v. Butterworth, 756 So. 2d 52, 54 (Fla. 2000).
55. See Yardley, supra note 53, at 5 (reporting Mr. Thomas's comments and quoting Democratic State Representative Chris Smith, who stated that Texas should be "our role model for killing people"); William Yardley, Bush's Adviser Key in Push for Quicker Death Row Appeals, St. Petersburg Times, Jan. 6, 2000, at 5B (describing Thomas's role in prompting Florida's overhaul of the death row appeals process).
56. Death Penalty Info. Ctr., Executions in the U.S. 1999, at http://www.deathpenaltyinfo.org/dpicexec99.html (last visited Jan. 26, 2001).
57. Death Penalty Info. Ctr., Executions in the U.S. 2000, at http://www.deathpenaltyinfo.org/dpicexec00.html (last visited Jan. 26, 2001).
58. Death Penalty Info. Ctr., Death Row USA, at http://www.deathpenaltyinfo.org/DRUSA-Stats.html (last modified Jan. 1, 2001).
59. For an excellent history of the role of the criminal justice system in maintaining the legalized oppression of African-Americans after emancipation, see David M. Oshinsky, Worse Than Slavery: Parchman Farm and the Ordeal of Jim Crow Justice (1996).
60. 60. See City of L.A. v. Lyons, 461 U.S. 95, 116 n.3 (1983) (Marshall, J., dissenting) (noting that although only nine percent of residents of Los Angeles are black males, they have accounted for seventy-five percent of deaths resulting from chokeholds by police).
61. See Charles J. Ogletree, Does Race Matter in Criminal Prosecutions?, Champion, July 1991, at 7, 10–12 (describing discriminatory practices by police against racial minorities); Mary Maxwell Thomas, The African American Male: Communication Gap Converts Justice Into "Just Us" System, 13 Harv. BlackLetter L.J. 1, 5 (1997).
62. See Ian Ayres & Joel Waldfogel, A Market Test for Race Discrimination in Bail Setting, 46 Stan. L. Rev. 987 (1994) (documenting discrimination in the setting of bail rates for African-Americans); Thomas, supra note 61, at 5.
63. Gerald W. Heaney, The Reality of Guidelines Sentencing: No End to Disparity, 28 Am. Crim. L. Rev. 161, 165 (1991) (arguing that "the most disturbing systemic disparity is the apparent disparate treatment of young, black males, who on the average receive guidelines sentences significantly longer than those received by their white counterparts for similar offenses"); see also The Real War on Crime: The Report of the National Criminal Justice Commission 99–129 (Stephen R. Donziger ed., 1996); Jerome G. Miller, Search and Destroy: African-American Males in the Criminal Justice System

(1996); Samuel L. Myers, Jr., Racial Disparities in Sentencing: Can Sentencing Reforms Reduce Discrimination in Punishment?, 64 U. Colo. L. Rev. 781 (1993).

64. Bill Rankin, Unequal Justice: Whites More Apt to Get Probation, Atlanta J. & Const., Feb. 8, 1998, at A1 (reporting that since 1990 white people convicted in Georgia were thirty to sixty percent more likely than blacks to get probation for various crimes even though prior criminal records were about same among blacks and whites); Keith W. Watters, Law Without Justice, Nat'l B. Ass'n Mag., Mar.-Apr. 1996 at 1, 23 (reporting that whites are more likely to be placed on probation than African-Americans, and that African-Americans make up only twelve percent of population and thirteen percent of drug users, but comprise fifty-five percent of drug convictions).
65. Jeffrey J. Pokorak, Probing the Capital Prosecutor's Perspective: Race of the Discretionary Actors, 83 Cornell L. Rev. 1811, 1817 (1998).
66. Id. at 1817–18.
67. See, e.g., David C. Baldus, Racial Discrimination and the Death Penalty in the Post-Furman Era: An Empirical and Legal Overview, with Recent Findings from Philadelphia, 83 Cornell L. Rev. 1638 (1998); U.S. Gen. Acct. Off., Rep. No. GGD-90–57, Death Penalty Sentencing: Research Indicates Pattern of Racial Disparities 5 (1990).
68. U.S. Dep't of Just., The Federal Death Penalty System: A Statistical Survey (1988–2000), available at http://www.usdoj.gov/dag/pubdoc/dpsurvey.html (Sept. 12, 2000).
69. Id.
70. Transcript of Hearing on Racial Discrimination held on Sep. 1–14, 1991, at 67–69, State v. Brooks, (Super. Ct. of Muscogee Co., Ga., Sep. 12, 1991) (Indictment Nos. 3888, 54606), on appeal 415 S.E.2d 903 [hereinafter Hearing on Racial Discrimination]. The evidence is described in David Margolick, In Land of Death Penalty, Accusations of Racial Bias, N.Y. Times, July 10, 1991, at A1 and Michael Kroll, Death Penalty Info. Ctr., Chattahoochee Judicial District: The Buckle of the Death Belt 10, available at http://www.deathpenaltyinfo.org/dpic.r11.html (1999).
71. Transcript of Hearing at 38, Davis v. Kemp (Super. Ct. of Butts Co., Ga., 1988) (No. 86-V-865) (testimony of James Isham, father of the victim).
72. Clint Claybrook, Slain Girl's Father Top Campaign Contributor, Columbus Ledger-Enquirer (Ga.), Aug. 7, 1988, at B1.
73. Davis v. State, 340 S.E.2d 869, 872, cert. denied, 479 U.S. 871 (1986).
74. Claybrook, supra note 72, at B1.
75. Id.
76. See, e.g., Phil Gast, District Attorney Criticizes Court for Rejecting Sentence, Columbus Enquirer (Ga.), Sept. 17, 1983, at A1.
77. Hearing on Racial Discrimination, supra note 70, at 178, 184–85, 192–93, 197, 199–200 (Sept. 12, 1991).
78. See Defense Exhibit 1A, admitted in Hearing on Racial Discrimination, supra note 70.
79. Richard Willing, Geography of the Death Penalty, USA Today, Dec. 20, 1999, at 1A.

80. Mike Tolson, A Deadly Distinction, Houston Chron., Feb. 23, 2001, at 1A (reporting that when Holmes left office, 61 people sentenced to death in Harris County had been executed and 150 were on death row).
81. Tina Rosenberg, The Deadliest D.A., N.Y. Times Mag., July 16, 1995, at 21.
82. Willing, supra note 79, at 1A.
83. U.S. Dep't of Just., Survey of the Federal Death Penalty System at T14, tbl.5A (2000), available at http://www.usdoj.gov/dag/pubdoc/dpsurvey.html.
84. Eddings v. Oklahoma, 455 U.S. 104, 112 (1982).
85. Chambers v. Florida, 309 U.S. 227, 241 (1940).
86. 351 U.S. 12 (1956).
87. Id. at 19.
88. 372 U.S. 335 (1963).
89. Id. at 344.
90. Id. In 1972, the Court held that the Constitution also requires counsel for poor people jailed for minor offenses. Argensinger v. Hamlin, 407 U.S. 25, 37 (1972).
91. Riles v. McCotter, 799 F.2d 947, 955 (5th Cir. 1986) (Rubin, J., concurring).
92. See, e.g., Frey v. Fulcomer, 974 F.2d 348, 359 (3d Cir. 1992) (allowing a lawyer in a Pennsylvania case to tailor his presentation of evidence and argument around a death penalty statute that had been declared unconstitutional three years earlier); Trial Record at 1875–76, State v. Smith, 581 So. 2d 497 (Ala. Crim. App. 1990) (No. 5 Div. 458) (allowing a defense lawyer to ask for time between the guilt and penalty phases so he could read the state's death penalty statute); Stephen B. Bright, Counsel for the Poor: The Death Sentence Not for the Worst Crime But for the Worst Lawyer, 103 Yale L.J. 1835, 1839 (1994) (describing a criminal defense attorney who, when asked to name the criminal law decisions with which he was familiar, could name only "Miranda and Dred Scott;" Dred Scott v. Sandford, 60 U.S. (19 How.) 393 (1857), was not a criminal case); Transcript of Habeas Corpus Hearing of Jan. 10–11, 1996, at 396–97, Fugate v. Thomas, (Super. Ct. Butts Co., Ga.) (Civ. No. 94-V-195) (parts of which are reprinted in A Lawyer Without Precedent, Harper's, June 1997, at 24) (lawyer unaware of any case).
93. See, e.g., Jeffrey L. Kirshmeier, Drink, Drugs, and Drowsiness: The Constitutional Right to Effective Assistance of Counsel and the Strickland Prejudice Requirement, 75 Neb. L. Rev. 425, 455–60 (1996) (citing cases in which convictions were upheld even though defense lawyers were intoxicated, abusing drugs, or mentally ill); People v. Garrison, 765 P.2d 419, 440–41 (1989) (upholding conviction even though counsel, an alcoholic, was arrested en route to court one morning and found to have a blood alcohol level of 0.27).
94. See, e.g., McFarland v. Texas, 928 S.W.2d 482, 505–06 (Tex. Crim. App. 1996) (upholding death sentence even though lead defense counsel slept during trial); Ex parte Burdine, 901 S.W.2d 456 (Tex. Crim. App. 1995) (Maloney, J., dissenting) (upholding

death sentence even though defense counsel slept during trial); David R. Dow, The State, the Death Penalty, and Carl Johnson, 37 B.C. L. Rev. 691, 694–95, 711 (1996) (describing the case of Carl Johnson, who was executed even though his defense counsel slept during portions of the trial).

95. Haney v. State, 603 So. 2d 368, 377–78 (Ala. Crim. App. 1991), affd, 603 So. 2d 412 (Ala. 1992), cert. denied, 507 U.S. 925 (1993).
96. Powell v. Alabama, 287 U.S. 45, 57 (1932).
97. Peter Applebome, Two Electric Jolts in Alabama Execution, N.Y. Times, July 15, 1989, at A6.
98. Affidavit of Charles Marchman, Jr. at 1–5, Young v. Kemp, (M.D. Ga. 1985) (No. 85-98-2-MAC).
99. John Makeig, Asleep on the Job: Slaying Trial Boring, Lawyer Says, Houston Chron., Aug. 14, 1992, at A35.
100. Id.
101. McFarland, 928 S.W.2d at 527 (Baird, J., dissenting).
102. Ex parte Burdine, 901 S.W.2d at 456.
103. Burdine v. Johnson, 66 F. Supp. 2d 854, 866 (S. D. Tex. 1999).
104. Burdine v. Johnson, 231 F.3d 950, 965 (5th Cir. 2000) (Benavides, J., dissenting).
105. Id. at 950.
106. Burdine v. Johnson, 234 F.3d 1339 (5th Cir. 2000).
107. Paul M. Barrett, On the Defense: Lawyer's Fast Work on Death Cases Raises Doubts About System, Wall St. J., Sept. 7, 1994, at A1 (reporting that Cannon is known for hurrying through capital trials like "greased lightening" and had ten clients sentenced to death).
108. David R. Dow, The State, the Death Penalty, and Carl Johnson, 37 B.C. L. Rev. 691, 711 (1996).
109. Transcript of Hearing of Sept. 12, at 2-3, Gibson v. Turpin, (Super. Ct. of Butts Co., Ga.) (No. 95-V-648).
110. Id.
111. Paul Duggan, On Death Row, Not Even Dying Is Certain, Wash. Post, Dec. 20, 1998, at A22, available at 1998 WL 22542235.
112. Transcript of Hearing of Aug. 15, 1997, at 26, State v. Cantu (104th Dist. Ct. of Taylor County, Tex.) (No. 10, 172-B) [hereinafter Cantu Transcript].
113. Bruce Tomaso, Change of Address: Death Row's New Home Offers Fewer Amenities for its Tenants, Dallas Morning News, June 9, 1999, at 25A, available at 1999 WL 4127009.
114. Pub. L. No. 104–132, 110 Stat. 1217 (codified in scattered titles of U.S.C.).
115. Id. 101, 105 (amending 28 U.S.C. 2244(d)(1)); Cantu Transcript, supra note 112, at 27–28 (testimony of the lawyer).

116. Cantu-Tzin v. Johnson, 162F.3d295 (5th Cir. 1998) stay denied, 525 U.S. 1132 (1999) (holding that because the habeas petition was time-barred, the district court was not required to appoint counsel pursuant to 21 U.S.C. 848(q)(4)(B)).
117. Rick Bragg, Killer Racked by Delusions is Put to Death in Alabama, N.Y. Times, May 13, 1995, at A7.
118. Rumbaugh v. Procunier, 753 F.2d 395, 397, 405–07 (5th Cir. 1985), cert. denied, 473 U.S. 919 (1985).
119. Id. at 403.
120. Steve Wiegand, Governor's Warning to 2 Justices, S.F. Chron., Mar. 14, 1986, at 1.
121. Stephen B. Bright & Patrick J. Keenan, Judges and the Politics of Death: Deciding Between the Bill of Rights and the Next Election in Capital Cases, 75 B.U. L. Rev. 759. 760–61 (1995) (describing campaigns against judges in California and other states).
122. Janet Elliott & Richard Connelly, Mansfield: The Stealth Candidate; His Past Isn't What It Seems, Tex. Law., Oct. 3, 1994, at 1, 32 (reprinting a campaign advertisement of a Texas Court of Criminal Appeals candidate that lists a series of pro-death penalty positions).
123. See Do It Now, Ft. Worth Star-Telegram, Nov. 12, 1994, at 32, available at 1994 WL 4033647 (calling for the reform of the judicial election system in Texas and for an immediate challenge to Mansfield's election because he had "shaded the truth of virtually every aspect of his career"); Q & A with Stephen Mansfield: "The Greatest Challenge of My Life," Tex. Law., Nov. 21, 1994, at 8 (printing a post-election interview with Mansfield in which he retracts a number of statements made before and during the election).
124. Janet Elliott, Unqualified Success: Mansfield's Mandate; Vote Makes a Case for Merit Selection, Tex. Law., Nov. 14, 1994, at 1 (stating that Mansfield's suspect past and poor qualifications make him a "poster boy" for advocates of nonpartisan judicial elections); Q & A with Stephen Mansfield, supra note 123, at 8.
125. John Williams, Election "94: GOP Gains Majority in State Supreme Court, Houston Chron., Nov. 10, 1994, at A29, available at 1994 WL 4602404.
126. See Elliott & Connelly, supra note 122, at 32 (reporting that Mansfield's writings consisted of a guest column in a local paper regarding a capital murder conviction, and two articles that appeared in a journal for charter life underwriters); Elliott, supra note 124 (reporting that Mansfield was unable to verify campaign claims regarding the number of criminal cases he had handled).
127. Elliott, supra note 124.
128. Id.
129. Child Support Allegations Threaten Judge Seat, Ft. Worth Star-Telegram, Dec. 10, 1994, at 29, available at 1994 WL 4037619 (outlining the allegations of back child support by Mansfield's ex-wife and his subsequent denial of the allegations).

130. Janet Elliott & John Council, Scalping Allegation Lands Mansfield in Hairy Situation, Tex. Law., Dec. 14, 1998, at 1 (outlining the controversies that have plagued Judge Mansfield); Claire Osborn, Judge Charged with Trespassing at UT, Austin Am.-Statesman, Dec. 5, 1998, at B2, available at 1998 WL 3633981 (outlining the circumstances surrounding Judge Mansfield's arrest at the University of Texas).
131. Pete Slover, Judge Reprimanded Over Ticket-Selling Incident, Dallas Morning News, May 14, 1999, at A31, available at 1999 WL 4120830 (reporting Judge Mansfield's reprimand by the Texas Conduct Commission).
132. State v. Odom, 928 S.W.2d 18, 33 (Tenn. 1996).
133. For a detailed discussion of the campaign against Justice White see Stephen B. Bright, Can Judicial Independence be Attained in the South? Overcoming History, Elections and Misperceptions About the Role of the Judiciary, 14 Ga. St. U. L. Rev. 817, 847–49 (1998) and Stephen B. Bright, Political Attacks on the Judiciary: Can Justice Be Done Amid Efforts to Intimidate and Remove Judges from Office for Unpopular Decisions?, 72 N.Y.U. L. Rev. 308, 313–15 (1997).
134. Amadeo v. Zant, 486 U.S. 214 (1988).
135. State v. Makwanyane, 1995 (3) SALR 391 (CC), reprinted in 16 Hum. Rts. L.J. 154, 190 (1995) (Langa, J., concurring).

Working Against the Past

The Function of American History of Race Relations and Capital Punishment in Supreme Court Opinions

Rita K. Lomio*

SUMMARY:
... McCleskey cited the Baldus study for the proposition that the race of the victim matters a great deal in determining who receives the death penalty: "The raw numbers collected by Professor Baldus indicate that defendants charged with killing white persons received the death penalty in 11% of the cases, but defendants charged with killing blacks received the death penalty in only 1% of the cases." ... The majority opinion, delivered by Justice Powell and joined by Chief Justice Rehnquist and Justices White, O'Connor, and Scalia, expressed concern that McCleskey's racial discrimination claim could be leveled against other penalties, extend to other "unexplained discrepancies that correlate to membership in other minority groups, and even to gender," and could prompt studies looking at the "race or sex of other actors in the criminal justice system." ... Responding to the "Times Have Changed" Argument A concern with the "times have changed" argument may explain why those Furman justices who supported abolition of the death penalty—Justices Brennan, Douglas, and Marshall—did not rely exclusively (or at all) on American history of race relations and capital punishment. ... By not voicing concerns with a troubling history of race and capital punishment, Justices White and Stewart, through their Furman opinions, narrowed the issues that states would have to confront in developing constitutional sentencing schemes. ... Presentation of American history of race and capital punishment may be intended to empower the reader with the information necessary to understand his or her society, encourage debate by provoking outrage, and shape debate by injecting content and defining the contours of the issue. ... The presentation of a history of racial injustice

* Law Clerk to the Honorable Ruggero J. Aldisert, United States Court of Appeals for the Third Circuit. Stanford University, B.A., 2004, Harvard Law School, J.D., 2007.

in capital punishment is rich and varied based on its doctrinal or advocacy function: focus may be on past state laws, statistics, anecdotes, or the testimony of individuals as to local county practices during their lifetimes.

INTRODUCTION

Memory of the past permeates criminal trials. This is particularly true in capital cases. In such cases, the history of capital punishment in America is ever-present, inevitably intertwined with a history of race relations.[1]

Physical trappings of the past can be found in courtroom paraphernalia. A history professor, for example, took the stand in Georgia to recite a history of the Confederate battle flag and racial violence in the South to support the argument that a black defendant, sentenced to death in a courtroom where the flag was displayed, was not given a fair trial.[2] History finds its way into sentencing. A defendant's background and victim impact statements provide frameworks for sentencing. When the jury deliberates, long-standing biases and prejudice may persist.[3] It is unsurprising, therefore, that history also finds its way into court opinions. This article examines the appearance of the American history of race relations and capital punishment in opinions of the United States Supreme Court: where history is used, how it is used, and why it is used or omitted.

This article will use the term "history" as defined by Charles A. Miller: "that which … is believed to be true about the past—about past facts and past thoughts."[4] In the context of this article, this history focuses on past race-based state criminal codes, racial composition of capital trial participants, extralegal capital punishment such as mob lynchings, and unequal application of the death penalty based on race.

Part II of this Article examines several cases in which Supreme Court justices documented and memorialized American history of race relations and capital punishment in a variety of forms and for various purposes. Part III then considers the many functions such history may serve in Court opinions and how it may sculpt criminal procedure.

II. EXAMPLES OF AMERICAN HISTORY OF RACE RELATIONS AND CAPITAL PUNISHMENT IN COURT OPINIONS

A. The "Cruel and Unusual Punishment" Clause of the Eighth Amendment

The "Cruel and Unusual Punishment" Clause of the Eighth Amendment lends itself to historical analysis. The clause is, as Chief Justice Burger observed, "less than self-defining" and "one of the most difficult [fundamental guarantees] to translate into judicially manageable terms."[5] It is therefore not surprising that courts turn to history when interpreting the meaning of the clause (by examining the framers' intent),[6] as well as when applying the clause (by ascertaining whether the "evolving standards of decency that mark the progress of a maturing society"[7] support outlawing a historically-permissible punishment).[8] Indeed, a general history of capital punishment runs throughout Eighth Amendment opinions on capital punishment.[9] The use of a race-conscious history of capital punishment in America, however, is less frequent.

1. Furman v. Georgia

In Furman, the Court was faced with three cases involving black defendants sentenced to death. The per curiam opinion, addressing whether "the imposition and carrying out of the death penalty in these cases constitute[s] cruel and unusual punishment in violation of the Eighth and Fourteenth Amendments," answered in the affirmative.[10] The reasoning behind the holding was splintered. Each justice wrote his own opinion, with five supporting the judgment (Justices Douglas, Brennan, Stewart, White, and Marshall) and four dissenting (Chief Justice Burger and Justices Blackmun, Powell, and Rehnquist).

In *Furman*, the justices were squarely confronted with America's troubled history of race and capital punishment. The National Association for the Advancement of Colored People (NAACP), the National Urban League, the Southern Christian Leadership Conference, the Mexican-American Legal Defense and Education Fund, and the National Council of Negro Women filed an amicus brief which focused on "the areas that bear with discriminatory harshness upon blacks, Mexican-Americans, the poor and other disadvantaged persons."[11] Half of the brief detailed the "Pre-1935 History of the Racially Discriminatory Use of Formal and Informal Capital Punishment by Whites Against Non-Whites," reviewing slavery from 1619 to 1865 and lynching and vigilantism from 1882 to 1935. The eleven-page appendix, entitled "Pre-Civil War History of Punishment for Rape in Southern States and Washington, D.C.," listed the disparate punishment for rape in each state for white defendants and for black defendants.[12]

The *Furman* opinions can be crudely divided into two categories: those that contain a race-conscious history and those that do not.[13] However, even those that mention such a history use it for different purposes (e.g., in support of or opposition to abolition) and present it in different forms (e.g., past official policy or statistics). The appearance of this racial history alone cannot be mapped to the outcome of the opinion as it is present in both concurring and dissenting opinions, and absent in both.

a. Silence to a Past of Racial Discrimination and Capital Punishment

The opinions of Justices Brennan, Rehnquist, and Blackmun do not include explicit race-conscious description of the past. Justice Brennan, for example, argues generally that the death penalty is cruel and unusual.[14] Yet only one of the four principles he articulates for determining whether a punishment is "cruel and unusual" arbitrary infliction of severe punishments—implicates racial discrimination. Even then, the only indication in the opinion that Brennan suspected a link between arbitrariness and racial discrimination appears in a footnote.[15] Instead, his opinion was meant to be a sweeping statement of societal norms to show that the gradual progression of society had resulted in a per se rejection of the death penalty. While inclusion of a history of slavery, racial hatred, and racially-discriminatory criminal codes may have served to demonstrate what Justice Brennan saw as the many defects of the death penalty, he may have been concerned that explicit ties to race would have turned his opinion into a defensive reaction against something, suggesting the death penalty would be allowed if only efforts were made to remove racial discrimination.

b. No Evidence of Continuing Racial Discrimination

Justice White, while concurring in judgment, did not address the constitutionality of the death penalty per se.[16] Instead, he focused on the arbitrariness and infrequency of its imposition. He did not rely on racial discrimination or history for support. Referencing "10 years of almost daily exposure to the facts and circumstances of hundreds and hundreds of federal and state criminal cases involving crimes for which death is the authorized penalty," he found "no meaningful basis for distinguishing the few cases in which it is imposed from the many cases in which it is not."[17]

c. "Times Have Changed"

Chief Justice Burger, in his dissent, acknowledged in a footnote claims of racial discrimination, but concluded that, while such discrimination might form the basis of a Fourteenth Amendment claim, it is irrelevant to the Eighth Amendment.[18] Even under the Fourteenth Amendment, however, "it is not enough to show how [the statutory authorization for the death penalty] was applied in the distant past" because racial segregation is no longer the official policy of many states.[19] Justice Powell also took a dismissive posture as to past racial discrimination, claiming that times have changed. He stated:

> The possibility of racial bias in the trial and sentencing process has diminished in recent years. The segregation of our society in decades past, which contributed substantially to the severity of punishment for interracial crimes, is now no longer prevalent in this country. Likewise, the day is past when juries do not represent the minority group elements of the community. The assurance of fair trials for all citizens is greater today than at any previous time in our history. Because standards of criminal justice have 'evolved' in a manner favorable to the accused, discriminatory imposition of capital punishment is far less likely today than in the past.[20]

Both Justice Powell and Chief Justice Burger, therefore, framed history by focusing on official policy and outward manifestations of the legal system (such as the racial composition of juries). This historical narrative of official policy, as well as reference to a "distant past" and "decades past," implied that such a history had only minimal if any bearing on current policies or construction of procedural safeguards because that "day is past."

d. A Legacy of Racial Discrimination

Justices Douglas and Marshall used evidence of past race relations and capital punishment in a limited manner to supply evidence of continuing discrimination, and presented it in the form of statistics, not narrative or past official policy.

Justice Douglas argued that the death penalty is "unusual" if it discriminates.[21] He was concerned with disproportionate application of the death penalty to unpopular groups, and surveyed history to provide troubling precedents. For example, he chronicled a history of using the death penalty against political dissenters, referencing the Bloody Assizes;[22] ancient Hindu law's inverse correlation between severity of punishment and level of social status;[23] and he drew from a book written by a warden, Lewis E. Lawes, in 1928, arguing that the death penalty is disproportionately distributed between the rich and poor.[24]

Justice Douglas briefly placed a history of racial discrimination within this framework of general discrimination. Justice Douglas introduced the defendants as "Jackson, a black," "Furman, a black," and "Branch, a black" and noted that Jackson and Branch were convicted of raping white women.[25] Justice Douglas' concern with a history of racial discrimination appears in statistical form. He documents the "ethnic disparities" revealed by a study of capital cases in Texas between 1924 and 1968.[26] In a footnote, Justice Douglas presents a table entitled "Race of the Offender by Final Disposition" which separates defendants into "negro" and "white" categories, and lists dispositions of "executed" and "commuted," revealing persistent racial discrimination.[27] For his assertion that "there is no permissible 'caste' aspect of law enforcement," Justice Douglas cites Guy B. Johnson, The Negro and Crime,[28] an article which argued that many aspects of blacks' behavior and situation can be traced to the institution and experience of slavery.[29]

Justice Marshall took a similar approach in using American history of racial injustice in capital punishment. Race is absent from his exhaustive review of the history of capital punishment in the United States.[30] Instead, he includes history of race and capital punishment at the conclusion of his opinion, as dicta, as facts that "would serve to convince even the most hesitant of citizens to condemn death as a sanction."[31] This evidence takes the form of statistics of the execution of white and black individuals since 1930.[32] However, Justice Marshall does not dwell on the racial element, and documents additional bases of impermissible discrimination.[33]

Both Justices Douglas and Marshall, therefore, condemn the more general discrimination that accompanies a system which gives broad discretion to the sentencer. Such discrimination could be premised on poverty, lack of political clout, membership in "a suspect or unpopular minority," or social position.[34] Historical and continuing racial discrimination was introduced as one "form" of discrimination which had taken hold in the United States.

The bleak narrative and anecdotal accounts of American history of race and capital punishment that appear in works cited by Justice Marshall for their statistics,[35] including Johnson's *The Negro and Crime* and Franklin H. Williams' *The Death Penalty and the Negro*,[36] are not recounted. Their descriptions of atmosphere[37] and reporting of sayings[38] are abandoned by Justices Marshall and Douglas in favor of recitation of statistics.

Viewed together, Justices Douglas' and Marshall's opinions tie the past closely to the present and show the continuing relevance of race. Their use of statistics provides a common measurement system for comparing the recent past with the present. Justice Marshall reports that since 1930, 405 of the 455 persons executed for rape have been black. Justice Douglas ties that statistical past with the present, observing that two of the three black defendants in *Furman* were sentenced to death for rape.

e. Avoiding Past Injustices

Interestingly, the closest race relations history comes to supporting a preventative doctrine in Furman comes in Justice Stewart's opinion, where lynch law makes a brief appearance.[39] Justice Stewart muses that retribution may be a constitutionally-permissible "ingredient in the imposition of punishment."[40] Were retribution, "part of the nature of man," not "channeled" through the criminal justice system, "people [might] begin to believe that organized society is unwilling or unable to impose upon criminal offenders the punishment they 'deserve,' [and as a result] there are sown the seeds of anarchy—of self-help, vigilante justice, and lynch law."[41]

Justice Stewart does not tie lynch law, self-help, and vigilante justice with race explicitly. However, vigilante justice and lynch law were prominent themes in the NAACP amicus brief filed with the Court. The brief noted that a majority of the lynchings between 1882 and 1903 involved non-whites.[42] The brief also observed that "[n]ot unmixed with vigilantism is frequently a fair share of racism."[43] The connection between race and lynching is widely reported in the media. The Los Angeles Times, for example, reported that "[d]uring Virginia's most recent execution in June, members of a cheering crowd hollered, 'Bring back lynching!' and carried signs saying, 'Fry the Nigger.'"[44] Further, lynching, when referenced by justices, is often associated with race.[45]

The fact that Justice Stewart mentions lynch law in passing in a part of his opinion that he views to be "in the abstract," counsels against affording it much weight. Nonetheless, its function in his argument is interesting. Justice Stewart references a historical evil which has strong racial overtones (lynching) in support of his argument that retribution may be a desirable "ingredient" in the imposition of punishment. Taken to the extreme, he suggests that the legislature should craft doctrine and punishment in order to prevent a historical evil from resurfacing. In this reading, Justice Stewart is responsive to history.[46] He addresses the history of race relations more directly than Justice Douglas (who uses racial discrimination as one piece of evidence of continuing discrimination) or Justice Marshall (who cites racial discrimination to convince "the most hesitant of citizens"). In addition, he sees past injustices as a source of insight into present challenges, an approach that Chief Justice Burger and Justice Powell were reluctant to take.

2. Post-*Furman* Capital Punishment Statutes

In 1976, in response to *Furman*, the Court reviewed statutes authorizing capital punishment as crafted by four states: Georgia, Texas, Florida, and North Carolina. In the Court's opinions, the concern of racial discrimination expressed by Justices Douglas and Marshall in *Furman* is absent. Instead, the Court defined "[t]he basic concern of *Furman*" to be the arbitrary and capricious imposition of the death penalty.[47] Part of this may be due to the facts of the cases: Of the four cases, three involved discretionary sentencing schemes,[48] each involving a white defendant.[49]

While concern for racial discrimination by a minority of the justices in *Furman* was not referenced in the opinions on the resulting state statutes, it may have influenced the Court in at least three respects.

First, the Court highlighted the importance of the statutory schemes' automatic appellate review to ferret out improper "passion" and "prejudice."[50] The Court cited approvingly the review of the Supreme Court of Florida, which had vacated eight of the twenty-one death sentences it had reviewed.[51] None of the eight cases, however, involved reversals due to racial discrimination or prejudice.[52]

Second, Justice Stewart's argument in *Furman* regarding "self-help, vigilante justice, and lynch law" is quoted in the Gregg plurality opinion (also written by Justice Stewart).[53] Third, an awareness of the history of capital punishment and race in the United States may have fueled the Court's distinction between permissible and impermissible discretion. For example, in Gregg, the Court addressed the petitioner's argument that impermissible discretionary opportunities were vested in the state prosecutor, jury, and governor, as all three could choose not to pursue the death penalty.[54] The Court responded that such discretion was permissible:

> At each of these stages an actor in the criminal justice system makes a decision which may remove a defendant from consideration as a candidate for the death penalty. ... Nothing in any of our cases suggests that the decision to afford an individual defendant mercy violates the Constitution.[55]

Therefore, while statutes mandating higher penalties for blacks than for whites are no longer permissible, decisions of criminal justice actors to extend mercy disproportionately to white individuals would be permissible. This occurs despite the fact that the "end result" more black defendants executed than whites would be the same. The Court's discussion reflects a concern with racially-discriminatory application of punishment. The same result of disproportionate executions but from a different source (mercy, not racial hatred), has not been a traditional historical concern.

3. McCleskey v. Kemp

In 1986, the Supreme Court was again confronted with evidence of racial discrimination in an Eighth Amendment challenge to the death penalty. In McCleskey v. Kemp, McCleskey, a black man, shot and killed a white police officer during a robbery.[56] McCleskey introduced a "complex statistical study," the Baldus study, "that examined over 2,000 murder cases that occurred in Georgia during the 1970s."[57] The crime McCleskey was charged with occurred in 1978. McCleskey cited the Baldus study for the proposition that the race of the victim matters a great deal in determining who receives the death penalty: "The raw numbers collected by Professor Baldus indicate that defendants charged with killing white persons received the death penalty in 11% of the cases, but defendants charged with killing blacks received the death penalty in only 1% of the cases."[58] McCleskey argued, among other things, "that the Georgia capital punishment system is arbitrary and capricious in application, and therefore his sentence is excessive, because racial considerations may influence capital sentencing decision in Georgia."[59] The Court rejected this argument, noting that while "we have engaged in 'unceasing efforts' to eradicate racial prejudice from our criminal justice system[,] … [t]he discrepancy indicated by the Baldus study is a far cry from the major systemic defects identified in *Furman*.'"[60]

In support of its holding that "the Baldus study does not demonstrate a constitutionally significant risk of racial bias affecting the Georgia capital sentencing process,"[61] the majority discussed "[t]wo additional concerns" that "inform[ed]" its decision: the specter of a slippery slope and the proper roles of the judiciary and legislature.[62] The majority and dissent both used history in their discussion of these concerns in strikingly different ways.

a. The Slippery Slope

(i) The majority: concern with a slippery slope

The first concern was based on an awareness that the Eighth Amendment applies to all penalties, not simply capital punishment.[63] The majority opinion, delivered by Justice Powell and joined by Chief Justice Rehnquist and Justices White, O'Connor, and Scalia, expressed concern that McCleskey's racial discrimination claim could be leveled against other penalties, extend to other "unexplained discrepancies that correlate to membership in other minority groups, and even to gender,"[64] and could prompt studies looking at the "race or sex of other actors in the criminal justice system."[65] The majority suggested that a white defendant, in a city where minorities constituted the majority of the population, might even attempt to mimic McCleskey's claim.[66] The majority was further concerned that defendants might challenge the system based on seemingly irrelevant factors such as the attractiveness of the defendant.[67] Tying all these concerns together, the majority declared, "[T]here is no limiting principle to the type of challenge brought by McCleskey."[68]

Reference to history was made in the abstract, with an exasperated tone, to highlight the fact "that populations change in composition, and many do so in relatively short time-spans."[69] The majority noted that "the national 'majority' is composed of various minority groups, most of which can lay claim to a history of prior discrimination at the hands of the State and private individuals."[70] History, then, not only did not provide the "limiting principle" the majority strove for but also was a cause of the potential overrun of the system. History is so laden with discrimination against various groups that to address the concerns of those discriminated against at some point in history would overwhelm the system.

(ii) The dissent: history as a limiting principle

The dissenting opinion of Justice Brennan, joined by Justices Marshall, Blackmun, and Stevens, approached history and the problem of a limiting principle differently. Instead of "a [general] history of prior discrimination" that "various minority groups" could "lay claim to," Justice Brennan exhaustively documented Georgia's past criminal laws that specifically impacted blacks: "The criminal law expressly differentiated between crimes committed by and against blacks and whites, distinctions whose lineage traced back to the time of slavery."[71] He detailed laws during the colonial period, the Civil War, and up to "recent times":[72]

> For many years, Georgia operated openly and formally precisely the type of dual system the evidence shows is still effectively in place. The criminal law expressly differentiated between crimes committed by and against blacks and whites, distinctions whose lineage traced back to the time of slavery. During the colonial period, black slaves who killed whites in Georgia, regardless of whether in self-defense or in defense of another, were automatically executed. By the time of the Civil War, a dual system of crime and punishment was well established in Georgia. The state criminal code contained separate sections for 'Slaves and Free Persons of Color' and for all other persons. The code provided, for instance, for an automatic death sentence for murder committed by blacks, but declared that anyone else convicted of murder might receive life imprisonment

> if the conviction were founded solely on circumstantial testimony or simply if the jury so recommended. The code established that the rape of a free white female by a black 'shall be' punishable by death. However, rape by anyone else of a free white female was punishable by a prison term not less than 2 nor more than 20 years. The rape of blacks was punishable 'by fine and imprisonment, at the discretion of the court.' A black convicted of assaulting a free white person with intent to murder could be put to death at the discretion of the court, but the same offense committed against a black, slave or free, was classified as a 'minor' offense whose punishment lay in the discretion of the court, as long as such punishment did not 'extend to life, limb, or health.' Assault with intent to murder by a white person was punishable by a prison term of from 2 to 10 years. While sufficient provocation could reduce a charge of murder to manslaughter, the code provided that '[o]bedience and submission being the duty of a slave, much greater provocation is necessary to reduce a homicide of a white person by him to voluntary manslaughter, than is prescribed for white persons.'[73]

"This historical review of Georgia criminal law," Justice Brennan wrote, "is not intended as a bill of indictment calling the State to account for past transgressions. Citation of past practices does not justify the automatic condemnation of current ones."[74] Instead, history was invoked by Justice Brennan to supplement statistical evidence presented by McCleskey:

> [I]t would be unrealistic to ignore the influence of history in assessing the plausible implications of McCleskey's evidence. Americans share a historical experience that has resulted in individuals within the culture ubiquitously attaching a significance to race that is irrational and often outside their awareness.[75]

That is, history could be used to support the validity of the statistics:

> History and its continuing legacy thus buttress the probative force of McCleskey's statistics. Formal dual criminal laws may no longer be in effect, and intentional discrimination may no longer be prominent. Nonetheless ... subtle, less consciously held racial attitudes continue to be of concern ... The conclusions drawn from McCleskey's statistical evidence are therefore consistent with the lessons of social experience.[76]

The past is relevant to judicial proceedings because it has a "continuing legacy": "[W]e ignore [McCleskey] at our peril, for we remain imprisoned by the past as long as we deny its influence in the present."[77]

In addition, Justice Brennan offered history as the "limiting principle" to Eighth Amendment challenges that the majority sought: "[The Court] must ... ask whether the conclusion suggested by [the statistics from the Baldus study are] consonant with our understanding of history and human experience."[78] History would serve to limit those claims that can be made. Claims grounded with a historical backing, such as in racial intolerance, will be allowed; those not so grounded, such as in discrimination based on hair color, will not be allowed:

> Certainly, a factor that we would regard as morally irrelevant, such as hair color, at least theoretically could be associated with sentencing results to such an extent that we would regard as arbitrary a system in which that factor played a significant role ... [H]owever, the evaluation of evidence suggesting such a correlation must be informed not merely by statistics, but by history and experience. One could hardly contend that this Nation has on the basis of hair color inflicted upon persons deprivation comparable to that imposed on the basis of race.[79]

b. Judicial and Legislative Roles

(i) The majority: deference to the legislature

The majority also noted that "McCleskey's arguments are best presented to the legislative bodies. It is not the responsibility—or indeed even the right—of this Court to determine the appropriate punishment for particular crimes."[80]

(ii) The dissent: the roles of the legislature and court in light of history

Justice Brennan, in his dissent, presented a different narrative of the role of courts. This narrative was grounded in a historical framework that emphasized what today are considered past judicial wrongdoings:

> At the time our Constitution was framed 200 years ago this year, blacks "had for more than a century before been regarded as beings of an inferior order, and altogether unfit to associate with the white race, either in social or political relations; and so far inferior, that they had no rights which the white man was bound to respect." *Dred Scottv. Sandford*, 19 How. 393, 407, 15 L.Ed. 691 (1857). Only 130 years ago, this Court relied on these observations to deny American citizenship to blacks. *Ibid.* A mere three generations ago, this Court sanctioned racial segregation, stating that "[i]f one race be inferior to the other socially, the Constitution of the United States cannot put them upon the same

plane." *Plessy v. Ferguson*, 163 U.S. 537, 552, 16 S.Ct. 1138, 1143, 41 L.Ed. 256 (1896).[81]

The "historical legacy spanning centuries,"[82] detailed by Justice Brennan, which has judicial sanction of a racist society as its theme, stands in stark contrast with the majority's abstract and brief mention of the judiciary's need to defer to the legislature. History, as used by Justice Brennan, argues for judicial involvement in correcting those injustices which in the past it had sanctioned. History, then, is used to counter the problem abolitionists often face: actors in the criminal justice system may be reluctant to take the initiative to address concerns with the death penalty.[83]

4. Thompson v. Oklahoma

Invocation of a history of race and capital punishment in America can serve more limited, rhetorical purposes. In *Thompson v. Oklahoma*, for example, the plurality and dissent disagreed sharply as to whether standards of decency had "evolved" to the extent that imposition of the death penalty on an individual who was under sixteen years of age when he committed the offense should be declared unconstitutional as violating of the Eighth Amendment.[84] The Court held that imposition under such circumstances was unconstitutional. Both the plurality and the dissent cited the same article on the history of the death penalty with respect to juveniles in the United States.[85] The plurality and dissent, however, related the article's historical information in different ways. Justice Scalia, in his dissenting opinion, cited the article from a race-neutral historical perspective: "One scholar has documented 22 executions, between 1642 and 1899, for crimes committed under the age of 16."[86] The plurality, by contrast, presented a race-conscious portrait of history when citing the article: "It is reported that a 10-year-old black child was hanged in Louisiana in 1855 and a Cherokee Indian child of the same age was hanged in Arkansas in 1885."[87]

The *Thompson* holding was not crafted around "righting" a race-based historical injustice. Instead, the Court argued that standards of decency had evolved and that juveniles as a class of offenders have capacity for growth and a reduced level of culpability. The plurality's emphasis on the children's ethnicity may therefore have served more modest, persuasive functions: For example, the plurality may have sought to counter the assumption that the death penalty only applies infrequently to "but a few of the vicious or the moronic"[88] by suggesting that sometimes it is applied to the vulnerable for impermissible (here, racist) reasons and highlighting the importance of correcting an infrequent practice by personalizing the defendants in a sympathetic manner. In addition, the plurality may have sought to emphasize its "evolving standards of decency" argument by providing a portrait of the past (execution of young, vulnerable, minority children) that was fundamentally at odds with current public sentiment.

B. The Equal Protection Clause of the Fourteenth Amendment

Judicial use of a history of race and capital punishment in the United States also arises in cases that do not challenge the constitutionality of the death penalty per se. Fourteenth Amendment doctrine and opinions are perhaps uniquely receptive to a history of race relations in the United States.[89] Even in such opinions, however, the role of history in supporting and crafting doctrine is disputed.

1. Imposition of the Death Penalty

The Court in McCleskey confronted the argument "that the Georgia capital punishment statute violated the Equal Protection Clause of the Fourteenth Amendment."[90] In order to prevail in his claim, McCleskey had to "prove that the decisionmakers in his case acted with discriminatory purpose."[91] The majority and dissent took different views as to the evidentiary value of the historical evidence proffered by McCleskey "Georgia laws in force during and just after the Civil War"[92] in meeting this purpose requirement.

The majority, in a footnote, rejected McCleskey's reliance on such "'historical evidence' to support the claim of purposeful discrimination by the State."[93] The Court noted that historical evidence, to have "probative value," must be "reasonably contemporaneous with the challenged decision ... Although the history of racial discrimination in this country is undeniable, we cannot accept official actions taken long ago as evidence of current intent."[94]

Justice Blackmun, in a dissenting opinion joined by Justices Marshall, Stevens and, in part, Justice Brennan, took a different approach. Instead of rejecting evidence of historical discrimination, as the majority did, Justice Blackmun suggested that "history of Georgia's racially based dual system of criminal justice ... gives rise to an inference of discriminatory purpose."[95]

2. Exclusion of Jurors

The McCleskey dissent's impulse to fold a history of racial injustice into an evidentiary source available to the defendant has been incorporated into doctrine surrounding exclusion of minorities from juries.

In *Norris v. Alabama*, the Court reversed the conviction and death sentence of one of the "Scottsboro Boys."[96] The Court permitted the use of a history of exclusion of blacks from juries as the basis for a prima facie case of impermissible discrimination.[97] The defendant's evidence was more localized and recent than the Civil War-era criminal codes of *McCleskey*, consisting of witness testimony by individuals who had lived in the particular county all their lives (to ages of fifty through seventy-six) and did not recall a black serving on a jury during their lifetimes.[98]

The Court addressed the issue again in *Batson v. Kentucky*, where it also allowed historical evidence to support a defendant's claim of impermissible use of peremptory challenges, holding that "a defendant may ... make a prima facie case [in part] by proving that in the particular jurisdiction members of his race have not been summoned for jury service over an extended period of time."[99]

III. THE DIFFERENT FUNCTIONS OF AMERICAN HISTORY OF RACE RELATIONS AND CAPITAL PUNISHMENT IN COURT OPINIONS

It is common understanding that the past informs our present. What function past injustices should have in judicial opinions and sculpting doctrine, however, is unclear. The Court's divergent use and presentation of American history of race relations and capital punishment reveals the varied roles the troubling memory of our past can play in Court opinions.

A. Abolition of the Death Penalty as a Statement Against Past Injustices

At the extreme, a history of injustice and violence against blacks might call for the abolition of the death penalty, with the idea of using the legal system to make a "statement against the past."[100] Judicial opinions might provide a unique forum for apology and action[101] where the judiciary had an active role in the past injustice and is therefore uniquely situated both symbolically and practically to make the apology.[102] Justice Brennan's use of history in McCleskey to emphasize the Court's historical role in sanctioning racial segregation suggests that the Court has a unique responsibility to speak out.

Problems associated with applying a "statement" approach are that it may be overbroad, underinclusive, and it could corrupt the role of the court and the law.[103] The legal system may be considered an inappropriate forum for such a statement where the injustice was not solely (or primarily) caused by the judiciary. Condemnation of past acts can and have come from the policy-oriented legislative and executive branches.[104]

Abolition as apology by the judiciary may be unnecessary: In 2005, the Senate passed a resolution, with explicit reference to the African-American experience, "[a]pologizing to the victims of lynching and the descendants of those victims for the failure of the Senate to enact anti-lynching legislation."[105] The Senate's apology, however, was not accompanied by remedial action.[106]

B. Abolition of the Death Penalty to Prevent Past Injustices

Alternatively, a history of injustice and violence against blacks might call for the abolition of the death penalty in order to prevent recurrence, or continuation, of past injustice. Such a use of history would be a broad implementation of the methodology of "identifying] the most grievous wrongs whose recurrence we seek to prevent, and then ask[ing] whether the absence of certain rights contributed to these wrongs."[107]

This position supports the "new abolitionist" view that the death penalty should be abolished, not because "it is immoral or cruel," but because "it has not been, and cannot be, administered in a manner that is compatible with our legal system's fundamental commitments to fair and equal treatment."[108] Proponents of such a view might combine a history of injustice with the failure of attempts to remedy the system's flaws to illustrate the permanent nature of capital punishment's failures.

1. Using History of Race and Capital Punishment to Argue Against Abolition

The main drawback with the position that the death penalty should be abolished in order to prevent recurrence and continuation of past injustices is that it may be both overbroad and nearsighted.[109] Racism has pervaded, and continues to pervade, many areas of the criminal justice system. Abolition may be overbroad as there is a certain range of cases where the imposition of the death penalty may not have been influenced by race.[110]

American history of race relations and capital punishment has also been used to highlight the fact that "times have changed"; therefore, it has been argued that the sweeping remedy of abolition is not a necessary response to past injustice. Chief Justice Burger and Justice Powell took such an approach by painting a portrait of the "distant" "decades past."[111] When arguing that past injustices do not require judicial action, the justices presented the past injustice in a form clearly distinct from the present day—by referring to "official policy" or state-sponsored segregation. Through this formulation, Chief Justice Burger and Justice Powell were able to assert that times have changed because those policies were no longer in existence, thus avoiding the argument that the past may have changed only to a degree.

a. Responding to the "Times Have Changed" Argument

A concern with the "times have changed" argument may explain why those *Furman* justices who supported abolition of the death penalty—Justices Brennan, Douglas, and Marshall—did not rely exclusively (or at all) on American history of race relations and capital punishment.[112]

A different presentation of history, however, can be used to argue that times have not changed. Justice Marshall and Douglas, for example, used statistics as a vehicle to compare the past and the present: Since 1930, 405 of 455 individuals executed for rape have been black.[113] In the case before them, two defendants sentenced to death for rape were black. Use of history through statistics, therefore, helped bridge the gap between the past and present.

In addition, the "times have changed" view does not necessarily render a history of past injustices irrelevant. Justice Brennan's reference to "experience" emphasizes the timelessness of lessons from the past. Furthermore, inherent in the idea that "times have changed" is the belief that times *can* change. One can acknowledge past injustice and believe that progress has been made, but still believe that some level of racial discrimination persists that must be addressed. Therefore, while past injustice may not necessitate abolition of capital punishment, it may support reform of lower levels of trial mechanics and procedure.[114]

b. Using "Times Have Changed" to Support Abolition

While the differences between the past and the present highlighted by Chief Justice Burger and Justice Powell were meant to suggest the irrelevance of that history in deciding the constitutionality of the death penalty, a different formulation of the past, with the similar design of stressing the differences between past and present times, can be used in support of abolition.

In *Thompson*, for example, by invoking two images—"a 10-year-old black child was hanged in Louisiana in 1855 and a Cherokee Indian child of the same age was hanged in Arkansas in 1885"[115]—the plurality provided a personalized, disturbing portrait of the past that was at odds with current public sentiment; thus dramatically illustrating its argument that standards of decency had evolved to the point where execution of minors was no longer permissible.[116]

2. The Inverse: The Death Penalty as Necessary to Prevent Past Injustices

The opposite view would argue that the death penalty must be retained to prevent recurrence of past injustices. This view finds life in Justice Stewart's Furman opinion, where Justice Stewart connects capital punishment with retribution, and suggests that were retribution, "part of the nature of man," not "channeled" through the criminal justice system, "people [might] begin to believe that organized society is unwilling or unable to impose upon criminal offenders the punishment they 'deserve,' [and as a result] there are sown the seeds of anarchy—of self-help, vigilante justice, and lynch law."[117]

C. Preventing Past Injustices by Crafting Procedural Safeguards

If abolition of the death penalty in response to past violence against minorities is too broad a stroke, the Court may still use lessons from past injustice to inform narrowly-tailored reform. The past then would be used to support more flexible "tinkering" instead of broad abolitionist mandates. History would be used to the extent it reveals or addresses defects in the current criminal justice system, both on a general level and on a case-by-case basis. To some extent, the Court appears to be using history in this manner.

1. General Lessons From History

A race-conscious historical appraisal of capital punishment in the United States may reveal deficiencies in the criminal justice system and argue for general safeguards. For example, a history of disproportionate application of the death penalty on the basis of race may call attention to a general concern with discretionless juries and argue for appellate review to ferret out continued discrimination—based on both racial and nonracial factors. History may also inform the general approach of the judiciary in evaluating performance. In Gregg, the American past of racial hatred supported judicial scrutiny of unequal application of the death penalty to blacks, but was silent to the act of pardoning unequally.[118]

2. "Historical Evidence"

a. Supplementing hard-to-prove and -explain claims

American history of race relations and capital punishment may additionally find case-specific relevance. It may become a form of admissible evidence. That is, history can be incorporated into the "critical subconstitutional rules"[119] and "fill in the gaps" of otherwise hard-to-prove or -explain claims.

(i) Narrow, specific accounts of history

Historical evidence may be used to supplement present intuitions. For example, persistent, purposeful discrimination is hard to prove.[120] Not surprisingly, then, the Court has allowed some defendants with claims arising under the Equal Protection Clause of the Fourteenth Amendment to use "historical evidence" to support otherwise hard-to-prove claims. For example, in peremptory challenge cases, the Court permitted defendants to use historical evidence to support prima facie showings of impermissible exclusion of blacks from juries.[121]

The Court has restricted the form of such historical support: Historical evidence in Fourteenth Amendment claims generally must have clear ties to the present day and the particular locality.[122] In Norris, for example, historical evidence presented through community members who testified to events during their lifetimes was permissible.[123]

(ii) General historical awareness

History may serve a more general purpose by providing insight into current realities and bridging the human gap in self-awareness. Psychologists have documented a disconnect between the "perceived norm" of racial equality and the reality of continued racism.[124] History could play a role in explaining what otherwise might seem irrational or insignificant, such as the Baldus study. As Justice Brennan observed, "Americans share a historical experience that has resulted in individuals within the culture ubiquitously attaching a significance to race that is irrational and often outside their awareness."[125] History, then, might be a vehicle to admit into law, courts, and individuals[126] "knowledge about hidden biases and subtle racism now studied most intensively by contemporary social scientists,"[127] through illustrating the "historical continuity"[128] of racial hostility.

Instead of mere "deficiencies" (the majority's characterization of the Baldus study's findings), Justice Brennan found the Baldus study to reveal broader systemic deficiencies by invoking a more amorphous history to supplement evidence of present reality, noting: "Close analysis of the Baldus study … in light of both statistics, principles and human experience, reveals that the risk that race influenced McCleskey's sentence is intolerable by any imaginable standard."[129] General history then served to complement and supplement statistical evidence that, standing alone, did not seem complete or indicative of a large-scale problem.

b. Limitation on Claims

American history of race relations and capital punishment may also enter a case as part of an evidentiary burden on the defendant to show the validity of the claim. In McCleskey, for example, Justice Brennan suggested that only those factors that were "morally relevant" would be considered and that general "history and experience" would assist in making that determination: "One could hardly contend that this Nation has on the basis of hair color inflicted upon persons deprivation comparable to that imposed on the basis of race."[130]

D. Role of Court as Educator and Mobilizer

The justices' varied use of history reflects the reality that opinions are written for a variety of audiences and for a variety of purposes. At the most basic level, opinions provide precedent to be followed by the legal profession. They also function, however, "to convince the judge, the parties, and the public that cases are rightly decided."[131] One underlying motivation for this is to buttress the authority[132] and public valuation of the courts and their work.[133] Opinions are guides for further action by courts, legislatures, the executive, and the public.[134] As a form of dialogue, opinions have sparked social movements and prompted legislative reform.[135] Embedding a history of race relations and capital punishment into an opinion may help meet some of these goals.

1. Improving Public Perception of the Courts and Their Work

It has long been observed that the public is dissatisfied with the administration of justice in America.[136] One reason that has been suggested is that the public often perceives the judiciary as "out of touch" with "the affairs of men"[137] and is dissatisfied with the "mechanical operation of legal rules."[138] The judiciary's awareness of, and concern with, historical injustice might suggest to the public that the law is not stagnant, not wedded to mechanical rules, but instead responds to and learns from the past in pursuit of a better system.

2. Opinions as a Guide for Future Action

a. Influencing Debate in the Public Arena

It has been suggested that Supreme Court Justices are "particularly effective as communicators; because of their prestige and visibility, they influence the moral attitudes of others more effectively than nearly anybody else."[139] Supreme Court decisions on the death penalty get particular attention from the media. The New York Times, for example, published excerpts of the Furman the day after it was decided.[140] Some Court opinions are narrowly limited to the particular facts of the case and are not likely to spark policy debate.[141] Mention of a history of injustice in an opinion, however, provides broad and fertile substance for debate by, for example, informing the public, prompting outrage, and redefining the debate.

(i) Informing the public

Many of the goals and values of teaching race relations history in the classroom are equally relevant to informing public debate.[142] Inclusion of race relations history in schools is considered beneficial for a number of reasons, including giving minority students pride[143] and an opportunity "to see themselves in history,"[144] providing a more comprehensive and accurate view of history, aiding students in "understand[ing] the role of the past in shaping current events,"[145] "sensitiz[ing] students to the lives and experiences of others,"[146] and training future social reformers.[147]

A race-conscious historical account in a judicial opinion might similarly reflect a desire to introduce a "usable past,"[148] providing the public with the background and tools necessary to understand current systems and practices and contribute effectively to policy debate.[149] Justice Marshall in particular included history in his opinions with the explicit goal of informing the public.[150] In his dissent in Gregg, he notes his belief that "the American people are largely unaware of the information critical to a judgment on the morality of the death penalty."[151] In Furman, he included a history of racially-disparate imposition of the death penalty because such evidence "would serve to convince even the most hesitant of citizens to condemn death as a sanction."[152]

(ii) Promoting involvement

Individuals often need a strong chain of causation and a blameworthy "bad actor" in narratives of injustice before they will react.[153] This need for a "bad actor" may explain why "the race-related criminal procedure cases of the interwar period were attractive candidates for Supreme Court intervention."[154] These cases provided a distinct "bad actor": Southern state courts that "operated under a different paradigm of legal justice from that of the High Court."[155] Scholars have suggested that one reason evidence of racial injustice has been largely immune from criticism is that popular conceptions of racism understand racism to be "intentional, conscious, deliberate, hate-inflected, or color-oriented prejudice."[156] The law similarly often requires a showing that discrimination is "intentional" before offering a remedy.[157]

The subtle but pervasive racial discrimination that persists in the American criminal justice system today, however, often does not have a prototypical, blameworthy "bad actor." Current procedures surrounding capital trials may not contain *intentional* racism. Instead, they may retain the vestiges of a racist nation: "The bias uncovered by the Baldus study [in *McCleskey*, for example,] was covert in nature and arose from the abuse of discretion, rather than from the application of an explicit racial classification."[158] Without a bad actor to assign the blame and responsibility, the McCleskey Court was reluctant to give the defendant relief.

History, with its wide array of "bad actor" lynch mobs, outspoken prosecutors,[159] and racist laws, might supply this motivating force.[160] The current criminal justice system might not seem an evil or discriminatory machine, but the dual criminal law statutes of Georgia that distinguished between crimes committed by blacks and those committed by whites provokes outrage.[161] Further, using the past as the bad actor has the advantage of mitigating direct criticism of current individuals, systems, and governments.[162] This may explain why Justice Brennan spent as much time detailing the flaws in the previous Georgia criminal justice system as he did the flaws in the current system at issue.[163]

History may be presented briefly through anecdotes and references to inject moral outrage into an argument. Justice Marshall, for example, dissenting from a denial of a writ of certiorari, argued that the defendant was entitled to an evidentiary hearing where, among other things, "a juror handed the bailiff a napkin with a drawing of a man on a gallows above the inscription 'Hang the Niggers.'"[164] Justice Marshall noted that the case involved "a vulgar incident of lynch-mob racism reminiscent of Reconstruction days."[165] In *Thompson*, the image of the hanging of two minority children may have served a similar purpose.[166]

In addition, intertwined with the goal of improving public perception of the criminal justice system is an interest in increasing public interest and involvement in the work of the judiciary. Embedding a history of race and capital punishment into a legal opinion might promote public involvement in the issue, as it would illustrate that the law is responsive and active. Michael Klarman, for example, has argued that "[o]ne of the most formidable challenges" to the social movement for civil rights in the interwar South "was simply convincing blacks that the status quo of racial subordination and oppression was not natural and inevitable, but rather contingent and malleable."[167]

(iii) Redefining the debate

Inclusion of history may be able to "shape" or focus public debate by redefining it. Scholars have suggested that public backlash against Furman was unsurprising, as "[p]otent symbols are relinquished only with some misgivings."[168] Franklin E. Zimring argues that the death penalty has undergone a "symbolic transformation" whereby execution is now considered "a victim-service program."[169] Inclusion of history might supply a replacement symbolic association and thereby transform what would otherwise be a simple "backlash" based on a narrow conception of a "zero-sum" game between a victim's relatives and the defendant to a more comprehensive debate placed in the context of racially-motivated vengeance, slavery, and segregation.[170]

b. Encouraging Judicial Action

In addition, referencing past bad acts may be an attempt to combat omission bias.[171] For example, Justice Brennan's dissent in McCleskey focused on past actions of the Court: "[T]his Court *den[ied]* American citizenship to blacks ... [and] *sanctioned* racial segregation."[172] Perhaps referencing historical acts was an attempt to "attribute," to some extent, "causal responsibility" to the judiciary and supply a motivating force for change.[173]

c. Debate in the Legislative Sphere

Judicial opinions serve to frame the scope of future discussion and debate not only in the public and judicial spheres, but also in the legislative sphere. The Court's ruling in McCleskey, for example, inspired the introduction of the Racial Justice Act in Congress.[174]

The presence or absence in Court opinions of a history of injustice can influence the parameters of legislative response. For example, the bases for striking down the death sentences in *Furman* were important, as states quickly responded by crafting new capital punishment statutes. The opinions of Justices White and Stewart, and the reasoning underlying them, took center stage, as both ruled to vacate the sentences but left open the possibility of permissible imposition of the death penalty.

By not voicing concerns with a troubling history of race and capital punishment, Justices White and Stewart, through their *Furman* opinions, narrowed the issues that states would have to confront in developing constitutional sentencing schemes. If it is true, as some have argued, that Justices Stewart and White's opinions were "an audacious gamble," made in the hopes that legislatures would "give up" and abandon attempts to rewrite death penalty statutes,[175] it seems odd that they would not include in their opinions an awareness of the racially-skewed history of capital punishment in the United States, as such concerns would further complicate state response.[176]

IV. CONCLUSIONS

Courts routinely take on, to a variety of degrees, the role of the historian.[177] Reliance on past decisions and investigation into the framers' intent, for example, all involve historical review. Memory of racial injustice and capital punishment pervades Supreme Court opinions and doctrine. The function of such national memory in opinions, however, is inconsistent and complex. Memory of past injustices can be used explicitly to define or guide doctrine, or it can be used more generally as an advocacy device.

American law is considered uniquely American.[178] It is not surprising, then, that American history of race relations and capital punishment should find itself shaping legal doctrine. Invocation of such a history may support both sides of the debate on the constitutionality of the death penalty. History can be used to support the argument that times have changed, and no remedial judicial action is needed or, conversely, that what was once permissible no longer should be. Such a history may be embedded into criminal procedure: it can provide general lessons of problematic areas in the criminal justice system (e.g., discretionless juries) or supplement evidence of otherwise subtle social realities (e.g., continuing racial discrimination in prosecutorial use of peremptory challenges).

But judicial opinions do not merely *dictate* the law—they are shaped by underlying motivations of persuasion, credibility, and encouraging future action. Presentation of American history of race and capital punishment may be intended to empower the reader with the information necessary to understand his or her society, encourage debate by provoking outrage, and shape debate by injecting content and defining the contours of the issue.

Where such a history is absent may also be telling: desire to abolish the death penalty outright may argue against relying on such a history for more than ancillary support, as use of such history is easily criticized as improper,[179] overbroad, overly-narrow, or outdated.

No single static form of memory takes hold in Court opinions. The presentation of a history of racial injustice in capital punishment is rich and varied based on its doctrinal or advocacy function: focus may be on past state laws, statistics, anecdotes, or the testimony of individuals as to local county practices during their lifetimes. Whatever form it takes, the appearance of such history in opinions forces the past to be remembered and, as a result, the past becomes a puzzle, a tool, a statement, that both author and reader must grapple with, expressly or not, consciously or not.

Legal Topics:

For related research and practice materials, see the following legal topics:
Criminal Law & Procedure Sentencing Appeals Capital Punishment Criminal Law & Procedure Sentencing Capital Punishment Cruel & Unusual Punishment Governments Courts Judges

NOTES:

1. *See generally* Stuart Banner, "Traces of Slavery: Race and the Death Penalty in Historical Perspective," in CHARLES J. OGLETREE, JR. & AUSTIN SARAT, FROM LYNCH MOBS TO THE KILLING STATE: RACE AND THE DEATH PENALTY IN AMERICA 96 (2006).
2. WILLIAM S. MCFEELY, PROXIMITY TO DEATH 31 (2000).
3. David B. Wilkins, *Straightjacketing Professionalism: A Comment on Russell*, 95 MICH. L. REV. 795, 808 (1997) ("Three hundred years of demonizing black male sexuality has left its mark on the consciousness of many whites, particularly in cases involving white women.").
4. CHARLES A. MILLER, THE SUPREME COURT AND THE USES OF HISTORY 20 (1969).
5. *Furman v. Georgia*, 408 U.S. 238, 375–76 (1972) (Burger, C.J., dissenting).
6. In 1965, the Supreme Court Review published Alfred H. *Kelly's Clio and the Court: An Illicit Love Affair*, a scathing attack on the Supreme Court's use of history. 1965 SUP. CT. REV. 119. Kelly distinguished two judicial uses of history: "judicial fiat" and "authoritative revelation." Id. at 122. Kelly focused on constitutional history being used by the Court for the purpose of constitutional continuity (used to ascertain the "aboriginal meaning of the constitution"). Id. at 131, 125. The Court's use of history in this paper is not so limited. Instead, inclusion of a race-conscious perspective of capital punishment in the United States resembles what Miller describes as a "use of continuing or 'ongoing' history [that] allows the Constitution to move with the prevailing temper of the country and may therefore be considered forward-looking." *See* MILLER, supra note 4, at 27("[Justice] Taney's theory of constitutional construction [in *Dred Scott*] was unequivocally historical, ongoing history played no role in his conception of how to use the past. He relied only on history as intent ... The example of *Dred Scott* apparently confirms that history as intent is a restraining force in constitutional law and that ongoing history is the champion of progress."); *Id.* at 25 (contrasting the use of "ongoing" history with "history concerned with the formation and ratification of the Constitution [that] serves to restrain the Court in its decisions [like constitutional text and precedent]").
7. *Furman*, 408 U.S. at 383 (Burger, C.J., dissenting) (quoting Trop v. Dulles, 356 U.S. 86, 101 (1958) (Warren, C.J., plurality opinion)).
8. *Id.* at 383–84. Punishments "commonplace at the time of the adoption of the Constitution," such as branding and cutting off ears, would today be found "excessively cruel because we

could say with complete assurance that contemporary society universally rejects such bizarre penalties." See Joseph L. Hoffmann, *The "Cruel and Unusual Punishment" Clause: A Limit on the Power to Punish or Constitutional Rhetoric?* in DAVID J. BODENHAMER & JAMES W. ELY, JR., EDS., THE BILL OF RIGHTS IN MODERN AMERICAN AFTER 200 YEARS 139, 139–154 (1993). Certain practices such as branding, pillorying, and ear-cropping have fallen out of use and law even without Eighth Amendment invocation.

9. *See, e.g., Furman*, 408 U.S. at 376–78 (Burger, C.J., dissenting). The selection, presentation, and interpretation of that history, however, vary. Some opinions find that history reveals trends or movements toward abolition, others deduce continued acceptance. A history of infrequent imposition is interpreted as either impermissible arbitrariness or laudable thoughtfulness. *See, e.g., Id.* at 412–13 (Blackmun, J., dissenting); *Id.* at 437, 441 (Powell, J., dissenting). For example, in 1971, the Court upheld sentencing schemes which provided juries with absolute discretion. McGautha v. California, 402 U.S. 183 (1971). To explain its holding, the majority relied primarily on legal history, reviewing "the salient features of the history of capital punishment for homicides under the common law in England, and subsequent statutory developments in this country," including the laws of Alfred, Exodus, and the thirteenth century Statute of Gloucester. id. at 197–201. Review of contemporary state statutes providing juries with absolute discretion revealed that legislatures were motivated to discourage jury nullification that had occurred under previous regimes where jury discretion had been limited. Id. at 199. The majority concluded that the "lesson taught by the history" was that there was no principled way to limit discretion. Id. at 204. Dissenting, Justice Douglas presented a different history—that of barbaric procedures—for a different purpose; namely, for the lesson that criminal procedure, and due process, ought to be recognized as an ever-changing and -expanding "stream." Furman, 408 U.S. at 241 (Douglas, J., dissenting).
10. *Furman*, 408 U.S. at 239 (plurality opinion).
11. Motion for Leave to File Brief as Amici Curiae and Brief Amici Curiae of the National Association for the Advancement of Colored People, National Urban League, Southern Christian Leadership Conference, Mexican-American Legal Defense and Educational Fund, and the National Council of Negro Women 2-M (filed August 31, 1971) [hereinafter "NAACP Brief1"]. See also NAACP Hails Ban On Death Penalty, 79 THE CRISIS 278 (1972) (quoting statement of Nathaniel R. Jones, general counsel of the NAACP: "The history of the administration of capital punishment clearly illustrates that it was applied in a way that discriminated against black Americans"). *See infra* text accompanying note 113.
12. NAACP Brief, supra note 11, at la. For example, Appendix A lists the following for Alabama:

Whites: An act of 1802 provided that rape shall be punishable by death. In 1841, the punishment for rape was changed to life imprisonment.

Slaves, free negroes, and mulattoes: An act of 1814 provided that a slave convicted of an attempt to rape a white woman shall suffer death. The 1841 Penal Code of Slaves and Free

Negroes provided that a slave, free negro or mulatto convicted of the crime of rape upon, or an attempt to rape upon, a white woman shall suffer death. (internal citations omitted).

13. Various questions are considered by each opinion, including what constitutes "cruel and unusual," the scope of judicial review, what justifications for punishment are acceptable, how to determine contemporary social standards, and the excessiveness of death as punishment for rape. This paper, however, focuses primarily on those sections that make a race-conscious reference to the past.
14. *Furman*, 408 U.S. at 305–06 (Brennan, J., concurring).
15. Id. at 294 n.48 (Justice Brennan criticized the argument that Furman's crime was "extreme" by detailing Furman's confession—accepted by the Georgia Supreme Court—that the murder was unintentional. He noted, "About Furman himself, the jury knew only that he was black and that, according to his statement at trial, he was 26 years old and worked at 'Superior Upholstery.' It took the jury one hour and 35 minutes to return a verdict of guilty and a sentence of death.") (internal citations omitted). In addition, Brennan referenced Justice Marshall's survey of English and American history of capital punishment when discussing his third principle, contemporary societal norms, *Id.* at 295, but did not discuss race in particular and focused instead on history as revealing a gradual restriction of permissible methods, *Id.* at 296–97, and a decrease in death sentences. *Id.* at 297–98.
16. *Id.* at 310–14 (White, J., concurring).
17. *Id.* at 313 (White, J., concurring). Justice Stewart echoed these sentiments. While Justice Stewart acknowledged the possibility of racial discrimination in imposition of the death penalty, he found that "racial discrimination has not been proved, and I put it to one side." *Id.* at 310 (Stewart, J., concurring) (citing the opinions of Justices Douglas and Marshall).
18. *Id.* at 389 n.12 (Burger, C.J., dissenting).
19. *Id.*
20. *Id.* at 450 (Powell, J., dissenting).
21. *Id.* at 242 (Douglas, J., concurring).
22. *Id.* at 253–55.
23. *Id.* at 255.
24. *Id.* at 251. Lawes' book did include a race-conscious history, albeit in a different form: he noted that the majority of cases of first and second degree murder were committed by foreigners, and argued that "the typical murderer of any given period comes from that race which is making a place for itself in a new environment." LEWIS E. LAWES, LIFE AND DEATH IN SING SING 148–49 (1929) (noting that, "MI-0m 1850 to 1870 the foreign-born Irish led in the number of commitments for murder ... [f]rom 1890 to 1927 those of Italian stock ... and now the Negro, who is migrating from the South"). Lawes' opposition to the death penalty, however, was not premised on racial concerns.
25. *Furman*, 408 U.S. at 252–53 (Douglas, J., concurring).
26. *Id.* at 250–51.
27. *Id.* at 250 n.15.

28. *Id.* at 255.
29. Guy B. Johnson, The Negro and Crime, 217 ANNALS OF THE AM. ACAD. OF POL. AND SOC. SCI. 93, 94 (1941).
30. *Furman*, 408 U.S. at 333–41 (Marshall, J., concurring). He surveys the basis of capital punishment in tribal private vengeance, the reign of Henry II, expansion of death-eligible offenses in England, transferral of capital punishment to the American colonies, eighteenth century abolitionist movements in Pennsylvania, state debates, the "rising tide of sentiment against capital punishment," Id. at 337, in the nineteenth century, state abolition, the effect of the Civil War on abolitionist sentiment, and World War I's effect on capital punishment, before concluding that "capital punishment was carried from Europe to America but, once here, was tempered considerably." *Id.* at 341.
31. *Id.* at 363–64.
32. *Id.* at 364 (illustrating racial discrimination; for example, of the 455 people executed for rape, 405 were black).
33. *Id.* at 365–66 (including gender, income, education, and privilege).
34. *Id.* at 255 (Douglas, J., concurring).
35. *Id.* at 364 n.152 (Marshall, J., concurring).
36. Franklin H. Williams, *The Death Penalty and the Negro*, 67 THE CRISIS 501 (1960).
37. *Id.* at 503–04 (describing the "lynch spirit" that "so permeated the atmosphere" surrounding one case).
38. Id. at 502–03 ("It is no coincidence that throughout the South many white persons see humor in the anecdote which to most Negroes is too true and tragic for laughter. You can often hear it said that if a Negro kills a white man, it is murder. If a white man kills a Negro, it is unfortunate. But, if a white man kills a white man it is probably in self-defense, unless the fight was over a woman, in which case death was caused by apoplexy.").
39. *Furman*, 408 U.S. at 308 (Stewart, J., concurring).
40. *Id.*
41. *Id.* Justice Stewart is not alone in suggesting a connection between legal executions and the decline of lynchings. See, e.g., Michael J. Klarman, The Racial Origins of Modern Criminal Procedure, 99 MICH. L. REV. 48, 55–56 (2000) ("[T]he decline in lynchings probably also was dependent on their being replaced by quick trials that reliably produced guilty verdicts, death sentences, and rapid executions. Arkansas actually enacted a law designed to prevent lynchings by providing for a special term of court in case of rape or other crimes likely to arouse the passions of the people; trial was to take place within ten days of the alleged crime.").
42. NAACP Brief, *supra* note 11 at 11–12.
43. *Id.* at 13 (quoting HUGH GRAHAM & TED GURR, VIOLENCE IN AMERICA—HISTORICAL AND COMPARATIVE PERSPECTIVES—A STAFF REPORT TO THE NATIONAL COMMISSION ON THE CAUSES AND PREVENTION OF VIOLENCE, Vol. 1, p. 105 (1969)). *See also* NAACP Brief, supra note 11 at 14 ("[H]

istorically, lynching and vigilantism ... performed the same function of domination and subjection on nonwhites by a white majority.").

44. Maura Dolan, *Executions*, Los ANGELES TIMES, Aug. 25, 1985 at 1, 20–21.
45. *See, e.g., Andrews v. Shulsen*, 485 U.S. 919, 922 (1988) (Marshall, J., dissenting from denial of petition of writ of certiorari) (noting that the case involved "a vulgar incident of lynch-mob racism reminiscent of Reconstruction days"). However, there are also seemingly race-neutral references to vigilante justice, although it is still difficult to disentangle connections with race. See Coleman v. Balkcom, 451 U.S 949, 961 (1981) (Rehnquist, J., dissenting from denial of petition for writ of certiorari) ("San Francisco experienced vigilante justice during the Gold Rush in the middle part of the last century; the mining towns of Montana experienced it a short time later; and it is still with us as a result of the series of unsolved slayings of Negro children in Atlanta.").
46. See Coleman, 451 U.S. at 960 (Rehnquist, J., dissenting from denial of petition for writ of certiorari) (citing Stewart's comments on "self-help, vigilante justice, and lynch law" in support of the proposition that "delay in the enforcement of capital punishment frustrates the purpose of retribution").
47. Gregg v. Georgia, 428 U.S. 153, 206 (1976) (plurality opinion).
48. Id. at 162–68; Jurek v. Texas, 428 U.S. 262, 269–74 (1976); Proffitt v. Florida, 428 U.S. 242, 247 -53 (1976). The fourth case addressed by the Court, Woodson v. North Carolina, involved a mandatory sentencing scheme which was struck down by the Court. 428 U.S. 280 (1976). James Tyrone Woodson and Luby Waxton, the petitioners, were both black. Death-Row Interviews: Five Under Sentence to Die Speak Out, U.S. NEWS & WORLD REPORT, July 12, 1976 at 51.
49. Death-Row Interviews, supra note 48, at 51.
50. Gregg, 428 U.S. at 204. See also Proffitt, 428 U.S. at 250–51.
51. Proffitt, 428 U.S. at 253.
52. Instead, they involved procedural concerns or instances where the trial judge declined to follow a jury's recommendation of mercy. Lamadline v. State, 303 So. 2d 17 (1974) (holding that a defendant must knowingly and intelligently waive the right to a sentencing jury); Messer v. State, 330 So. 2d 137 (1976) (holding that evidence was improperly excluded); Taylor v. State, 294 So. 2d 648 (1974); Tedder v. State, 322 So. 2d 908 (1975); Slater v. State, 316 So. 2d 539 (1975); Thompson v. State, 328 So. 2d 1 (1976). In the eighth case, Halliwell v. State, 323 So. 2d 557 (1975), the Supreme Court of Florida reweighed the mitigating and aggravating factors and overturned a death sentence.
53. Gregg, 428 U.S. at 183 (quoting Furman, 408 U.S. at 308 (Stewart, J., concurring)).
54. *Id.* at 199.
55. *Id.*
56. 481 U.S. 279 (1986).
57. *Id.* at 282, 286.
58. *Id.* at 286.

59. *Id.* at 308.
60. *Id.* at 309, 313 (quoting Pulley v. Harris, 463 U.S. 37, 54 (1984)).
61. *Id.* at 313.
62. *Id.* at 314.
63. Id.
64. Id. at 316–17.
65. Id. at 317.
66. Id. at 316n.39.
67. Id. at 318.
68. Id. at 318.
69. Id. at 316 n.39.
70. Id.
71. Id. at 329 (Brennan, J., dissenting).
72. Id. at 328–30.
73. Id. at 328–30 (internal citations omitted).
74. Id. at 332.
75. Id.
76. Id. at 334 (internal quotation marks and citations omitted).
77. Id.
78. Id. at 328.
79. Id. at 341 (internal citation omitted).
80. Id. at 319.
81. Id. at 343–44 (Brennan, J., dissenting).
82. Id. at 344.
83. See, e.g., MICHAEL MELTSNER, CRUEL AND UNUSUAL: THE SUPREME COURT AND CAPITAL PUNISHMENT 60 (1973) ("Legislators did not feel responsible for the death penalty because the law rarely required it; selection of the condemned was left to juries and judges. Prosecuting attorneys told themselves that they only presented the state's case in the courts. Jurors often believed that trial judges would correct matters if they acted improperly. The trial judge, on the other hand, felt that the life-death decision was in the hands of the jury. If he did make an error in handling the case, surely the appellate courts would set it right. Courts of review conventionally complained that they had limited power and capacity to upset the verdict of a jury or the rulings of a judge who had observed the trial testimony. At any rate, executive clemency was available. But governors pointed to the jury verdict, the trial judge who could have set it aside, and the appellate courts that had declined to interfere; jurors and judges had agreed on a death sentence, and the power to commute was narrow."). Cf. Jon Hanson & Kathleen Hanson, The Blame Frame: Justifying (Racial) Injustice in America, 41 HARV. C.R.-C.L. L. REV. 413, 423 (2006) ("As part of a group, a team, or a shared project, we can maintain our favorable self-image by imagining ourselves to be just one component in a bigger situation over which we have no control.").

84. 487 U.S. 815 (1988).
85. See Id. at 828 n.27 (plurality opinion); 864 (Scalia, J., dissenting) (both citing Victor L. Streib, Death Penalty for Children: The American Experience with Capital Punishment for Crimes Committed While under Age Eighteen, 36 OKLA. L. REV. 613 (1983)).
86. Id. at 864 (Scalia, J., dissenting).
87. Id. at 828 n.27 (plurality opinion). This information was included in two amicus briefs. See Brief for National Legal Aid and Defender Ass'n et al. as Amici Curiae in Supporting Petitioner at 3-4, Thompson v. Oklahoma, 487 U.S. 815 (1987) (No. 86-6169), 1987 WL 881441 ("The youngest children known to have been executed in the United States were two ten-year-olds: A Black child, whose name has been lost to history and who was hanged in Louisiana in 1855, and James Arcene, a Cherokee Indian child hanged in Arkansas in 1885."(citing Streib)); Brief for the Child Welfare League of America et al. as Amici Curiae in Support of Petitioner at 10 n.2, Thompson, 487 U.S. 815 (No. 86-6169), 1987 WL 864198).
88. MELTSNER, supra note 83, at 37 ("[T]he unmasking and delegitimizing of American racism undermined the public's sense … of the culpability of criminals.").
89. See, e.g., Batson v. Kentucky, 476 U.S. 79, 85 (1986) (observing that "the central concern" of the Fourteenth Amendment "was to put an end to governmental discrimination on account of race"). In McCleskey, Justice Blackmun cited the legislative history of the Fourteenth Amendment as a reminder "that discriminatory enforcement of States' criminal laws was a matter of great concern for the drafters." 481 U.S. at 346 (Blackmun, J., dissenting). For example, he quoted Brev. Maj. Gen. Wager Swayne as having testified in 1866 that "I have not known, after six months' residence at the capital of the State, a single instance of a white man being convicted and hung or sent to the penitentiary for crime against a negro, while many cases of crime warranting such punishment have been reported to me." Id. at 347 n.2.
90. 481 U.S. at 291.
91. Id. at 292.
92. Id. at 298 n.20.
93. Id.
94. Id.
95. Id. at 359 (Blackmun, J., dissenting).
96. Norris v. Alabama, 294 U.S. 587 (1935).
97. Id. at 598–99.
98. Id. at 591.
99. Batson, 476 U.S. at 94. See also Swain v. Alabama, 380 U.S. 202, 223—24 (1965) ("We have decided that it is permissible to insulate from inquiry the removal of Negroes from a particular jury on the assumption that the prosecutor is acting on acceptable considerations related to the case he is trying, the particular defendant involved and the particular crime charged. But when the prosecutor in a county, in case after case, whatever the circumstances, whatever the crime and whoever the defendant or the victim may be, is responsible for the

removal of Negroes who have been selected as qualified jurors by the jury commissioners and who have survived challenges for cause, with the result that no Negroes ever serve on petit juries, the Fourteenth Amendment claim takes on added significance. ... Such proof might support a reasonable inference that Negroes are excluded from juries for reasons wholly unrelated to the outcome of the particular case on trial and that the peremptory system is being used to deny the Negro the same right and opportunity to participate in the administration of justice enjoyed by the white population.") (ultimately finding that "the record in this case is not sufficient to demonstrate that the rule has been violated by the peremptory system as it operates in Talladega County.").

100. "Abolition as statement" differs from Justice Brennan's observation that "[c]itation of past practices does not justify the automatic condemnation of current ones" in that with "abolition as statement," citation of past practices is used as an automatic condemnation of past practices and does not speak directly to current practices. McCleskey, 481 U.S. at 332 (Brennan, J., dissenting). The "statement" approach combines at least three themes commonly associated with formal "apologies" for past actions. First, by including action (abolition) with the statement, it is an acknowledgment that in some instances a mere verbal apology for the past is insufficient. Melissa Nobles, Official Apologies and Their Effects on Political Membership in Democracies 5 (2003), http://web.mit.edu/polisci/research/mobles/official_apologies_in_democracies.pdf ("African-American leadership and publics have responded tepidly to the idea of apology alone [for slavery]. However, support for apology increases once it is coupled with reparations for slavery, Jim Crow segregation, and race riots."). See also Roy L. Brooks, The New Patriotism and Apology for Slavery, in TAKING WRONGS SERIOUSLY: APOLOGIES AND RECONCILIATION 213, 228 (Elazar Barkan & Alexander Karn eds., 2006) (Moral apology requires that "the perpetrator government ... provide meaningful reparations. Apology standing alone does not demonstrate sufficient remorse. As an example, many Native Hawaiians correctly rejected President Clinton's expression of apology made on behalf of the federal government for the United States' overthrow of the Hawaiian sovereign nation in the late nineteenth century. President Clinton's apology ... was empty; it was not backed up with anything tangible."). Second, by documenting history as its base, it reflects the notion that "an apology ratifies certain reinterpretation(s) of history." Nobles, supra. at 11. See also Rebecca Tsosie, The BIA's Apology to Native Americans: An Essay on Collective Memory and Collective Conscience, in TAKING WRONGS SERIOUSLY: APOLOGIES AND RECONCILIATION, supra, at 185, 191 -93 (noting that the apology of the Bureau of Indian Affairs to the Indian nation and people on September 8, 2000 was "intended to issue a corrective history to evaluate past conduct"). Third, it reflects the idea that demand for and offering of an apology may implicate a desire for "concrete political [and legal] alterations." Nobles, supra, at 8. See also Tsosie, supra, at 195 (noting that BIA apology was "intended to inspire a policy template to deal with legal and political redress for past wrongs. ...

101. See infra text accompanying note 103.

102. Cf Tsosie, supra note 100, at 185–186 (describing Assistant Secretary for Indian Affairs Kevin Gover's "formal apology to Indian people for the historical conduct of this agency."); Id. at 189 ("[T]he acknowledgment of historical harm by a representative of the culpable party appears central to the integrity of the apology.") (internal parenthetical omitted). That it was the Senate that issued a formal apology for failing to enact anti-lynching legislation was considered particularly salient. Senator Mary Landrieu (D-La.), for example, observed, "[t]here may be no other injustice in American history for which the Senate so uniquely bears responsibility." Avis Thomas-Lester, A Senate Apology for History on Lynching; Vote Condemns Past Failure to Act, WASH. POST, June 14, 2005, at A12.
103. See Furman, 408 U.S. at 450 (Powell, J., dissenting) ("I agree that discriminatory application of the death penalty in the past, admittedly indefensible, is no justification for holding today that capital punishment is invalid in all cases in which sentences were handed out to members of the class discriminated against."). With respect to a possible argument of abolition-as-reparation, abolition of the death penalty may be too sweeping and lack the asymmetry some scholars believe reparations require. See Brooks, supra note 100, at 229 (finding civil rights legislation insufficient as reparation for slavery because it does not apply only to blacks). Some might argue that reparations must serve broader social goals and that abolition as "reparation" does not seem to have a purpose other than symbolic: abolition alone would not necessarily promote education, improve economic viability, or reduce crime rates of the harmed class. See generally Carlton Waterhouse, Avoiding Another Step in a Series of Unfortunate Legal Events: A Consideration of Black Life Under American Law From 1619 to 1972 and a Challenge to Prevailing Notions of Legally Based Reparations, 26 B.C. THIRD WORLD L.J. 207 (2006).
104. For example, President Ronald Reagan signed the Civil Liberties Act of 1988, and President George H.W. Bush signed its 1992 amendment, as well as issuing a formal apology for the internment of Japanese and Japanese-Americans during World War II. See supra text accompanying note 102.
105. S. Res. 39, 109th Cong., 151 Cong. Rec. 6364 (2005) (enacted) ("Whereas the crime of lynching succeeded slavery as the ultimate expression of racism in the United States following Reconstruction. …").
106. See, e.g., Thomas-Lester, supra note 102, at A12 ("Several advocates would like to see lawmakers do more. The Committee for a Formal Apology would like to see [the name of Richard B. Russell (D-Ga.), who had previously filibustered the resolution,] stripped from the Senate building.").
107. ALAN DERSHOWITZ, RIGHTS FROM WRONGS: A SECULAR THEORY OF THE ORIGINS OF RIGHTS 82 (2004).
108. Austin Sarat, The Rhetoric of Race in the "New Abolitionism," in FROM LYNCH MOBS TO THE KILLING STATE: RACE AND DEATH PENALTY IN AMERICA 260, 263 (Charles J. Ogletree, Jr. & Austin Sarat eds., 2006).

109. DERSHOWITZ, supra note 107, at 114 ("Rights, thus defined, will expand, contract, and change over time. ... They will also have to be continually defended and explained by reference to our ever-changing experiences.").

110. See McCleskey, 481 U.S. at 367 (Stevens, J., dissenting) ("One of the lessons of the Baldus study is that there exist certain categories of extremely serious crimes for which prosecutors consistently seek, and juries consistently impose, the death penalty without regard to the race of the victim or the race of the offender.").

111. Justice Powell's Furman opinion also reflects a reaction against the general argument that constitutional rights should derive from past injustices. In particular, he argues that social and economic factors "have plagued humanity since the beginning of recorded history" and "[t]he causes underlying this problem are unrelated to the constitutional issue before the Court." Furman, 408 U.S. at 447 -48 (Powell, J., dissenting). Other justices have been similarly unwilling to craft legal doctrine in response to historical evidence. For example, Eric. W. Rise has argued that the Supreme Court, under Chief Justice Vinson, was unwilling to assume the mantle of "accomplishing social reform through legal means" in response to "empirical, historical, and other extralegal methods of proof." ERIC W. RISE, THE MARTINSVILLE SEVEN: RACE, RAPE, AND CAPITAL PUNISHMENT 130 (1995).

112. See Coker v. Georgia, 433 U.S. 584 (1977) (declaring unconstitutional capital punishment imposed for the rape of an adult woman, while no reference to an American history of race relations and capital punishment was made).

113. Furman, 403 U.S. at 364.

114. See infra Part III.C. The "rights from wrongs" model articulated by Professor Dershowitz is inherently malleable, premised on "an ongoing process of trial and error." DERSHOWITZ, supra note 107, at 123.

115. Thompson, 487 U.S. at 828 n.27.

116. In the Furman amicus brief the amici used a history of slavery and racially-motivated extra-legal violence to sketch a "trend away from the imposition of formal and informal punishment on alleged black offenders," arguing that "any lingering executions which 'prima facie' have been affected by racial discrimination, violated contemporary American standards for civilized criminal justice; thereby constituting cruel and unusual punishment." Brief for NAACP et al. as Amici Curiae Supporting Petitioners at 7, Furman v. Georgia, 408 U.S. 238 (1971) (Nos. 68–5027, 69–5030, 69–5003, and 69–5031), 1971 WL 134376. See also Brief for Petitioner, supra, at 20 ("Amici curiae assert that the clear sweep of American history, running from the period of slavery through the extra-legal and racially motivated lynchings, vigilantism and race riots shows an unmistakable and contemporary trend toward disuse and relinquishment of race as a basis for taking a man's life.").

117. Furman, 408 U.S. at 308 (Stewart, J., concurring).

118. Gregg, 428 U.S. 153.

119. Klarman, supra note 41, at 65.

120. Justice Marshall has observed: "A little over a century ago, this Court invalidated a state statute providing that black citizens could not serve as jurors. State officials then turned to somewhat more subtle ways of keeping blacks off jury venires." Batson, 476 U.S. at 103 (Marshall, J., concurring) (internal citation omitted).
121. See, e.g., Id. at 93–94.
122. See McCleskey, 481 U.S. at 298 n.20 (historical evidence must be "reasonably contemporaneous"); Furman, 408 U.S. at 389 n.12 (Burger, C.J., dissenting) ("[I]t is not enough to show how [the statutory authorization for the death penalty] was applied in the distant past.").
123. Norris, 294 U.S. at 586–587.
124. Martha Chamallas, Deepening the Legal Understanding of Bias: On Devaluation and Biased Prototypes, 74 S. CAL. L. REV. 747, 775 (2001).
125. McCleskey, 481 U.S. at 332 (Brennan, J., dissenting) (internal quotation marks and citation omitted). See also Charles J. Ogletree, Jr., Making Race Matter in Death Matters, in FROM LYNCH MOBS TO THE KILLING STATE: RACE AND THE DEATH PENALTY IN AMERICA, supra note 100, at 55–56 ("Many of the effects of race felt within the criminal justice system, however, are elusive and intangible; they stem from years of history that cannot easily be calculated or analyzed.").
126. See Chamallas, supra note 123, at 805 ("'[L]ow prejudice' persons who desire to act fairly can sometimes check the effects of unconscious stereotyping and biased prototypes on their decisions once they are alerted to the potential for bias.").
127. Id. at 775 (discussing limiting the legal definition of discrimination to "international disparate treatment"). Professor Jody David Armour has observed "that, like all bad habits, the habit of prejudice is hard, but not impossible, to break and doing so requires a conscious effort. He argues in favor of bringing hidden biases out in the open in the course of litigation and permitting lawyers to appeal to the jury's sense of fairness and commitment to equality." Id. at 806 (citing JODY DAVID ARMOUR, NEGROPHOBIA AND REASONABLE RACISM: THE HIDDEN COSTS OF BEING BLACK IN AMERICA 133–39 (1997)). History might serve to explain the basis for, or serve to illustrate, many such biases in tandem with social science research.
128. See NAACP Brief supra note 11, at 14.
129. McCleskey, 481 U.S. at 325 (Brennan, J., dissenting) (emphasis added).
130. Id. at 341.
131. MILLER, supra note 4, at 11–12.
132. See Id. at 28 ("It is the reasoning of the Supreme Court, not the bare decisions, which imparts meaning to constitutional law. It is the validity of that reasoning which in large part determines the authority of the Constitution and the Court in the public mind.").
133. See Id. at 11 ("Judicial opinions are the most permanent and public manifestation of the work of the courts …"). See also Philip B. Kurland, The Court Should Decide Less and Explain More, NEW YORK TIMES 35 (June 9, 1968) ("[A] deeper and wider credibility

gap [is] created by the Supreme Court. The inadequate reasons put forth by the Court in support of its judgments are the cause of this second gap, or gulch.").

134. MILLER, supra note 4, at 13 (quoting Justice Harlan Stone as remarking, "I can hardly see the use of writing judicial opinions unless they are to embody methods of analysis and of deposition which will serve the profession as a guide to the decision of future cases").

135. Klarman, supra note 41, at 88 (suggesting that interwar criminal procedure cases had effects of "convincing blacks that the racial status quo was not impervious to change; educating them about their rights; providing a rallying point around which to organize a protest movement; and perhaps even instructing oblivious whites as to the egregious nature of Jim Crow conditions"); Jack M. Balkin, How Social Movements Change (Or Fail to Change) the Constitution: The Case of the New Departure, 39 SUFFOLK U. L. REV. 27, 35–36 (2005) ("Roe v. Wade energized new conservative social movements that portrayed the Supreme Court as a symbol of liberal elitism and judicial usurpation of democracy.").

136. Roscoe Pound, "The Causes of Popular Dissatisfaction with the Administration of Justice" (Aug. 29, 1906), in A. LEO LEVIN & RUSSELL R. WHEELER, EDS., THE POUND CONFERENCE: PERSPECTIVES ON JUSTICE IN THE FUTURE 337 (1979) (discussing civil justice).

137. Id.

138. Id. at 339.

139. JAN GORECKI, CAPITAL PUNISHMENT: CRIMINAL LAW AND SOCIAL EVOLUTION 111 (1983).

140. Excerpts From Opinions on Death Penalty, N.Y TIMES, June 30, 1972, at A14. See also Death is Not the Answer, BAY ST. BANNER, Mar. 22, 1973, at 4 (arguing against the death penalty and describing each justice's position in Furman); Linda Mathews & Ronald J. Ostrow, Supreme Court Strikes Down Most Death Penalty Laws, L.A. TIMES, June 30, 1972, at A1, A20 (noting that Justice Douglas "said he found that punishment unconstitutional because it had been applied selectively to minorities," and reporting the racial make-up of the death row prisoners affected by Furman).

141. See, e.g., Klarman, supra note 41, at 79 ("Justice Sutherland's Powell opinion was written as narrowly as was humanly possible. Not only did the ruling cover only capital cases, but it seemed to be limited to the precise facts of Scottsboro—'the ignorance and illiteracy of the defendants, their youth, the circumstances of public hostility, the imprisonment and the close surveillance of the defendants by the military forces …'") (citing Powell, 287 U.S. 45, 71 (1932)).

142. In addition, the public audience of judicial opinions, and the unique position of the Supreme Court in reaching this audience, may impose upon justices a responsibility to ensure that their presentation of history is accurate and complete. That is, [b]y writing history into its opinions the Court contributes to the public's view of the American past as much as, and sometimes even more than, professional historians and other historical writers do." MILLER, supra note 4, at 25. See also Klarman, supra note 41, at 92 ("As Ralph Bunche

pointed out. … '[c]ourt decisions, favorable or unfavorable, serve to dramatize the plight of the race more effectively than any other recourse; their propaganda and educative value is great.'"). Thus, "[w]hen the Supreme Court has the chance to tell us what American history is, history becomes more than a tool of decision. It affirms or denies the significance of past events for the activities of the present." MILLER, supra note 4, at 25. Miller has suggested that, "[w]ith the increased scope and power granted the Court by the use of history goes the increased responsibility in handling of historical materials." Id.

143. Walter G. Daniel, Editorial Comment: Black Studies in American Education, 39 J. NEGRO EDUC. 189, 191 (1970).

144. John S. Wills, Who Needs Multicultural Education? White Students, U.S. History, and the Construction of a Usable Past, 27 ANTHROPOLOGY & EDUC. Q. 365, 366 (1996).

145. Id. at 370.

146. Id. at 377.

147. Daniel, supra note 139, at 189. See generally P. Rudy Mattai, Rethinking the Nature of Multicultural Education: Has it Lost its Focus or is it Being Misused? 61 J. NEGRO EDUC. 65 (1992); Terrie Epstein, Adolescents' Perspectives on Racial Diversity in U.S. History: Case Studies From an Urban Classroom, 37 AM. EDUC. RES. J. 185 (2000).

148. Wills, supra note 140, at 385.

149. Such a use of history may be found particularly in dissenting opinions, as such opinions often hope to sway future courts and the public to their position, with the desire to provoke debate to challenge the law as it stands. Justice Marshall's dissenting opinions have been considered, in part, "blueprints for corrective influences on the law of criminal justice." Daniel, supra note 139, at 62.

150. Such an approach would also reflect the early methods of the NAACP, for whom Justice Marshall worked before joining the bench: "[l]obbying, education, and publicity." RISE, supra note 109, at 58. Indeed, the lawyers of the NAACP Legal Defense and Educational Fund, Inc., "fully intended to use the courts as a forum for the purpose of educating the public." RANDALL WALTON BLAND, JUSTICE THURGOOD MARSHALL: CRUSADER FOR LIBERALISM, HIS JUDICIAL BIOGRAPHY (1908–1993) 35 (2001) (internal quotation marks and citation omitted). Prior to joining the Supreme Court, Justice Marshall, explaining NAACP's legal strategy, observed of housing discrimination that "the only method of counteracting this vicious practice is by means of educating the general public, from which juries are chosen, to the plight of the Negro." NAACP Wartime Conference, reprinted in BLACK PROTEST THOUGHT IN THE TWENTIETH CENTURY 250, 260 (August Meier, Elliott Rudwick & Francis L. Broderick, eds., 1980).

151. Gregg, 428 U.S. at 232 (Marshall, J., dissenting). A professor of Political Science and a professor of psychology tested Marshall's assertion that, if the public knew about various aspects of capital punishment, they would oppose it. They provided individuals with either utilitarian information on the death penalty, humanitarian information, both, or neither. They found that when exposed to information about the utilitarian aspects of capital punishment,

"a substantial proportion of the subjects altered their opinions toward it," with the trend of opposing its application. Austin Sarat & Neil Vidmar, Public Opinion, the Death Penalty, and the Eighth Amendment: Testing the Marshall Hypothesis 176 Wis. L. REV. 171, 195 (cited in Gregg, 428 U.S. at 232 n.1 (Marshall, J., dissenting)). Interestingly, however, the researchers found that "presentation of humanitarian information had minimal effects on death penalty support, either singly or in combination with utilitarian information." Id. at 190. The humanitarian information presented to subjects included several paragraphs devoted to discussion of studies that indicated "that the death penalty is applied disproportionately to black defendants" but did not include a historical review of segregation, lynch mobs, or state-created race-specific capital sentencing statutes. Id. at 203 (appendix).

152. Furman, 408 U.S. at 363–64 (Marshall, J., concurring).
153. See generally Jon Hanson & David Yosifon, The Situation: An Introduction to the Situational Character, Critical Realism, Power Economics, and Deep Capture, U. PA. L. REV. 129 (2003); Chamallas, supra note 120, at 788 (discussing the "rape prototype," the circumstances under which we acknowledge a rape has occurred, as requiring "labeling the rapist as crazy or a bully," otherwise there is no rape perceived, and the "victim" is cast into the role of the bad actor—"promiscuous or vindictive"); Adam Benforado, Jon Hanson & David Yosifon, Broken Scales: Obesity and Justice in America, 53 EMORY L.J. 1645, 1776 -81 (2004) (discussing the rhetoric of personal responsibility in the obesity debate).
154. Klarman, supra note 41, at 69.
155. Id.
156. Hanson & Hanson, supra note 83, at 477.
157. See generally Chamallas, supra note 120, at 748–55. In McCleskey, the Court noted that McCleskey's Equal Protection Clause claim required "the existence of purposeful discrimination." McCleskey, 481 U.S. at 292 (quoting Whitus v. Georgia, 385 U.S. 545, 550 (1967)). The format of the doctrine itself, then, requires a "bad actor."
158. Id. at 762.
159. Batson, 476 U.S. at 104 n.3 (Marshall, J., concurring) ("An earlier jury-selection treatise circulated in [Dallas County, Texas,] instructed prosecutors: 'Do not take Jews, Negroes, Dagos, Mexicans or a member of any minority race on a jury, no matter how rich or how well educated.'").
160. History can be presented in such a way that a person or system "bad actor" is not explicitly formulated. See, e.g., Swain, 380 U.S. at 226 (acknowledging that "there has not been a Negro on a jury in Talladega County since about 1950," but finding such evidence insufficient because "the responsibility of the prosecutor is not illuminated in [the] record [before the Court]").
161. McCleskey, 481 U.S. at 329 (Brennan, J., dissenting).
162. Klarman, supra note 41, at 71 ("It is, perhaps, a natural human tendency to react defensively toward criticism by outsiders."). While it is true that history is a part of self-identity, and

criticism of the past may be taken as criticism of the present, few today would defend the mob lynchings of the late nineteenth and early twentieth centuries.

163. McCleskey, 481 U.S. at 328 (Brennan, J., dissenting).
164. Andrews, 485 U.S. at 920 (Marshall, J., dissenting).
165. Id. at 922.
166. Thompson, 487 U.S. at 828 n.27.
167. Klarman, supra note 41, at 88.
168. FRANKLIN E. ZIMRING & GORDON HAWKINS, CAPITAL PUNISHMENT AND THE AMERICAN AGENDA 40 (1987).
169. FRANKLIN E. ZIMRING, THE CONTRADICTIONS OF AMERICAN CAPITAL PUNISHMENT 62 (2003) (arguing that this transformation "provides three powerful functions for the death penalty in the United States. First, it gives the horrifying process of human execution a positive impact that many students can identify with: closure, not vengeance. Second, this degovernmentalization of the rationale of the death penalty means that citizens do not have to worry about executions as an excessive use of power by and for the government ... The third function ... is that it links the symbolism of execution to a long American history of community control of punishment. The United States is not far removed from its age of vigilante punishment, and the nostalgia for many of the symbols and sentiments of punishment as a community rather than a government enterprise is quite powerful in many parts of the modern United States.").
170. Id. at 55 ("The symbolic transformation of the death penalty trial into a private competition between the claims of those hurt by murder and appeals to mercy for the murderers makes a number of assumptions about the relationship between criminal punishment and the well-being of those who suffered a loss as a result of the crime. It is assumed that there is a 'zero-sum' relationship between the welfare of the victim's relative and that of the offender. ...").
171. Hanson & Hanson, supra note 83, at 421 ("When individual action is salient, we seen choice and attribute causal responsibility accordingly, but where individuals fail to act, the omissions tend to fade into the surrounding situation.") (internal parenthetical omitted).
172. McCleskey, 481 U.S. at 344 (Brennan, J., dissenting) (emphasis added).
173. Hanson & Hanson, supra note 83, at 421.
174. Michael L. Radelet & Marian J. Borg, The Changing Nature of Death Penalty Debates, 26 ANN. REV. Soc. 43, 48 (2000) ("[T]he 'Racial Justice Act,' which would have required courts to hold hearings to examine statistical patterns of disparities in capital cases, failed to gain congressional approval.").
175. See JOHN C. JEFFRIES, JR., JUSTICE LEWIS F. POWELL, JR. 413 (2001) (Justices Stewart and White "wanted to [be] done with capital punishment but without taking on themselves the responsibility for ruling it unconstitutional. They hoped a nudge would be sufficient. Executions were increasingly rare, and popular support seemed on the wane.

If the Court struck down existing death-penalty statutes, exposed the defects in current practice, and made legislatures start over, perhaps they would simply give up.").

176. It would also pose a potential political difficulty for legislators who would have to tackle the issue of race before their constituents.

177. Courts, though, are perhaps not very good historians. "The object of [the legal system] is not objective truth, historical or otherwise, but advocacy," whereas the scholar-historian resides in a world of complexity, investigation, reflection, and ambiguity. Kelly, supra note 6, at 156.

178. Cf. Roper v. Simmons, 543 U.S. 551, 622–29 (2005) (Scalia, J., dissenting).

179. More generally, today there may be skepticism of "playing the race card." Cf. Margaret M. Russell, Beyond "Sellouts" and "Race Cards": Black Attorneys and the Straitjacket of Legal Practice, 95 MICH. L. REV. 766, 801 (1997) ("The attitude that we have 'gotten beyond' race is applied with special force to the law."); Id. at 802 ("[A]ttorneys are under pressure to suppress or deny instances in which race affects the administration of justice. Those who defy the pressure and bring race into the courtroom force other participants in the proceedings and the public at large to confront the discomforting extent to which the ideals of American justice remain unfulfilled. Accusing these lawyers of 'playing the race card' is one way to deflect attention from this uncomfortable reality."); Hanson & Hanson, supra note 83, at 473–77 (discussing the backlash against vocalization of concerns about "race" and "racism" in the wake of Hurricane Katrina); Batson, 476 U.S. at 129 (Burger, C.J., dissenting) ("A further painful paradox of the Court's holding is that it is likely to interject racial matters back into the jury selection process, contrary to the general thrust of a long line of Court decisions and the notion of our country as a 'melting pot.'").

DISCUSSION QUESTIONS

1. What is it about American culture and history that causes us to continue to cling to the death penalty when practically every other country has abandoned it?
2. What suggestions do you have to improve the quality of representation in capital cases?
3. What can be done to prevent capital punishment from being used as a political tool?
4. What role, if any, does the race of the victim and defendant play in capital punishment?

DISPARITIES

Introduction

Race, Region, and Death Sentencing in Illinois, 1988–1997
By Glenn L. Pierce and Michael L. Radelet

Racial Disparities in the Capital of Capital Punishment
By Scott Phillips

This chapter presents two readings on the topic of disparities in the death penalty system. The basic questions concern whether there is bias in the procedures through which criminal justice professionals (e.g., police, prosecutors, judges) pursue the death penalty, and whether bias is evident in executions. The two readings present research and data analysis aimed at answering specific questions regarding the administration and application of the death penalty. While each reading presents credible statistical evidence regarding disparities in the application of the death penalty, we are left with a sense of frustration, partly because time, resources, and available data restrict the extent to which we can delve deeply in to the many questions that exist regarding administration of the death penalty in America, and partly because scientific research cannot answer all questions with absolute certainty. For all the evidence that exists regarding disparities, questions remain.

Pierce and Radelet (2002) present the results of a statistical analysis of death eligible cases in Illinois relying on data for over 5,000 first degree murder cases from 1988 to 1997. They focus on two specific research questions: Is the death penalty reserved for the more grievous and heinous cases (those with more aggravating factors, the worst of the worst)?, and is there a correlation between extra legal factors and imposition of the death penalty, when seriousness of the crime (aggravating factors) is held constant? To their credit, Pierce and Radelet point out several limitations to their research and analysis. For example, the lack of a longitudinal design, one that tracks murder cases through the justice system from initial investigation to final case outcome, precludes investigating sources of bias that might occur during early stages of case processing, while still being evident when data is analyzed for closed cases. Simply put, the chain of decisions that might contribute to biased outcomes in sentencing cannot be analyzed with existing data resources. Additionally, the authors' analysis concerns those sentenced to death (on death row), not those spared the death penalty post sentencing. Finally, and perhaps most importantly, it is impossible to tease out from administrative data (criminal justice system records) whether individual or institutional racism (or other biases) are the true causes of observed disparities in death sentences.

With these limitations acknowledged, Pierce and Radelet present a series of data tables and statistical calculations suggesting that geographical (regional) and racial disparities exist in death sentencing in Illinois (at least for the 10 years covered in their analysis). The authors found that some of the legally defined aggravating factors allowing imposition of the death penalty in Illinois (e.g., prior murder conviction, contemporaneous murder) correlated with the imposition of the death penalty, while some other aggravating factors did not (e.g., contemporaneous armed violence, prior Class 1 felony offense, prior Class 4 felony offense). They also found evidence that race and region (county or type of county) have significant independent statistical influences on the imposition of the death penalty in Illinois. Regarding the race variable, the authors found no significant difference in the race of the offender, but they did find a significant difference regarding the race of the victim (offenders convicted of murdering whites are more likely to receive the death penalty, and blacks who kill whites are more likely to receive the death penalty compared to blacks who kill blacks). Readers should note that this analysis by Pierce and Radelet factored into the decision by former Illinois Governor George Ryan to commute the death sentences of over 200 individuals to life without parole in 2003.

Phillips draws our attention to the "capital of capital punishment" (Houston, Texas). He notes that most research on death sentence disparities has focused on states that do not utilize the death penalty option much, at least not in comparison to Houston, and that this represents a limitation in the research on disparities. Data available to Phillips allowed him to examine disparities in prosecutor charging decisions (something Pierce and Radelet could not examine), as well as other process and case outcome variables. Phillips conducted an analysis of data pertaining to over 500 defendants indicted for murder in Harris County, Texas from 1992 to 1999, and he used a statistical analysis technique (logistic regression) similar to the technique utilized by Pierce and Radelet. Phillips finds, consistent with other research, that race does emerge as a statistically significant factor in the imposition of the death penalty (after controlling for other factors), and the data available to him suggest that race factors into death penalty decisions differently depending on the stage of processing in the criminal justice system.

> " … death is more likely to be imposed against black defendants than white defendants, and death is more likely to be imposed on behalf of white victims than black victims. The central pattern stems from an intriguing interplay between race, the seriousness of a murder, and the stages of capital litigation (Phillips, 2008, p. 838).

Phillips points to several findings suggesting that the district attorney in Harris County made case processing decisions in murder cases that reflect a racial bias. He also suggests that juries' decisions reflect attempts to attenuate the biased decisions of the district attorney. Phillips notes several limitations to his analysis and the data available, citing in particular the lack of information regarding the strength of evidence in the capital cases analyzed.

Readers should note, as do the authors of the studies presented here, that there have been numerous studies examining whether there is evidence of bias (racial and other sources of bias) in death penalty sentencing. While many argue the results are mixed, the preponderance of evidence seems to point in the direction of support for the bias hypotheses (there is less, and less consistent evidence, of the lack of bias across all studies). Still, the research studies represent a series of different methodologies, utilizing disparate data sources, and concerning qualitatively different jurisdictions. Thus, we are left to conclude that it is plausible that biases exist in the administration of the death penalty, but that it is not a statistical certainty. We may never achieve that level of confidence in our research findings on this matter.

Race, Region, and Death Sentencing in Illinois, 1988–1997

Glenn L. Pierce and Michael L. Radelet

II. INTRODUCTION AND STATEMENT OF RESEARCH QUESTIONS

Along the long and complicated path to an execution in Illinois, many are called, but few are chosen. Before an execution can occur, law enforcement officials must first devote ample resources to collecting the type of high-quality evidence that prosecutors and jurors would usually like to see before agreeing on a capital sentence. Prosecutors must decide both to seek a death sentence and to steadfastly stand by that decision, even if the defendant seeks some sort of plea bargain. Resources must be available for defense attorneys, regardless of the region of the state or the racial attributes of the defendant or victim. Jurors must unanimously agree that a given defendant, convicted of first-degree murder, should be executed rather than live the rest of his life in prison. The Illinois Supreme Court must concur. The governor, if asked to consider executive clemency (whereby the death sentence can be commuted to a prison term), must also give a green light. Clearly, not everyone sentenced to death will be executed. Nonetheless, examining who is sentenced to death is a useful starting spot from which to begin studying who is executed.

According to data collected by the Center for Wrongful Convictions at Northwestern University, between mid-1977, when the current Illinois death penalty statute took effect, and December 31, 2001, some 289 people were sentenced to death in Illinois. Of these, 173 remained on death row on December 31, 2001[1]; the other 116 had been resentenced to prison terms, died from natural deaths or execution, or otherwise had been released from death row. This is a tiny fraction of the state's 12.4 million residents. In their seminal study of death sentencing in Illinois, Gross and Mauro found that in the 3.5 years ending

1 NAACP Legal Defense and Educational Fund, Inc., Death Row, USA. (unpublished document) (Winter 2002), at 40.

in December 1980, only one percent of homicides, and 1.4 percent of those with a known suspect, resulted in a death sentence for the perpetrator. Hence, the death penalty has been infrequently imposed.

The goal of the present study is quite narrow. Using ten years of data, we compare characteristics of cases in which the death penalty was imposed with the characteristics of other Illinois cases in which defendants were convicted of first-degree murder. Are cases in which the death penalty is imposed more "aggravated" than cases in which it is not? Among cases with similar levels of aggravation, do extra-legal factors, such as race or region, correlate with who is sentenced to death?

The decision to start with a sample of cases where people have already been convicted of first-degree murder is not the ideal way to shed light on what we refer to as the "continuous chain" of decisions, from the initial police investigation through appellate and clemency decisions, that result in (some) executions. Law enforcement officials, prosecutors, judges, and juries are all involved in deciding who to send to death row. Ideally, we would want to start a study such as this by initially focusing on how the race of defendant or victim might correlate with the amount of resources that law enforcement devotes to gathering evidence. Then, we would isolate and look solely at prosecutorial behavior, examining all cases (or a sample of cases), which, on the basis of their characteristics, were eligible for the death penalty, and then comparing them with cases in which the prosecutor originally sought death—whether or not a death sentence was ultimately imposed. We would like to know in which cases the prosecutor was willing to accept a guilty plea in exchange for a prison term. However, limitations on data for Illinois homicides would make such a study a long-term and extremely high-cost project. In short, since death sentencing involves a chain of decisions, one dependent on another, any decisions made before the point at which data are gathered, whether or not infected by improper bias, are invisible.

Similarly, in this study we do not focus attention on what happens after a death sentence is imposed. We do not explore any differences that may or may not exist between who is on death row (the 173 cases) and who has been sentenced to death but, for whatever reason, is no longer on death row (the 116 cases).

Some questions can be raised by comparing those sentenced to death with the demographic characteristics of the state as a whole. Estimates by the U.S. Bureau of Census put the population of Illinois on April 1, 2000, at 12.42 million, of whom 75.1 percent are white and 15.6 percent black.[2] While blacks are 15.6 percent of the population, the Northwestern data indicate that 58.5 percent of those sentenced to death are black (169/289), 3.75 times more than their representation in the population. Whites account for 75.1 percent of the Illinois population, but only 34.9 percent (101/289) of those sentenced to death. And, while 40.8 percent of the African Americans sentenced to death were convicted of killing whites (69/169), only 3 of the 100 whites sentenced to death

2 See http://www.nipc.cog.il.us/GDP-counties/gdp17.pdf

were convicted of killing blacks.[3] Of the twelve men executed in Illinois since 1977, eleven were convicted of killing at least one white victim.

Similarly, the racial makeup of inmates currently on death row in Illinois is quite different than the racial characteristics of the state's population as a whole. Today, some 63 percent of the 173 condemned inmates in Illinois are African American.[4]

Such comparisons between census data and the racial characteristics of those sentenced to death or those on death row raise interesting questions. As those comparisons do not control for differential involvement in, or victimization from, homicides (much less the most aggravated homicides), in and of themselves they do not, and cannot, prove racial disparities. Instead, they simply challenge the researcher to examine, or "control for," legally-relevant factors that might explain the disparities. For example, to say that African Americans are 15.6 percent of the population and 58.5 percent of those sentenced to death leads to no conclusions; it simply invites one to see if the disparity is "explained" by such factors as the possibility that African Americans are more likely to be involved in highly-aggravated homicides than are whites.

The same can be said about characteristics of homicide victims. As mentioned, between the time the Illinois death penalty statute took effect in 1977 and the end of 2001, 289 people were sentenced to death, of whom 173 remained on death row at the end of 2001. Table 1 displays the racial breakdowns of the homicide victims of the 289 death-sentenced defendants are:

Table 1. Race-of-Victim Among Those Sentenced to Death in Illinois

	1977–2001 (N=289)	
White	165	(57.1%)
Black	97	(33.6%)
Latino	12	(4.2%)
Black & White	10	(3.5%)
Asian & White	1	(.3%)
Other	5	(1.7%)

3 Center for Wrongful Convictions, *Illinois Death Penalty Fact Sheet—1977–2001*. Unpublished Report, School of Law, Northwestern University (Nov. 9).

4 NAACP Legal Defense and Educational Fund, Inc., *Death Row, USA*. (unpublished document) (Winter 2002), at 40. The precise count of inmates varies depending on whether one includes inmates who are awaiting resentencing.

Thus, among the 289 Illinois death sentences, 173, or 60 percent, were imposed on defendants who were convicted of killing at least one white victim. But if homicides with white victims are more aggravated or otherwise more death-eligible than homicides with black victims, this disparity can be explained by legally-relevant variables.

While the above patterns may raise important questions, they do not at all "prove" that racial bias is present in death sentencing in Illinois. It is entirely possible, for example, that African Americans are more likely than whites to be arrested for and convicted of criminal homicides. If true, this would explain at least some of the above disparities. Even given a conviction for homicide, it is possible that whites tend to be convicted of homicides committed in the heat of passion (such as an argument with a friend or loved one), while blacks are more likely to be convicted of homicides which more closely match the statutory requirements for the imposition of a death sentence, such as homicides accompanied by a robbery or rape. In addition, it could be that the racial differences above are, in part, a reflection of defendants' prior records of violent criminality. Given identical homicides, if black defendants tend to have longer records of prior arrests than white defendants, at least some of the racial differences in death sentences would be explained by perfectly appropriate, non-racial factors.

Hence, to rigorously assess whether race, gender, region, or other inappropriate factors are associated with death sentencing, researchers need to "statistically control" for legally-relevant factors that appropriately influence death sentencing. Accordingly, in this study, to assess whether these appropriate factors can account for any initial correlations observed between extra-legal factors (e.g., race) and death sentencing, we have secured data that allow us to measure a broad range of such factors. This allows us, for example, to first examine only those homicides accompanied by additional felonies. But if blacks are more likely than whites to be sentenced to death (or those who kill whites are more likely to be sentenced to death than those who kill blacks) for similar homicides (e.g., among those with accompanying felonies), then the conclusion that race does indeed affect death sentencing would be supported. As additional legally-relevant variables are statistically controlled, any race differences that remain serve to buttress the conclusion of racial bias.

After controlling for legally-relevant factors—that is, assessing the effect of race and region among homicides with roughly similar levels of aggravation—there are three possible outcomes. First, if the death sentencing system operates in a fair manner, cases that have the highest level of aggravation would be those most likely to result in a death sentence, regardless of race or region. Cases with similar levels of aggravation would have roughly equal probabilities of resulting in a death sentence. A second possible outcome might be that even after taking into account legally-relevant factors, it is difficult or impossible to figure out who has been sentenced to death and who was not among similar homicides. This result would lend support to the conclusion that death sentencing is affected by arbitrariness. Third, even after controlling for legally-relevant factors, race or region may still predict who is, and who is not, sentenced to death. This is not arbitrariness in a strict sense—who is sentenced to death can be predicted, so it is not random or arbitrary—but death sentences are predicted on the basis of legally irrelevant factors.

Both arbitrariness and racial disparities, if found, have policy implications. For example, Walter Berns, one of the nation's most articulate supporters of the death penalty, points out that support for the death penalty in principle is quite different than support for the death penalty as it is actually applied. He argues that regardless of how strong a person may support the death penalty in theory, its propriety in practice "depends on our ability to restrict its use to the worst of our criminals and to impose it in a nondiscriminatory fashion."[5] Any penalty that is justified on the basis of its "justness" or on "just desserts" is undermined by injustices in its application.

If racial disparities in death sentencing remain after statistically controlling for legally-relevant factors, the conclusion that race indeed affects death sentencing gains significant strength. Such a finding, however, does not mean that race necessarily operates in a given individual case. Thus, in the seminal 1987 decision in McCleskey v. Kemp, the U.S. Supreme Court held that such statistical evidence of racial disparities in death sentencing cases was not legally sufficient for a defendant (McCleskey) to challenge his death sentence.[6] Written by Justice Lewis Powell, who later called the decision the worst decision he made while sitting on the Court,[7] this 5–4 ruling placed major blockades in the path of defendants alleging that race affected their death sentences.[8] This is because any race effect found in statistical studies of death sentencing can be either intentional or non-intentional (or, more likely, some combination of the two), and the Court held that, to prevail, a defendant must show intentional racial discrimination in his or her specific case.[9] Intentional racial discrimination is extremely difficult to prove; one would need to have a prosecutor who, in public, states (for example) that the death penalty was sought in a specific case because the defendant was black or the victim was white.[10] Instead, the

---

5 Walter Berns, *Defending the Death Penalty*, 26 CRIME & DELINQUENCY 503, 511 (1980).

6 McCleskey v. Kemp, 481 U.S. 279 (1987).

7 JOHN C. JEFFRIES, JUSTICE LEWIS F. POWELL, JR.: A BIOGRAPHY 451 (1994).

8 "In this century, no American court has upheld a legal claim alleging racial discrimination in the use of the death penalty." David C. Baldus, George Woodworth, David Zuckerman, Neil Alan Weiner, & Barbara Broffitt, Racial Discrimination and the Death Penalty in the Post-Furman Era: An Empirical and Legal Overview, with Recent Findings from Philadelphia, 83 CORNELL 1. REV. 1638, 1643 (1998).

9 It is for that reason that Illinois courts have not been receptive to previous studies that have examined race and death sentencing in Illinois, most notably the work published by Gross and Mauro (1984; 1989). However, the lack of interest expressed by the courts in their work has nothing to do with its quality. See, e.g., People v. Davis, 119 Ill.2d 61, 65 (1987); People v. Stewart, 121 Ill.2d 93 (1988).

10 Although rare, it is not unheard of for judges or prosecutors to use racially derogatory language when referring to minority defendants. For example, in a Florida death penalty case in the mid-1980s, the trial

Court in McCleskey said that statistical patterns of racial bias were within the province of the executive and legislative branches of the government to correct. Thus, any statistical demonstration of disparities is of relevance to legislative and gubernatorial decisions, not judicial decisions.

"Nonintentional discrimination is more insidious and difficult to prove or measure than overt racial bias. The racial disparities observed by researchers who have studied modern death penalty systems do not necessarily reveal, or even suggest, that the individual actors (judges, jurors, prosecutors, and defense attorneys) in the system act with conscious discriminatory intent.[11] Statistical patterns of racial biases in the application of the death penalty cannot be attributed solely (or even primarily) to "bad apples" in decision-making positions. Instead, the enormous costs of seeking a death penalty and securing an execution force prosecutors and other decision-makers to make very difficult decisions about which first-degree murders are "normal" and which are "worse." In making those decisions, the race, ethnicity, and social class of the victim, while inappropriate, may be part of the ingredients used to determine which human lives are more valuable. As such, the decision becomes political.

We now turn our attention to studies that have examined the application of the death penalty in Illinois since 1977 (similar research from other states is reviewed in Appendix I).

III. PRIOR RESEARCH ON POST-FURMAN[12] DEATH SENTENCING IN ILLINOIS

A. Gross and Mauro

The only post-Furman scholarly study to assess the possibility of racial disparities in death sentencing in Illinois was conducted by Samuel Gross and Robert Mauro.[13] Their study, which also examined seven other states, focused on the five-year period, January 1, 1976 through December 31, 1980, or, as they note, "for that portion of that period during which the state in question had a capital sentencing statute in force."[14] Because Illinois did

judge referred to the African-American defendant's family with a racially derogatory term. See Peek v. State, 488 So.2d 52, 56 (Fla. 1986).

11 Sheri Lynn Johnson, *Unconscious Racism and the Criminal Law*, 73 Cornell Law Review (1016 (1988).

12 Furman v. Georgia, 408 U.S. 238 (1972).

13 Samuel R. Gross & Robert Mauro, Patterns of Death: An Analysis of Racial Disparities in Capital Sentencing and Homicide Victimization, 37 STANFORD LAW REVIEW 27 (1984); SAMUEL R. GROSS & ROBERT MAURO, DEATH & DISCRIMINATION: RACIAL DISPARITIES IN CAPITAL SENTENCING (1989).

14 GROSS & MAURO, *supra* note 12 (1989), at 35.

not have an active death penalty statute until mid-1977, Gross and Mauro confined their attention in Illinois to the period July 1, 1977 through 1980.[15]

Special attention was given to death sentencing in Florida, Georgia, and Illinois—the three states with the largest death row populations at the time. Among the three states, Illinois had the lowest death sentencing rate. There, 1.4 percent of all homicides with known offenders were sentenced to death, compared to 3.7 percent in both Georgia and Florida.[16] Their study included 45 death sentences in Illinois, which is approximately 15 percent of all death sentences imposed in Illinois between mid-1977 and the end of 2001. These 45 death sentences (out of 3,115 homicides) provide sufficient data to ascertain several statistically significant patterns (e.g., a correlation between victim's race and death sentencing in several subsamples), but not enough data to draw conclusions about other patterns (e.g., whether blacks convicted of killing whites during robberies are treated differently than whites convicted of killing whites).

The homicide data used by Gross and Mauro came from the Supplemental Homicide Reports, which are compiled by local police departments and filed with the Uniform Crime Reports division of the Federal Bureau of Investigation. They obtained data on the:

1. sex, age, and race of the victim or victims;
2. sex, age, and race of the suspected killer or killers;
3. date and place of the homicide;
4. weapon used;
5. commission of any separate felony accompanying the homicide; and
6. relationship between the victim(s) and the suspected killer(s).

To determine which of these homicides resulted in a death sentence, Gross and Mauro used data on death penalty cases collected by the NAACP Legal Defense Fund. That death row data set also included data on such characteristics as the location, month, year, and county, and sex, age, and race of both the defendant and victim. Hence, by comparing these items in both the LDF and the SHR data, it became possible to "match" cases and identify those that resulted in a death sentence.

According to the 1980 Census, the population of Illinois was 11.5 million, 80 percent of whom were white, 14.5 percent black, and 5.5 percent Hispanic.[17] Despite the fact that blacks were only 14.5 percent of the total population, Gross and Mauro note that some 58.6 percent of the homicides in Illinois during the 3.5-year study period took the lives of blacks. Thus, blacks were four times more likely to be victims of homicides than their

---

15 *Id.* at 233.

16 *Id.* at 43.

17 U.S. BUREAU OF THE CENSUS, STATISTICAL ABSTRACT OF THE UNITED STATES: 1981 (102d edition), at 33.

representation in the population would suggest. As we have noted earlier in this report, however, comparison of the demographic characteristics of death row inmates and the larger state population can raise questions, but not offer conclusions.

Gross and Mauro then demonstrated that race was clearly associated with the imposition of death sentences. Among those suspected of killing whites, 2.9 percent went to death row, compared to 0.5 percent of those suspected of killing blacks. In cases where a black was suspected of killing a white, 7.5 percent were sentenced to death, compared to 1.9 percent of the whites killing whites and 0.6 percent of the blacks killing blacks. None of the 56 whites suspected of killing blacks during the study period were sentenced to death.

What accounts for these racial disparities? One hypothesis might be that homicides that victimize whites are generally more serious or "death penalty eligible" than those that victimize blacks. But if it was found that among only those highly-aggravated cases (such as rape murders or multiple murders) those who victimize whites are still more likely to be sentenced to death, then solid evidence of racial disparities—or even racial discrimination—would remain. After all, in Illinois only 27.1 percent of the homicides involved an accompanying felony, but 75 percent of the death penalty cases involved accompanying felonies. If felony circumstances were more prevalent in white-victim cases, then a race-neutral and legally-relevant explanation for the racial differences in death sentencing would be suggested.

Nonetheless, the presence of felony circumstances (i.e., a murder in the course of another felony) did not explain the racial disparities. In Illinois, 9.4 percent of the white victim cases with felony circumstances ended in a death sentence, compared to only 3.0 percent of similar cases with black victims. Nor did the relationship between defendant and victim, where 22 percent of all homicides, but 70 percent of death penalty cases, involved strangers. Here 5.8 percent of those suspected of killing white strangers were sentenced to death, compared to only 1.5 percent of those suspected of killing black strangers. Similarly, 4 percent of all murders, but 44 percent of the death penalty cases, involved multiple murders. But when the victims of those multiple murders included at least one white, 22.5 percent ended in a death sentence, compared to 6.8 percent of the cases where the victims were black.

In the end, these "control variables" failed to explain the racial disparities in death sentencing. Among all homicides, those suspected of killing whites were 5.8 times more likely to be sentenced to death than those who kill blacks (2.9/0.5). Among those with accompanying felonies, the ratio is 3 to 1 (9.4/3.0). Among those suspected of killing strangers, the ratio was 3.9 (5.8/1.5). Among those suspected of multiple murders, the ratio was 3.3 (22.5/6.8).

To conclude their study, Gross and Mauro developed an Aggravation Scale by assigning each homicide one point for each of three factors: 1) it involved accompanying felonies, 2) the suspect and victim were strangers, or 3) there were multiple victims. This aggravation scale does a good job in predicting who is sentenced to death. Only 0.1 percent of the homicides with "0" on this aggravation scale ended in a death sentence, 1.0 percent of those with a "1," 7.4 percent of those coded as "2," and 22.6 percent of those coded as "3." However, within each level of aggravation, those suspected of killing whites were more likely than other homicide suspects to be sentenced to death. For example, among those with a "2" or "3" level of aggravation, 12.4 percent of those suspected of killing whites in Illinois and 4.4 percent of those suspected of killing blacks were sentenced to death. When all the variables were entered into a logistic regression model, it was found "In Illinois the overall odds of an offender receiving the death penalty for killing a white were 4.0 times greater than for killing a black."[18]

B. Chicago Tribune

In a 1999 analysis of 285 death penalty cases in Illinois, journalists Ken Armstrong and Steve Mills found that 33 included defense attorneys who were subsequently disbarred or suspended, 46 where the conviction rested on the testimony of jailhouse informants, 20 that included controversial hair analysis, and 25 where black defendants were convicted and sentenced to death by all-white juries.[19] They concluded that the findings "reveal a system so plagued by unprofessionalism, imprecision and bias that they have rendered the state's ultimate form of punishment its least credible."

We now turn our attention to the methodology we employed to more thoroughly examine these issues.

IV. Methodology

A. Data Sources

The data used in this report is a subset of conviction data from the cases of all defendants convicted of first-degree murder in Illinois who were formally sentenced during the ten-year period, January 1, 1988 through December 31, 1997. The cases included in this study are analyzed in terms of sentencing events. As used in this report, the term "sentencing event" refers to a judicial proceeding in which a sentence is imposed. A defendant may be sentenced in one judicial proceeding for the murders of multiple victims where those murders occurred as part of the same course of conduct. Or, where multiple murders occur in separate events, a defendant is more likely to be sentenced in separate judicial proceedings for each murder. As a result, defendants in the latter category appear in our data set on more than one occasion. A total of 5,310 cases or sentencing events in the study time

18 GROSS & MAURO, *supra* note 12 (1989), at 66.

19 Ken Armstrong & Steve Mills, *Death Row Justice Derailed,* CHICAGO TRIBUNE, Nov. 14–18, 1999 (five-part series).

frame were identified from IDOC records, of which 115 ended with a death sentence. The subset of cases for which there is no missing data for any of the 27 independent variables used in this analysis (see Table 2) is 4,182 cases, which contain 76 death sentence cases.

As we will discuss further in our conclusions section, the focus on only those convicted of first-degree murder introduces a conservative bias into our results. Race or region, for example, might be correlated with which types of homicide cases (other factors constant) are most likely to result in a conviction for first-degree murder. It may correlate with the amount of effort made by the prosecutor to find mitigation sufficient to justify offering to reduce the penalty for first-degree charges. Or, once a prosecutor brings a defendant charged with first-degree murder before a jury, race may correlate with the probability the defendant is found guilty. Illinois is among several states that have been criticized for the unbridled discretion that prosecutors have in deciding in which cases the death penalty will be sought.[20]

However, the multitude of decisions made before a defendant is convicted of first-degree murder are not examined in this project, so any possible impact on these decisions by political and extra-legal factors cannot be exposed. Again we refer to the "continuous chain" of decisions that are necessary before a person is executed, with police, prosecutors, jurors, judges, appellate courts, and governors all involved. The individual decisions may be invisible (that is, detailed data are not collected that would allow one to show consistency), but their effects are not. Therefore, if extra-legal factors are shown to correlate with sentencing decisions among those convicted of first-degree murder, the results will be conservative because these earlier decision points are not studied, and whatever improper biases may or may not exist will not be spotted. In addition, our data measure only whether or not the death penalty was imposed. This sentence reflects decisions made not only by prosecutors, but also by judges and juries. To pinpoint any political influences in prosecutors' decisions, the ideal research project would examine cases where the death penalty was sought, not only where it is imposed.

Several sources of official data were supplied to the researchers to develop the analytic database for this analysis. The final database for this analysis was based exclusively on data supplied and/or collected by the State of Illinois. The specific data used in this study are outlined below.

1. <u>Department of Corrections:</u> Our "master list" of cases was obtained from the Illinois Department of Corrections (IDOC). This is a confidential, non-public database that was made available to us solely for purposes of this study. That office maintains an "Offender Tracking System" (OTS) data file that contains a wide array of information about the offender and the offense/s for which she or he was convicted. Included are only those

20 William G. Potratz, *The Prosecutor's Discretionary Power to Initiate the Death Sentencing Hearing*, 29 DEPAUL L. REV. 1097 (1980).

cases where defendants were sentenced for first-degree murder, where the sentencing date occurred between 1/1/88 through 12/31/97.

In addition to providing the sample of events that are the basis for this study, IDOC data also allowed us to construct a broad range of variables that measure the potential seriousness of a homicide(s) associated with the first-degree homicide offenders in our sample. This is possible because IDOC data provide information on all previous and contemporaneous offenses for which a first-degree homicide offender has been convicted and incarcerated in Illinois Department of Corrections. Two types of indicators of legally-relevant factors were developed from IDOC data on offenses for which defendants were incarcerated: indicators of 1) death sentence eligibility and 2) aggravating facts for the death sentencing proceeding. Finally, IDOC data also provides information on the race and sex of offenders and on the county from which offenders in this study were sentenced.

While the IDOC data provide detailed information on the offense, we turned to three additional sources of data to obtain information about the victims.

2. Chicago Homicide Data: Approximately three-quarters of Illinois homicides occur in Cook County, and almost all of those take place in the City of Chicago. Detailed data on Chicago homicides has been collected by the Chicago Police Department, on and off, for at least 130 years. Data from cases during the study period were obtained from the Illinois Criminal Justice Information Authority (ICJIA). The data give important information about the circumstances of the crime and characteristics of the victim. Of special importance is that the Chicago Police data also contain a unique number that we used to link the case with the information on the offender in the IDOC database.[21] Using the unique Chicago case number we were able to link information on the victims of homicide to 2,898 (or 54.7 percent) of the offenders in the sample.

3. Victim Data from Selected State and Local Records: Information on the race, ethnicity and sex of victims for non-Chicago first-degree murders in the study sample was obtained primarily by the Illinois Criminal Justice Information Authority, a state agency responsible for research on the criminal justice system in Illinois. This information was gathered by ICJIA through a search of a variety of official records, both state and local, including some law enforcement records. Information was gathered on the age, gender, and race of victims of non-Chicago first-degree murder offenders in the study sample. Data was gathered on the race of victims for an additional 1,091 (or 20.6 percent) first-degree murder offenders in the sample.

4. Supplemental Homicide Reports Data: For offenders in the study for which no victim information was available from the search of state records or from linking to

21 The Chicago Police Department's unique identifying link, which the Department provided to connect IDOC case numbers to victim information, was provided by the Chicago Police Department. These linking identifiers are generally not available to the public. They were obtained for this study pursuant to a confidentiality agreement.

Chicago police data, a final search for victim information was conducted through use of the Supplemental Homicide Report (SHR) data. SHRs represent homicide data gathered by local police departments and forwarded to the Federal Bureau of Investigation for national tabulations. While the data do not give the name of the victim or offender, or the specific date of the offense, they do contain information on the county, month, and year of the offense, the gender, race, and age of the defendant and victim, and information on 1) the victim–defendant relationship, 2) the method of killing, and 3) information on the type of felony (if any) that accompanied the homicide. There was sufficient SHR information on the race, age, and sex of offenders, as well as on the date and county of offense to "match" SHR victim data with comparable information from the Department of Corrections. Using SHR data we were able to link homicide victim information to 263 additional offenders in the sample that did not already have victim data from the state or Chicago Police sources. Linking to SHR data added an additional 4.9 percent of offenders where the victim information was available. Overall race of victim information was matched to 80.1 percent of the offenders in our sample.

B. Variables Used for the Analysis

Two major categories of variables were developed for this analysis; legally-relevant factors that could be expected to affect the likelihood of a first degree murder offender receiving a death sentence, and extra-legal factors which should not affect whether an offender receives a death sentence. Among the legally-relevant factors two types of indicators were developed for the first degree murder offenders in this study: 1) indicators of death sentence eligibility, and 2) indicators of aggravating facts. Below the specific variables used in the analysis are reviewed within their major substantive categories.

1. <u>Indicators of Death Sentence Eligibility</u>: Illinois has a bifurcated death-sentencing proceeding. The first part focuses on the question of whether the defendant is eligible for the death penalty. Here the State must prove, beyond a reasonable doubt, that the defendant is at least age 18, and prove the existence of at least one of the twenty death penalty eligibility factors provided for under Illinois law. Using IDOC offender data, we developed indicators for two major classes of death penalty eligibility; specifically, indicators were developed for "multiple-murder factor" first-degree murders and "in the course of another felony" first-degree murders. Under the multiple-murder factor a defendant may be eligible for the death penalty if s/he has been convicted of murdering two or more individuals. Case law indicates that these contemporaneous and/or prior convictions must be for intentional murder or for knowing murder (not for felony murder) to qualify as a multiple murder eligibility factor. Variables 1 and 2 in Table 2 present the indicators of contemporaneous and prior multiple murder eligibility factors used in this analysis. Appendix II presents the specific Illinois statutory citations for convictions that define these factors in the present study.

Under the "in the course of another felony" factor a defendant is eligible for the death penalty where the murder has occurred in the course of any one of several statutorily specified felonies. Using IDOC data a number of specific "in the course of another felony" eligibility indicators were developed, based on convictions for felonies that occurred within the same sentencing event as the first-degree murder for which the defendant was incarcerated. Variables 3 through 12 in Table 2 present the indicators of "in the course of another felony" eligibility factors used in this study. Appendix II presents the specific Illinois statutory citations that identify crimes as potential contemporaneous felonies. There is a requirement that, in addition to a contemporaneous felony offense,[22] there be some element of intentional or knowing conduct on the part of offender. This element cannot be measured with IDOC data.

Finally, three additional indicators of death penalty eligibility were developed from victim information that we obtained from the Chicago Police Department, state records, or SHR data sources. Specifically indicators for the murder of an elderly person (over age 59), for the murder of a young person (under age 12), and for multiple-victim murders (contemporaneous murders, but not necessarily "intentional or knowing") were developed from victim data. For the age of the victim to qualify as death penalty eligibility factors requires "brutal and heinous" conduct, which are factors that we were unable to measure. Variables 13 through 15 in Table 2 present these indicators.

2. Indicators of Aggravating Facts: After the defendant is determined to be eligible for the death penalty, then proceedings move on to the "aggravation/mitigation" phase. At that point, the state provides evidence in aggravation (prior criminal history, etc.) and defendant provides mitigation evidence. In theory those defendants with the worst set of aggravating facts (e.g., the worst criminal history) should be more likely to receive the death penalty (assuming level of culpability, etc., is constant).

IDOC data provides information on evidence in aggravation in the form of measures of contemporaneous or prior other serious murder convictions (e.g., solicitation for murder, conspiracy to murder, attempted murder, etc.), and in the form of measures of offender's prior criminal history that go beyond the offender's prior history of murder. In terms of prior criminal history, IDOC provides information on the number of prior IDOC incarcerations for all Class X, 1, 2, 3, and 4 offenses for the first-degree offenders in our sample (see variables 16 through 22 in Table 2 for the indicators of other serious murder convictions and prior criminal history). Appendix II presents the specific Illinois statutory citations that identify other serious murder convictions and other felony convictions.

3. Indicators of Extra Legal Factors: Information on the race, ethnicity and sex of victims was provided from victim information that we acquired from the Chicago Police

22 An actual conviction for the contemporaneous felony is not required for an offense to serve as a death sentence eligibility factor. Since we can only measure the cases where there was an actual conviction, that makes our data more conservative.

Department, selected state records, or SHR data sources (see variables 23 and 24). IDOC data provides information on the race and sex of offenders (see variables 25 and 26 in Table 2) and on the county from which offenders in this study were sentenced (see variable 27). Information on offender's trial court sentencing county allows us to investigate the possibility of geographic disparities in death penalty sentencing. The county of offender's sentencing was coded into four standard Illinois sub-regions used by the Illinois Criminal Justice Authority (ICJIA), specifically; Cook County, "Collar" counties, other urban counties, and rural counties. Because of its size, Cook County is its own category. The Collar counties are the five counties which border Cook County (DuPage, Lake, Kane, McHenry and Will). Urban and rural counties are defined by whether or not they lay within a Metropolitan Statistical Area (MSA). Based on this definition, there are 28 counties in Illinois that are part of a MSA (Cook, Collar and urban counties) and 74 counties that are not part of a MSA (in other words, rural).

A number of obvious potential extra legal factors are not included in the analysis, such as the social class of the victim, whether the victim was a member of the community, adequacy of legal counsel, and the quality of police/forensic investigative work on the case. In addition to these more obvious factors, this class of variables has the peculiar quality of containing information that may seemingly be far removed from the legal process of a given case, but may nevertheless sometimes have a direct and significant effect on the imposition of a death sentence. Such factors may include events such as violent crime waves or spectacular media coverage of violent crime, and/or they may include organizational/political phenomena, such as political campaigns or local community pressures. Very little is known about the influence of these types of factors on processes in the criminal justice system, because they are very difficult to study. Nevertheless they do provide some examples of types of extra legal factors that are potentially useful to examine in death penalty research and may be important in the monitoring of the death sentencing process.

Table 2
Independent Variables for Death Sentence Analysis

1. MPMFM1
   Prior Intentional/Knowing Murder (no=0; yes=1)
2. MCMFACTR
   Contemporaneous Intentional/Knowing Murder (no=0; yes=1)
3. MCGRPA1
   Contemporaneous Armed Robbery (no=0; yes=1)
4. MCGRPB1
   Contemporaneous Aggravated Criminal Sexual Assault (no=0; yes=1)
5. MCGRPC1
   Contemporaneous Home Invasion (group 3c) (no=0; yes=1)

6. MCGRPD1
   Contemporaneous Aggravated Kidnapping (group 3d) (no=0; yes=1)
7. MCGRPE1
   Contemporaneous Arson (no=0; yes=1)
8. MCGRPF1
   Contemporaneous Simple Robbery (no=0; yes=1)
9. MCGRP3BR
   Contemporaneous Residential Robbery (no=0; yes=1)
10. MCGRP3CR
    Contemporaneous Armed Violence (no=0; yes=1)
11. MCGRP3DR
    Contemporaneous Vehicular Hijack (no=0; yes=1)
12. MCBFCTR1
    Contemporaneous Burglary (no=0; yes=1)
13. VCCNTT4
    Number of Homicide Victims (1, 2, 3, 4+)
14. VICGT59D
    Homicide Victims Over Age 59 (no=0; yes=1)
15. VICLT12D
    Homicide Victims Under Age 12 (no=0; yes=1)
16. MCSM2
    Contemporaneous Other Serious Murder Convictions (0, 1, 2+)
17. MPSM2
    Prior Other Serious Murder Convictions (0, 1, 2+)
18. MPCLAS12
    Prior Class 1 Offenses (0, 1, 2+)
19. MPCLAS22
    Prior Class 2 Offenses (0, 1, 2+)
20. MPCLAS32
    Prior Class 3 Offenses (0, 1, 2+)
21. MPCLAS42
    Prior Class 4 Offenses (0, 1, 2+)
22. MPCLASX2
    Prior Class X Offenses
23. VICSEXD
    One or more female victims (none, 1+)
24. VICRACE
    Victim's Race (1 only white, 2 only black, 3 only Hispanic, 4 only other race, 5 victims from more than one race)

24a. VICBLKD
At least one black victim (none, 1+)—This is a dichotomous variable version of variable 24.

25. MIRSEX
Offender's sex is female (0 not female, 1 female)

26. OFFRACE
Offender's Race (1 white, 2 black, 3 Hispanic, 4 other race)

26a OFFBLACK (0 not black, 1 black)—This is a dichotomous variable version of variable 26.

27. COUNTY
County of Trial (1 Cook County, 2 Collar Counties, 3 Other Urban Counties, 4 Rural Counties)

27a. COOKOTH
County of Trial (0 Not Cook County, 1 Cook County)—This is a dichotomous variable version of variable 27.

27b. CNTYCOUR
County of Trial (0 Not Collar or Other Urban counties, 1 collar of Other Urban Counties)—This is a dichotomous variable version of variable 27.

C. Statistical Approach

The analysis first examines the bivariate relationships between sentencing and 22 indicators of legally relevant factors that are potential determinants of death sentencing in Illinois. These indicators include measures of death penalty eligibility factors (variables 2–15 in Table 2), and measures of facts of aggravation (variables 16–22 in Table 2). The analysis also examines the bivariate relationship between death sentencing and three potential extra-legal factors including, the race and sex of victims, the race and sex homicide offenders, and the county where the offender were sentenced (variables 23–27 in Table 2).

After presenting the results of these cross-tabulations, we then assess the unique ability of each of these variables to explain who is and who is not sentenced to death. That is, we assess the potential impact of extra-legal factors on death sentencing while statistically controlling for legally relevant factors. To do this, logistic regression analysis was employed. Logistic regression models estimate the average effect of each independent variable (predictor) on the odds that a convicted felon would receive a sentence of death. An odds ratio is simply the ratio of the probability of a death sentence to the probability of a sentence other than death. Thus, when one's likelihood of receiving a death sentence is .75 (P), then the probability of receiving a non-death sentence is .25 (1-P). The odds ratio in this example is .75/25 or 3 to 1. Simply put, the odds of getting the death sentence in this case are 3 to 1.

The dependent variable is natural logarithm of the odds ratio, y, of having received the death penalty. Thus, y = P / 1–P and;

$$(1)\ln(y) = \hat{a}_0 + X\hat{a} + E_i$$

where $\hat{a}_0$ is an intercept, $\hat{a}_i$ are the i coefficients for the i independent variables, X is the matrix of observations on the independent variables, and E_i is the error term.

Results for the logistic model are reported as odds ratios. Recall that when interpreting odds ratios, an odds ratio of 1 means that someone with that specific characteristic is just as likely to receive a capital sentence as not. Odds ratios of greater than one indicate a higher likelihood of the death penalty for those offenders who have a positive value for that particular independent variable. When the independent variable is continuous, the odds ratio indicates the increase in the odds of receiving the death penalty for each unitary increase in the predictor.

V. FINDINGS

A total of 5,310 cases in the study time frame were identified from IDOC records, of which 115 ended with a death sentence. Of the 5,310 total cases, there was county of trial information on 5,300. We were able to match 4,252 cases with race of victim information (80.1 percent). Of the cases we were able to match to race of victim, 84.1 percent of the cases in Cook County were matched, 60.8 of the cases in the collar county region were matched, 72.9 percent of the cases in the urban county region were matched, and 66.1 percent of the cases in the rural county region were matched. The subset of cases for which there is no missing data for any of the 27 independent variables used in this analysis (see Table 2) is 4,182 cases, which contain 76 death sentence cases.

1. Bivariate Analysis of Death Sentence Eligibility. Tables 3 through 17 are presented in Appendix III. They examine the imposition of the death penalty by the indicators of death sentence eligibility. These include indicator for "multiple murder factor" (i.e., conviction for a contemporaneous or prior "intentional or knowing murder" in addition to the offender's first-degree murder conviction), and for "in the course of another felony" murders. In addition, death sentence eligibility indicators are examined for the murder of an elderly person (over age 59), the murder of a young person (under age 12), and for multiple victim murders.[23]

Tables 3 and 4 examine the imposition of a death sentence by convictions for prior and contemporaneous murder. Both variables show a statistically significant relation with

---

23 It should be noted that the multiple murder conviction factor and the multiple victim murder indicator are not duplicative since one depends almost entirely prior murder convictions and one relates to the number of victims in a single incident.

death sentencing. Under the "in the course of another felony" factor, a defendant is eligible for the death penalty when the murder has occurred in the course of any one of several statutorily specified felonies. Tables 5 through 14 examine the imposition of the death penalty by our indicators of "in the course of another felony" eligibility factors. Of the ten accompanying felony indicators examined, nine showed a statistically significant relationship with imposition of the death sentence based on the Pearson chi-square test, and six showed a significant relation base on the Yates Continuity Correction for the chi-square test.[24] Some of these indicators may not have achieved a statistically significant relationship with death sentences due to the low frequency of their occurrence in the sample. In addition, the magnitude of the relationships between the "in the course of another felony" factors and imposition of a death sentence shows considerable variability across the ten indicators. Among the indicators showing a statistically significant effect on death sentencing, the percent of death sentences imposed where one of these eligibility factors is present varies from a low of 4.1 percent for the armed robbery indicator (Table 5) to a high of 15.7 percent for the aggravated kidnapping indicator (Table 8). Since these variables represent indicators of death penalty eligibility, the data indicate that the eligibility factors vary considerably in their overall importance in death penalty decisions.

Tables 15 through 17 examine imposition of the death penalty by the three indicators of death sentence eligibility derived from homicide victim data: the murder of an elderly person (over age 59), the murder of a young person (under age 12), and for multiple victim murders. As would be expected, each of these indicators shows a statistically significant correlation with imposition of the death sentence, with the multiple victims murder indicator showing the largest effect on death sentencing.

2. <u>Bivariate Analysis of Facts of Aggravation.</u> As noted, after a defendant is determined to be eligible for the death penalty, the judicial proceedings then move on to the "aggravation/mitigation" phase. At that point, the state provides evidence in aggravation (e.g., prior criminal history), and defendant provides mitigation evidence. IDOC data provides information on evidence in aggravation in the form of measures of contemporaneous or prior "other serious murder convictions" (e.g., solicitation for murder, conspiracy to murder, attempted murder, etc.), and in the form of measures of offender's prior criminal history that go beyond the offender's prior history of murder.

Tables 18 and 19 examine imposition of the death penalty by contemporaneous and prior "other serious murder convictions." Convictions for contemporaneous offenses are not statistically related to the imposition of a death sentence. Cases with one or more convictions for prior "other serious murder offenses" show a statistically significant

24 In using the chi-square as a test for statistical significance care must be taken if in a given table some of the expected frequencies are very low (under 10). In this case the Yates continuity correction reduces the difference between the observed and expected frequencies by .5. This reduces the overall size of the chi-square and provides a more conservative estimate of statistical significance.

relationship with imposition of the death sentence only using the Pearson Chi-square test, but not with the Continuity Correction.

In terms of prior criminal history, IDOC provides information on the number of prior IDOC incarcerations for all Class X, 1, 2, 3, and 4 offenses for the first-degree offenders in our sample. Tables 20 through 24 examine the relationship between offenders' prior criminal record and imposition of the death sentence. Of the five indicators of prior criminal record examined, three show a statistically significant relationship with death sentencing. The indicators not statistically related to the death sentence were 1) an offender's prior record of incarcerations of Class 1 offenses (Table 21), and 2) their prior record of Class 4 offenses (Table 24).

3. Bivariate Analysis of Extra Legal Factors. Extra legal factors represent those factors that should not affect whether an offender receives a death sentence. A major objective of this study is to examine the potential impact of extra legal factors on death sentencing in Illinois. Factors we examined include geographic region of the state, the race and sex of the first-degree murder victims and offenders.

Geographic Region. Information on county of sentence allows us to investigate the possibility of geographic disparities in death penalty sentencing decisions. To this end, offender's county of trial was coded into the four standard Illinois sub-regions used by the Illinois Criminal Justice Information Authority: Cook County, Collar counties, other urban counties, and rural counties. Table 25 shows patterns of death sentencing in these four regions. In Cook County, 1.5 percent the first-degree murders ended with a death sentence, versus 3.3 percent of the cases in the Collar counties, 3.4 percent of the cases in other urban counties, and 8.4 percent of the cases in rural counties. The cross regional differences were statistically significant at < .001 level of significance.

Sex and Race of Victim. Table 26 examines the imposition of the death sentences by the sex of the homicide victims. Examination of Table 26 shows that the sex of murder victims is significantly related to imposition of the death sentence. Specifically, 4.3 percent of the offenders who were convicted of killing one or more females received the death penalty, versus 1.2 percent of the offenders who were convicted of killing solely male victims.

Table 27 reveals statistically significant differences in the imposition of the death penalty by race of first-degree murder victims. Specifically, 3.8 percent of the first-degree murder cases where the victim(s) was white resulted in a death sentence, versus 1.1 percent of the cases where the murder victim(s) was black, and 1.5 percent of the cases where the victim(s) was Hispanic.[25] Where the victim was "other" race or was part of a mixed race multiple homicide case, the death sentence was imposed 5.7 and 4.0 percent of the

25 No information on ethnicity was available on the 263 cases that were matched to SHR for race of victim data. For these 263 cases victims who were Hispanic would have been coded as white or possibly black victims depending on their race.

time respectively. This disparity in the imposition of the death sentence was statistically significant at a < .001 level of significance.

Sex and Race of Offender. Table 28 examines the imposition of death sentences by the sex of the offender. Examination of Table 28 shows that 1.3% of the women and 2.2% of the men in our sample were sentenced to death. This difference, however, is not statistically significant.

Examination of Table 29 reveals statistically significant differences in the imposition of the death penalty by race of offender. Specifically, 4.5 percent of the first-degree murder cases where the offender was white resulted in a death sentence, versus 1.8 percent of the cases where the offender was black, and .7 percent of the cases where the offender was Hispanic.[26] None of the 23 cases where the offender's race was listed as "other" ended in a death sentence. However, as we will discuss below, focusing simply on the race of offender without also including race of victim can be very misleading. This disparity in the imposition of the death sentence was statistically significant at a < .001 level of significance.

Race of Victim and Offender Combinations. Initial examination of Table 29 shows that black offenders are less likely to receive the death penalty than white offenders, given a conviction for first-degree murder. We also know, however, that most murders are intra-racial incidents and that (as Table 27 shows) first-degree murders with black victims are the least likely to receive the death sentence. Thus, in order to examine the imposition of the death penalty by the race of offender, it is important to also control for the race of victim. In comparing white and black homicide offenders, we must control for the race of the victim because our data show that blacks are most likely to be convicted for killing other blacks and the murders of black victims are the least likely to receive a death sentence.

Table 30 examines the imposition of the death sentence by race-of-victim and offender combinations for white and black victims and offenders. Examination of this Table shows that when race of victim is taken into consideration, the offender race differences largely disappear. Thus, among offenders convicted of killing white victims, 4.5 percent of the black offenders received a death sentence, versus 4.8 percent of the white offenders. In contrast, only 1.1 percent of the black offenders who killed black victims were sentenced to death. Finally, 4.8 percent of the whites who were convicted of killing blacks received the death sentence, but this percent is based on only 62 cases in this category.

4. Multivariate Analysis of Indicators of Death Eligibility. Aggravating Facts, and Extra Legal Factors. In the final stage of our analysis, we assess the potential impact of extra-legal factors on death sentencing while statistically controlling for legally relevant factors. To do this, as noted above, logistic regression analysis was employed. Logistic regression models estimate the effect of each independent variable (predictor) on the odds that a convicted felon would receive a sentence of death while controlling for the other variables in the equation.

---

26 See note 24.

Logistic regression is the preferred statistical approach for analysis of dichotomous dependent variables such as the dependent variable in this study that measures the presence or absence of a death sentence. Nevertheless, any multivariate statistical technique will be limited by the quality and scope of available data. As noted, despite extensive efforts to obtain data, there may be important legal and/or extra legal factors that have not been included in the present analysis. In addition, although most of the independent variables in the study have very little missing data, there are some missing data on race and sex of victims.

Finally, we have limited the scope of the analysis to more recent first-degree murder cases (i.e., cases that were sentenced between 1/1/88 and 12/31/97). By doing so we assume that these more recent cases better reflect the death penalty today than do pre-1988 cases that we did not examine.

Table 31a presents the results of the logistic regression analysis. The logistic analysis shows that two important extra-legal factors identified in the bivariate analysis: race-of-victim and sentencing county/region are statistically significant predictors of imposition of the death sentence after controlling for the 22 indicators of legally relevant factors developed for this study. Of the statutorily defined indicators of death penalty eligibility (variables 1-12 in Table 2 and in the logistic regression) introduced into the analysis, 7 out of 12 indicators remained statistically significant predictors of death sentencing when the effects of all the other variables were controlled.

Comparison across all the variables in the logistic regression analysis shows that sentencing county/region (i.e., Cook County) and race of victim (one or more black victims versus all other race of victim categories, variable 24a, Table 2) are among the five independent variables (out of 27 variables) that achieved the highest level of statistical significance (see the Wald statistic in Table 31a). To examine the estimated effect of an independent variable, controlling on the other variables, we use the exponentiated value of the Beta (B) coefficient, which is the logistic regression beta coefficient, Exp(B)(see the Table 31a for these coefficients). The Exp(B) coefficient is the B coefficient expressed as an odds ratio.

Examination of the Exp(B) coefficients in Table 31a shows that the odds of receiving a death sentence for killing a black victim(s) decrease by a factor of .404, controlling on the other 26 independent variables. As noted, .404, (the Exp(B) value for black victim) is the odds ratio of a first-degree murder offender who killed a black victim being sentenced to death. An odds ratio of exactly 1.0 would mean that the likelihood of receiving the death sentence changed by a factor of 1, or not at all. In this case, the results indicate that the odds of receiving a death sentence, if a first-degree murder offender kills a black victim, are on average 59.6 percent lower (i.e., 1–.404 = .596 or 59.6%) controlling for the other 26 variables in the analysis.

Turning to the question of geographic region, Table 31a indicates that the odds of receiving a death sentence for killing a victim(s) in Cook County decease by a factor of .164 (i.e., the Exp(B) value for Cook County in Table 31a). Likewise, the odds of receiving a death sentence for killing a victim(s) in Cook County are on average 83.6 percent lower than for killing a victim(s) in the airal county region of Illinois controlling for the other 26 variables in the analysis.

Readers of this report will disagree among themselves about the policy implications suggested by our finding of geographic disparities. Some will say that the finding that first-degree murder offenders in Cook County are less likely to receive the death sentence than offenders in other counties may mean that the Cook County criminal justice system is not pursuing potential death sentence cases with sufficient rigor. Others will argue that rural counties are imposing the death sentence too liberally and/or without sufficient oversight. However, one consequence to carefully consider in proposing that Cook County is not rigorously and/or properly pursuing death sentences, is that a more rigorous application of the death sentence by Cook County, on the order of the rural county region or even the other urban county region, would result in dramatically higher numbers of offenders sentenced to death in Illinois.

Overall, the statistical analysis reveals some surprises about what factors correlate with death sentences in Illinois. Some of the predictor variables that would be expected to affect death sentencing do not show statistically significant relationships with sentence outcomes. For example, of the 12 indicators of statutorily-defined death eligibility included in the analysis, only seven were significantly related to death sentencing, even though each one of the twelve are legally relevant in identifying which first-degree murder cases are eligible for a death sentence. These 12 indicators represent two (i.e., the multiple murder factor and in the course of another felony factor) of the twenty death eligibility factors identified in Illinois statues. Nonetheless, these two factors are the most commonly used factors in death sentence cases, and thus account for a high proportion of death eligible cases.

VI. CONCLUSIONS AND POLICY RECOMMENDATIONS

A. Limits to this Study

The results of this study are limited by both scope and data. First, the goal of this study was to examine only those cases that involved a conviction for first-degree murder, comparing cases that resulted in a death sentence with those that did not. Our study examines only sentencing decisions, not charging decisions or a wide array of other decisions involved in sending a defendant to death row. It is quite possible that disparities correlated with extra-legal factors (e.g., race, social class, region, or gender) also exist, either at a greater or lesser strength, in decisions in the criminal justice system that are not examined in this research.

Critics of this study who point to its limited scope and limited number of variables should realize that the addition of more data could very well increase the power of non-legal explanatory variables. Baldus et al, for example, point to nine states where both well-controlled and less-well-controlled studies of death sentencing have been conducted. In two-thirds of these states, the racial disparities were stronger in the well-controlled studies than in the less complex work.[27] Certainly the data we have gathered for this research is strong enough to raise serious concerns in the minds of both those who support and oppose the death penalty about whether it is being equitably applied in Illinois.

A second limitation of this research is missing victim data on cases included in our analysis. As noted, we were able to match 4,252 cases with race of victim information (80.1 percent) to form the final sample for our analysis. However, missing data is only a problem if the cases excluded are somehow different than the cases for which we do have complete data. We see nothing to indicate that the cases with missing data in this study are significantly different than the cases for which there are data.

B. Summary of Major Conclusions

Indicators of two extra legal factors, the race of first-degree murder victims and geographic region, were found to be statistically related to the imposition of the death sentence in Illinois controlling on the other variables in this study. Although there are limitations to the present study, these findings on race and geography are consistent with those reported in many other studies. This pattern of findings raises important concerns about how the death sentence is imposed in Illinois.

A major limitation of this study is the lack of high-quality data that is needed to measure additional factors that may affect death penalty decision making. A great deal of time and effort was expended to acquire data necessary for the present study, and despite these efforts, the present study's data is limited in both scope and completeness. The data problems encountered in this study are not the responsibility of the Illinois state and local agencies that participated in this study. They provided extensive support and consultation (at no cost) to the project. The problem arises because present criminal justice information systems were designed primarily to support administrative functions of the agencies they assist. These systems were not designed to support research activities and, equally important, judicial monitoring activities. Thus the limitations of data and information encountered by this study directly mirror the limitations that any death sentencing monitoring system would encounter in Illinois. Indeed, properly conducted assessments of death sentences in Illinois would resemble smaller scale projects of the type conducted for this project. Critically, today's criminal justice information systems are entirely inadequate to collect, manage and integrate the range and quality of information on criminal cases necessary to support a reliable criminal justice monitoring system. As

---

27 Baldus et al., *supra* note 7 (Cornell), at 1661–62.

a result, the quality of available criminal data will greatly limit the integrity of any death sentencing monitoring system for the foreseeable future.

C. Recommendations

The results of our analysis lead us to suggest two policy recommendations.

1. Proportionality Review. The data suggest the necessity for the Illinois Supreme Court, as the body responsible for reviewing death penalty cases, to pay special attention to issues of proportionality.[28] Like New Jersey, they might consider a comparison between cases in which the death penalty was imposed and other death-eligible cases with equal levels of aggravation and mitigation in which the defendant was sentenced to a prison term.[29] This type of review, however, will be very limited if only cases that end with a death sentence are examined and information and cases from prior stages of the criminal justice system decision-making process are not available.

2. Monitoring. To conduct a meaningful proportionality review, officials will need to construct, maintain, and use a database on Illinois homicides. As criminologists, one of the most important lessons we have learned from this research is that data on Illinois homicides is fragmented, difficult to obtain, and often of poor quality. It has been gathered not for purposes of ensuring even-handedness in sentencing, but rather for unique needs of individual state agencies (e.g., local police departments, Department of Corrections). If the death penalty is to be continued, comprehensive high-quality data needs to be gathered and made available to a diverse group of researchers so that issues of equity can be monitored.

A monitoring system built on a foundation of comprehensive high-quality data can be used both to help ensure that race and other inappropriate factors are not involved in death sentencing decisions, and to help ensure that pure arbitrariness (inequities not attributable to either legal or not-legal factors) does not permeate sentencing. While it is beyond the mandate given to the current authors to design a comprehensive monitoring system, it is clear that there must be an intensive effort by all parties involved in capital cases in Illinois to gather detailed data on all aspects of homicide cases. Here we are not suggesting data collection on decisions made from charging through sentencing, but, rather, going back to the day of the homicide and beginning with measures of the quality of the investigation

---

28 For an elaboration on this and on other ideas to improve the administration of the death penalty, see THE CONSTITUTION PROJECT, MANDATORY JUSTICE: EIGHTEEN REFORMS TO THE DEATH PENALTY 27 (2001).

29 This proportionality review has the added advantage of alerting prosecutors and trial courts to the importance of issues of proportionality, which in turn may affect decisions on when to seek a death sentence. The New Jersey Supreme Court, for example, has struck down only one death sentence because of issues of proportionality. State v. Papasavvas, 2002 N.J. LEXIS 51 (Feb. 14, 2002).

by the police. If the police devote more resources to the investigation of the murders of prominent white victims than to other cases, even if all other decision-makers (e.g., prosecutors, judges, jurors, and governors) are fair, racial bias will still permeate the system. In addition, a database needs to be constructed to follow all cases from the time a death sentence is imposed to the time the person exits death row (via court or gubernatorial action, natural death, suicide, or execution). All links in the "continuous chain" of decision makers need to be involved in gathering data, which they can use to monitor their own performance.[30]

In some cases, data gathering itself may add an element of fairness in the system. For example, a study that examines charging decisions would most certainly remind prosecutors of their duty to be even-handed. But even if they were, decisions made at earlier points (e.g., by police) would remain invisible. Gathering data at all decision-points on the chain of decisions makes the decisions more transparent, more accountable, and reminds everyone that their work is no longer invisible.

Those designing such a database would need input from prosecutors, defense attorneys, judges, law enforcement investigators, forensic experts and other criminal justice personnel, as well as scholars and other more disinterested parties. To be sure, there will undoubtedly be differences in informed opinion between various parties in the debate, but if all cooperate in data gathering, the system will be made much more transparent.

Recent research has also shown the importance of gathering data on the racial characteristics of potential jurors in capital cases, and on how (and why) jurors are excused through peremptory challenges. The most thorough research to address this issue focused on 317 capital prosecutions in Philadelphia, 1981–1997. The authors found that "discrimination in the use of peremptory challenges on the basis of race and gender by both prosecutors and defense counsel is widespread."[31] They found that prosecutors are more successful than defense attorneys in controlling jury composition, and that these biases tend to increase the number of death sentences and the degree of racial discrimination in death sentencing decisions. The opportunity for prosecutors and defense attorneys to interview jurors after they have completed their service and rendered their verdicts might reveal occasional acts of overt racism that may have infected their work.

30 The racial and ethnic backgrounds of these decision-makers are one example of data needed (as well as continued efforts to bring more diversity into the decision-making circle).

31 David C. Baldus, George Woodworth, David Zuckerman, Neil Alan Weiner, & Barbara Brottiff, The Use of Peremptory Challenges in Capital Murder Trials: A Legal and Empirical Analysis, 3 U. OF PENN. 1. OF CONSTITUTIONAL LAW 3 (2001); *see also* William J. Bowers, Benjamin D. Steiner, and Marla Sandys, *Death Sentencing in Black and White: An Empirical Analysis of the Role of Jurors' Race and Jury Racial Composition*, 3 U. OF PENN. J. OF CONSTITUTIONAL LAW 171 (2001).

D. A Final Note

In conclusion, the unique character of homicide in general and the death penalty in particular raises the distinct possibility of powerful political and psychological factors intruding on and interfering with the criminal justice and judicial decision process and with the goal of equity in administration of the death penalty. Hence the importance of vigilant monitoring. When a murder occurs, all who hear about it—citizens, prosecutors, jurors—feel a threat and a need to confront, to varying degrees, personal fears of death. One way to deal with the threat is to retreat to the comfort of people who are familiar to us. When the murder victim is among those communities with which we are most familiar (and race and social class are part of the victim's social or human capital that can make them part of that familiar community) and the killer is more of an outsider (both in social and geographic sense), the fear and outrage grow.

And in the past thirty years, the potential for death penalty decisions to become more political has grown like never before. One reason for this is media pressure—the media can sensationalize homicides and prioritize them in terms of outrage and threat (not all murders are given equal media coverage), and it can put pressure on decision-makers to accept those priorities. In addition, all of the reforms in the death penalty in the past three decades have made it extremely costly and time-consuming to pursue. Especially in these days where state budgets are constrained, prosecutors must make priority decisions. There may be pressure from one source to pursue death (e.g., from the media), but also pressure from the office accountant not to do so.

Rational and informed citizens will continue to disagree on the death penalty, but certainly one point on which all interested parties can agree is that if we are going to make these life and death decisions, we need to make them as carefully and equitably as possible.

APPENDIX I:

Post 1990 Research on Race and Death Sentencing Outside Illinois

In 1990, the U.S General Accounting Office examined some 28 studies that had studied issues of race and arbitrariness in death sentencing in various American jurisdictions since 1972. The year 1972 was chosen as a beginning because that year the Supreme Court invalidated all existing death penalty statutes, and legislatures began to enact the new wave of death statutes, some of which remain in effect today. The GAO synthesis of the 28 studies revealed:

> a pattern of evidence indicating racial disparities in the charging, sentencing, and imposition of the death penalty after the Furman decision. In 82 percent of the studies, race-of-victim was found to influence the likelihood of being charged with capital murder or receiving the death penalty ... This finding was

remarkably consistent across data sets, data collection methods, and analytic techniques.

The GAO found the evidence for a race-of-defendant impact was less clear, and hence the evidence supporting a victim's race effect was "equivocal." Since that report, additional high-quality studies have investigated the relationship between race and death sentencing in a) Arizona, b) Florida, c) Indiana, d) Kentucky, e) Maryland, f) Nebraska, g) New Jersey, h) North Carolina, i) Philadelphia, and j) Virginia, and we now briefly review those studies as well as an ongoing study of death sentencing under federal statutes.

A. Arizona

In September 2000, Arizona Attorney General Janet Napolitano appointed a 30-member Commission to prepare recommendations on how to "streamline the process," to examine legal representation, and to collect data on what types of homicides are most likely to result in a death sentence. She prohibited the Commission from examining whether a moratorium should be declared on executions, and from debating the issue of whether the death penalty should be abolished. "One of the things I want to ensure as the chief legal office (sic) of Arizona is that we do not become another Illinois."

Researchers from Arizona State University retained by the Commission began their work by examining the characteristics of 230 Arizona cases in which the death penalty was imposed (involving 228 defendants) between 1974 and July 1, 2000. This report was presented to the Commission in March 2001. Based on it, in July 2001, the Commission put forward three recommendations: additional resources for defense attorneys, commutation of death sentences for mentally ill death row inmates, and a ban on executing minors.

Next, the researchers built a database that included all cases (N=871) in which there was an indictment for first-degree murder in four Arizona counties, January 1, 1995, through December 31, 1999. Three groups of cases were compared: 1) the cases that ended with a death sentence (N=29), 2) the cases in this sample that were "death-noticed" (cases where the prosecutor announced that s/he would seek the death penalty) (N=343), and 3) the non-death noticed cases. Because the data from this analysis was presented to the Commission only recently (January 2002), no final conclusions or recommendations have yet been released. In its present state, only cross-tabulations have been calculated; no multivariate statistics were given to the Commission so they could pinpoint the effects of one variable (e.g., race of defendant) net of the effects of other factors. No data on race of victim is contained in the January 2002 report, and the restriction of the sample to four counties will restrict any possible conclusion about regional variation in death sentencing. Hence, at this date, no statement can be made about death sentencing patterns in Arizona.

A third data set being compiled by the Commission will attempt to measure the costs of the death penalty vs. the costs of the alternative sentence of "life without parole." No date has yet been announced for when these data will be released.

B. Florida

Of the 28 studies reviewed by the GAO in 1990, four were authored or coauthored by the two authors of the present report. The first study examined Florida, Georgia, Ohio, and Texas, while the other three studies examined patterns solely in Florida. Shortly after the GAO study was released, Radelet and Pierce released the results of their most recent Florida study.

Commissioned by the Florida Supreme Court's "Racial and Ethnic Bias Study Commission," the study examined some 15,000 Florida homicides, covering the years 1976 through 1987. After correcting for missing data, the final sample analyzed included 10,142 cases, 3.6 percent of which resulted in a death sentence. Initially, it was found that 5.9 percent of those who killed whites and 1.0 percent of those who killed blacks were sentenced to death. This was not because of any greater probability for whites to be victims of murders with additional felony circumstances present. Among the homicides with accompanying felonies, 16.2 percent of those who killed whites and 3.3 percent of those who killed blacks were sentenced to death. Radelet and Pierce went on to examine the effects of defendant–victim relationship, number of victims, victim's sex, type of weapon, and location of crime—none of which could explain the race effects. Overall, when all the explanatory variables were assessed with a linear equation, the authors found that the odds of a death sentence for those suspected of killing whites were 3.42 times higher than the odds of a death sentence for those suspected of killing blacks.

C. Indiana

While final results have not yet been released, a 26-member "Indiana Law Study Commission" was appointed by Governor Frank O'Bannon in March 2000 to study the administration of the death penalty in Indiana. Although the primary question investigated was whether Indiana needed additional safeguards to protect itself against the execution of the innocent, the effects of race on death sentencing were also examined. Preliminary results indicate that the race of victim is strongly associated with Indiana death sentencing, although it is unknown how detailed the data collection effort that underlies this conclusion has been.

D. Kentucky

The death penalty in Kentucky has been studied for many years by University of Louisville criminologists Thomas Keil and Gennaro Vito. Their latest work examines death sentencing from the time that Kentucky's current capital statute took effect in December 1976, through 1991. All 577 homicides that occurred in Kentucky during this study period were examined.

After statistically controlling for legally relevant factors such as concurrent felonies, history of violence, number of victims, and the existence of multiple aggravating factors, Keil and Vito found that black defendants charged with killing white victims were more likely to be charged with a capital crime (by the prosecutor) and more likely to be sentenced to death (by jurors) than other homicide defendants. As a direct result of this work, Kentucky legislators passed a "Racial Justice Act," allowing capital defendants to use statistical evidence to support a challenge their death sentences were inappropriately sought on the basis of race. Kentucky remains the only state to have enacted such legislation.

E. Maryland

A major study of race and death sentencing in Maryland is currently being undertaken by University of Maryland criminologist Ray Paternoster. Regional disparities in death sentencing in Maryland are already obvious. That state currently houses 13 death row inmates, 9 of whom were sentenced from Baltimore County. Baltimore County records approximately 10 percent of the state's homicides, but defendants from Baltimore County make up nearly 70 percent of the state's death row. Homicide rates are ten times higher in the City of Baltimore (averaging 390 per year since 1990) than in Baltimore County (averaging 31 homicides per year since 1990), but only one person is on death row from Baltimore City. There are two reasons for this disparity. First, over the past two decades the state attorney in Baltimore County, Sandra A. O'Connor, has sought the death penalty in virtually every case possible. Her only exceptions are when the family of the victim stands opposed to the death penalty or when the sole evidence against the defendant comes from the testimony of a co-defendant. Second, the County is overwhelmingly white, and white Americans tend to show more support for the death penalty than blacks.

Nine of the 13 inmates on death row in Maryland are black. Whether this disparity can be attributed to legally relevant factors will be revealed by the Paternoster study, due for completion in late 2002.

F. Nebraska

By any measure, the most comprehensive study of death sentencing in the past decade was that undertaken by David Baldus and his colleagues in Nebraska. This study was released in 2001. The study focused on all 177 Nebraska homicides, 1973–1999, that were eligible for the death penalty. Twenty-seven cases resulted in a death sentence. Despite these low numbers, there were several patterns that were strong enough to attain statistical significance.

Of the 177 cases, 17 percent of the white victim cases and 11 percent of the black victim cases resulted in a death sentence. Of the 177 death-eligible cases, 81 included a penalty trial, in which the death penalty was considered. Of those 81, 36 percent of the white victim cases and 21 percent of the black victim cases ended with a death sentence.

However, these race-of-victim differences were overshadowed by regional and social class differences in death sentencing. Prosecutors in the two urban areas of the state, Lincoln and Omaha, were much more likely than their counterparts in other areas of the state to seek death sentences. Because most minorities in Nebraska live in the urban areas, the death penalty has a differential impact on minorities, although there is no evidence that they are subjected to differential treatment. "The data indicate that the differences between charging and plea bargaining practices of prosecutors in the major urban counties and those in greater Nebraska produce a statewide "adverse disparate impact" on racial minorities."

Finally, prosecutors sought the death penalty in 37 percent of cases with low-status victims (33 cases), 50 percent of the cases with middle-status victims (32 cases), and 65 percent of the cases with high-status victims (15 cases).

G. <u>New Jersey</u>

Since 1989, the New Jersey Supreme Court has sponsored a rigorous effort to collect high-quality data on New Jersey homicides. Such data are necessary for the court to conduct a "proportionality review" in death penalty cases, whereby death-sentenced inmates can challenge their sentences by pointing to similar cases of other convicted murderers where the death penalty was not imposed. Both prosecutors and defense attorneys have had ample opportunities to critique the methodology of this work, and the database is publicly available so attorneys and researchers from a wide array of backgrounds can easily access it. Consequently, "no other empirical study of the death penalty's administration has received such close and sophisticated scrutiny."

Three "Special Masters" have been appointed by the Supreme Court to assist their study. The first, David Baldus, found some evidence of racial disparities, but sample sizes were too small for a thorough analysis. The second and the third Special Masters, Richard Cohen and David S. Baime, found no racial disparities in New Jersey death sentencing.

Judge Baime's most recent report (282 pages), submitted June 1, 2001, found that neither race of defendant nor race of victim played any significant role in death sentencing in New Jersey. However, some evidence "strongly suggests" that those who kill whites are more likely than those who kill blacks to advance a penalty phase (where death vs. life sentence is considered). Judge Baime attributes this to regional disparities in death prosecutions: counties with a large number of African American murder victims are less vigorous in their pursuit of the death penalty than less urban counties where there are a higher proportion of white-victim murders. Such regional disparities, however, are beyond the scope of Judge Baime's inquiry.

H. North Carolina

A 2001 study released by University of North Carolina–Chapel Hill researchers Isaac Unah and Jack Boger found that race "infects and undermines" the capital punishment system of that state. The researchers looked at the effects of 113 potential factors in 502 cases in which the death penalty was imposed, 1993 through 1997. "The odds of receiving a death sentence rose by 3.5 times or more among those defendants (regardless of the defendant's race) who murdered white persons."

I. Philadelphia

The death penalty in Pennsylvania is largely a "Philadelphia death penalty." At the end of 2000, there were more people on death row from Philadelphia—135—than on the death rows of 42 states. Ninety percent of these prisoners are racial or ethnic minorities. Not surprisingly, Philadelphia has become the site for the most comprehensive study of death sentencing that any city in the U.S. has ever received.

David Baldus and his colleagues analyzed eleven years of homicide data from Philadelphia, 1983–1993. It is a complex piece of scholarship; the effects of several variables, including race, were examined at six crucial decision points. They began with 707 homicide cases, 157 of which ended when the prosecutor accepted a guilty plea and waived a death sentence. In 125 other cases, the defendant did have a guilt trial, but the prosecutor waived the death penalty. A third stage is penalty phase bench trial; 41 defendants had a penalty trial before a judge only (only four of whom were sentenced to death), while 384 had a penalty trial before a jury. Next, the researchers differentiated those cases where aggravating factors were and were not found, and those cases where mitigating circumstances were and were not found (in 63 cases where no mitigation was found, the death penalty was automatically imposed). Finally, they compared 180 cases where the aggravators were found to not outweigh the mitigators with 51 cases in which the death penalty was imposed after this weighing procedure (i.e., the aggravating circumstances outweighed the mitigating circumstances).

The researchers found widespread race-of-defendant and race-of-victim disparities, with the former, in most analyses, stronger than those exerted by race-of-victim. For example, among defendants who have a penalty trial, the odds of a death sentence for black defendants are 9.3 times higher than the odds faced by nonblack defendants, or, restated in another way, the odds of a death sentence for black defendants are 1.6 times greater than the odds for a similarly-situated nonblack defendant. In addition, cases in which the homicide victim has a low socioeconomic status were less likely to end with a death sentence. The race effects were strongest in cases with a midrange level of aggravation.

J. Virginia

Capital sentencing in Virginia was the subject of a one-year study conducted by the Virginia General Assembly's "Audit and Review Commission," the state's "watchdog" agency. Their report was released December 10, 2001. The study included data from only a five-year period (1995–1999), and focused on cases in which the prosecutor sought the death penalty (not the larger universe of cases that were potentially eligible for the death penalty). The data indicate that in cases where at least one of the victims is female, the defendant's odds of being indicted for capital murder "were over six times greater than for those defendants whose alleged victims were all male." In addition, Virginia prosecutors were three times more likely to seek the death penalty when the victim was white rather than black, but the small sample size meant that this difference, even large, was not statistically significant. An earlier, and larger 20-year study in Virginia found that African Americans were 58 percent of those murdered in Virginia, 41 percent of the victims of potentially capital crimes, but only 19 percent of those sent to death row were convicted of killing blacks.

Most importantly, the Audit and Review Commission's data indicated a strong regional disparity in death sentencing, with prosecutors in high-density jurisdictions 87 percent less likely to seek the death penalty than prosecutors in medium-density locations. Overall, defendants are twice as likely to face a death sentence in rural areas than they are for the same crimes in an urban area. Hence, the researchers concluded that "significant inconsistencies are evident in the statewide application of capital punishment in Virginia."

K. The Federal System

Concern over the impact of race and geography on federal death sentencing was raised in a front-page New York Times article in June 2000. At that time, 17 of the 21 prisoners on federal death row were minorities, and half of all the cases in which the death penalty was sought originated from southern states. During the four years of George H.W. Bush's presidency (1989–1993), the administration sought the death penalty against 27 defendants for drug-related killings, 23 of whom were minorities. At that time the federal government has sought the death penalty against 199 defendants since 1988, 76 percent of whom were minorities.

Later in 2000, the Justice Department released a comprehensive study of decisions surrounding the federal death penalty. They found that three-quarters of the times in which a death sentence had been sought over the previous five years involved cases with minority defendants. In more than half the cases, the defendants were black. Furthermore, political factors appeared to influence the decision to seek a death sentence: a "handful" of the 93 U.S. attorneys accounted for some 40 percent of the death penalty prosecutions, while 20 U.S. attorneys had never sought death. However, within eight months after that report was released, a new administration was seated in Washington, and a new Justice Department report was released that concluded that the disparities were not the result of racial or ethnic bias, but instead a consequence of "the representation of minorities in the pool of potential federal capital cases." With that green light, the first two executions under federal authority since 1963 were quickly carried out during the Summer of 2001. During the Fall of 2001, the Justice Department solicited research proposals to stimulate further research on the issue.

APPENDIX II: INDICATORS OF DEATH SENTENCE ELIGIBILITY AND AGGRAVATING FACTS DOCUMENTATION

Indicators of Death Penalty Eligibility and Facts in Aggravation

This appendix identifies the specific Illinois statues and amendments to statues that were used to develop indicators of death penalty eligibility and also facts in aggravation from Illinois Department of Corrections records for the first-degree murder offenders in our sample. Below are presented the specific indicators that were developed and their accompanying statutory citations. Statutory citations include references to Chapter 38 of the Criminal Code of 1961 and to the Illinois Compiled Statutes (ILCS), a comprehensive renumbering of the Illinois statutes, which took effect in 1993.

I. Indicators of Death Penalty Eligibility Factors

In Illinois, there are 20 statutory eligibility factors. Two commonly used eligibility factors could be identified in this database by virtue of information about convictions: the Multiple Murder factor (720 ILCS 5/9-l (b)(3)) and the Course of a Felony factor (720 ILCS 5/94 (b)(6)).

Under eligibility factor (b)(3), a defendant may be eligible for the death penalty if he has been convicted of intentionally murdering two or more individuals. Illinois law recognizes three varieties of first degree murder: intentional murder, murder where the person knows or should know death is the probable result and felony murder. Case law suggests that the prior murder conviction must be for intentional murder or for knowing murder in order to make the defendant eligible for the death penalty. Generally speaking, a prior conviction for felony murder would not satisfy this requirement without proof of a separate intent to murder. This item is a factor in demonstrating that the defendant is actually eligible for the death penalty. The fact of multiple murder convictions may also be considered as an aggravating factor when the jury makes a determination of whether or not to impose the death penalty.

A defendant may also be eligible for the death penalty if he has been convicted of first degree murder "in the course of another felony." 720 ILCS 5/9-1 (b)(6). This factor makes a person eligible for the death penalty when the murder has occurred in the course of any one of several specified felonies. Illinois law also imposes the requirement that there be some element of intentional or knowing conduct by the defendant; those who are only tangentially involved in the criminal enterprise would not likely be eligible under this factor.

1.1. As a proxy for death eligibility under the Multiple Murder eligibility factor, we identified any offender in our sample with a prior conviction and incarceration in the Illinois Department of Corrections on one of the following:

MPMFM1, Table 2 ***Number of occurrences = 176***

Label	*Statutory cite*
1st Deg.	*38/9-1*
1st Deg.	*38/9-1A*
1st Deg.	*720 ILCS 5/9-1A1*
1st Deg.	*720 ILCS 5/9-1A*
1st Deg.StrongPr	*38/9-1 (A)(2)*
1st Deg.StrongPr	*720 ILCS 5/9-1(A)(2)*

This covers the range of intentional or knowing first-degree murders.

1.2. As a proxy for death eligibility under the Multiple Murder factor, we also identified any offender in our sample with a contemporaneous conviction and incarceration in Illinois Department of Corrections on one of the following:

MCMFACTR, Table 2 ***Number of occurrences = 6***

Label	*Statutory cite*
1st Deg.	*38/9-1*
1st Deg.	*38/9-1A*
1st Deg.	*720 ILCS 5/9-1Al*
1st Deg.	*720 ILCS 5/9-1A*
1st Deg.StrongPr	*38/9-1 (A)(2)*
1st Deg.StrongPr	*720 ILCS 5/9-1 (A)(2)*

1.3 Indicators of "in the course of another felony" eligibility factor

As a proxy for this eligibility factor, we identified persons convicted of first-degree murder (720 ILCS 5/9-1) who were also convicted contemporaneously for certain felonies. As of 1984, the last year amendments were made before the study period, the statute made the following felonies eligible: armed robbery, robbery, rape, deviate sexual assault, aggravated kidnapping, forcible detention, arson, burglary, taking indecent liberties with a child, aggravated arson, home invasion, aggravated criminal sexual assault, or the attempt of any of these. Between 1988 and 1996 (which is the period of the study) additional felonies were added to the eligibility factor, on almost a yearly basis.

Group 1 below includes the original felonies contained when the death penalty statute was enacted in 1977, and also the amendments to the statue between 1982 and 1984, which added additional felonies. As a result, Group 1 represents the felonies that could make a defendant eligible for the death penalty at the beginning of the study period in 1988. Group 2 represents the amendments between 1988 and 1997, with the effective dates of the statutes. The Illinois Compiled Statutes (ILCS), a comprehensive rewrite and reorganization of all Illinois statutes, took effect in January of 1993. Finally, we included among felony factors only those that occurred in this sample 5 or more times.

1.3.1 Group 1

Below are listed the felonies included in (b)(6) "in the course of a felony" prior to 1985.

Group 1 A
<u>Armed Robbery Group</u>

MCGRPA1, Table 2	***Number of occurrences = 723***
<u>Label</u>	*<u>Statutory Cite</u>*
Armed Robbery	*38/18-2<X>*
Armed Robbery	*720 ILCS 5/18-2(A)<X>*
Armed Robbery	*720 ILCS 5/18-2<X>*
Attempt Armed Robbery	*38/18-2,8-4<1>*
Attempt Armed Robbery	*720 ILCS 5/18-2,8-4<1>*

Group 1 B
<u>Aggravated Criminal Sexual Assault Group</u>

MCGRPB1, Table 2	***Number of occurrences = 99***
Rape	*38/11-KX>*
Attempt Rape	*38/11-1,8-4< 1 >*
AggCrimSexAss/BodHarm	*38/12-14(A)(2)<X>*
AggCrimSexAss/BodHarm	*720 ILCS 5/12-14(A)(2)<X>*

AggCrimSexAss/ThreatLif	*720 ILCS 5/12-14-(A)(3)<X>*
AggCrimSexAss/Felony	*38/12-14(A)(4)<X>*
AggCrimSexAss/Felony	*38/12-14<X>*
AggCrimSexAss/Felony	*720 ILCS 5/12-14<X>*
AggCrimSexAss/Weapon	*38/12-14(A)(1)<X>*
AggCrimSexAss/Weapon	*720 ILCS 5/12-14(A)(1)<X>*
AttAggCrimSexAss/F	*38/12-14,8-4<1>*
AttAggCrimSexAss/F	*720 ILCS5/12-14, 8-4<1>*

Group 1 C
Home Invasion Group

MCGRPC1, Table 2 ***Number of occurrences = 139***

Home Invasion	*38/12-11<X>*
Home Invasion	*720 ILCS5/12-11<X>*
Home Inv/Armed/Force	*720 ICLS5/12-11(A)(1)<X>*
Home Inv/Cause Injury	*720 ILCS5/12-U(A)(2)<X>*

Group 1 D
Aggravated Kidnapping Group

MCGRPD1, Table 2 ***Number of occurrences = 70***

Label	*Statutory cite*
AggKidnapping/InflHarm	*720 ILCS 5/10-2(A)(3)<1>*
AggKidnapping/No Rans.	*38/10-2<1>*
AggKidnapping/No Rans.	*720 ILCS 5/10-2<1>*
AggKidnapping/Armed	*720 ILCS 5/10-2(A)(5)<1>*
AggKidnapping/Ransom	*38/10-2<X>*
AggKidnapping/Ransom	*720 ILCS 5/10-2<X>*
Attempt AggrKidNoRans.	*38/10-2,8-4<2>*

Group 1 E
Arson/Aggravated Arson Group

MCGRPE1, Table 2 ***Number of occurrences = 70***

Arson	*38/20-1<2>*
Arson	*720 ILCS 5/20-1*
Aggr Arson	*38/20-1.1<X>*
Aggravated Arson	*720 ILCS 5/20-1.1<X>*
Attempt (Arson)	*38/20-1,8-4<3>*

Group 2 F
<u>Simple Robbery Group</u>

MCGRPFl, Table 2 ***Number of occurrences = 65***

Robbery	*38/18-1<2>*
Robbery	*38/18-1<X>*
Robbery	*720 ILCS 5/18-1<2>*
Robbery/VicHand, 60+	*38/19-1<2>*
Robbery/VicHand, 60+	*720 ILCS 5/18-1<2>*
Attempt Robbery	*38/18-1,8-4<3>*
Attempt Robbery	*720 ILCS 5/18-1,5/8-4<3>*
AttemptRob/VicHand, 60+	*38-18-1,8-4<2>*

Group 1 G
<u>Burglary and Attempted Burglary</u>

MCBFCTR1, Table 2 ***Number of occurrences = 294***

Label	*Statutory cite*
Burglary	*38/19-1<2>*
Burglary	*720 ILCS 5/19-1<2>*
Attempt Burglary	*38/19-1,8-4 <3>*
Attempt Burglary	*720 ILCS 5/19-1,5/8-4<3>*

1.3.2 Group 2

Group 2 contains the felonies added to (b)(6) "in the course of a felony" statute along with the effective date of the amendment.

Group 2 A
<u>Calculated Criminal Drug Conspiracy</u>

Effective September 7, 1989; adds calculated criminal drug conspiracy as defined in Section 405 of the Illinois Controlled Substances Act. There were no instances of an offender having calculated criminal drug conspiracy as a contemporaneous offense in the sample. As a result this variable was not included in the analysis.

Group 2 B
Residential Burglary

Effective **July 1, 1990;** adds residential burglary.

MCGRP3BR, Table 2	**Number of occurrences = 67**
Label	*Statutory cite*
Residential Burglary	*38/19-3<1>*
Residential Burglary	*720 ILCS 5/19-3<1>*
AttResidential Burglary	*38/19-3,8-4<2>*
AttResidential Burglary	*720 ILCS 5/19-3,8-4<1>*

Group 2 C
Armed Violence

Effective **December 15, 1994**; adds armed violence

MCGRP3CR, Table 2	**Number of occurrences = 15**
Label	*Statutory cite*
Arm Viol/Categ.I Weap.	*38/33A-2<X>*
Arm Viol/Categ.I Weap.	*720 ILCS 5/33A-2<X>*
Arm Viol/Categ.II Weap/1st	*38/33A-2<2>*
Arm Viol/Categ.II Weap/1st	*720 ILCS5/33A-2<2>*
Arm Viol/Categ.II Weap/2nd+	*38/33A-2<1>*
Arm Viol/Categ.II Weap/2nd+	*720 ILCS 5/33A-2<1>*
Arm Viol/Categ.II Weap.	*720 ILCS 5/33A-2*1 <X>*
Arm Viol/Categ.III Weap.	*720 ILCS 5/33A-2*1<2>*

Group 2 D
Armed Violence, Aggravated Vehicular Hijacking, and Aggravated Stalking

Effective **July 1, 1995;** adds Armed Violence, Aggravated Vehicular Hijacking, and Aggravated Stalking.

MCGRP3DR, Table 2	***Number of occurrences = 6***
Label	*Statutory cite*
AggVehicularHijack	*38/18-4<X>*
AggrVehicularHijack	*720 ILCS 5/18-4<X>*
AggVeh.Hijack/Weapon	*720 ILCS 5/18-4(A)(3)<X>*

[Agg.Stalking does not appear in database]

Group 2 E

Predatory Criminal Sexual Assault of a child

Effective ***December 13, 1995****; adds Predatory Criminal Sexual Assault of a child. There was only one instance of an offender having a predatory criminal sexual assault of a child as a contemporaneous offense in the sample. As a result this variable was not included in the analysis.*

II. INDICATORS OF FACTS IN AGGRAVATION

In addition to providing indicators of death sentence eligibility IDOC data can also provide information about the defendant that would be considered during the "aggravation" phase of the sentencing trial. While a variety of facts might be submitted at this time, the DOC data only provides information with respect to the defendant's prior criminal history, generally considered to be an important factor in the imposition of the death penalty. **2.1.** As a proxy for other, serious murder convictions (as opposed to just other serious felony convictions) the following were used:

MPSM2, Table 2 ***Number of occurrences = 133***

Label	*Statutory cite*
Vol. Manslaughter	*38/9-2<1>*
Vol. Mans.prior 1/82	*38/9-2<2>*
2nd Deg. M.	*38/9-2D<1>*
2nd Deg. M.	*38/9-2D-553C8<X>*
2nd Deg. M.	*720 ILCS 5/9-2D<1>*
Att. M., Intent	*38/9-1,8-4 <X>*
Att. M., Intent	*38/9-1A,8-4<X>*
Att. M., Intent	*720 ILCS 5/9-1 (A)(1),8-4<X>*
Att. M., Intent	*720 ILCS 5/9-1A,8-4<X>*
Att. M., StrngPro	*720 ILCS 5/9-1 (A)(2),8-4<X>*
Consp.M., Intent	*38/9-1(A)(1), 8-2<X>*
Consp.M., Intent	*38/9-1,8-2<2>*
Consp.M., Intent	*38/9-1,8-2<4>*
Consp.M., Intent	*38/9-1A,8-2<2>*
Consp.M., Intent	*720 ILCS5/9-1A,8-2<2>*
Sol.M., Intent	*38/9-1,8-KX>*
Sol.M., Intent	*38/9-1A,8-KX>*
Sol.M., for Hire	*38/8-1.2<X>*
Sol.M., for Hire	*720 ILCS 5/8-1.2<X>*

2.2. As a proxy for other contemporaneous serious murder convictions (as opposed to just other serious felony convictions) the following were used:

MCSM2, Table 2	***Number of occurrences = 527***
Label	*Statutory cite*
Vol. Manslaughter	*38/9-2<1>*
Vol. Mans.prior1/82	*38/9-2<2>*
2nd Deg.M.	*38/9-2D<1>*
2nd Deg.M.	*38/9-2D-553C8<X>*
2nd Deg. M.	*720 ILCS 5/9-2D<1>*
Att. M., Intent	*38/9-1,8-4 <X>*
Att. M., Intent	*38/9-1A,8-4<X>*
Att. M., Intent	*720 ILCS 5/9-1 (A)(1),8-4<X>*
Att. M., Intent	*720 ILCS 5/9-1 A,8-4<X>*
Att. M., StrngPro	*720 ILCS 5/9-1 (A)(2), 8-4<X>*
Consp.M., Intent	*38/9-l(A)(1),8-2<X>*
Consp.M., Intent	*38/9-1,8-2<2>*
Consp.M., Intent	*38/9-1,8-2<4>*
Consp.M., Intent	*38/9-1A,8-2<2>*
Consp.M., Intent	*720 ILCS5/9-1A,8-2<2>*
Sol.M., Intent	*38/9-1,8-1 <X>*
Sol.M., Intent	*38/9-1A,8-KX>*
Sol.M, for Hire	*38/8-1.2<X>*
Sol.M., for Hire	*720 ILCS 5/8-1.2<X>*

2.3 Other felony convictions

Illinois also ranks felony convictions for purposes of sentencing by a classification system. Under that system, a felony may be ranked as **Class X (MPCLASX2, Table 2),** the most serious non-murder felony carrying a mandatory minimum sentence, or ranked as Class 1 through 4 **(MPCLAS12, MPCLAS22, MPCLAS32, and MPCLAS42, Table 2).** Of the felonies ranked **Class 1 through 4, Class 1** felonies are the most serious for purposes of sentence determination, and **Class 4** are the least serious. Armed Robbery, for example, is a Class X felony, while Robbery is a **Class 1** felony. The conviction data provided by IDOC contains information as to the classification of all felony convictions. As a consequence, measures could be developed in the database with respect to the seriousness of the felony record for an individual defendant.

Appendix III: Tables 3 Through 31 of the Findings

Table 3. Death Sentence by Conviction for Prior Intentional or Knowing Murder

Sentence		Conviction for Prior Murder None	One +	Total
Other	N	5043	152	5195
	%	98.3%	85.4%	97.8%
Death	N	89	26	115
	%	1.7%	14.6%	2.2%
Total	N	5132	178	5310
		100.0%	100.0%	100.0%

	Value	df	Sign.
Pearson Chi-Square	134.538	1	.000
Continuity correction	128.531	1	.000
Number of Cases	(5310)		

Table 4. Death Sentence by Contemporaneous Intentional or Knowing Murder

Sentence		Contemporaneous Intentional or Knowing Murder None	One +	Total
Other	N	5191	4	5195
	%	97.9%	80.0%	97.8%
Death	N	114	1	115
	%	2.1%	20.0%	2.2%
Total	N	5305	5	5310
	%	100.0%	100.0%	100.0%

	Value	df	Sign.
Pearson Chi-Square	7.513	1	.006
Continuity correction	1.450	1	.229
Number of Cases	(5310)		

Table 5. Death Sentence by Contemporaneous Armed Robbery

Sentence		Contemporaneous Armed Robbery None	One +	Total
Other	N	4501	694	5195
	%	98.1%	95.9%	97.8%
Death	N	85	30	115
	%	1.9%	4.1%	2.2%
Total	N	4586	724	5310
	%	100.0%	100.0%	100.0%

	Value	df	Sign.
Pearson Chi-Square	15.478	1	.000
Continuity correction	14.416	1	.000
Number of Cases	(5310)		

Table 6. Death Sentence by Contemporaneous Aggravated Criminal Sexual Assault

Sentence		Aggravated Sexual Assault None	One +	Total
Other	N	5111	84	5195
	%	98.1%	84.0%	97.8%
Death	N	99	16	115
	%	1.7%	14.6%	2.2%
Total	N	5210	100	5310
	%	100.0%	100.0%	100.0%

	Value	df	Sign.
Pearson Chi-Square	92.061	1	.000
Continuity correction	85.527	1	.000
Number of Cases	(5310)		

Table 7. Death Sentence by a Contemporaneous Home Invasion

Sentence		Contemporaneous Home Invasion None	One +	Total
Other	N	5069	126	5195
	%	98.0%	90.6%	97.8%
Death	N	102	13	115
	%	2.0%	9.4%	2.2%
Total	N	5171	139	5310
	%	100.0%	100.0%	100.0%

	Value	df	Sign.
Pearson Chi-Square	34.795	1	.000
Continuity correction	31.399	1	.000
Number of Cases	(5310)		

Table 8. Death Sentence by Contemporaneous Aggravated Kidnapping

Sentence		Aggravated Kidnapping None	One +	Total
Other	N	5136	59	5195
	%	98.0%	84.3%	97.8%
Death	N	104	11	115
	%	2.0%	15.7%	2.2%
Total	N	5240	70	5310
	%	100.0%	100.0%	100.0%

	Value	df	Sign.
Pearson Chi-Square	61.454	1	.000
Continuity correction	55.145	1	.000
Number of Cases	(5310)		

Table 9. Death Sentence by a Contemporaneous Arson

Sentence		Contemporaneous Arson None	One +	Total
Other	N	5134	61	5195
	%	98.0%	87.1%	97.8%
Death	N	106	9	115
	%	2.0%	12.9%	2.2%
Total	N	5240	70	5310
	%	100.0%	100.0%	100.0%

	Value	df	Sign.
Pearson Chi-Square	38.268	1	.000
Continuity correction	33.326	1	.000
Number of Cases	(5310)		

Table 10. Death Sentence by a Contemporaneous Simple (Unarmed) Robbery

Sentence		Contemporaneous Simple Robbery None	One +	Total
Other	N	5133	62	5195
	%	97.9%	93.9%	97.8%
Death	N	111	4	115
	%	2.1%	6.1%	2.2%
Total	N	5244	66	5310
	%	100.0%	100.0%	100.0%

	Value	df	Sign.
Pearson Chi-Square	4.785	1	.029
Continuity correction	3.105	1	.078
Number of Cases	(5310)		

Table 11. Death Sentence by Contemporaneous Burglary

Sentence		Contemporaneous Burglary None	One +	Total
Other	N	5175	20	5195
	%	97.9%	90.9%	97.8%
Death	N	113	2	115
	%	2.1%	9.1%	2.2%
Total	N	5288	22	5310
	%	100.0%	100.0%	100.0%

	Value	df	Sign.
Pearson Chi-Square	5.000	1	.025
Continuity correction	2.257	1	.133
Number of Cases	(5310)		

Table 12. Death Sentence by Contemporaneous Residential Burglary

Sentence		Contemporaneous Residential Burglary None	One +	Total
Other	N	5160	35	5195
	%	97.9%	87.5%	97.8%
Death	N	110	5	115
	%	2.1%	12.5%	2.2%
Total	N	5270	40	5310
	%	100.0%	100.0%	100.0%

	Value	df	Sign.
Pearson Chi-Square	134.538	1	.000
Continuity correction	128.531	1	.000
Number of Cases	(5310)		

Table 13. Death Sentence by Contemporaneous Armed Violence

Sentence		Contemporaneous Armed Violence None	One +	Total
Other	N	5181	14	5195
	%	97.8%	93.3%	97.8%
Death	N	114	1	115
	%	2.2%	6.7%	2.2%
Total	N	5295	15	5310
	%	100.0%	100.0%	100.0%

	Value	df	Sign.
Pearson Chi-Square	1.438	1	.230
Continuity correction	.097	1	.756
Number of Cases	(5310)		

Table 14. Death Sentence by Contemporaneous Vehicular Hijacking

Sentence		Contemporaneous Vehicular Hijacking None	One +	Total
Other	N	5190	5	5195
	%	97.9%	83.3%	97.8%
Death	N	114	1	115
	%	2.1%	16.7%	2.2%
Total	N	5304	6	5310
	%	100.0%	100.0%	100.0%

	Value	df	Sign.
Pearson Chi-Square	5.961	1	.015
Continuity correction	1.078	1	.299
Number of Cases	(5310)		

Table 15. Death Sentence by Number of Victims

Sentence		Number of Victims One	Two	Three	Four +	Total
Other	N	4017	169	18	4	4208
	%	98.7%	90.4%	75.0%	44.4%	98.1%
Death	N	53	18	6	5	82
	%	1.3%	9.6%	25.0%	55.6%	1.9%
Total	N	4070	187	24	9	4290
	%	100.0%	100.0%	100.0%	100.0%	100.0%

	Value	df	Sign.
Pearson Chi-Square	273.787	3	.000
Continuity correction	88.127	3	.000
Number of Cases	(4290)		

Table 16. Death Sentence by One or More Victims over 59

Sentence		Victims over 59 None	One +	Total
Other	N	3839	286	4125
	%	98.2%	96.3%	98.1%
Death	N	70	11	81
	%	1.8%	3.7%	1.9%
Total	N	3909	297	4206
	%	100.0%	100.0%	100.0%

	Value	Df	Sign.
Pearson Chi-Square	5.348	1	.021
Continuity correction	4.383	1	.036
Number of Cases	(4206)		

Table 17. Death Sentence by One or More Victims Under 12

Sentence		Victims Under 12: None	One +	Total
Other	N	3909	216	4125
	%	98.3%	94.3%	98.1%
Death	N	68	13	81
	%	1.7%	5.7%	1.9%
Total	N	3977	229	4206
	%	100.0%	100.0%	100.0%

	Value	df	Sign.
Pearson Chi-Square	18.042	1	.000
Continuity correction	16.003	1	.000
Number of Cases	(4206)		

Table 18. Death Sentence by Contemporaneous Other Serious Murder Conviction

Sentence		Contemporaneous Other Serious Murder Conviction: None	One	Two +	Total
Other	N	4677	482	36	5195
	%	97.8%	98.4%	97.3%	97.8%
Death	N	106	8	1	115
	%	2.2%	1.69%	2.7%	2.2%
Total	N	4783	490	37	5310
	%	100.0%	100.0%	100.0%	100.0%

	Value	df	Sign.
Pearson Chi-Square	.765	2	.682
Continuity correction	.821	2	.663
Number of Cases	(5310)		

Table 19. Death Sentence by Prior Other Serious Murder Conviction

Sentence		Prior Other Serious Murder Conviction None	One	Two +	Total
Other	N	5069	116	10	5195
	%	97.9%	95.1%	90.9%	97.8%
Death	N	108	6	1	115
	%	2.1%	4.9%	9.1%	2.2%
Total	N	5177	122	11	5310
	%	100.0%	100.0%	100.0%	100.0%

	Value	df	Sign.
Pearson Chi-Square	7.006	2	.030
Continuity correction	4.779	2	.092
Number of Cases	(5310)		

Table 20. Death Sentence by Prior Class X Offenses

Sentence		Prior Class X Offenses None	One	Two +	Total
Other	N	4739	320	136	5195
	%	98.2%	94.7%	92.5%	97.8%
Death	N	86	18	11	115
	%	1.8%	5.3%	7.5	2.2%
Total	N	4825	338	147	5310
	%	100.0%	100.0%	100.0%	100.0%

	Value	df	Sign.
Pearson Chi-Square	38.888	2	.000
Continuity correction	27.016	2	.000
Number of Cases	(5310)		

Table 21. Death Sentence by Prior Class 1 Offenses

Sentence		Prior Class 1 Offenses None	One	Two +	Total
Other	N	4890	261	44	5195
	%	97.9%	97.4%	95.7%	97.8%
Death	N	106	7	2	115
	%	2.1%	2.6%	4.3%	2.2%
Total	N	4996	268	46	5310
	%	100.0%	100.0%	100.0%	100.0%

	Value	df	Sign.
Pearson Chi-Square	1.331	2	.514
Continuity correction	1.085	2	.581
Number of Cases	(5310)		

Table 22. Death Sentence by Prior Class 2 Offenses

Sentence		Prior Class 2 Offenses None	One	Two +	Total
Other	N	4600	361	234	5195
	%	98.2%	95.8%	94.7%	97.8%
Death	N	86	16	13	115
	%	1.8%	4.2%	5.3%	2.2%
Total	N	4686	377	247	5310
	%	100.0%	100.0%	100.0%	100.0%

	Value	df	Sign.
Pearson Chi-Square	21.285	2	.000
Continuity correction	16.602	2	.000
Number of Cases	(5310)		

Table 23. Death Sentence by Prior Class 3 Offenses

Sentence		Prior Class 3 Offenses None	One	Two +	Total
Other	N	4962	172	61	5195
	%	98.2%	93.0%	87.1%	97.8%
Death	N	93	13	9	115
	%	1.8%	7.0%	12.9	2.2%
Total	N	5055	185	70	5310
	%	100.0%	100.0%	100.0%	100.0%

	Value	df	Sign.
Pearson Chi-Square	60.933	2	.000
Continuity correction	33.681	2	.000
Number of Cases	(5310)		

Table 24. Death Sentence by Prior Class 4 Offenses

Sentence		Prior Class 4 Offenses None	One	Two +	Total
Other	N	4899	244	52	5195
	%	97.9%	96.4%	96.3%	97.8%
Death	N	104	9	2	115
	%	2.1%	3.6%	3.7	2.2%
Total	N	5003	253	54	5310
	%	100.0%	100.0%	100.0%	100.0%

	Value	df	Sign.
Pearson Chi-Square	3.094	2	.213
Continuity correction	2.621	2	.270
Number of Cases	(5310)		

Table 25. Death Sentence by Region

Sentence		Trial Court Region Cook County	Collar Counties	Urban Counties	Rural Counties	Total
Other	N	3948	348	659	230	5185
	%	98.5%	96.7%	96.6%	91.6%	97.8%
Death	N	59	12	23	21	115
	%	1.5%	3.3%	3.4%	8.4%	2.2%
Total	N	4007	360	682	251	5300
	%	100.0%	100.0%	100.0%	100.0%	100.0%

	Value	df	Sign.
Pearson Chi-Square	61.528	3	.000
Continuity correction	42.877	3	.000
Number of Cases	(5300)		

Table 26. Death Sentence by Sex of Victim

Sentence		Sex of Victim is Female No Females	One + Females	Total
Other	N	3235	973	4208
	%	98.8%	95.7%	98.1%
Death	N	38	44	82
	%	1.2%	4.3%	1.9%
Total	N	3273	1017	4290
	%	100.0%	100.0%	100.0%

	Value	df	Sign.
Pearson Chi-Square	41.467	1	.000
Continuity correction	39.796	1	.000
Number of Cases	(4290)		

Table 27. Death Sentence by Race of Victim

Sentence		Race of Victim Only White	Only Black	Only Hisp.	Only Other	One + races	Total
Other	N	996	2656	464	33	24	4173
	%	96.2%	98.9%	98.5%	94.3%	96.0%	98.1%
Death	N	39	30	7	2	1	79
	%	3.8%	1.1%	1.5%	5.7%	4.0%	1.9%
Total	N	1035	2686	471	35	25	4252
	%	100.0%	100.0%	100.0%	100.0%	100.0%	100.0%

	Value	df	Sign.
Pearson Chi-Square	36.640	4	.000
Continuity correction	28.131	4	.000
Number of Cases	(4252)		

Table 28. Death Sentence by Sex of Offender

Sentence		Sex of Offender Male	Female	Total
Other	N	4896	299	5195
	%	97.8%	98.7%	97.8%
Death	N	111	4	115
	%	2.2%	1.3%	2.2%
Total	N	5007	303	5310
	%	100.0%	100.0%	100.0%

	Value	df	Sign.
Pearson Chi-Square	1.084	1	.298
Continuity correction	.702	1	.402
Number of Cases	(5310)		

Table 29. Death Sentence by Race of Offender

Sentence		Race of Offender White	Black	Hisp.	Asian/Am Indian	Total
Other	N	883	3604	683	23	5193
	%	95.5%	98.2%	99.3%	100.0%	97.9%
Death	N	42	67	5		114
	%	4.5%	1.8%	.7%		2.1%
Total	N	925	3671	688	23	5307
	%	100.0%	100.0%	100.0%	100.0%	100.0%

	Value	df	Sign.
Pearson Chi-Square	34.128	3	.000
Continuity correction	30.935	3	.000
Number of Cases	(5307)		

Table 30. Death Sentence by Race of Victim/Offender Combination for Whites and Blacks

Sentence		White Black Victim Offender Combination Black kills White	White kills White	Black kills Black	White kills Black	Total
Other	N	363	458	2526	59	3406
	%	95.5%	95.2%	98.9%	95.2%	98.0%
Death	N	17	23	27	3	70
	%	4.5%	4.8%	1.1%	4.8%	2.0%
Total	N	380	481	2553	62	3476
	%	100.0%	100.0%	100.0%	100.0%	100.0%

	Value	df	Sign.
Pearson Chi-Square	44.665	3	.000
Continuity correction	38.304	3	.000
Number of Cases	(3476)		

Table 31a. Logistic Regression of Legally Relevant and Extra-legal Indicators with Death Sentence

	B	S.E.	Wald	Sig.	Exp(B)
MPMFM1	1.954	.391	25.031	.000	7.059
MCMFACTR	2.918	1.390	4.406	.036	18.498
MCGRPA1	-.018	.384	.002	.963	.983
MCGRPB1	1.193	.522	5.214	.022	3.297
MCGRPC1	1.351	.487	7.687	.006	3.862
MCGRPD1	2.669	.531	25.264	.000	14.429
MCGRPE1	.917	.629	2.123	.145	2.501
MCGRPF1	-1.766	1.337	1.744	.187	.171
MCBFCTR1	.360	1.144	.099	.753	1.433
MCGRP3BR	1.435	.737	3.790	.052	4.200
MCGRP3CR	1.452	1.585	.840	.359	4.273
MCGRP3DR	2.101	1.352	2.417	.120	8.176
VICCNTT4	1.636	.232	49.733	.000	5.136
VICGT59D	.338	.423	.636	.425	1.402
VICLT12D	.037	.547	.005	.946	1.038
MCSM2	-1.034	.640	2.608	.106	.356
MPSM2	.043	.674	.004	.949	1.044
MPCLAS12	-1.040	.478	4.733	.030	.353
MPCLAS22	.531	.242	4.793	.029	1.700
MPCLAS32	.703	.311	5.121	.024	2.020
MPCLAS42	-.002	.409	.000	.997	.998
MPCLASX2	.504	.298	2.863	.091	1.655
COOKOTH	-1.808	.413	19.136	.000	.164
CNTYCOUR	-.805	.426	3.563	.059	.447
VICSEX_D	.368	.310	1.411	.235	1.445
MI_RSEX	-1.002	1.046	.918	.338	.367
VICBLK_D	-.907	.348	6.778	.009	.404
OFFBLACK	.191	.348	.302	.582	1.211
Constant	-4.137	1.194	12.010	.001	.016

Table 31b. Omnibus Tests and Model Summary for Logistic Regression of Legally Relevant and Extra-legal Indicators with Death Sentence

Case Processing Summary

	N	Percent
Selected Cases*	4182	78.8%
Missing Cases	1128	21.2%
Total	5310	100.0%

*The number of cases selected is that set of cases for which there is valid data for all 27 of the variables included in the logistic regression analysis.

Omnibus Tests of Model Coefficients

	Chi-square	df	Sig.
Model	255.036	28	.000

Model Summary

-2 Log likelihood	Cox & Snell R Square	Nagelkerke R Square
504.762	.059	.356

Classification Table (The cut value is .500)

		Predicted: Death Sentence .00	Predicted: Death Sentence 1.00	Percentage Correct
Observed				
Death Sentence	.00	4099	7	99.8
	1.00	63	13	17.1
Overall Percentage				98.3

APPENDIX IV: ACKNOWLEDGEMENTS

The authors would like to express their appreciation to the Governor's Commission on Capital Punishment for the invitation to study Illinois sentencing outcomes. Our special thanks go to Deputy Governor Matthew R. Bettenhausen, both a member of the Commission and its Executive Director, for facilitating the cooperation of state agencies with respect to collection of data and providing other support for this study.

In addition, the authors would like to acknowledge the many contributions made by Jean M. Templeton, the Research Director for the Governor's Commission on Capital Punishment, to the materials in Appendix II, which defined the variables used in the study. Ms. Templeton, an attorney in Illinois since 1981, also provided extensive and valuable advice to the authors on many points of Illinois law that appear in this report.

The authors would also like to thank the Illinois Department of Corrections, the Illinois Criminal Justice Information Authority, the Illinois State Police, and the Illinois Department of Public Health, whose employees contributed significant time and effort to provide the data without which this study would not have been possible.

The authors wish to thank Alan Saiz, of the College of Criminal Justice at Northeastern University for his database management support and consultation throughout this project. In addition, we wish to thank Raymond Hyatt of the Department of Sociology at Brown University for his statistical consultation and also David Baldus of the School of Law at the University of Iowa for his advice and consultation.

Finally, the authors would like to acknowledge the support provided by the Institute on Race and Justice and the College of Criminal Justice at Northeastern University and the Sociology Department at the University of Colorado.

Funding support for this study was provided by the State of Illinois.

Racial Disparities in the Capital of Capital Punishment

Scott Phillips

ABSTRACT

Despite decades of research on race and capital punishment, "reasonably well-controlled" studies have not been conducted in the five most active death states: Texas, Virginia, Oklahoma, Missouri, and Florida. To begin to address this limitation, the current research examines the impact of race on the District Attorney's (DA) decision to pursue a death trial and the jury's decision to impose a death sentence against adult defendants indicted for capital murder in Harris County (Houston), Texas from 1992 to 1999 (n = 504). The findings challenge conventional wisdom by suggesting that the race of the defendant and victim are both pivotal in the capital of capital punishment: death was more likely to be imposed against black defendants than white defendants; death was more likely to be imposed on behalf of white victims than black victims. The black–white disparities stem from an intriguing interplay between race, the seriousness of a murder, and the stages of capital litigation. The current research also represents one of the few attempts to extend traditional black–white comparisons to include Hispanics; no Hispanic-white disparities were observed. The research concludes with a call to action for scholars to initiate "reasonably well-controlled" studies in the most active death jurisdictions in the United States.

Please direct correspondence to: Scott Phillips, Department of Sociology and Criminology, University of Denver, 2000 E. Asbury Avenue, Denver, CO 80208-2948, Scott.Phillipsfgtdu.edu. I am indebted to Scott Durfee, Chief Counsel to the Harris County District Attorney, who explained numerous office processes and provided archival data. I am also indebted to Kim Bohannon from the Harris County District Clerk's office who made the research possible through complete assistance with the JIMS database. I would like to thank Russ Curtis for discussions about capital punishment in Texas during the earliest stages of the project. For providing comments on drafts, I thank Paul Colomy, Mark Cooney, Jim Coverdill, David Dow, Mike Radelet, and Nancy Reichman. Most importantly, I could not have completed the project without help from the following undergraduate Research Assistants: Shaefali Pillai Rogers, Breck Garrett, Mor Regev, and Ivan Zapata. The research was financed in part through funding from Rice University.

Racial Disparities in the Capital of Capital Punishment

Justice is supposed to be blind—meted out according to the legal characteristics of a case rather than the social characteristics of the defendant and victim. Decades of research on race and capital punishment, however, demonstrate that blind justice is a mirage (United States General Accounting Office 1990; Baldus and Woodworth 2003a, 2003b; Paternoster, Brame, and Bacon 2008).

Ironically, the most rigorous research on race and capital punishment has not been conducted in the jurisdictions that execute the most offenders. In a recent comprehensive review of the literature, David Baldus and George Woodworth, leading scholars in the field, argue that "reasonably well-controlled" studies have been conducted in the following jurisdictions: California, Colorado, Georgia, Kentucky, Maryland, Mississippi, Nebraska, New Jersey, North Carolina, Philadelphia, and South Carolina (2003a:519). The list of jurisdictions with "reasonably well-controlled" studies is striking due to glaring omissions—the list does not include the five most active death states: Texas, Virginia, Oklahoma, Missouri, and Florida. Such states account for 719 of the 1,099 executions in the modern era, defined as the Supreme Court's reinstatement of capital punishment in 1976 to the present.

The current paper advances the field of race and capital punishment by conducting "reasonably well-controlled" research in one of the most active death jurisdictions in the United States. To do so, I examine whether race influenced the District Attorney's (DA) decision to pursue a death trial or the jury's decision to impose a death sentence against adult defendants indicted for capital murder in Harris County, Texas from 1992–1999 (n = 504).[1]

Though the entire state of Texas has earned a reputation for execution, Harris County —home to Houston and surrounding areas—is arguably the capital of capital punishment. With 102 executions in the modern era, Harris County has often captured the national and international spotlight in the death penalty debate (see e.g. Amnesty International, 2007). Table 1 demonstrates three compelling patterns: if Harris County were a state it would rank second in executions after Texas, recently passing Virginia; Harris County has executed more offenders than all the other major urban counties in Texas, combined; and Harris County has executed more than twice as many offenders as the top death jurisdiction that has been subject to "reasonably well-controlled" research on race and capital punishment. The period from 1992 to 1999 is also critical because

1 Baldus and Woodworth define "reasonably well-controlled" studies as those including "statistical controls for 10 or more legitimate non-racial case characteristics" (2003 a: 519). The current research meets the Baldus/Woodworth standard of being "reasonably well-controlled." To be clear, the current research does not claim to be in the same league as Baldus and colleagues' seminal research. The Baldus study remains the most rigorous research on race and capital punishment by far, and arguably the most impressive research on any topic in the field of Criminology.

the number of death sentences in Harris County climbed to historic highs. From 1976 to 1991, Texas' death row received an average of six offenders per year from Harris County. But from 1992 to 1999, the average almost doubled to 11 offenders per year—about one a month. The average dropped to 5 offenders per year from 2000 to 2007 (Texas Department of Criminal Justice, 2008).

Table 1. Number of Executions in Selected Jurisdictions, 1976 to Present

Top 10 States		**Texas' Urban Counties**		**Jurisdictions with "Reasonably Well-Controlled" Research**	
Texas	405	Harris County (Houston)	102	Harris County (Houston)	102
Harris County (Houston)	102	Dallas County (Dallas)	34	North Carolina	43
Virginia	98	Tarrant County (Fort Worth)	27	Georgia	40
Oklahoma	86	Bexar County (San Antonio)	26	South Carolina	37
Missouri	66	Travis County (Austin)	7	California	13
Florida	64			Mississippi	8
North Carolina	43			Maryland	5
Georgia	40			Philadelphia	3
Alabama	38			Nebraska	3
South Carolina	37			Kentucky	2
Louisiana	27			Colorado	1
				New Jersey	0

Notes:
1. Current as of March 27, 2008.
2. Data on Texas come from the Texas Department of Criminal Justice website. Data for the remaining states come from the Death Penalty Information Center website.
3. Numbers for Philadelphia represent Pennsylvania.

To anticipate, the results challenge conventional wisdom regarding the basic relationship between race and capital punishment. Conventional wisdom holds that the race of the victim is pivotal, but the race of the defendant is not (United States General Accounting Office 1990). The current research suggests that the race of the defendant and victim are both pivotal in the capital of capital punishment: death was more likely to be imposed against black defendants than white defendants, and death was more likely to be imposed on behalf of white victims than black victims. No Hispanic-white disparities were observed.

Before proceeding it is important to note that the central claim of the research—racial disparities exist—does not insinuate that judicial actors intend to discriminate. Because human motivations are unobservable, scientific methods cannot be used to determine whether disparities are intentional or unintentional, conscious or unconscious (Black 1995). The word "disparities" is used throughout the research to denote aggregate numerical differences, while the word "discrimination" has been avoided because it unfairly impugns motives.

I. RACE AND CAPITAL PUNISHMENT

Rather than attempt to summarize the immense body of scholarship on race and capital punishment, the following review focuses on five issues that are relevant to the current project: (1) landmark Supreme Court cases, (2) seminal research conducted by Baldus and colleagues, (3) existing reviews of the literature, (4) prior research in Texas, and (5) the limitations of prior research in Texas.[2, 3]

In *Furman v. Georgia* (1972), the Supreme Court ruled on a 5–4 vote that capital punishment was administered in an arbitrary manner that constituted cruel and unusual punishment. Most of the justices in the majority used the word "arbitrary" to refer to numerical disparities, arguing that there was no legal basis for distinguishing the handful of defendants who were sentenced to death from the large number of defendants

---

2 One could argue that it is inaccurate to call Harris County the "capital of capital punishment." In an important article that provides the first comprehensive examination of death sentences for the entire nation, Blume and colleagues (2004) demonstrate that the death sentence rate in Texas is below the national average (the death sentence rate is defined as the number of death sentences divided by the number of murders). In fact, the death sentence rate in Texas ranks 16th among the 31 states that sent more than 10 offenders to death row from 1977 to 1999. The authors also note in a New York Times article that the death sentence rate in Harris County is average for Texas (Liptak 2004). Thus, the considerable number of executions in Texas is not a product of a high death sentence rate, but rather a large number of murders coupled with the state's propensity to execute inmates who are sentenced to death (Blume, Eisenberg, and Wells 2004). Given Blume and colleagues' (2004) findings, how can Harris County be called the capital of capital punishment? Consider the following: (1) The execution rate is arguably more important than the death sentence rate—a death sentence is a pivotal and crucial moment in a capital case, but execution is the quintessence of capital punishment. Calculating the execution rate reveals that Texas catapults from 16th to 3rd in the national rankings (the execution rate is defined as the number of executions divided by the number of murders). (2) Raw numbers and rates both matter. The following example from baseball illustrates the point. Barry Bonds holds the career homerun record at 762 even though Bonds hit a homerun in 7.7 percent of at bats (762/9,847) compared to Babe Ruth who hit a homerun in 8.5 percent of at bats (714/8,398). Ty Cobb holds the career batting average record at .366 even though Cobb had a total of 4,189 hits compared to Pete Rose who had 4, 256 hits www.baseball-reference.com/leaders/). Bonds' raw number of homeruns is not diminished by Ruth's homerun rate, nor is Cobb's batting rate diminished by Rose's raw number of hits. In most areas of life, including baseball and capital punishment, raw numbers and rates both contain important information needed to determine rankings. (3) The phrase "capital of capital punishment" is not meant to suggest that Harris County would be rated as the most prolific death penalty jurisdiction under any possible standard. Rather, the phrase is a heuristic device used to call attention to the indisputable fact that Harris County is one of the most active death jurisdictions in the nation.

3 The annual number of death sentences from Harris County was calculated from the Texas Department of Criminal Justice website which lists the county of conviction for each offender and the date the offender was received on death row.

who committed equally reprehensible crimes but were not condemned. But two justices, Douglas and Marshall, also used the word "arbitrary" to refer to racial disparities in the imposition of capital punishment.

After the Supreme Court's decision in *Furman*, states began to revise their laws and reinstate capital punishment. Some states eliminated arbitrariness by making the death penalty mandatory for defendants convicted of certain crimes. Other states adopted "guided discretion," an approach that narrowed and specified the range of crimes eligible for death, separated the guilt and sentencing phases of a capital trial (allowing the prosecution and defense to introduce evidence of aggravating and mitigating circumstances during the sentencing phase that could not have been introduced during the guilt phase), and required automatic appellate review of death sentences. In *Woodson v. North Carolina* (1976) and the companion case of *Roberts v. Louisiana* (1976), the Supreme Court struck down mandatory death statutes arguing that the protection of human dignity required individual consideration of each case. But the Supreme Court upheld guided discretion statutes in *Gregg v. Georgia* (1976) and the companion cases of *Proffitt v. Florida* (1976) and *Jurek v. Texas* (1976), beginning the modern era of capital punishment. Guided discretion statutes soon proliferated as states passed legislation that would comply with the ruling in Gregg.

Following the Supreme Court decision in Gregg (1976), social scientists began to examine whether guided discretion eliminated the influence of race on capital punishment. Baldus and colleagues' Procedural Reform Study (PRS) and Charging and Sentencing Study (CSS) remain the most important and rigorous research on the topic (Baldus, Woodworth, and Pulaski 1990). The PRS includes 750 (156 pre-*Furman* and 594 post-*Furman*) murder convictions in Georgia spanning 1970 to 1978, and the CSS includes 1,066 defendants convicted of murder or voluntary manslaughter in Georgia from 1973 to 1979. Both studies control for an enormous number of potential confounders. The statewide post-*Furman* findings reveal that the race of the defendant was not a significant predictor, but the race of the victim was crucial: defendants who killed white victims were 4.3 times more likely to be sentenced to death. Moreover, black defendants who killed white victims were more likely to be sentenced to death than any other racial combination.

The results of the CSS, and to a lesser degree the PRS, became the basis for the most important Supreme Court decision on race and capital punishment: *McCleskey v. Kemp* (1987). McCleskey argued that racial disparities in the administration of capital punishment rendered the ultimate sanction unconstitutional. The Supreme Court did not contest the empirical patterns, but nonetheless rejected McCleskey's challenge on a 5–4 vote. Most centrally, the court argued that statistical evidence of racial disparities alone, without evidence of discrimination in the particular case at hand, does not establish a constitutional violation. The court was also reluctant to open Pandora's box, reasoning that if social science research regarding racial disparities invalidated capital punishment then social science research could ultimately undermine the entire criminal justice system.

Two comprehensive reviews of research on race and capital punishment have been conducted since the Supreme Court decision in *McCleskey*. The United States General Accounting Office reviewed the 28 studies published from 1972 to 1990, and, more recently, Baldus and Woodworth reviewed the 18 studies reported or published from 1990 to 2003 (United States General Accounting Office 1990; Baldus and Woodworth 2003a, 2003b). Both reviews reach the same conclusion: (1) The race of the defendant does not have a consistent influence on capital punishment: some studies suggest the disparate treatment of black defendants, but most do not. (2) The race of the victim has a consistent and robust influence on capital punishment: almost all studies suggest that death is more apt to be imposed on behalf of white victims.

Drawing on Supplemental Homicide Reports (SHR), scholars have also examined the relationship between race and capital punishment in Texas. The SHR data are used to examine whether race distinguishes the large number of defendants arrested for murder from the small number sentenced to death. The post-*Furman* findings in Texas mirror established patterns: the race of the defendant does not seem to matter; death is more apt to be imposed on behalf of white victims; and minorities who kill whites are more apt to be sentenced to death than any other racial combination (Bowers and Pierce 1980; Ekland-Olson 1988; Sorensen and Marquart 1990–1991; Marquart, Ekland-Olson, and Sorensen 1994; Brock, Cohen, and Sorensen 2000; for pre-*Furman* patterns see e.g. Koeninger 1969; Ralph, Sorensen, and Marquart 1992; Hunter, Ralph, and Marquart 1993).

Existing research in Texas suffers from five important limitations, most of which stem from a reliance on SHR data: (1) SHR data cannot control for critical confounders such as the defendant's prior criminal record or the heinousness of the crime. Hence, no study in Texas meets the Baldus/Woodworth standard for "reasonably well-controlled" research enumerated above. (2) SHR data cannot isolate murder defendants who were eligible for capital punishment under Texas law, so the imperfect comparison includes defendants who were not eligible for death and/or excludes defendants who were eligible for death. (3) If racial disparities emerge, SHR data cannot identify the stage of the process that produced the disparities. Disparities may originate in the decision to charge a defendant with capital murder, the decision to indict a defendant for capital murder, the DA's decision to pursue a death trial, or the jury's decision to impose a death sentence. (4) SHR data are sometimes problematic due to missing values. (5) Existing studies tend to examine the entire state of Texas (for an exception see Brock, Cohen, and Sorensen 2000). Because capital punishment in Texas is the aggregation of capital punishment in 254 counties with different histories, cultures, political climates, and legal actors—including different DA's who decide whether to pursue a death trial—an investigation of race and capital punishment across the state of Texas cannot account for local conditions.

The current research overcomes such limitations by: controlling for critical confounders, focusing exclusively on defendants who were eligible for death, identifying the stage of the process that produced racial disparities, including complete data for all cases, and examining patterns for a single county.

II. RESEARCH METHODS

A. Dependent Variables: Trajectory and Disposition

In Harris County, the path from the commission of a murder to the pronouncement of a death sentence includes four major decisions: the intake prosecutor's decision to charge a defendant with capital murder, the grand jury's decision to indict a defendant for capital murder, the District Attorney's decision to pursue a death trial, and the jury's decision to impose a death sentence. Because the charging and indictment decisions do not appear to exhibit enough variation to warrant an investigation, the current research focuses on whether race influenced the DA's decision to pursue death or the jury's decision to impose death—the trajectory and disposition of a case.[4,5,6]

The data include the population of adult defendants indicted for capital murder in Harris County, Texas from 1992 to 1999 (n = 504).[7] The Harris County District Clerk (HCDC) used the Harris County Justice Information Management System (JIMS) to

---

4 John Holmes Jr. was the DA in Harris County during the time period under consideration.

5 The Harris County intake division prosecutor must determine whether a homicide can be charged under the Texas capital murder statute. Despite repeated attempts, collecting the data needed to examine the impact of race on the charging decision proved impossible. But the charging decision does not appear to exhibit much variation. To begin, the Texas capital murder statute delineates narrow categories of murder that are death-eligible. The precision of the statute simplifies the charging decision, as opposed to states that define heinous murders as death eligible (see Texas Penal Code, title 5, chapter 19, section 19.03). Moreover, The Houston Chronicle reports in a February 2001 special series that the intake prosecutor has "standing orders" to file capital murder charges in all possible cases (Tolson and Brewer, February 4, 2001:Al; the remaining segments in the special series are listed in the reference section for the interested reader). Nonetheless, the inability to examine the charging decision remains a potential weakness of the current research.

6 The grand jury must return a "Bill of Indictment" for capital murder in order for the DA to pursue a death trial. This step borders on a formality, as data from the Harris County district clerk indicate that grand juries returned a "No Bill" in just seven capital cases from 1992 to 1999.

7 Defendants were excluded if the case was dismissed, the case was disposed but expunged, the defendant was never arrested, the victim's remains could not be identified, or the case had not been disposed at the time the list of cases was requested from the Harris County District Clerk in December 2001. The two Native American defendants were also excluded.

identify the defendants. The HCDC also provided a JIMS file that contained public information about each case, including whether the case resulted in a plea bargain or trial and the disposition. The Harris County District Attorney's office provided archival documents that were used to verify the list of defendants and determine if the DA pursued a death trial.

Figure 1 traces the trajectory, disposition, and current status of the 504 defendants who murdered 614 victims (defendants age 17 or older at the time of the crime were considered adults in Texas during the time period under consideration). The figure reveals that the DA pursued a death trial against 129 of the 504 defendants. Of the 129 defendants who advanced to a death trial, 98 were sentenced to death, 29 were sentenced to life imprisonment, one was sentenced to confinement in the Texas Department of Corrections (TDC) for some period of time less than life, and one was acquitted.[8] Of the

Figure 1: Trajectory, Disposition, and Status of Adult Defendants Indicted for Capital Murder in Harris County, Texas from 1992 to 1999 (status current as of March 27, 2008).

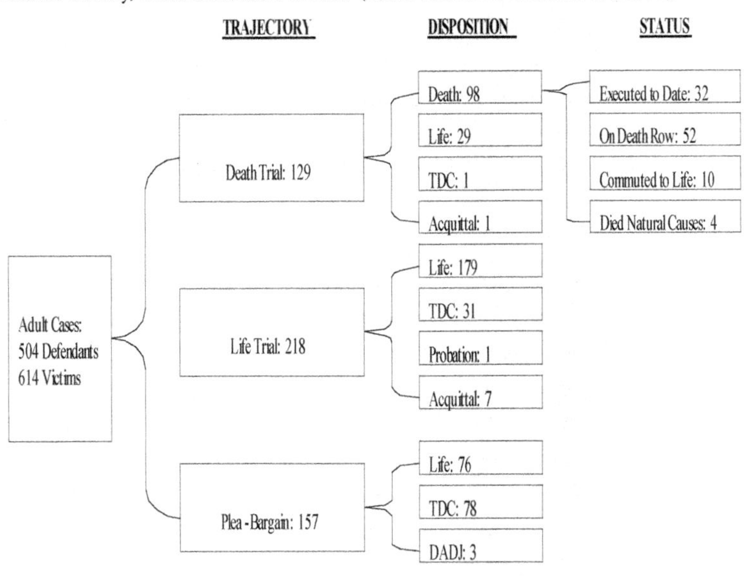

Abbreviations: TDC = Texas Department of Corrections; DADJ = Deferred Adjudication.

8 The inmates sentenced to life imprisonment are eligible for parole because Texas did not pass a life without parole (LWOP) statute until 2005 (defendants in the data who were convicted in 1992 must serve 35 years before becoming eligible for parole; defendants in the data who were convicted between 1993 and the passage of LWOP must serve 40 years before becoming eligible for parole).

98 condemned defendants, 32 have been executed to date, 52 remain on death row, and 14 will not be executed (10 were commuted to life imprisonment due to the Supreme Court's 2005 decision regarding juveniles in *Roper v. Simmons*; four died of natural causes on death row). The figure also reveals that the DA pursued a life trial against 218 defendants and reached a plea bargain with 157 defendants.

B. Race/Ethnicity

Table 2 describes measurement strategies, data sources, and means for the race/ethnicity of the defendant and victim. Though the terms "race" and "ethnicity" are not interchangeable, in the interest of brevity the generic term "race" is used throughout the remainder of the paper.

Data regarding the defendant's race were obtained from JIMS. The JIMS file included separate indicators for race (white, black, Asian) and ethnic origin (Hispanic). But important clues suggested that JIMS did not distinguish between Hispanic defendants and non-Hispanic defendants in a consistent manner. An examination of defendants' names suggested a problem of under-inclusion: defendants coded as Hispanic tended to have Spanish surnames, but some defendants with Spanish surnames were not coded as Hispanic. The same defendants who appeared to be miscoded tended to murder Hispanic victims, a pattern that supports the presumption of coding errors in JIMS considering the intra-racial nature of most murder. The problem was addressed with a two-pronged approach: (1) If a defendant was coded as Hispanic in JIMS then the original code remained the same. (2) If a defendant was coded as non-Hispanic in JIMS then the defendant's name was compared to the U.S. Census Bureau's 1990 Spanish Surname List (Word and Perkins 1996). The list classifies 12, 215 surnames as "Heavily Hispanic," meaning more than 75 percent of Census respondents with the surname reported being Hispanic. Using a conservative standard, capital murder defendants were recoded as Hispanic if at least 80 percent of Census respondents with the same surname reported being Hispanic. After correcting Hispanic origin, the defendants are distributed as follows: 24 percent white, 23 percent Hispanic, 49 percent black, and 3 percent Asian.

Data regarding the victim's race were obtained from a name-identified version of the Texas Department of Health's Vital Statistics Mortality File (VSMF).[9] Coding the race of the victim required a procedure that could accommodate cases with multiple victims: 75 cases include multiple victims of the same race; 11 cases include multiple victims of different races. If multiple victims are the same race, then one dichotomous indicator represents the victims (if a white defendant murders two Hispanic victims then the indicator for Hispanic victim is coded 1). If multiple victims are of different races, then multiple

---

9 If data were missing in the VSMF, then Harris County Medical Examiner records were used to code the race of the victim.

Table 2. Measurement Strategies, Data Sources, and Means for the Independent Variables

Variable	Measurement	Data Source[1]	Mean
Defendant Race			
White	1 = yes	JIMS	.24
Hispanic	1 = yes	JIMS	.23
Black	1 = yes	JIMS	.49
Asian	1 = yes	JIMS	.03
Victim Race			
White	1 = yes	VSMF	.41
Hispanic	1 = yes	VSMF	.24
Black	1 = yes	VSMF	.28
Asian	1 = yes	VSMF	.10
Controls			
Legal Dimensions of Case			
Heinous Level 1	1 = yes	HC	.27
Heinous Level 2	1 = yes	HC	.51
Heinous Level 3	1 = yes	HC	.22
Multiple Defendants Indicted on Case	1 = yes	GJI	.49
Form of Capital Murder: Robbery	1 = yes	GJI	.72
Form of Capital Murder: Burglary	1 = yes	GJI	.10
Form of Capital Murder: Multiple Victims	1 = yes	GJI	.17
Form of Capital Murder: Kidnapping	1 = yes	GJI	.10
Form of Capital Murder: Rape	1 = yes	GJI	.06
Form of Capital Murder: Remunerate	1 = yes	GJI	.05
Form of Capital Murder: Child	1 = age 0 to 5	GJI	.03
Form of Capital Murder: Other	1 = yes	GJI	.02
Method of Murder: Shot	1 = yes	HCME	.74
Method of Murder: Beaten	1 = yes	HCME	.14
Method of Murder: Stabbed	1 = yes	HCME	.10
Method of Murder: Asphyxiated	1 = yes	HCME	.09
Defendant Social Characteristics			
Teen	1 = 17 to 19	JIMS	.37
Young Adult	1 = 20 to 29	JIMS	.44
Adult	1 = ≥ 30	JIMS	.19
Sex	1 = male	JIMS	.95
Prior Violent Conviction	1 = yes	JIMS	.19
Prior Non-Violent Conviction	1 = yes	JIMS	.45
Appointed Attorney	1 =appointed only	JIMS	.73
Victim Social Characteristics			
Vulnerable Age	1 = age 6-16 or > 60	VSMF	.12
Sex	1 = female	VSMF	.27
Prior Conviction	1 = yes	www.publicdata.com	.14

Note:
1. Abbreviations: JIMS = Justice Information Management System; VSMF = Vital Statistics Mortality File; HC = *The Houston Chronicle*; GJI = Grand Jury Indictment; HCME = Harris County Medical Examiner.

dichotomous indicators represent the victims (if a white defendant murders a Hispanic victim and a black victim then the indicators for Hispanic victim and black victim are both coded 1). The dichotomous indicators capture the presence or absence of victims of each race. The victims are distributed as follows: 41 percent white, 24 percent Hispanic, 28 percent black, and 10 percent Asian (percentages do not sum to 100 because the dichotomous indicators for each case are not mutually exclusive).

C. Controls

To control for potential confounders, the models also examine the social characteristics of the defendant, the social characteristics of the victim, and the legal dimensions of the case. Table 2 also reports measurement strategies, data sources, and means for the controls.

1. Defendant Social Characteristics

Data regarding defendant social characteristics were drawn from the JIMS file. The multivariate models control for the defendant's sex (1 = male), age (dichotomous indictors for teen 17 to 19, young adult 20 to 29, and adult 30 or more), whether the defendant had a prior violent conviction (discussed below), whether the defendant had a prior non-violent conviction (discussed below), and the defendant's form of legal counsel (discussed below). Measurement of the defendant's prior record and legal counsel require elaboration.

Controlling for the defendant's criminal record is crucial because of the special sentencing issues considered during the punishment phase of a Texas capital murder trial. To sentence a defendant to death, jurors must answer two or three questions depending on whether the defendant was a lone actor or a party to the case: (1) Does the defendant pose a continuing threat to society? (2) If the defendant is a party to the case, did the defendant cause the death of the victim, intend to cause the death of the victim, or anticipate that a life would be taken? (3) Do mitigating circumstances warrant a life sentence? If the jurors unanimously answer the questions in the following order—yes, yes, no—then the defendant is sentenced to death (Texas Statutes: Code of Criminal Procedure, 2007: Chapter 37, Article 37.071).[10] Research suggests that future dangerousness is the most critical sentencing consideration in Texas: most defendants sentenced to life were spared because jurors concluded that the defendant did not pose a continuing threat, not because jurors concluded that mitigating circumstances warranted mercy (Sorensen and Marquart 2003: 286; Sorensen and Pilgrim 2006:53). Thus, to pursue a death trial the DA must decide if

---

10 Prior to 1991, jurors considered three different special sentencing issues: (1) Did the defendant deliberately kill the victim? (2) Does the defendant pose a continuing threat to society? (3) If relevant, was the defendant's behavior an unreasonable response to the victim's provocation? If the jury unanimously answered yes to all the questions then the defendant was sentenced to death. The second question regarding future dangerousness was meant to allow the defense to present the types of mitigating circumstances that the Supreme Court required for a statute to pass constitutional muster. However, Penry, a mentally retarded defendant who was a victim of child abuse, maintained that the second special sentencing issue did just the opposite in his case. Specifically, Penry claimed that if he presented the issues of retardation and abuse as mitigating circumstances the jury might conclude that he was more of a future danger, thereby transforming mitigating circumstances into aggravating circumstances. In the 1989 case of Penry v. Lynaugh, the Supreme Court upheld the defendant's challenge, leading to the adoption of the current special sentencing issues which explicitly require consideration of mitigating circumstances (Sorensen and Pilgrim 2006:1–8).

the defendant's criminal record (or some other aspect of the case) supports a prediction of future dangerousness. Although the DA has access to national criminal record data, JIMS criminal record data are limited to Harris County. To address the problem, JIMS data were supplemented with information from the website: www.publicdata.com. The website charges users a fee to access public criminal record data compiled from 45 states, including Texas. Searches were conducted on all defendants. The inquiries revealed that among defendants who had a clean record in JIMS, 13 had a prior violent conviction and 32 had a prior non-violent conviction on the public data website. Merging data from JIMS and the public data website, the indicators for prior violent conviction and prior non-violent conviction are coded 1 = yes, 0 = no.

Controlling for the defendant's form of legal counsel is also important, particularly because Harris County does not have a Public Defender's Office; if a defendant is indigent then the judge appoints defense counsel from a list of qualified attorneys. The JIMS file indicates that 369 defendants were appointed counsel, 31 defendants hired counsel, and 104 defendants had both hired and appointed counsel at different stages of the case. Legal counsel is measured through a dichotomous indicator coded 1 = appointed only, 0 = hired counsel at some point during the case.[11,12]

2. Victim Social Characteristics

Data regarding victim social characteristics were drawn from the Vital Statistics Mortality File and www.publicdata.com.[13] The multivariate models control for the victim's sex (1 = female), whether the victim was vulnerable due to age (1 = 6 to 16 or over 60; children 0 to 5 considered below), and whether the victim had a prior violent or non-violent conviction (1 = yes; searches were conducted on all victims on the public data website). Coding the victims' characteristics required a procedure that could accommodate cases with multiple victims. Because each of the characteristics is thought to influence the chance of a death trial and a death sentence—more on behalf of female victims and vulnerable victims, but less on behalf of disreputable victims with a prior criminal record–a case is coded 1 if one or more of the victims meet the specified criterion.

---

11 Legal counsel could also be measured through three dichotomous indicators: appointed, hired, and both. But this approach poses the problem of quasi-complete separation: 1 of the 31 defendants with hired counsel advanced to a death trial; 0 of the 31 defendants with hired counsel received a death sentence (for more on quasi-complete separation see Allison 1999).

12 The JIMS file does not indicate whether defendants who had both changed from appointed to hired, or hired to appointed (or the date of the change).

13 If data were missing in the VSMF, then Harris County Medical Examiner records were used to code the age and sex of the victim.

3. Legal Dimensions of Case

Data regarding the legal dimensions of the case were obtained from Grand Jury indictments, the Harris County Medical Examiner (HCME), and The Houston Chronicle. The multivariate models control for the heinousness of the crime (discussed below), whether multiple defendants were indicted (1 = yes), the form of capital murder (discussed below), and the method of murder (dichotomous indicators for shot, stabbed, beaten, and asphyxiated). Controls for heinousness and the form of capital murder require elaboration.

To measure the heinousness of the crime, newspaper articles about each case were collected from The Houston Chronicle online archive (an average of 6.75 articles per case, for a total of more than 3,400 articles). The aggravating and mitigating circumstances in each case were coded based on a list drawn from Baldus and colleagues' research on race and capital punishment (1990:526–535). Table 3 lists the aggravating and mitigating circumstances in question. The following formula was used to construct a scale of heinousness: number of aggravating circumstances minus number of mitigating circumstances (the scale ranged from –3 to +7). The original scale was transformed into three dichotomous indicators: Level 1 Heinousness (bottom quartile of scores ranging from –3 to 0), Level 2 Heinousness (middle 50 percent of scores ranging from 1 to 2), and Level 3 Heinousness (top quartile of scores ranging from 3 to 7).

Table 3. Aggravating and Mitigating Circumstances used to Construct Measure of Heinousness

Aggravating Circumstances	Mitigating Circumstances
∞ Victim vulnerable (e.g. handicapped, mental retardation, frail, pregnant, etc.)	∞ Defendant showed remorse
∞ Victim suffered physical torture (methodical infliction of severe pain)	∞ Victim aroused defendant's sexual desire at time of homicide
∞ Victim suffered mental torture (e.g. hostage informed of impending death before homicide)	∞ Victim aroused defendant's fear for life at time of homicide
∞ Unnecessary pain (pain that is not necessary to kill the victim given the method of killing)	∞ Victim provoked defendant – verbal abuse or physical attack at time of homicide
∞ Victim suffered lingering death	∞ Victim provoked defendant – verbal abuse or physical attack of someone defendant cares about
∞ Victim suffered brutal beating – stomping, clubbing, etc	∞ Victim aroused defendant's hate on a previous occasion
∞ Victim bound/gagged	∞ Victim had used alcohol or drugs immediately prior to crime
∞ Victim ambushed	∞ Victim showing or talking about large amounts of money
∞ Execution style murder (methodical, passionless killing of subdued/defenseless victim)	∞ History of bad blood between defendant and victim
∞ Killing unnecessary to complete felony (e.g. store-keeper turns over money and then shot)	∞ Victim consents to killing
∞ Victim plead for life	∞ Victim was a participant in the crime
∞ Defendant expressed pleasure regarding killing	∞ Victim engaged in questionable behavior
∞ Defendant violated victim's dead body (e.g. mutilation, sexual assault)	∞ Defendant mental impairment
∞ Victim disrobed	
∞ Defendant engaged in significant planning for murder	
∞ Defendant attempted to dispose/conceal body of the victim	
∞ Victim killed in presence of family members or friends	
∞ Defendant used multiple methods for killing	
∞ Overkill	

The list of aggravating and mitigating circumstances was derived from Baldus et al. (1990: 526-535).

The heinousness measure included missing data because The Houston Chronicle did not report on 28 cases. To address the problem, missing cases are assumed to be Level 1. This assumption is based on compelling patterns. To begin, the cliche "if it bleeds it leads" encapsulates the media's obsession with sensational crimes. Considering the fact that The Houston Chronicle reported on 476 of the 504 cases, the 28 capital murders that did not attract media attention are almost sure to be the least heinous of all. In fact, the DA did not pursue a death trial against any of the 28 defendants, bolstering the assumption of minimal heinousness. Because the substantive results are the same regardless of whether the missing cases are excluded or coded as Level 1, the models presented in the results section use the revised indicator of heinousness to ensure complete data for all cases. Thus, the original scale was transformed into three dichotomous indicators to facilitate a solution to the missing data problem (also because several values on the original scale had no cases or just one case).[14]

Grand Jury indictments were used to determine the form of capital murder. Of the forms delineated in the Texas capital murder statute, the following appear in the data: robbery, burglary, multiple victims, kidnapping, rape, remuneration, child 0 to 5 years old, police officer, arson, and obstruction/retaliation. The form of capital murder is measured through dichotomous indicators coded 1 = yes, 0 = no (other includes police officer, arson, and obstruction/retaliation). Because a case can be a capital murder for multiple reasons, the indicators are not mutually exclusive.

D. Modeling

Logistic regression is used to estimate the impact of race on the odds of a death trial (1 = death trial; 0 = all other trajectories) and a death sentence (1 = death sentence; 0 = all other dispositions). In a logistic model, odds ratios represent the effect of a unit change in the independent variable on the odds of the outcome occurring—a death trial or a death sentence. An odds ratio greater than 1 denotes a direct relationship, an odds ratio less than 1 denotes an inverse relationship, and an odds ratio of 1 suggests that the independent variable has no influence on the outcome. So, for example, an odds ratio of 1.5 would suggest that being a black defendant, relative to the reference of being a white defendant, increases the odds of a death trial by 50 percent (or, the odds of a death trial are 1.5 times greater for black defendants than white defendants). An odds ratio of

---

14 Heinousness was also coded based on a visceral reaction to the facts of the crime, just as a DA or juror would do. Each case was assigned to Level 1 (relative minimal), Level 2 (intermediate), or Level 3 (extreme). The Baldus measure of heinousness (based on coding of aggravating and mitigating circumstances) and the visceral measure of heinousness produce the same substantive results. The Baldus measure is used here because it provides slightly more conservative estimates of the impact of race on capital punishment.

.7 would suggest that being a black defendant, relative to the reference of being a white defendant, reduces the odds of a death trial by 30 percent (1–.7 = .3).

Because the data include a population rather than a random sample, statistical significance becomes meaningless (Cowger 1984, 1985).[15] Tests of statistical significance examine a narrow question: the probability of making a Type 1 or Type 2 error in generalizing from a sample to a population. The current research does not generalize from a sample to a population, but rather describes the impact of race on capital punishment for a population of cases. The critical issue in the current research is substantive significance, not statistical significance. Thus, I focus on the magnitude of population parameters (Bollen 1995:468). Specifically, regression coefficients are converted to predicted probabilities in order to examine the cost of racial disparities in human lives. Ignoring statistical significance also eliminates the need to correct for non-independent observations (clustering occurs because multiple defendants are often indicted for the same crime). Non-independent observations can produce correlated error terms leading to biased standard errors and inaccurate tests of statistical significance (McClendon, 1994). But correlated error terms do not influence population parameters.

It is important to note that the data do not include enough Asian defendants or Asian victims to produce robust parameters (for defendants the DA pursued a death trial in 4 of 15 cases and jurors imposed death in 3 of 15 cases; for victims the DA pursued death in 8 of 48 cases and jurors imposed death in 6 of 48 cases). To preserve the population of cases, Asian defendants and Asian victims are included in the multivariate models. But the parameters for Asian defendant and Asian victim are reported in table footnotes and should not be interpreted.[16]

E. Limitations

The most significant limitation is the inability to control for the strength of evidence in each case, an important consideration in the DA's decision to pursue a death trial and the jury's decision to impose a death sentence. This is not a fatal flaw. The only reason to control for a potential confounder is if the confounder is correlated with both race and the trajectory or disposition of cases. Strength of evidence could be related to race if members of certain racial groups tend to be defendants/victims in capital murders that naturally produce more evidence. If, for example, beating a rape victim to death produces more evidence than shooting a robbery victim, and if certain racial groups are more

---

15 For more on the topic of statistical significance and population data see: Berk, Western, and Weiss 1995a, 1995b; Firebaugh 1995; Rubin 1995.

16 Because Asians are often considered the "model minority," whites and Asians could be combined into a single category. But whites and Asians are treated differently (see Table 4), so combining the groups would dilute black–white and Hispanic-white comparisons.

apt to be defendants/victims in the former murder than the latter, then apparent racial disparities might be a legitimate response to differences in the strength of evidence across cases. But the models control for the form and method of murder, so the data include proxies for strength of evidence. Strength of evidence could also be related to race if the police conduct more thorough investigations against certain racial groups, or on behalf of certain racial groups. If so, then controlling for strength of evidence might locate the source of racial disparities in the police department rather than the DA's office or the jurors' deliberation room, but would not eliminate the existence of racial disparities. It is also worth noting that the only study to measure strength of evidence in capital cases found that inclusion of the evidence variable did not change the race findings (Nakell and Hardy 1987). Moreover, in the current data 496 of the 504 defendants were convicted, suggesting that insufficient evidence was rarely a problem for the Harris County DA.

III. RESULTS

A. Bivariate Patterns

Table 4 presents percentage distributions for case trajectory and case disposition by race. Panel A demonstrates the equal treatment of defendants: the DA pursued a death trial against 27 percent of white defendants, 25 percent of Hispanic defendants, and 25 percent of black defendants; a death sentence was imposed against 21 percent of white defendants, 19 percent of Hispanic defendants, and 19 percent of black defendants.

Panel B demonstrates the relatively equal treatment of Hispanic and white victims, but suggests disparities in the treatment of black victims compared to white victims: the DA pursued a death trial on behalf of 30 percent of white victims and 26 percent

Table 4: Case Trajectory and Case Disposition by Race (N=504)

	Trajectory (in percentages)			Disposition (in percentages)						(N)
	Plea Bargain	Life Trial	Death Trial	Acquit	Deferred Adjudication	Probation	TDC	Life	Death Sentence	
Panel A: Defendant Race										
White	38	35	27	2	2	0	24	52	21	122
Hispanic	31	45	25	1	1	1	23	56	19	118
Black	28	47	25	2	0	0	22	57	19	249
Asian	33	40	27	0	0	0	0	80	20	15
Panel B: Victim Race										
White	30	40	30	1	1	1	22	53	23	205
Hispanic	30	45	26	3	1	0	21	55	21	121
Black	29	48	23	2	0	0	24	56	18	141
Asian	42	42	17	0	2	0	13	73	13	48

Notes:
1. Abbreviation: TDC refers to a period of confinement in the Texas Department of Corrections for some period less than life.
2. Panel A has 504 cases because the data include 504 defendants. Panel B has 515 cases because 11 defendants killed multiple victims of two different races.

of Hispanic victims, but just 23 percent of black victims; a death sentence was imposed on behalf of 23 percent of white victims and 21 percent of Hispanic victims, but just 18 percent of black victims.

B. Multivariate Patterns: Death Trial

Do the bivariate patterns regarding death trials hold in a multivariate context? Table 5 reports odds ratios from the logistic regression of death trial on race. The results present a surprising twist. The bivariate comparison of Hispanics to whites holds: Hispanic and white defendants and victims are treated the same. But the bivariate comparison of blacks to whites does not.

1. Black and White Defendants

The percentage distribution suggested that the DA pursued death against black defendants and white defendants at the same rate, but controlling for confounders reveals disparities in the treatment of black defendants: the odds ratio for black defendant changes from .91 in the bivariate logistic model (available upon request) to 1.75 in the multivariate logistic model. The transformation occurs because black defendants committed murders that were less "serious." Here, the term "serious" refers to the features of a murder that increase the chance of a death trial at the bivariate level in the current data. Table 6 demonstrates that black defendants were less likely than white defendants to:

- ∞ murder white victims;
- ∞ commit the most heinous murders;
- ∞ commit murders involving burglary, kidnapping, rape, remuneration, or a child;
- ∞ commit murder by beating, stabbing, or asphyxiating the victim;
- ∞ commit murder as an adult;
- ∞ murder victims who were vulnerable due to age;
- ∞ murder women.

So the DA pursued death against black defendants and white defendants at the same rate despite the fact that black defendants committed less serious murders along several dimensions—meaning black defendants committed murders that were less likely to include the features that tend to increase the chance of a death trial in Harris County. Put differently, the bar appears to have been set lower for pursuing death against black defendants. Comparing the percentage distribution to the multivariate finding leads to the following conclusion: to impose equal punishment against unequal crimes is to impose unequal punishment.

Table 5. Odds Ratios from the Logistic Regression of Case Trajectory on Race (n = 504)	
	Death Trial
Defendant Race	
Hispanic	1.043
Black	1.752
Victim Race	
Hispanic	1.045
Black	.565
Control	
Legal Dimensions of Case	
Heinous Level 2	1.890
Heinous Level 3	2.285
Multiple Defendants Indicted On Case	.268
Type of Capital Murder: Burglary	.497
Type of Capital Murder: Multiple Victims	2.508
Type of Capital Murder: Kidnapping	2.235
Type of Capital Murder: Rape	2.565
Type of Capital Murder: Remunerate	11.900
Type of Capital Murder: Child	.794
Type of Capital Murder: Other	10.376
Method of Murder: Beaten	1.031
Method of Murder: Stabbed	1.617
Method of Murder: Asphyxiated	1.103
Defendant Social Characteristics	
Young Adult	1.056
Adult	1.050
Male	5.822
Prior Violent Conviction	2.030
Prior Non-Violent Conviction	1.278
Appointed Attorney	1.237
Victim Social Characteristics	
Vulnerable Age	1.748
Female	2.697
Prior Conviction	.511

Notes:
1. Reference categories: defendant race = white; victim race = white; heinousness = level 1; type of capital murder = robbery; method of murder = shot; defendant age = teen.
2. Other type of capital murder includes arson, obstruction/retaliation, and killing a police officer.
3. The odds ratio for Asian defendant is 1.773. The odds ratio for Asian victim is .853.

2. Black and White Victims

The percentage distribution suggested that the DA was less likely to pursue death on behalf of black victims than white victims, but controlling for confounders amplifies the original disparity: the odds ratio for black victim changes from .75 in the bivariate logistic model (available upon request) to .57 in the multivariate logistic model. The transformation occurs because black victims were twice as likely to be killed in murders

Table 6. Explaining the Relationship Between Black Defendant and Case Trajectory			
	Black Defendant (in percentages)	**White Defendant (in percentages)**	**Death Trial (in percentages)**
Victim Race			
White	26	77	30
Hispanic	16	13	26
Black	53	3	23
Asian	8	8	17
Heinousness			
Level 1	28	22	14
Level 2	54	55	26
Level 3	18	23	38
Type of Capital Murder			
Robbery	79	61	19
Burglary	8	12	24
Child	2	7	35
Multiple Victims	15	16	38
Kidnapping	8	14	41
Remunerate	4	9	50
Rape	4	6	63
Other	1	2	75
Method of Murder			
Shot	86	47	23
Beaten	8	25	29
Stabbed	7	20	35
Asphyxiated	6	16	46
Defendant Age			
Teen	37	27	18
Young Adult	49	36	26
Adult	14	37	39
Victim Vulnerable Age			
17 to 60	89	79	23
6 to 16 or > 60	9	15	46
Victim Gender			
Male	74	62	17
Female	26	38	49

with multiple victims: 24 percent of black victim cases had multiple victims compared to just 11 percent of white victim cases. So the DA pursued death less on behalf of black victims than white victims despite the fact that black victims were killed in more serious murders with multiple victims. Put differently, the bar appears to have been set higher for pursuing death on behalf of black victims.

C. Multivariate Patterns: Death Sentence

The DA decides whether to pursue a death trial, but jurors decide whether to impose a death sentence. If jurors treated all cases the same regardless of race, then disparities in death trials would be duplicated in death sentences. But jurors could also strengthen, attenuate, or eliminate disparities that originate in the DA's office. Table 7 reports odds ratios from the logistic regression of death sentence on race.

The results suggest duplication and slight attenuation. Duplicating the existing patterns, Hispanic and white defendants and victims are treated the same. But jurors attenuate the differential treatment of blacks and whites: the odds of a death trial are 1.75 times higher against black defendants than white defendants, but drop to 1.49 times higher for a death sentence; the odds of a death trial are 43 percent lower on behalf of black victims relative to white victims, but drop to 38 percent lower for a death sentence. Presumably,

Table 7. Odds Ratios from Logistic Regression of Case Disposition on Race (N = 504)	
	Death Sentence
Defendant Race	
Hispanic	.966
Black	1.491
Victim Race	
Hispanic	1.186
Black	.615
Controls	
Legal Dimensions of Case	
Heinous Level 2	1.162
Heinous Level 3	2.793
Multiple Defendants Indicted On Case	.316
Type of Capital Murder: Burglary	.621
Type of Capital Murder: Multiple Victims	1.886
Type of Capital Murder: Kidnapping	1.474
Type of Capital Murder: Rape	2.104
Type of Capital Murder: Remunerate	7.166
Type of Capital Murder: Child	.523
Type of Capital Murder: Other	2.964
Method of Murder: Beaten	1.038
Method of Murder: Stabbed	1.803
Method of Murder: Asphyxiated	1.624
Defendant Social Characteristics	
Young Adult	.997
Adult	.940
Male	3.816
Prior Violent Conviction	1.966
Prior Non-Violent Conviction	.908
Appointed Attorney	2.154
Victim Social Characteristics	
Vulnerable Age	1.505
Female	2.044
Prior Conviction	.569

Notes:
1. Reference categories: defendant race = white; victim race = white; heinousness = level 1; type of capital murder = robbery; method of murder = shot; defendant age = teen.
2. Other type of capital murder includes arson, obstruction/retaliation, and killing a police officer.
3. The odds ratio for Asian defendant is 1.518. The odds ratio for Asian victim is .865.

the partial correction by jurors is a response to the DA occasionally overreaching against black defendants and on behalf of white victims. But the correction is partial—disparities in death sentences remain.[17]

17 The multivariate models for death trial and death sentence were also run controlling for the relationship between the defendant and victim. Data regarding the defendant–victim relationship were drawn from newspaper articles about each case (stranger = 1, non-stranger = 0). If the newspaper did not mention a relationship then the defendant and victim were considered to be strangers. Controlling

D. Using Predicted Probabilities to Examine the Magnitude of Black-White Disparities

The results suggest that capital punishment in Harris County is stratified according to race—Hispanics and whites are treated the same, but blacks and whites are not. How substantial are the black–white disparities? To provide a more interpretable metric, Table 8 presents predicted probabilities of death trials and death sentences (confounders held constant at the mean). The predicted probabilities are then used to calculate the conditional probability of juries imposing a death sentence against defendants who advance to a death trial. To illustrate the calculation of conditional probabilities, consider the following example. For black defendants, the predicted probability of a death trial is .23 and the predicted probability of a death sentence is .17. Thus, the conditional probability of juries imposing a death sentence is: .23x = . 17; x = .17/.23; x = .74.

Table 8. Using Predicted Probabilities (PP) to Illuminate Black-White Disparities

	Death Trial	Conditional Probability: Death Sentence if Death Trial (PP Death Trial)(X) = PP Death Sentence X = (PP Death Sentence) / (PP Death Trial)	Death Sentence
Panel A. Race of Defendant			
Black	.23	.74	.17
White	.15	.80	.12
Panel B. Race of Victim			
White	.22	.68	.15
Black	.13	.77	.10

Panel A examines the impact of defendant race. Assume, hypothetically, that 100 black defendants and 100 white defendants were indicted for capital murder. The predicted probabilities suggest the following: the DA would pursue death against 23 black defendants and jurors would impose death in 74 percent of the cases, so 17 black defendants would be condemned; the DA would pursue death against 15 white defendants and jurors would impose death in 80 percent of the cases, so 12 white defendants would be condemned. The probabilities translate abstract numbers into human lives: five black defendants would be sentenced to the ultimate state sanction because of race.

Panel B examines the impact of victim race. Here, assume, hypothetically, that 100 defendants murdered white victims and 100 defendants murdered black victims. The predicted probabilities suggest the following: the DA would pursue death on behalf of 22 white victims and jurors would impose death in 68 percent of the cases, so 15 defendants would be condemned; the DA would pursue death on behalf of 13 black victims and jurors would impose death in 77 percent of the cases, so 10 defendants would be condemned. The impact in terms of human lives is the same: five defendants would be sentenced to the ultimate state sanction because the victim is white.

---

for the defendant–victim relationship did not change the substantive results. However, the relationship variable is not included in the tables due to missing data and the obvious problems of relying on the newspaper for such information.

The predicted probabilities also demonstrate how jurors provide a partial correction to disparities that arise in the DA's decision to pursue a death trial. The DA is considerably more likely to pursue death against black defendants and on behalf of white victims, but jurors are slightly more likely to impose death against white defendants and on behalf of black victims. The net effect is that jurors attenuate but do not eliminate the overall black–white disparities—black defendants and defendants who kill whites are still more likely to be sentenced to death, all else equal. The bottom line is clear: race continues to shape case outcomes decades after the Supreme Court declared in *Gregg v. Georgia* (1976) that guided discretion would eliminate arbitrariness in the administration of capital punishment.

IV. CONCLUSION

The race and capital punishment literature is somewhat paradoxical. Numerous studies have been conducted over the years, but no "reasonably well-controlled" research has been done in the five most active death states: Texas, Virginia, Oklahoma, Missouri, and Florida. The current research begins to address this paradox by focusing on the capital of capital punishment. Harris County is exceptional in the modern era of execution. Not only has the county executed 102 inmates, 123 more inmates from Harris County are currently awaiting execution on Texas' death row. Because the pipeline is full, Harris County will probably continue to be one of the most active death jurisdictions in the United States for the foreseeable future.

Some might consider the focus on Harris County to be a limitation rather than an asset—because Harris County is exceptional the findings do not tell us much about the relationship between race and capital punishment in a broader context. But this potential critique misses the mark. No research on race and capital punishment can be generalized to other places or time periods. Seminal research in Georgia (Baldus et al. 1990) and Maryland (Paternoster et al. 2004), for example, cannot be generalized to Harris County, nor can research in Harris County be generalized to Georgia or Maryland. Research in Harris County cannot even be generalized to the rest of Texas—Texas does not have a singular capital punishment regime, but rather 254 capital punishment regimes operating in separate counties authorized by state law. The fact that all research on the topic is confined to particular places and time periods might seem dire, but such a pessimistic conclusion is unwarranted. Our understanding of the relationship between race and capital punishment has always expanded through individual studies that cannot be generalized, but nonetheless combine to form a composite picture—the current research adds an important pixel.

How does the current pixel sharpen the existing image? The findings challenge conventional wisdom by suggesting that the race of the defendant and victim are both pivotal in the capital of capital punishment: death is more likely to be imposed against black defendants than white defendants, and death is more likely to be imposed on behalf of white victims than black victims. The central pattern stems from an intriguing interplay between race, the seriousness of a murder, and the stages of capital litigation. Defendants and victims are considered in turn.

- ∞ Defendants: The DA pursued death against black defendants and white defendants at the same rate, but controlling for confounders revealed disparate treatment because black defendants committed murders that were less "serious" along several dimensions. Although the DA was considerably more likely to pursue death against black defendants, juries were slightly more likely to impose death against white defendants. Presumably, the jurors' behavior is a response to the DA's occasional overreaching against black defendants, a possibility that should be investigated in future research. The net effect is that juries attenuate but do not eliminate disparities between black and white defendants that originate in the DA's office.

- ∞ Victims: The DA was considerably more likely to pursue death on behalf of white victims than black victims, particularly given the fact that black victims tended to be killed in murders that were more serious due to the presence of multiple victims. But jurors were slightly more likely to impose death on behalf of black victims. Again, the jurors' behavior is assumed to be a response to the DA's occasional overreaching on behalf of white victims. The net effect is that juries attenuate but do not eliminate disparities between black and white victims that originate in the DA's office.

Perhaps surprisingly, the findings also suggest that Hispanics and whites are treated the same. This pattern could be a product of the demographic landscape: whites and Hispanics represent an equal share of Harris County residents at 38 percent each, compared to 18 percent for blacks. Such numbers suggest that Hispanics wield more political power and are a greater presence within criminal justice, such as on juries (U.S. Census Bureau 2007). More research is needed to understand the juxtaposition of black–white disparities but Hispanic-white parities.

The capital punishment literature is marked by exemplary research (see e.g. Bowers and Pierce 1980; Radelet 1981; Foley and Powell 1982; Paternoster 1984; Nakell and Hardy 1987; Gross and Mauro 1989; Keil and Vito 1989; Baldus et al. 1990; Paternoster et al. 2004; Blume et al. 2004; Pierce and Radelet 2005; Hindson et al. 2006). The current research contributes to a crowded field by: focusing on the capital of capital punishment; challenging conventional wisdom regarding the basic relationship between race and capital punishment; demonstrating the nuanced interplay between race, the seriousness of a murder, and the stages of capital litigation; translating abstract odds ratios into interpretable predicted probabilities that are accessible to policymakers; and serving as a call to action for scholars to initiate "reasonably well-controlled" studies in the most active death jurisdictions in the United States.

REFERENCES

Allison, Paul D. 1999. Logistic Regression Using the SAS System: Theory and Application. Cary, NC: SAS Institute Inc.

Amnesty International. 2007. http://www.amnesty.org/en/report/info/AMR51/125/2007

Baldus, David C. George Woodworth, and Charles A. Pulaski Jr. 1990. Equal Justice and the Death Penalty: A Legal and Empirical Analysis. Boston: Northeastern University Press.

Baldus, David C. and George Woodworth. 2003a. "Race Discrimination and the Death Penalty: An Empirical and Legal Overview." Pp. 501–551 in America's Experiment with Capital Punishment edited by James R. Acker, Robert M. Bohm, and Charles S. Lanier. Durham. North Carolina: Carolina Academic Press.

Baldus, David C. and George Woodworth. 2003b. "Race Discrimination in the Administration of the Death Penalty: An Overview of the Empirical Evidence with Special Emphasis on the Post-1990 Research." Criminal Law Bulletin 39: 194–226.

Berk, Richard A., Bruce Western, and Robert E. Weiss. 1995a. "Statistical Inference for Apparent Populations." Sociological Methodology 25:421–458.

Berk, Richard A., Bruce Western, and Robert E. Weiss. 1995b. "Reply to Bollen, Firebaugh, and Rubin." Sociological Methodology 25:481–485.

Black, Donald. 1995. "The Epistemology of Pure Sociology." Law and Social Inquiry 20 (3):829–870.

Blume, John, Theodore Eisenberg, and Martin T. Wells. 2004. "Explaining Death Row's Population and Racial Composition." Journal of Empirical Legal Studies 1(1): 165–207.

Bollen, Kenneth A. 1995. "Apparent and Nonapparent Significance Tests." Sociological Methodology 25:459–468.

Bowers, William J. and Glenn L. Pierce. 1980. "Arbitrariness and Discrimination under Post-Furman Capital Statutes." Crime and Delinquency 26:563–635.

Brock, Dean, Nigel Cohen, and Jonathan Sorensen. 2000. "Arbitrariness in the Imposition of Death Sentences in Texas: An Analysis of Four Counties by Offense Seriousness, Race of Victim, and Race of Offender." American Journal of Criminal Law 28:43–71.

Cowger, Charles D. 1984. "Statistical Significance Tests: Scientific Ritualism or Scientific Method?" Social Services Review 58:358–371.

Cowger, Charles D. 1985. "Reply to Allen Rubin's Significance Testing with Population Data." Social Services Review 59:521–522.

Death Penalty Information Center. 2007. http://www.deathpenaltyinfo.org/. Retrieved September 17, 2007.

Ekland-Olson, Sheldon. 1988. "Structured Discretion, Racial Bias, and the Death Penalty: The First Decade after Furman in Texas." Social Science Quarterly 69(4):853–873.

Firebaugh, Glenn. 1995. "Will Bayesian Inference Help? A Skeptical View." Sociological Methodology 25:469–472.

Foley, Linda and Richard Powell. 1982. "The Discretion of Prosecutors, Judges, and Juries in Capital Cases." Criminal Justice Review 7(2): 16–22.

Gross, Samuel R. and Robert Mauro. 1989. Death and Discrimination: Racial Disparities in Capital Sentencing. Boston: Northeastern University Press.

Hindson, Stephanie, Hillary Potter, and Michael L. Radelet. 2006. "Race, Gender, Region, and Death Sentencing in Colorado, 1980–1999." University of Colorado Law Review 77(3):549–594.

Houston Chronicle. Allan Turner. February 4, 2001. Harris County is a Pipeline to Death Row. A Four-Part Series Examines Why, and Explores Whether Justice is Served. A Deadly Distinction: Bloodthirsty Image at Odds with Local Poll. A1.

Houston Chronicle. Mike Tolson. February 5, 2001. A Deadly Distinction: Part II. Between Life and Death: Borderline Capital Cases Raise Questions of Justice. A1.

Houston Chronicle. Steve Brewer and Mike Tolson. February 6, 2001. A Deadly Distinction: Part III. Debate Fervent in Mental Cases: Johnny Paul Penry Illustrates a Lingering Capital Conundrum. A6.

Houston Chronicle. Mike Tolson. February 7, 2001. A Deadly Distinction: Part IV. Death Penalty Reforms Sought: Life Without Parole Has Chance to Pass in this Legislature. A1.

Hunter, Robert J., Paige Heather Ralph, and James Marquart. 1993. "The Death Sentencing of Rapists in VtQ-Furman Texas (1942–1971): The Racial Dimension." American Journal of Criminal Law 20(3):313–337.

Keil, Thomas J. and Gennaro F. Vito. 1989. "Race, Homicide Severity, and Application of the Death Penalty: A Consideration of the Barnett Scale." Criminology 27(3):511–536.

Koeninger, Rupert C. 1969. Capital Punishment in Texas, 1924–1968." Crime and Delinquency 15:132–141.

Marquart, James W., Sheldon Ekland-Olson, and Jonathan R. Sorensen. 1994. The Rope, the Chair, and the Needle: Capital Punishment in Texas. 1923–1990. Austin, Texas: University of Texas Press.

McClendon, McKee J. 1994. Multiple Regression and Causal Analysis. F.E. Peacock Publishers: Itasca, Illinois.

Nakell, Barry and Kenneth A Hardy. 1987. The Arbitrariness of the Death Penalty. Philadelphia, Pennsylvania: Temple University Press.

New York Times. Adam Liptak. February 14, 2004. Study Revises Texas' Standing as a Death Penalty Leader.

Paternoster, Raymond. 1984. "Prosecutorial Discretion in Requesting the Death Penalty: A case of Victim-Based Racial Discrimination." Law and Society Review 18(3):437–478.

Paternoster, Raymond, Robert Brame, Sarah Bacon, and Andrew Ditchfield. 2004. "Justice by Geography and Race: The Administration of the Death Penalty in Maryland, 1978–1999." Margins: University of Maryland Law Journal on Race. Religion. Gender and Class 4(1): 1–97.

Paternoster, Raymond, Robert Brame, and Sarah Bacon. 2008. The Death Penalty: America's Experience with Capital Punishment. New York: Oxford University Press.

Pierce, Glenn L. and Michael L. Radelet. 2005. "The Impact of Legally Inappropriate Factors on Death Sentencing for California Homicides, 1990–1999." Santa Clara Law Review 46(1): 1–47.

Radelet, Michael L. 1981. "Racial Characteristics and the Imposition of the Death Penalty." American Sociological Review 46(6):918–927.

Ralph, Paige H., Jonathan R. Sorensen, and James W. Marquart. 1992. "A Comparison of Death Sentenced and Incarcerated Murderers in VtQ-Furman Texas." Justice Quarterly 9(2): 185–209.

Rubin, Donald B. 1995. "Bayes, Neyman, and Calibration." Sociological Methodology 25:473–479.

Sorensen, Jonathan R. and James W. Marquart. 1990–1991. "Prosecutorial and Jury Decision-Making in Vost-Furman Texas Capital Cases." NYU Review of Law and Social Change 18(3):743–776.

Sorensen, Jon and James Marquart. 2003. "Future Dangerousness and Incapacitation." Pp. 283–300 in America's Experiment with Capital Punishment edited by James R. Acker, Robert M. Bohm, and Charles S. Lanier. Durham. North Carolina: Carolina Academic Press.

Sorensen, Jon and Rocky Leann Pilgrim. 2006. Lethal Injection: Capital Punishment in Texas During the Modern Era. Austin, Texas: University of Texas Press.

Texas Department of Criminal Justice. 2007. http://www.tdcj.state.tx.us/stat/deathrow.htm. Retrieved September 17, 2007.

Texas Statutes: Code of Criminal Procedure. 2007. http://tlo2.tlc.state.tx.us/statutes/cr.toc.htm. Retrieved September 19, 2007.

Texas Statutes: Penal Code. 2007. http://tlo2.tlc.state.tx.us/statutes/petoc.html. Retrieved September 17, 2007.

United States Census Bureau. 2007. http://quickfacts.census.gov/qfd/states/48/48201.html. Retrieved September 17, 2007.

United States General Accounting Office. 1990. "Death Penalty Sentencing: Resource Indicates Pattern of Racial Disparities. Washington, D.C.: U.S. General Accounting Office.

Word, David L. and R. Colby Perkins. 1996. "Building a Spanish Surname List for the 1990's—A New Approach to an Old Problem."

http://www.census.gov/population/documentation/twpno13.pdf. Retrieved September 17, 2007.

CASES CITED

Furman v. Georgia, 408 U.S. 238 (1972).
Gregg v. Georgia, 428 U.S. 153 (1976).
McCleskey v. Kemp, 481 U.S. 279 (1987).
Penry v. Lynaugh, 492 U.S. 302 (1989)
Proffitt v. Florida, 428 U.S. 242 (1976).
Roberts v. Louisiana, 428 U.S. 325 (1976).
Roper v. Simmons, 543 U.S. 551 (2005).
Woodson v. North Carolina, 428 U.S. 280 (1976).

DISCUSSION QUESTIONS

1. Review and describe the different data sets used by Pierce and Radelet, and Phillips, to test their disparity hypotheses. Discuss also the data and methodological limitations noted in each study. In your opinion, are these limitations so damaging as to render the findings presented useless? Explain your answer.
2. What are the potential sources of bias in the capital punishment system (limit your answer to the top three or four sources, if possible)? Is it possible to measure the extent to which these various sources of bias exist, with confidence and statistical certainty? If so, why does it not happen with more regularity? If not, why do you think people continue to make such measurements and make policy-related arguments based on their analyses?
3. Consider the argument that we can never eliminate bias from the capital punishment system—so long as humans administer the system, it will reflect human failings, including prejudice and violence. If this is true, how can we reconcile living with a biased system that makes systematic mistakes regarding a penalty as serious as death? Under what conditions are you willing to tolerate such a system (you can consider this question even if you are an abolitionist, because the same mistakes would likely be made in life without parole sentences)?
4. Pierce and Radelet note that region (e.g., type of county—urban vs. rural) has a statistically significant influence on the imposition of the death penalty, and they suggest that this is an unacceptable situation. Many agree. Others argue that local or regional culture should rightly influence the administration of justice. After all, the justice system should reflect community norms. Is there a resolution to this dilemma, or should we think of the capital punishment system as a constant struggle to find balance between universal rights and local determination? Consider whether you would have the same opinion regarding capital cases and lesser offenses (e.g., simple assault or shoplifting)? Are there other criterion that influence your opinion on this matter?

DETERRENCE

Introduction

Capital Punishment and Deterrence: Some Further Thoughts and Additional Evidence

By Isaac Ehrlich

Death and Deterrence Redux: Science, Law and Causal Reasoning on Capital Punishment

By Jeffrey Fagan

This chapter presents two readings on deterrence that span almost thirty years—beginning with Isaac Ehrlich's influential 1977 article, "Capital Punishment and Deterrence: Some Further Thoughts and Additional Evidence," in which he expands on some of his own earlier research (Erlich 1973, 1975) and claims that capital punishment has "... a substantial deterrent effect of punishment on murder and related violent crimes ..." The second reading comprises Professor Jeffrey Fagan's 2005 Walter C. Reckless lecture at Ohio State University. He takes on the deterrence theorists, old and new, with a blistering critique of the underpinnings of deterrence theory—theoretical assumptions, conceptualization, model specification, replication, faulty data, and more. Note that he does not specifically argue for or against deterrence theory, rather he provides a compelling statement regarding what the data and research do or do not support regarding deterrence theory.

We include these two articles because of their importance to understanding deterrence theory and how knowledgeable researchers address the task of theory development and theory testing, in deductive fashion. Ehrlich's article, debatable points aside, had a dramatic impact on deterrence research, and was a catalyst for pro-deterrence and pro-death penalty advocates. Indeed, his work was cited in the Gregg v. Georgia Supreme Court case that paved the way for the reinstatement of the death penalty in the U.S. (Fagan 2005). Fagan's article arrives several decades after Ehrlich's, and was written, not in response to Ehrlich but in response to a stream of pro-deterrence research and theorizing that followed Ehrlich's work, and particularly in response to several studies published in the five years preceding his 2005 lecture (Fagan 2005). Thus, the reader should not approach these readings as a "Ehrlich v. Fagan" standoff, but as a contrast between two serious scholars writing at two different historical times on a critical theme in the death penalty debate—deterrence.

Readers should take note of several differences between these two articles. We draw the reader's attention to these differences to aid in the interpretation of these complex arguments, not to suggest that either is better than the other in any aspect. Ehrlich, obviously, produced his work almost 30 years ago, when knowledge of, and access to, sophisticated statistical analysis techniques was more limited than it is now. It will be difficult for the reader to comprehend the tremendous effort Ehrlich must have made at the time to complete a long series of statistical econometric analyses such as those presented in his paper. Fagan, on the other hand, had more sophisticated analytical techniques and computer programs at his disposal, and was able to conduct an impressive array of tests and replications that Ehrlich might not have been able to imagine in his day. Fagan also had the benefit of 30 years of research and theorizing about deterrence to draw from. To his credit, however, Fagan presents an equally impressive series of specific analyses aimed at testing numerous individual assumptions and questions about deterrence theory. Fagan did not directly test Ehrlich's analysis, though he did test the assumptions and conclusions of some of the more recent research on deterrence theory, and in one case actually obtained one of the researcher's data sets for re-analysis.

Ehrlich's article presents a limited test of deterrence theory, compared to the broader approach taken by Fagan. As Fagan points out, Ehrlich's work is almost exclusively in the realm of econometrics (to the exclusion of more useful and appropriate methods), whereas Fagan uses several different statistical techniques to test deterrence theory. Finally, Fagan addresses much broader issues than Ehrlich, such as: the political context within which death penalty research, and specifically deterrence research, takes place; and the questionable, as Fagan argues, editorial decisions by scholarly journals that publish some research with obvious flaws and omissions.

Capital Punishment and Deterrence

Some Further Thoughts and Additional Evidence

Isaac Ehrlich

Investigation of the deterrent effect of capital punishment has implications far beyond the propriety of execution as punishment since it concerns the general question of offenders' responsiveness to incentives. This study challenges popular allegations by earlier researchers denying the deterrence hypothesis. The empirical analysis based on cross-sectional data from the U.S. corroborates my earlier analysis of the time series. Findings indicate a substantial deterrent effect of punishment on murder and related violent crimes and support the economic and econometric models used in investigations of other crimes. Distinctions between classes of executing and nonexecuting states are also examined in light of theory and evidence.

Author's Note: I am indebted to my colleagues Lawrence Fisher, Ronald Gallant, James Heekman, Sam Peltzman, George Stigler, and to two anonymous referees for numerous comments and suggestions. I am particularly grateful to Randall Mark for his general research assistance and suggestions and to Joel Gibbons for useful comments on a previous draft. I also wish to acknowledge the competent computational assistance of Linda Moy and Vasant Sukhatme. I am also indebted to Kenneth R. Brimmer of the National Prisoner Statistics of the Bureau of the Census for his help in obtaining execution data for the years 1936–40. I alone am responsible for errors. Financial assistance for this study has been provided by a grant from the National Science Foundation to the National Bureau of Economic Research for research in law and economics. The financial support of the Charles C. Walgreen Foundation is also gratefully acknowledged. The paper is not an official NBER publication.

The importance of determining the deterrent effect on crime of various punishments is one of the few issues concerning deterrence that is not controversial. The problem of deterrence is encountered in all socially disapproved behavior, but it has a natural and dramatic significance with respect to the crime of murder. The present essay will examine the evidence on the cross-sectional patterns of murder and execution in 1940 and 1950, both as an illuminating source of information on the problem of deterrence and as a supplement to my earlier study of the time series.[1] The cross-sectional studies on balance reinforce the findings of the substantial restraining effect on murders of punishment in general and capital punishment in particular. The specific results obtained are consistent with sharp predictions emanating from the deterrence theory.

I deal here with the relationship between estimates of the murder rate and the conditional probability of execution, but the present investigation explores more fully than the previous study the nature of deterrence. The time-series analysis was based on a small number of observations, whereas the present analysis uses a larger body of independent, cross-sectional data relating to different states in the United States. The cross-sectional data include estimates of severity of imprisonment for murder and other crimes, missing from the time series, and provide useful information on additional relevant variables. While the time-series analysis deals with aggregate data relating to both executing and nonexecuting states, the cross-sectional statistics allow separate investigation of the subsets of executing and nonexecuting states and other groupings. The more complete data on punishments imposed for other crimes also permit a partial investigation of the interaction between murder and related violent crimes and thus provide for a somewhat more complete assessment of specific deterrent effects. The cross-sectional data from 1940 and 1950 are advantageous also because they relate to years in which the level of enforcement of capital punishment in executing states appears to have been sufficiently high and variable to permit a meaningful statistical test of the hypothesis of no deterrence. And the general uniformity in the reporting of crime rates in 1940 and 1950 permits some testing of temporal as well as cross-sectional homogeneity. In contrast, however, data exigencies unique to the cross-sectional samples have at this stage precluded utilization of the relatively more sophisticated estimation techniques employed in my earlier investigations.

Some economists may feel that a study of murder is of little relevance for the purpose of testing the economic approach to criminality. Indeed, my main concern is the general question of offenders' responsiveness to incentives, an issue I have investigated in earlier studies by stressing other crimes and different punishments (see Ehrlich 1974). I return to the seemingly narrower study of murder both because of the presumed relative superiority of murder statistics and because I find no compelling reason to expect perpetrators of crimes of passion necessarily to be less responsive to incentives than perpetrators of crimes involving material gains only. Those with a greater proclivity or "taste" for violence are indeed more likely to commit assault or murder than others, given the same objective motives and equal prospects of punishment. However, they need not be less responsive to changes in these factors. Inelasticity of demand is not necessarily an increasing function of the extent of demand at given income and prices. Being emotional does not preclude the ability to make self-serving choices. Even if control over actions is foregone temporarily during the commission of crime, the prospect of punishment through public or private sanctions still may prevail upon individuals to avoid situations in which "loss of control" is likely to occur. And if rational people fear death more than other punishment, the death penalty should have the greatest deterrent effect. Conclusions reached in research concerning the abhorrent crime of murder, which some criminologists consider a special form of deviance, thus can shed important light on the relevance of the economic approach to crime and to human behavior in general.

The plan of the paper is as follows: Section I discusses some analytical issues unique to this study. Section II presents an econometric investigation of cross-state variations in murder and related crimes and analyzes the results. Section III examines data on differences in offense rates, conviction risks, and sanction levels across executing and non-executing states and analyzes these data in light of a model of optimal demand for public law enforcement. A brief comparison with previous findings is offered in the concluding section.

[...]

II. EMPIRICAL IMPLEMENTATION

A. Introduction

The supply-of-offenses functions relating to murder and other crimes are estimated in this investigation using cross-state data from 1940 and 1950. These years are chosen because the level of enforcement of capital punishment in individual executing states appears to have been sufficiently high and variable to permit a meaningful test of the hypothesis of no deterrence. Due to data exigencies, the parameters of the supply functions are estimated via classical least-squares and seemingly un-related simultaneous-equations techniques rather than the two-stage least-squares procedure employed in my related works. Because the preferred regression format is found to be logarithmic and the estimated levels of conditional risks of execution in nonexecuting states are "zero," supply-of-offenses functions are estimated separately in executing states as well as in the full samples comprised of executing and nonexecuting states. In the full-sample regressions estimated via the approximate logarithmic transformation, statistical considerations dictate allowance for separate constant terms in each class of states. Following tests for homoscedasticity, generalized least-squares estimates are achieved by weighting all variables by the square roots of either urban, state, or (when available) the relevant sample populations.

B. Analysis of Regression Results

1. Analysis of FBI (UGR) Data

FBI statistics on murder and other felonies are available in 1940 and 1950 only as crime rates in samples of urban areas covering, on average, 49 percent of the states' residential population in 1940 and 45 percent in 1950 (see U.S. Department of Justice, Uniform Crime Reports, 1940, 1950–51, 1960, 1970). Crime statistics are based on complaints of crime, subject to police verification procedures, and are recorded according to Uniform Crime Reports (UCR) classifications. The category "murder" refers to all willful felonious homicides.

a) Subsets of states with positive executions.—The basic regression model used in the analysis is linear in the logarithms of all relevant variables:[8]

$$E(\ln q^{o}) = a + b_1 \ln T + b_2 \ln P^{o}c + b_3 \ln P^{o}e|c + b_4 \ln NW + b_5 \ln X + b_6 \ln W + b_7 \ln \mathrm{AGE} + b_8 \ln \mathrm{URB}$$

Table 3 presents estimates of regression coefficients and the ratios of these coefficients to their standard errors. Magnitudes of the "R^2" statistics reported in connection with weighted regressions are the conventional R^2 measures obtained after multiplying the variables in equation (5) by a weighting factor. These "R^2" measures thus may serve merely as indicators of goodness of fit in the transformed regression equations.

Results obtained in connection with the three deterrence variables, T, P°c, and measures of P°e|c, exhibit a consistent pattern throughout the regression analysis. The estimated regression coefficients associated with these variables are all negative, with magnitudes generally well above twice the values of corresponding standard errors. More important, with no exception, the estimated elasticities of the murder rate, with respect to the probability of conviction (P°c), exceed those with respect to the conditional probability of execution, given conviction (P°e|c). In all of the cases reported in tables 3 and 4, the differences between the magnitudes of the latter elasticities are significant at the 5 percent level for a two-tail test.[10] As for the effect of T, it should be recalled that the variable used in both the 1940 and the 1950 regressions is the median length of time served by those released from prisons in 1951. In spite of potential biases which may be injected into regression estimates in 1940 as a result, estimates of deterrence effects are statistically indistinguishable across different regressions and do not depend on the inclusion of T_{50} in the 1940 regressions (see Part 5 below).

TABLE 2

LIST OF VARIABLES USED IN THE REGRESSION ANALYSIS

q_i^o = urban crime rate (per 100,000 population) for offense category i, based on *UCR* samples;

h^o = homicide rate (per 100,000 population), based on *VS* data;

$P^o c_i = \frac{C_i^o}{Q_i^o}$ = estimate of probability of conviction: the ratio of prisoners received in state prisons to the estimated (state) total numbers of offenses in category i;

$P^h c = \frac{C^o}{H^o}$ = corresponding estimate of probability of conviction for murder using *VS* data on the number of homicides in a state;

T_i† = median time spent in state prisons by offenders prior to first release;

$PX5 = \frac{\sum_{j=0}^{4} E_{t-j}^o/5}{C_t^o}$ = the ratio of the average number of executions in years t to $t - j$ to the estimated number of convictions for murder in sample year t;

$PX4 = \frac{\sum_{j=0}^{3} E_{t-j}^o/4}{C_t}$ $PXQ1 = \frac{E_{t+1}^o}{C_t^o}$ $PXQ2 = \frac{E_t^o}{C_t^o}$ $PXA = \frac{E_{t+1}^o + E_t^o/2}{C_t}$

$PXQ1Q - PX5Q$‡ = same as the preceding ratios but with E_t^o defined to include only executions for murders;

W§ = median income of families in year $t - 1$: a census estimate;

X = percentage of families with income below one-half of W;

NW = percent of nonwhites in the population;

AGE = percent of population in the age group 15–24;

A_{25-34} = percent of population in the age group 25–34;

URB = percent of urban population in the total state population;

EPOS = a dummy variable distinguishing executing states (1) from states (0) with $P^o e | c = 0$;

N_s = state population in 100,000s;

N_{URB} = urban population in 100,000s;

N_{REP} = size of population (in 100,000s) in *UCR* samples reporting q_i^o in 1951;

NOTE.—Due to data exigencies, UCR murder regressions omit from the full samples in 1940 and 1950 the following states: 1940—Georgia, Maine, Mississippi, Nevada, and Vermont; 1950—Georgia, Michigan, North Dakota, and Vermont.

† In the 1940 regressions data exigencies dictated the use of the corresponding variable from 1950 (7*50). The actual data are for prisoners released in 1951 (1952 for TMUR in Idaho, Michigan, Rhode Island, South Dakota, and Vermont) because 1950 figures are not available.

‡ In 1940 PX5Q cannot be computed because execution data for 1936 are not available by crime category.

§ In 1940 available only as median earnings of a sample of wage and salary workers.

In contrast to time-series estimates of the simple correlation between measures of the murder rate and the conditional probability of execution, these simple correlations are found to be negative in all the relevant subsets of executing states.[11] In addition, estimates of deterrent effects derived from regressions in which only the three deterrence variables, T, P°c, and P°e|c, served as regressors show similar qualitative results, with estimates of deterrent effects actually larger in absolute magnitudes.

Except for estimates derived from unweighted regressions in 1950, virtually all 95 percent confidence intervals associated with the estimated elasticities of the murder rate with respect to alternative measures of the conditional risk of execution include only negative values. Nevertheless, the quantitative differences observed among the point estimates of elasticities associated with other measures of P°e|c (not reported here due to lack of space) indicate the inherent limitations of these measures, resulting from the rather sizable

TABLE 3

MURDER SUPPLY FUNCTIONS: GLS (Weighted) AND OLS REGRESSIONS, LOGARITHMIC FORM

Eq.	Year	N	"R^2"	Constant	T	P_c^o	$P^o{}_{e\|c}$	NW	X	W	AGE	URB
Weight = $\sqrt{N_{URB}}$:												
							$PX5$					
1.	1940	33	.9539	7.372 (1.89)	−0.292 (−2.35)	−0.673 (−4.70)	−0.339 (−3.48)	0.508 (7.26)	. . .	0.436 (1.21)	−2.101 (−2.23)	−0.982 (−4.43)
							$PX4Q$					
2.	1940	33	.9565	5.466 (1.44)	−0.232 (−1.93)	−0.709 (−4.99)	−0.389 (−3.79)	0.468 (6.58)	. . .	0.505 (1.44)	−1.741 (−1.92)	−0.993 (−4.63)
Weight = $\sqrt{N_s}$:												
							$PX5$					
3.	1940	33	.9518	5.757 (1.37)	−0.320 (−2.45)	−0.682 (−4.44)	−0.366 (−3.46)	0.487 (6.20)	. . .	0.480 (1.26)	−1.691 (−1.58)	−0.928 (−4.01)
							$PX4Q$					
4.	1940	33	.9585	4.259 (1.09)	−0.249 (−2.03)	−0.725 (−5.07)	−0.430 (−4.23)	0.438 (5.79)	. . .	0.469 (1.33)	−1.393 (−1.41)	−0.882 (−4.08)
Weight = $\sqrt{N_{REP}}$:												
							$PX5$					
5.	1950	35	.9581	−4.622 (−1.17)	−0.459 (−3.59)	−0.687 (−5.23)	−0.272 (−4.74)	0.496 (7.13)	1.200 (2.22)	1.226 (2.65)	0.274 (0.44)	−0.742 (−2.08)

							PX5Q					
6.	1950	35	.9588	−4.690 (−1.20)	−0.422 (−3.35)	−0.670 (−5.15)	−0.270 (−4.81)	0.487 (7.01)	1.143 (2.12)	1.256 (2.74)	0.177 (0.29)	−0.783 (−2.21)
Weight = $\sqrt{N_s}$:												
							PX5					
7.	1950	35	.9503	−3.024 (−0.84)	−0.507 (−3.87)	−0.719 (−5.30)	−0.324 (−5.04)	0.468 (6.23)	0.904 (1.52)	0.921 (1.99)	0.374 (0.63)	−0.703 (−1.94)
							PX5Q					
8.	1950	35	.9512	−3.101 (−0.87)	−0.460 (−3.53)	−0.694 (−5.18)	−0.324 (−5.13)	0.456 (6.13)	0.834 (1.41)	0.940 (2.06)	0.282 (0.48)	−0.738 (−2.05)
Unweighted:												
							PX4Q					
9.	1940	33	.9087	5.633 (1.19)	−0.152 (−0.98)	−0.792 (−6.11)	−0.509 (−5.48)	0.312 (4.89)	... ...	−0.064 (−0.18)	−1.062 (−0.80)	−0.705 (−2.79)
							PX5Q					
10.	1950	35	.8394	−2.201 (−0.50)	−0.490 (−2.39)	−0.595 (−3.33)	−0.145 (−1.38)	0.460 (4.40)	0.945 (1.07)	0.793 (1.32)	0.192 (0.37)	−0.364 (−0.74)

NOTE.—$\hat{\beta}/S_{\hat{\beta}}$ in parentheses.

relative fluctuations in the small numbers of executions carried out in a given state over successive years.[12] Indeed, the reported measures of $P^{\circ}e|c$ based on 4-or 5-year averages of the yearly number of executions generally yield more consistent and pronounced results across the 1940 and 1950 samples. The apparent superiority of PX4Q, PX5Q, and PX5 as measures of execution risk may also be due to the fact that the regressions utilizing these variables include a larger number of observations. Thus the results are based on a larger number of degrees of freedom.

The estimated effects of measures of income (W) and income inequality (X) may reflect the influence of different and possibly even conflicting factors.[13] The variables W and X may serve as indicators of the potential gains and the differential gains from property crimes relative to legitimate earning activities (see Ehrlich [1974, section IIIB] and the results in connection with robbery and assault in tables 6 and 7). The generally positive effects of these variables on the murder rate may be due to the fact that murder is often a by-product of these crimes. The direct partial effects of W and X on the incentive to commit acts of malice are more ambiguous, however (see Ehrlich 1975*a*). Presumably, the incentive effects of wealth on crime outweigh the effect of medical care available to victims of aggravated assault. Note, however, that the observed positive effects of X and NW on q" may partly be due to the effect of inferior medical care services available to relatively low-income persons.

The percent of urban population in the total state population (URB) is found to be negatively associated with the (urban) murder rate in both 1940 and 1950. The result might suggest that the magnitudes of some explanatory variables computed from statistics relating to the entire state population differ by constant proportions across urban and rural areas, and, consequently, that URB serves as a "correcting factor." The net effect of URB then would not be clear a priori since it would depend on the direction of specific differences. Alternatively, the degree of urbanization of a state may serve as a proxy for other relevant factors, such as access to relevant medical services, the partial effect of which on the murder rate is expected to be negative.[14]

The percent of young age groups (15–24) in the state population (AGE) is not always found to have a systematic association with the murder rate, whereas the effect of the percent of nonwhites in the population (NW) is generally positive and significant in all regressions. As in the case of URB, AGE may perform the role of a "correcting factor" which allows derivation of unbiased estimates of the effects of deterrence variables. Presumably, magnitudes of these variables differ across different age brackets because of the differential treatment of young offenders under the law. While this consideration alone might lead to the expectation that q" and AGE would be positively correlated, other differences in determinants of murder and acts of malice across different age groups may give rise to different associations. According to information compiled from the Vital Statistics of the United States (see Klebba 1975), the homicide victimization rate for nonwhites and for the total population has tended to peak at the age group 25–34 (A_{25-34}) in the period under study. Indeed, estimates of equation (5) with A_{25-34} replacing AGE reveal a positive association between A_{25-34} and the murder rate, especially in 1950, contrary to the inconclusive effect of AGE in these regressions. Generally, estimates of deterrent effects in (5) obtained with A_{25-34} as a measure of age composition did not differ markedly from the estimates discussed in the preceding analysis: the effects of $P^{o}c$ and $P^{o}e|c$ were found somewhat higher in absolute values, and that of T somewhat lower. The main change was observed in 1950 regressions in connection with the effect of the percent of nonwhites in the population, which decreased in magnitude although it remained statistically significant.[15] It thus appears that the positive and significant association of NW and q^{o} may be, at least in part, the result of its relatively high partial correlation with A_{23-34}. However, homicide victimization data reveal that nonwhites face a much higher risk of victimization than do their white counterparts in all age and sex groups. This evidence is not inconsistent with the hypothesis that the higher frequency of murder among nonwhites is the result of relatively low general (and age-specific) earning opportunities which reduce potential incarceration costs and access to relevant medical services at all ages.[16]

b) Full-sample results.—The basic regression equation estimated using the full set of observations available in 1940 and 1950 is a modified version of the regression model specified in equation (5),

$$E[q^{o(\lambda)}] = a + b_1 T^{(\lambda)} + \bullet\bullet\bullet + b_8 \text{URB}^{(\lambda)} + b_9 \text{EPOS}, \quad (6)$$

where EPOS is a dummy variable distinguishing the relevant executing (1) and nonexecuting (0) states, and the transformation (λ) is defined in Section IC. Because the values of measured execution risks in nonexecuting states are zero, the log-linear regression format specified in equation (5) is here approximated by setting $\lambda = 0.001$. The results for the simple linear and the approximate log-linear transformations are reported in equations lb, 1c, 2b, and 2c in table 4, parts A and B.

The full-sample results which allow for separate constant terms in executing and nonexecuting states via EPOS, especially those derived through the approximate logarithmic transformation, are essentially the same as the corresponding results based on subsamples of executing states. The point estimates of the elasticity of the murder rate with respect to estimates of $P^{o}e|c$ are virtually identical. More important, application of Chow's test of equality between the comparable regression coefficients associated with variables entering the approximate logarithmic analog of equation (5) in executing and nonexecuting states, except for the constant terms of the separate equations, shows that the hypothesis of equality for that set of regression coefficients cannot be rejected at the 5 percent, and generally much higher, level of significance. This is evident in tests relating to both the 1940, 1950, and pooled samples (see below) and for regressions using alternative measures of execution risk or different weighting factors.[17]

TABLE 4

A. MURDER SUPPLY FUNCTIONS: 1940, 43 STATES

Eq.	λ	$L(\lambda)$*	Constant	T	$P^{o}c$	$P^{o}e\|c$	NW	W	AGE	URB	EPOS
						$\overline{PX5}$					
1a......	$0.100 = \hat{\lambda}$	−5.0524	0.918	−0.231	−0.885	−0.481	0.531	0.370	−1.510	−0.756	4.217
			(0.268)	(−3.026)	(−5.645)	(−3.920)	(9.332)	(2.032)	(−2.057)	(−5.212)	(4.257)
1b......	0.001	−6.2315	−331.71	−0.324	−0.664	−0.338	0.535	0.635	−1.888	−0.963	337.16
			(−3.706)	(−3.014)	(−5.482)	(−3.764)	(9.367)	(2.030)	(−2.160)	(−5.032)	(3.768)
1c......	1.0	−47.1601	−10.22	−0.017	−13.184	−9.992	0.314	−0.002	−0.011	−0.083	3.313
			(−0.806)	(−1.742)	(−2.898)	(−1.888)	(3.880)	(−0.365)	(−0.022)	(−2.252)	(2.421)
						$\overline{PX4Q}$					
2a......	$0.175 = \hat{\lambda}$	−13.6604	−3.538	−0.149	−1.013	−0.777	0.391	0.138	−0.046	−0.414	3.680
			(−0.700)	(−1.805)	(−5.285)	(−4.470)	(5.643)	(0.849)	(−0.044)	(−2.602)	(5.333)
2b......	0.001	−15.4821	−426.98	−0.254	−0.624	−0.429	0.358	0.212	−0.192	−0.529	428.44
			(−4.081)	(−1.665)	(−4.994)	(−4.106)	(5.304)	(0.535)	(−0.130)	(−2.121)	(4.112)
2c......	1.0	−46.9512	−12.76	−0.019	−9.272	−9.363	0.265	−0.002	0.310	−0.068	4.246
			(−0.933)	(−1.892)	(−2.949)	(−2.628)	(2.949)	(−0.426)	(0.453)	(−1.502)	(2.820)

B. MURDER SUPPLY FUNCTIONS: 1950, 44 STATES

Eq.	λ	$L(\lambda)$*	Constant	T	$P^o c$	$P^o e\|c$	NW	X	W	AGE	URB	EPOS
						$\overline{PX5}$						
1a........	0.225 $= \hat{\lambda}$	−2.3101	−5.088	−0.149	−0.975	−0.776	0.410	2.905	0.193	0.726	−0.151	2.285
			(−1.722)	(−2.790)	(−4.792)	(−4.849)	(6.405)	(2.689)	(1.708)	(1.623)	(−0.878)	(5.009)
1b........	0.001	−4.5945	−278.12	−0.294	−0.538	−0.274	0.445	1.545	0.881	0.853	−0.342	273.11
			(−4.421)	(−2.439)	(−4.588)	(−4.309)	(6.118)	(2.711)	(1.811)	(1.374)	(−1.020)	(4.313)
1c........	1.0	−25.3507	−4.491	−0.013	−7.475	−25.780	0.207	41.665	0.001	0.485	0.014	3.292
			(−0.291)	(−2.419)	(−3.017)	(−3.903)	(4.287)	(2.234)	(0.466)	(1.703)	(0.444)	(3.119)
						$\overline{PX5Q}$						
2a........	0.15 $= \hat{\lambda}$	−12.5914	−1.481	−0.152	−0.568	−0.268	0.381	1.969	0.151	0.375	−0.022	1.334
			(−0.386)	(−1.412)	(−2.885)	(−1.289)	(3.893)	(1.387)	(0.645)	(0.850)	(−0.084)	(1.421)
2b........	0.001	−13.2404	−157.87	−0.239	−0.401	−0.158	0.375	1.280	0.264	0.403	−0.004	157.57
			(−1.358)	(−1.299)	(−2.941)	(−1.364)	(3.759)	(1.432)	(0.451)	(0.753)	(−0.011)	(1.365)
2c........	1.0	−32.9919	27.257	−0.015	−4.298	0.478	0.147	40.613	0.000	0.301	0.030	1.238
			(1.192)	(−2.109)	(−1.763)	(0.069)	(2.336)	(1.264)	(0.071)	(1.188)	(0.721)	(0.996)

NOTE.—GLS and OLS regressions, selected transformations of linear form, results from Box and Cox tests on full observation set ($\hat{\beta}/S_{\hat{\beta}}$ in parentheses). Eqq. 1a–1c in part A are weighted by $\sqrt{N_{URB}}$; eqq. 1a–1c in part B are weighted by $\sqrt{N_{REP}}$; eqq. 2a–2c are unweighted throughout.

* $L(\lambda)$ is the magnitude of the estimated log-likelihood function at the given value of λ, as defined in eqq. (A2) and (A4) in Appendix A.

The effect of the dummy variable EPOS, in turn, is found to be significant in all the regressions using the approximate logarithmic transformation and in the weighted regressions using the simple linear specifications. Indeed, the elimination of EPOS from the regression equation is found to have a drastic effect on the standard error and even the sign of the coefficient associated with $P°e|c$ measures. In the approximate log specification of equation (6) the signs of the latter are positive and sometimes significant with magnitudes very nearly zero, whereas in the simple linear specification the coefficients have the expected negative sign and are occasionally significant as well.[18] The technical explanation is straightforward: EPOS is very highly correlated with $P°e|c$, extremely so in the approximate logarithmic versions of equation (6). Thus, its absence from the regression equation produces the expected "specification bias" resulting from a missing variable, and the magnitude of the quantitative change in the coefficient associated with $P°e|c^{(\lambda)}$ is expected to equal the product of the true partial regression coefficient associated with EPOS and the relevant partial regression coefficient relating EPOS to $P°e|c^{(\lambda)}$. Indeed, it is estimated that the extent of "specification bias" resulting from the omission of EPOS is likely to outweigh the magnitude of the true partial coefficient associated with measures of $P°e|c^{(\lambda)}$ in the approximate logarithmic regressions but not in most of the simple linear runs.[19] It is important to stress, however, that the *magnitude* of the coefficient associated with EPOS is an arbitrary number by definition. It is but an artifact of two related factors: the transformation applied to the dependent and independent variables in the regression and the range of the dummy variable measuring EPOS. If the value of EPOS is transformed, for example, by the same value of λ (0.001) used to transform all other variables in the approximate logarithmic regressions, then the quantitative magnitude of the coefficient associated with EPOS in these regressions would be reduced by precisely 1,000-fold. The only valid inference to be drawn from the estimated effect of EPOS is that it indicates the existence of a statistically significant difference between the mean rates of murder in executing and nonexecuting states after the effects of other variables entering equation (6) have been accounted for. This does not mean, necessarily, that the mean rate of murder in nonexecuting states is lower than the rate in executing states where the level of $P°e|c$ is lowest. More important it cannot be determined whether the observed significant difference between the estimated constant terms in equations relating to executing and nonexecuting states is the result of "missing variables" that differ significantly across these subsets of states or because of the arbitrary values assigned to measures of the perceived risk of execution in nonexecuting states: if the true risks were higher than "zero" in these states, then the assignment of zero values to estimates of $Pe|c$ will necessarily bias the constant terms of the corresponding regression equations toward negative values, especially in the approximate logarithmic format. That the effect of EPOS sometimes is found to be statistically insignificant in regressions based on the simple linear specification indicates the relative importance of this consideration (see also n. 27).

3. VITAL STATISTICS DATA ON HOMICIDE

The Vital Statistics of the United States (VS) (U.S. Bureau of the Census 1943; U.S. Department of Health, Education, and Welfare 1953) provides alternative data on homicides. For the purpose of an empirical implementation of the theory, however, the FBI data are conceptually superior to the Vital Statistics series because the latter includes justifiable and excusable homicides, whereas the FBI murder category is defined to include only willful felonious homicides.[20] The VS data may also under-state the true number of homicides, because death certificates on which these statistics are based sometimes reflect classification of death by medical causes alone, especially in those instances when death from homicidal assaults lags the actual time of assault. The cross-sectional information in the Vital Statistics in 1950 is also somewhat noncomparable because in 1940 homicide statistics are reported by the place of the occurrence of homicide, which is the desired statistic, whereas in 1950 these statistics are reported by the place of the victim's residence. Also, only the 1950 data permit homicides caused by the legal intervention of police to be separated from the total homicide counts. One clear advantage of the VS data over the UCR statistics, however, is that the VS information is based on a count of homicides in the entire state, whereas the FBI data are based on samples of urban areas.

The regression models applied to the VS data are the models summarized in equations (5) and (6) with the following modifications: the dependent variable now is the homicide rate defined as $h^{\circ} = (H^{c} | N_{S})$, where H° stands for the *VS* total homicide counts[21] and N_{S} is the state population. The conviction risk is now defined as $P^{h}c = (C^{\circ} | H^{\circ})$. A sample of the regression results is summarized in table 5.

The results are qualitatively the same as those discussed in connection with the FBI data. The quantitative results differ mainly in connection with the estimated deterrent effect of the probability of conviction measures used in the separate analyses which is here smaller in magnitude and less precise. This result is not entirely surprising given that the VS data on homicide may not be as clearly related to the relevant concept of murder as are the FBI statistics. It indicates that the efficiency of empirical measures of conviction risk depend heavily on the relevance of the crime statistics used in their construction.

The pattern of results reported in table 5 generally is quite consistent with the pattern observed in the analysis of the FBI data. Weighted regressions, here executed only with $\sqrt{N_{S}}$ as a weighting factor, yield regression coefficients with lower standard errors than unweighted regressions in both 1940 and 1950. Furthermore, the log-linear regression format is found to be decisively superior to the simple linear format. A Box and Cox test performed on the full observation set in 1940, for example, shows that the approximate logarithmic transformation, unlike the simple linear transformation, cannot be rejected as an optimal regression form.

TABLE 5

HOMICIDE SUPPLY FUNCTIONS: 1940 AND 1950, GLS REGRESSIONS

Eq.	Year	N	"R^2"	Constant	T	$P^h c$	$P^o e\|c$	NW	X	W	AGE	URB	EPOS
Results from subsets of states with positive executions:*													
							$\overline{PX4Q}$						
1........	1940	33	.9527	9.036 (2.42)	−0.226 (−2.07)	−0.562 (−4.26)	−0.341 (−3.54)	0.432 (6.73)	... ...	0.262 (0.82)	−2.446 (−2.69)	−0.877 (−4.56)	... ...
							$\overline{PX5Q}$						
2........	1950	36	.9555	−2.106 (−0.71)	−0.271 (−2.15)	−0.253 (−1.45)	−0.196 (−3.21)	0.401 (6.68)	1.617 (2.92)	0.827 (2.14)	0.098 (0.20)	−0.284 (−0.85)	... ...
Results from full-observation set:†													
							$\overline{PX4Q}$						
3........	1940	44	.9526	−326.5 (−3.45)	−0.276 (−2.73)	−0.551 (−4.60)	−0.333 (−3.56)	0.467 (8.51)	... ...	0.483 (1.59)	−2.098 (−2.37)	−0.818 (−4.41)	333.0 (3.57)
							$\overline{PX5Q}$						
4........	1950	46	.9523	−194.8 (−2.95)	−0.154 (−1.36)	−0.211 (−1.52)	−0.194 (−2.94)	0.335 (5.38)	1.982 (3.51)	0.348 (0.86)	0.303 (0.59)	0.236 (0.82)	194.0 (2.94)

NOTE.—All eqq. are weighted by $\sqrt{N_S}$.
* All variables measured in natural logarithms.
† All variables except EPOS transformed via $x^* = (x^\lambda - 1/\lambda)$, where x denotes the natural value of a variable and $\lambda = 0.001$.

4. Murder, Aggravated Assault, and Robbery—Further Analysis of FBI Data

A complete implementation of the analysis of interrelationships among murder, aggravated assault, and robbery developed in Section IA could not be pursued because of the absence of published data on all the specific conditional probabilities and severities of punishment entering equation (3). Introduction in the regression analysis of deterrence variables associated with a specific crime ($P^\circ c_i$, T_i) along with corresponding variables associated with interrelated crimes ($P^\circ c_j$ T_j, $j \neq i$) generally has been found to yield insignificant estimates of the effects of $P^\circ c_j$ and T_j on q°_i, possibly because the latter are not efficient measures of the relevant conditional probabilities or due to a high degree of partial correlation between estimates of probability and severity of imprisonment for different crimes. Only the murder equations reported in table 6, lines 4 and 5, show some evidence for complementarity relations. The bulk of the analysis on interdependencies among these crimes has been conducted through implementation of the restricted model:

$$q_i^{o(\lambda)} = a + b_{i1} T_i^{(\lambda)} + b_{i2} P^\circ c_i^{(\lambda)} + b_{i3} P^\circ e|c^{(\lambda)} + \bullet \bullet \bullet, \qquad (7)$$

where i = assault and robbery, $P^\circ e|c$ is the conditional probability of execution for murder, and the remaining relevant variables are those introduced in equations (5) or (6). In this model all the relevant probabilities and severities of punishment for related crimes (j) are identified with, or assumed to be proportionally related to, $P^\circ c_i$ and T_i, and the coefficient b_3 indicates the direction of interdependencies between murder and robbery or assault. In analyses of subsets of executing states the transformation employed in estimating equation (7) is logarithmic. The results are reported in table 6, equations 1–3. (The murder regression is shown for comparison.) Difficulties in the estimation of cross-deterrence effects of probability and severity of punishment notwithstanding the interdependencies among the three crimes examined may still be reflected in systematic correlations among the residual terms associated with each crime. Indeed, analysis of residuals estimated from the single equations reveals sizable *positive* correlations[22] indicating complementary effects. To take account of these correlations in deriving efficient estimates of the interrelated regressions, both the subsets of executing states and the full observation sets have been estimated simultaneously via Zellner's seemingly unrelated regression method (SUR). The results are reported in table 7.[23]

The regression results are highly consistent with previously reported findings. The main novel finding is that the elasticities of robbery and aggravated assault, as well as of murder, with respect to measures of the conditional risk of execution are negative. Execution risk has the most sizable effect on the murder rate and the least sizable effect on the frequency of assault. The interpretation may be that aggravated assault is more of a "substitute" for murder than is robbery. This pattern of the results is seen more convincingly in the results derived from the application of the SUR method. The standard errors of SUR estimates

TABLE 6

INTERRELATED CRIMES: SELECTED RESULTS FOR 1950 SINGLE EQUATIONS, LOGARITHMIC FORM

Eq.	Dependent Variable	N	"R^2"	Constant	T_i	$P^o c_i$	$P^o e \mid c$	NW	X	W	AGE	URB		
					T_{MUR}	P^o_{MUR}	$PX5$							
1	$q^o_{(murder)}$*	35	.9581	−4.622 3.950 (−1.17)	−0.459 0.128 (−3.59)	−0.687 0.131 (−5.23)	−0.272 0.057 (−4.74)	0.497 0.070 (7.13)	1.200 0.541 (2.22)	1.226 0.463 (2.65)	0.274 0.623 (0.44)	−0.742 0.357 (−2.08)		
					T_{ASS}	P^o_{ASS}	$PX5$							
2	$q^o_{(assault)}$	35	.9818	−5.854 5.707 (−1.03)	−0.416 0.209 (−2.00)	−0.429 0.098 (−4.37)	−0.024 0.108 (−0.22)	0.761 0.110 (6.89)	0.175 0.879 (0.20)	1.694 0.701 (2.42)	−0.173 0.889 (−0.19)	−1.160 0.507 (−2.29)		
					T_{ROB}	P^o_{ROB}	$PX5$							
3	$q^o_{(robbery)}$	35	.9819	−6.534 5.672 (−1.15)	−0.570 0.219 (−2.60)	−0.887 0.123 (−7.20)	−0.146 0.091 (−1.61)	0.266 0.105 (2.54)	0.932 0.746 (1.25)	1.309 0.772 (1.69)	−0.593 0.868 (−0.68)	0.439 0.519 (0.85)		
					T_{MUR}	P^o_{MUR}	$PX5Q$						T_{ASS}	P^o_{ASS}
4	$q^o_{(murder)}$	35	.9633	−3.013 (−0.75)	−0.424 (−3.43)	−0.640 (−4.92)	−0.204 (−2.99)	0.466 (6.25)	0.854 (1.35)	1.062 (2.29)	0.093 (0.15)	−0.841 (−2.33)	−0.063 (−0.45)	−0.098 (−1.55)
					T_{MUR}	P^o_{MUR}	$PX5Q$						T_{ROB}	P^o_{ROB}
5	$q^o_{(murder)}$	35	.9671	−3.777 (−1.01)	−0.398 (−3.20)	−0.670 (−4.86)	−0.224 (−3.98)	0.515 (7.63)	0.822 (1.59)	1.073 (2.11)	0.192 (0.33)	−0.730 (−1.92)	−0.189 (−1.25)	−0.167 (−2.13)

NOTE.—All eqq. are weighted by $\sqrt{N_{REP}}$; reported statistics are $\hat{\beta}$, $S_{\hat{\beta}}$, and $\hat{\beta}/S_{\hat{\beta}}$ in parentheses.

* From table 3, line 5.

of regression coefficients, without exception, are lower than the corresponding estimates derived from application of the single-equation least-squares procedure.[24]

III. EXECUTING AND NONEXECUTING STATES

The murder rate has been shown to depend, in part, on the risks of conviction and execution and on the severity of imprisonment for murder, each of which, in turn, is subject to the control of public authorities.

The magnitudes of these variables may be the result, rather than the cause, of the relevant crime rates. In particular, the tendency of state courts, juries, and other relevant authorities to retain or impose the death penalty is expected to be responsive to the perceived social costs of capital crimes. The purpose of this section is to compare some crime and punishment data across executing and nonexecuting states in light of theoretical expectations.

In the analysis of optimal defense against crime, law enforcement agencies are assumed to behave in accordance with the expectation that certainty and severity of imprisonment and the risk of execution have restraining (i.e., deterrent and incapacitating) effects on the frequency of crime. The agencies are assumed to set optimal penalties and produce optimal values of the probability of conviction and the conditional probabilities of specific penalties so as to minimize the net per capita social losses from crime, including the costs of all law enforcement activities. The components of the social loss function are identified in equation (8) below:[28]

$$L = D(q) + C(q, Pc) + y_1 Pc\, Pe|c\, qd + y_2 Pc(1 - Pe|c)m. \qquad (8)$$

In equation (8) q is the crime rate, D(q) designates the net direct social damage from crime, C (q, Pc) represents the costs of apprehending and convicting offenders, and the last two terms represent the social costs associated with executing and incarcerating convicted persons, respectively. The terms d (treated as a parameter at a point in time) and m measure the discounted value of the private costs of execution and imprisonment per convict, and y_1 and y_2 are positive coefficients "translating" private into social (deadweight) costs and augmenting the relevant public expenditures in administering penalties. Both D(q) and C(q, Pc) are assumed to be convex functions.

In terms of the social loss function introduced in equation (8), optimal (cost-minimizing) values of the risk or status of execution as well as the other deterrence variables must equate the marginal cost of deterrence with the marginal revenue from the expected decrease in crime levels. An important implication of the optimality conditions is that the optimal risk of execution could be considerably below unity even if on the margin the death penalty has a differential restraining impact on murder over and above that of imprisonment because executions entail a larger deadweight loss on society (the difference between $y_1 d$ and $y_2 m$ is assumed positive). Variations in the enforcement level of capital punishment, including its abolition, as well as changes in the magnitudes of other deterrence variables generally can be explained as a consequence of shifts in three basic sets of parameters: the level of the marginal harm from murder and related crimes, the social cost of capital punishment relative to other sanctions, and the technology of producing means of deterrence and incapacitation. The first two sets of factors appear to be especially relevant for analysis of data relating to the classes of executing and nonexecuting states.

A central behavioral implication of the model is that the optimal magnitudes of all three deterrence variables generally must rise as a result of an increase in the marginal social damages from crime due to exogenous factors. Since stability conditions for optimal law enforcement are satisfied if, among other related conditions, the marginal damages from crime are monotonically related to the rate of crime in the population,[29] an increase in the crime rate due to exogenous factors would require that the optimal values of deterrence variables be increased. A decrease in the crime rate then would have the reverse effects. While the theory does not predict that each of the three deterrence variables would be reduced as a consequence, it suggests that both certainty of conviction and severity of punishment would tend to decline if "punishment" were defined as a single-choice variable. More generally, $Pe|c$ and m always are expected to move in the same direction if y_1 and y_2 remain constant. In particular, it follows that those states where murder rates have traditionally been exceptionally low due to factors exogenous to the law enforcement system (such as demographic and general economic variables) are more likely to minimize the application of, or abolish, the death penalty either legally or in practice. These states also are expected to impose relatively short imprisonment terms and possibly to have relatively low conviction risks.

The theory allows for corner solutions in the risk of execution across states to occur not only, however, as a consequence of autonomous changes in the crime rate, but also as a result of changes in factors determining the "social cost" of execution. For example, changes in political factors strengthening the influence of groups interested in greater emphasis on rehabilitation or reformation of offenders, federal judicial or administrative rulings, or increased social aversion toward harsh punishments would either raise the magnitude of the coefficient y_1 in equation (8) or might lead directly to a decrease in the magnitude of $Pe|c$. Under such circumstances, if a corner solution occurs so that execution is abolished de facto, the theory predicts that either the probability of conviction or the severity of punishment by imprisonment or both will be increased. The intuitive reason is that to the extent that cessation of execution is not motivated by a low level of crime, relinquishing the practice of execution must be "compensated" through greater reliance on alternative instruments of law enforcement in order to bring about an optimal level of deterrence and incapacitation.

Both predictions appear to be compatible with data on the mean value of crime and deterrence variables across various subsets of executing and nonexecuting states in 1940,

TABLE 9

MEANS OF ESTIMATED CRIME RATES, PROBABILITIES OF CONVICTION, AND IMPRISONMENT TERMS IN EXECUTING AND NONEXECUTING STATES, 1940–60

Subsets Compared by Year and Mean*	Execution Status in t: $E_t > 0$ (1)	Execution Status in t: $E_t = 0$ (2)	Execution Status in 5 Years: $\sum_{j=0}^{4} E_{t-j} > 0$ (3)	Execution Status in 5 Years: $\sum_{j=0}^{4} E_{t-j} = 0$ (4)	Legal Status of Death Penalty: Legal (5)	Legal Status of Death Penalty: Illegal (6)
1940:						
q^o (murder)	9.9069	2.0947	8.5583	1.5833	7.6048	1.2833
$P^o{}_c$ (murder)†	0.2074	0.3438	0.2338	0.3523	0.2597	0.2739
T_{50} (murder)	119.759	158.105	130.222	149.083	135.143	133.500
q^o (assault)	87.0034	17.6421	75.0028	13.1833	66.0595	13.9667
q^o (robbery)	60.0414	29.0737	55.6083	24.3083	51.0309	25.0500
$PX5$‡	...	...	0.1552	...	...	...
No. of states	29	19	36	12	42	6
1950:						
q^o (murder)	8.5291	2.3752	6.3541	1.8591	5.8679	1.5167
$P^o{}_c$ (murder)§	0.2324	0.3106	0.2595	0.3183	0.2735	0.2514
T (murder)	117.696	150.800	135.676	132.445	135.143	133.500
q^o (assault)	105.004	27.0960	76.0486	25.3363	69.8405	26.5333
q^o (robbery)	49.6522	31.1000	43.1378	29.4000	42.3809	23.2500
$PX5$‖	...	...	0.0809	...	...	...
No. of states	23	25	37	11	42	6
q^o (murder)	7.1050	3.3857	6.2492	2.2750	5.3397	2.3857
$P^o{}_c$ (murder)††	0.4548	0.4830	0.4542	0.5034	0.4776	0.4330
T (murder)††	134.890	169.104	131.361	199.642	144.277	213.214
q^o (assault)	71.9200	40.7849	69.8000	21.7875	58.6103	25.4428
q^o (robbery)	40.1300	33.2727	43.4018	21.7875	38.1927	24.4857
$PX5$‡‡	...	...	0.0195	...	...	...
No. of states	20	28	32	16	41	7

* Simple means of the state statistics; number of states compared dictated by the availability of relevant data.
† Cols. 1 and 3 exclude Georgia, Mississippi, and Nevada; cols. 2 and 4 exclude Maine and Vermont; col. 5 excludes Georgia, Mississippi, Nevada, and Vermont; col. 6 excludes Maine.
‡ Col. 3 estimate excludes Georgia and Mississippi.
§ Col. 1 excludes Georgia; col. 2 excludes North Dakota, Michigan, and Vermont; cols. 3 and 5 exclude Georgia and Vermont; cols. 4 and 6 exclude Michigan and North Dakota.
‖ Col. 3 estimate excludes Georgia.
** Data for 1960 exclude Alaska and Hawaii. The data for 1960 are not comparable to the 1940 and 1950 data due to the following differences: (1) In 1960 q^o is based on total reported crimes in each state, whereas q^o in 1940 and 1950 is based on a state sample of urban areas. (2) Commitments to state prisons in 1960 are convicts of homicide whereas in 1940 and 1950 commitments are for murder convicts. Commitments in 1960 include only convicts with definite sentences. To estimate convictions, E_{60} is added to commitments. Also, $P^o{}_c$ in 1960 is based on total reported crimes, Q^o, whereas in 1940 and 1950 $P^o{}_c$ is based on $Q^o = q^o \times N_s$. (3) T in 1960 is average time served whereas median time served measures T in 1950.
†† Cols. 2, 3 and 5 exclude New Jersey.
‡‡ Col. 3 estimate excludes New Jersey.

1950, and 1960. As table 9 demonstrates, in all 3 years analyzed, the murder rate is found to be lowest in states which abolish the death penalty in law, somewhat higher in states which persistently refrain from enforcing the death penalty, and is even higher in states which only intermittently refrain from executing convicts. In addition, the murder rate is always higher in the corresponding subsets of executing states which complement the three subsets of legally or practically nonexecuting states discussed above. Moreover, subsets of abolition states having exceptionally low murder rates not only choose to refrain from using the death penalty, they also tend to set somewhat lower values of conviction risks and imprisonment terms.[30] Indeed, there is a strong indication—apart from the regression results in Section II—that the relatively low magnitudes of the execution risk variables in these subsets are the result rather than the cause of low murder rates. As table 9 shows, the subsets of persistently nonexecuting states are characterized by much lower frequencies of assault and robbery relative to the corresponding executing or retentionist states in all 3 years considered. Given the regression results, the differences between the crime levels in the two classes of states may be ascribed, in part, to the substantial differences in demographic variables, such as the percentage of nonwhites, and possibly to other "missing" or misspecified factors.[31] To some extent, the relatively low frequencies of assault and robbery may even be contributing causes for the legal or practical abolition of the death penalty, because murder is often a by-product of assault and robbery and the enforcement of capital punishment may have restraining effects on these crimes as well (see Section II). Thus the incentive to enforce the death penalty might be monotonically related to the frequencies of assault and robbery as well as of murder. Again, there is some evidence that at least severity of imprisonment for assault and robbery tends to be lower in abolitionist than in retentionist states.

At the same time, table 9 reveals that in the set of states which refrain from enforcing the death penalty in a given year, but not necessarily over a greater period, and in which murder rates are found to be higher than in the relatively smaller subset of persistently nonexecuting states, both probability and severity of imprisonment for murder appear to be higher than in the complementary set of executing states. This is the case in all 3 years considered. Furthermore, in 1960 even the set of persistently nonexecuting states, considerably larger in 1960 than in 1950, is characterized by higher values of probability and severity of imprisonment for murder relative to the complementary set of executing states.[32] This tendency for greater reliance on certainty and severity of imprisonment in specific subsets of nonexecuting states, especially in more recent years, is compatible with the theoretical expectation that reductions in execution risk prompted by an increase in the social cost of execution and related exogenous factors would result in compensatory changes in certainty and severity of alternative punishments. The existence of such a tendency is not inconsistent with the hypothesis that capital punishment and other penalties do exert a restraining effect on the murder rate. It is at least compatible with the assumption that law enforcement bodies behave in accordance with that hypothesis.[33]

IV. SUMMARY AND CONCLUSION

Contrary to strong inferences of many death-penalty researchers who interpreted their evidence as a categorical denial of the deterrence hypothesis, this study as well as a related analysis based on time-series data develop evidence not inconsistent with that hypothesis.

The case for the deterrence theory is based, in part, on a critical evaluation of earlier works (see n. 1). In the main, the case is based on new empirical findings and their compatibility with a set of predictions derived from the theory. Before summarizing the main findings of the empirical investigation, some of its inherent limitations must be stressed. The present analysis does not account systematically for potential simultaneity relations between crime rates and deterrence variables—especially the risks of execution and conviction. Although the simple remedies to the problem invoked here may lead to an understatement of the true effect of execution risk, the net direction of the bias cannot be ascertained with confidence because the estimates of effects associated with other deterrence variables may not be statistically consistent. There are many imperfections associated with measures of the probabilities of conviction and execution and the severity of imprisonment as viewed by potential offenders. The regression equations do not include estimates of the extent and quality of medical services available across states, and the interdependencies among murder, robbery, and aggravated assault are dealt with only in a partial manner. While the present investigation deals with the choice of an optimal regression format, it does so only in the context of restricted families of "power transformations." All the statistical tests conducted are conditional upon the validity of the assumptions concerning disturbance terms.

At the same time the consistency and stability in the results obtained upon application of efficient estimation procedures, given the sample limitations, and their consistency with specific theoretical predictions and previous findings seem remarkable. Indeed, it is noteworthy that all the deterrence variables examined in this analysis yield the expected results in connection with murder and other crimes, and that the coefficients associated with explanatory variables other than constant terms appear statistically indistinguishable across different samples as well as across subsets of executing and nonexecuting states. In particular, the subsets based on data from executing states indicate that when enforced the death penalty exerts a restraining effect on the frequency of murder and possibly robbery as well. The investigation shows the existence of distinct execution and imprisonment effects: both $P^{\circ}e|c$ and T appear to exert a deterrent effect on murder. Indeed, because the effect of imprisonment is accounted for explicitly in the analysis, this investigation, more directly than the earlier time-series study, indicates that capital punishment has a differential deterrent effect over and above the actually enforced imprisonment terms. The effects of execution risk and other deterrence variables are largely unaffected by the introduction of additional explanatory variables, including the "prices" associated with related crimes and other indicators of relative rewards. Even introduction of risk of death through police intervention (see n. 24) does not affect the regression results. Moreover, as predicted by the theory, the estimated elasticities of murder rates with respect to measures of conviction risk are significantly larger than the estimated elasticities associated with measures of the conditional risk of execution. Also, that the estimated elasticity of the murder rate with respect to conviction risk exceeds the corresponding elasticity with respect to imprisonment severity is not inconsistent with the analysis of optimal public defense against murder (see

n. 28). The joint estimation of "supply functions" associated with murder, robbery, and aggravated assault, as well as the pooling of the 1940 and the 1950 samples, narrow the confidence intervals associated with point estimates. Furthermore, the analysis of changes in murder rates within states between 1940 and 1950 produces results which corroborate the general cross-sectional findings.

More important, the basic set of results derived in this cross-sectional investigation is in essence the same as that derived from analysis of time-series data on murder, although the results have been obtained through different estimation procedures and although the time-series analysis did not account for possible variations in imprisonment severity and other relevant variables. The corroborating independent evidence from the 1940 and the 1950 cross sections does not support the proposition that the time-series results on deterrence are merely artifacts of the 1960s or the result of "missing factors" such as the Vietnam War or the proliferation of handguns. Despite statistical differences, point estimates of the elasticity of the murder rate with respect to measures of unconditional probabilities of conviction in the time-series and cross-section analyses lie within each other's confidence intervals (compare, e.g., the results in Ehrlich [1973, table 7] and the results reported above in tables 3, 4, and 8). The larger point estimates of the effect of the unconditional risk of execution on the extent of the murder rate in the cross-sectional analysis may be the result of the fact that the data permit the estimation of such an effect within the set of states with positive executions, whereas the aggregate data used in the time-series analysis have not allowed for a separate estimation of deterrence effects within strictly execution states.[34] Tentative estimates of the average trade-offs between executions and murders computed via the method employed in the time-series study (Ehrlich 1975*a*, section IIIB) on the basis of the GLS results reported in equations 1–4 in table 8, for example, range between 20 and 24 murders for one execution. It is important to stress that these estimates are based upon regression coefficients derived through the GLS estimation procedure which does not insure consistent estimates. They also are conditional upon specific data limitations.[35]

One of the conspicuous results of the cross-sectional investigation is the strong statistical association between crime rates, especially murder and assault, and the percent of nonwhites in the population. However, the NW effect may, in part, reflect the roles of other demographic variables not fully analyzed in this paper. Its magnitude is reduced when A_{25-34} replaces the usual AGE (15–24) variable. The NW effect in the cross section may largely reflect the effect of low earnings opportunities, specific to nonwhites, which are not accounted for directly in this analysis. The relevance of the latter factor is indicated by the fact that both my time-series analysis and the examination of murder changes between 1940 and 1950 fail to uncover any significant association between NW and murder over time.

Another intriguing issue concerns interdependencies between levels of crime rates and deterrence measures in executing and nonexecuting states. Consistent with analysis of optimal social defense against crime, the persistently nonexecuting states face substantially lower risks of victimization through murder and related crimes than do the persistently executing states. The low crime levels in the former class of states, in turn, can be partly attributed to factors whose influence is reflected by the percentage of nonwhites in the population and related demographic variables. Some of the apparent differences in crime levels across the two classes of states, as revealed through the regression model, also may result from understatement of the true (perceived) risks of execution in states classified as "zero" execution risk states. A fuller analysis of the differences in crime levels across these classes and of the variations in execution policy across states and over time must await future research.

Hopefully, the main contribution of this research lies in the suggestion that the basic economic and econometric frameworks used by economists to explain behavior in the marketplace can also be applied in explaining criminal and perhaps some other behavior traditionally labeled as "deviant." The regularities uncovered in connection with movements in crime rates and law enforcement activities pose a challenge for future research. The economic approach might prove useful in analyzing recidivism by offenders, the impact of legitimate employment and training opportunities, apparent racial and sex differences in participation in specific crimes, international variations in crime rates, and public and private protection against crime. As to the policy implications emanating from the new findings, however, basic theoretical and methodological questions remain unanswered because of the complexity of the range of choices available and the difficulties associated with quantifying basic parameters affecting the social costs from offenses and other targets of social policy (see n. 33). Estimates of the restraining effect of the risk of execution in terms of the implied trade-offs between lives sacrificed and lives saved, though apparently not negligible, must be viewed as tentative and imprecise also because they may not represent the relevant marginal trade-offs. But even if the estimates were accurate, they simply might indicate the extent of the full social costs associated with sacrifices of the lives of convicted persons for the lives of potential victims, assuming that the actual policy toward capital punishment has reflected a local social optimum. Perhaps the main policy implication of the present study lies in the support it lends to the general deterrence hypothesis. Indeed, if punishment did not deter offenders, then incapacitation and reformation of those apprehended and convicted would become the sole means of crime control. Not only would such means be of limited usefulness because of the small fraction of potential offenders who would be incapacitated or reformed at a point in time given the relevant costs, but incapacitating penalties are intrinsically inefficient modes of taxing illegitimate behavior from a social point of view. In contrast, if offenders do respond to incentives, punishment and law enforcement become more expedient means of crime control independently of any incapacitating or reformatory benefits of sanctions. Indeed, incapacitation and related "cruel" punishment, in principle, can be replaced by more "humane" penalties involving smaller deadweight losses. Moreover, crime control could be achieved through an optimal balance between both negative and positive incentives.

REFERENCES

Aday, L. A., and Anderson, R. Access to Medical Care. Ann Arbor, Mich.: Health Admin. Press, 1975.

Becker, Gary S. "Crime and Punishment: An Economic Approach." J.P.E. 78, no. 2 (March/April 1968): 169–217.

Box, G. E. P., and Cox, D. R. "An Analysis of Transformations." J. Royal Statis. Soc. 26, Ser. B (1964): 211–43.

Ehrlich, Isaac. "Participation in Illegitimate Activities: An Economic Analysis." Ph.D. dissertation, Columbia Univ., 1970.

——. "The Deterrent Effect of Capital Punishment: A Question of Life and Death." Working Paper no. 18, Nat. Bur. Econ. Res., 1973.

——. "Participation in Illegitimate Activities: An Economic Analysis." In Essays in the Economics of Crime and Punishment, edited by G. S. Becker and W. M. Landes. New York: Columbia Univ. Press, 1974.

——. "The Deterrent Effect of Capital Punishment: A Question of Life and Death." A.E.R. 65 (June 1975): 397–417. (a)

——. "Deterrence: Evidence and Inference." Yale Law J. 85 (December 1975) :
209–27. (b)

——Goldfeld, S. M., and Ouandt, R. E. "Some Tests for Homoscedasticity." J. American Statis. Assoc. 60 (June 1965): 539–47.

Klebba, A. J. "Homicide Trends in the United States, 1900–74." Public Health Reports 90, no. 3 (May–June 1975): 195–204.

Pashigian, B. Peter. "The Hill-Burton Program: The Effects of the Federal Subsidy in Kind on the Hospital Industry." Report no. 7346, Center Math. Studies Bus. and Econ., Univ. Chicago, 1973.

Schuessler, Karl F. "The Deterrent Influence of the Death Penalty." Ann. American Acad. Polit, and Soc. Sci. 284 (November 1952): 54–62.

U.S. Bureau of the Census. Prisoners in State and Federal Prisons and Reformatories. Washington: Government Printing Office, 1936–41, 1946.

——. Vital Statistics of the United States, 1940. Pt. 1. Washington: Government Printing Office, 1943.

——. Statistical Abstract of the United States. Washington: Government Printing Office, 1945, 1946, 1953.

——. U.S. Census of the Population: 1950. Vol. 2. Washington: Government Printing Office, 1952.

——. Historical Statistics of the United States from Colonial Times to 1957. Washington: Government Printing Office, 1960.

U.S. Department of Health, Education, and Welfare, Public Health Service. Vital Statistics of the United States, 1950. Vol. 3. Washington: Government Printing Office, 1953.

——. Vital Statistics of the United States, 1971. Vol. 2. Washington: Government Printing Office, 1975.

U.S. Department of Justice, Bureau of Prisons. National Prisoner Statistics: Prisoners Released from State and Federal Institutions. Washington: Government Printing Office, 1951, 1952–53.

——. National Prisoner Statistics: Prisoners in State and Federal Institutions, 1950. Leavenworth, Kans., 1954.

U.S. Department of Justice, Federal Bureau of Investigation. Uniform Crime Reports. Washington: Government Printing Office, 1940, 1950–51, 1960, 1970.

Wolfgang, Marvin. "A Sociological Analysis of Criminal Homicides." Federal Probation 25 (March 1961): 48–55.

NOTES

1 Ehrlich (1975a, 1975). A more complete critical review of the literature on the deterrent effect of capital punishment will be included in a forthcoming monograph on the topic.

7 This result, which is "forced" by the logarithmic specification, is, of course, consistent with the theoretical analysis itself (see n. 4 above).

8 The set of variables included in equation (5) generally yielded consistent and significant results in the different regressions performed. Other variables tested are measures of unemployment and labor-force participation rates. As in my previous cross-sectional investigations, these variables have not been found to have a systematic impact on the extent of crime rates across states, although both variables did appear to have such effects in my related time-series analysis (see the discussion in Ehrlich [1975a]). Their exclusion from the regression equations did not have any significant impact on the regression results reported here.

10 All tests of significance reported in this investigation are conditional on the assumption that the error terms satisfy all the standard conditions of the regression model.

11 The simple (unweighted) correlation coefficients between natural values of q^{o} and the measures of the conditional risk of execution listed below are:

1940	1950
$PXQ_1 = -.13697$	$PXQ_1 = -.11230$
$PXQ_2 = -.27668$	$PXQ_2 = -.17299$
$PX5 = -.18251$	$PX5 = -.00605$
$PX4Q = -.24158$	$PX5Q = -.10576$

The simple regression coefficients associated with these same measures of execution risk in weighted logarithmic regressions were always negative, and higher in absolute value than the coefficients reported in table 3 and n. 12. Note that the cross-state measures of the risk of execution given conviction of murder are based on independently reported conviction (prison commitments for both imprisonment and execution) data, which do not depend on the FBI estimates of murder rates.

12 A sample of results associated with alternative measures of P°e|c defined in table 2 substituted for the measures used in equations 1–2 and 5–6 in table 3 relating to 1940 and 1950, respectively, is as follows (ßjSA in parentheses) :

Measure	PXQ_1	PXQ_2	PXA	PXQ_1Q	PXQ_2Q	PXAQ
1940 (set 1–2) ...	–.132	–.212	–.160	–.118	–.267	(–.151)
	(–2.42)	(–3.36)	(–2.62)	(–2.02)	(–4.03)	(–2.39)
1950 (set 5–6) ...	–.152	–.335	–.332	–.177	–.327	–.340
	(–2.05)	(–2.92)	(–4.50)	(–2.25)	(–2.25)	(–4.70)

The magnitudes of estimates of other deterrence variables do not change appreciably and remain statistically significant as alternative estimates of P°e|c are substituted. However, standard errors tend to be lowest with the measures presented in table 3.

13 In the 1940 regressions, X_{40} yielded insignificant and inconsistent results across equations including a different measure of P°e|c. However, both W_{40} and X_{40} are based on a sample of employed wage and salary workers with positive earnings in 1939 rather than on a sample of family income in 1949, including families with no income, from which W_{50} and X_{50} are computed. The exclusion of X_{40} from the regression equations had little impact on the estimated magnitudes of other regressors.

14 This tentative interpretation is not incompatible with the fact that URB is found to be negatively associated also with a total homicide measure based on state statistics, especially in 1940 (see table 5). Differences in availability of medical services across urbanized and less-urbanized states may have been particularly high in 1940.

15 For example, when A_{25-34} replaces AGE in equation 7 of table 3, the nonwhite coefficient drops by nearly half and the effect of W becomes insignificant. However, substituting A_{25-34} for AGE in the 1940 murder regressions does not have any marked effects on other variables' coefficients. Using A_{25-34} in the murder regressions yields somewhat higher "R^2" values than AGE in 1950 and slightly lower ones in 1940. Also, substituting A_{25-34} in tune 1950 robbery and assault regressions (e.g., eqq. 2 and 3 of table 6 and in table 7) hardly affects the robbery regression, while the assault equation is affected much the same way as were the (1950) murder regressions.

16 For some initial attempts to arrive at a methodology for testing for racial differences in criminal activity see Ehrlich (1970). A fuller investigation requires data concerning the level of law enforcement activity directed against specific groups in connection with crimes against the person and efficient measures of group-specific earning (and medical care) opportunities.

17 For example, the F-statistics based on the sum of squared residuals estimated from equations 1 and 2 in table 8 (with k = 0.001), its counterpart in nonexecuting states, and equation 4 in table 8 are $F_{5,74} = 0.686$ and $F_{6,72} = 1.260$, respectively.

18 Estimates of the elasticity of the murder rate with respect to measures of execution risk in equations 1b, 1c, 2b, and 2c in table 4, parts A and B, which were estimated without introducing EPOS in the regression equation (be), are reported in their respective order: 1940: 0.0003 (2.28), –4.491 (–0.88),

0.0006 (3.23), –6.963 (–1.84); 1950: 0.0003 (1.11), –17.35 (–2.58), 0.0001 (0.59), 3.124 (0.49). The numbers in parentheses are the ratios of the coefficients to their respective standard errors.

19 The estimated regression coefficient associated with P°e|c in the regressions excluding EPOS $\hat{b}_e$ would be given by plim ($\hat{b}_e$) = $b_3 + b_9 b_{93}\ldots$ where b_3 and b_9 are the partial (population) regression coefficients associated with P°e|c and EPOS in equation (6) and $b_{93}\ldots$ is the partial (population) regression coefficient associated with P°e|c in a regression of EPOS on P°e|c and all other regressors entering (6). Since b_3 is expected to be negative, and b_3 and $b_{93}\ldots$ are found to be positive, the sign of plim ($\hat{b}_e$) would reverse in those transformations where the term $b_9 b_{93}\ldots$ outweighs the absolute magnitude of b_3. Indeed, LS estimates of $b_{93}\ldots$ verify that $\hat{b}_9\hat{b}_{93}\ldots$ tends to exceed $|\hat{b}_3|$ in the approximate log-linear transformations but that it falls short of $|\hat{b}_3|$ in the simple linear transformations, with $\hat{b}_3 + \hat{b}_9\hat{b}_{93}\ldots$, virtually identical to $\hat{b}_e$.

20 For an elaboration of this point see Ehrlich (1975b, pp. 212–13). The conceptual superiority of police-gathered data is generally recognized in the criminology literature; see, e.g., Wolfgang (1961, p. 49).

21 Legal executions are excluded as are, in 1950 only, homicides through legal intervention of police.

22 The correlation matrix of residuals associated with murder, robbery, and assault shows that the correlation coefficients between paired crimes range between + .35 and + .5.

28 In a more general formulation of the model, one may wish to define casa vector of interrelated crimes such as murder, robbery, and assault. Similarly, Pc, m, and Pe|c could be defined as vectors of corresponding deterrence variables. Such generalization would complicate the derivations of the basic behavioral implications discussed but would not change their basic thrust. Behavioral implications following from the formulation adopted in equation (8) are formally developed in the mathematical Appendix to this paper, omitted here for lack of space. One important implication of that model, which is compatible with the empirical findings reported in Section II, is that the elasticity of the murder rate with respect to Pc exceeds the corresponding elasticities with respect to both Pe|c and the cost of imprisonment m, or $e_{Pe|c} < e_{Pc} > e_m$.

29 This assumption can be justified partly on the grounds that the resource costs expended by offenders in the course of their criminal activity rise with the frequency of crime committed (especially by new "entrants") and because the marginal costs of apprehending and convicting offenders are expected to be an increasing function of the frequency of offenses committed (both C_{qq} and C_{qPc} are positive). Indeed, it can be shown that if both the production function of law enforcement activity implicit in C(q, Pc) and the supply-of-offenses function are of the Cobb-Douglas variety, then an exogenous increase in q will necessarily lead to an increase in the magnitudes of severity and certainty of punishment even if D_{qq} = 0. Of course, the marginal social valuation of the human and nonhuman assets destroyed through crime must eventually rise as their "stocks" are depleted with more crimes committed at a point in time.

30 Due to the small number of states included in the subsets of states where execution is illegal, the means of the state statistics based on single-years data must be viewed with caution. (See also n. 32 below.)

31 The simple mean levels of NW in executing (cols. 3 and 5 in table 9) and non-executing (cols. 4 and 6 in table 9) subsets are 12.3 and 11.0 as against 2.0 and 2.2 in 1950, and 12.9 and 11.4 as against 2.2 and 1.6 in 1940, respectively. The corresponding mean levels of A_{25-34} also are slightly lower in

nonexecuting states in both years. It also seems that abolitionist states tend to be more urbanized than retentionist states in both 1940 and 1950. Other variables examined in the regression analysis do not differ markedly between the two subsets.

32 Average and median imprisonment terms served for murder in nonexecuting states may be higher than those in executing states simply because murder convicts liable for capital punishment receive long prison sentences in the former class. That this technical consideration may not provide the main explanation for the observed differences in actual imprisonment terms between executing and nonexecuting states is apparent from the fact that states where the death penalty was illegal in 1950 did not have a higher median imprisonment term than states which still retained the death penalty in that year.

33 Although this analysis of optimal law enforcement against murder has been applied here in explanation of changes in execution status across different states, it also can be applied in explanation of trends in the enforcement and status of capital punishment in connection with murder and other "capital crimes" over time. An attempt along these lines is included in a related unpublished paper where the social loss from offenses is generalized to incorporate a criterion of "equity" in addition to that of efficiency.

34 See the discussion in Ehrlich (1975<z, p. 408). It is possible that the cross-sectional elasticities are biased upward relative to the time-series results due to "spillover effects" (see Ehrlich 1974, n. 25) that result from interstate movements of offenders in response to interstate variations in deterrence variables. However, the results show that the estimated elasticities associated with conviction risk are much more similar across the time-series and the cross-section analysis. More generally, it seems unlikely that "spillover effects" would be empirically important in connection with crimes against the person. It should be pointed out that the estimated elasticity of the murder rate with respect to Pe|c, in principle, includes both deterrent and incapacitation effects. An estimate of the latter derived through a procedure similar to that used in Ehrlich (1975a, p. 413) indicates that the magnitude of the incapacitation effect is at most 0.08, much lower than the estimated elasticities.

35 It should be emphasized that in 1940 and 1950 there do not exist estimates of the total number of murders within individual states so that even tentative tradeoffs cannot be calculated without additional assumptions. The numbers mentioned above are implied by the relevant elasticities associated with measures of execution risk on the assumption that urban and rural murder rates were identical in the states included in the general sample underlying table 8.

43 Data sources not previously cited include U.S. Bureau of the Census, Prisoners in State and Federal Prisons and Reformatories (1936–41, 1946) and U.S. Department of Justice (1954) for E°; U.S. Bureau of the Census, Prisoners in State and Federal Prisons and Reformatories (1940) and U.S. Department of Justice (1954) for C_i°; U.S. Bureau of the Census, Statistical Abstract of the United Stales (1945) and U.S. Census of the Population: 1950 (1952) for the variables P K and X; and U.S. Bureau of the Census, Statistical Abstract of the United States (1946, 1953) for N_5, NW, AGE, A_{25-34}., N_{URB}, and URB.

44 The implicit assumption in the regression analysis is that the proportion of under-reported offenses is constant across states. However, the incentive to report a crime is affected by the relevant costs and gains associated with reporting. To the extent that explanatory variables introduced in the regression also affect the incentive to report, their estimated effects would be a mix of their effects on the incentive to commit as well as to report offenses. For example, individuals may be more willing to report an offense

if the probability that the offender will be apprehended and punished and the severity of punishment are high. Persons with low opportunity cost of time may be more likely to bear the costs of reporting a crime of given severity, including the costs of filing a complaint and appearing as witnesses in court. The estimated effects of $P^{\circ}c$, T, and X, for example, might therefore be biased in a positive direction and that of IT in a negative direction relative to their true effects.

Death and Deterrence Redux

Science, Law and Causal Reasoning on Capital Punishment

Jeffrey Fagan*

"Things are seldom what they seem ... Skim-milk masquerades as cream ..."
—Gilbert and Sullivan

I. THE CURRENT CONTROVERSY

Long before the U.S. Supreme Court restored capital punishment in 1976, proponents of the death penalty claimed that executions save lives by deterring would-be murderers from lethal violence. The more recent ascension of deterrence as a rationale for capital punishment in the 1970s coincided with a series of landmark Supreme Court cases that first abolished and then reinstated the death penalty (a list of cases is available), and with the publication of a series of articles that claimed a scientific basis for the assertion that potential murderers can be deterred from homicide by the threat of execution. The originator of these claims was economist Isaac Ehrlich, who (inspired by the theoretical work of the University of Chicago's Gary Becker[1]) developed a theoretical model that explained crime as a process of rational choice between illegal

---

* Professor of Law and Public Health, Columbia University. Outstanding research assistance was provided by Arie Rubinstein, Ethan Jacobs, Michel Werschtenschlag, David Finkelstein and Jason Stramaglia. Amanda Beth Geller provided excellent assistance in the empirical analyses. I am indebted to the Criminal Justice Research Center at The Ohio State University for their invitation to deliver the Walter C. Reckless Lecture in April 2005, which was the basis for this essay. I am also indebted to Brandon Garrett, Michael Maltz, Christopher Maxwell, Justin Wolfers, Avery Katz and Franklin Zimring who provided helpful comments and advice on earlier versions of the article.

1 See generally Gary S. Becker, *Crime and Punishment: An Economic Approach*, 76 J. POL. ECON. 169 (1968) [hereinafter Becker, *Crime and Punishment*]; GARY S. BECKER, THE ECONOMIC APPROACH TO HUMAN BEHAVIOR (1976) [hereinafter BECKER, ECONOMIC APPROACH].

and legal behavior; the choices were shaped by how law enforcement reacted to illegal activities.[2] Such rationality, Ehrlich argued, would influence would-be offenders to avoid punishment and forego crime.

Ehrlich published a highly influential article in 1975 that tested this model in the case of murder and capital punishment. It was a technical piece using econometric methods, but its influence went way beyond the economics profession. Ehrlich's work was cited in *Gregg v. Georgia*,[3] the landmark U.S. Supreme Court decision restoring capital punishment. No matter how carefully Ehrlich qualified his conclusions, his article had the popular and political appeal of a headline, a sound bite and a bumper sticker all rolled into one: "One execution saves eight innocent lives." Ehrlich's work was cited favorably in *Gregg*, and it was later cited in an amicus brief filed by the U.S. Solicitor General in *Fowler v. North Carolina*.[4] Even though Ehrlich's findings were disputed in academic journals such as the *Yale Law Journal*,[5] the proponents of deterrence had gained the upper hand in how this research was interpreted and how its findings were applied.[6]

Ehrlich's work became the focal point for research on deterrence and the death penalty, launching an era of contentious arguments in the press and in professional journals.[7] Over

---

2 Isaac Ehrlich, *The Deterrent Effect of Capital Punishment: A Question of Life and Death*, 65 AM. ECON. REV. 397 (1975); Isaac Ehrlich, *Capital Punishment and Deterrence: Some Further Thoughts and Additional Evidence*, 85 J. POL. ECON. 741 (1977).

3 428 U.S. 153 (1976).

4 428 U.S. 904 (1976).

5 See Editors' Introduction, *Statistical Evidence on the Deterrent Effect of Capital Punishment*, 85 YALE L.J. 164 (1975); David C. Baldus & James W.L. Cole, *A Comparison of the Work of Thorsten Sellin and Isaac Ehrlich on the Deterrent Effect of Capital Punishment*, 85 YALE L.J. 170 (1975); William J. Bowers & Glenn L. Pierce, *The Illusion of Deterrence in Isaac Ehrlich's Research on Capital Punishment*, 85 YALE L.J. 187 (1975); Isaac Ehrlich, *Deterrence: Evidence and Inference*, 85 YALE L.J. 209 (1975).

6 For critiques of Ehrlich's work, see Michael McAleer & Michael R. Veall, *How Fragile Are Fragile Inferences? A Re-Evaluation of the Deterrent Effect of Capital Punishment*, 71 REV. ECON. & STATISTICS 99 (1989); Edward E. Leamer, *Let's Take the Con out of Econometrics*, 73 AM. ECON. REV. 31 (1983); Walter S. McManus, *Estimates of the Deterrent Effect of Capital Punishment: The Importance of the Researcher's Prior Beliefs*, 93 J. POL. ECON. 417 (1985); Jeffrey Grogger, *The Deterrent Effect of Capital Punishment: An Analysis of Daily Homicide Counts*, 85 J. AM. STATISTICAL ASSOC. 295 (1990).

For support and extensions of Ehrlich's work, see Stephen A. Layson, *Homicide and Deterrence: A Reexamination of the United States Time-Series Evidence*, 52 S. ECON. J. 68 (1985) [hereinafter Layson, *Homicide and Deterrence*]; James P. Cover & Paul D. Thistle, *Time Series, Homicide, and the Deterrent Effect of Capital Punishment*, 54 S. ECON. J. 615 (1988); George A. Chressanthis, *Capital Punishment and the Deterrent Effect Revisited: Recent Time-Series Econometric Evidence*, 18 J. BEHAV. ECON. 81 (1989).

7 For an excellent summary of the critique of Ehrlich's article, see John Lamperti, *Deter Murder? A Brief Look at the Evidence*, 17, available at http://www.math.dartmouth.edu/~lamperti/capitalpunishment.html (last visited Aug. 18, 2006).

the next two decades, economists and other social scientists attempted to replicate Ehrlich's results using different data, alternative statistical methods, and other twists that tried to address glaring errors in Ehrlich's techniques and data.[8] Yet the accumulated scientific evidence from these later studies also weighed heavily against the claim that executions deter murders.[9] Ehrlich's findings were challenged by many scholars as to the sample period and/or the variables he chose, and the murder supply equation and the functional form of the equations he estimated.[10] Also, under Ehrlich's methodology, the aggregation of data from all U.S. states led to his conclusion that "a decrease in the execution risk in one State combined with an increase in the murder in another State would, all other things being equal, suggest a deterrent effect that quite obviously would not exist."[11] Within three years of the publication of Ehrlich's study, an expert panel appointed by the National Academy

8 See, e.g., Layson, *Homicide and Deterrence, supra* note 6, at 75, 80; Stephen Layson, *United States Time-Series Homicide Regressions with Adaptive Expectations*, 62 BULL. N.Y. ACAD. MED. 589 (1986).

9 For example, Peter Passell and John Taylor showed that Ehrlich's result relied heavily on movements from 1963 to 1969. They focused on Ehrlich's observed negative relation between executions and homicide rates, and analyzed the impact of a change in the time period chosen for the model or a change in the assumptions as to the model's functional form. Both changes showed that the broad aspects of the model were unchanged, but that the evidence suggesting a particular deterrent effect from executions had totally vanished. See Peter Passell & John B. Taylor, *The Deterrent Effect of Capital Punishment: Another View*, 67 AM. ECON. REV. 445, 450 (1977):

> First, we have shown that Ehrlich's model does not satisfy the statistical requirement of temporal homogeneity and that the results are sensitive to specification of the variables and transformation of the data. ... Second, ... it is not possible to infer from [Ehrlich's murder rate regression function] that a change in legal institutions ... would reduce murder rates. ... [I]t is prudent to neither to accept nor reject the hypothesis that capital punishment deters murder.

See also Bowers & Pierce, *supra* note 5, at 187; Richard M. McGahey, *Dr. Ehrlich's Magic Bullet: Economic Theory, Econometrics and the Death Penalty*, 26 CRIME & DELINQ. 485 (1980); Stephen A. Hoenack & William C. Weiler, *A Structural Model of Murder Behavior and the Criminal Justice System*, 70 AM. ECON. REV. 327 (1980); McAleer & Veall, *supra* note 6, at 99. See *generally* Grogger, *supra* note 6, at 295; See *also* William C. Bailey, *Deterrence, Brutalization, and the Death Penalty: Another Examination of Oklahoma's Return to Capital Punishment*, 36 CRIMINOLOGY 711 (1998); Jon Sorenson et al., *Capital Punishment and Deterrence: Examining the Effect of Executions on Murder in Texas*, 45 CRIME & DELINQ. 481 (1999).

10 H. Naci Mocan & R. Kaj Gittings, *Getting Off Death Row: Commuted Sentences and the Deterrent Effect of Capital Punishment*, 46 J. L. & ECON. 453 (2003).

11 Craig J. Albert, *Challenging Deterrence: New Insights on Capital Punishment Derived from Panel Data*, 60 U. PITT. L. REV. 321, 356 (1999) (citing *Gregg* v. Georgia, 428 U.S. 153, 235 (1976) (Marshall, J., dissenting)). Later in the article, the author also adds, after analyzing the same data as Ehrlich's, "the data do not support any conclusion that executions deter homicides." *Id.* at 363.

of Sciences issued strong criticisms of his work.[12] Despite the weight of technical economic and other social science evidence condemning Ehrlich's work, each new study that followed supporting the deterrence conclusion found uncritical acceptance among proponents of the death penalty, while the critiques failed to get popular or political traction.

History is now repeating itself. In the past five years, a new wave of a dozen or more studies have appeared, reporting deterrent effects of capital punishment that go well beyond Ehrlich's findings. The new deterrence studies analyze data that spans the entire period since the resumption of executions in the U.S. following the 1973 decision in *Furman v. Georgia*.[13] The new studies go further, though, claiming that pardons, commutations, and exonerations cause murders to increase.[14] Some say that even murders of passion, among the most irrational of lethal acts, can be deterred.[15]

At least one study, by Professor Zhiqiang Liu, claims that executions not only deter murders, but they also increase the deterrent effects of other punishments.[16] Following this logic, the new deterrence research has been applied to justify punitive criminal justice policies in several areas: mandatory minimum sentences and "three strikes" laws, zero tolerance policies for school children and drug offenders, and mandatory transfer of adolescent offenders from the juvenile court to the criminal court. Thus, the deterrent effects of capital punishment are apparently indefinite and offer execution as a cure-all for everyday crime.[17]

Many of these studies have already appeared in leading academic journals, while others are working their way through the review process. These studies have been reported favorably and uncritically by leading newspapers (e.g., *Washington Post, Boston Globe, Wall Street Journal*), and they have been broadcast widely by pro-death penalty advocacy groups to state legislators.[18] Many were cited in major newspapers even before their papers under-

---

12 See Lawrence R. Klein et al., *The Deterrent Effect of Capital Punishment: An Assessment of the Estimates, in* DETERRENCE AND INCAPACITATION: ESTIMATING THE EFFECTS OF CRIMINAL SANCTIONS ON CRIME RATES 336, 336–60 (Alfred Blumstein et al. eds., 1978).

13 408 U.S. 238 (1972).

14 See Mocan & Gittings, *supra* note 10.

15 Joanna M. Shepherd, *Murders of Passion, Execution Delays, and the Deterrence of Capital Punishment*, 33 J. LEGAL STUD. 283 (2004) [hereinafter Shepherd, Murders of Passion].

16 Zhiqiang Liu, *Capital Punishment and the Deterrence Hypothesis: Some New Insights and Empirical Evidence*, 30 E. ECON. J. 237 (2004).

17 *Id.*

18 For example, Mocan's article received media coverage in *inter alia* Gene Koretz, *Equality? Not on Death Row*, BUSINESS WEEK, June 30, 2003, at 28; Jeff Jacoby, *Execution Saves Innocents*, BOSTON GLOBE, Sept. 28, 2003 at H11; Kieran Nicholson, *Study: Race, Gender of Governors Affect Death-Row Decisions*, DENVER POST, Dec. 19, 2002, at A17; Richard Morin, *Lame Ducks and the Death Penalty*, WASH. POST, Jan. 20, 2002, at B05; Richard Morin, *Murderous Pardons?*, WASH. POST, Dec. 15, 2002, at B05. See *also* Mocan & Gittings, *supra* note 10.

went some major changes after comments and critiques of their peers, while newspapers of record, such as The Washington Post, quoted in their headlines findings that were later proven to be wrong.[19] Pro-death penalty advocacy groups including *Justice for All, The Criminal Justice Legal Foundation* and *American Voice*, are widely disseminating the results of the new studies as scientific evidence of the deterrent effects of capital punishment. State groups in California and North Carolina also are citing this evidence to oppose local moratorium efforts. As in the *Gregg* era, these studies have been cited without challenge in amicus briefs in recent capital cases including *Schirro v. Summerlin*.[20] In April 2004, Professor Joanna Shepherd, coauthor of some of these studies, summarized the new deterrence evidence in testimony before the federal House Judiciary Committee, claiming that there is sound scientific evidence that each execution deters between three and eighteen murders.[21]

Accordingly, the reach of the new deterrence research seems quite long, and its potential impact on criminal justice politics and policies extends well beyond the death penalty. This new deterrence research also benefits advocates of capital punishment by competing with death penalty opponents who cite high rates of errors in capital cases and wrongful convictions as arguments for state moratoria or abolition.[22] If these claims

---

19 George Lardner, *The Role of the Press in the Clemency Process*, 31 CAP. U. L. REV. 179 (2003) (pinpointing all the mistakes made in the Mocan's article and taken at face value by the Washington Post, without any due review by professional criminologists).

20 Summerlin v. Stewart, 341 F.3d 1082 (9th Cir. 2003), rev'd, Schirro v. Summerlin, 542 U.S. 348 (2004).

21 Joanna Shepherd has recently argued before Congress that recent research has created a "strong consensus among economists that capital punishment deters crime," going so far as to claim that "[t]he studies are unanimous." *Terrorist Penalties Enhancement Act of 2003: Hearing on H.R. 2934 Before the Subcomm. on Crime, Terrorism, and Homeland Security of the H. Comm. on the Judiciary*, 108th Cong. 23–28 (2004) (statement of Joanna M. Shepherd, Visiting Assistant Professor, Emory Law School) [hereinafter Shepard Statement]. This consensus was repeated in recent testimony by Professor Paul Rubin, co-author on several recent studies also reporting deterrent effects from executions. *An Examination of the Death Penalty in the United States: Hearing Before the Subcommittee on the Constitution, Civil Rights and Property Rights of the Senate Committee on the Judiciary*, 109th Cong. (2006) (statement of Paul H. Rubin, Samuel Candler Dobbs Professor of Economics and Law, Emory), available at http://judiciary.senate.gov/testimony.cfm?id=1745&wit_id=4991 (last visited Mar. 10, 2006) [hereinafter Rubin Statement].

22 See, *e.g.*, Lawrence C. Marshall, *The Innocence Revolution and the Death Penalty*, 1 OHIO ST. J. CRIM. L. 573 (2004); Robert Warden, *Illinois Death Penalty Reform: How it Happened, What it Promises*, 95 J. CRIM. L. & CRIMINOLOGY 381 (2005). See *generally* DAVID L. PROTESS & ROBERT WARDEN, A PROMISE OF JUSTICE (1998) (documenting the media reactions to the exonerations of the four death row inmates).

are true, the new evidence would not only fundamentally change the roiling discourse on capital punishment, it could have influence on both the politics and substance of criminal law and policy.

What are we to make of these claims? I answer this question in three ways. First, we will look at the evidence itself. What claims are made in the various studies, and what might we conclude about executions and deterrence scanning across the new body of evidence? What is the structure of the data and what does the data tell us, even before we look at the modeling process itself? What cautions should we place on the interpretation and application of this information?

Second, we ask how well these claims stand up to scientific scrutiny. Have these analyses asked too much of the data? What happens when the data are subject to alternatives in measurement and analysis? Do the studies pay sufficient attention to the conceptual details of deterrence, murder itself, and alternate explanations for the complex relationships that influence changes in murder rates over time? Here, we consider some serious omissions in the construction of this theoretical framework, both conceptually and in the details of some modeling decisions.

Third, can the causal modeling approach of these studies justify the claims they make?[23] In this section, we offer secondary analyses of data from one of the new deterrence studies, authored by Professors Naci Mocan and Kaj Gittings,[24] in an effort to replicate the findings.[25] Replication is one of the cornerstones of the scientific process,[26] and is essential to vetting the types of claims of causal inference that are deeply embedded in the new deterrence studies. In this spirit, the re-analyses in this article apply alternate measurement

---

23 For discussion of the complexity of causal analysis in estimating the effects of social interventions with observational data, see Martin Rein & Christopher Winship, *The Dangers of 'Strong' Causal Reasoning in Social Policy*, 36 SOCIETY 38 (July/August 1999); Michael E. Sobel, *An Introduction to Causal Inference*, 24 SOC. METHODS & RES. 353 (1996); Richard A. Berk & David A. Freedman, *Statistical Assumptions as Empirical Commitments*, in PUNISHMENT AND SOCIAL CONTROL 235 (2d ed.) (Thomas G. Blomberg & Stanley Cohen eds., 2003); PAUL R. ROSENBAUM, OBSERVATIONAL STUDIES (1995).

24 Mocan & Gittings, *supra* note 10, at 454.

25 Another re-analysis of the Mocan and Gittings data also reported instability in these results. See John Donohue & Justin Wolfers, *Uses and Abuses of Empirical Evidence in the Death Penalty Debate*, 58 STAN. L. REV. 791 (2005) [hereinafter Donohue & Wolfers, *Uses and Abuses*](reviewing the main studies cited by Sunstein and Vermeule and finding the empirical support for the claim that the death penalty deters ... to be unstable and too unreliable to inform either law or policy).

26 Lee Epstein & Gary King, *The Rules of Inference*, 69 U. CHI. L. REV. 1 (2002) [hereinafter Epstein & King, *The Rules of Inference*]. For examples of how data sharing and independent replication can advance the scientific process, see Lee Epstein & Gary King, *Building an Infrastructure for Empirical Research in the Law*, 53 J. LEGAL EDUC. 311 (2003).

strategies and model forms to establish the robustness or fragility of these findings. Already, at least one re-analysis has shown that the estimates are unstable when re-analyzed under different measurement and analysis conditions.[27] The analysis in this article goes further by re-specifying these models using analytic strategies that account for the unique temporal dependence in murder rates. Based on the results, I draw conclusions about the status of this evidence and its utility both in law and policy.

Finally, we consider the tensions at the intersection of science and law that these episodes raise. Here, we examine the recurring phenomenon of what we might conveniently call a "rush to judgment" when science—whether behavioral or natural—dangles the promise of simple answers to urgent but very complex questions.

The essay shows that the new deterrence studies are fraught with numerous technical and conceptual errors: inappropriate methods of statistical analysis, failures to consider several relevant factors that drive murder rates such as drug epidemics, missing data on key variables in key states, the tyranny of a few outlier states and years, weak to non-existent tests of concurrent effects of incarceration, statistical confounding of murder rates with death sentences, failure to consider the general performance of the criminal justice system, artifactual results from truncated time frames, and the absence of any direct test of the components of contemporary theoretical constructions of deterrence. Social scientists have failed to replicate several of these studies, and in some cases have produced contradictory or unstable results with the same data, suggesting that the original findings are unreliable and perhaps inaccurate. The central mistake in this enterprise is one of causal reasoning: the attempt to draw causal inferences from a flawed and limited set of observational data, and the failure to address important competing influences on murder. Murder is a complex and multiply-determined phenomenon, with cyclical patterns for over forty years of distinct periods of increase and decline that are not unlike epidemics of contagious diseases. There is no reliable, scientifically sound evidence that pits execution against a robust set of competing explanations to identify whether it can exert a deterrent effect that is uniquely and sufficiently powerful to overwhelm these consistent and recurring epidemic patterns. These flaws and omissions in a body of scientific evidence render it unreliable as a basis for law or policy that generate life-and-death decisions. To accept it uncritically invites errors that have the most severe human costs.

II. THE NEW DETERRENCE LITERATURE

Over a dozen new studies appeared since the mid-1990s, mainly in economics journals, with most claiming new evidence that executions have strong and powerful deterrent

27 Donohue & Wolfers, *Uses and Abuses*, *supra* note 25, at 791.

effects on homicide.[28] The studies have quickly found their way into the courts. Similar to the immediate citations of Ehrlich's work in *Gregg* and other cases, the new deterrence studies were cited in Schirro v. Summerlin[29] in an amicus brief in a certiorari petition to the United States Court of Appeals for the Ninth Circuit.[30] The studies gained attention in Congress,[31] in the popular press,[32] among death penalty advocates,[33] and now, among legal scholars.[34] Professors Sunstein and Vermeule find the new deterrence evidence

---

28 For a compilation of recent studies, along with abstracts, see CRIMINAL JUSTICE LEGAL FOUNDATION, ARTICLES ON DEATH PENALTY DETERRENCE, http://www.cjlf.org/deathpenalty/DPDeterrence.htm (last visited Nov. 11, 2005).

29 542 U.S. 348 (2004).

30 Arguing that "[t]here is grave danger that the 'annually improvised' jurisprudence of capital punishment is killing innocent people through lost deterrence" and that "that a death penalty which is actually enforced saves innocent lives in large numbers." Brief of Amici Curiae Criminal Justice Legal Foundation at 23–24, Schirro v. Summerlin, 542 U.S. 348 (2004) (No. 03–526), available at http://www.cjlf.org/briefs/Summerlin.pdf.

31 See Shepherd Statement, *supra* note 21; Rubin Statement, *supra* note 21.

32 See, e.g., Jacoby, *supra* note 18; see also John Hood, *A Deadly Moratorium?*, CAROLINA J. ONLINE, (2004), http://www.carolinajournal.com/jhdailyjournal/display_jhdailyjournal.html?id=13 91. Studies such as Mocan & Gittings, *supra* note 10, were discussed in the Washington Post even before their publication in peer-reviewed journals. Several of the unreviewed papers received broad media coverage in, inter alia, BUSINESS WEEK, *supra* note 18; BOSTON GLOBE, *supra* note 18; DENVER POST, *supra* note 18; and WASH. POST, *supra* note 18. See also Hashem Dezhbakhsh et al., *Does Capital Punishment Have a Deterrent Effect? New Evidence from Postmoratorium Panel Data*, 5 AM. L. & ECON. REV. 344 (2003), was discussed uncritically in, Jerry Seper, *Garza Executed for Drug Killings: Murderer Makes Deathbed Apology*, WASH. TIMES, June 20, 2001, at A3; Paul H. Rubin, *Study: Death Penalty Deters Scores of Killings*, ATLANTA J. CONST., Mar. 14, 2002, at 22A, which led to Professor Shepherd's testimony before the U.S. House of Representatives, *supra* note 31. None of these papers sought opinions from criminologists who might have raised questions about the reliability of many of the new deterrence studies. See, e.g., George Lardner, *supra* note 19 (pinpointing mistakes made in Mocan & Gittings, *supra* note 10).

33 See, e.g., CRIMINAL JUSTICE LEGAL FOUNDATION, *supra* note 28.

34 Cass R. Sunstein & Adrian Vermeule, *Is the Death Penalty Morally Required? Acts, Omissions, and Life-Life Tradeoffs*, 58 STAN. L. REV. 703 (2005). See also Richard Posner, *The Economics of Capital Punishment*, http://www.becker-posner-blog.com/archives/2005/12/the_economics_o.html (last visited Dec. 18, 2005); Gary Becker, *More on the Economics of Capital Punishment*, http://www.becker-posner-blog.com/archives/2005/12/more_on_the_eco.html (last visited Dec. 18, 2005).

But see Carol S. Steiker, *No, Capital Punishment Is Not Morally Required: Deterrence, Deontology, and the Death Penalty*, 58 STAN. L. REV. 703 (2005) (responding to claim of the "moral requirement" of Sunstein and Vermeule by stating that " … executions constitute a distinctive moral wrong (purposeful as opposed to non-purposeful killing), and a distinctive kind of injustice (unjustified punishment)" and "powerful"[35] and "impressive,"[36] and they couple it with "many decades of reliable data about [capital punishment's] deterrent effects"[37] as the "foundation" of their argument that since "capital punishment powerfully deters killings,"[38] there is a moral imperative to aggressively prosecute capital crimes.

The studies use several designs that conceptualize capital punishment as a "treatment" that would deter homicides. The studies include classical panel designs that co-vary homicide rates and deterrence measures that incorporate executions, quasi-experiments testing the effects of moratoria, natural experiments comparing homicide rates in death penalty and non-death penalty states, nested (hierarchical) designs of counties within states that provide more fine-grained analyses of local homicide rates, and instrumental variables designs that attempt to disentangle spurious effects due to factors other than deterrence. The estimation techniques vary from standard Ordinary Least Squares models to complex equilibrium models with simultaneous equations, to negative binomial estimators of homicides. Several have used a relatively new dataset on death sentences and executions to operationalize and measure deterrence. The data are produced by the U.S. Department of Justice,[39] and are updated and revised annually. They include all death sentences and their dispositions following the resumption of capital punishment following *Furman*. The conclusions these studies derive are wedded to the methods and sources that are used to compile these data. The studies have appeared both in peer-reviewed journals, primarily in economics, and in law reviews; a few have been published online as working papers.

The studies are listed in Appendix A. Their claims are strong, far stronger than results produced in most social policy experiments on education, welfare, or crime control. A detailed analysis of the methods and results of these studies is not the purpose here; instead, here is a representative sampling of the results and claims made by these authors.

---

concluding that. ... "acceptance of 'threshold' deontology in no way requires a commitment to capital punishment even if. ... deterrence is proven").

35 Sunstein & Vermeule, *supra* note 34, at 745.

36 *Id.* at 713.

37 *Id.* at 751.

38 *Id.* at 738.

39 BUREAU OF JUSTICE STATISTICS, U.S. DEP'T OF JUSTICE, CAPITAL PUNISHMENT IN THE UNITED STATES, 1973–2002, http://webapp.icpsr.umich.edu/cocoon/ICPSR-DAS/03958.xml). See THOMAS P. BONCZAR & TRACY L SNELL, CAPITAL PUNISHMENT (2002), at www.ojp.usdoj.gov/bjs/pub/pdf/cp02.pdffor illustrations of the components of the dataset and trends and patterns over time.

- Mocan & Gittings: "[A]n additional execution generates a reduction in homicide by five, an additional commutation increases homicides by four to five, and an additional removal brings about one additional murder."[40]
- Dezhbakhsh et al.: "Our results suggest that capital punishment has a strong deterrent effect; each execution results, on average, in eighteen fewer murders—with a margin of error of plus or minus ten."[41]
- Shepherd (Murders of Passion): "[E]ach execution results in, on average, three fewer murders. ... [C]apital punishment deters murders previously believed to be undeterrable: crimes of passion and murders by intimates. ... [L]onger waits on death row before execution lessen the deterrence. ... [O]ne less murder is committed for every 2.75–year reduction in death row waits. Thus, recent legislation to shorten the wait should strengthen capital punishment's deterrent effect."[42]
- Dezhbakhsh & Shepherd: "Our results indicate that capital punishment has a deterrent effect, and the moratorium and executions deter murders in distinct ways. This evidence is corroborated by both the before-and-after comparisons and regression analysis."[43]
- Cloninger and Marchesini: As a result of the unofficial moratorium on executions during most of 1996 and early 1997, the citizens of Texas experienced a net 90 additional innocent lives lost to homicide.[44]
- Liu: From the econometric standpoint, the structure of the murder supply function depends on the status of the death penalty, which is in itself endogenous. Liu goes on to claim that executions deter crimes other than murder, suggesting collateral benefits of capital punishment for public safety more broadly.[45]
- Shepherd (Deterrence Versus Brutalization): The impact of executions differs substantially among the states. Executions deter murders in six states, executions have no effect on murders in eight states, and executions increase murders in thirteen states. Additional empirical analyses indicate that there is a threshold effect that explains the differing impacts of capital punishment. On average, the states with deterrence execute many more people than do the states where executions increase crime or have no effect. To achieve deterrence, states must execute several people.[46]

---

40 Mocan & Gittings, *supra* note 10, at 469.

41 Dezhbakhsh et al., *supra* note 32.

42 Shepherd, *Murders of Passion, supra* note 15.

43 Hashem Dezhbakhsh & Joanna M. Shepherd, *The Deterrent Effect of Capital Punishment: Evidence from a "Judicial Experiment,"* 44 ECON. INQUIRY 512, 517–26 (2006).

44 Dale O. Cloninger & Roberto Marchesini, *Execution and Deterrence: A Quasi-Controlled Group Experiment*, 33 APPLIED ECON. 568, 575 (2001).

45 Liu, *supra* note 16, at 238.

46 Joanna M. Shepherd, *Deterrence Versus Brutalization: Capital Punishment's Differing Impacts Among States*, 104 MICH. L. REV. 203, 205 (2005) [hereinafter Shepherd, *Deterrence Versus Brutalization*].

Readers can easily see the appeal of these findings. Just as the Ehrlich findings were quickly embraced in popular and political culture, these new studies make strong claims that have similar appeal. It is not surprising that they have been quickly embraced and disseminated as a counterweight against the cultural and political narratives of innocence[47] and errors.[48]

---

47 See, e.g., BARRY SCHECK ET AL., ACTUAL INNOCENCE: FIVE DAYS TO EXECUTION, AND OTHER DISPATCHES FROM THE WRONGLY CONVICTED (2000) (citing numerous exonerations from death row as evidence of the risks of wrongfully executing an innocent person); see also Samuel R. Gross et al., *Exonerations in the United States, 1989 Through 2003,* 95 J. CRIM. L. & CRIMINOLOGY 523 (2005); RICHARD C. DIETER, DEATH PENALTY INFORMATION CENTER, INNOCENCE AND THE CRISIS IN THE AMERICAN DEATH PENALTY (2004), available at http://www.deathpenaltyinfo.org/article.php?scid=45&did=1149#ExSum (last visited Aug. 18, 2006) (showing that the number of innocence cases increased by more than fifty percent in an eight year period, from thirty-two in 1989–1996 to forty-nine in 1997–2004); STAFF OF S. COMM. ON THE JUDICIARY, SUBCOMM. ON CIVIL AND CONSTITUTIONAL RIGHTS, 103D CONG., INNOCENCE AND THE DEATH PENALTY: ASSESSING THE DANGER OF MISTAKEN EXECUTIONS (OCT. 21, 1993); Joshua Herman, Comment, *Death Denies Due Process: Evaluating Due Process Challenges to the Federal Death Penalty Act,* 53 DEPAUL L. REV. 1777 (2004); Joseph L. Hoffmann, *Protecting the Innocent: The Massachusetts Governor's Council Report,* 95 J. CRIM. L. & CRIMINOLOGY 561 (2005); Evan J. Mandery, *Innocence as a Death Penalty Issue,* 40 CRIM. L. BULL. 78 (2004); Evan J. Mandery, *Massachusetts and the Changing Debate on the Death Penalty,* 40 CRIM. L. BULL. 518 (2004); Michael L. Radelet, William S. Lofquist & Hugo A. Bedau, *Prisoners Released from Death Rows Since 1970 Because of Doubts About Their Guilt,* 13 T. M. COOLEY L. REV. 907 (1996); Rob Warden, *Illinois Death Penalty Reform: How it Happened, What it Promises,* 95 J. CRIM L. & CRIMINOLOGY 381 (2005); Laurie A. Whitt et al., *Executing the Innocent: The Next Step in the Marshall Hypotheses,* 26 N.Y.U. REV. L. & SOC. CHANGE 309 (2001– 2002); Laurie A. Whitt et al., *Innocence Matters: How Innocence Recasts the Death Penalty Debate,* 38 CRIM. L. BULL. 670 (2002). Newspaper accounts also show that growing support for moratoria on executions is animated by fears of wrongful executions. See Ken Armstrong & Steve Mills, *O'Connor Questions Fairness of Death Penalty Justice Rethinking Laws She Shaped,* CHIC. TRIB., July 4, 2001, at 1; Helen Dewar, *Support Grows for Execution Safeguards: Exonerations Spur Bills in Congress,* WASH. POST, June 16, 2000, at A1; Sara Rimer, *Support for a Moratorium in Executions Gets Stronger,* N.Y. Times, Oct 31, 2000, at A18; Jodi Wilgoren, *Citing Issue of Fairness, Governor Clears Out Death Row in Illinois,* N.Y. TIMES, Jan 12, 2003, at A1. In addition to Illinois, popular and political concerns over innocence have generated creation of an innocence commission in North Carolina. See Phoebe Zerwick, *Innocence Commission: N.C. Creates First In Nation To Backstop Courts,* WINSTON-SALEM JOURNAL, Aug. 20, 2006, at A1.

48 James S. Liebman et al., *Capital Attrition: Error Rates in Capital Cases,* 1973–1995, 78 TEX. L. REV. 1839 (2000) (showing that 68% of all death sentences since *Furman* v. Georgia were reversed either on direct appeal, state direct appeal, or federal habeas review; most (82%) of those reversed were re-sentenced to non-capital punishments, 7% were exonerated, and the remainder were re-sentenced to

III. SOCIAL SCIENCE REASONING

These strong claims of powerful deterrent effects are not without contradictions and serious limitations. When the elements of this scientific enterprise are decomposed and evaluated, we can identify a series of recurring challenges in their conceptualization, model specification, measurement, and causal reasoning. The totality and cumulative weight of these challenges yields strong reasonable doubts about the reliability of these claims. There are errors both of commission and omission in this oeuvre of research, as I discuss below. In addition, some simple empirical exercises reveal problems in the sensitivity of the results to alternate measurement and model specification assumptions, producing different results whose instability and fragility undermine the strong claims of death penalty proponents.

A. The Structure of the Data

The findings of a negative correlation between executions and murder seem to be structured into the data in a way that weakens generalizations or predictions. Indeed, executions in most states in most years since *Gregg* are very rare. According to the Death Penalty Information Center, there have been 1045 executions since 1976; more than one in three (366) have been in Texas.[49] A simple average of executions per state per year would be deceptive, since state laws were enacted in different years, but even a simple estimate—there are thirty-eight death penalty states, each with a valid law in effect for an average of twenty years since *Gregg*—suggests that on average, there is fewer than one execution per year per state. In states other than Texas, the median state-year average is far lower.

In Mocan and Gittings,[50] for example, executions between 1976 and 1997 range from 0 to 18, with 859 of the 1000 over the 21 years (86%) equal to 0. As a result, the median is also 0. There are 78 values (8%) equal to 1. There are but 11 values (1%) larger than 5, ranging from 7 to 18 executions. Obviously, the distribution is highly skewed, and the mean is dominated by a few extreme values. Most states in most years execute no one.

---

death). See, e.g., David Broder, *Broken Justice*, WASH. POST, June 18, 2000, at B7; see also Jonathan Alter, *The Death Penalty on Trial: Special Report: DNA and Other Evidence Freed 87 People from Death Row; Now Ricky McGinn is Roiling Campaign 2000. Why America's Rethinking Capital Punishment*, NEWSWEEK, June 12, 2000, at 24, 26–34 (noting changes in political rhetoric concerning the death penalty); Alan Berlow, *The Broken Machinery of Death*, AM. PROSPECT, July 30, 2001, at 16; David Gergen, *Death by Incompetence*, U.S. NEWS & WORLD REP., June 26, 2000, at 76; James Liebman, *The Condemned, and the Mistakes*, N.Y. TIMES, July 12, 2000, at A20; *Murder One*, THE ECONOMIST, June 17, 2000, at 33.

49 DEATH PENALTY INFORMATION CENTER, available at http://www.deathpenaltyinfo.org/article.php?scid=8&did=146 (last updated Sept. 1, 2006).

50 Mocan & Gittings, *supra* note 10, at 458 fig. 1.

Accordingly, the low number of events in most states suggests that there is hardly enough signal to reach a disparate and heterogeneous population of would-be murderers.[51]

The problems of both low base rates and the hegemony of Texas in the new deterrence studies have been illustrated by Professor Richard Berk, who reanalyzed data from Mocan and Gittings to show some simple trends and empirical facts in the data.[52] Berk constructed a simple deterrence measure, lagging executions one year behind homicides, to show several underlying trends in these data. First, a deterrent effect—that is, a negative slope in the murder rate relative to the execution rate—occurs when the number of executions within a state over a single year is five or more. Figure 1, from Professor Berk's analysis, illustrates this point. But even at this extreme tail of the distribution, the confidence intervals are so large as to render a claim of prediction meaningless.

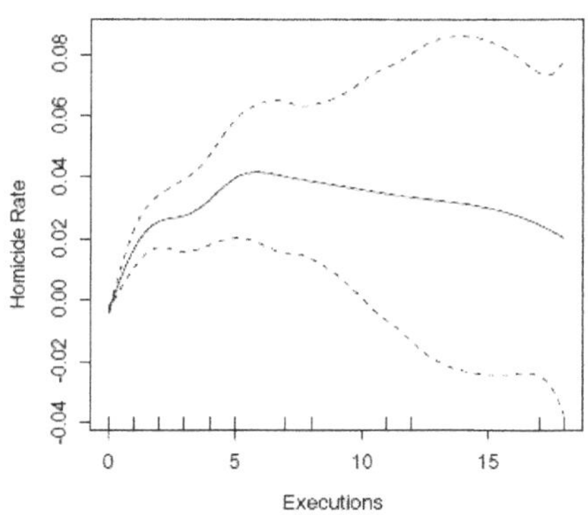

Figure 1. Homicide rate as a function of the number of executions lagged by one year, 1976–1997.[53]

---

51 Richard Berk, *New Claims About Executions and General Deterrence: Déjà Vu All Over Again?*, 2 J. EMPIRICAL LEGAL STUD. 303 (2005) [hereinafter Berk, New Claims]. Not only are executions clustered in Texas, but most states in most years have no executions, a statistical burden that none of the new deterrence studies competently address. To address this problem statistically, one must first estimate a model that explains which states have any executions, and then a second model to show the factors that predict the frequency of its use. Such models are called "hurdle" regressions. See, e.g., Christopher J. W. Zorn, *An Analytic and Empirical Examination of Zero-Inflated and Hurdle Poison Specifications*, 26 SOC. METHODS & RES. 368 (1998); see also Yin Bin Cheung, *Zero-Inflated Models for Regression Analysis of Count Data: A Study of Growth and Development*, 21 STAT. IN MED. 1461, 1462–67 (2002). Statistical methods that fail to account for this two part process will produce unreliable and inflated results.

52 Berk, *New Claims, supra* note 51, at 304.

53 *Id.* (reanalyzing data from Mocan & Gittings, *supra* note 10). Note: Solid line is smoothed fitted values. The dotted lines contain the approximate 95% confidence interval. The relationship between the

Second, Professor Berk shows that after controlling both for the initial and average murder rate per state over the full twenty-one year study interval and state population size over time, the trends become unstable and unpredictable.[54] Third and most important, he shows that once Texas is removed from the analysis, all deterrent effects disappear.[55]

These extremes have undue "leverage" and "influence" on the data.[56] Most of the model-fitting methods in these studies tend to weigh these skewed observations very heavily, giving them undue leverage in the regression coefficients in complex models. According to Professor Berk, claims of a deterrent effect reflect these extreme cases, not the mass of the data.[57] The leverage of these cases is transformed into influence when extreme values of a predictor—executions—are likely to be paired with extreme values of a response variable—homicides. By "influence" one means that the potential impact of leverage in a model's fit becomes a reality, reinforcing the illusion of a statistical relationship which—in this case—actually is simply a product of one small set of observations. When he eliminates Texas, where these extremes are concentrated, Professor Berk shows that the relationship between execution and homicide disappears.[58]

Some analysts have tried to overcome these difficulties by disaggregating murders to the county level,[59] but the extreme cases still unduly influence the execution-homicide trends. No matter how deterrence is measured, the analyses remain captives of the structure of the data, and that structure ordains a particular result. If there is an effect of executions on homicides, it is the result of eleven extreme values, and from the influence of Texas. Generalizations from the eleven observations to the remaining ninety-nine percent would be unstable and inappropriate.

---

homicide rate and the lagged number of executions is generally positive for up to five executions and uncertain thereafter.

54 *Id.* at 319 fig.13.

55 *Id.* at 321–24 figs.15–18.

56 *Id.* at 305.

57 *Id.* at 318.

58 *Id.* at 322 fig. 16. The confidence intervals in Figure 16 suggest that there may be a positive relationship between the homicide rate and the lagged number of executions when Texas is removed from the data set.

59 Shepherd, *Deterrence Versus Brutalization, supra* note 46, at 223. One of the problems that Shepherd faced in this analysis was disaggregating death sentences and executions to the county level. Her solution was to apply the statewide measures for each year to each county within the state, creating an ecological fallacy that biases estimates of deterrence.

B. Theory and Specifications

The current set of deterrence tests typically takes the form of a regression model predicting murder rates. The predictors include measures of deterrence in the form of executions per death sentence, a lag function expresses assumptions about the delay from sentence to execution; and from execution to the deterrent effect on murder. At least one study includes "announcement effects" of executions by including newspaper reports of executions.[60] Controls are sometimes introduced to account for different assumptions about the production of the "supply" of offenders eligible for execution: murder arrests, population size and demography. Rarely are there measures that capture the punitiveness of the criminal justice system or its incapacitative effects. Some try to estimate the risks of detection by indexing the number of police. Few estimate the aggressiveness of law enforcement by looking at the general behavior of legal institutions toward crime generally. Socio-economic contexts associated with homicide appear via measures of the age distribution of the population, poverty and unemployment rates, and the extent of urbanization of the population. These structural factors have been identified as homicide risks over time and across different units of analysis including states, cities, and neighborhoods.[61] Most of the new deterrence studies measure both murder and social structural risk at the state level, but others are based on a county-within-state analysis.[62]

The typical approach in the new deterrence studies involves estimation of regressions with different combinations of predictor variables, with sensitivity or robustness estimated from variation in the size of the regression coefficient for execution or the statutory presence of the death penalty in different configurations of predictors. Covariates associated with the production of homicides are included, but often are manipulated to form a sensitivity test for the specifications. However, these predictor sets often omit a range of other important factors that have stable and recurring effects on murder rates. These omissions in turn create specification errors that tend to inflate the significance of the deterrence factors. As we shall see below, some omissions are more important than others, but the cumulative effect of these omissions is a distortion and inflation of execution effects.

---

60 *Id.* at 253.

61 See, e.g., Kenneth C. Land et al., *Structural Covariates of Homicides Rates: Are There Any Invariances Across Time and Social Space?* 95 AM. J. SOC. 922 (1990); Robert J. Sampson & Janet Lauritsen, *Violent Victimization and Offending: Individual-, Situational-, and Community-Level Risk Factors*, in UNDERSTANDING AND PREVENTING VIOLENCE: SOCIAL INFLUENCES 1, 48–63 (A. Reiss & J. A. Roth eds., 1994); Lauren J. Krivo & Ruth D. Peterson, *The Structural Context of Homicide: Accounting for Racial Differences in Process*, 65 AM. SOC. REV. 547 (2000).

62 Shepherd, *Deterrence Versus Brutalization*, *supra* note 46.

1. Deterrence, Incapacitation, and Life Without Parole

Perhaps the most important theoretical misspecification in the new deterrence studies is the omission of the incapacitative effects of imprisonment generally, and Life Without Parole (LWOP) sentences in particular. Of the thirty-eight states that currently have valid death penalty statutes, thirty-seven also have LWOP statutes. Only New Mexico does not. Of the twelve states without the death penalty, eleven have life without parole. Only Alaska does not.[63] Even if LWOP were available as a sentencing option in cases other than capital trials, incarceration of persons with lengthy histories of violent crimes for non-capital offenses would likely exert some prophylactic effect on murder, given the prevalence of felony murders such as robbery-homicides.[64] Accordingly, the omission of LWOP from research on legal interventions to reduce homicide is a potentially biasing omission.

But how much of an effect might LWOP have on homicide rates? Systematic data on the extent to which juries return LWOP sentences capital cases is difficult to obtain; when available, it often is only for periods beginning in 1990 or later. Information is available on when each state passed its LWOP statute or modified it to make it a sentencing alternative in capital cases,[65] so the effects at least of the availability of LWOP as a sentencing option could be modeled and estimated. None of the new deterrence studies do so.

Yet data from a small number of states shows ample evidence that LWOP is used far more often than are death sentences in capital cases and cannot be ignored in estimating reasons for the decline in homicide rates.[66] For example, data from the Pennsylvania Department of Corrections shows that there were 139 LWOP sentences in Pennsylvania in 1999, compared to 15 death sentences.[67] In 2000, there were 121 life sentences compared to 12 death sentences.[68] In California, there were 3163 inmates serving life without parole

---

63 Julian H. Wright, Jr., *Life-Without-Parole: An Alternative to Death or Not Much of a Life at All?*, 43 VAND. L. REV. 529, 546 (1990); J. Mark Lane, *"Is There Life Without Parole?" A Capital Defendant's Right to a Meaningful Alternative Sentence*, 26 LOY. L.A. L. REV. 327 (1993); DEATH PENALTY INFORMATION CENTER, LIFE WITHOUT PAROLE (2000), available at http://www.deathpenaltyinfo.org/article.php?did=555&scid=59 [hereinafter DPIC]; BUREAU OF JUSTICE STATISTICS, U.S. DEP'T OF JUSTICE, STATE COURT ORGANIZATION (1998), available at http://www.ojp.usdoj.gov/bjs/pub/pdf/sco9807.pdf.

64 Jeffrey Fagan et al., *Capital Punishment and Capital Murder: Market Share and the Deterrent Effects of the Death Penalty*, 84 TEX. L. REV 1803 (2006) [hereinafter Fagan et al., *Capital Punishment and Capital Murder*].

65 DPIC, *supra* note 63.

66 *Id.*

67 PA. DEP'T OF CORRECTIONS, ANNUAL STATISTICAL REPORT 18 (1999), available at http://www.cor.state.pa.us/stats/lib/stats/ASR1999.pdf.

68 PA. DEP'T OF CORRECTIONS, ANNUAL STATISTICAL REPORT 19 (2000), available at http://www.cor.state.pa.us/stats/lib/stats/Annual%20Report%202000.pdf.

on February 29, 2004, compared to 635 on death row, and zero executions.[69] In South Carolina, 485 defendants have received LWOP sentences since 1996, compared to 27 executions.[70] One final illustration comes from Georgia. Georgia has sentenced 369 persons to death since passing its LWOP statute in 1993, while death sentences have declined from about ten per year to four during this time.[71] Georgia has executed 21 persons since passing its LWOP statute.[72] Overall, data from the National Judicial Reporting Program in 2002 shows that LWOP sentences were more than three times more frequent in murder cases than were death sentences, and nearly ten times more common than executions.[73]

Obviously, LWOP has incapacitative effects, as does execution, and the two are difficult to disentangle empirically. The 1978 National Research Council Panel on Research on Deterrence and Incapacitation noted the complex relationship between the two and the difficulty of separating the effects of each.[74] Using a lengthy time series, Professors Katz, Levitt and Shustarovich compared deterrence (executions per 1000 prisoners) with incapacitation and conclude that the death rate among prisoners, which they view as a proxy for prison conditions, has a significant deterrent effect on violent crime rates, but they find no robust evidence of a deterrent effect of capital punishment.[75] And in one study that does compete incarceration and deterrence, Mocan and Gittings report larger regression coefficients for incarceration (–.0354) than executions (–.006).[76] Mocan and

---

69 CAL. DEP'T OF CORRECTIONS, FACTS AND FIGURES (Third Quarter 2004), available at http://www.corr.ca.gov/DivisionsBoards/AOAP/FactFiguresArchive/FactsFiguresArchive.html. Fewer than 100 of the LWOP sentences were "Three Strikes Convictions." See FRANKLIN ZIMRING ET AL., PUNISHMENT AND DEMOCRACY: THREE STRIKES AND YOU'RE OUT IN CALIFORNIA (2001).

70 S.C. DEP'T OF CORRECTIONS, INMATE POPULATION STATISTICS AND TRENDS, SENTENCE LENGTH DISTRIBUTION FY-01-05 (2005), available at http://www.doc.sc.gov/PublicInformation/StatisticalReports/InmatePopulationStatsTrend/AsOfTrendSentenceLengthDistributionFY01-05.pdf. For sentence length distributions for 1996–2001, data are available from the author at http://www2.law.columbia.edu/fagan/researchdata/osjcl_deter/.

71 Associated Press, *Georgia: Number of Death Penalty Cases Decline*, Dec. 28, 2003, available at http://www.democracyinaction.org.dia/organizations/ncadp/news.jsp?key=374&t=.

72 GA. DEP'T OF CORRECTIONS, INMATE STATISTICAL PROFILE, available at http://www.dcor.state.ga.us/pdf/lwop04-10.pdf (last visited Oct. 21, 2004).

73 U.S. DEP'T. OF JUSTICE, BUREAU OF JUSTICE STATISTICS NATIONAL JUDICIAL REPORTING PROGRAM 2002, INTER-UNIVERSITY CONSORTIUM FOR POLITICAL SCIENCE AND SOCIAL RESEARCH, http://www.icpsr.com.

74 *See generally* Klein et al., *supra* note 12.

75 Lawrence Katz et al., *Prison Conditions, Capital Punishment, and Deterrence*, 5 AM. L. & ECON. REV., 318, 327 (2003) [hereinafter Katz et al., *Prison Conditions*].

76 Mocan & Gittings, *supra* note 10, at 464 tbl. 2 col. 1.

Gittings call no attention to this very interesting finding that competes well with execution as an explanation for the decline in murders. Few other studies in the new deterrence literature report incarceration effects, and when they do, the effects either compete with or overwhelm execution effects.

To claim that executions deter homicides when there may be equally strong simultaneous effects from incarceration—whether incapacitative or deterrent—introduces an omitted variable bias that potentially inflates the effects of execution. Indeed, with the exceptions noted above, most of the new deterrence studies simply ignore incarceration or understate its effects.[77] Incarceration effects argue against the *marginal* deterrent effects of execution threats. Felony murder offenders should be deterred both by the threat of prison and the threat of execution. But when both are included in multivariate models, there seems to be no greater marginal threat from execution than from a generalized effect from incarceration. Indeed, one sensitivity test that was not conducted by Mocan and Gittings is a model that includes incarceration but not execution.

Parsing the deterrent effects of incarceration from its incapacitative effects is a task for another article. But for this essay, it is important to note that high incarceration rates across most states are exerting a significant downward pressure on homicide rates.[78] Moreover, these rates are highest for violent crimes.[79] This is important for two reasons. First, most capital-eligible homicides are felony murders: homicides committed in the course of other crimes, specifically robbery and rape.[80] No offense category has grown faster in the run-up of incarceration than violent crimes.[81] Removing a segment of serious

---

77 For example, Shepherd's analysis of state-by-state "Deterrence Versus Brutalization" effects includes prison admissions in one of the estimating equations in her model of deterrence, but the effects are not reported. See Shepherd, *Deterrence Versus Brutalization*, *supra* note 46.

78 Prison sentences and prison populations have been increasing dramatically since 1978. See Alfred Blumstein & Allen J. Beck, *Population Growth in U.S. Prisons, 1980–1996*, 26 CRIME & JUST. 17 (1999). The largest segment of the prison population is inmates convicted of violent crimes. See PAIGE M. HARRISON & ALLEN J. BECK, BUREAU OF JUSTICE STATISTICS, U. S. DEP'T OF JUSTICE, PRISONERS IN 2004 (2005), available at http://www.ojp.usdoj.gov/bjs/pub/pdf/p04.pdf. At year end in 2004, there were 2.1 million persons incarcerated in state prisons, including an estimated 624,900 prisoners serving time for a violent offense, and the nationwide incarceration rate in state prisons was 486 per 100,000 population. See, e.g., MARK R. DUROSE & PATRICK A. LANGAN, BUREAU OF JUSTICE STATISTICS, U. S. DEP'T OF JUSTICE, FELONY SENTENCES IN STATE COURTS, 2002 (2005), available at http://www.ojp.usdoj.gov/bjs/pub/pdf/fssc02.pdf. In 2002, the average state prison sentence for a violent offense was eighty-four months, a rate that excludes life sentences. The average time served was 5.4 years. *Id.*

79 See Durose & Langan, *supra* note 78.

80 See Fagan et al., *Capital Punishment and Capital Murder*, *supra* note 64.

81 See Durose & Langan, *supra* note 78.

offenders through incarceration inevitably will reduce the base rate of robbery and assault, and reduce the portion of such crimes that escalate to homicides. While Shepherd controls for the robbery rate in one of the new deterrence studies, she does not control for robbery incarcerations or any other incarceration category.[82] Second, the high rate of incarceration and the increasingly lengthy sentences imposed for violent offenses may leave little margin for additional deterrent effects from the threat of execution. Certainly, a robust test of deterrence, as well as a fully specified conceptual theory, would address the separate if not conditional effects of incarceration on murder rates. Unfortunately, the current crop of deterrence studies overlooks this question.

2. Policing and Deterrence

Deterrence theorists emphasize the importance of perceived punishment risk in dissuading would-be offenders from committing crimes. Such risks depend on the efficiency of the police in detecting wrongdoing and responding quickly and efficiently, or alternately, the risk of punishment after having been caught and prosecuted. Research both with offenders and general population samples suggests that (subjectively) perceived risk weighs heavily on the decisions of would-be offenders to engage in or avoid crime.[83] But only a small minority of the new deterrence studies include measures of risk of detection, especially as constructed through effective and efficient policing.

For example, Mocan and Gittings include "the subjective probabilities that potential offenders are apprehended, convicted, and executed" in their estimation models, but restrict their policing and conviction estimates to murders.[84] This is a fairly typical strategy in the few studies that do consider policing. Others focus on police expenditures,[85] or the number of police officers.[86] But with the exception of Katz and his colleagues, there is little attention to the contributions of policing to reductions or variations in homicide rates.

This is an error not just in understanding how crime rates vary, but also it mis-specifies the theoretical pathway and mediating effects of how policing affects deterrence and homicide. The locus of deterrent effects may reside either in the threat of execution or in the threat of apprehension and punishment. A century of deterrence theory and research shows that punishment risk outweighs punishment costs in a general deterrence heuristic,[87] sug-

---

82 Shepherd, *Deterrence Versus Brutalization*, *supra* note 46, at 225.

83 Daniel S. Nagin, *Criminal Deterrence Research at the Outset of the Twenty-First Century*, 23 CRIME & JUST. 1(1998).

84 Mocan & Gittings, *supra* note 10, at 457–58.

85 See Shepherd, *Murders of Passion*, *supra* note 15; Shepherd, *Deterrence Versus Brutalization*, *supra* note 46.

86 See, e.g., Dezhbakhsh et al., *supra* note 32.

87 Nagin, *supra* note 83.

gesting that the margin for deterrence from execution may be rather thin when compared to punishment risks that have a higher present-value to offenders. Clearance rates for murder are a simple metric for establishing these risks. Clearance rates usually are expressed as the percent of homicides that result in an arrest of a suspect leading to a prosecution. Although plea bargaining often reduces the conviction charge and punishment cost for the offense, homicide arrests are still quite likely to generate a sentence of some lengthy spell of incarceration, achieving either a deterrent or incapacitative effect, if not both. The question, then, is whether there is a marginal deterrent effect of execution.

The clearance rate for felonies that creates punishment risk also attenuates the supply of potential homicide offenders. The ability of local law enforcement to identify homicide offenders or high rate offenders generally will reduce their prevalence and in turn the risks of homicides, especially felony murders. Examining errors in capital sentences, Professor James Liebman and his colleagues showed that from 1976 to 1995 inefficient criminal justice systems seemed to overly rely on the death penalty to respond to homicides compared to jurisdictions with more efficient and effective policing regimes.[88] This signals that the death penalty was compensatory in these locales for poor policing. The court jurisdictions that used the death penalty more often were prone to higher rates of serious reversible error.[89]

Recent studies also show that the police have a prophylactic effect on crime.[90] This effect goes beyond simply the expenditure on policing or the number of police. Police efficiency and strategy exert strong influences on crime rates, including gun-related crimes that carry a special risk of escalating to lethality. For example, Professor Jacqueline Cohen's analysis of aggressive police interdiction strategies in Pittsburgh showed strong reductions in gun crimes and gun injuries.[91]

---

88 JAMES S. LIEBMAN ET AL., A BROKEN SYSTEM, PART II: WHY THERE IS SO MUCH ERROR IN CAPITAL CASES, AND WHAT CAN BE DONE ABOUT IT (2002), available at http://www2.law.columbia.edu/brokensystem2/report.pdf [hereinafter LIEBMAN ET AL., A BROKEN SYSTEM, PART II].

89 *Id.*

90 See, e.g., Hope Corman & H. Naci Mocan, *A Time-Series Analysis of Crime, Deterrence, and Drug Abuse in New York City*, 90 AM. ECON. REV. 584 (2000); Steven D. Levitt, *Using Electoral Cycles in Police Hiring to Estimate the Effect of Police on Crime*, 87 AM. ECON. REV. 270 (1997); Jeffrey Grogger, *Certainty vs. Severity of Punishment*, 29 ECON. INQUIRY 297 (1991); Jonathan Klick & Alexander Tabarrok, *Using Terror Alert Levels to Estimate the Effect of Police on Crime*, 48 J. L. & ECON. 267 (2005); Steven D. Levitt, *Understanding Why Crime Fell 1990s: Four Factors that Explain Decline and Six that Do Not*, 18 J. ECON. PERSP. 163 (2004).

91 Jacqueline Cohen & Jens Ludwig, *Policing Crime Guns*, in EVALUATING GUN POLICY: EFFECTS ON CRIME AND VIOLENCE 217 (Philip J. Cook & Jens Ludwig eds., 2003). *See generally* FAIRNESS AND EFFECTIVENESS IN POLICING: THE EVIDENCE (Wesley Skogan & Kathleen Frydl eds., 2004) (citing empirical evidence that specialized policing targeting specific crime problems is

Local police departments allocate and deploy their resources to reflect strategic analyses of crime problems and the tactics best suited to their control. These decisions, and policing effects generally, are not accurately captured through measures of police force size or police expenditures that are typically used in the new deterrence studies. In general, the inconsistent and atheoretical attention to policing as a competing source of deterrence or crime control is another form of omitted variable bias that weakens the claims of the new deterrence studies.

3. Co-Morbid Epidemics

Homicide was not the only epidemic social problem in the United States in the years following *Furman*. *Furman* was decided just as a five year epidemic of heroin use had begun to wane in the United States in the early 1970s,[92] an era when homicide rates also rose sharply across American cities.[93] The sharp rise in homicides was linked temporally and spatially to an epidemic of heroin use.[94] Over the next two decades, homicide rates rose and fell concurrently with other drug epidemics. Homicide rates spiked again from 1979 to 1981, concurrent with the emergence of street drug markets in major cities where

---

more effective than general reactive policing, and discounting evidence reporting that larger police forces are more effective at crime deterrence).

92 See DAVID F. MUSTO, THE AMERICAN DISEASE: ORIGINS OF NARCOTIC CONTROL (3d ed. 1987). *See generally* David F. Musto, *Perception and Regulation of Drug Use: The Rise and Fall of the Tide*, 123 ANNALS INTERNAL MED. 468 (1995).

93 See FRANKLIN ZIMRING & GORDON HAWKINS, CRIME IS NOT THE PROBLEM: LETHAL VIOLENCE IN AMERICA (1997); see also Alfred Blumstein & Richard Rosenfeld, *Explaining Recent Trends in U.S. Homicide Rates*, 88 J. CRIM. L. & CRIMINOLOGY 1175 (1998); Richard Rosenfeld, *Patterns in Adult Homicide: 1980–1995*, in THE CRIME DROP IN AMERICA 130 (Alfred Blumstein & Joel Wallman eds., 2000).

94 See LEON G. HUNT & CARL D. CHAMBERS, THE HEROIN EPIDEMICS: A STUDY OF HEROIN USE IN THE UNITED STATES, 1965–1975, 73–113 (1976); James A. Inciardi, *Heroin Use and Street Crime*, 25 CRIME & DELINQ. 335 (1979); D.J. Egan & D.O. Robinson, *Models of a Heroin Epidemic*, 136 AM. J. PSYCHIATRY 1162 (1979); Michael Agar & H.S. Reisenger, *A Heroin Epidemic at the Intersection of Histories: The 1960s Epidemic Among African Americans in Baltimore*, 21 MED. ANTHROPOL. 115 (2002).

powdered cocaine was openly sold.[95] Record homicide rates in American cities in the early 1990s coincided with the crack epidemic that lasted nearly a decade after 1986.[96]

The temporal and spatial dependence of murder and drugs is an epidemiological fact that deserves serious attention as a competing influence on the murder rate. One might see drug epidemics and murder as simply co-morbid problems that share common etiologies or that combine to weaken the resources needed to resist such social problems. Or, one might see them as causally related, in which case the rise and fall of one epidemic would predict concurrent or closely spaced changes in the other.[97] The latter view dominated criminological research through the 1990s. Through mechanisms that connect drug sales and gun violence, the crack epidemic exerted a strong push on murder rates and spread across American cities in a pattern similar to a contagious disease.[98]

---

95 See, e.g., Bruce D. Johnson et al., *Drug Abuse in the Inner City: Impact on Hard Drug Users and the Community*, in DRUGS AND CRIME 9 (Michael Tonry & James Q. Wilson eds., 1990); TERRY WILLIAMS, THE COCAINE KIDS (1989); Audio Tape: Lloyd Johnston et al., National Trends in Drug Use and Related Factors Among American High School Students and Young Adults, 1975–86 (1987) (DHS ADM 87–1535); LYNN ZIMMER, OPERATION PRESSURE POINT: THE DISRUPTION OF STREET-LEVEL DRUG TRADE ON NEW YORK's LOWER EAST SIDE (1987); Lynn Zimmer, *Proactive Policing Against Street-Level Drug Trafficking*, 9 AM. J. POLICE 43 (1990).

96 Eric Baumer et al., *Poverty, Crack, and Crime: A Cross-City Analysis*, 31 J. RES. CRIME & DELINQ. 311 (1994); Eric Baumer et al., *The Influence of Crack Cocaine on Robbery, Burglary and Homicide Rates: A Cross-City Longitudinal Analysis*, 35 J. RES. CRIME & DELINQ. 316 (1998); Jeff Grogger & Michael Willis, *The Emergence of Crack Cocaine and the Rise in Urban Crime Rates*, 82 REV. ECON. & STAT. 519, 526 (2000); Roland G. Fryer et al., *Measuring the Impact of Crack Cocaine* 1–65 (Nat'l Bureau of Econ. Research, Working Paper No. 11318, 2005), available at http://papers. nber.org/papers/w11318. pdf (last visited Mar. 13, 2006).

97 See, e.g., Jan M. Chaiken & Marcia R. Chaiken, *Drugs and Predatory Crime*, in DRUGS AND CRIME 203 (Michael Tonry & James Q. Wilson eds., 1990); ROBERT J. MACCOUN & PETER REUTER, DRUG WAR HERESIES: LEARNING FROM OTHER VICES, TIMES AND PLACES (2003).

98 See Alfred Blumstein, *Youth Violence, Guns, and the Illicit-Drug Industry*, 86 J. CRIM. L. & CRIMINOLOGY 10 (1995); Daniel Cork, *Examining Space-Time Interaction in City-Level Homicide Data: Crack Markets and the Diffusion of Guns Among Youth*, 15 J. QUANTITATIVE CRIMINOLOGY 379 (1999); see also Paul J. Goldstein et al., *Crack and Homicide in New York City, 1988: A Conceptually Based Event Analysis*, 16 CONTEMP. DRUG PROBS. 651 (1989) (showing that in 1988 in New York City, 85% of crack-related crimes were caused by the market culture associated with illicit crack sales, primarily territorial disputes between rival crack dealers); Roland G. Fryer et al., *supra* note 96. The Fryer crack index is specific to cocaine and specifically crack, and emphasizes homicide victimization and drug overdose deaths. However, since most drug-related violence, including homicide, is associated with drug trafficking, the index is of less utility in explaining long-term variation in drug market trends and their effects on homicides. See Jeffrey Fagan, *Intoxication and Aggression*, in DRUGS AND CRIME 241

The decline in homicides through the late 1990s and into the early part of this decade has been linked to the decline in the crack epidemics, specifically changes in street markets where drugs had been openly sold amidst much violence a decade earlier.[99] Drug sales declined in volume and moved indoors as demand shrunk and also as police focused on drug sales. Competition between sellers waned, reducing the incidence of disputes implicated in many murders during the height of the epidemic.[100]

None of the new deterrence studies consider the epidemics of drug use and related violence, especially murder. Perhaps the declines in drug markets were due to police efforts to deter drug selling through intensive drug enforcement and high volumes of drug arrests, or to sentencing laws that targeted drug sellers. But these direct or indirect effects of policing were also not given close attention. As in policing, the inattention to the effect of drug epidemics on violence is an omission that challenges, if not impeaches, the conclusions of the new deterrence studies of a singular effect of execution on homicide.

4. Are All Homicides Deterrable?

Most of the new deterrence studies regard homicide as a homogeneous criminal behavior. With one exception, these studies make no distinctions between homicides committed in varying contexts or with different motivations. The assumption is that all are equally deterrable. This logic is challenged in at least two different ways. First, several decades of empirical research on homicide that cut across the social sciences suggests that homicides are variably rational; some, such as crimes of jealousy or unplanned and highly contingent events, are simply poor candidates for deterrence. Second, the law makes these distinctions explicit in felony murder rules, and carves out a particular set of homicides—such as homicides committed in the course of other crimes—as eligible for capital punishment. The most accurate test of the underlying rationale for deterrence would be the sensitivity of these homicides to the threat of execution.

(Michael Tonry & James Q. Wilson eds., 1990). *See generally* U.S. SENTENCING COMMISSION, *Chapter 5: Cocaine and Crime*, in REPORT ON COCAINE AND FEDERAL SENTENCING POLICY, available at http://www.ussc.gov/crack/chap5.htm (last visited Mar. 22, 2006).

99 See, e.g., Richard Curtis, *The Improbable Transformation of Inner-City Neighborhoods: Crime, Violence, Drugs and Youth in the 1990s*, 88 J. CRIM. L. & CRIMINOLOGY 1233 (1998).

100 *Id.* See also NAT'L INSTITUTE OF JUSTICE, 1998 ANNUAL REPORT ON COCAINE USE AMONG ARRESTEES, NCJ 175657, available at http://www.ncjrs.gov/pdffiles1/175657.txt (last visited Mar. 16, 2006).

Only one among the new studies, by Professor Joanna Shepherd,[101] offers estimates of the deterrent effects of execution on specific categories of homicide.[102] Shepherd reports that executions deter all types of murder, including domestic or marital homicides, or other "crimes of passion" that so often are considered to be irrational and spontaneous acts that are beyond the rational reach of execution threats.[103]

The high rate of murder-suicides in domestic homicides is one clue to the irrationality if not mental illness of this subset of murderers, limiting the prospects for deterrence.[104] The gradient of uncontrolled rage that precedes many domestic homicides also suggests the inelasticity of motivation and arousal among men who kill or nearly kill their intimate partners.[105] The steady decline over nearly 30 years in "domestic" or intimate partner homicides[106] suggests a secular trend that is insensitive to fluctuations in the number of executions since capital punishment was reinstated following *Gregg*.

---

101 Shepherd, *Murders of Passion*, *supra* note 15.

102 Information about the circumstances of events is provided by the Federal Bureau of Investigation in the Supplemental Homicide Reports, a data file of homicide records that includes information on victims, offenders (where known via arrest), and the circumstances of the homicide event. See BUREAU OF JUSTICE STATISTICS, U.S. DEP'T OF JUSTICE, HOMICIDE TRENDS IN THE U.S., available at http://www.ojp.usdoj.gov/bjs/homicide/homtrnd.htm#contents (last visited Sept. 1, 2006); JAMES A. FOX, INTER-UNIVERSITY CONSORTIUM FOR POLITICAL SCIENCE AND SOCIAL RESEARCH, UNIFORM CRIME REPORTS [UNITED STATES]: SUPPLEMENTARY HOMICIDE REPORTS, 1976–2003 (2005), available at http://webapp.icpsr.umich.edu/cocoon/ICPSR-STUDY/04351.xml.

103 Shepherd, *Murders of Passion*, *supra* note 15.

104 See, e.g., Jacquelyn C. Campbell et al., *Risk Assessment for Intimate Partner Homicide*, in CLINICAL ASSESSMENT OF DANGEROUSNESS: EMPIRICAL CONTRIBUTIONS 136 (Georges-Franck Pinard & Linda Pagani eds., 2001); Lauren Bennett et al., *Risk Assessment Among Batterers Arrested for Domestic Assault: The Salience of Psychological Abuse*, 6 VIOLENCE AGAINST WOMEN 1190 (2000); Arlene N. Weisz et al., *Assessing the Risk of Severe Domestic Violence: The Importance of Survivors' Predictions*, 15 J. INTERPERSONAL VIOLENCE 75 (2000).

105 See KENNETH POLK, WHEN MEN KILL: SCENARIOS OF MASCULINE VIOLENCE (1994); see also Jeffrey Fagan & Angela Browne, *Violence toward Spouses and Intimates: Physical Aggression between Men and Women in Intimate Relationships*, in 3 UNDERSTANDING AND PREVENTING VIOLENCE 115 (Albert J. Reiss, Jr., & Jeffrey A. Roth eds., 1994); Angela Browne et al., *Homicide Between Intimate Partners*, in HOMICIDE: A SOURCEBOOK OF SOCIAL RESEARCH 149 (M. Dwayne Smith & Margaret A. Zahn eds., 1999).

106 See, e.g., Laura Dugan et al., *Explaining the Decline in Intimate Partner Homicide: The Effects of Changing Domesticity, Women's Status, and Domestic Violence Resources*, 3 HOMICIDE STUD. 187 (1999) (attributing the two-decades-long decline in the intimate partner homicide rate in the United States as a function of three factors that reduce exposure to violent relationships: shifts in marriage, di-

The literature on homicide events shows that many homicide offenders are simply unresponsive to punishment threats.[107] Professor Jack Katz offers an analysis of homicide events and offenders that portrays some as "stone cold killers" while others simply take pleasure from killing, even as they remain indifferent to punishment threats or even death by retaliation in the moment of the homicide.[108] Using a social interactionist framework, several sociologists conclude that most homicide events are largely unplanned products of complicated social interactions—disputes that escalate from minor conflicts into threatening conflicts where the fear of injury or death motivates lethally violent responses to even minor provocations.[109] Deanna Wilkinson and I suggest that the presence of firearms short circuits the decision stages where the perceived cost of not killing a possibly armed opponent is one's own death from the opponent's firearm.[110] There is no planning in these events; the emotional arousal in the moment trumps all restraint and compromises the type of reasoning and calculation necessary for deterrence.[111]

The use of total homicides has always been an aggregation error in the deterrence debate in the United States.[112] Under common law, only the top grade of murder was ever

---

vorce, and other factors associated with declining domesticity; the improved economic status of women; and increases in the availability of domestic violence services).

107 See JACK KATZ, SEDUCTIONS OF CRIME: THE MORAL AND SENSUAL ATTRACTIONS OF DOING EVIL (1988) [hereinafter KATZ, SEDUCTIONS OF CRIME] (describing "stone cold killers" who are insensitive to punishment threats, and whose homicides can only be described as the pursuit of domination and pleasure); see also NATHANIEL J. PALLONE & JAMES J. HENNESSY, TINDER-BOX CRIMINAL AGGRESSION: NEUROPSYCHOLOGY, DEMOGRAPHY, PHENOMENOLOGY (1996).

108 KATZ, SEDUCTIONS OF CRIME, *supra* note 107.

109 See Richard B. Felson & Henry J. Steadman, *Situational Factors in Disputes Leading to Criminal Violence*, 21 CRIMINOLOGY 59, 59–60 (1983); David F. Luckenbill, *Criminal Homicide as a Situated Transaction*, 25 SOC. PROBS. 176 (1977); Richard B. Felson, *Impression Management and the Escalation of Aggression and Violence*, 45 SOCIAL PSYCHOLOGY Q. 245 (1982); David F. Luckenbill & Daniel P. Doyle, *Structural Position and Violence: Developing a Cultural Explanation*, 27 CRIMINOLOGY 422, 422–23 (1989); WILLIAM OLIVER, THE VIOLENT SOCIAL WORLD OF BLACK MEN 138–40 (1994).

110 Deanna L. Wilkinson & Jeffrey Fagan, *A Theory of Violent Events*, in THE PROCESS AND STRUCTURE OF CRIME: CRIMINAL EVENTS AND CRIME ANALYSIS 169 (Robert F. Meier & Leslie Kennedy eds., 2001). See also DEANNA L. WILKINSON, GUNS, VIOLENCE, AND IDENTITY AMONG AFRICAN AMERICAN AND LATINO YOUTH (2004); Jeffrey Fagan & Deanna L. Wilkinson, *Guns, Youth Violence, and Social Identity in Inner Cities*, in YOUTH VIOLENCE 105 (Michael Tonry & M.H. Moore eds., 1998) [hereinafter Fagan & Wilkinson, *Guns, Youth Violence*].

111 PALLONE & HENNESSY, *supra* note 107.

112 See THORSTEN SELLIN, THE DEATH PENALTY: A REPORT FOR THE MODEL PENAL CODE PROJECT OF THE AMERICAN LAW INSTITUTE (1959). Sellin's classic studies of more

eligible for the death penalty. However, the traditional legal framework on the criteria that made criminal homicide potentially capital was far from clear until the U.S. Supreme Court imposed minimum constitutional standards for death eligibility in *Gregg v. Georgia* and its companion 1976 cases.[113] Shepherd's was one of the few projects to attempt to disaggregate homicides into separate categories to assess their deterability. However, she did not use legally relevant categories; her partitioning of the data was not indexed to statute, but to a set of categories descriptive of "different types of murders"[114] that were defined neither by statute nor, with the exception of "crimes of passion," by theory. More importantly, none of these categories were narrowed according to statutory criteria that bound the circumstances and conditions that qualify a murder as "capital."[115]

In fact, when one narrows the search for deterrence by focusing not on general homicide trends and rates, but on the subset of homicides that are eligible for the death penalty, any evidence of deterrence disappears. If execution risk is the core element in deterrence, these types of homicides should provide a more sensitive test than the overall homicide rate index for detecting a deterrent effect from execution.[116] After all, felony murder carries strict liability, a consequence of the intent-based retributivism that guides most of the capital murder statutes in effect in 38 states today.[117]

However, when partitioned according to these legal categories, there seems to be no evidence of deterrence based on lagged executions. Analyses of homicide trends from 1976 to 2003 in death penalty states, using a variety of econometric models, show that there is no significant effect of executions on the rate of capital-eligible murders.[118] One deterrence story is that the threat of execution should affect the subset of homicides eligible for executions more than other homicides. Accordingly, the "market share" of homicides that are capital-eligible should decline as the overall homicide rate declines, while non-capital homicides should remain unaffected by the threat of execution. But, together with colleagues Franklin Zimring and Amanda Geller, I find just the opposite: the market share

---

than 50 years ago included particularly high risk categories of homicides, such as killings of police officers and prison guards.

113 *Gregg v. Georgia*, 428 U.S. 153 (1976).

114 Shepherd, *Murders of Passion*, *supra* note 15, at 292 (sorting murders into categories of victim-offender relationship including intimates, acquaintances, and strangers, crime-of-passion murders and murders committed during other felonies, and murders of African-American and white people).

115 For the distinction between felony murder and capital murder, see 40A AM. JUR. 2D *Homicide* § 551 (2006).

116 See, e.g., Franklin Zimring & Gordon Hawkins, *Deterrence and Marginal Groups*, 5 J. RES. CRIME & DELINQ. 100 (1968).

117 Kevin Cole, *Killings During Crime: Toward a Discriminating Theory of Strict Liability*, 28 AM. CRIM. L. REV. 73 (1990).

118 Fagan et al., *Capital Punishment and Capital Murder*, *supra* note 63.

is rising, since capital-eligible homicides remain stable over time while the rate of other homicides declines. This also is true when we isolate county-level trends in Texas, the state that has carried out more than one third of all executions in the United States since *Gregg*.[119] This is the opposite of what would be predicted from economic theories of death penalty deterrence.

If capital eligible homicides are insensitive to deterrent threats, even as other homicides are declining, then the prospects for a more generalized pattern of deterrence of homicide are not good. As non-capital eligible homicides decrease in number, it would be logical that police and prosecutors would devote more attention to the smaller number of capital-eligible cases. Greater resources would be available for police investigations and clearance rates should improve. Prosecutors also would have more time and greater resources to devote to these cases, increasing the likelihood of lengthy prison sentences, if not capital sentences. Yet even this concentration of criminal justice resources on capital-eligible cases has not leveraged the rate of capital-eligible homicides.

C. Measurement and Specification Errors

Three types of measurement error undermine the claims of the new deterrence studies: large amounts of missing data on key indices of murder, over-inclusion of persons who are eligible for capital punishment in the estimates of deterrence, and arbitrary and artifactual temporal truncation in the panel designs. Each source of error independently leads to inflated estimates of deterrence.

1. Missing Data

To measure both homicides and homicide arrests, most of the new deterrence studies rely on data published by the Federal Bureau of Investigation through its Uniform Crime Reporting (UCR) program.[120] However, the UCR data have large amounts of missing data from critical states. For example, data on homicide and robbery arrests in Florida are missing for many local police departments in 1988 and 1989 and again in 1997 through 2002.[121] A more recent analysis by Professors Michael Maltz and Harald Weiss of monthly data on crimes reported to the police shows that many years have only partial data: reports

---

119 *Id.*

120 FED. BUREAU OF INVESTIGATION, UNIFORM CRIME REPORTS DEP'T OF JUSTICE, UNIFORM CRIME REPORTS FOR THE UNITED STATES: CRIME IN THE UNITED STATES, 1973–2003, available at http://bjsdata.ojp.usdoj.gov/dataonline/(last visited Aug. 18, 2006).

121 See, e.g., INTER-UNIVERSITY CONSORTIUM FOR POLITICAL SCIENCE AND SOCIAL RESEARCH, UNIFORM CRIME REPORTING PROGRAM DATA [UNITED STATES]: OFFENSES KNOWN AND CLEARANCES BY ARREST (1999) available at http://www.icpsr.

in fewer than the full twelve months of the calendar year.[122] For example, Florida reported homicides to the UCR system for no months in 1988, five months in 1989, and no more than two months in 1997 through 1999.[123] Yet Florida is one of the nation's most active death penalty states, with fifty-seven executions from *Gregg* through 2003, so the importance of its omission and the potential bias in estimating the deterrent effects of execution due to incomplete data is obvious. In general, non-reporting by police agencies is a recurring problem in the UCR program. For example, from 1992–1994, 3516 of the 18,413 (19%) agencies participating in the UCR system made no reports at all to the UCR program.[124] According to Professor Michael Maltz, the non-reporting agencies included the primary police agencies in three counties and cities with populations greater than 100,000, and also the primary agencies in 200 cities with populations greater than 10,000. By 1995, the percent of the U.S. population covered by agencies reporting crimes to the UCR system declined from nearly 100% in 1980 to less than 90%.[125] By 1997, the percent of the U.S. population covered by agencies reporting UCR arrest records had declined from 95% in 1977 to 73%.[126]

The new deterrence studies are generally silent on the patterns of missing data and offer no adjustments that might compensate the biases from excluding key states and years. When not silent, the adjustments for missing data are often puzzling, but more worrisome is their potential for introducing bias. In one study, Professor Shepherd takes heart in the fact that over 90% of the homicides are reported by the FBI, ignoring the weighting and distribution of the missing homicide statistics. Instead, she simply dropped those data points "so that the missing data do not bias my results."[127] Quite the contrary, simply leaving out these state-months raises doubts about the accuracy and absence of bias in her results. The 10% of the population that is not included in the UCR's crime reports is not normally distributed, nor is the 27% that is not included in the arrest statistics. The bias

---

umich.edu/cgi-bin/bob/newark?study=3158&path=NACJD (last visited July 21, 2006). Data for each state and year are available at http://www.icpsr.umich.edu/NACJD/ucr.html (last visited July 21, 2006).

122 MICHAEL D. MALTZ & HARALD E. WEISS, CREATING A UCR UTILITY: FINAL REPORT TO THE NATIONAL INSTITUTE OF JUSTICE (2006), available at http://www.ncjrs.gov/pdffiles1/nij/grants/215341.pdf.

123 *Id.* Data for Florida and all other states from 1960–2002 are available in spreadsheets from http://sociology.osu.edu/people/mdm/UCR_Utility.zip.

124 See MICHAEL MALTZ, BUREAU OF JUSTICE STATISTICS, U.S. DEP'T OF JUSTICE, BRIDGING GAPS IN POLICE CRIME DATA (1999), available at http://www.ojp.usdoj.gov/bjs/pub/pdf/bgpcd.pdf, at 9 tbl.1 and accompanying text. The percent of the population covered by police agencies reporting arrests statistics declined from 95% in 1977 to 73% by 1997. *Id.* at fig. 10.

125 *Id.* at fig. 3.

126 *Id.* at fig. 10.

127 Shepherd, *Murders of Passion*, *supra* note 15, at 304.

from ignoring the processes generating such large amounts of missing data is potentially quite large.

Even within states, the omission of these key agencies and years in places like Florida introduces a selection bias that is likely to distort both the regression coefficients and the standard errors. Professor Jon Sorenson showed an undercounting of 137 homicides in a two year span from 1996 to 1997 by Cloninger and Marchesini[128] in their analysis of the impacts on homicide of the short moratorium on executions in Texas in the mid-1990s.[129] Similarly, Mocan and Gittings use a substitution algorithm to replace cases where division by zero (in computing executions per lagged death sentence) with .99, a decision that increases the size of the deterrence coefficient by approximating a value of one rather than a value of zero.[130] In Section IV, I show that when I run the Mocan and Gittings regression models correcting this coding decision, the deterrence variable is no longer statistically significant.[131]

The new deterrence studies also fail to address the missing data problems or investigate alternate data sources that might fill in important gaps in annual homicide rates. One such data set is available from the mortality and morbidity files of the National Center for Health Statistics (NCHS).[132] Information on all deaths classified as homicides by local coroners or medical examiners are compiled by NCHS and reported annually. The data are available for counties as well as states, and have been used in research on capital punish-

---

128 Cloninger & Marchesini, *supra* note 44.

129 Jon Sorensen et al., *Capital Punishment and Deterrence: Examining the Effect of Executions on Murder in Texas*, 45 CRIME & DELINQ. 481 (1999) (finding no evidence of deterrence resulting from capital punishment using Texas execution and murder rate data from 1984 through 1997); see also JON SORENSON & ROCKY LEANN PILGRIM, LETHAL INJECTION: CAPITAL PUNISHMENT IN TEXAS DURING THE MODERN ERA (2006) (re-analyzing claim that the moratorium resulted in an increase in homicides).

130 Mocan & Gittings, *supra* note 10. See also Donohue & Wolfers, *Uses and Abuses*, *supra* note 25.

131 *See infra* Part IV. A., tbl. 1; see also Donohue & Wolfers, *Uses and Abuses*, *supra* note 25.

132 State homicide and victimization data, including by race, are from the Vital Statistics of the United States or other data compilations generated by the Centers for Disease Control and Prevention National Center for Health Statistics. Data for 1973–1992 are from Vital Statistics of the United States, Mortality Detail Files, 1968–1992, Inter-University Consortium for Political Science and Social Research, Study No. 7632, 6798. Data for 1993–1998 are from Centers for Disease Control and Prevention National Center for Health Statistics, Compressed Mortality File, 1989–98 CD-ROM Series 20, No. 2C ASCII Version. Data after 1998 are from CDC Wonder, the Centers for Disease Control data extraction engine at http://wonder.cdc.gov. Through 1992, the relevant data sources list homicide victims by State of death. After 1993, the relevant data source lists homicide victims by state of residence. Data for 2001 excludes all victims from the events of September 11, 2001.

ment to develop a metric of the use of the death penalty relative to local homicide rates.[133] The extent of the missing data bias is evident when we substitute a complete record of homicides in regression models estimating the deterrent effects of capital punishment. For example, when the complete NCHS homicide victimization data set is substituted for the incomplete FBI homicide data in the Mocan and Gittings data set, regression model results change dramatically and the magnitude of a putative deterrent effect is significantly reduced.[134]

2. Deterring Which Murders?

Most of the new deterrence studies use global measures of murder that include persons or types of murders that are ineligible for execution. For example, global measures of homicide offenses include murders committed by persons whose ages are below the threshold of eligibility for capital punishment in most death penalty states. Since *Gregg*, only eleven persons below the age of sixteen at the time of their crime were sentenced to death, and none were executed.[135] Moreover, the practice was barred by the 1988 U.S. Supreme Court decision in Thompson v. Oklahoma[136] exempting juveniles below the age of sixteen from capital punishment. Yet despite the exclusion (at first by socio-legal norm and later by law) of youths below the age of sixteen from capital punishment, the new deterrence studies include all homicides in their estimates. Yet between 1976 and 2003, 8312 of the 339,187 homicides since *Gregg* (where the offender's age is known) were committed by persons below the age of sixteen.[137] In Texas, where more than one in three executions in the U.S. have taken place of the homicides (of the 36,630 where information is available on the offender's age) during these years were committed by persons below the age of sixteen.

---

133 John Blume & Theodore Eisenberg, *Judicial Politics, Death Penalty Appeals, and Case Selection: An Empirical Study*, 72 S. CAL. L. REV. 465 (1999); LIEBMAN ET AL., A BROKEN SYSTEM, PART II, *supra* note 88.

134 *See infra* Part IV. & tbl. 1.

135 VICTOR STREIB, THE JUVENILE DEATH PENALTY TODAY: DEATH SENTENCES AND EXECUTIONS FOR JUVENILE CRIMES, JANUARY 1, 1973—FEBRUARY 28, 2005 (2005), available at http://www.law.onu.edu/faculty/streib/documents/juvdeath.pdf.

136 487 U.S. 815 (1988) (plurality opinion).

137 See INTER-UNIVERSITY CONSORTIUM FOR POLITICAL SCIENCE AND SOCIAL RESEARCH, UNIFORM CRIME REPORTING PROGRAM DATA [UNITED STATES]: SUPPLEMENTARY HOMICIDE REPORTS, 1976–2003, available at http://webapp.icpsr.umich.edu/cocoon/ICPSR-STUDY/04351.xml (last visited Dec. 15, 2005). The Supplementary Homicide Reports are filtered to exclude the deaths in New York associated with the attacks of September 11, 2001, but include those associated with the Oklahoma City bombing of April 19, 1995.

During the years of the highest homicide rates in the United States, juveniles were the fastest growing group of homicide offenders from 1985 through 1993.[138]

The extent of potential bias depends on several factors. If the number of juvenile homicide offenders is small and stable over time, then this poses little threat. From 1976–2003, among homicides where the offender's age was known, a small subset of homicides (2.6%) were committed by persons under the age of sixteen.[139] But offender age is unknown in about one in three cases in this interval,[140] and there is no reliable way to estimate the age distribution of offenders in unknown cases. Yet, assuming that the age distribution of the unknown cases approximates the age distribution of the known cases, there may be no reason to suspect that the parameter estimates of deterrence are inflated due to the inclusion of murders by very young offenders in the homicide rate. Whatever noise these cases introduce into the econometric models is negligible and unlikely to be correlated with any of the predictors. But this is obvious neither empirically nor theoretically, especially since homicides by and of adolescents increased more rapidly than every other category of homicides for nearly a decade beginning in 1985.[141]

The instability over time in the number of homicides committed by persons below sixteen, and also instability over time in the number of cases where the offender age is unknown, create measurement problems that invalidate the invariance assumptions needed to ignore such trends. If these two parameters are fluctuating over time, and their correlation with other predictors is changing simultaneously, then we have to ask additional questions to assess whether these shifts are inconsequential in their effects on the estimates of the homicide rates.[142]

First, is the timing of the fluctuations related to the peaks and valleys in the homicide rate, and second, is the timing of these changes correlated with any of the control variables that also are predictors of homicide? For example, if the number of homicide offenders

---

138 Philip J. Cook & John H. Laub, *The Unprecedented Epidemic of Youth Violence*, in 24 CRIME AND JUSTICE: A REVIEW OF RESEARCH 27 (Michael Tonry & Mark H. Moore eds., 1998).

139 Fagan et al., *Capital Punishment and Capital Murder*, *supra* note 64, at tbl.1.

140 *Id.*

141 Cook & Laub, *supra* note 138.

142 For example, these correlates were changing simultaneously with the changes in homicide rates by adolescents. From 1985–1992, the percentage of homicides committed by firearm rose more quickly among adolescents than other population groups. So too did the demography of homicide: the concentration of perpetrators and victims among African Americans rose steadily throughout this period. *Id.* See also Lois A. Fingerhut et al., *Firearm and Nonfirearm Homicide Among Persons 15 Through 19 Years of Age: Differences by Level of Urbanization*, United States, 1979 Through 1989. 267 J. AM. MED. ASS'N 3048 (1992); Lois A. Fingerhut et al., *Firearm Homicide Among Black Teenage Males in Metropolitan Counties: Comparison of Death Rates in Two Periods, 1983 Through 1985 and 1987 Through 1989*, 267 J. AM. MED. ASS'N 3054 (1992).

below sixteen rises during periods of intense drug activity and increases in the violence associated with drug markets, then the error terms in the homicide estimates and the predictors may be correlated, biasing the standard errors and distorting the significance of the estimates of the size of a putative deterrent effect of execution. At the least, the timing and magnitude of increases in the youth homicide rate and increases in the number of offenders whose ages are unknown should raise cautions in interpreting the magnitude of deterrent effects in the types of panel series econometrics that populate the new deterrence studies.

3. Early Cutoffs in Panel Designs

A third concern is the artifactual truncation of observations that excludes data points where execution and homicide show no relationship. What would happen if there were five to eight more years added to these panels, years when homicide rates were stable while executions were sharply declining? That is the case in the new deterrence studies, and the result is that the current estimates suffer from period effects that produce artifactual and elevated estimates of deterrence.

Many of the studies include data from 1977 through 1996[143], 1997[144], or 1999.[145] Only one panel study extended the observational window through 2000.[146] But the pattern of executions and homicides in the five years following these studies suggests that murder was insensitive to the levels of execution in this interval: executions declined nationwide from ninety-eight in 1999 to fifty-nine in 2004, but the murder rate remained nearly stable, varying between 5.5 and 5.6 per 100,000 population. Perhaps there were changes in the predictors of homicide in that period that helped stabilize the murder rate, such as shifts in demography, incarceration patterns, drug epidemics, or other factors such as the robbery rate that influences the crimes that typically lead to capital-eligible felony murders. But there is no reason to believe that homicide rates had become insensitive to the pace of change in these externalities. Nor did these factors decline at a rate greater than the 40% decline in executions. If homicides were sensitive to executions, we would expect an uptick in the homicide rate as executions declined. But this distinctive footprint of deterrence is not evident in the patterns of murder through 2004, which remained nearly flat across the nation since 1999.

---

143 Shepherd, *Deterrence Versus Brutalization*, *supra* note 46.

144 See, e.g., Mocan & Gittings, *supra* note 10; Paul R. Zimmerman, *State Executions, Deterrence, and the Incidence of Murder*, 7 J. APPLIED ECON. 163 (2004); James A. Yunker, *A New Statistical Analysis of Capital Punishment Incorporating U.S. Postmoratorium Data*, 82 SOC. SCI. Q. 297 (2001).

145 Shepherd, *Murders of Passion*, *supra* note 15.

146 Zimmerman, *supra* note 144.

The flat pattern of homicides and executions since 1999 is likely to influence both the regression coefficient for any of the measures of execution-based deterrence, as well as the standard errors of the estimates. Whatever the form of the model before 2000, it is now different. Throughout the late 1990s, as executions increased while homicides declined, there was nearly a linear relationship between execution and murder. But the addition of five more years with a different pattern of executions and homicides, where the relationship is no longer tightly defined, makes the earlier model at a minimum less accurate because the overall fit of the trend line is no longer comfortable. In other words, the shape of the curve is now different, and so too should be the functional form of the equation that predicts it.

4. Computation and Model Specification Errors

Other computational and model specification errors have been noted in two articles by Professors John Donohue and Justin Wolfers,[147] including conceptual and measurement errors in the selection of instrumental variables by Dezhbakhsh et al.[148] Instrumental variables should be correlated with the predictor—in this case, executions—but not with the dependent variable murders. This technique allows analysts to conduct quasi-experiments that simulate the conditions of true experiments. Dezhbakhsh and colleagues use instruments that are in all likelihood correlated with executions: prison admissions, Republican voters, and police payrolls. It is hard to imagine that the same social and political dynamics, including higher crime rates, that contribute to higher prison admissions do not also contribute to harsher criminal justice policies including the aggressive application of the death penalty. Indeed, Professor Liebman and his colleagues show that these measures—political dynamics, punitive criminal justice policies, high murder rates, and aggressive use of the death penalty—are correlated with errors in death sentences.[149]

When Donohue and Wolfers make minor adjustments to avoid the confounding of the instruments with the other design elements, the estimates of deterrence become very unstable and range so widely (from 429 lives saved per execution to 86 lives lost) as to become meaningless.[150] They also show, as I do in Section IV of this article, that when computational errors by Mocan and Gittings are corrected, their estimates are no longer statistically significant. Overall, these types of computational errors lead to biased if not

---

147 Donohue & Wolfers, *Uses and Abuses*, *supra* note 25; John Donohue & Justin Wolfers, *The Death Penalty: No Evidence for Deterrence*, THE ECONOMIST's VOICE 1 (2006), available at http://bpp.wharton.upenn.edu/jwolfers/Press/DeathPenalty(BEPress).pdf [hereinafter Donohue & Wolfers, *The Death Penalty*].

148 Dezhbakhsh et al., *supra* note 32.

149 LIEBMAN ET AL., A BROKEN SYSTEM, PART II, *supra* note 88.

150 Donohue & Wolfers, *The Death Penalty*, *supra* note 147, at 3.

inaccurate estimates. The biases affect both the size of the regression coefficients and the standard errors. Both biases suggest that the published estimates are unacceptably sensitive to even minor modifications in measurement and, as we see below, estimation techniques. This is the opposite of robustness, and shows the risks of a utilitarian approach to vetting claims of deterrence.

D. Estimation Techniques

The new deterrence studies share a common econometric language and preferences for analytic strategies. All the studies use panel data examining murder rates over time within states or counties over a number of years. The general analytic form is a regression equation where the murder rate in each state and year in the time series (or panel) is the dependent variable, and the predictors are a linear combination of factors including the presence of a death penalty law in a given state, the predictability of execution given a death sentence in some previous era, state effects that account for differences between the states, and year effects that account for national time trends that affect the states. Most studies estimate models with states as the unit of analysis, while others include models where county murder rates are predicted from a combination of state-and county-level predictors.[151]

As discussed earlier, most designs include statistical controls or covariates that represent factors within states or counties that may affect both the homicide rate including demographic and socio-economic conditions, law enforcement indicia and political forces that may encourage use of the death penalty. But these factors also influence the presence and use of the death penalty, introducing an analytic confound that can bias results and give misleading and inflated estimates of deterrence.[152] To avoid this, and to approximate an experiment where experiments are not possible, some studies use instrumental variables designs, where variables are included that might affect the use of the death penalty but not necessarily murder.[153] These studies assume that this strategy can produce accurate

---

151 See, e.g., Dezhbakhsh et al., *supra* note 32.

152 For a discussion of how this endogeneity problem affects estimates of deterrence, see Richard A. Berk, *Knowing When to Fold 'Em: An Essay on Evaluating the Impact of CEASEFIRE, COMPSTAT, and EXILE*, 4 CRIMINOLOGY & PUB. POL'Y 451 (2005).

153 Instrumental variables or instruments are necessary when the predictors or independent variables are correlated with the error terms of the dependent variable. A valid instrument is a variable that would be correlated with the explanatory variable (in this case, executions or the presence of a death statute) and is uncorrelated with the error term of the dependent variable, or the murder rates. See, e.g., Dezhbakhsh et al., *supra* note 32 (using several instruments including prison admissions, police payrolls, judicial expenditures, and the statewide Republican vote). Misspecification of instruments can produce misleading results by introducing factors that might be correlated not just with the execution rate, but also with the error term in the crime rate. Donohue and Wolfers point out that Republican voters are more likely to

and unbiased results, however, we saw earlier that measurement and model specification errors can produce misleading, if not inaccurate, results regardless of how sound the instruments may be.[154]

Put that aside for the moment, and consider the analytic strategy on its own terms. Two connected assumptions in this strategy may undermine the stability and accuracy of the claims of the new deterrence studies. First, the state-fixed effects strategy assumes that any variance that is not accounted for by the covariates remains stable over time. In other words, state-or county-level factors that might produce initial differences are assumed to be invariant. This is probably incorrect, especially for longer time periods: the assumption that the states or counties are invariant with respect to stability in these exogenous factors places a huge burden on the covariates to do all the work in accounting for meaningful change within the states over time. Accordingly, the assumption of stability is only as good as the selection of the covariates. Earlier, I discussed limitations and errors in these predictors and covariates that are likely to produce biased and inaccurate estimates. So, analytic strategies that rely on the assumptions of stability (or the absence of cross-sectional heteroskedacity) in the unmeasured variance in the predictors are quite risky and probably wrong.

Second, using fixed effects for years treats each year as a separate experimental period that is independent from the previous year's outcomes. The year-fixed effects may account for national trends over time, but it ignores the effects of time within states. In effect, this approach to understanding time in panel data ignores the fact that murder rates within states vary through time, and that murder rates within states or counties are serially correlated over time. This is the problem of autoregression, or serial correlation.[155] Autoregression is the tendency of trends in longitudinal or time series data to be heavily influenced by the trends in preceding years.[156] In other words, the best predictor of what the murder rate will be next year is what it was last year. Statistically and conceptually, it is unlikely that effects of extremely rare events, such as executions, can impact trends that are

---

elect legislators who will pass tough-on-crime measures such as mandatory minimum sentences, which would also affect the murder rate. See Donohue & Wolfers, *The Death Penalty*, *supra* note 147, at 3. In classic experimental terms, this is an endogeneity problem, where the "treatment" condition (in this case, executions) is correlated with other predictors (Republican votes) of the dependent variables (murders). See, e.g., PAUL ROSENBAUM, OBSERVATIONAL STUDIES (2d ed. 2002).

154 See discussion *supra* Parts III. C. 1–3.

155 County murder rates are also spatially correlated. The murder rates in a particular county, may reflect processes that are taking place in the adjacent counties, such that they are simply picking up the effects of causal factors operating nearby but not necessarily within the county itself. See SPATIAL STATISTICS: METHODOLOGICAL ASPECTS AND APPLICATIONS (Marc Moore ed., 2001).

156 See, e.g., WILLIAM GREENE, ECONOMETRIC ANALYSIS (5th ed. 2003).

so heavily influenced by their own history.[157] The problem is compounded when there are patterns of missing observations in time series models when the data evidence autoregressive structures.[158] The problem is compounded again when there is serial correlation in the treatment variable, as is the case when estimating the effects of the presence of a death penalty statute, which nearly always is constantly present from year to year once a valid statute passes and goes into effect.[159]

Many of the studies underplay the question of when and where executions take place and the differences between death penalty and non-death penalty states. Several of the studies include non-death penalty states as comparisons, but fail to address statistically the differences between the two groups of states. Simple contrasts between death penalty and non-death penalty states, even with covariates that characterize some of the differences, make strong identifying assumptions that in the absence of a treatment, the average murder rates for states in each group would have followed parallel paths over time. But if the murder rates are higher in death penalty states, then the antecedents of homicides are probably unbalanced in the two groups, and the estimates of treatment effects are biased. Simply controlling for state differences via state fixed effects, or inserting a variable for whether a valid death penalty statute was in effect in any year, raises a series of connected endogeneity problems that require an integration of econometrics with methods more familiar in the analysis of data in natural experiments.[160]

Most of the new deterrence studies use standard errors computed from simple Ordinary Least Squares (OLS) regressions, but without correcting for autoregression, the standard errors in the estimates of the effects of execution are well understated.[161] In at

157 See Berk, *New Claims*, *supra* note 51; see also BADI H. BALTAGI, ECONOMETRIC ANALYSIS OF PANEL DATA (2001); Badi H. Baltagi & Qi Li, *Testing AR(1) Against MA(1) Disturbances in an Error Component Model*, 68 J. ECONOMETRICS 133 (1995); Robert C. Jung & A.R. Tremayne, *Testing for Serial Dependence in Time Series Models of Counts*, 24 J. TIME SERIES ANALYSIS 65 (2003).

158 K.D.S. Yound & L.I. Pettit, *The Effect of Observations on Bayesian Choice of an Autoregressive Model*, 27 J. TIME SERIES ANALYSIS 41 (2006).

159 See JEFFREY M. WOOLDRIDGE, ECONOMETRIC ANALYSIS OF CROSS SECTION AND PANEL DATA (2002); see also Marianne Bertrand et al., *How Much Should We Trust Differences-in-Differences Estimates?*, 119 Q. J. ECON. 249 (2004).

160 See, e.g., Alberto Abadie, *Semiparametric Difference-in-Differences Estimators*, 72 REV. ECON. STUD. 1 (2005). For classic examples of the use of natural experiments to detect the presence of deterrent effects of executions, see Hans Zeisel, *The Deterrent Effect of the Death Penalty: Facts v. Faiths*, 1976 SUP. CT. REV. 317 (1976). See also Thorsten Sellin, *Homicides in Retentionist and Abolitionist States*, in CAPITAL PUNISHMENT 135 (Thorsten Sellin ed., 1967); Thorsten Sellin, *Experiments with Abolition*, in CAPITAL PUNISHMENT 122 (Thorsten Sellin ed., 1967).

161 See, e.g., Bertrand et al., *supra* note 160. In general, to produce accurate standard errors when there is serial correlation or autoregression in the outcome variables, we need to estimate standard errors

least two studies in the new deterrence literature, when the standard errors are corrected for autoregression, the standard errors increase, and the execution variable is no longer statistically significant.[162] Such instability in the coefficients under different measurement and analytic conditions should be a serious warning sign to those who would uncritically embrace the new deterrence evidence. In section IV., I show that statistical modeling techniques that account for the strong year-to-year correlation of murder rates over time produces dramatic changes in the statistical significance and effect size of executions on murder rates.[163]

E. Deterrence

Death sentences are rare, as are executions. One reason is that capital punishment is limited by a jurisprudence that recognizes that "death is different" and should, therefore, be reserved for only the most heinous murders.[164] This jurisprudence leads to a necessary scarcity: most states have narrowly tailored capital punishment laws to constrain the number and types of homicides that are eligible for the death penalty.[165] This scarcity undermines the logic of deterrence: is it reasonable to expect that rare execution events will have salience across large heterogeneous pools of potential offenders?

---

that are robust to autocorrelation as well as heteroskedasticity, otherwise known as Heteroskedasticity and Autocorrelation-Consistent (HAC) standard errors, or Newey-West standard errors. See Whitney Newey & Kenneth D. West, *A Simple, Positive Semi-Definite, Heteroskedasticity and Autocorrelation Consistent-Covariance Matrix*, 55 ECONOMETRICA 703 (1987); see also WOOLDRIDGE, *supra* note 160.

162 See Donohue & Wolfers, *Uses and Abuses*, *supra* note 25, at 835 (reporting that when they correct Zimmerman's (2004) analysis for serial clustering or correlation, the confidence interval on his estimates widens to a range of twenty-three homicides caused by each execution to fifty-four homicides prevented by each execution); see also *infra* Part IV.

163 *See infra* Part IV. B; see also Donohue & Wolfers, *Uses and Abuses*, *supra* note 25, at 835.

164 HUGO ADAM BEDEAU, DEATH IS DIFFERENT: STUDIES IN THE MORALITY, LAW, AND POLITICS OF CAPITAL PUNISHMENT 55–59 (1987); Jeffrey Abramson, *Death-is-Different Jurisprudence and the Role of the Capital Jury*, 2 OHIO ST. J. CRIM. L. 117 (2004).

165 But see Jonathan Simon & Christina Spaulding, *Tokens of Our Esteem: Aggravating Factors in the Era of Deregulated Death Penalties*, in THE KILLING STATE: CAPITAL PUNISHMENT IN LAW, POLITICS, AND CULTURE 81 (Austin Sarat ed., 1999) (showing that state legislatures steadily expanded death penalty eligibility for two decades starting in the early 1980s by adding a wide range of aggravators). Scarcity has been eroded by a gradual expansion of the categories of murders that are subject to felony murder rules and classification as capital-eligible. Simon and Spaulding note that these elements of homicides provide a "currency through which states seek to recognize various concerns and valorize certain kinds of subjects and situations." *Id.*

This problem is not just a matter of social science, but also of law. The Supreme Court concluded in *Furman* that when only a tiny fraction of persons who commit murder are sentenced to death, capital punishment is unconstitutionally irrational because it serves no identifiable penal function.[166] Assuming rationality, for the moment, rare executions are unlikely to influence decision processes by motivating would-be killers to adjust to these punishment threats. A death penalty that is almost never used serves no deterrent function, because no would-be murderer can reasonably expect to be executed.[167] In his concurrence in *Furman*,[168] Justice White recognized that:

> [A] major goal of the criminal law—to deter others by punishing the convicted criminal—would not be substantially served where the penalty is so seldom invoked that it ceases to be the credible threat essential to influence the conduct of others. ... [C]ommon sense and experience tell us that seldom-enforced laws become ineffective measures for controlling human conduct and that the death penalty, unless imposed with sufficient frequency, will make little contribution to deterring those crimes for which it may be exacted.[169]

The heart of the matter, then, is whether the criminal law can deter murder and if so, under what conditions. The contours of the modern deterrence argument in capital punishment were constructed by Professor Gary Becker in theoretical work that preceded and informed Ehrlich's 1975 empirical application to the death penalty.[170] Becker's framework was a decision heuristic informed by rational choice and information processing: "All human behavior can be viewed as involving participants who (1) maximize their utility (2) form a stable set of preferences and (3) accumulate an optimal amount of information and other inputs in a variety of markets."[171] In the decades following Ehrlich's publication, these theoretical propositions formed the core of discourse, theory and research on

---

166 408 U.S. 238 (1972).

167 See, e.g., Paul Slovic et al., *Decision Processes, Rationality and Adjustment to Natural Hazards*, in PERCEPTION OF RISK 1 (Paul Slovic ed., 2000).

168 408 U.S. 238 (1972).

169 *Id.* at 312 (White, J., concurring).

170 Becker, *Crime and Punishment*, *supra* note 1.

171 *Id.* See also BECKER, ECONOMIC APPROACH, *supra* note 1, at 14. Becker continues to advance price theory as a supplement to, if not a substitution for, the limitations of the new deterrence research, noting that "most people have a powerful fear of death" that ultimately will deter their homicidal behavior. See Gary S. Becker, *On the Economics of Capital Punishment*, 3 THE ECONOMIST'S VOICE 1166 (2006), available at http://www.bepress.com/ev/vol3/iss3/art4 (last visited April 16, 2006) [hereinafter Becker, *On the Economics of Capital Punishment*].

deterrence. Accordingly, the new deterrence studies are minor extensions of Becker's and Ehrlich's original theoretical formulations that lean heavily on price theory.[172]

Until recently, the crossfire between death penalty deterrence advocates and opponents focused not on the moving parts of deterrence theory, but on three methodological concerns: the econometrics to estimate deterrence, data and measurement concerns, and model specification problems such as those discussed earlier.[173] Despite advances in theorizing deterrence in the context of public enforcement of law, including the addition of constructs such as tastes for risk or imperfect knowledge,[174] empirical research on capital punishment has not been updated to test these propositions. In fact, there still have been no direct tests of deterrence among groups whose responses could be reasonably generalized to violent offenders. No studies have shown that murderers are aware of executions in their own state, much less in far-away states, and that they rationally decide to forego homicide and use less lethal forms of violence in the face of risk of execution.

No one doubts that the criminal law, as well as other types of legal sanctions, have deterrent effects, but the evidence suggests that such effects may be confined to risk groups atypical of homicide offenders.[175] Deterrence research in the last half century is equivocal on the robustness of deterrent effects, and quite modest when extending deterrence

---

172 When confronted with unstable and noisy data from the current studies, proponents of deterrence, such as Becker, lean on price theory, claiming that since most people have a strong fear of death, they will avoid murder. See Becker, *On the Economics of Capital Punishment*, *supra* note 172.

173 For example, one of the primary critiques of Ehrlich's 1975 article was the leverage that was exerted on homicide trends by the final seven years of his time series (1963–1969), while ignoring contemporaneous trends in non-death penalty states. See, e.g., Peter Passell & John B. Taylor, *The Deterrent Effect of Capital Punishment: Another View*, 67 AM. ECON. REV. 445 (1977); see also Walter S. McManus, *Estimates of the Deterrent Effect of Capital Punishment: The Importance of the Researcher's Prior Beliefs*, 93 J. POL. ECON. 417 (1985); Zeisel, *supra* note 161, at 317.

174 See A. Mitchell Polinsky & Steven Shavell, *The Theory of Public Enforcement of Law*, in 1 HANDBOOK OF LAW AND ECONOMICS (forthcoming 2006); see also Owen Bar-Gill & Alon Harel, *Crime Rates and Expected Sanctions: The Economics of Deterrence Revisited*, 30 J. LEGAL STUD. 485 (2001).

175 Nagin, *supra* note 83. See, e.g., Jeff T. Casey & John T. Scholz, *Beyond Deterrence: Behavioral Decision Theory and Tax Compliance*, 25 LAW & SOC'Y REV. 821 (1991); Karly A. Kinsey et al., *Framing Justice: Taxpayer Evaluations of Personal Tax Burdens*, 25 LAW & SOC'Y REV. 845 (1991); Greg Pogarsky & Alexis R. Piquero, *Can Punishment Encourage Offending? Investigating the "Resetting" Effect*, 40 J. RES. CRIME & DELINQ. 95 (2003) (exploring the relevance of judgment and decision making research on gambler's fallacies in probabilistic reasoning for crime decision making); see also D.L. McArthur & J.F. Kraus, *The Specific Deterrence of Administrative Per Se Laws in Reducing Drunk Driving Recidivism*, 16 AM. J. PREVENTIVE MED. 68 (Supp. 1999); Donald S. Kenkel & Steven F. Koch, *Deterrence and Knowledge of the Law: The Case of Drunk Driving*, 33 APPLIED ECON. 845 (2001).

rationales to groups of high-rate or serious offenders.[176] Professor Daniel Nagin's detailed review shows that deterrent effects in the criminal law are conditioned on the social position of the person and the type of crime. The evidence cannot be reliably extended to murderers, since the more persuasive deterrence experiments have been done using experimental paradigms with lower risk groups.[177] Obviously, in experimental paradigms, it is unrealistic to simulate the contexts where lethal aggression tends to occur. But one could doubt that extreme violence might be deterred: Nagin reports no evidence of valid tests for deterrence of injury aggression.

With these limitations in mind, what conditions are necessary to reliably extend deterrence theory to the case of murder and capital punishment? Professors Paul Robinson and John Darley identify three conceptual and practical prerequisites to deterrence that are necessary to establish a plausible link between punishment contingencies and behavioral outcomes: rationality, knowledge, and choice.[178] They characterize each as a conceptual hurdle that deterrence theory must overcome to attain empirical validity and conceptual legitimacy.

1. Rationality

The rationality test asks whether offenders, assuming they possess knowledge of the risks of detection and punishment, will apply their understanding to the decision to engage in homicide at the moment when they are making the choice. Studies that directly examine the reactions of individuals to punishment threats consistently show the limits of rationality, especially in the case of aggression or violence. For example, violence often is embedded in the contexts of the moment, where choices among alternatives are skewed by the demands of the situation. For murder, these contingencies include revenge, retaliation, fear of lethal attack, and nonnegotiable demands of peers or network cohorts.[179]

---

176 See Nagin, *supra* note 83; see also Daniel S. Nagin & Greg Pogarsky, *Integrating Celerity, Impulsivity, and Extralegal Sanction Threats into a Model of General Deterrence: Theory and Evidence*, 39 CRIMINOLOGY 865 (2001).

177 See, e.g., Daniel Nagin & Raymond Paternoster, *Personal Capital and Social Control: The Deterrence Implications of Individual Differences in Criminal Offending*, 32 CRIMINOLOGY 581, 584 (1994) (reporting results of research with a sample of college students showing that "individuals who commit crimes place little weight on the future consequences of their actions").

178 Paul H. Robinson & John M. Darley, *Does Criminal Law Deter? A Behavioral Science Investigation*, 24 OXFORD J. LEGAL STUD. 173 (2004) (reviewing evidence from criminology and other behavioral sciences and concluding that the deterrent effects of the criminal law are quite limited).

179 See, e.g., LEE ROSS & RICHARD NISBETT, THE PERSON AND THE SITUATION: PERSPECTIVES OF SOCIAL PSYCHOLOGY (1991). See also Luckenbill & Doyle, *supra* note 109; Andrew V. Papachristos, *Murder Markets: Network Contagion and the Social Order of Gang Homicide*,

Consequently, many situations that could end in lethal violence are highly volatile, where decisions are made under conditions of arousal, whether anger or fear.[180] Rationality may be further impaired by cognitive, organic and neuropsychological factors that may occlude punishment risk from rational calculations.[181]

The underlying assumptions of rationality depend on clarity and objectivity among offenders in cognition, risk analysis, cost measuring, future orientation and premeditation.[182] Such attributes are unknown in research on murder and murderers, except perhaps among the very small percentage of murder-for-hire and premeditated killings.[183] Rather, murderers are more likely to discount punishment risks, and inflate the present value of whatever gains the crime may offer.[184] This amounts to economics minus the rationality assumptions.[185]

The limitations in unreconstructed rationality lead Professors Russell Korobkin and Thomas Ulen to recommend replacing the rationality assumption with a multidisciplinary understanding of human behavior, drawing from such fields as cognitive psychology, sociology, and decision sciences.[186] Along the same lines, Professor

---

Abstract, available at http://ssrn.com/abstract=855304 (last visited May 15, 2006) [hereinafter Papachristos, *Murder Markets*].

180 See, e.g., PALLONE & HENNESSY, *supra* note 107; Fagan & Wilkinson, *Guns, Youth Violence*, *supra* note 110.

181 See, e.g., Adrian Raine et al., *Reduced Prefrontal and Increased Subcortical Brain Functioning Assessed Using Positron Emission Tomography in Predatory and Affective Murderers*, 16 BEHAV. SCI. & L. 319 (1998); Lisa M. Gatzke-Kopp et al., *Temporal Lobe Deficits in Murderers: EEG Findings Undetected by PET*, 13 J. NEUROPSYCHIATRY & CLINICAL NEUROSCI. 486 (2001); Dorothy Otnow Lewis et al., *Ethics Questions Raised by the Neuropsychiatric, Neuropsychological, Educational, Developmental, and Family Characteristics of 18 Juveniles Awaiting Execution in Texas*, 32 J. AM. ACAD. PSYCHIATRY & L. 408 (2004); Dorothy Otnow Lewis et al., *Neuropsychiatric, Psychoeducational, and Family Characteristics of 14 Juveniles Condemned to Death in the United States*, 145 AM. J. PSYCHIATRY 584 (1988); D. Michael Bitz & Jean Seipp Bitz, *Incompetence in the Brain Injured Individual*, 12 ST. THOMAS L. REV. 205, 260 (1999).

182 Jon Elster, *When Rationality Fails*, in THE LIMITS OF RATIONALITY 19 (Karen Schweers Cook & Margaret Levi eds., 1990).

183 KATZ, SEDUCTIONS OF CRIME, *supra* note 107 (citing anecdotal evidence to build a theory of criminal motivation in killings).

184 See, e.g., PALLONE & HENNESEY, *supra* note 107; see also KATZ, SEDUCTIONS OF CRIME, *supra* note 107; POLK, *supra* note 105; ELIJAH ANDERSON, THE CODE OF THE STREET (1999) [hereinafter ANDERSON, CODE OF THE STREET].

185 Christine Jolls, Cass R. Sunstein & Richard Thaler, *A Behavioral Approach to Law and Economics*, 50 STAN. L. REV. 1471 (1998).

186 Russell Korobkin & Thomas S. Ulen, *Law and Behavioral Science: Removing the Rationality Assumption from Law and Economics*, 88 CAL. L. REV. 1051 (2000).

Robert Cooter says that economic theories of deterrence need a theory of endogenous preferences that will integrate cognitive psychology to incorporate motives and values into the deterrence calculus.[187] These theories are unified in prospect theory, an alternate decision framework that describes how people actually make decisions.[188] Like rational choice theory, prospect theory assumes that decision makers will seek to maximize their outcomes, but in unpredictable ways. The theory assumes that people will make risk-averse decisions when deciding among options that seem to be gains, but will make risk-seeking decisions when faced with losses.[189] Offenders will value losses more than gains of a similar magnitude, and they will overvalue certainty.[190] In other words, most people, perhaps including criminal offenders, are more likely to take risks to avoid losses than to accumulate gains.

This challenge to rationality and the movement toward disciplinary integration exposes the fault lines in assumptions of rationality among criminal offenders. As a group, offenders often are risk-seekers and prone to thrill seeking,[191] and their impulsivity tends to be significantly higher than non-offenders.[192] They value social rewards and status from crime over the social rewards of conventional roles and behaviors,[193] and they often are impaired cognitively from extensive careers of drug and alcohol abuse.[194] Future consequences are either ignored or postponed, giving way to an orientation to consider only present contingencies.[195] In one of the few studies with samples of criminal offenders, Professor Charles Dean and his research collaborators report that the stability of present orientation over a

---

187 Robert Cooter, *Treating Yourself Instrumentally: Internalization, Rationality and the Law*, in THE LAW AND ECONOMICS OF IRRATIONAL BEHAVIOR 95 (Franco Parisi & Vernon L. Smith eds., 2005).

188 Chris Guthrie, *Prospect Theory, Risk Preference, and the Law*, 97 NW. U. L. REV. 1115, 1116–19(2003).

189 *Id.* at 1116.

190 Daniel Kahneman & Amos Tversky, *Prospect Theory: An Analysis of Decisions Under Risk*, 47 ECONOMETRICA 263 (1979) [hereinafter Kahneman & Tversky, *Prospect Theory*].

191 Nagin & Paternoster, *supra* note 178.

192 But see Cooter, *supra* note 188.

193 Jeffrey Fagan & Deanna L. Wilkinson, *Social Contexts and Functions of Adolescent Violence*, in VIOLENCE IN AMERICAN SCHOOLS: A NEW PERSPECTIVE 55 (D.S. Elliott, B. Hamburg & K.R. Williams eds., 1998) [hereinafter Fagan & Wilkinson, *Social Contexts*]; Deanna L. Wilkinson & Jeffery Fagan, *The Role of Firearms in Violence "Scripts": The Dynamics of Gun Events Among Adolescent Males*, 59 LAW & CONTEMP. PROBS. 55 (1996) [hereinafter Wilkinson & Fagan, *Role of Firearms*].

194 Chaiken & Chaiken, *supra* note 97.

195 Nagin & Paternoster, *supra* note 178.

long developmental period explains long criminal careers.[196] These irrational orientations tend to co-exist in a cascade of organic and cognitive impairments to further weaken cognition and decision making.[197]

Under these conditions, when faced with uncertainty, decision makers are likely to systematically depart from the rational actor model.[198] Nevertheless, rationality is a familiar comfort zone for the law.[199] But rationality as a descriptive term for cognition has given way in social science to the concept of "bounded rationality."[200] Professor Herbert Simon uses "bounded rationality" to describe the process of making decisions using decision making heuristics, limited time, and incomplete information. A rational choice would be one which maximizes utility, but Simon points out that in many cases the decision maker will aim to make only a satisfactory choice (Simon calls this "satisficing").[201]

---

196 Charles Dean, Robert Brame & Alex Piquero, *Criminal Propensities, Discrete Groups of Offenders, and Persistence in Crime*, 34 CRIMINOLOGY 547 (1996).

197 But see Stephen J. Morse, *Brain Over Claim Syndrome and Criminal Responsibility: A Diagnostic Note*, 3 OHIO ST. J. CRIM. L. 397 (2006) (facetiously addressing the tendency among some social scientists and legal scholars to apply limited research from neuroscience to explain a wide range of antisocial and violent behaviors).

198 Amos Tversky & Daniel Kahneman, *Rational Choice and the Framing of Decisions*, 59 J. BUS. S251, S251–54 (1986) [hereinafter Tversky & Kahneman, *Rational Choice*]. The failure of rationality under conditions of uncertainty suggests the need to distinguish between rationality and rational choice. The latter is the topic of later sections in this essay. See infra Part III.E.3–4.

199 See, e.g., Richard A. Posner, *The Economic Approach to Law*, 53 TEX. L. REV. 757, 761 (1973) ("The basis of an economic approach to law is the assumption that the people involved with the legal system act as rational maximizers of their satisfactions"); see also Richard A. Posner, *Values and Consequences: An Introduction to Economic Analysis of Law*, in CHICAGO LECTURES IN LAW AND ECONOMICS 189, 191 (Eric A. Posner ed., 2000) ("Most economic analysis consists of tracing out the consequences of assuming that people are more or less rational in their social interactions"); Jeanne L. Schroeder, *Rationality in Law and Economics Scholarship*, 79 OR. L. REV. 147 (2000) (providing an alternate foundation for the basis of rationality in the law while critiquing Posner's model of rationality); Herbert Hovenkamp, *Rationality in Law & Economics*, 60 GEO. WASH. L. REV. 293 (1992); MELVIN ARON EISENBERG, THE NATURE OF THE COMMON LAW (1988) (setting forth the case for internal rationality in the common law).

200 Herbert A. Simon, *Theories of Bounded Rationality*, in 2 MODELS OF BOUNDED RATIONALITY: BEHAVIORAL ECONOMICS AND BUSINESS ORGANIZATION 408 (1982).

201 Herbert A. Simon, *Rational Choice and the Structure of the Environment*, in MODELS OF MAN: SOCIAL AND RATIONAL 261, 270–71 (1957). The difference between "satisficing" and optimizing can be understood by the following analogy: optimizing is searching for the sharpest needle in the haystack, and satisficing is searching for a needle that is sharp enough for sewing. See Melvin Aron Eisenberg, *The Limits of Cognition and the Limits of Contract*, 47 STAN. L. REV. 211, 214 (1995).

These shortcomings in rationality remind us that even when facts are known, they may be neither recalled in a particular event nor mobilized accurately as part of a decision heuristic. The facts themselves may or may not be relevant to the situation,[202] and even if recalled, they may be interpreted incorrectly given the context. If a criminal offender is prone to discounting costs that create cognitive dissonance with the perceived benefits or their preferences, the facts that communicate those costs will be distorted if not ignored.[203]

2. Knowledge

The second hurdle is knowledge: does the offender know and understand the implications of the law?[204] Does the offender know which actions are criminalized and at what schedule, or which actions will excuse one's crime or otherwise mitigate one's culpability?

There is little attention to this question in the new deterrence literature. For example, Professor Joanna Shepherd elaborates on the early deterrence theoretical framework, maintaining that executions deter all types of murder by allowing all would-be murderers to update their expectations of punishment risk, compensating for the uncertainty about whether the murder they are about to commit would be charged and prosecuted capitally.[205] Such uncertainty, she claims, has less to do with the motivations of murderers than with their capacity to internalize exogenous factors such as prosecutorial discretion, quality of defense counsel, and juror preferences. There are no assumptions in her study nor in the other studies in this oeuvre about where or how potential murderers acquire the information to do so.

Instead, the new deterrence studies seem to assume, incredibly, that murderers have perfect knowledge about the probability and magnitude of sanctions, and that their decisions about risk are neither discounted nor variable. One study, for example, includes measures of newspaper stories and other media reports of executions.[206] It is a causal story that assumes much about the reading habits and television viewing preferences of would-be murderers. Quite the opposite is probably true given literacy levels among most prison inmates. The new studies fail to show that murderers are aware of executions in their own state, much less in far-away states, and that they rationally decide to forego homicide and use less lethal forms of violence.

---

202 See ROSS & NISBETT, *supra* note 180.

203 See, e.g., David Anderson, *The Deterrence Hypothesis and Picking Pockets at the Pickpocket's Hanging*, 4 AM. L. & ECON. REV. 295 (2002), cited in Robinson & Darley, *supra* note 179, at 176.

204 Robinson & Darley, *supra* note 179, at 176.

205 Shepherd, *Murders of Passion*, *supra* note 15, at 292.

206 Shepherd, *Deterrence Versus Brutalization*, *supra* note 46.

The rules—whether one faces execution for one type of murder versus another, or whether one faces execution at all given the circumstances producing a death—are too abstract and removed from the moment to be salient, even assuming that there is a small number of murderers or would-be murderers who have such knowledge. There is no evidence that information markets among would-be murderers are dense, efficient, or fueled by accurate information.[207] First, there is no evidence to suggest that there are networks among persons who commit murder. They may be embedded in social networks where violence is common—for example, in street gangs or drug selling networks—but homicide is far from a primary motivator of social cohesion in these groups.[208] Cass Sunstein also claims that in such markets, competition among group members may lead to gaming where some may withhold information or not disclose what they know. This has the unfortunate effect of propagating errors and corroding group cohesion.

While experience—whether direct or vicarious—may substitute for knowledge, these experiences may not be transferable to the specific situations that may lead to murder. Robinson and Darley suggest that offenders are unlikely to do the calculations necessary to decide correctly which rules apply in which situations.[209] Indirect or vicarious knowledge is prone to error as well, as it is fueled by gossip and misinformation about the rules of law and the probabilities of detection and punishment.

3. Choice and Preferences

Assuming knowledge and rationality, will an offender make a behavioral choice consistent with deterrence? Robinson and Darley refer to this as the Perceived Net Cost Hurdle.[210]

Decisions themselves—as a matter of human development and not just antisocial behavior—suggest that even in a "rational" estimation of costs and benefits, decision makers are more likely to use intuitive heuristics, shortcuts which may or may not result in wise decision making.[211] Professors Amos Tversky and Daniel Kahneman note that although heuristics sometimes work well, they can also lead to irrational decisions or decisions that may not maximize utility but instead maximize short-term preferences that are framed by

207 See, e.g., Cass R. Sunstein, *Group Judgments: Deliberations, Statistical Means, and Information Markets*, 80 N.Y.U. L. REV. 962 (2005) (showing that network connectedness and group deliberation are prerequisites for efficiency in information markets and in both individual and collective decisions).

208 See, e.g., Papachristos, *supra* note 180.

209 Robinson & Darley, *supra* note 179, at 178.

210 *Id.* at 182.

211 RICHARD THALER, QUASI RATIONAL ECONOMICS (1991).

situational contingencies and present circumstances.[212] "In general, these heuristics are quite useful, but sometimes they lead to severe and systematic errors."[213] The moving parts in biased decision making heuristics include two dimensions: fallacies and skewed adjustments.[214] Additionally, decisions are skewed by emotions. Preferences for utility, cognition and heuristics under conditions of arousal are all vulnerable to distortion under conditions of arousal or fear.

a. Availability, Representativeness and the Base Rate Fallacy

Tversky and Kahneman suggest that rational decision makers would take into account general information about population characteristics, and especially information about the chance of a specific event occurring, but rarely do. The failure to consider relevant information to make a probability judgment is a logical fallacy known as the base rate fallacy.[215] The representativeness fallacy refers to the tendency of decision makers to ignore base rates and overestimate the correlation between what something is and what it appears to be. The availability heuristic, like the representativeness heuristic, can lead to irrational decision making in ignoring base rates.[216] The availability heuristic, on the other hand,

---

212 Kahneman & Tversky, *Prospect Theory*, *supra* note 191, at 263–91; Daniel Kahneman, *Reference Points, Anchors, Norms, and Mixed Feelings*, 51 ORG. BEHAV. & HUM. DECISION PROCESSES 296 (1992).

213 Amos Tversky & Daniel Kahneman, *Judgment Under Uncertainty: Heuristics and Biases*, 185 SCI. 1124 (1974).

214 See Korobkin & Ulen, *supra* note 187, at 1086; see also Pamela K. Lattimore et al., *The Influence of Probability on Risky Choice: A Parametric Estimation*, 17 J. ECON. BEHAV. & ORG. 377 (1992) (applying the prospect theory principle of nonlinear probability weighting to crime decision making).

215 See Daniel Kahneman & Amos Tversky, *On the Psychology of Prediction*, 80 PSYCHOL. REV. 237 (1973); see also Maya Bar-Hillel, *The Base-Rate Fallacy in Probability Judgments*, 44 ACTA PSYCHOLOGICA 211 (1980); Matthew C. Schneider, *Deterrence and the Base Rate Fallacy: An Examination of Perceived Certainty*, 18 JUST. Q. 63 (2001).

216 See Korobkin & Ulen, *supra* note 187, at 1087. For example, most people believe that there are more words that begin with the letter "k" than words in which "k" is the third letter. This is probably because it is easier to think of words beginning with "k"; i.e., such words are more readily available. However, there are actually two times as many words that have "k" in the third letter than in the first. Similarly, most people believe that homicides and car accidents kill more people in the United States than diabetes and stomach cancer, because the former events receive more media attention and are thus more available.

refers to the tendency of decision makers to overestimate the relevance of significant or memorable incidents, and underestimate the base rates.[217]

b. Anchoring and Adjustment

In the estimating process, decision makers are likely to form an arbitrary "anchor" that serves as the starting point for estimation, and then adjust from this anchor but still remain too close to it.[218] Professors Russell Korobkin and Chris Guthrie conducted a series of experiments to show, among other things, how this irrational tendency to anchor and adjust can affect settlements in litigation.[219] In one experiment, subjects were assigned to two groups and were given almost identical scenarios, at the end of which they were asked whether they would settle with the defendant, or go to trial (with the prospect of winning more but the risk of losing everything). The only difference in the scenarios was the anchor—one group was given an extremely low settlement offer (the "low ball initial offer" group) and the other was given a reasonable settlement offer (the "reasonable initial offer" group)—but both groups were given an identical "final" settlement offer.[220]

Rational choice theory would predict that, given identical choices, the two groups would either accept the settlement offer or reject it and proceed to trial in the same proportions. However, the initial settlement offer had a strong effect on the option chosen by subjects in each group. Subjects who were made the reasonable initial offer were more likely to reject it than to accept it, whereas subjects who were made the low initial offer were more likely to accept it. This difference between the groups was statistically significant.[221] Thus, as Korobkin and Guthrie note, "When choosing between a concrete settlement offer and an uncertain trial result, our subjects faced cognitive biases that prevented at least some of them from acting in what decision theorists would consider a rational manner. ...Together, the results suggest that litigants—who are not always rational actors—may fail to reach settlement on some occasions when settlement makes good economic sense."[222]

---

217 See, e.g., REID HASTIE & ROBYN M. DAWES, RATIONAL CHOICE IN AN UNCERTAIN WORLD: THE PSYCHOLOGY OF JUDGMENT AND DECISION MAKING, 112–13 (2001).

218 Tversky & Kahneman, *Rational Choice*, *supra* note 199.

219 Russell Korobkin & Chris Guthrie, *Psychological Barriers to Litigation Settlement: An Experimental Approach*, 93 MICH. L. REV. 107,139–42 (1994).

220 *Id.*

221 *Id.*

222 *Id.* at 142.

c. Emotion

One's emotional state plays a role in decision making, and can influence a person to act in ways that are not maximally optimal (or rational).[223] Obviously, anger and other forms of arousal can skew judgment in several ways, changing both rationality and also reshaping the estimation of costs and benefits. Professor Anne Dailey argues that lawyers should focus more on the source of an individual's needs, feelings, and motives, which may be unconscious, irrational, or both.[224] One example of how emotions can lead to irrational decision making is illustrated by the finding that, in general, people are willing to pay more for an emotionally meaningful item than for an equally valuble but emotionally neutral item. Professor Russell Korobkin calls this the endowment effect.[225]

d. Weighing Net Costs

Assume that knowledge is internalized and a would-be murderer will put this information to work accurately and rationally. Theorists from Becker[226] to Polinsky and Shavell[227] have posited a calculus of decision making where actors weigh costs and benefits prior to action (or inaction). The decision making is complex, of course, with different actors assigning different utilities and preferences to the components of cost and return. For example, postponing reward is an expression of preference, as is discounting past (sunk) costs or postponing present costs. Deterrence will take place, to put it simply, when punishment is a cost worth avoiding—that is, when the costs of punishment outweigh the perceived rewards of the act. Put another way, is the offender likely to choose compliance as the more beneficial option?

Beginning with Bentham, deterrence theorists have disaggregated costs into three dimensions: probability, severity, and delay.[228] While there is no debate on severity,[229] there is

---

223 Anne C. Dailey, *The Hidden Economy of the Unconscious*, 74 CHI.-KENT L. REV. 1599, 1604–06 (2000).

224 *Id.* at 1606–08.

225 Russell Korobkin, *The Endowment Effect and Legal Analysis*, 97 NW. U. L. REV. 1227, 1228 (2003). This also is an example of risk aversion. See also Richard Birke, *Reconciling Loss Aversion and Guilty Pleas*, 1999 UTAH L. REV. 205, 212.

226 Becker, *Crime and Punishment*, *supra* note 1.

227 Polinsky & Shavell, *supra* note 175.

228 JEREMY BENTHAM, AN INTRODUCTION TO THE PRINCIPLES OF MORALS AND LEGISLATION (1789). See also Robinson & Darley, *supra* note 179.

229 Although there may be some debate on the severity of life imprisonment without the possibility of parole compared to execution, and the marginal deterrence of capital punishment relative to such life sentences is unknown. See *supra* Part III.B. 1.

strong evidence that death is delayed punishment owing to due process and the numerous errors in capital sentences.[230] Probability also is low: no more than one homicide in four is capital-eligible,[231] few of these are selected for prosecution,[232] and the percentage of death row cases that proceed to execution for states other than Texas remains very low.[233] As mentioned earlier, scarcity undermines the deterrent threat of death, and the marginal deterrence from this weak threat compared to the certainty and harshness of incarceration undermines this utilitarian argument for capital punishment.

The benefit side of the equation is more complex. Together with Professor Richard Freeman, I analyzed a series of empirical studies on the tradeoffs between legal work and

230 See JAMES LIEBMAN ET AL., A BROKEN SYSTEM, PART I: ERROR RATES IN CAPITAL CASES, 1973–1995 (2000), available at http://www2.law.columbia.edu/instructionalservices/liebman/ [hereinafter LIEBMAN ET AL., A BROKEN SYSTEM, PART I] (citing the average time from sentence to execution of 9 years for death sentences imposed between 1973 and 1995, and an average of 7.6 years until death sentences are reversed and defendants are re-sentenced, exonerated, pardoned or their sentences commuted). See also Alex Kozinski & Sean Gallagher, *Death: The Ultimate Run-On Sentence*, 46 CASE W. RES. L. REV. 1, 2, n.10 (1995).

231 See Fagan et al., *Capital Punishment and Capital Murder*, *supra* note 64.

232 See, e.g., Raymond Paternoster et al., *Justice by Geography and Race: The Administration of the Death Penalty in Maryland*, 1978–99, 4 MD. L.J. RACE, RELIGION, GENDER & CLASS 1 (2004) (examining 1311 death-eligible cases from 1978 to 1999 based on the Maryland statute, MD. CODE ANN., CRIM. LAW § 2-201 & 2-205m, which defines murder in the first degree as: (a) a deliberate, premeditated, and willful killing, (b) committed by lying in wait, (c) committed by poison, (d) committed in the perpetration of or an attempt to perpetrate arson, burglary, carjacking, escape from prison, kidnapping, mayhem, rape, robbery, sexual offense, sodomy, bomb-making, and (e) if they willfully, deliberately, and with premeditation intended the death of a law enforcement officer.) Although the Maryland study generated statistical information on which statutory aggravating factors were most often present among cases selected for capital prosecution: murders committed during other crimes, murders with multiple victims, murders committed while the perpetrator was in a correctional institution, contract killings, and murders committed while fleeing capture by police. *Id.*

233 As a simple index for comparison, Texas courts have issued 776 death sentences since 1976 and executed 364 inmates, nearly half those sentenced. In Florida, Pennsylvania, and California, three states whose courts also issue high numbers of death sentences, the comparable number of death sentences and executions are: 60 of 235 (Florida), 13 of 652 (California), and 3 of 316 (Pennsylvania). See DEATH PENALTY INFORMATION CENTER, DEATH SENTENCING RATE BY STATE, available at http://www.deathpenaltyinfo.org/article.php?scid=67&did=915 (last visited May 15, 2006); DEATH PENALTY INFORMATION CENTER, NUMBER OF DEATH EXECUTIONS BY STATE AND REGION SINCE 1976, available at http://www.deathpenaltyinfo.org/article.php?scid=8&did=186 (last visited May 15, 2006).

illegal income-producing criminal activity for young men in inner cities.[234] When faced with sharply escalating incarceration risks throughout the late 1980s and 1990s, robbers and drug dealers consistently valued the economic returns of illegal work over either the foregone opportunities for legal income or the punishment costs that jail would exact. Similar tradeoffs were reported by burglars[235] and robbers[236] in ethnographic studies of their crime decision making. Other studies have shown that drug offenders will heavily value the combined reward of relief from withdrawal symptoms and the pleasure of addiction over the risk of detection and punishment.[237]

Scholars of homicide have long known that murder is the result of complex social interactions that increase the present value of benefits and push costs to the background.[238] Recent studies on violence in situ confirm the salience of reward, and introduce an element of risk that attaches when extreme violence is not used. In interviews with 125 young males ages sixteen to twenty-four who were involved in over 300 incidents of gun violence in New York City from 1995–1997, I collaborated with Professor Deanna Wilkinson to understand decision making within violent events where guns were used, and other events where guns were almost used but avoided at some point during a confrontation.[239] In these settings, lethal violence has both instrumental and intrinsic rewards that trumped what these young men perceived inaccurately as a distal risk of detection and punishment. In fact, there was greater fear of retaliation from victims' families or friends than from what was perceived as the remote possibility of police involvement. Extreme violence was an expected and valued behavior and, for some, thought to be necessary to ensure their

---

234 Jeffrey Fagan & Richard B. Freeman, *Crime and Work*, in 25 CRIME AND JUSTICE: A REVIEW OF RESEARCH 225 (1999).

235 RICHARD T. WRIGHT & SCOTT H. DECKER, BURGLARS ON THE JOB: STREETLIFE AND RESIDENTIAL BREAK-INS (1994).

236 RICHARD T. WRIGHT & SCOTT H. DECKER, ARMED ROBBERS IN ACTION: STICKUPS AND STREET CULTURE (1997) [hereinafter WRIGHT & DECKER, ARMED ROBBERS IN ACTION]. Wright and Decker interviewed men whose criminal careers included repeated robberies. Robbers were committed to a street culture that emphasized the materials rewards and social status attendant to being a successful "stickup boy," while minimizing or heavily discounting punishment risk.

237 JOHN KAPLAN, THE HARDEST DRUG: HEROIN AND PUBLIC POLICY (1983).

238 See, e.g., MARVIN E. WOLFGANG, PATTERNS IN CRIMINAL HOMICIDE (1958); KATZ, SEDUCTIONS OF CRIME, *supra* note 107; POLK, *supra* note 105; JAMES O'KANE, WICKED DEEDS: MURDER IN AMERICA (2005).

239 Fagan & Wilkinson, *Guns, Youth Violence*, *supra* note 110. See also KATZ, SEDUCTIONS OF CRIME, *supra* note 107.

survival.[240] Chance encounters with others in these neighborhoods were seen as potentially threatening or lethal—unknown others were widely thought to harbor hostile intentions and capacity to inflict harm. Extreme violence and toughness was the currency of respect, and respect had both strategic value and offered strong social reward. Violence was a public performance, designed to maintain a social identity that deters attack and reinforces a self-presentation of "toughness." Other acts of violence also were pathways to social status. For example, robbery not only generated material goods or cash and was helpful in sexual conquests, but it also established one's status in a social hierarchy where respect was a finite commodity.[241] Of course, the danger that a robbery could escalate into a homicide was always present. Violence also functions as social control in these contexts, redressing grievances or peremptorily ending them before they ever begin.

In a similar study, Andrew Papachristos interviewed gang members in the Austin and North Lawndale neighborhoods of Chicago.[242] Most had been involved either as witnesses or accomplices in murders committed in gang disputes. The risk of a death sentence was simply not a reality among gang members despite Illinois' high rate of death sentences prior to 2000. This is not to say that rationality is not part of their decisions about crime and violence: gang members often think rationally about crimes, especially drug dealing, but usually as a matter of business details such as packaging, marketing and selling drugs to maximize their returns. Their knowledge of law clearly passed the knowledge hurdle.[243]

---

240 WILKINSON, GUNS, VIOLENCE, AND IDENTITY, *supra* note 110 (illustrating the dynamics of violent events, including their "spark" or motivation, and their ending). In social interactions in this context, violence is an expected and valued behavior, shaped by a normative code. It is but one response in a toolkit of behaviors and responses to danger that evolves within these social worlds. Teenagers select from this toolkit according to their cognitive reading of a situation, with the level of danger and lethality their primary consideration. The presumption of hostile intent is both an accurate reading of potential danger and a reflection of socialization within this ecology. Cognitive appraisals occur within a setting of witnesses (bystanders) who judge and announce the actor's level of toughness under conditions of arousal, perhaps while high or drunk, very likely while armed, and with an adversary whose intentions are either hostile or unknown. See also Jeffrey Fagan, *Context and Culpability in Violent Events*, 6 VA. J. SOC. POLY & L. 507 (1999).

241 See ANDERSON, CODE OF THE STREET, *supra* note 185; ELIJAH ANDERSON, STREETWISE: RACE, CLASS AND CHANGE IN AN URBAN COMMUNITY (1990).

242 Andrew V. Papachristos, *Gang Violence as Social Control* (unpublished manuscript, on file with the University of Chicago, Department of Sociology). See also Papachristos, *Murder Markets*, *supra* note 180.

243 See Papachristos, *Murder Markets*, *supra* note 180. In one organized drug location, Papachristos observed an intricate ten man selling system that used walkie-talkies, look-outs, and multiple "drive-through" locations. Moreover, the "leaders" of this operation had detailed knowledge of gun and narcotic laws. They made sure that the guns and dope were kept separately to ensure that, in the possibility of

But the perceptions of risk and benefit were different for interpersonal violence, including murder. Compared with drug selling, gang members do not necessarily act "rationally" or weigh the prospects of execution in the course of violence. Although most of these gang members had been in and out of jail quite often, very few know anyone on "death row" or who has been executed. Rather, the greatest risk in murder was retaliation by members of rival gangs, not retribution by the state. A much broader and more pressing "threat of violence" looms over the gang world. Even more so than in "street culture" more generally, the consequences of victimization is the chief concern and is to be avoided at all costs. Self-protection and mutual protection are often key determinants in carrying weapons and engaging in violence. Violence was often reactionary and retaliatory, serving as a deterrent against future victimization, a form of self-protection, or a mechanism of social control. State sanctions, and especially the death penalty, rarely entered into the means–ends calculus of gang members on the street. Quite the opposite was true: gang members see prison sentences as "worth it" in order to maintain face and self-respect to deter the possibility of victimization. Often, receiving a prison sentence for maintaining personal honor can, in fact, increase one's personal reputation.[244]

There are numerous other examples of perceived benefits eclipsing risk in homicide: murders by violent spouses aimed at dominating and controlling intimate partners, retaliation and reprisal, or even robbery-homicides.[245] In fact, punishment costs may be discounted even more in the modal category of capital-eligible crimes: felony murders—homicides committed in the course of other crimes, especially robbery. Robbery is not a crime that is committed casually, nor are robbers a random sample of the criminal population: most have prior arrest records and many have completed spells in prison.[246] In felony murders, especially robbery-homicides which are more than half the capital-eligible murders,[247] struggles for weapons or fear of identification may escalate the crime to a homicide. There is a weak prospect that a risk heuristic of punishment will enter into the volatile and unpredictable street dynamics of robbery interactions to reduce the risk

---

an arrest, they would not get enhanced sentences for "criminal conspiracy cases" (in Cook County, the presence of weapons and drugs implies on on-going drug operation and carries stiffer penalties). In one instance, a gang leader made sure that any members carrying weapons near his drug operation were juveniles to ensure that the leaders could avoid gun charges if caught. See also Steven Levitt & Sudhir A. Venkatesh, *Growing Up in the Projects: The Economic Lives of a Cohort of Men Who Came of Age in Chicago Public Housing*, 91 AM. ECON. REV. 79 (2001).

244 *Id.*

245 KATZ, SEDUCTIONS OF CRIME, *supra* note 107.

246 See, e.g., WRIGHT & DECKER, ARMED ROBBERS IN ACTION, *supra* note 237. Most acknowledge the risk of punishment as intrinsic to their work, yet tend to either discount the cost of punishment or over-value the present benefits of the robbery, or both.

247 Fagan et al., *Capital Punishment and Capital Murder*, *supra* note 64.

of lethality,[248] especially when a gun is present. Accordingly, the presence of a gun in a robbery further increases not just the risk of lethality but the decision by the robber to use it.[249] In other words, there is a strong risk of cognitive errors in situations of intense arousal, errors that are likely to overwhelm the evaluations of the benefits of crime and the risks and costs of punishments.[250]

4. Cumulative and Conditional Corrosion

In the Robinson-Darley framework, "[s]etting any one of the variables to zero means that there is no deterrent effect whatever."[251] Of course, none of these values reach zero in reality, except perhaps in the case of the mentally ill.[252] Nevertheless, the parts of this framework are neither exchangeable nor separate. Rather, they interact conditionally and multiplicatively to produce a robust deterrent effect, and weakness in any one domain will drag down the salience of the others. So, for example, prison may be worth avoiding if there is a positive benefit from compliance. If detached from conventional social worlds via joblessness or addiction, the exposure of violent offenders to the actuarial benefits of compliance declines, and their perception of detection risks—not inaccurately, from their perspective—declines with it.[253] The scarcity of execution, however salient executions may be, is unlikely to disturb their risk assessment. How deterrence works in this social system and in skewed information markets is uncharted territory. Having said that, there is a large body of social science evidence that in the case of murder, each of the three hurdles in this framework becomes far higher than in the case of less complex or serious crimes, and their reciprocal and multiple effects are likely to militate against deterrence. That is, the cumulative effect of these hurdles

---

248 *Id.* See also Franklin Zimring, *Determinants of the Death Rate from Robbery: A Detroit Time Study*, 6 J. LEGAL STUD. 317 (1977); Franklin Zimring & James Zuehl, *Victim Injury and Death in Urban Robbery: A Chicago Study*, 15 J. LEGAL STUD. 1 (1986) [hereinafter Zimring & Zuehl, *Victim Injury and Death*]; Jack Katz, *The Motivation of the Persistent Robber*, in 14 CRIME AND JUSTICE: A REVIEW OF RESEARCH 277 (1991).

249 Zimring & Zuehl, *Victim Injury and Death*, *supra* note 249; Fagan & Wilkinson, *Social Contexts*, *supra* note 194; Wilkinson & Fagan, *Role of Firearms*, *supra* note 194.

250 See, e.g., Daniel Kahneman & Amos Tversky, *Choice, Values, and Frames*, 39 AM. PSYCHOLOGIST 341 (1984).

251 Robinson & Darley, *supra* note 179, at 196.

252 See, e.g., Bruce G. Link et al., *Psychotic Symptoms and Violent Behaviors: Probing the Components of "Threat/Control-Override" Symptoms*, 33 SOC. PSYCHIATRY & PSYCHIATRIC. EPIDEMIOLOGY S55 (Supp. 1998).

253 Robinson and Darley tell a similar story. See Robinson & Darley, *supra* note 179, at 197.

Table 1. Original and Alternate Specifications for Analysis of Deterrent Effects of Execution from Mocan and Gittings Data[a]

Model	*B*	*SE*	*p(t)*	*Exp B*	*CI* *Lower*	*CI* *Upper*	*N*
1. Original Specification	- .006	.003	.028	.994	-.011	-.001	680
2. Alternate Data Sources[1]	-.004	.001	.004	.996	-.007	-.001	682
3. Original Specification, Recoding[2]	.000	.000	.762	1.000	.000	.000	680
4. Original Specification without Texas	-.005	.003	.074	.995	-.010	.000	666
5. Original Specification without Texas, Recoding[2]	-.00002	.000	.639	1.000	-.0001	.0001	666
6. Alternate Data Sources[1], Recoding[2]	.000	.000	.340	1.000	.000	.000	682
7. Original Specification, Recoding 0=0	-.006	.004	.084	.994	-.014	.001	359
8. Alternate Data Sources[1], Recoding, 0=0	-.003	.001	.048	.997	-.006	.000	364
9. Alternate Data Sources, No Texas	-.003	.001	.021	.997	-.006	-.001	668
10. Original Specification without state-time trend	-.002	.003	.497	.998	-.008	.004	680
11. Original Specification, Alternate Deterrence Index[3]	-.001	.000	.065	.999	-.002	.000	879

[a] Source: Naci Mocan & Kai Gittings, *Getting Off Death Row: Commuted Sentences and the Deterrent Effect of Capital Punishment*, 46 J.L. & ECON. 453 (2003).

[1] Homicides: NAT'L CTR. FOR HEALTH STATISTICS, MORBIDITY FILE; Death Sentences: BUREAU OF JUSTICE STATISTICS, U.S. DEP'T OF JUSTICE, CAPPUN2003; Executions: DEATH PENALTY INFORMATION CENTER.

[2] Recoding years with zero death sentences to .01 instead of .99.

[3] Executions lagged one year and Death Sentences lagged two years.

Table 2. Growth Curve Models of Effects of Execution and Incarceration on Murder Rates, Using Mocan and Gittings Execution Index and Incarceration Data[a]

	Time		*Time and Time^2*	
Effect	***B***	***p(t)***	***B***	***p(t)***
Execution	-.003	.826	-.007	.829
Custody	-.004	.797	.051	.088
Time * Execution	-.0003	.677	.0005	.916
Time * Custody	-.002	.016	-.010	.018
Time^2 * Execution			-.00003	.853
Time^2 * Custody			.0003	.030
Ratio of Custody to Execution Coefficients				
β (Custody) | β (Execution)	1.50		-6.99	
β (T*Custody) | β (T*Execution)	7.13		-19.72	
β (T^2*Custody) | β(T^2 * Execution)			-10.37	
Model Fit				
-2LL	-3404		-3342	
AIC	-3398		-3336	
BIC	-3385		-3323	

[a] All models estimated with random intercepts and both fixed and random effects for time. Estimates are population-averaged with AR(1) covariance structure. Execution measure derived from H. Naci Mocan & R. Kaj Gittings, *Getting off Death Row: Commuted Sentences and the Deterrent Effect of Capital Punishment*, 46 J.L. & ECON. 453, tbl.2, panel A (2003).

for deterring murder is considerable, and their height casts doubt on the streamlined version of deterrence argued in the new deterrence studies.

IV. RE-ESTIMATING DETERRENCE

One of the highest hurdles of causal inference is the replication requirement.[254] In the conduct of social inquiry, it is commonplace if not imperative for investigators to subject their data to testing under alternate measurement and analytic conditions. Obtaining

254 Epstein & King, *The Rules of Inference*, *supra* note 26.

consistent evidence is a sign of reliability and robustness[255] of the central theoretical and empirical finding. Some of the researchers whose work is central to the claims of the "new deterrence" have followed these norms and made not only their data available for further testing and replication, but also their statistical programming that produced the results they reported. To assess the robustness and stability of the empirical deterrence claims, I chose one of these datasets, from Mocan and Gittings[256] (hereafter, MG), for statistical analyses with a set of alternate measurement and analytic specifications. The results are shown in Tables 1 and 2.

The replication is done in two steps. The first set of analyses accepts the functional form of the regressions that are reported by MG in their 2003 article, but substitutes alternate data sources and also makes a series of adjustments to handle missing data in ways that differ from MG's strategies. In the second set of analyses, reported in Table 2, I vary the functional form of the regression equation and adopt an analytic strategy that responds to concerns discussed earlier about the panel structure of the data and appropriate statistical tests to detect changes over time when observational data are heavily correlated from one year to the next.

A. Sensitivity Tests

The columns in Table 1 show the results of estimates for the deterrence measure reported by MG in Table 2. In the original MG analysis, the deterrence measure is computed as the ratio of executions in the past year to death sentences six years preceding. Table 1 shows only the regression results for that deterrence variable, using the original code and data generously provided by Professors Mocan and Gittings.[257] The columns include a standard set of statistics to characterize the results in each model. Of particular interest is the regression coefficient, the standard error, the probability or statistical significance of the estimate (p(t)), and the number of cases included in the analysis.[258]

255 A finding is considered to be robust when it is insensitive to variation among the inputs and can be reproduced under a variety of sampling and measurement conditions.

256 Mocan & Gittings, *supra* note 10.

257 Mocan and Gittings include several other predictors simultaneously with the deterrence variable. So, these results show the estimated effects of the deterrence variable, controlled statistically for other variables including population characteristics and urbanization, incarceration rates, income and unemployment, infant mortality, other causes of removal from death row (commutations and pardons), prison death rates, the presence of a Republican governor in the state, and state minimum drinking age laws. They also include a dummy variable to account for the spike in homicides in Oklahoma City in 1995 from the bombing of the Murrah Federal Office Building.

258 Readers familiar with regression analyses will be interested in the confidence intervals, which show the range in which the coefficient could vary, and the exponentiated coefficient, which describes the

The first step is a replication of the original MG analysis. Model 1 shows results identical to those reported by MG in several regression estimates in Table 2, row 1. Model 2 uses the original MG specification, but substitutes alternate data sources to measure homicides and executions. MG used homicide statistics obtained from the Uniform Crime Reports, a crime accounting system maintained by the Federal Bureau of Investigation, U.S. Department of Justice. There are well-known limitations in that system, including large amounts of missing data.[259] We use data from the Morbidity and Mortality Files of the National Center for Health Statistics. Homicide counts are generated from death certificates filed by each county's coroner or medical examiner. Cases are classified as homicides pursuant to a separate investigation and decision making process. More important, there is complete coverage in these records for all years in the time series (1976–1998). The second alternate measure is the count of executions in each state. MG used reports of executions obtained from the U.S. Justice Department in an archive that is updated each year based on death row cases. The current version of this dataset is publicly available as Capital Punishment 2003,[260] and is updated annually with new information supplied by the states. The alternate data source is a count of executions generated by the Death Penalty Information Center,[261] a private not-for-profit organization that closely monitors capital punishment legislation and activity across the states and in the federal courts. With these alternate data, the results are again statistically significant, though the regression coefficient is smaller compared to Model 1.

Model 3 uses the original MG data, but applies an alternate computation to estimate deterrence for cases when the denominator in the original measure was zero. Recall that deterrence is measured as the number of executions in a given state divided by the number of death sentences six years earlier. For some observations, this required division by zero, which would produce an infinite result. For these observations, MG replaced the incomputable zero value with .99. The alternate measure was to replace the problem observation with .01, a value that is closer to the true value of zero in the denominator.[262] The result

---

magnitude of the effects of the deterrence variable.

259 See Maltz, *supra* note 124.

260 BUREAU OF JUSTICE STATISTICS, U.S. DEP'T OF JUSTICE, CAPITAL PUNISHMENT IN THE UNITED STATES, 1973–2003 (2004).

261 DEATH PENALTY INFORMATION CENTER, EXECUTIONS IN THE UNITED STATES, 1976–2006 (2006), available at http://www.deathpenaltyinfo.org/article.php?did=414&scid=8.

262 MG recode all state-years with 0 death sentences as having 0.99 death sentences. Thus for non-executing states, the probability of execution is 0.99. When there are zero executions, there is no difference whether one uses 0.99 or 0.01, because the ratio of executions to death sentences remains zero. However, they intended to drop those cases, based on their computer code, so there is no effect on their estimates when they substitute for zero. For the state-years when there are positive (greater than zero) executions, they assume that the denominator is 0.99, but it does influence their estimates because they

here is a dramatic change from Models 1 and 2. The coefficient is now close to 0 (it is rounded to .000 in the table), and deterrence is no longer statistically significant.

Model 4 repeats Model 1—a replication of the original MG analysis—but excludes Texas. The hegemony of Texas in the estimates of deterrence was discussed earlier, and its influence on the distributions suggests that specifications without Texas might show different results. The results here are mixed. The coefficient is in the same range as in Models 1 and 2, but it no longer is statistically significant (p=.074) at the conventional p<.05 threshold.[263] Model 5 repeats Model 4, excluding Texas while adopting the alternative coding procedures of Model 3. The results closely resemble the results in Model 3, and deterrence here is not statistically significant (p=.639). Model 6 repeats Model 2, but adopting the recoding conventions of Model 3; deterrence again is not statistically significant (p=.340).

Models 7 and 8 use a different strategy for addressing the problem of division-by-zero, this time by substituting a true zero for the zero value. The deterrence estimate in Model 7 is the same as in the original MG analysis, but it no longer is statistically significant, with (p=.084). In Model 8, using the alternate data sources, the coefficient is smaller but it once again is significant (p=.048). However, note the sample size is nearly halved: the decrease in the number of cases that are eliminated when true zeros replace the artifactual values of either .01 or .99 for the cases with division-by-zero. In Model 9, using alternate data sources but excluding Texas, the coefficient is half of the original estimate (Model 1), and it is significant (p=.021).

Model 10 omits one predictor from the MG models—a within-state time parameter that is meant to capture variance in the models that is attributable to state-specific time trends within each death penalty state.[264] The contribution of this time trend is not obvious, and possibly is redundant with the linear time trend for the aggregate panel, with state and year fixed effects in the original MG model. Without this time trend, the coefficient for deterrence in Model 10 is not significant (p=.497).

Finally, Model 11 replicates Model 1 but shortens the time lag for executions. Here, deterrence is computed as the number of executions in the previous year divided by the number of death sentences two years prior. This specification emphasizes the temporal proximity of punishment by assuming a shorter duration between death sentences and

---

dropped cases at a lag of six years, not seven. See Donohue & Wolfers, *Uses and Abuses*, *supra* note 25. In the estimates in this article, both these errors are corrected, and several models are estimated with full data and a denominator of 0.01 for years when there are no executions.

263 See Epstein & King, *The Rules of Inference*, *supra* note 26 for a discussion of this convention.

264 See Mocan & Gittings, *supra* note 10, at 461 (providing a more detailed explanation of this time trend).

executions. MG assume that six years[265] temporal proximity brings the importance of the celerity of punishment to the forefront in estimating deterrent effects, since offenders may be less likely to discount punishments that are not postponed far into the future; in other words, celerity increases the present value of a deterrent threat. It also provides a better approximation of how offenders update their information, since they are unlikely to recall the frequency of death sentences in their state from six or seven years earlier. When we substitute this measure, the coefficient becomes very small (β=-.001) and is not statistically significant (p=.065).[266]

The sensitivity of these analyses to alternate specifications undermines the claims by MG of robust deterrence findings. The coefficient for deterrence varies from 0 to -.006 in the 10 alternate models, and only four of the 10 are statistically significant at the conventional threshold of $p<.05$. Note also that in Models 3 through 8 and again in Model 10, the upper bound on the confidence interval is zero or above. This suggests that it is possible that the regression coefficients may be zero or positive, suggesting either no deterrent effect, or a positive or "brutalization" effect of executions. The sensitivity of these analyses to wide swings in the estimates of deterrence when alternate data sources are used and when coding errors are corrected weakens the case for deterrence and introduces uncertainty and fragility when the policy questions demand stability and consistency.

B. A Different Accounting of Time

The panel structure of the data in most of the deterrence studies lends itself to a class of statistical models that explicitly examine change over time and identify the effects of time-varying events that may alter trajectories of homicide. Earlier, I noted the advantages and appropriateness of such models for data with repeated measures over time, where the events in one year are highly correlated with the events in both the preceding and the following years. In this section, I use this functional form to re-estimate the effects of deterrence using the MG dataset.[267]

---

265 In some models, they intended to estimate a seven year lag, although close inspection of the MG programming code shows that they actually estimated a six year lag. Both time intervals are well shorter than the measured lag between sentence and execution, averaging approximately nine years for death sentences handed out from 1973–1995. See LIEBMAN ET AL., A BROKEN SYSTEM, PART II, *supra* note 88.

266 We also increase the sample size in this model to 879 cases, since the shorter lag time means that fewer years are censored due to truncation from lagged denominator in the MG deterrence measure.

267 The models were estimated using the MIXED procedure in SPSS 13.0. The programming commands and the output are available at http://www2.law.columbia.edu/fagan/researchdata/osjcl_deter/. This package was selected because it offered options to specify an autoregressive covariance structure. See *supra* Part III. D. and notes 155–58. Other options to adjust regression estimates in analyses of

One class of models that is designed for these circumstances is hierarchical or mixed effects regressions. These regression models can identify the parameters that shape a trajectory or pattern or sequence of behaviors over time, and estimate the effects of interventions or treatments that might influence these patterns.[268] The models are "mixed" in the sense that some variables are considered fixed and others random. Variables are "fixed" when we assume that they are measured without error, or that they are constant across studies. So, for example, variables such as population, the number of executions or death sentences, or the incarcerated population are fixed effects. We assume that "random" variables have measurement error, and that models with random effects are making inferences or generalizations within some probability distribution.

In mixed effects growth curve modeling, time is usually modeled as both a fixed effect, to control for the effects of specific years in the time series, and a random effect, to estimate change over time in the dependent variable. Of particular interest in this class of models is the interaction of time with each of the fixed effects. This interaction allows the influence of a fixed effect to vary over time as the fixed effect itself changes. Accordingly, the interactions show whether and how the rate of change in the dependent variable over time is affected by the values of the predictor or independent variable at different points in time. Finally, because of "serial correlation," the estimates in Table 2 use an adjustment for autoregression.[269]

The general composite two-level model follows the form:

$$Y_{ij} = \gamma_{00} + \gamma_{10}\text{TIME} + \gamma_{01}\text{EXECUTION} + \gamma_{11}(\text{EXECUTION* TIME}) + \gamma_{02}\text{CUSTODY} + \gamma_{21}(\text{CUSTODY * TIME})] + [\zeta_{01} + \zeta_{1i}\text{TIME} + \varepsilon_{ij}]$$

---

panel data include the use of Newey-West standard errors. Since observations in panel data often are highly correlated over time, this temporal dependence results in serial correlation and thus downwardly biased standard errors. For an illustration using crime data, see Klick & Tabarrok, *supra* note 90. For the derivation of Newey-West standard errors, see Newey & West, *supra* note 162, at 703–08. See also Jeremy Smith & Michael McAleer, *Newey-West Covariance Matrix Estimates for Models with Generated Regressors*, 26 APPLIED ECON. 635 (1994).

268 See, e.g., ANTHONY BRYK & STEPHEN RAUDENBUSH, HIERARCHICAL LINEAR MODELS: APPLICATIONS AND DATA ANALYSIS METHODS (1992); JUDITH SINGER & JOHN B. WILLETT, APPLIED LONGITUDINAL DATA ANALYSIS: MODELING CHANGE AND EVENT OCCURRENCE (2003); Sophia Rabe-Hesketh et al., *Maximum Likelihood Estimates of Limited and Discrete Dependent Variables with Nested Random Effects*, 128 J. ECONOMETRICS 301 (2005).

269 Panel data often are troubled by correlated error terms over time in the relationships between the dependent variables and the predictors. To adjust for this problem, the models are estimated using AR(1) covariance structures. See, e.g., GREENE, *supra* note 157; SINGER & WILLETT, *supra* note 269.

where EXECUTION is the deterrence measure in MG, and CUSTODY represents the incarceration parameter. The cross-level interactions of each predictor with TIME identify whether the effects of TIME differ by levels of the theoretical predictors—i.e., whether EXECUTION or DETERRENCE variables are, in fact, associated with a decrease in homicide rates. This is the critical test. The models are specified with the same time-varying covariates as in MG, Table 2. Estimates are population-averaged, and an autogressive (AR[1]) covariance structure is assumed.

Table 2 shows the results of models that apply mixed effects regressions to the MG data. The models included two expressions of time: a linear measure and a second order polynomial (time and $time^2$). The latter expression of time reflects the actual pattern of change in homicide rates over time during the study interval: rising through 1993 followed by a relatively steep decline through the end of the study period.[270] To illustrate the importance of such assumptions on how we assess deterrence, I compare the results of a model using only a linear measure of time with a model using this second order polynomial change. Although all the variables in the MG analysis were included in these models, Table 2 shows only the results for two predictors: deterrence (EXECUTION) and incarceration (CUSTODY). Incarceration is shown because it is an important counterfactual to the claim of deterrence.[271] Both the main effects for each predictor and the interactions of time with each predictor are shown. The models also include random intercepts, a technique that controls for differences between the states in their initial starting points at the outset of the time series in 1977.[272] As in Table 1, the regression estimate (coefficient) is shown together with the standard error and the statistical significance (probability) for that parameter. To further assess the relative contributions of deterrence and incarceration to changes in homicide rates, Table 2 shows the ratio of the coefficients for the two measures, including the coefficients for their interactions with time.

The left half of Table 2 shows that when we estimate the effects of deterrence using a linear time parameter, deterrence is not statistically significant (p=.677) but incarceration is (p=.016). The ratio of the interactions of TIME * EXECUTION to TIME * CUSTODY is 7.13, suggesting a strong difference in the relative contributions of the two variables to homicide rates. The right half of Table 2 repeats this analysis but with a second order polynomial term to model the effects of the predictors over time. The non-linear term better reflects the actual distribution of homicide over time. The results are the same. The important parameter is the line for the interaction of $TIME^2$ * EXECUTION and $TIME^2$ * CUSTODY. The effects for deterrence are not statistically significant (p=.853), but the

270 See, e.g., Richard Rosenfeld, *Patterns in Adult Homicide: 1980–1995*, in THE CRIME DROP IN AMERICA 130 (Alfred Blumstein & Joel Wallman eds., 2005).

271 Katz et al., *Prison Conditions*, *supra* note 75.

272 See SINGER & WILLETT, *supra* note 269 (discussing the use and interpretation of random intercepts).

effects of incarceration are (p=.030). The ratio of incarceration to executions for this model is 10.37, again suggesting that the contributions of incarceration to declining homicide rates are far greater than the contributions of execution.

The story told by Table 2 is that an alternate functional form, one designed explicitly to account for serial correlation (autoregression) in homicide rates within states over time, produces estimates of deterrence that are not significant. We are unable to reproduce the estimates of deterrence once we correct for this centrally important feature in homicide trends and patterns. The regression coefficients in the model on the left side of Table 2 are similar in size and range to the estimates obtained using the fixed effects regression models in Table 1, but the standard errors are far higher and the results not statistically significant. There is greater range in the estimates of deterrence in the models using the polynomial term on the right side of Table 2. In this model, we find significant effects only for the custody variables while execution remains not significant.

C. Instability and Robustness

These analyses were designed neither to contradict the results shown by MG, nor were they intended as a critique of MG. Rather, these results illustrate the sensitivity and volatility of estimates of the deterrent effects of capital punishment on homicide.[273] The analyses do show the uncertainty and lack of robustness for this one study of the effects of capital punishment on murder. Simple adjustments in measurement, coding, and in the functional form of the regressions all introduce not consistency in the findings of deterrence, but consistency only in the volatility of the critical finding. Moreover, any effects on the murder rate are small, and depending on the model specification and other plausible empirical decisions, also could appear to be a counter-deterrent. But I take no more faith in that finding than I do in deterrence, simply because of the poor conceptual specification of the factors that produce murders in this study and the others in the new deterrence literature, and the numerous limitations in measurement and method that were discussed earlier.

The limitations identified here are not likely to be an artifact of the decisions of MG: that many of the problems identified and addressed in these analyses are also plainly evident in other datasets used in the new deterrence literature.[274] The cyclical movements of homicide over the three decades since *Furman* and *Gregg* are simply too large to be influenced by small numbers of executions that are widely scattered across the states and so heavily concentrated in one state as to make executions in the others appear to be anomalies. Legal

---

273 Donohue and Wolfers have also shown the uncertainty of estimates of the deterrent effects of capital punishment in other studies in the new deterrence literature. See Donohue & Wolfers, *Uses and Abuses*, *supra* note 25.

274 For example, Shepherd's decision to drop cases with missing data on homicide rates in high murder and high execution states such as Florida. See Shepherd, *Murders of Passion*, *supra* note 15, at 304.

scholars and legislators makers should take note of this uncertainty before taking what amounts to a leap of faith rather than an extension of scientific fact.

V. CONCLUSION: A CAUTIONARY TALE

The new deterrence studies claim that each execution prevents anywhere from three to thirty two murders. This is hardly a new claim: about 30 years ago, similar claims about the death penalty were made just before executions resumed following the post-*Furman* moratorium. One thousand executions later, the claim has been revived by a small group of researchers touting advances in econometric techniques and new data sources that resolve technical problems in the earlier work. Endorsing these claims, Sunstein and Vermeule suggest that this evidence "morally" requires executions, a conclusion echoed by Becker and Posner. These arguments too are neither new nor correct.

The new deterrence literature fails to provide a stable foundation of scientific evidence on which to base law or policy. Nor can this evidence be used to calibrate the normative implications of new "facts" about lives saved or lost. As in the debate over Ehrlich's findings, simple but necessary changes in the functional form of regression equations, combined with measurement strategies that provide more complete and accurate data, produce different results that differ from the current crop of studies, results that are far more equivocal. Even more significant modifications to these studies, such as using research designs that more closely approximate quasi-experiments that account for murder trends in states with no executions, also produce different and equivocal results.[275] Conceptual errors and omissions in specifying the multiple influences on murder rates seriously bias the estimates of deterrence.

The wide range of results, and the sensitivity of findings to even the most minor tweaks, introduces model uncertainty. Each study in the new deterrence literature, both those that confirm and those that challenge the deterrence claims, uses a particular model of crime that embodies a choice of data, time period, control variables, and statistical specifications. Variation in these choices is part of a vigorous scientific vetting of a theoretical proposition. While model uncertainty is endemic to this process, the uncertainty here is so wide and so profound as to raise strong cautions on reaching any conclusion about deterrence, much less policy. At the end of the day, econometric "pyrotechnics"[276] may dazzle, but they are diversions that fail to advance the debate on capital punishment.

Sunstein and Vermeule embrace these findings, and use the evidence to animate their calls for a more vigorous use of the death penalty. Sunstein and Vermeule are willing to tolerate error in the estimates of deterrence, arguing that doubts about their robustness should not stand in the way of increasing the use of execution if executions can avoid harm.[277]

275 See Donohue & Wolfers, *Uses and Abuses*, *supra* note 25.

276 *Id.*

277 Sunstein & Vermeule, *supra* note 34.

The problem for them is that the fragility of the new deterrence evidence, a function of the fundamental empirical and theoretical errors in this body of work, raises concerns greater than simply just "doubt": the conclusions in this body of work are wrong, there is no reliable evidence of deterrence. The only scientifically and ethically acceptable conclusion from the complete body of existing social science literature on deterrence and the death penalty is that it is impossible to tell whether deterrent effects are strong or weak, or whether they exist at all.[278]

Social science sets a high bar for causal inference, demanding caution until such claims can be replicated under a variety of experimental conditions. Several such replication efforts, facilitated by generous sharing of data and statistical programs, suggest that these claims of deterrence are volatile and inconsistent, sensitive to alternate ways to measure murder rates and decisions on how to account for anomalies such as missing information and years with no homicides.[279] Depending on commonplace methodological adjustments, regression models can just as easily show that executions increase murder or reduce murder.[280] In fact, this work fails the tests of rigorous replication and robustness analysis that are the hallmarks of good science. And the analyses here and elsewhere suggest that the prospect for replications that will produce a range of estimates that can confirm the core finding of deterrence are not forthcoming.

As a matter of social science, it is important to ask how this debate, in reality the second round in the debate over deterrence and the death penalty, arrived at this point. Like the cold fusion scandal in the 1980s,[281] when bold scientific claims were greeted with wide-

---

278 Donohue & Wolfers, *The Death Penalty*, *supra* note 147.

279 Donohue & Wolfers, *Uses and Abuses*, *supra* note 25.

280 *Id.*

281 For a thorough account of the cold fusion episode, see Michele Landis Dauber, *The Big Muddy*, 57 STAN. L. REV. 1899 (2005). When Stanley Pons and Martin Fleischmann announced at a press conference in March 1989 that they had achieved cold fusion, their news was wildly embraced by the public and the media as a scientific breakthrough that promised to transform the nation's protracted and contentious debate over energy policy. (Cold fusion is defined by Wikipedia as "a sustained nuclear fusion in a beaker of water at room temperature that would produce vast quantities of energy at little cost and with few environmental risks." For a general description of cold fusion, see Cold Fusion on Wikipedia, at http://en.wikipedia.org/wiki/Cold_Fusion). But the scientific community greeted the news with skepticism and caution. The discovery came not through a process of vetting via scientific publication and replication, but instead was presented to the scientific community via the news media. Although they invited peer review and replication, they pre-empted scientific testing by claiming that other scientists had already "repeated his experiments with success." FRANK CLOSE, TOO HOT TO HANDLE: THE RACE FOR COLD FUSION 335 (1991). The claim that other scientists had vetted the Pons and Fleischmann finding was untrue. Although some scientists reached similar conclusions, others were skeptical and suspected several methodological flaws. It took some time, since these other researchers

spread enthusiasm by the public that fueled a sharp mobilization of academic and political institutions, there was a quick and passionate embrace of the new deterrence claims by a small community of legal scholars and death penalty advocates. As the new evidence leeched into the mainstream media and eventually into political discourse and appellate arguments, the evidence was reified as scientifically rigorous. And as with the cold fusion episode, these claims seem to be unable to withstand scientific vetting.

There are several distinctions between cold fusion and the current deterrence debate. Cold fusion was the work of two scientists. The new deterrence is the work of several researchers, nearly all economists, using core elements of identical data sets on executions, death sentences, and murders, and submitting their papers to peer reviewed journals in economics and non-peer reviewed law reviews. One can only speculate about what happens between submission of an empirical article to a good journal and an editorial decision. But Walter McManus showed that it is not unreasonable to assume that a reviewer's priors influence her posteriors.[282] When McManus introduced the priors of researchers into a representative regression model of murders and executions, he showed that "significant conflicts remain over the estimated deterrent effect of an additional execution, even after the researchers have confronted the same data. The conflicting interpretations of the data evidence are serious."[283] Model uncertainty would be large in a condition such as this.[284] The priors of the researchers, in other words, overwhelm the data, and the data simply are not strong enough to lead researchers to a consensus or convergent conclusion. It is not hard to see, given McManus' demonstration, how like-minded researchers would reach similar conclusions.

But understanding the priors of researchers can not explain how reviewers and journal editors would overlook the same flaws that are apparent to many others who have critiqued this body of work. One assumes that reviewers and editors have a wider distribution of priors, but whether the priors of reviewers and editors enter into peer review decisions is unknowable for the moment. I suspect a different dynamic: a set of papers about murder were reviewed as part of an interior conversation among economists who have little or no familiarity with the dynamics of murder, murderers, and criminal legal institutions.

---

were starting from scratch, but eventually, physicists rejected the cold fusion claims as soon as mistakes were uncovered and published. According to John Huizenga, one physicist said of their research, "If you got a paper like that from an undergraduate, you would give it an F." JOHN HUIZENGA, COLD FUSION: THE SCIENTIFIC FIASCO OF THE CENTURY 24 (1992). Sadly, as evidence mounted that the results could not be replicated, Pons and Fleishmann refused to admit that there were problems in the initial research that undermined their claims.

282 McManus, *supra* note 6.

283 *Id.* at 423.

284 Leamer, *supra* note 6.

Other opinions seem to be unwelcome in this literature.[285] Editors and reviewers alike seem impervious to the kind of intellectual humility that would sustain a result at dissonance with the dominant paradigm of price theory. When discussing the study of deterrence as carried out by economists, Coase[286] notes in Economics and Contiguous Disciplines that:

> Punishment, for example, can be regarded as the price of crime. An economist will not debate whether increased punishment will reduce crime; he will merely try to answer the question, by how much? The economist's analysis may fail to touch some of the problems found in the other social systems. ... [287]

Indeed, potentially the most disturbing concerns in this interlude reside not just in the willingness (or preference) of good journals to publish stylized econometrics over substantive social science theory. Rather, these decisions also are rooted in the striking absence of either critical commentary or substantive contributions by scholars from other disciplines since the initial publication of these articles over the past decade.[288] In fact, these other disciplines are marginalized or dismissed in the current debate. Nor do editors or reviewers challenge this self-referential group with concerted attempts to test more rigorously for the immediate impact of a change in threatened punishment with more detailed crime data and a better causal theory. Unfortunately for anyone interested in the deterrent impact of harsher sentences, several of the built-in safeguards for self-correction within the social sciences have clearly failed in this instance. Whether the explanation resides in orthodox beliefs, lack of critical skepticism, or whatever else may be responsible, the failure to maintain scientific and intellectual rigor is particularly disturbing. Indeed, any study which is not adequately challenged by one's scholarly peers can only hinder rather than help the credibility of scholarly contributions to either side of the deterrence debate.

As a regulatory matter, embracing the new deterrence findings ignores risks of error that would have serious consequences. As a normative matter, the implications are dangerous.

---

285 Sorensen et al., *supra* note 129, at 569 (showing that Cloninger and Marchessi fail to cite one article on the deterrent effects of the death penalty authored by a sociologist). My own reading of these articles shows similar omissions in several articles. Shepherd breezily dismisses the contributions of sociologists to the empirical literature on the death penalty as insubstantial and perhaps ideologically motivated. See Shepherd, *Murders of Passion*, *supra* note 15; Shepherd, *Deterrence Versus Brutalization*, *supra* note 46.

286 Ronald H. Coase, *Economics and Contiguous Disciplines*, 7 J. LEGAL STUD. 201 (1978).

287 *Id.* at 210.

288 In fact, concern with declining critical commentary has also been raised by others. For an empirical illustration of the problem in major economic journals, see, for example, Philip R.P. Coelho et al., *Decline in Critical Commentary*, 1963–2004, 2 ECON. J. WATCH 355 (2005), available at http://www.econjournalwatch.org/pdf/CoelhoetalEconomicsInPracticeAugust2005.pdf.

Research at Columbia Law School on reversals in capital sentences from 1973–1995 showed that the number of serious errors leading to reversal in capital sentences increased sharply with higher rates of death sentences per murder.[289] More than two death sentences in three during this time were reversed, and at resentencing, approximately five percent were exonerated.[290] Even the harshest critics of the Columbia studies acknowledge that the lower bound on error rates is four in ten.[291] Making more people eligible for execution increases the risks of horrific errors of wrongful conviction that are far more likely in states that execute "many people." The clamor to make policy if not law under these conditions of uncertainty is expensive and dangerous.

In this episode, a group of scholars combine some sophisticated empirical strategies to compare the use of the death penalty with a sample of state murder rates. They introduce a set of theoretically tangential controls, and reach a conclusion of deterrence that fails to replicate when more complete data are applied, when unsustainable coding decisions are corrected, and when the functional form is modified to account for the rigid structure of the data. The appeal of this simple story of deterrence is obvious. Sadly, though, "it is easier to muddy the waters than it is to calm them,"[292] especially in the midst of recent erosion in popular support for the death penalty that followed the moratorium on executions in Illinois,[293] the exoneration of the 100th person from death row,[294] and the revelations of widespread reversals and errors in capital sentences.[295] Complexity and uncertainty, though, are what the data say. Until this research survives the rigors of replication and thorough testing of alternative hypotheses, this research provides no basis for decisions to take many more lives.

This cohort of studies and researchers, like Ehrlich before them, has created unjustified confidence in the minds of legislators, death penalty advocates, and a small group of legal scholars about the capacity of death sentences and executions to deter murder. They raise their concerns to a high moral ground, and brush off evidentiary doubts as unreasonable cautions that place potential beneficiaries at risk of severe harm. Although rebukes like this

---

289 See LIEBMAN ET AL., A BROKEN SYSTEM, PART II, *supra* note 88.

290 LIEBMAN ET AL., A BROKEN SYSTEM, PART I, *supra* note 231.

291 Joseph L. Hoffman, *Violence and the Truth*, 76 IND. L.J. 939, 946 (2001).

292 Dauber, *supra* note 282.

293 See Rob Warden, *Illinois Death Penalty Reform: How it Happened, What it Promises*, 95 J. CRIM. L. & CRIMINOLOGY 381, 406 (2005). See *generally* DAVID L. PROTESS & ROBERT WARDEN, A PROMISE OF JUSTICE (1998) (documenting the media reactions to the exonerations of the four death row inmates).

294 Samuel R. Gross et al., *Exonerations in the United States*, 1989 Through 2003, 95 J. CRIM. L. & CRIMINOLOGY 523, 527 (2005).

295 See LIEBMAN ET AL., A BROKEN SYSTEM, PART I, *supra* note 231; LIEBMAN ET AL., A BROKEN SYSTEM, PART II, *supra* note 88.

and others may put the brakes on the rush to once again embrace deterrence as the cure for murder, interludes such as this one also remind us to invoke the tough, neutral social science standards and commonsense causal reasoning before taking a path that can do far more harm than good.

APPENDIX A. PARTIAL LIST OF STUDIES PUBLISHED AFTER 1990 ON DETERRENT EFFECTS OF THE DEATH PENALTY

Harold J. Brumm & Dale O. Cloninger, *Perceived Risk of Punishment and the Commission of Homicides: A Covariance Structure Analysis*, 31 J. ECON. BEHAV. & ORG. 1 (1996).

Dale O. Cloninger, *Capital Punishment and Deterrence: A Portfolio Approach*, 24 APP. ECON. 645 (1992).

Cloninger, Dale O. & Roberto Marchesini, *Execution and Deterrence: A Quasi-Controlled Group Experiment*, 35 APPLIED ECON. 569 (2001).

Dale O. Cloninger & Roberto Marchesini, *Executions, Moratoriums, Commutations, and Deterrence: The Case of Illinois* (June 2005), available at http://econwpa.wustl.edu:8089/eps/le/papers/0507/0507002. pdf.

Hashem Dezhbakhsh et al., *Does Capital Punishment Have a Deterrent Effect? New Evidence from Postmoratorium Panel Data*, 5 AM. L. & ECON. REV. 344 (2003).

Hashem Dezhbakhsh & Joanna M. Shepherd, *The Deterrent Effect of Capital Punishment: Evidence from a "Judicial Experiment,"* 44 ECON. INQUIRY 512 (2006)

Lawrence Katz et al., *Prison Conditions, Capital Punishment, and Deterrence*, 5 AM. L. & ECON. REV. 318 (2003).

Zhiqiang Liu, *Capital Punishment and the Deterrence Hypothesis: Some New Insights and Empirical Evidence*, 30 E. ECON. J. 237 (2004)

H. Naci Mocan & R. Kaj Gittings, *Getting Off Death Row: Commuted Sentences and the Deterrent Effect of Capital Punishment*, 46 J.L. & ECON. 453 (2003).

Joanna M. Shepherd, *Deterrence Versus Brutalization: Capital Punishment's Differing Impacts Among States*, 104 MICH. L. REV. 203 (2005).

Joanna M. Shepherd, *Murders of Passion, Execution Delays, and the Deterrence of Capital Punishment*, 33 J. LEGAL STUD. 283 (2004).

Jon Sorenson et al., *Capital Punishment and Deterrence: Examining the Effect of Executions on Murder in Texas*, 45 CRIME & DELINQ. 481 (1999).

Paul R. Zimmerman, *Estimates of the Deterrent Effect of Alternative Execution Methods in the United States: 1978–2000*, 65 AM. J. ECON. & SOC. 909 (2006).

Paul R. Zimmerman, *Executions, Deterrence, and the Incidence of Murder*, 7 J. APPLIED ECON. 163 (2004).

James A. Yunker, *A New Statistical Analysis of Capital Punishment Incorporating U.S. Postmoratorium Data*, 82 SOC. SCI. Q. 297 (2002).

DISCUSSION QUESTIONS

1. Drawing primarily from the Fagan article, trace the history of deterrence research. What have been the primary arguments, research methods, conclusions, and limitations? Where does Fagan leave us (or the field of deterrence research)? Is there a roadmap to follow into the future? If not, what should it be?
2. What claims have been made in support of the deterrent effect (consider the magnitude of the effect, the different variables influencing or determining the effect, the types of crimes that the effect does or does not apply to), and what are some of the specific tests or comparisons that have been made to support these arguments?
3. Review the various facets of Fagan's critique of deterrence theory research. Consider, for example: methodological narcissism, faulty data sets, the "Texas effect," poor modeling, and more. Do you think that some of his arguments carry more weight than others? Explain your answer.
4. Fagan suggests that there is a vexing problem with deterrence research because once any research (supportive or non-supportive of deterrence or the death penalty in general), the media, political groups, and advocacy groups will seize on the information to support their vision or their agenda. When research is flawed, this presents serious problems according to Fagan. How do you respond to this argument? Can we prevent 'research abuse' in a democratic society? If peer-reviewed publications don't prevent these problems, what can or should be done to promote "truth" in research regarding the death penalty?

THE COST OF THE DEATH PENALTY

Introduction

Starving the Death Penalty: Do Financial Constraints Limit Its Use?
By James W. Douglas and Helen King Stockstill

Potential Savings from Abolition of the Death Penalty in North Carolina
By Philip J. Cook

This chapter presents two readings pertaining to the cost of the death penalty. In recent years abolitionists have seized the cost issue as a means of driving home their argument. While such an argument may be compelling to some, it is fraught with methodological complications. Estimating the cost of the death penalty is difficult for a number of reasons. For example, many individuals from different sectors of the justice system become involved in capital cases, so information is needed from many different sources; most capital cases take many years to bring to a conclusion, so costs are ongoing and inflationary adjustments are needed; there are different types of costs to account for, such as direct costs and indirect (e.g., social costs); and a number of different estimates and assumptions are required (in some cases very crude estimates and methods are used in the haste to publish reports on costs). Still, death penalty costs studies are likely to increase in number in the upcoming years, and they will undoubtedly produce a number of different findings using a number of different methodologies, and the debates will continue.

The two articles included in this chapter represent recent cost studies (Douglas and Stockstill, 2008; Cook, 2009), and they provide us with two distinctly different approaches to studying the cost of the death penalty. Douglas and Stockstill's article primarily concerns the extent to which local prosecutors in South Carolina factor in costs associated with death penalty prosecutions in their decisions to file capital charges. There concern, then, is more with how the cost factor affects prosecutorial decision making in capital cases rather than with figuring out just how much it costs to prosecute capital cases. Cook tackles the cost estimation issue in a more direct manner. His primary concern is to estimate how much the death penalty cost the state of North Carolina in a two-year span (2005 to 2006), compared with the costs the state would have incurred (or the savings it would have realized) if the death penalty had been abolished during that time period.

Douglas and Stockstill use two research methods to estimate the extent to which cost considerations affect prosecutors' decisions to file capital charges–interviews with solicitors (chief prosecutors) in South Carolina (nine out of 16, 56%, completed the survey), as well as an interview with the state's executive director of prosecution coordination; and a statistical analysis (at the county level) of the relationship between county wealth (measured as median household income) and the number of death penalty cases filed in each county between 2005 and 2007, controlling for such factors as county population, percent African-American, Index Crime Rate, and partisan identification of the prosecutors (Douglas and Stockstill, 2008, pp. 333–334). Briefly, their findings suggest that prosecutors do not consider costs when deciding to file capital cases, and all respondents "... maintained that cost issues would never dissuade them from pursuing the death penalty in a case" (ibid., p. 330). Three of the nine respondents said they considered costs when deciding whether to file capital charges, and three respondents mentioned that they had heard of other prosecutors avoiding capital prosecutions because of cost considerations (ibid., pp. 330–331). On the other hand, the authors found a significant relationship between county wealth and the number of capital charges filed, and the only other factor (out of the four control variables mentioned above) with a significant relationship to number of capital charges filed was county population. Thus, the Douglas and Stockstill article both supports and challenges their hypothesis that cost considerations affect decisions to file capital charges in South Carolina.

Readers should be mindful of several limitations to the Douglas and Stockstill study. As they acknowledge (p. 335), their study includes only one state, funding for capital cases comes from both county and state sources (they measured only county wealth), and they did not address how funding affects the quality of defense in capital cases. Other concerns about this study include the small sample of prosecutors and the low response rate, as well as the county-level analysis. While county wealth and resources may factor into decisions to file capital charges, the factors that prosecutors include in their decisions to file capital charges (such as quality of evidence, victims' wishes, and aggravating factors, to mention a few) largely come into play at the case or individual level; thus the statistical analysis of county wealth and number of capital cases filed my suffer from the ecological fallacy problem (Robinson, 1950); that is, a county-level analysis of an individual level phenomenon may produce inaccurate estimates of the relationship between the independent and dependent variables. A case-level analysis, or a multi-level analysis, may have produced more accurate findings.

Cook (2009) presents a more detailed analysis of death penalty costs by developing a comparison of the cost of the death penalty in North Carolina to the likely costs in the absence of the death penalty, covering a two-year period (2005–2006). In order to conduct this analysis, Cook made the assumption that most savings realized would result from fewer government activities required by capital cases and would free up resources for other cases in the court system (thus, abolition would not likely produce lower agency budgets). Cook suggested that this would produce an improvement in the quality of justice overall, since there would be more resources available for non-capital cases (Cook, 2009, p. 8). Other assumptions made by Cook include: abolition of the death penalty would not affect the murder rate (the flow of cases into the system, essentially a rejection of the deterrence argument), murder cases that would have been handled as capital cases would proceed in the system similar to the way that non-capital cases proceed; offenders on death row, upon abolition, would be assigned to incarceration conditions in a manner similar to those sentenced to life without parole (LWOP); post-conviction activity after abolition would proceed in a manner similar to post-conviction activity for individuals sentenced to LWOP.

Following his discussion regarding assumptions, Cook provides a detailed description of the data used for his analysis (1,034 murder cases in 2005–2006). He also distinguishes between "cash costs" (specific, measurable payments for private attorneys paid to represent indigent defendants, for expert witness, to select and convent juries, for example) and "in-kind costs" (" … diversion of resources … that would be available for other criminal cases within the same criminal justice agency") (ibid., pp. 17–18).

Cook includes 592 cases in his final analysis (murder cases in 2005–2006 that did not end in dismissal or conviction for less than second degree murder). Cook estimates costs associated with the trial phase, appeal and resentencing phases, prison costs, and appeals at the end of the trial phase. He concludes that if capital punishment had been abolished in North Carolina, state expenditures on murder cases would have been reduced by $21.6 million, or $10.8 million per year (ibid., 29). Cook points out that his analysis does not factor in social costs associated with abolition (e.g., affects on victims' families and others, other costs to society produced by murders). Since he assumes that abolition would have little or no impact on the murder rate, he suggests that a calculation of social costs in this analysis would not have been very illuminating (ibid., p. 30). In addition, like the Douglas and Stockstill research, his analysis represents only one state and only two years, so it is difficult to generalize the findings.

Students and readers who pursue further inquiry into cost issues pertaining to the death penalty will likely encounter some frustrations. The two articles presented here represent reasonable attempts to estimate cost issues using accepted research methods. Still, they have significant limitations and rely on assumptions that may produce spirited debate (e.g., Cook's assumption that the death penalty has no affect on the murder rate). We should appreciate the articles because they at least describe in detail the methods, data, and assumptions used, which will allow for replication, further testing of assumptions by future research, and methodological refinements in death penalty cost analyses, all of which are needed in order to further this avenue of inquiry.

Starving the Death Penalty

Do Financial Constraints Limit Its Use?

James W. Douglas and Helen King Stockstill

Death penalty cases are expensive for judicial systems to administer, in terms of both time and money. This is a potential problem for the equitable administration of justice when such cases are financed by local governments. The relative wealth of local jurisdictions varies, giving some a greater ability to raise revenues for public purposes. Given the scarcity of resources, especially in poorer jurisdictions, it is possible that cost considerations play a part in the decision over whether to file capital charges. We explore this issue in South Carolina through both interviews of local prosecutors and analysis of death penalty caseloads for 2005–07. While local prosecutors recognize that cost can be a concern, they claim that money issues do not influence their decisions regarding whether to file capital charges. In contrast, we find in our quantitative analysis a positive relationship between county wealth and death penalty caseloads.

One argument by opponents of the death penalty is that the money needed to prosecute capital cases is simply too much to justify seeking that penalty (see Dieter, 1994). The American Civil Liberties Union (ACLU, 2007) maintains that capital-punishment cases waste scarce public resources, costing as much as 70 percent more than life imprisonment. Former California judge Donald McCartin complains: "It costs 10 times more to kill these guys than to keep them alive in prison. It's absurd. And imagine the poor victims' families having to go through this again and again" (Dillow, 2008). There is little doubt that death penalty cases are very expensive, and thus it is important to examine the extent to which cost affects prosecutors' decisions to file capital charges. This is an especially salient question for states where trial court operations are dependent upon local governments for funding. If officials in jurisdictions with fewer resources are unwilling or unable to finance capital cases, then there is the potential for serious inequities in the administration of justice within a state. We address whether the death penalty has become an option that only wealthy jurisdictions can afford by examining the decisions of solicitors to file capital charges within their judicial circuits in South Carolina.

We chose South Carolina for study because it is one of twenty-one states where local counties pay for a majority of trial-court expenses.[1] This reliance on local funding makes south Carolina a good case through which to assess the extent to which the disparities between counties' ability to pay for court activities are affecting judicial decision making. Another obviously important characteristic that makes South Carolina appropriate for this study is that certain crimes within the state are in fact subject to the death penalty. South Carolina law permits use of the death penalty in cases involving either murder with aggravating circumstances or criminal sexual conduct with a minor with aggravating circumstances (BJS, 2007). At the time of this study in 2008, South Carolina had a total of 58 inmates on death row, ranking it fourteenth in this regard among the thirty-eight states where the death penalty is legal (median number of death-row inmates = 38) (DPIC, 2008a). So, the death penalty option is both available and used in South Carolina. South Carolina has executed thirty-seven people since 1976, including one as recently as 2007 (DPIC, 2008b).

LOCAL FUNDING AND THE ADMINISTRATION OF JUSTICE

Advocates of the judiciary have long argued that unequal funding across the judicial system risks inequality in the administration of justice (Tobin, 1999). The problem for the courts is not unlike that faced by local school systems. Because school funding in many states is dependent upon local resources, poorer jurisdictions have complained about their inability to match the lavish spending on education in high-income areas. The resulting imbalance negatively affects the quality of education for children in the former. Empirical evidence makes clear that differences in funding levels affect academic achievement across schools (Condron and Roscigno, 2003:18–36; Murray, Evans, and Schwab 1998:789–812). Similarly, funding disparities among court systems can have a negative effect on court performance, particularly in the area of case-processing times, in jurisdictions with less wealth (Wolfson, 1994; Tobin, 1999).

To reduce financial inequities, reformers have pushed states to take over the funding of trial court systems to create more uniform quality of justice across local jurisdictions (Baar, 1975; Hays, 1978; Tobin, 1999). If local funding does result in inequities in the administration of justice, we should expect to see the wealth of local jurisdictions influence

---

1 Those states are Arizona, Arkansas, California, Florida, Georgia, Idaho, Illinois, Indiana, Louisiana, Michigan, Minnesota, Mississippi, Montana, Nevada, Ohio, Pennsylvania, South Carolina, Tennessee, Texas, Washington, and Wisconsin (Tobin, 1996).

the willingness of prosecutors to file capital charges. Studies have shown that death penalty cases are more expensive than cases in which only life imprisonment is sought (Ehrmann, 1952; Costanzo, 1997; Radelet and Borg, 2000). This being the case, local officials have to ask themselves if there are not better ways to spend their finite resources. They have to ask whether they can afford the death penalty.

JUDICIAL CIRCUIT FUNDING IN SOUTH CAROLINA

Trial courts in South Carolina are organized into sixteen circuits, each composed of between two and five counties (median number of counties = 2.5). Each county has its own courthouse for cases originating within its borders. Judicial agencies, including the solicitors' offices, receive funding from the state based upon a number of formulas, principally on a per-capita basis; factors such as the caseloads or crime rates are not considered in the formula, placing pressure on circuits with heavy workloads to ask for more resources from their counties.

A special fund does exist to help finance death penalty cases. The fund automatically provides $25,000 to courts where death penalty charges have been filed. Trial court officials can request additional money from this fund, but the entire fund holds only $500,000. The South Carolina Commission on Indigent Defense also provides money to help pay death penalty expenses for the local public defenders' offices.

Despite the resources provided by the state, trial court circuits are dependent upon their local counties for a significant portion of their funding. The solicitors interviewed indicated that an average of 60.4 percent of their budgets were received from their counties (range = 35 to 75 percent). Only two solicitors reported relying on their counties for less than 60 percent of their funding, and both stated that local money financed only 35 percent of their budgets. These two circuits had the lowest median household income, which provides a crude indicator that richer counties are appropriating more for their judicial systems while poorer counties depend more heavily on state funds.

THIS STUDY

As the chief prosecutors in South Carolina's sixteen judicial circuits, the solicitors are responsible for making decisions on which charges to file against defendants. The decision to seek the death penalty rests with them; how capital punishment is administered across South Carolina is shaped largely by their attitudes about the circumstances that justify the death penalty's use (Songer and Unah, 206:60). They are, therefore, the appropriate officers to query about the factors taken into account in the decision whether to bring capital charges in a particular case. We therefore sought to interview the solicitors, and nine agreed, a 56.3 percent participation rate.[2] The individuals who agreed to be interviewed had an average of 5.7 years of experience as solicitors and 16.6 years as prosecutors. There were no systematic differences along the dimensions of median household income, population, percent African-American, and crime rate between participating and nonparticipating circuits.

To help reduce selection bias further, we interviewed the executive director of the South Carolina Commission on Prosecution Coordination, who could provide a broad understanding of our research questions because his office is responsible for coordinating the administrative operations of the sixteen solicitors' offices and lobbying the state legislature on the solicitors' behalf. Interviews allowed us the flexibility to tease out differences between rich and poor counties within each circuit. Solicitors serving both rich and poor counties were able to discriminate between those counties when answering the questions.

Our interview format consisted of open-ended questions, which asked the respondents to provide some background on the use of the death penalty in their circuits, describe the factors most important in determining whether to bring capital charges against a defendant, and provide information about budgetary issues related to death penalty cases. All interviews were conducted by telephone by the senior author. Each participant was promised that responses would not be attributed to individuals, particularly important because solicitors are elected. Because seven of the sixteen solicitors did not consent to interviews despite the promise of anonymity, we supplemented our qualitative analysis with statistical analysis of data concerning county wealth and capital caseloads.

SOLICITORS' COMMENTS REGARDING THE DEATH PENALTY

Use of the Death Penalty. To ascertain the extent to which death penalty cases occurred in each circuit of the state, we asked respondents about the last time that a capital charge was filed in their jurisdictions and how often such charges were filed. All but one of the solicitors interviewed reported that their circuits either were prosecuting a death penalty case or had done so at least once in the past four years. However, the frequency with which they claimed to prosecute such cases differed substantially across circuits. Three reported that no more than one case appeared in their circuits every ten years; three reported at least one every five years; two reported that they averaged about one per year; and one reported two to three cases per year. **Decision Calculus.** One would like to believe that the decision to use the death penalty is not entered into lightly. After all, the authority of the government to take a human life is its most extreme power. The solicitors universally described sets of rigorously defined factors they use when deciding whether to pursue the death penalty. Of course, all respondents indicated that they first make sure potential cases

2 Three solicitors referred us to their deputy solicitors. For simplicity, we refer to all respondents as "solicitors."

meet the legal criteria for capital charges, but none believed that meeting the legal requirements alone was sufficient to warrant capital charges. Eight commented that they would consider only cases in which the crime was egregious in nature. Examples given included the murder of someone who was particularly vulnerable, such as a child or elderly person; multiple homicides; crimes that "terrorize" the community; crimes that put large numbers of innocent people at risk, such as a shoot-out in public; the murder of a law-enforcement officer; and murder combined with rape.

For five solicitors, the quality of evidence is extremely important. They generally remarked that they do not simply want to be confident that they will win their cases. They maintained that the severity of the death penalty is so great that guilt must be absolutely certain. One solicitor stated, "It is not enough to have evidence that will convict someone beyond a reasonable doubt. It must be beyond any doubt," and another said, "The evidence of guilt must be ironclad. The quality of evidence is vital to my decision."

For five solicitors, the wishes of victims' families are important when they consider the death penalty. Families may ask prosecutors not to pursue capital charges because they are morally opposed to capital punishment or they do not want to go through the emotional strain of a capital case. One solicitor summed up the issue:

> Capital cases are a lengthy process. They take 20 years. Family members must live with the case as long as it is going on. There are many appeals. Many family members ask me to go for life without parole instead because those types of cases take less time and are more likely to get a plea.

The background of the defendant is an important factor for four of the respondents. They stated that individuals with long criminal records or violent histories were more likely to be candidates for the death penalty. As one solicitor commented, "We try to separate bad people from normal people who do bad things." However, these solicitors claimed that they are not just looking for signs that an individual is a "bad" person; they are also looking for indicators of the defendants' culpability, particularly whether defendants knew that what they did was wrong. One solicitor went so far as to disqualify individuals who had below-average IQs from capital charges.

Cost as a Factor. Only three solicitors stated that they considered the cost associated with death penalty cases when deciding whether to file capital charges. Each, however, maintained that cost issues would never dissuade them from pursuing the death penalty in a case. Instead, they claimed that cost in both time and money was more a matter of which they needed to be acutely aware, rather than a factor that could eliminate the death penalty as a possibility. We queried each of the other six solicitors who did not mention cost as a factor in their decision calculus about whether it might affect their decision making. Each responded that they had never considered cost. However, one admitted that it was not beyond the realm of possibility for cost issues to affect decision making regarding the death penalty in the future. Two solicitors also indicated that county council members in their circuits have become concerned over the high cost of certain cases and made comments to them in that regard. They both argued, however, that no council member had ever tried to pressure them to avoid the death penalty for a case.

When asked about the specific costs associated with death penalty cases, all of the respondents indicated that the majority of the expenses fall on the defense and the court system more generally, not on their offices. A typical response was:

> It is not more expensive for my office in terms of trial costs. My staff is all on salary, so my expenses are relatively constant. Jury costs can go up more because they are often sequestered; so hotel, meal, and police overtime to guard them runs costs up. Costs for expert witnesses might be higher. Most expert witness costs fall on the defense though because they are trying to show they did everything possible to defend their clients. Overall, the costs for a capital case are very high. These cases take 20 years. It is cheaper to put someone in prison for life than to try someone for the death penalty.

The solicitors reported a multitude of factors that drive up the costs of capital cases. These include a state requirement that all defendants be represented by two lawyers, increased use of investigators and expert witnesses by the defense, overtime pay for court officials such as clerks and deputies, the length of the cases, and appeals. They also stated that jury expenses are much higher for capital cases because they often have to go out of their jurisdictions to find a jury, the jury pool needs to be larger, jury consultants are generally used by the defense, the jury is automatically sequestered, and the length of the trial tends to be much longer than for a regular murder case. Moreover, the position of the court tends to be one of caution. One solicitor pointed out that judges in South Carolina are very willing to support defense attorneys' requests for resources and time and that providing a thorough defense is not cheap.

The solicitors did admit that death penalty cases do not come without costs for their offices, but these costs come more in the form of case backlogs and overworked staff than in direct financial costs. Only two solicitors claimed that death penalty cases impose no extra costs on their offices; they stated that the counties in their circuits were relatively wealthy and provide them with all the resources they need. The remaining seven solicitors asserted that the tremendous amount of time involved in trying a capital case limited their offices' abilities to process other cases on their dockets. For example, one remarked, "I have a small staff. I only have one attorney for one of my counties and only two each for the others. Capital cases tax our resources. Who handles all the other cases while we work on the capital case?" And still another observed,

> The cases are time consuming and stressful. If we have a capital case, besides myself, I need at least one lawyer working on it full-time. Since I only have a few prosecutors, cases get backed up. For the county where I only have one prosecutor, who is going to handle the rest of the caseload? This raises costs for the counties because many of the defendants for these other cases are locked-up while awaiting trial.

Thus, despite capital cases imposing relatively small monetary costs on solicitors' offices in South Carolina, it appears that these cases do limit the ability of some offices to administer the rest of their caseloads efficiently.

Perceptions of the Local Funding System. As to the realities of forcing judicial circuits to rely upon county funding for parts of their budgets, we asked the solicitors if they believed that lower-income jurisdictions were constrained in their ability to administer justice. Six answered in the affirmative, two in the negative, and one did not know. Among those responding in the affirmative, one, who noted being in a poor circuit, said, "The most I have ever gotten from my counties is $100,000, while others get millions. Of course, they often have more cases because of their larger populations. In general though, poorer counties have larger backlogs in South Carolina." And another reported:

> Yes, it creates problems if you have poor counties. It would definitely be the case for me if my counties did not fund me so well. I would have to think long and hard about the circumstances of a case before bringing capital charges. I don't know how they can handle it with more limited staffs. I have never heard of a solicitor not going for the death penalty because of money, but they are probably thinking about it. I know I would be thinking about it if I were in a poor circuit.

Interestingly, one solicitor who answered "no" believed that low-income jurisdictions were often more efficient: "Inefficiencies can be brought about by size. The smaller the system, the more efficient it is. If you only have court three times a year, it is easy to coordinate everyone's schedules—police, lawyers, judges, staff vacations, etc."

Next, because solicitors might be reluctant to admit that cost issues deterred them from bringing capital charges, we asked if the solicitors had heard of other jurisdictions avoiding capital cases because of cost considerations. Six said they were not familiar with such decisions, but the other three did. One reported knowing of "a very poor county where death penalty cases do not happen. I think they just can't afford them," while another had heard of "other counties putting pressure on solicitors to not bring expensive cases to trial. There are certainly some poor counties which just don't have the resources to invest in expensive trials." In a more extensive comment, the third said,

> It's hard to say. The poorer circuits tend to bring fewer capital charges. However, they tend to be more heavily African American. African Americans are less supportive of the death penalty than whites. So, are there fewer capital cases because of resources or because the communities take a more negative view of the death penalty?

Finally, we explained that many states had moved away from local funding for their trial-court systems to provide their citizens with a more uniform quality of justice and asked the solicitors if they thought such a system would be good for South Carolina and would make it easier to file capital charges. Two solicitors did not know how a unified budget system would affect the circuits, and another argued that it would be better to reform the current system for allocating state money, saying, "Some circuits don't try a lot of cases but they still get the same per capita allowance. Circuits should be funded based on how much work they are doing. Right now some get more than they need, while others go without."

The remaining solicitors were split over whether full state funding was a good idea. Three argued for state funding, complaining that they should not have to "go begging" to counties for the money to do their jobs, with one saying, "Decisions about how many cases to bring to trial or the charges to bring should not be based on how wealthy a jurisdiction is." Not surprisingly, the three solicitors opposed to full state funding worked in relatively wealthy jurisdictions. One summed up their argument nicely:

> I am happy with the generosity of my counties. I believe that wealthier counties such as mine would be opposed to full state funding. They want to make sure they get high quality. South Carolina just passed a law preventing the property tax from being used for education and they are paying for it by an increase in the sales tax. This has upset a lot of school districts because now they are stuck with the sales tax money the state gives them. If their citizens want to pay more money for better schools they don't really have any options now that the property tax is off the table. I think the same thing would happen if local funding were taken off the table for the courts.

Such comments comport with Tobin's (1999) findings that wealthier jurisdictions tended to be at the forefront of resistance to moves by states to eliminate local funding.

By and large, our interviews reveal that cost issues do not play a role in solicitors' decisions over whether to file capital charges. There is some speculation by the respondents that cost might be influencing solicitors' decisions in other jurisdictions, particularly in poorer areas. However, there are no concrete examples of solicitors shying away from the death penalty due to cost considerations.

COUNTY WEALTH AND CAPITAL CASES

Data and Measurement. Because South Carolina counties are expected to help pay for cases originating within their borders, we focus on the county level to ascertain whether the wealth of local jurisdictions affects the number of capital cases filed in their trial courts. A focus on the circuit would be inappropriate, because, if cost affects the decision to file capital charges, a judicial circuit comprising a large rich county and a small poor county might produce a large number of death penalty cases that all occur in the richer county.

To supplement what we have learned from our interviews, we analyzed data that allow us to test the relationships between county wealth and the number of capital cases filed in a county. Because the high cost of capital cases places wealthier jurisdictions in a better position to seek the death penalty, our hypothesis is that the number of capital charges filed in a county will be positively related to the county's median household income.

Data on the number of death penalty cases filed in each county between 2005 and 2007 were acquired from the South Carolina Judicial Department, which, although it began keeping a record of each judge assigned to a death penalty case in 1999, did not begin to record the location of each case until 2005. Thus, we are limited to data for 2005 to 2007.

To measure county wealth, we use median household income from the U.S. Census Bureau (as reported at http://www.ors2.state.sc.us). Median household income is a good proxy for resource availability for county governments. The higher the median income, the more revenue a county can draw from its citizens to finance important functions, such as trial court operations. To control for other factors that might affect the relationship, we employ county population, percent of the population that is African-American, the Index Crime Rate per 10,000 population, and partisan identification of the solicitors. We expect population and crime rate to be positively related to the number of death penalty cases.[3]

Findings. The relationship between median household income and the number of capital charges filed in a county is statistically significant (p-value = 0.01), thus providing support for our hypothesis. Wealthier counties in South Carolina had more death penalty cases than less-wealthy counties. This finding seems to conflict with the solicitors' comments that resource availability does not affect decisions over whether to file capital charges. The only other variable that was statistically significant in our model was county population (p-value = 0.02); as population increases, the number of death penalty cases

3 A separate analysis using individual cases as the unit of analysis would be useful. Doing so would allow us to control for important variables, such as the nature of the case, the quality of evidence, wishes of victims' families, and criminal records. Unfortunately, collecting these data would be exceedingly difficult.

The model used here is appropriate given that we are not attempting to measure all determinants for bringing capital charges in each case but are instead attempting to ascertain whether county wealth plays a role in the decision-making process as a whole. Thus, using cases as the unit of analysis would not address our research question.

increases. Crime rate, percent African-American, and party identification of the solicitors did not appear to affect death penalty caseloads.[4]

DISCUSSION AND CONCLUSION

Were interview respondents hiding the fact that they use cost in their decision calculus when deciding whether to file capital charges? The solicitors claimed that their decisions were based upon the egregious nature of the crimes, defendants' backgrounds, wishes of victims' families, and quality of evidence. While they admitted that death penalty cases are expensive relative to other murder cases, they maintained that cost issues played no role in their decision processes. These claims lie in sharp contrast to the quantitative evidence that county wealth is related to death penalty caseloads. It appears that wealthier counties, because they can better afford to finance expensive cases, try more capital cases.

A closer inspection of the interview data reveals that the solicitors' comments may not be as inconsistent with the quantitative analysis as first appears. The solicitors recognized that richer counties were better able to provide for local trial court functions. Solicitors working in counties that provided them with ample resources questioned how their counterparts in less-wealthy jurisdictions could afford to file capital charges very often. Some solicitors also revealed that they knew of pressures put on other prosecutors to avoid expensive cases. Finally, three solicitors admitted that more state funding would make it "easier" for them to file capital charges.

There are several reasons why it should not be surprising that none of the respondents stated directly that money issues affect their decision-making processes regarding the death penalty. First, solicitors whose offices are well financed by their local governments do not experience this constraint. Therefore, we should not expect them to cite it as a problem. Second, because solicitors are elected in South Carolina, they have a strong incentive not to admit that money issues affect their decisions regarding cases. This may have caused solicitors who are more likely to consider cost to select themselves out of the interview process. Third, it is possible that solicitors do not recognize the extent to which a lack of resources is affecting the decisions they make.

Whatever the reason that no solicitors interviewed stated that cost had a direct effect on their death penalty decisions, our findings—both qualitative and quantitative—suggest that quality in the administration of justice is influenced by the availability of resources. This conclusion by itself is not earth shattering. However, ours is the first study to show systematically that resource availability affects the extent to which the most extreme power of government is utilized. While the death penalty may not be an option that only wealthy counties can afford, our evidence indicates that it is an option that wealthy counties can afford to use more often. This finding has serious implications for equality

4 Detailed results of the statistical test and method used can be obtained from the lead author.

across jurisdictions in the administration of justice. It may be an inconvenience if low funding causes long delays. However, it is an injustice if low funding is the difference between life and death.

There are, of course, limitations to our findings that call for future research. We examined only one state, and that state does indeed provide some additional funding to judicial circuits to help defray the cost of death penalty cases. Our data analysis is based on death penalty cases for only a three-year period, and we lack data on how finances affect the quality of defense. Longer term, multistate studies would be ideal, perhaps with the present study as the groundwork for such efforts.

REFERENCES

ACLU (2007). "National Death Penalty Fact Sheet: Death Penalty 101." American Civil Liberties union, Capital Punishment Project, Durham, N.C. http://www.aclu.org/images/asset_upload_file758_29292.pdf

Baar, C. (1975). Separate but Subservient: Court Budgeting in the American States. Lexington, MA: Lexington Books.

Bureau of Justice Statistics (2007). "Capital Punishment, 2006." Bureau of Justice Statistics, Washington, D.C.

Condron, D. J., and V. J. Roscigno (2003). "Disparities Within: Unequal Spending and Achievement in an Urban School District," 76 Sociology of Education18.

Costanzo, M. (1997). Just Revenge: Costs and Consequences of the Death Penalty. New York: St. Martin's Press.

DPIC (2008a). "Death Row Inmates by State." Death Penalty Information Center, Washington, D.C. http://www.deathpenaltyinfo.org/article.php?did=188 (2008b). "Number of Executions by State and Region Since 1976." Death Penalty

Information Center, Washington, D.C. http://www.deathpenaltyinfo.org/article.php?scid=8&did=186.

Dieter, R. S. (1994). "Millions Misspent: What Politicians Don't Say About the High Costs of the Death Penalty." Death Penalty Information Center, Washington, D.C. http://www.deathpenatyinfo.org/article.php?scid=45&did=385#fn100

Dillow, G. (2008). "Judge McCartin Turns Against Death Penalty," Orange County Register, March 2. http://www.ocregister.com/column/death-judge-mccartin-1990936-penalty-ramirez

Ehrmann, H. B. (1952). "The Death Penalty and the Administration of Justice," 284 Annals of the American Academy of Political and Social Sciences 73.

Hays, S. W. (1978). Court Reform. Lexington, MA: Lexington Books.

Murray, S. E., W. N. Evans, and R. M. Schwab (1988). "Education-Finance Reform and the Distribution of Education Resources," 88 American Economic Review 789.

Radelet, M. L., and M. Borg (2000). "The Changing Nature of Death Penalty Debates," 26 Annual Review of Sociology 43.

Songer, M. J., and I. Unah (2006). "The Effects of Race, Gender, and Location on Prosecutorial Decisions to Seek the Death Penalty in South Carolina," 58 South Carolina Law Review 161.

South Carolina Law Enforcement Division. 2004 Crime in South Carolina, as reported at http://www.ors2.state.sc.us/abstract/chapter1/countyrank10.asp.

Tobin, R. W. (1999). Creating the Judicial Branch: The Unfinished Reform. Williamsburg, VA: National Center for State Courts.

(1996). Funding the State Courts: Issues and Approaches. Williamsburg, VA: National Center for State Courts.

Wolfson, B. (1993). Preserving the Independence of the Judiciary: The Dual Challenge of Democracy and the Budget Crisis. Washington, DC: Roscoe Pound Foundation.

United States Census Bureau. 2000 Census of Population and Housing, as reported by the South Carolina State Budget Control Board, Office of Research and Statistics: http://www.ors2.state.sc.us/abstract/chapter1/countyrank3.asp, http://www.ors2.state.sc.us/abstract/chapter1/countyrank1.asp, http://www.ors2.state.sc.us/abstract/chapter14/pop13.asp.

Appendix A: Descriptive Statistics

Variable	**Minimum**	**Maximum**	**Mean**	**Standard Deviation**
Number of Death Penalty Cases	0	7	0.96	1.46
Median Household Income	$20,898	$46,992	$33,597	$5,757
Population	10,108	407,383	92,502	96,477
% Black	6.7	72.3	37.1	16.4
Crime Rate	175.3	858.5	466.3	160.4

Potential Savings from Abolition of the Death Penalty in North Carolina

Philip J. Cook

Despite the long-term decline in the number of death sentences and the lack of executions, the cost of the death penalty in North Carolina remains high. To document this cost, the empirical analysis here focuses on a recent two-year period, comparing actual costs associated with capital proceedings, with likely costs in the absence of the death penalty. The conclusion: the state would have spent almost $11 million less each year on criminal justice activities (including appeals and imprisonment) if the death penalty had been abolished. Additional criminal justice resources would have been freed up and available to be redirected to other cases.

1. INTRODUCTION

In line with a nationwide trend, the death penalty has become quite rare in North Carolina. During 2007 and 2008 there were no executions and just twenty-five capital trials with four death penalties imposed, compared with over 1000 murders. Yet the cost of the death penalty to state government remains high. The state's payments for representation of capital defendants at trial and during post-conviction appeals add up to millions of dollars per year over and above what it would cost if these cases had proceeded noncapitally. This analysis provides an estimate of cost savings and other consequences, for better or worse, that would result if North Carolina abolished the death penalty.

The empirical analysis focuses on a two-year period, fiscal years 2005 and 2006, comparing actual costs to the state during that period that were associated with capital proceedings, with likely costs in the absence of the death penalty. The answer serves as a guide to what is at stake in considering abolition for sometime in the future.

The conclusion of the analysis is that North Carolina would have spent almost $11 million less each year on criminal justice activities (including imprisonment) without the death penalty. In addition, substantial resources would have been freed up within the courts and district attorneys offices that could have been used to prosecute other criminal cases more fully. But these budgetary and resource savings would not have been the whole story. The outcomes of some of the murder cases would have been different in the absence of the death penalty—not only the eleven cases in which a jury actually imposed the death penalty during the two-year window, but also some other cases that resulted in a plea to first-degree murder. There is reason to believe that some of those defendants would have pled out to a lesser offense—second-degree murder, say—if the district attorney had lacked the leverage provided by the death penalty. On the other hand, the resources freed up by not proceeding capitally could have been redeployed by the district attorneys to prosecute other cases more fully. The net effect of these changes may have had some effect on the murder rate in either direction—there is no firm basis in logic or empirical evidence to predict, except to say that any such effect would likely be small.

The focus here on the costs of the death penalty does not reflect a value judgment that cost considerations should be paramount. Clearly, there are questions of justice and crime prevention that are vitally important as well. Nevertheless, especially in this time of fiscal stringency, it is hard to claim that the effects of the death penalty on the state government budget are not relevant to an ethical debate on this subject. Extra expenditures on capital proceedings compete with other functions of state government, such as education and health care. Certainly, the debate in other states that have considered ending the death penalty has included a discussion of cost. That was true in the two states that actually did decide to abolish, New Jersey and New Mexico, and elsewhere. For example, the Maryland Commission on Capital Punishment recommended abolition of the death penalty in 2008, arguing its conclusion in part on the cost study by the Urban Institute (Roman et al., 2008).

The estimates of potential savings from abolition are developed here as follows. The next section provides background information on the recent changes in the law, policy, and practice of capital litigation in North Carolina, and documents the declining rate of capital trials and death sentences. Section 3 explains the accounting method used to estimate the extra costs associated with the death penalty. Here I discuss the question of whether the death penalty has a deterrent effect on murder, and how it is used by prosecutors in plea negotiations. Section 4 then tabulates the estimated savings from abolition, including the impacts in the trial courts, appellate process, and prisons. The final section provides a sensitivity analysis, caveats, and conclusion.

2. RECENT HISTORY OF LAW AND PRACTICE

North Carolina reserves the death penalty for murder cases in which there are aggravating circumstances. Imposition of a death sentence requires that the defendant be convicted of first-degree murder, either in a capital trial or following a guilty plea. The death sentence may only be imposed by a jury. Each jury member in a sentencing proceeding is to determine individually whether the State has proven one or more aggravating circumstances beyond a reasonable doubt, and then determine whether those aggravating circumstances outweigh any mitigating circumstances. If the jury is not unanimous in recommending death, then the judge is to sentence the convicted defendant to life without possibility of parole (LWOP).

North Carolina reinstated the death penalty in 1977 following clarification by the Supreme Court of the United States (SCOTUS) of what procedures would pass constitutional muster in capital cases. Capital defendants are accorded special due-process protections, reflecting the fundamental view that "death is different" (Cook and Slawson, 1993; Fry and Humphries, 2009). Defendants are entitled to two defense attorneys from the time that the district attorney first gives notice of intent to proceed capitally. Best practice requires a vigorous motion litigation by the defense, which includes some pretrial motions that are specific to capital cases. In a capital trial, the jury must be death qualified, which is to say that each juror is determined during *voir dire* to be open to the possibility of voting for a death sentence. If the trial results in conviction for first-degree murder, then the same jury is retained for the sentencing phase, where evidence is presented on aggravating and mitigating circumstances. If the jury does impose the death sentence, the defendant is entitled to continuing representation by two attorneys during post-conviction appeals.

Defendants sentenced to death have the right of direct appeal to the North Carolina Supreme Court. (Murder defendants sentenced to LWOP after a jury trial have a right to appeal to the Court of Appeals rather than the Supreme Court.) If the Supreme Court does not provide relief, then attorneys file a certiorari petition with the SCOTUS. If that is denied, as it usually is, then lawyers investigate and present a Motion for Appropriate Relief (MAR) in NC Superior Court. There may be a hearing, and a review by certiorari to the NC Supreme Court. The defendant then has the right to file a habeas petition in federal district court, with review by the Fourth Circuit Court of Appeals and certiorari petition to SCOTUS. Cases often return to state courts for additional litigation. The various channels for review are depicted in Figure 1.

Over the last three decades, appellate courts have vacated numerous death sentences due to a finding of Constitutional error or a change in the legal scope of the death sentence. (In recent years, two new bars to execution have been imposed, for mental retardation and for crimes committed before the age of 18.) A successful post-conviction process may result in an order for a retrial, a resentencing hearing, or simply a substitution of a life sentence for death. In any event, implementing these special due process protections is

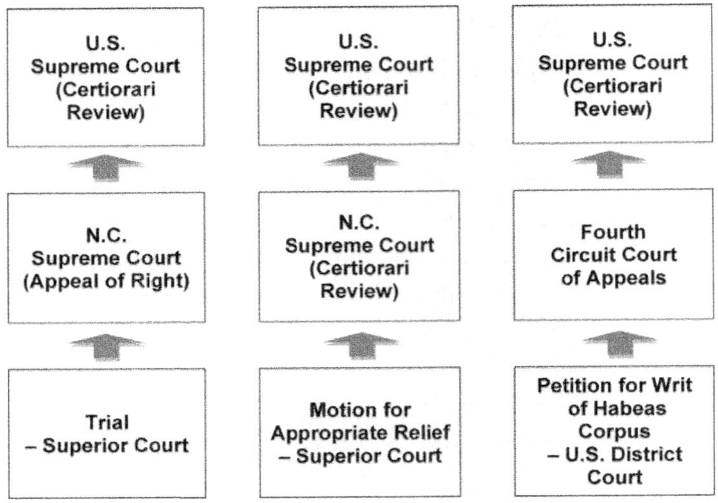

Figure 1. *Channels of Review in a Capital Case.*

Table 1. Recent History of Death Penalty in North Carolina

Calendar year	Change in policy or law in North Carolina	Capital trials	Death sentences
1993		[a]	32
1994	LWOP mandated for first-degree murder convictions	[a]	27
1995		[a]	34
1996	Open-file discovery in post-conviction proceedings mandated	[a]	25
1997		[a]	22
1998		[a]	20
1999		[a]	24
2000		[a]	18
2001	IDS given responsibility to appoint defenders in first-degree murder proceedings; Prosecutors given right to negotiate plea in capital cases Capital punishment outlawed for mentally retarded	50	14
2002		36	7
2003		22	6
2004	Pretrial open file discovery mandated in felony cases	24	4
2005	Supreme Court bars application of death penalty for crimes committed while under the age of 18	19	6
2006		24	5
2007		11	3
2008		14	1

Source: Policy and law: Fry and Humphries (2009). Counts of capital trials and death sentences provided by Center for Death Penalty Litigation.

Note: Capital trials include retrials and resentencing hearings resulting from successful appeals, as well as second trials following an earlier mistrial.

[a]No data are available.

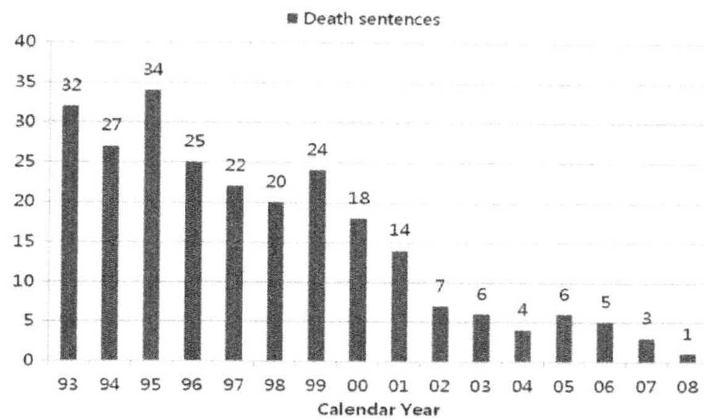

Figure 2. *Trends in Death Sentences since 1993.*
Source: Table 1 of this paper.

costly to the state and federal government, since in practice both sides of the adversarial process are publicly financed.

A previous analysis of the costs of processing murder cases in North Carolina found that the extra costs to the state accrued due to capital cases amounted to $4 million per year (Cook and Slawson, 1993). That study is out of date for a variety of reasons, as suggested by the time line in Table 1 and the trend depicted in Figure 2. Since 1993, North Carolina eliminated the parole possibility for life sentences given in first-degree murder cases, and more recently allowed district attorneys to accept a plea of guilty to first-degree murder in exchange for a LWOP sentence. The Office of Indigent Defense Services was created and assigned responsibility for appointing defense counsel in murder cases rather than leave this vital function to local judges; this change was an important step in ensuring a high-quality defense. These and other changes help explain the dramatic drop in the number of capital trials and in the number of defendants sentenced to death each year. However, a complete explanation for this drop in the use of the death penalty must take account of the national trend. The death row population in the United States peaked in 2000 and has declined every year since then. Two states, New Mexico and New Jersey, have recently abolished the death penalty, and repeal has been seriously debated in Maryland and other states. Concerns about the cost of the death penalty have figured quite prominently in the debate.[1]

Meanwhile, the distinctive pattern of flows into and out of death row has continued. Most departures from death row have not been due to execution, but rather to a successful appeal that has resulted in retrial, resentencing, commutation, or judicially vacated sentences (see Table 2).

1 Ian Urbina, "Citing Cost, States Consider End to Death Penalty," *New York Times* February 24, 2009; Tim Jones, "Resistance to Death Penalty Growing," *Chicago Tribune* April 8, 2007; David Von Drehle, "Death Penalty Walking," *Time* January 4, 2008; Corrina Barrett Lain, "The New Case against the Death Penalty," *Christian Science Monitor* May 11, 2009.

Table 2. Persons Removed from Death Row since NC Reinstated Death Penalty in 1977

	Successful appeal	Death (suicide or natural causes)	Execution
1977–1984	20	2	2
1985–1989	20	1	2
1990–1994	47	1	3
1995–1999	10	3	9
2000–2004	44	5	19
2005–2008	18	7	9[a]
Total	**159**	**19**	**44**

Source: http://www.doc.state.nc.us/DOP/deathpenalty/removed.htm (accessed 7/14/09).

Note: Cases in which the death penalty was reinstated following a resentencing hearing are not included as "removals."

[a]There have been no executions since August 2006.

The current situation (as of July, 2009) is that capital trials continue to occur, although at a low rate by recent historical standards. There have been no executions since August, 2006 due to litigation concerning the use of lethal injection as the means of execution. The death row population stands at 163.

3. ACCOUNTING METHODS AND ASSUMPTIONS

The main question investigated here is what savings North Carolina state government could expect if the death penalty were abolished. (The abolition of the death penalty in North Carolina would also have cost implications for the federal court system due to federal post-conviction proceedings, but these are not included in what follows.) Much of the savings to the state would come in the form of reduced expenditures for specific government-sponsored activities that are affected by the special requirements of capital cases. The bulk of the savings of this sort would come in the defense representation of indigent murder defendants during the trial phase, and both the defense and state representation during appeals and post-conviction phases. There would also be budget implications for the prisons, since prisoners on death row would be resentenced to life, in which case they could eventually be eligible for transfer from close security to less expensive, medium security. On the other hand, the prison population would be somewhat larger because executions would cease. The goal here is to estimate the net savings, taking account of such additional costs.

The abolition of the death penalty would have other consequences that are unlikely to be reflected in agency budgets. In the trial courts, the main consequence of abolition would likely be to free up resources that could be devoted to other cases, rather than to reduce trial court budgets. In particular, I assume that the number of courtrooms, judges, prosecutors, and support staff would not be affected by the abolition of the death penalty, nor would the budget of the NC Supreme Court. If correct, then the resources that would be freed up within the criminal justice system by abolition are an opportunity cost of the death penalty—or more precisely, that opportunity cost should be defined as the potential improvement in the quality of justice for the entire flow of criminal cases. In principle it is possible to put a price on the resources that would be freed up by abolition (Cook and Slawson, 1993), under the dubious assumption that the public value of their contribution is exactly equal to the amount they are actually paid.[2] No attempt to monetize the in-kind savings is made in what follows; rather the in-kind savings in resources are kept separate from the direct reductions in expenditures for particular activities.

To be more precise, the goal here is to estimate the hypothetical financial and in-kind consequences of abolishing the death penalty on July 1, 2004. Abolition is then the counterfactual scenario, against which the observed flow of costs is compared. This comparison requires a number of assumptions about the consequences of abolition; these assumptions are spelled out at each step of the way, and summarized here.

The financial consequences of North Carolina's abolishing the death penalty would extend far into the future, but the analysis here focuses on the first two years of the counterfactual (fiscal years 2005 and 2006). Subsequent savings would depend on such unknowns as future legislation and litigation that will have the effect of changing the scope of the death penalty and due process requirements; popular sentiment regarding the death penalty (which may influence juries' decisions as well as choices made by district attorneys); state programs for funding capital cases; and trends in the murder rate. All of these areas have been in flux during recent decades, and there is every reason to believe that law and practice regarding the death penalty will continue to evolve. Lacking a crystal ball, I make estimates for the recent past and offer the result as a best guess about the flow of savings in the future, with the proviso that there is considerable uncertainty around this steady-state assumption.[3]

In summary form, the principal assumptions made in this analysis include the following:

2 There is reason to believe that a dollar spent in the public sector has substantially greater value than a dollar spent in the private sector. Public expenditures are financed by taxes, and taxes distort economic choices and are costly to collect. Estimates of the full cost of collecting an additional dollar of taxes range from $0.33 to $0.46 (Boardman et al., 2006, p. 429). If public expenditures are subjected to a cost-benefit test, then the marginal dollar expended would therefore have to generate $1.33 to $1.46 in public benefit.

3 It should be pointed out that my steady-state assumption informs my accounting method for trial costs. Instead of attempting to estimate the extra costs of proceeding capitally for all cases during the two-year window, I instead compute the extra costs associated with those cases that were disposed of during that window. In fact, some of the costs for these cases were incurred prior to July 1, 2004, so attributing the full costs to the "window" overstates the true cost for that period; on the other hand, my approach neglects the costs associated with cases that were ongoing during the window but not

1. The flow of murder indictments would be unaffected by abolition.
2. Murder cases that in fact proceeded capitally would instead have proceeded much like the serious murder cases that in fact proceeded non-capitally. In particular, I assume that the relevant counter factual for the cases that proceeded capitally is a subset of the cases where the district attorney chose to proceed non-capitally. That subset includes those murder cases that were not dismissed, and which were disposed of either by guilty plea to murder or murder trial.
3. All offenders on death row on July 1, 2004 would be (costlessly) resentenced to life without possibility of parole, and assigned to incarceration conditions on the same basis as other prisoners sentenced to LWOP.
4. Post-conviction activity for those who had been sentenced to death would follow the same course as those who in fact were sentenced to LWOP.

The first of these assumptions is particularly contentious, since it requires a judgment about the deterrent effect of the death penalty. The remaining assumptions are developed in the context of the empirical work that follows.

How would abolition affect the murder rate? A common belief that the death penalty reduces the murder rate begins with the presumption that some would-be killers are deterred by the possibility of being executed.[4] My assumption that the murder rate would be unaffected by abolition does not deny the possibility that some would-be murderers consider the consequences, and would be more likely to desist in the face of greater expected punishment. Rather, this assumption is motivated by two arguments, one theoretical and one empirical: (1) It is not at all clear as a theoretical matter that abolition would reduce expected punishment for murder in North Carolina—only a minuscule percentage of murderers are executed under the current regime, and abolition would free up resources that could actually be used to increase the punishment for other defendants; (2) The econometric evidence on the deterrent effect of the death penalty provides little guidance, leaving it an open statistical question whether the effect is to reduce or increase the murder rate.

Turning to the first point, the potential importance of the deterrence mechanism is undercut by the fact that in practice the likelihood of execution for murder is vanishingly small. The 11 murder defendants who were sentenced to death during FY 2005 and 2006 can be compared with over 1000 criminal homicides in North Carolina during that

---

disposed of by June 30, 2006, and in that respect understates the total. In a steady-state situation, the out-of-window costs would balance out.

4 The belief in the extra deterrent effect of the death penalty (over and above the deterrent effect of life imprisonment) is not shared by leading criminologists, for whom the consensus is that there is no deterrent (Radelet and Lacock, 2009).

period. The historical record predicts that just two or so of those eleven will actually be executed.[5] A reasonable estimate, then, is that the probability that any given murderer will be arrested, indicted, convicted, sentenced to death, and executed in North Carolina is on the order of one in 500 (0.2%).

Given this reality, a calculating killer would consider not just the logical possibility of being put to death, but also the array of other (far more likely) legal consequences. The death penalty may affect which sentence is ultimately imposed through its influence on plea negotiations and other mechanisms. During FY 2005 and 2006, those who were indicted for murder were either sentenced to LWOP (16%) or a less severe sentence (56%), or were not convicted (27%). It can be argued that the most severe of these penalties, LWOP, is imposed more frequently than it would be in the absence of the death penalty as a result of the fact that the death penalty provides leverage to prosecutors in plea negotiations. Some defendants who plead guilty to first-degree murder (and hence are sentenced to LWOP) in the face of the district attorney's threat to take them to trial, might otherwise hold out for a better deal.

But while the death penalty strengthens the prosecutor's bargaining position in some cases, it comes at a cost in terms of the additional resources required to proceed capitally. Capital proceedings divert the resources of trial courts that could instead be utilized to prosecute other defendants more vigorously, including other murder defendants—almost half of whom currently have their cases dismissed or are convicted of a relatively minor crime (see below). The net effect of the death penalty on the average severity of sentence for murder defendants is hence ambiguous.

To be more precise, suppose that a rational actor is considering the possibility of committing murder under one of two regimes, distinguished by whether or not a possible consequence for murder is a death sentence followed by execution. The decision of whether to commit murder for this rational actor is guided by an expected utility calculation, with the following parameters in the death-penalty regime:

$U = C$ if does not commit murder
$U = 1$ if commits murder and gets away with it (probability P)
$U = 0$ if executed (probability conditional on conviction of P_D)
$U = A$ if sentenced to life (with conditional probability P_L)[6]
$U = B$ if sentenced to lesser penalty (with conditional probability P_S)

5 Since the death penalty was reinstated in 1977, 222 individuals have been removed from death row: just forty-four (20%) have been executed. If that fraction is applied to the eleven death penalties imposed during FY2005 and 2006, then two is the best guess of the number of individuals who will be executed.

6 A sentence of "Life" should be understood to include both the mandatory sentence for first-degree murder (LWOP) and the sentence for second-degree murder (life).

Assume: $0 < A < B < C < 1$.

Then he will commit murder in the death-penalty regime if:

$$P + (1 - P)\ [P_L A + P_S B] > C.$$

Assuming other things equal, he will commit murder in the abolition regime if:

$$P + (1 - P)\ [q_L A + q_S B] > C$$

where $q_L \geq P_L + P_D$, and $P_S \geq q_S$.

The assumption here is that the cases that would have resulted in execution are instead sentenced to life imprisonment, and the court resources freed up by ending capital prosecutions could be used to convert some of the cases that were disposed of with a lesser penalty to life imprisonment. An increase in the overall conviction rate, 1 -P, is also a possible consequence of abolition, but is not considered here.

The prospect of committing murder is less attractive in the abolition regime than the death-penalty regime if:

$$P_L A + P_S B > q_L A + q_S B, \text{ which simplifies to}$$

$$A(q_L - P_L) - \mathrm{B}(P_S - q_S) < 0.$$

Because the overall probability of conviction remains unchanged,

$$P_L + P_S + P_D = q_L + q_S. \text{ Rearranging terms, we have}$$

$$q_L - P_L > P_D B/(B - A) \qquad (1)$$

as the condition under which murder is less attractive under the abolition condition.

Condition (1) requires that in moving from the death-penalty regime to the abolition regime, the probability of a life sentence must increase by more than the original probability of execution: that is, $q_L - P_L > P_D$. But that is not sufficient. Sufficiency depends on the relative magnitudes of A and B. If the offender views life imprisonment as almost as aversive as execution, and the lesser penalty as more attractive, $B >> A \approx 0$, then (1) will be satisfied if relatively few lesser penalties are converted to life imprisonment in the abolition regime.

The conclusion, then, is that abolition may have the effect of either increasing or reducing the attractiveness of murder for the rational offender, depending on the extent to which the likelihood of life imprisonment is increased under abolition, and the relative utility values of execution, life imprisonment, and a lesser penalty.

The econometric evidence on the effect of the death penalty is also relevant. Numerous economists and criminologists have attempted to determine whether the death penalty (as utilized in the modern era in the United States) has a deterrent effect on murder. The statistical analyses of this issue have often employed state-level panel data to determine whether changes in law and practice of the death penalty generate changes in the criminal homicide rate. One systematic review of the available evidence concludes that despite various claims to the contrary, this evidence tends to be very weak. The probability that a murderer will be put to death is slight (even in Texas). Thus the effect of these executions, if any, tends to be obscured by the natural variation in homicide rates, and, as noted in point 1, by the potential counterbalancing effect of the capital cases tying up resources that instead could go to fuller prosecution of other murder cases. Unsurprisingly, the econometric analysis of the deterrent effect of the death penalty provides little guidance even as to the basic question of whether the death penalty as practiced tends to result in fewer or more criminal homicides (Donohue and Wolfers, 2006a, 2006b).

Of course there are economists who disagree. Isaac Ehrlich's research in this regard has received the most attention, motivating the creation of an expert panel of the National Academy of Sciences—whose report was skeptical of Ehrlich's findings (Blumstein et al., 1978). Ehrlich himself offered this summary statement in 1996: "... in all studies supporting the deterrence hypothesis, the conditional risk of execution, while having a significant deterrent effect, has the least impact on the incidence of murder relative to equal percentage changes in apprehension, conviction or punishment risks, and that the alternative, and most frequently used sanction for murder—the length of imprisonment—also exerts a statistically significant discouraging effect on murder (Erhlich, 1996, p. 63)." This summary suggests that the overall deterrent effect of the criminal justice system on murder depends on the distribution of prosecution resources among cases—the concentration of resources on a few cases is likely to be less effective with respect to deterrence than a more even distribution that raises the likelihood of conviction and a long prison term.

Summing up, the death penalty in North Carolina has been applied in such a small percentage of murder cases that the threat of execution is likely to play a small role, if any, in the decisions made by would-be murderers. There may be ancillary effects of the death penalty on the actual severity of noncapital punishment due to leverage in plea bargaining or the opportunity cost of capital prosecutions, but it is not clear whether the net effect is to make the average punishment more or less severe. The econometric evidence provides no clear guidance on whether the death penalty tends to reduce or increase the homicide rate. Given the ambiguous conclusions from both logic and evidence, I proceed on the assumption that abolition of the death penalty in North Carolina would not affect the homicide rate, and that abolition would not have affected the flow of murder cases through the North Carolina trial courts in FY 2005 and 2006.

4. DATA ON MURDER CASES DURING TRIAL PHASE

To understand how capital punishment is influencing the flow of murder cases through the trial courts, I compiled information on all cases in which the defendant was indicted and arraigned for murder, and which were disposed of (by trial, guilty plea, or dismissal) during a particular two-year period, fiscal years 2005 and 2006.[7] The data indicate that of the 1034 defendants arraigned for murder, a total of just twenty-nine were tried capitally and eleven were sentenced to death (including two who were sentenced by a jury after pleading guilty). But for 274 (27%) cases the district attorney indicated early in the proceeding that he intended to seek the death penalty. That is relevant since the decision to proceed capitally engenders extra costs, whether or not the defendant is ultimately tried capitally.

The district attorney may formally indicate that he has evidence of an aggravating circumstance and intends to seek the death penalty either at arraignment or at a "Rule 24" conference before a judge. If the district attorney is proceeding capitally, then the defendant is entitled to the "super due process" protections that have been put in place by state law and constitutional precedent. In particular, the defendant is to be represented by two attorneys, and since most defendants are unable to pay for this assistance, the usual practice is for the State to appoint both attorneys. Those appointments are made and financed by the Office of Indigent Defense Services (IDS).

The analysis uses two sources of administrative data to track murder cases through the trial phase, combining the computerized files kept by the Administrative Office of the Courts (AOC) with the files kept by IDS (which include data on payments to attorneys and experts).[8] While neither file includes an explicit indication of whether a murder case was prosecuted capitally, the IDS data do indicate whether a defendant was represented by two attorneys at state expense. That indicator serves to identify most of the cases that ever proceeded capitally.[9] Additional information on capital prosecutions was provided by the Center for Death Penalty Litigation, which keeps a record of all capital trials. Those cases are a subset of the cases that proceeded capitally following arraignment—most capital cases end with a guilty plea or a noncapital trial rather than a capital trial.

The flow chart (Figure 3) follows the 1034 murder cases that were disposed of during FY 2005 or 2006. Of these cases, 274 proceeded capitally, as indicated by the IDS record that two attorneys had been appointed to represent the defendant. Most of those cases resulted in a guilty plea to first- or (more commonly) second-degree murder, but fifty-eight went to trial. Of those trials, twenty-nine were capital, resulting in nine death sentences. Including those cases, forty-nine of the fifty-eight trials resulted in conviction

---

7 If a case ended in mistrial, it was excluded unless it was disposed of later (by a successful trial or other means) within the two-year window.

8 Details on the construction of this dataset are available from the author on request.

9 The recent study of defense costs by the Office of Indigent Defense Services (2008) utilizes a similar approach.

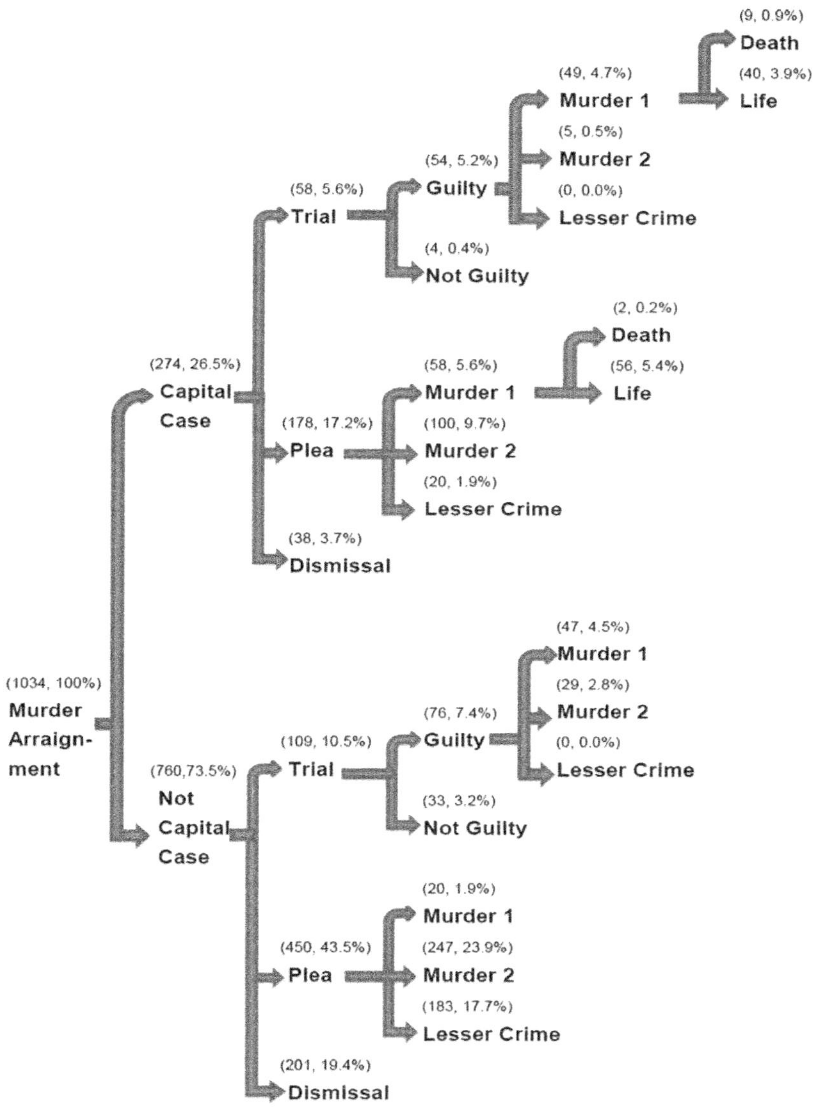

Figure 3. *Flow Chart of Murder Cases During Trial Phase.*

for first-degree murder, and only four resulted in a finding of not guilty. Two additional death sentences were imposed following guilty pleas.

The noncapital cases included the bulk of the weaker cases, as indicated by the fact that they ended up being dismissed by the prosecutor or a judge: of the 239 dismissals, 201 were never capital. It is also true that trials in cases that were never capital were more likely to result in a not-guilty verdict (30%) than was true in trials for cases that proceeded capitally (7%).

Guilty pleas for cases that proceeded capitally were much more likely to be for first-degree murder (33% of all pleas) than was true for noncapital cases (4% of pleas). Recalling that first-degree noncapital murder carries a mandatory sentence of LWOP, it is surprising that any defendant would decide to plead guilty instead of going to trial, where there is a chance of a better outcome—unless a trial also creates the possibility of a worse outcome. Presumably most of the first-degree murder pleas for the capital cases occurred in the shadow of a threatened capital trial with the possibility of death sentence.[10] (Since 2001, prosecutors who had evidence of an aggravating circumstance in a murder case have been given discretion of whether to pursue the death penalty. In practice, that discretion allows them to use the death sentence as a bargaining tool.) On the other hand, two of the pleas to first-degree murder included no such bargain, and in fact were followed by a sentencing hearing that resulted in the death penalty. It was also true that twenty of the noncapital cases resulted in a first-degree plea.

Figure 4 provides another representation of the distribution of outcomes for capital and noncapital cases. The third bar showing the combined distribution of cases demonstrates the large drop off between indictment and final disposition. Of the over 1000 cases indicted for murder, only 174 were actually convicted of first-degree murder (including the eleven death sentences). On the other hand, 276 of these cases resulted in dismissal or a jury verdict of not guilty. The most common outcome, with 381 cases, was conviction for second-degree murder.

4.1. Cash Costs versus In-kind Costs

When a district attorney elects to proceed capitally in a murder case, there are extra costs incurred by the state. These costs can be divided into two categories, referred to here as "cash costs" and "in-kind cost." The "cash cost" includes such items as payments by IDS for private attorneys retained to represent indigent defendants, payments by IDS for expert witnesses on behalf of the defense, and payments to jurors for cases that go to trial. For each of these cost items, there is a reasonable presumption that if the expenditures for any one case were reduced, the overall state expenditures on criminal justice would be reduced correspondingly. For example, if IDS is not required to appoint a second defense attorney for a murder defendant (because the district attorney decides to proceed noncapitally), and as a result avoids paying $50,000 in attorney's fees, that $50,000 would not be reallocated

10 Kuziemko (2006) analyzed the effect of the introduction of the death penalty in New York State in 1995. She found evidence that the threat of the death penalty persuaded some defendants to accept plea bargains with harsher terms, but did not increase defendants' overall propensity to plead guilty (p. 116).

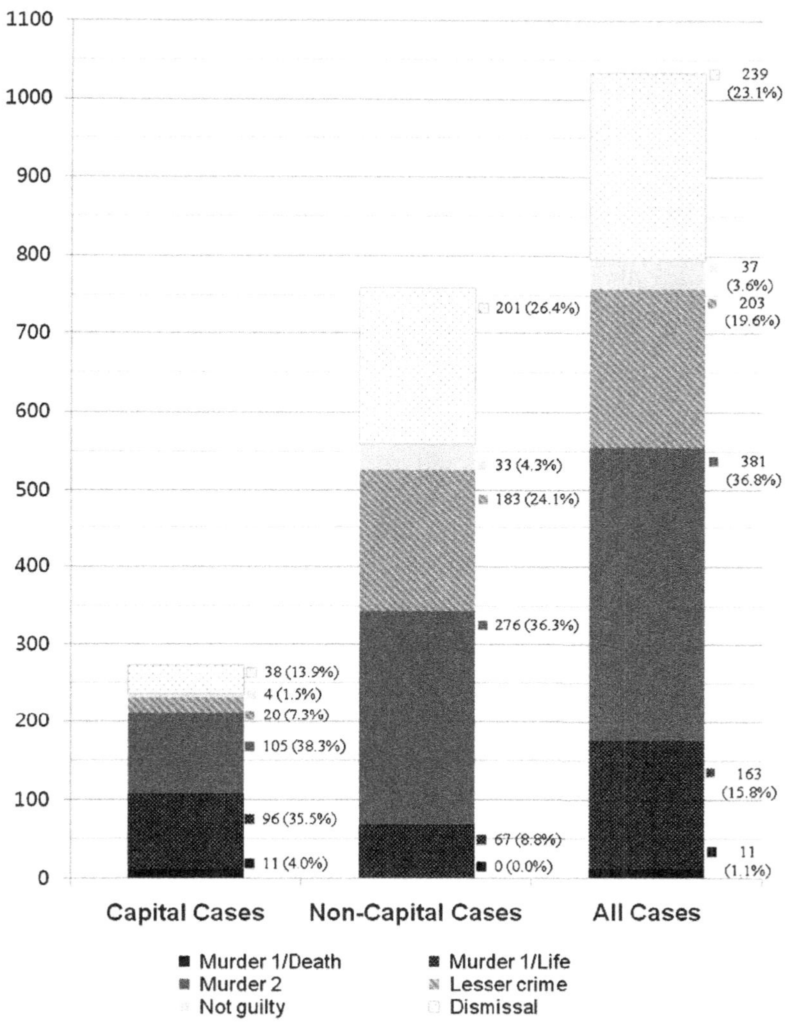

Figure 4. *Outcomes of Capital versus Noncapital Cases, FY2005–2006.*

to another IDS case, but rather could be used for other state government programs (education, Medicaid) or returned to the taxpayers in the form of lower tax rates.[11]

On the other hand, "in-kind costs" include the diversion of resources to a particular murder case that would otherwise be available for other criminal cases within the same criminal justice agency. Examples include the time spent by attorneys and other staff in

11 Additional savings would come from the fact that in North Carolina, appointed attorneys in capital cases are paid more than in noncapital cases. The rate for capital cases is currently $95 per hour, and was increased from $85 per hour on August 1, 2006. The rate for noncapital cases is just $75 per hour.

the district attorney's office, and the use of courtrooms, judges' time, and all the associated personnel required for hearings and trial days.[12] A reduction in the use of courtroom and prosecution resources for some cases is not likely to change the overall budgets and fixed resources available to the trial courts and district attorneys. Rather, those resources could be redeployed to other criminal cases being handled by the same office, with the result that those cases could then be prosecuted more fully.

If the death penalty were abolished, there would be cost savings of both types—cash and in-kind costs. The discussion begins with the trial phase.

4.2. Cash Costs in the Trial Phase

Murder defendants are in most cases unable to finance their own defense, and so the state must provide them with attorneys and pay the expense of any investigations or expert witnesses. In about one-fifth of murder cases a public defender has a role in the defense; unfortunately, there are no records on the public defender's use of time.[13] But most of the costs of the defense of murder defendants are expenditures for private attorneys appointed and compensated by IDS. Payments to private attorneys and expert witnesses for indigent defendants are recorded in IDS files. I also include here the costs associated with other agencies that have a role in the administration of the death penalty, and costs incurred by the prison system.

IDS expenditures on defense. As a start, all murder cases are divided into five categories according to whether they went to trial and whether they proceeded capitally at any point. Table 3 provides information on IDS expenditures in these cases. The highest expenditures by far are for cases that are disposed of by capital trial, averaging $116,400. Other cases that proceeded capitally result in expenditures averaging $67,800 (noncapital trial) or $43,200 (no trial). Far less expensive are cases that were never capital, whether or not they were disposed of by trial ($18,600 average) or by plea or other means ($8,300). Remarkably, noncapital cases that went to trial had lower defense expenditures by IDS than capital cases that were disposed of by pleas.

---

12 Another form of in-kind cost stems from the fact that expert witnesses for the prosecution are in most cases state employees; time they spend preparing testimony and testifying would come at the cost of discharging their other responsibilities.

13 IDS records indicate some involvement by public defenders in 19.5% of the murder cases. Margaret Gressens, IDS Research Director, suggested in an e-mail dated July 15, 2009, that the relevant margin for understanding the cost of public defenders is dictated by the practice of appointing additional private defense counsel if the attorneys in the public defender's office are working at capacity. Thus, if a capital case increases the workload in a county public defender's office, the result may well be an increase in cash costs associated with the necessity of making additional appointments of attorneys to represent other defendants.

Table 3. *Average Payments by IDS for Murder Cases Disposed of in FY2005 and 2006*

Category of case	Number	Attorneys fees ($1,000s)	Expert fees ($1,000s)	Total fees[b] ($1,000s)
A. Capital trial[a]	32	$79.8	$35.7	$116.4
B. Noncapital trial for capital case	29	$46.9	$20.9	$67.8
C. Other noncapital trial	109	$13.2	$5.4	$18.6
D. Capital case, no trial	213	$29.5	$13.7	$43.2
E. Noncapital case, no trial	651	$5.7	$2.6	$8.3

Source: Original computations from data provided by IDS.
Notes: When there is no record of IDS payment, it is assumed that there was no invoice submitted and hence no cost to the state.
[a]The capital trials include two cases when there was a sentencing hearing following a guilty plea, and one case in which a mistrial was followed by guilty plea.
[b]Includes some other fees paid by IDS.

These statistics confirm the special costs associated with super due process, including the appointment of a second defense attorney, the motions practice that is part of a capital proceedings, and the extra costs of a capital trial resulting from the extra time required to select a qualified jury and to conduct the sentencing phase.[14] Recall that the goal here is to estimate the expenditures in the counterfactual case in which the death penalty was not available to prosecutors for this two-year period, during which time everything remained the same in other respects, including the number and identity of murder cases. In that counterfactual scenario, there would be no capital trials and, indeed, no capital proceedings. Any estimate of counterfactual costs requires some assumptions about how capital cases would have proceeded if there were no death penalty.

One possible assumption is that the average expenditures for the noncapital cases actually observed provide a reasonable estimate for the expenditures that would have been made on the cases that in fact proceeded capitally. But that assumption would ignore the fact that the noncapital cases as a group are systematically different from the capital cases in at least one way that is relevant to cost—most of the weaker cases were noncapital, including the cases for which the judge or prosecutor ended up dismissing the charge. For that reason, a counterfactual was constructed using only those noncapital cases that were not dismissed and were convicted of murder (either first or second degree) or at least went to trial for murder (even if found not guilty). That approach should eliminate the weakest cases from both groups, thus making the two groups more comparable.

14 The average length of a capital trial in our sample was 19.1 days, compared to an average of 7.4 days for noncapital trials of cases that had proceeded capitally. (The medians are 18.0 and 5.5 days, respectively.) These figures are calculated based on data extracted from paper invoices in the files of IDS.

Even with this "pruning" of the noncapital cases, it is still possible that they do not provide a reliable counterfactual. It is possible, for example, that the average capital case was intrinsically more complex to prosecute than the average noncapital case. However, by one test at least that was not true in practice. There was not much difference in the duration of noncapital trials between cases in category B (cases that were initially prosecuted capitally) and category C (cases that were never capital), suggesting that on average these two groups of cases were quite similar with respect to what was required to try them before a jury.[15] This assumption receives further support from the analysis of capital-case costs in Maryland (in this issue), which finds that adjusting for the observable characteristics of capital and noncapital murder cases has little effect on the estimated difference in costs of processing (Roman et al., this issue).

Given this counterfactual, it is possible to estimate the extra expenditures on private attorneys associated with proceeding capitally in murder cases disposed of in FY2005 and 2006. There were 216 cases that were not dismissed, with an extra cost of $43,300 per case, for a total of $9,560,000 (see Table 4).

Note that the effects of the leverage that the death penalty may give the prosecutor during plea negotiations is incorporated in these calculations. While it may be true that some of the cases resulted in a plea rather than a trial as a result of this leverage, that savings, if any, is included.[16] After stripping away the weaker cases (that were dismissed or convicted of crimes other than first-or second-degree murder), the comparison is between all cases that proceeded capitally with all cases that did not, regardless of whether the cases ended with a trial or a plea.

---

15 Noncapital trials following capital proceedings lasted one more day on average than noncapital trials following noncapital proceedings (6.6 days versus 5.5 days). These estimates are based on data obtained from invoices to IDS by defense attorneys, which usually indicated days in trial. (AOC does not keep a record of courtroom usage or the duration of trials.)

16 Again, it should be noted that the likelihood of a plea may not be affected by the death penalty. Kuziemko (2006) found that the introduction of the death penalty in New York State did not affect the likelihood of a murder case going to trial, although the threat of the death penalty engendered more pleas to first-degree murder in particular.

Table 4. *Average Payments by IDS for Murder Cases (Excludes Cases Ending in Dismissal or Conviction for Less than Second Degree Murder)*

Category of case	Number	Attorneys fees ($1,000s)	Expert fees ($1,000s)	Total fees[a] ($1,000s)
Ever-capital cases	216	$38.7	$18.0	$56.9
Noncapital cases	376	$8.6	$4.0	$12.6
Difference	592	$30.1	$14.0	$43.3

Source: Original computations from data provided by IDS.
[a]Includes some other fees paid by IDS.

In addition to expenditures on private attorneys who are appointed by IDS to represent defendants in capital cases, the IDS Office of the Capital Defender has a staff of full-time attorneys and investigators who assist with capital cases and other murder cases around the state. The budget for this office totaled $3,296,795 for the two years under consideration. IDS officials estimated that 23.8% of the office's budget currently goes to noncapital murder cases.[17] The remainder is treated here as a potential savings from abolition.

Finally, the Center for Death Penalty Litigation (CDPL) helps recruit and train defense attorneys for capital case representation, and consults on specific cases. While CDPL is a private nonprofit agency, it receives part of its budget from the state, amounting to $1,187,482 during the two years.

In sum, the state's extra expenditures on defense in trial phase of capital cases amounted to the following:

$9,560,181	"Extra" payments to private attorneys and other fees
2,432,722	IDS Office of the Capital Defender
1,187,482	Center for Death Penalty Litigation
$13,180,385	Total, two years

An additional savings from abolishing the death penalty would be a reduction in jury costs. The thirty-two capital cases concluding in the two-year window (FY 2005 and 2006) lasted an average of 11.7 days longer than noncapital trials of cases that had once proceeded capitally. Given that North Carolina pays jurors $40 per day after the first five days, I esti-

17 Margaret A. Gressens (IDS Research Director) and Robert M. Hurley (Capital Defender) provided the estimate of the savings in the Office of the Capital Defender Budget if the death penalty did not exist. They believe that the office would be disbanded, and administrative positions within the office eliminated. The estimate includes the cost of experts as well as investigators and attorneys (e-mail from Margaret Gressens, dated July 17, 2009).

mate $224,640 of extra juror payments.[18] That figure does not include the extra payments for the jury pool during *voir dire*, or the reimbursement for parking and meals.

4.3. In-kind Costs During the Trial Phase

If the death penalty had been abolished on July 1, 2004, it is likely that the $13 million in extra expenditures on defense in capital cases would have been available to fund other activities of state government or to be returned to taxpayers over the subsequent two years. That is not likely to be true for costs incurred by the district attorneys' offices and courts. The extra resources used in processing capital cases would be freed up and could be used to prosecute other criminal cases more fully.[19] Rather than estimate a dollar value of these resources, I report some statistics on the extra resources absorbed by capital cases.

A rough estimate of the number of extra hours required from prosecution attorneys for capital cases may be generated on the assumption that the prosecution effort tends to be proportional to that of the defense. Table 5 indicates that private defense attorneys spent nearly three times as many hours if a murder case proceeded capitally (in part due to the appointment of a second defense attorney). (As before, this comparison excludes murder cases that were ultimately dismissed or resulted in conviction for a relatively minor crime.) The extra time utilized in the capital cases amounts to 63,526 hours. In the previous study of the costs of processing murder cases in North Carolina, I found that the prosecution devoted somewhat less than half as many hours to murder cases as did the attorneys for the defense. Assuming based on these older data that the ratio of prosecution to defense time is 42%, the implication is that extra time associated with capital proceedings amounted to 26,680 hours over the two years, which is about nine FTEs each year.[20] The support staff assigned to assistant district attorneys should also be included in this calculation. A second in-kind cost is the extra time in the courtroom required for capital cases. Each extra day in the courtroom, for the trial or for a hearing, requires the presence of a judge and other court officers and staff. The extra 3.2 days per case multiplies up to 691 days over the two years—time that could have otherwise been spent on other cases.

---

18 This figure assumes twelve jurors and three alternatives for each trial.

19 Some of the opportunity costs are to agencies outside the courts. To the extent that a capital trial requires greater use of expert witnesses by the prosecution as well as by the defense, that practice contributes to the cost. Since ordinarily expert witnesses for the State are salaried professionals working for state government (in mental health, the crime lab, or another agency) their involvement comes at the cost of their other responsibilities. No central record is kept on the use of such experts.

20 The estimate of 42% is based on the figures in Cook and Slawson (1993, Table 6.2). The FTE calculation assumes that an assistant district attorney has 1500 hours per year available for case processing after deducting vacation time, sick days, training and continuing education, and administration.

Table 5. *Average Time for Murder Cases during Trial Phase (Excludes Those Ending in Dismissal or Conviction for Less Than Second Degree Murder)*

Category of case	Number	Private defense attorneys (hours)	Courtroom use (days)
Ever-capital cases	216	451.5	6.3
Noncapital cases	376	157.4	3.1
Difference	592	294.1	3.2

Source: Original computations from data provided by IDS and AOC.
Note: Some cases have no data because the defense attorney was not paid by IDS. In these calculations those cases are treated as missing rather than as zeros.

It is also true that public defenders were involved in many of these murder cases. While there is no record of how much time they spent, it is possible to infer the extent of their role by comparing murder cases in districts that have public defenders and those that do not. Twenty-six of the one hundred counties in North Carolina employ public defenders. Average IDS payments to private defense attorneys were about the same in public defender and non-PD counties for both capital and noncapital cases, suggesting that PDs had a relatively minor role.[21]

4.4. Cash Cost Savings on Appeals and Resentencing

During the two-year window (FY 2005 and 2006), prisoners sentenced to death pursued a variety of appeals, including direct appeal to the NC Supreme Court following sentencing and subsequent appeals in state and federal courts. IDS reimbursed private attorneys who represented these death-row clients in state courts.

If these cases had been sentenced to LWOP rather than death, the opportunities to pursue post-conviction appeals would have been sharply curtailed. IDS does pay for defense attorneys who represent convicted murderers sentenced to LWOP, who if they are convicted by a jury (rather than pleading guilty) have the right of direct appeal to the NC Court of Appeals.[22] These appeals are typically less time consuming than capital appeals. The total expenditure on defense representation for LWOP appeals during the two-year

21 Using the same breakdown as in Table 5, I find that for ever-capital cases, the average payment for appointed attorneys was $38,000 in PD counties compared to $43,000 in non-PD counties. For noncapital cases, the average payments are essentially the same, just $100 higher in the PD counties.

22 While an automatic appeal is only available to defendants sentenced after trial, in some cases where the defendant pled guilty to first-degree murder and was sentenced to LWOP, there may be grounds for appeal as well.

window was $648,309.[23] Comparing that flow of expenditures with the flow of LWOP sentences during the same period (163 cases), and assuming steady state, the average payment for direct appeal per LWOP works out to $3,977. The eleven death-sentenced cases during that window, if they had been sentenced to LWOP instead, would then have cost about $43,750 in defense charges on direct appeal.[24]

In sum, here are the relevant payments for defense representation of defendants during post-conviction proceedings:

Capital appeal	$249,166
Estimated cost of appeal if noncapital	$(43,750)
Capital post-conviction	$4,087,448
Total	**$4,292,864**

During the same time frame, successful appeals resulted in new trial-court proceedings for three defendants who had been on death row. These three resentencing hearings resulted in total expenditures for the defense by IDS of $594,216. These hearings would not have occurred if the death penalty had been abolished.

Representing the state during capital post-conviction proceedings are the lawyers on salary with the NC Department of Justice, Capital Litigation Section. Based on the annual budget for this office, and the estimate by Barry McNeill (head of the office) that 90% of attorney time in the office is spent on state and federal capital post-conviction litigation, I estimate that $3,180,692 can be attributed to the death penalty during the two-year window.[25]

Here is the summary for expenditures on appeals and resentencing associated with capital cases, which total $8.1 million:

23 This figure was computed by IDS research director Margaret Gressens and conveyed by e-mail on August 25, 2009.

24 Another potential savings from the abolition of the death penalty would result from the fact that currently many of the LWOP sentences are the result of capital trials, and hence produce a longer transcript and more bases for appeal than would be true if the sentence had resulted from a noncapital trial. This additional savings are not estimated here.

25 Mr. McNeill estimated that the other 10% was devoted to direct appeal of noncapital cases. While budget information was not available for 2005 and 2006, I was advised by Nels Roseland, a budget officer in DOJ, to discount the 2008 budget by 4% for 2006 and 8% for 2005. The expenditure figure includes operating expenses of 12.5% of salaries.

IDS payments to private defense attorneys for appeals and post-conviction proceedings	$4,292,864
Net payments by the Capital Litigation Section	$3,180,692
IDS payments for resentencing of capital case following successful appeal	$594,216
Total	**$8,067,772**

4.5. Cash Costs in Prison

On July 1, 2004, there were 151 people on death row in North Carolina, Since reinstatement of the death penalty in 1977, thirty-one others had been executed. During the subsequent two years there were four more people sentenced to death and eleven executions. The expenditure implications for a repeal of the death penalty are of several sorts when compared with the counterfactual.

If the death penalty had been abolished before July 1, 2004, then the 151 inmates would have been moved off the death row and there would have been no executions during the next two years (or thereafter). The prisoners moved off the death row would have been resentenced to LWOP, and most of them placed in close security, for which the daily cost of maintenance is similar to death row. However, some would have been eligible for transfer to medium security, which is less costly. For example, thirty-seven death row inmates had served more than 10 years, and if they were transferred to medium security the savings would have been $196,000 for the next two years. On the other hand, the eleven inmates who were in reality executed would have remained in prison in the counterfactual circumstance, for a total cost (if they remained in close security) of $206,400.[26] The executions themselves were costly, and that expenditure would have been avoided: based on a study of execution costs in a fiscal note for the General Assembly, the cost per execution is $16,369, which for eleven executions totals to $180,059.

In summary, the net savings in expenditures in prison if the death penalty had been abolished at the beginning of our window is as follows:

26 26. According to the NC Department of Corrections annual reports, the cost of a day in close security was $74.52 in 2005 and $79.72 in 2006. The cost of a day in medium security was $68.90 in 2005 and $70.83 in 2006. The savings from the eleven executions is based on the days remaining during the two-year window following the exact dates of those executions. Incidentally, the *total* cost savings resulting from executions in the modern era (since the first in 1984) during any one year is rather small compared to the costs of the death penalty. During the two-year window, that savings was about $2 million after a small adjustment for the likelihood that, based on life expectancy, several of those who were executed would have died of natural causes by 2004. Thus the annual savings from all prior executions is on the order of $1 million per year.

Move death-row inmates to medium security after 10 years	$195,958
House an additional 11 inmates who were executed	($206,400)
Cost of 11 executions	$180,059
Total	**$169,617**

4.6. In-kind Costs for Appeals

Death sentences are appealed as a matter of right to the North Carolina Supreme Court, where they occupy about 10% of the courts' time and resources.[27] It is also true that the Office of the Appellate Defender has some role in capital cases, including coordinating capital defense after the end of the trial phase, assigning attorneys (in some cases providing direct representation), and consultation. Appellate Defender Staples S. Hughes conducted a survey and estimated that 10% of staff attorneys' time is spent on these functions on average, although it is variable year to year.

4.7. Summing Up

Bringing together the expenditures for the two-year window, FY 2005 and 2006, yields the following sum of extra expenditures that a repeal of the death penalty would have avoided:

Extra defense costs for capital cases in trial phase	$13,180,385
Extra payments to jurors	$224,640
Capital post-conviction costs	$7,473,556
Resentencing hearings	$594,216
Prison system	$169,617
Total	**$21,642,414**

Thus abolition of the death penalty would have reduced state expenditures on murder cases by about $10.8 million per year.

Abolition would also have freed up resources in the courts and district attorneys' offices, as well as the Office of the Appellate Defender and the North Carolina Supreme Court. These in-kind costs include freeing up the equivalent of nine assistant prosecutors each year, as well as 345 days of trial court time and something like 10% of the resources of the Supreme Court and the Office of the Appellate Defender.

As discussed above, there is a possibility that repeal of the death penalty would have influenced the outcomes of plea bargains for some of the cases on which the prosecutor

27 An informal survey by Christie Cameron found that NC Supreme Court justices spend 10–15% of their time on capital cases. Capital cases take longer to dispose of on average than the typical case coming before the Court.

proceeded capitally. The result would likely have been that some of the pleas to first-degree murder would have been replaced by a trial or a plea to second-degree murder. Over the long run (*not* in the two-year window) that shift would begin to be reflected in the prison population, causing some additional savings to the state. On the other hand, additional resources freed up and applied to some of the weaker murder cases might have increased the murder-conviction rate and thereby added to the prison population.

5. Sensitivity Analysis, Caveats, and Conclusions

If the death penalty had been abolished on July 1, 2004, state government expenditures for processing murder cases would have fallen by $10.8 million per year. Beyond that budgetary savings, resources within the trial courts, NC Supreme Court, and Attorney General's Office would have been freed up for redeployment to other cases. The ultimate effect on the crime rates could well depend on just how state officials chose to reallocate those resources.

Currently most murder cases do not proceed capitally and are generally disposed of at relatively low cost. Three of four murder cases were prosecuted noncapitally during FY 2005 and 2006, and together they accounted for only one-third of the expenditures on defense. Over half of all murder cases were dismissed, found innocent, or convicted of a relatively minor crime.[28] If the effect of eliminating the death penalty were to increase the prosecutorial effort allocated to routine murder cases, the net result may be to enhance the deterrent effect of the law and reduce the murder rate. That outcome is every bit as plausible as the reverse.

This analysis has focused on budgetary and resource savings for state government. The conclusion that abolition would save the state money indicates that the various changes in capital procedure and practice that have occurred over the last 15 years have not changed that basic conclusion (Cook and Slawson, 1993).

Note that the bottom line of this analysis rests on certain assumptions about how the relevant actors would respond to the abolition of the death penalty. The true cost consequences of abolition would depend on such factors as how district attorneys responded to the loss of leverage in plea bargaining, how they chose to utilize the resources freed up if no more cases were prosecuted capitally, and how potential killers would respond to the new regime—whatever shape that it took. One of the key assumptions in the analysis above is that the murder rate would be unaffected by the abolition of the death penalty.

---

28 In a study of homicide cases in Philadelphia, Franklin Zimring and his colleagues observed that most were disposed of "wholesale" with lenient sentences or dismissals, while a relative few were given "retail" treatment (Zimring, Eigen, and O'Malley, 1976): "An important minority of killings—the 'retail' cases—receive more attention, more complete due process, and penalties close to an order of magnitude higher than the low-visibility wholesale cases (p. 237)."

The conclusion that abolition would save the state money and resources is sensitive to that assumption. If in fact the murder rate increased by as much as 10% as a result of abolition, that cash savings would eventually be eliminated and even reversed.[29] But as explained above, it is as likely that abolition would reduce the murder rate as increase it—and a 10% change in either direction is highly unlikely.

5.1. Social Cost

It is important to recall that this analysis does not provide a complete accounting of social costs, but rather is narrowly focused on the costs to the state of processing cases. A complete accounting would consider a broader set of concerns. How murder cases are processed through the courts and corrections may have considerable impact on the well-being of victims' families and loved ones. Other citizens have a stake in how cases are processed to the extent that they are concerned about justice and fairness. There is little consensus. Some strongly believe that justice requires that especially heinous crimes be punished with death, while for others, the deliberate taking of life is immoral even if it is the life of a convicted murderer.

There is probably more of a consensus that murder cases deserve high priority in the courts, if for no other reason so as to incapacitate dangerous offenders and deter others from choosing to kill. The social costs of murder have been estimated as amounting to millions of dollars per death (Cook and Ludwig, 2000; Ludwig and Cook, 2001; Cohen et al., 2004). As a result, the impact of the criminal law and procedure on murder rates is of paramount concern. That fact was not ignored in this analysis; rather, it was set aside on the grounds that there is no basis for predicting whether abolition of the death penalty would increase or reduce the murder rate, and good reason to believe that the effect in either direction would be small.

The bottom line is that the death penalty is a financial burden on the state and a resource-absorbing burden on the trial courts. That conclusion is relevant to the debate over whether preserving the death penalty is in the public interest but surely not among the most important considerations.

---

29 Here is a back-of-the-envelope calculation. An increase of 10% would result in fifty additional murder indictments per year at current rates. Based on the analysis above, about half of these would end up with a life sentence, either for first-or second-degree murder, and one-quarter a short sentence, while the rest would be dismissed or found innocent. The result would be a gradual increase in the prison population. By the 12th year, if nothing else changed, there would be 320 prisoners more than there would have been otherwise (not counting executions), and that number would continue to grow. The extra costs of imprisonment, together with the extra costs of processing these cases, would exhaust the annual savings at about that point.

Author's note: Special thanks for the extraordinary assistance of Margaret Gressens of Indigent Defense Services, and to a number of other state agencies and offices that provided data and guidance. Anca Grozav took the lead in collecting and analyzing data. Other research assistants include Grace Stephens Eileen Ahlin, Jennifer Gibbs, Chris Nida, Emily Loney, Elizabeth Bruns, Chetan Jhaveri, Anu Madan, and Manoushka Germain. Seunghoon Han helped analyze the data and prepare the diagrams in this manuscript.

Send correspondence to: Prof. Philip J. Cook, Sanford School of Public Policy, Duke University, Durham, NC 27708, USA; Telephone: 919-613-7360; Fax: 919-681–8288; E-mail: pcook@duke.edu.

REFERENCES

Blumstein, Alfred, Jacqueline Cohen, and Daniel Nagin, eds. 1978. *Deterrence and Incapacitation: Estimating the Effects of Criminal Sanctions on Crime Rates.* Washington, DC: National Academy Press.

Boardman, Anthony E., David H. Greenberg, Aidan R. Vining, and David L. Weimer. 2006. *Cost-Benefit Analysis: Concepts and Practice.* Upper Saddle River, NJ: Pearson Prentice Hall.

Cohen, Mark A., Roland Rust, Sara Steen, and Simon Tidd. 2004. "Willingness-to-Pay for Crime Control Programs." 42 *Criminology* 86–106.

Cook, Philip J., and Jens Ludwig. 2000. *Gun Violence: The Real Costs.* New York: Oxford University Press.

Cook, Philip J., and Donna Slawson. 1993. *The Costs of Processing Murder Cases in North Carolina.* Sanford School of Public Policy, Duke University.

Donohue, John J., III, and Justin Wolfers. 2006a. "The Death Penalty: No Evidence for Deterrence," *Economists' Voice* April 1–6.

Donohue, John J., III, and Justin Wolfers. 2006b. "Uses and Abuses of Empirical Evidence in the Death Penalty Debate." NBER Working Paper w1 1982.

Ehrlich, Isaac. 1996. "Crime, Punishment, and the Market for Offenses," 10 *Journal of Economic Perspectives* 43–67.

Fry, David, and Tabitha Humphries. 2009. *Capital Procedure in North Carolina: Changes since 1993.* Durham, NC: Duke School of Law.

Kuziemko, Ilyana. 2006. "Does the Threat of the Death Penalty Affect Plea Bargaining in Murder Cases? Evidence from New York's 1995 Reinstatement of Capital Punishment," 8 *American Law and Economics Review* 116–42.

Ludwig, Jens, and Philip J. Cook. 2001. "The Benefits of Reducing Gun Violence: Evidence from Contingent-Valuation Survey Data," 22 *Journal of Risk and Uncertainty* 207–26.

N.C. Office of Indigent Defense Services. 2008. *FY07 Capital Trial Case Study: PAC and Expert Spending in Potentially Capital Cases at the Trial Level.* Durham, NC: Office of Indigent Defense Services.

Radelet, Michael L., and Traci L. Lacock. 2009. "Do Executions Lower Homicide Rates? The Views of Leading Criminologists," 99 *Journal of Criminal Law & Criminology* 489–508.

Roman, John, Aaron Chalfin, Aaron Sundquist, Carly Knight, and Askar Darmenov. 2008. *The Cost of the Death Penalty in Maryland.* Washington, DC: Urban Institute Justice Policy Center.

———. 2009. "The Cost of the Death Penalty in Maryland," *American Law and Economics Review* 10.1093/aler/ahp023.

Zimring, Franklin E., Joel Eigen, and Sheila O'Malley. 1976. "Punishing Homicide in Philadelphia: Perspectives on the Death Penalty" 43 *University of Chicago Law Review* 227–52.

DISCUSSION QUESTIONS

1. Is it a good idea to introduce costs into the death penalty debate? How is cost related to justice in the death penalty debate?
2. Is it fair to introduce the cost issue in the death penalty debate in a time when most states are experiencing severe financial hardship (would the cost argument be less compelling during fiscal good times)?
3. Is it reasonable to assume that, if substantial costs savings do result from abolition of the death penalty, the savings will be passed on to education, health care, infrastructure and other important cost centers?
4. Assume that a very wealthy benefactor made $100,000,000 available for research into the death penalty, in the hopes of bringing to closure some of the debates that have plagued us for decades. First, pick one issue that should receive all of these funds (deterrence, racial disparities, costs, issues in forensic science, etc.), and justify your selection. Next, divide the money up among three issues that you think are in the direst need for additional research, and justify your choices. Finally, explain how you would set up an independent organization to fairly allocate and monitor the expenditure of these funds.

EYEWITNESS IDENTIFICATION

Introduction

Eyewitness Identification: A Policy Review

By The Justice Project

Model Policy and Procedure for Eyewitness Identification

By Wisconsin Department of Justice, Office of the Attorney General

What could be more compelling than to have a victim stand up in court and point to the defendant as "the one who did it"? As far as evidence goes, this type of eyewitness identification can be conclusive and a major factor leading to a finding of guilt. After all, isn't it reasonable to assume that the victim knows who the perpetrator is? While at first blush this presumption seems more than reasonable, upon closer examination it may not be so. Eyewitness misidentification is widely recognized as the leading cause of wrongful convictions in the United States, accounting for more wrongful convictions than all other causes combined.

It is critical for the integrity of our criminal justice system that we thoroughly investigate the causes of wrongful convictions and substantially reduce them across all cases. Implementing some basic standards could go a long way toward accomplishing this goal. The authors suggest that the following be used in eyewitness administration:

Cautionary instructions: Prior to presenting line-ups, the witness should be instructed that the perpetrator may or may not be in the line up and he/she should not feel compelled to make an identification.

Use of fillers: Only one suspect should appear in each lineup. When used properly, fillers allow authorities to judge the reliability of an eyewitness.

Double blind administration: The person administering the line-up should not know the identification of the suspect. This prevents inadvertent clues or favoring one line-up member over another.

Sequential presentation: It is suggested that line-up members be presented one at a time (sequentially) rather than all at once (simultaneously). This prevents what the authors term "comparison shopping."

The foregoing recommendations represent practical strategies for minimizing eyewitness error. The Justice Project points out that there are several natural psychological phenomena which can undermine the accuracy of eyewitness identifications. Such factors as "confidence malleability" and "relative judgment" are explained as factors which can significantly reduce the reliability of eyewitness identification.

Perhaps, the most compelling portion of this report are the heart-rending stories of the victims of misidentification and wrongful convictions. Calvin Johnson, for example, spent 19 years in prison based upon no other significant piece of evidence other than the inconsistent identification of the victim identifying him as the culprit. This conviction stood despite ample evidence to the contrary. Equally compelling are the profiles of John Willis and Larry Fuller who spent 8 and 18 years in prison respectively, and who may have never been exonerated but for the advent of DNA testing which completely excluded them as suspects.

The State of Wisconsin has formally recognized the problem of eyewitness misidentification and through the Wisconsin Attorney General's Office has developed model legislation to address this issue. This model includes provisions for cautionary instructions, assessment of witness confidence immediately after identification, proper selection of fillers, double blind administration and sequential presentation of lineups. It also includes a simple procedure for administration of line-ups using the 'folder method,' a blind method of administration that can be used when a blind line-up administrator is not available (e.g., in a small jurisdiction). Additionally, the Wisconsin Department of Justice developed a training program to educate law enforcement across the state of Wisconsin on the need to change procedures to lessen the risk of misidentification and wrongful convictions. The program has trained over 800 investigators on this new procedure and has been incorporated into the training program for new investigators.

While not mandatory, the Wisconsin guidelines represent a model for implementation of the "best practices" in eyewitness identification.

Eyewitness Identification

A Policy Review

The Justice Project

INTRODUCTION

A measure of fairness and accuracy in the criminal justice system

Eyewitness identification is critical to the apprehension and prosecution of criminals. Eyewitness evidence can also be an important tool for exonerating innocent suspects. Groundbreaking research on eyewitness memory over the past three decades, as well as increasing attention to the problems in the cases of wrongfully convicted individuals, has brought the fallibility of eyewitness memory to the fore.

Eyewitness misidentification is widely recognized as the leading cause of wrongful conviction in the United States, accounting for more wrongful convictions than all other causes combined.[1] Since 1989, DNA evidence has been used to exonerate nearly 200 individuals who were wrongfully convicted. Of those, approximately 75 percent were convicted on evidence that included inaccurate and faulty eyewitness identifications.[2] In some cases, these innocent individuals were misidentified by more than one eyewitness.

In the vast majority of criminal cases, however, DNA or other biological evidence is not available to establish guilt or innocence. Given the persuasive nature of eyewitness evidence, as well as the inherent danger of misidentifications—both in convicting the innocent and allowing the true perpetrator to go free—it becomes imperative that we take stock of the procedures within the control of the criminal justice system that contribute to these problems in order to ensure that the most reliable evidence possible makes it into a courtroom and before a jury.

A number of challenges emerge in pursuit of a more accurate protocol, none more prevalent than an historical lack of communication between scientists and law enforcement.[3]

Decades of empirical research have proven that a number of small changes to identification procedures can help improve the accuracy and reliability of eyewitness identifications, and help ensure that the highest quality of eyewitness evidence is collected.

What's more, when put to the test in numerous jurisdictions throughout the country, these reforms have met with real-life success. Thus, it may seem surprising that these reforms have not been implemented in police districts across the board.

While much of the research has been extensively documented and peer-reviewed within the scientific community, and the recommendations for reform are widely accepted by experts in the field, these reforms were initially discussed and developed outside the realm of law enforcement.

Starting in the late nineties, however, leading researchers joined with law enforcement and legal practitioners to bridge the gap and comprehensively address eyewitness identification issues at the intersection of the two fields. As a result, guidelines and best practices for law enforcement were developed with the science in mind.

In October 1999, the Department of Justice released a comprehensive guide for law enforcement on procedures for obtaining more accurate eyewitness evidence.[4] However, there is no current national program or federal agency responsible for educating local departments about these reforms—or in assisting with their practical implementation.[5]

Eyewitness misidentification is widely recognized as the leading cause of wrongful conviction in the U.S., accounting for more wrongful convictions than all other causes combined.

Moreover, as reforms are implemented on a jurisdiction-by-jurisdiction basis in some states, there continues to be little opportunity for sharing information and perhaps even less incentive, given the already overloaded criminal caseloads of police, prosecutors and defenders, and the lack of leadership from the courts or legislature on the issue.

This policy review has been designed to facilitate communication among local law enforcement agencies, policymakers, and others regarding the best practices and methods for enhancing the evidentiary value of correct identifications and at the same time reducing the risk of erroneous identifications. By presenting many of the successful methods employed in local jurisdictions, as well as the science behind them, we hope to create a dialogue around recommendations that will enhance the quality of evidence relied upon in criminal trials, as well as confidence in our system of justice.

RECOMMENDATIONS & SOLUTIONS

Getting it right the first time

A handful of specific improvements have emerged as pragmatic strategies for minimizing eyewitness error. While modernizing identification procedures to incorporate advances in eyewitness memory science requires retooling long-standing lineup methods engrained in police culture, the substantial benefits of implementing the protocol are leading more jurisdictions to update their procedures to catch up with the science.

Because eyewitness evidence, much like trace evidence, is susceptible to contamination, some eyewitness identification procedures actually increase the risk of false identification. By improving these procedures in subtle ways, the actual quality of eyewitness evidence can be improved.

The following recommendations reflect the consensus in the scientific community—confirmed by successful implementation in numerous jurisdictions—as to the procedural changes that will enable law enforcement to extract the most reliable evidence from eyewitnesses for use in a criminal investigation.

These practical changes to the identification process help increase the likelihood of identifying the true culprit while enhancing protections for innocent people accused of crimes.

These reforms are equally effective for photographic lineups and live lineups.

CAUTIONARY INSTRUCTIONS

Prior to presenting the lineup members, the eyewitness should be instructed that the perpetrator may or may not be included in the lineup, and that she should not feel compelled to make an identification.

Cautionary instructions respond, in part, to the tendency of witnesses to make a relative judgment by removing some of the pressure on the eyewitness to choose a suspect when the culprit may not be in the lineup.

EFFECTIVE USE OF FILLERS

Only one suspect should appear in each lineup. In addition, at least five fillers should be included in a photo lineup, and at least four fillers in a live lineup. The fillers should resemble the witness' description of the perpetrator, and the suspect should not unduly stand out.

Fillers, if chosen correctly, allow authorities to judge the reliability of an eyewitness. The effective use of fillers is critical to ensuring that an innocent individual is not identified simply because of the composition of the lineup.

DOCUMENTATION

The identification procedure should be carefully documented. Documentation includes preservation of photos in a photo array or photographs taken of a live lineup, recording all individuals present at the lineup, documentation of the witness' statements regarding the lineup members during the procedure, and, if an identification is made, documentation of the witness' degree of confidence in the identification, in the witness' own words, prior to any feedback from authorities.

Careful documentation of the lineup procedures, including a witness' level of certainty that she has correctly identified the perpetrator, when taken immediately following the identification, helps the jury to assess the eyewitness evidence appropriately and minimizes the effects of reinforcing feedback that can distort the confidence level of an eyewitness between the time of the identification and the trial.

DOUBLE-BLIND ADMINISTRATION

The person who administers the lineup should not know the identity of the suspect. This procedure prevents well-intentioned officials from giving inadvertent clues to the witness as to which person in the lineup is the police suspect.

SEQUENTIAL PRESENTATION

The lineup members should be presented to the witness "sequentially" (one at a time) rather than simultaneously (all at once). Sequential presentation should only occur, however, if the identification procedures comply fully with the double-blind administration recommendation.

Presenting the lineup members one at a time to the witness reduces the tendency for witnesses to engage in "comparison shopping." Rather, an eyewitness must judge whether each lineup member matches her memory of the perpetrator, as opposed to making a relative judgment.

PSYCHOLOGICAL FACTORS

Preventing unreliable evidence in the courtroom

Reliable eyewitness evidence is critical to criminal investigation and prosecution, and it plays a powerful role within the criminal justice system. The repeated discovery of misidentifications contributing to wrongful convictions, however, has prompted inquiries into the nature of eyewitness evidence used to convict criminal suspects, and the problems that arise in utilizing human memory in criminal investigations.

The scientific community has brought the knowledge built through decades of research and experiments to bear on eyewitness identification procedures. Important lessons learned in the laboratory, and in the decades of research devoted to eyewitness memory science, are of enormous value in the legal and law enforcement communities. This substantial body of research has revealed that several natural psychological phenomena can undermine the accuracy of eyewitness identification, and that these psychological factors, left unchecked, can lead to unreliable evidence being presented in the courtroom.

LINEUPS AS EXPERIMENTS

Just as trace physical evidence (such as DNA or fingerprints) can be contaminated if it is not collected precisely and carefully, so too eyewitness evidence can be spoiled if it is gathered in ways that do not properly control for known sources of error.[8]

As some researchers have described, a lineup is essentially an experiment designed to test a hypothesis: whether the suspect matches the witness' memory of the perpetrator.[9] Like scientific experiments, careful controls must be put in place to ensure accuracy and prevent the witness' memory from being contaminated or skewed.

Essentially, the lineups as experiments analogy suggests that the logic used to conduct experiments—i.e., isolating variables and implementing careful control conditions—can and should be applied to the legal system when conducting lineups. Using some of the tried and true scientific methods for conducting experiments when conducting a lineup greatly reduces, or in some cases eliminates, the risk of contamination of the data (i.e., eyewitness identification evidence).

RELATIVE JUDGMENT

Relative judgment refers to the natural tendency of a witness to consider lineup participants in comparison with one another, as opposed to a more direct comparison of each lineup member with the witness' memory of the culprit. A witness viewing a lineup will thus tend to identify the person who looks most like the perpetrator in comparison to the other members in the lineup.[10] While, at face value, this process seems unproblematic, it can actually lead to inaccurate and unreliable identifications under certain conditions—namely, when the police suspect is innocent.

Several natural psychological phenomena can undermine the accuracy of eyewitness identification, and these psychological factors, left unchecked, can lead to unreliable evidence being presented in the courtroom.

The purpose of a lineup is to differentiate innocent suspects from those who actually committed crimes using an eyewitness' memory of an event. Thus, when conducting a lineup, law enforcement officers do not know if a suspect included in a lineup is, in fact, the true perpetrator or simply an innocent person suspected of a crime. If the lineup is full of innocent people (an innocent suspect and a group of innocent fillers), however, relative judgment would mean that an innocent person may be identified, because it is likely that there will always be someone in the lineup who looks more like the person who committed the crime than the other members of the lineup.

Sometimes this person will be a filler, and a witness identification will be dismissed. But sometimes an innocent suspect will be the victim of this tendency toward "comparison shopping," because the witness is always making a relative judgment—the witness is always picking the person who looks closest to the culprit relative to the other lineup members, even if the lineup is full of innocent people.

Take for example a six-person lineup that contains the actual culprit. It has been proven that witnesses who saw the same event will often pick someone out of a lineup when the culprit is removed. In other words, regardless of whether a culprit is in a lineup, witnesses tend to pick the person who looks closest to the culprit, even when the culprit is not present. As leading researchers have noted, "The problem with the relative judgment process, therefore, is that it includes no mechanism for deciding that the culprit is none of the people in the lineup."[11]

MALLEABILITY OF WITNESS CERTAINTY

Traditionally, a witness' self-reported degree of certainty in an identification was considered a good indicator of accuracy. Unfortunately, a great deal of research in recent decades has proven this intuitive assumption false. The level of certainty a witness expresses in her eyewitness testimony does not necessarily correlate with the level of accuracy of the identification. An eyewitness' confidence that she has identified the culprit can fluctuate as a result of factors that occur after the identification and have little to do with memory. This is what is referred to as confidence malleability.[12]

For example, experiments have been conducted in which witnesses were shown a staged crime and asked to identify the culprit from a lineup. The lineup they were shown, however, did not contain the culprit. After the witnesses unknowingly made false identifications, they were then asked their level of confidence. Before doing so, however, some of the witnesses were given various types of reinforcing feedback. Those witnesses who received some confirmation of their false identification, whether the information that a co-witness identified the same individual or some other confirming feedback, were far more confident in their identifications than other witnesses who were given no feedback—despite having given false identifications. These witnesses also distorted and exaggerated certain details, such as how good their view was, how much of an opportunity they had to view the culprit, etc.[13] Our new and better understanding of the influence feedback plays on a witness' self-described level of confidence strongly suggests that measures that control for this influence be adopted in our identification procedures.

THE SCIENCE

Demanding changes in eyewitness identification procedures

Scientific treatments of eyewitness evidence began over 100 years ago, most notably with Harvard Professor Hugo Munsterberg's 1908 book, On the Witness Stand.[14] While Munsterberg established that eyewitness evidence was much more fallible than previously thought, his research did not show a way forward. Based on the science of the day, the legal system had no capacity for dealing with these mistakes, and the system could not sort the mistakes from the true identifications.[15] The science, at first, only documented the problem, but it could provide no solutions.

In the late 1970s, however, eyewitness memory scientists began to zero-in on the particular sources of eyewitness error and test revised identification procedures that reduced the risk of mistakes. The guiding principle of this new research was that we must do all we can to ensure good quality evidence on the front end of the process, rather than trying to second guess identifications after the fact. For the research on eyewitness fallibility to be useful, it had to be applied to the criminal justice system in a way that allowed the system to prevent or reduce future mistakes. Scientists thus focused on the ways that the system of collecting eyewitness evidence could itself cause mistakes, in hopes that these mistakes could be prevented before they occurred.[16]

The past three decades of eyewitness research and discussion have coalesced around this purpose—preventing false identifications with research-based improvements to the system. Largely, these improvements focus on controlling the suggestiveness of the lineup procedures themselves. A discussion of the science behind these improvements follows.

CAUTIONARY INSTRUCTIONS

Regardless of whether the true perpetrator is in a lineup, an eyewitness may feel pressure to make an identification. Witnesses know that, at the very least, a lineup contains a police suspect. When the culprit is not, in fact, present in the lineup, this perception, combined with the natural tendency to compare lineup participants and make a relative judgment, may influence an eyewitness to identify an innocent person.

Cautioning an eyewitness that the offender may or may not be in the lineup reminds witnesses that the answer may be "none of the above."[17]

Research has shown that this extra step, while on its face pointing out a fact that should be obvious, significantly lowers the rate of inaccurate identifications without reducing the number of true identifications.[18]

EFFECTIVE USE OF FILLERS

Relative judgment theory means that an eyewitness viewing a simultaneous lineup tends to make a judgment about which individual in the lineup looks most like the perpetrator relative to the other members of the lineup. This is particularly problematic when a lineup only contains innocent people (i.e., a number of fillers and an innocent suspect).

Research has shown, however, that the effective use of fillers when composing a lineup can help combat the tendency for the relative judgment process to lead to the identification of an innocent suspect.[19]

First, ensuring that the suspect in the lineup does not stand out, or that the fillers resemble the witness' prior description of the culprit at least as much as the suspect does,

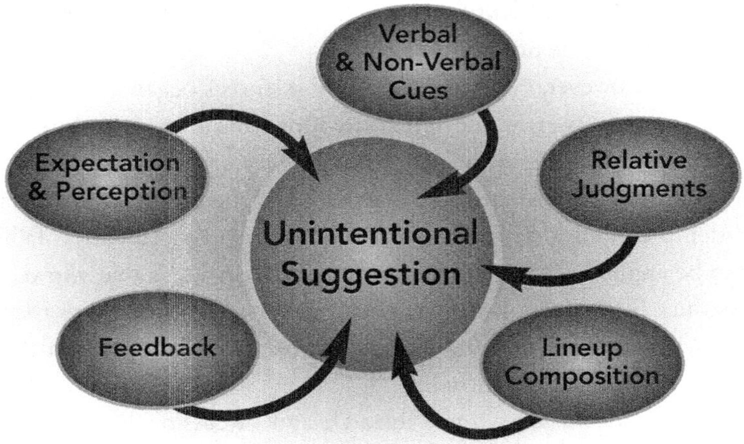

guards against the eyewitness choosing an innocent suspect simply because the suspect is the only lineup member that resembles the perpetrator.

For example, if the eyewitness describes the perpetrator as an Asian man with a mustache, and there is only one man in the lineup who is Asian and has a mustache, then the lineup is obviously suggestive, and the evidentiary value of any identification is nil. In contrast, if all of the lineup members resemble the prior description of the culprit (or all of the lineup members are Asian men with mustaches), then the eyewitness will have to rely more on comparisons to her own memory of the culprit. In short, no lineup participant can unduly stand out for a lineup to be effective. This holds true in general, but especially with regard to features of the witness' description of the culprit. For example, if a witness describes the perpetrator as having a particular feature such as a mustache, the lineup must be composed with all members sharing that feature.

There are certainly cases where selecting fillers is not as clear-cut. For example, if the suspect does not fit the witness' prior description of the suspect but other evidence creates suspicion of guilt, then it may be appropriate to place that suspect in the lineup, as witness descriptions can sometimes be off the mark. If so, however, the fillers must be chosen to be similar to the appearance of the suspect.[20] There are methods for dealing with contingencies, but the true test of this rule is whether the suspect stands out relative to the other fillers.[21] In other words, if a person who is not involved in the case is given a description of the perpetrator, would she be able to pick the suspect out of the lineup? Including only one suspect in a lineup is also a fundamental safeguard against misidentification. Lineups not only allow police to judge whether a suspect is innocent, they also allow investigators to judge the reliability of an eyewitness. If a lineup contains more than one suspect, however, its ability to test reliability is diminished. This is because it increases the likelihood that a witness would select a suspect based on a guess rather than recognition. The more choices in the lineup test that could be considered "correct" (i.e., suspect identification), the less the lineup can control for witnesses with weak memories or those who guess. The same considerations underpin the need to include an adequate number of fillers. Doing so also reduces the likelihood of an eyewitness identifying an innocent suspect based on a guess. For example, if there is only one suspect and one filler, the likelihood that an innocent suspect will resemble the culprit more than the other lineup members is 50%. If three fillers and one suspect, the likelihood is 25%; and so on.[22] While there is no magic number of fillers that should be used, the science has shown that the greater the number of fillers, the greater the reliability of the procedure.

DOCUMENTATION

Lineup identifications are a critical component of the investigation of criminal cases. Given the overwhelming importance of eyewitness testimony and the weight afforded to it by juries, it is essential to provide sufficient contextual information about an identification in order for fact-finders to evaluate its evidentiary weight correctly. Careful documentation of lineup procedures, where possible, means that a complete and accurate record of the methods used to obtain an identification is preserved for review. Recording the identification and the non-identification results, the dialogue between witnesses and police, and the photos themselves (or photographs of a live lineup), serves as much to protect the police from false claims of influencing a witness as it does to preserve the integrity of the evidence. Thorough documentation has the power to put an identification beyond reproach.

Scientists have shown that a number of procedures within the system actually contribute to misidentifications. Complete documentation allows any suggestiveness in the procedure to be considered by judges and juries in deciding how to weigh the evidence and, when reliable procedures are used, it strengthens the evidentiary value of an identification.

A critical component of appropriate documentation is recording an eyewitness' statement of confidence (or self-assessment of certainty) immediately after an identification. This guards against the confidence malleability problem—when an eyewitness' confidence that she has identified the culprit fluctuates as a result of factors that occur after the identification. To document a witness' confidence, the witness is asked her level of certainty that the person being identified is the true perpetrator prior to receiving any feedback from authorities or other witnesses. The witness' confidence level should be recorded in her own words in order to allow judges and juries to evaluate eyewitness testimony in an informed manner.

Studies have shown that information provided to an eyewitness after an identification can influence the witness' level of confidence, and thus skew a juror's assessment of the accuracy of the identification. For example, if an eyewitness makes an identification of a suspect, and that same witness later learns that the person identified also has a criminal record, the witness' confidence level may become artificially inflated.

A critical component of appropriate documentation is recording an eyewitness' statement of confidence (or self-assessment of certainty) immediately after an identification.

Confirmatory feedback oftentimes occurs without the knowledge or intent of investigators in the case or even the eyewitness, and if a confidence statement is not taken directly after the identification, the window of opportunity for protecting the integrity of the identification evidence as an indicator of accuracy is lost.

DOUBLE-BLIND ADMINISTRATION

The "double-blind" rule applies the scientific method to lineups, and is rooted in a general strategy for ensuring the objectivity of data collection and interpretation. The purpose of keeping the administrator "blind" as to which person in the lineup is the suspect is to prevent the administrator from unintentionally influencing the results through inadvertent cueing of the witness toward the suspect. A double-blind protocol also eliminates the problem of interpreting ambiguous witness comments and other behaviors through the lens of the theory that the suspect in a lineup is guilty.

Double-blind protocols are familiar to many in the context of pharmaceutical studies to test a new drug. Not only is the patient unaware of whether she received the drug or the placebo, but the doctor who examines the patient during the study is also "blind" to this fact. If the tester knew that the patient had taken the placebo, the tester might unknowingly skew the examination as a result.[23] Double-blind protocols are standard practice in such contexts not because we distrust the integrity of the medical and scientific professionals involved, but because we understand the risk of natural human psychological factors that can undermine objectivity. We control for such factors because there is much at stake.

Similarly, if a lineup administrator knows which member of the lineup is the suspect, she might unintentionally influence the identification through verbal or non-verbal cues. A cue can be a statement to the witness or even an administrator's posture or facial expression. Verbal and non-verbal cues are examples of suggestive procedures that can suggest to the witness where a suspect is in the lineup.

Verbal and non-verbal cues can also influence or inflate the certainty of the witness. Given that eyewitness confidence is weighed heavily in the legal system, and given that it has been shown to be highly malleable and particularly susceptible to feedback, it is important to design lineup procedures that eliminate the risk of over-inflating confidence through unintentional suggestion.

SEQUENTIAL PRESENTATION

Relative judgment theory also serves as the basis for the sequential presentation recommendation. Traditionally, eyewitnesses are shown a lineup or photo array in which the lineup members are presented as a group. This type of presentation actually encourages an eyewitness to "comparison shop" or to judge the lineup members against each other through a process of elimination.

On the other hand, sequential presentation, first articulated by researchers in the 1980s, is a process where the witness is shown the lineup members one by one and asked to decide if the lineup member presented is the perpetrator. By forcing witnesses to consider the lineup members individually, sequential presentation favors a direct and independent assessment of whether each lineup member matches a witness' actual memory of the perpetrator.

Researchers have shown that the sequential presentation, if implemented in tandem with the double-blind procedure, results in fewer false identifications.[24] It is important to note that if the administrator is not "blind," however, the sequential procedure can actually produce higher rates of false identifications, as witnesses may be more susceptible to unintentional feedback from the administrator when considering one lineup member at a time.

While eyewitnesses have been shown to make fewer choices when viewing a sequential lineup, the research suggests that this is due, in part, to fewer guesses on the part of eyewitnesses with a weak memory of the culprit.[25] A comparison of the accurate and mistaken identifications also suggests that a sequential presentation yields a higher probability that a suspect, if identified using this procedure, is in fact the culprit.[26] In short, the sequential lineup creates a higher threshold for identification by reducing the influence of the tendency to make relative judgments. As a result, the evidentiary value of identifications gained through sequential lineups is much higher, at the cost of some identifications based on weaker witness memory or witness guesses.

The "double-blind" rule applies the scientific method to lineups, and is rooted in a general strategy for ensuring the objectivity of data collection and interpretation.

Taking this research into the field has shown a generally positive effect. In a pilot project on the sequential procedures in Hennepin County, Minnesota, (Minneapolis) for example, eyewitnesses picked fewer fillers. Such a decrease in known errors confirmed the value of sequential procedures for officials in that jurisdiction.[27] In addition, New Jersey implemented sequential procedures statewide in 2000. A pilot project conducted by the Chicago Police Department in 2006, however, raised concerns that sequential double-blind lineups were less accurate than conventional methods.[28] Nonetheless, the Chicago study was criticized as having design problems that undermined the study's ability to yield reliable comparisons.[29] Researchers are currently pairing with other jurisdictions to add to the credible literature on the topic. While some questions have been raised about the value of sequential presentation, on balance, most experts believe that it has proven to be superior in both experimental research and in the field.

BENEFITS & COSTS

Investing in a fair and accurate criminal justice system

The benefits of improved eyewitness identification procedures are perhaps best conceived of in terms of the avoided costs. When an eyewitness mistakenly identifies the wrong individual, the costs to public safety are great. Scarce resources in the criminal justice system are misdirected toward investigating and perhaps even trying an innocent person, and not toward convicting and jailing criminals.

"The cost to society of inaccurate eyewitness identifications is twofold," notes psychologist Rod Lindsay of Queens University in Kingston, Ontario. "It's a double error. Not only are you convicting the innocent—or at least putting them through the process of having to get out of the situation—but the guilty are still out there doing the crimes."[31]

A pointed reminder of the costs of misidentification is the case of Clarence Harrison. Wrongfully convicted of a brutal rape in Decatur, Georgia, Clarence Harrison spent nearly 18 years in prison before DNA testing proved his innocence—and showed the eyewitness evidence in his case to be false. After the exoneration, the District Attorney relayed that while the victim was upset by the DNA results, "she is more upset that this means the person who raped her is yet to be identified."

When there are stronger identifications, the benefits to law enforcement and prosecutors, as well as to public safety, are increased, and we can be more confident that the right person is being prosecuted for the crime. In fact, with improved identification procedures, those in law enforcement can ensure that the quality of evidence they are collecting from eyewitnesses is higher than before. Prosecutors are also able to convey to jurors the steps taken to ensure accuracy, placing their evidence on a firm, scientific foundation. And when identifications are better, prosecutions are stronger, and convictions are more solid. By avoiding wrongful convictions, we also avoid the costs of needlessly and unjustly imprisoning an innocent person, as well as the costs of restitution and, in some cases, expensive civil judgments against local governments.

BENEFITS TO INNOCENT SUSPECTS

There can be no question that the conviction of the innocent is a profound injustice. By better protecting the innocent from wrongful conviction, we spare people the devastating ordeal of unjust incarceration that tears apart the families of innocent people and deprives them of their most fundamental liberties. To do justice to our respect for liberty, it is incumbent upon us to do all we can to enhance the accuracy of the criminal justice system.

"LEGAL SAFEGUARDS"

The U.S. Supreme Court has identified five criteria for evaluating the accuracy of eyewitness evidence—"opportunity of witness to view criminal at time of crime, witness' degree of attention, accuracy of witness' prior description of the criminal, level of certainty demonstrated by witness at the confrontation, and length of time between the crime and the confrontation" (Neil v. Biggers, 1972). Unfortunately, although a witness' level of certainty or confidence in her identification is one of the most powerful factors judges and juries consider when assessing eyewitness accuracy, a witness' high level of confidence in an identification does not necessarily mean that the identification is more accurate. In fact, oftentimes the opposite is true.

A number of other procedural protections in place in the legal system to assist in protecting against inaccurate eyewitness evidence have also proven to be starkly inadequate. At last count, more than 75 percent of the nearly 200 wrongfully convicted individuals later exonerated by DNA evidence were convicted on the basis of one or more eyewitness identifications, all with the benefits of legal safeguards to protect against inaccurate identification testimony, such as motions to suppress, cross examination of eyewitnesses and the (limited) admissibility of expert testimony on eyewitness error. Thus, without improvement to the actual quality of the identification procedures themselves, the ability of the legal system to screen out unreliable eyewitness testimony is in grave doubt.

COSTS OF IMPROVED LINEUP PROCEDURES

Reforming eyewitness identification procedures would incur relatively nominal monetary costs or expenditure of departmental time and resources. For example, instructing an eyewitness prior to the lineup, which has been shown to dramatically increase protections for innocent suspects, requires very little training and can be read from a script—it is simply a matter of a change in process. While more careful documentation of identification procedures may seem burdensome, the use of audio or video recording devices can make preservation of the record much easier at nominal cost.

> "The costs of changing procedures are minimal when compared with the benefits. The costs are really a matter of some extra training for our officers. The benefits are stronger, more accurate eyewitness IDs that ultimately make it easier for police and prosecutors to do our jobs."
>
> John Laux
> Chief of Police, Bloomington, Minnesota

While some costs may be incurred from implementing a "double-blind" procedure in terms of personnel, alternatives to using an additional officer to administer the lineup can be implemented by using alternative presentation methods that achieve the same result. For example, computer programs that can generate a photo array, and present it to a witness in random order, are increasingly available. Other "low-tech" options include a "folder method," in which the lineup administrator places photos in folders that are shuffled and presented to a witness such that the administrator cannot see the photos while the witness is studying them.[32] When weighed against the tremendous costs to the taxpayer in terms of lawsuits and compensation to the wrongfully convicted, as well as the very real costs in terms of human lives, the minimal procedural costs associated with these procedures are negligible. Ultimately, the benefits of implementation far outweigh the costs.

PROFILES OF INJUSTICE

Evidence of a broken criminal justice system

Calvin Johnson's Story

Wrongfully convicted at age 25, Calvin Johnson received a life sentence for the rape of a Georgia woman. Four different women identified him. Exonerated in 1999, he walked out of prison a 41-year old man. The true rapist has never been found.

On March 9, 1983, an African-American man entered the apartment of a 30-year old white woman through an unlocked door while she was sleeping in College Park, Georgia. The assailant tightened a belt around her neck until she passed out and then raped her. The victim told police that the attacker turned on the light and that she was able to get a good look at him. Two days earlier, a second woman in College Park had been raped in a remarkably similar manner. College Park straddles the county line between suburban Clayton County and Atlanta's Fulton County. The March 9 attack occurred in Clayton County, and the March 7 rape occurred in Fulton.

THE INVESTIGATION AND EYEWITNESSES

Authorities soon focused on 25-year-old Calvin C. Johnson, Jr., a college graduate recently released from prison for a 1981 burglary. He had readily confessed and pled guilty to the burglary of a College Park man's apartment, and served 20 months. While in jail on that charge, however, police came to suspect Johnson of a sexual assault that occurred the same night of the burglary.

While Johnson was in jail, one of the detectives who worked the burglary went to his cell with a young white woman. He said they wanted to talk to him about other crimes in the neighborhood, but Johnson refused, telling him he didn't know about any other crimes.

Shortly thereafter, Johnson was charged with the 1981 rape—based on the young woman's identification of his voice during the brief jailhouse exchange with the detective. All the rape-related charges were dismissed, however, due to what the prosecutor later characterized as problems with the investigation.

An all-white jury took 45 minutes to find Johnson guilty. On the day of his conviction, he told the judge, "As God is my witness, you've got the wrong man."

Johnson's lawyer later learned that the victim, who had been forced to have oral sex during the attack, stated several times that her assailant was uncircumcised, a fact that clearly ruled out Johnson. When the College Park rapes occurred 2 years later, however, suspicions lingered, and Johnson quickly became the target of the investigation.

The same detective from the 1981 cases presented photo arrays, which included Johnson's picture, to both rape victims. The Clayton County victim picked Johnson, but the Fulton County victim picked out another man.

The investigators also showed the photo lineup to two other women who experienced incidents that may have been related to the rapes, as the incidents occurred in the same vicinity and around the same time period. One witness picked Johnson's photo as the man she discovered in her living room when she came out of the shower. The other witness identified his photo as the man who tried to enter her apartment.

The photo of Johnson used in the line-up was from his 1981 arrest, showing him clean-shaven. The perpetrator had been described as clean-shaven, or perhaps having some stubble. At the time of the attacks, however, Johnson had a full beard and moustache—a fact his boss and other witnesses corroborated.

Based on the photo line-ups, police arrested Johnson for rape on March 14, 1983. A search of his home turned up no physical evidence linking him to the crime, but prosecutors later claimed that a jacket of his was similar to one described by one of the victims.

Two days after the arrest, detectives arranged a live line-up that included Johnson. This time, with Johnson's lawyer present, the Clayton rape victim did not pick Johnson, but identified a "filler" instead. The two other women who had picked out his photo also failed to pick him out of the live line-up (one identified a filler and the other picked no one). The Fulton rape victim, however, did identify Johnson at the live line-up, though she had failed to identify him from the photo array.

One of the few pieces of physical evidence in the case was a pubic hair found on the Clayton rape victim's sheets. After comparing it with numerous hairs plucked from all over Johnson's body, the state's own forensic experts determined that the hair did not match Johnson. Prosecutors ordered another set of hairs collected from Johnson, but the results were the same—no match.

THE TRIALS

Johnson went to trial for the Clayton County rape on November 2, 1983. Both rape victims identified him in court as their assailant, despite their inconsistent line-up performance.

The two other women who identified Johnson's photo but failed to pick him out of the live line-up also identified him in court as the man from their encounters. As the

Fulton rape victim left the witness stand, she lunged at Johnson and cursed him in front of the jury.

Johnson's lawyer presented the testimony of four witnesses who supported his alibi. In addition to the inconsistencies in the photo and live line-up identifications, the defense highlighted the discrepancy between descriptions of a clean-shaven assailant and evidence that proved Johnson had a full beard at the time of the crimes.

The defense also called a state crime lab expert, who testified that the pubic hair found on the victim's bed could not have been Johnson's. The prosecutor argued that the hair must have gotten on the sheet at a public laundry.

After a three-day trial, an all-white jury took 45 minutes to find Johnson guilty. On the day of his conviction, he told the judge, "As God is my witness, you've got the wrong man." Johnson received a sentence of life plus 15 years.

The following year, Johnson was brought to trial for the rape of the woman in Fulton County. This time, after hearing the same evidence from the same witnesses (plus his conviction for the Clayton County rape), a racially mixed jury unanimously acquitted him. Authorities had virtually no doubt that the same assailant committed both rapes, but the Fulton County acquittal had no effect on Johnson's life sentence.

During those 16 years, Johnson had several opportunities for parole, but the board rejected parole each time because he refused to formally admit guilt and participate in a sex offender program.

THE EXONERATION

With the help of James Bonner, an attorney at the Prisoner Legal Counseling Project at the University of Georgia Law School, Johnson located the evidence from his trial, including a semen sample, though no state law at the time required that the biological evidence be preserved.

According to the prosecutor, when the trial judge retired, a court clerk threw out many old evidence boxes, but someone had pulled Johnson's evidence out of the trash bin and placed it back in storage. In 1994, Johnson wrote to the Innocence Project, and they agreed to take his case.

The Innocence Project arranged to have the remaining evidence sent to Dr. Edward Blake, the nation's foremost forensic DNA expert. Dr. Blake reported that the DNA testing positively excluded Johnson as the source of the semen collected in the rape kit.

Testing of the pubic hair recovered from the victim's sheet also excluded Johnson as the source of the hair, showing a match with the DNA from the rape kit.

On June 15, 1999, the state vacated Johnson's conviction, and Clayton County District Attorney Robert Keller, who had prosecuted the case 16 years earlier, agreed to drop all charges. The true perpetrator has never been found.

In 2000, the Georgia legislature awarded Johnson $500,000 compensation for his wrongful imprisonment.

John Willis' Story

Misidentified by 11 different eyewitnesses for a pattern of crimes involving robbery and rape, John Willis spent over eight years in prison before missing forensic evidence was uncovered that conclusively exonerated him.

Between December 1989 and September 1990, a man the media dubbed the "beauty shop rapist" terrorized the Chatham neighborhood on Chicago's south side.

In the first of a string of remarkably similar and unusual crimes, a man entered a beauty salon brandishing a pistol. He ordered the women in the shop to a back room, forced the women to undress, and robbed them of money and jewelry.

Four crimes of this pattern occurred in beauty shops, and in two of these incidents, on May 2 and September 7, 1990, the man sexually assaulted a female victim. A fifth crime following the pattern of the beauty shop incidents occurred in a store.

THE INVESTIGATION AND EYEWITNESSES

With the help of multiple victim eyewitnesses, police produced and widely distributed a composite sketch.

On September 14, 1990, police arrested John Willis based on an anonymous tip. Though Willis, then 42, had a job cleaning up at a tavern, he had a criminal record of theft and was a self-described "career tire thief and gambler." Willis had no record of violent crime, however, and consistently and emphatically maintained his innocence.

Both of the victims of the sexual assaults identified Willis in photographic lineups as their attacker, as did most of the other witnesses from the salons. A total of 11 eyewitnesses identified Willis as the perpetrator.

THE TRIALS

In 1992, Willis was tried separately for the two crimes that included rapes. In the first case, while no fingerprints or other physical evidence tied Willis to the crime, physical evidence had been collected from the crime scene, including the perpetrator's semen.

The state's forensic analyst from the Chicago Crime Lab, Pamela Fish, testified that her analysis of semen from the crime scene was "inconclusive"—the tests could neither exclude Willis, nor identify him as the source of the semen. In the absence of conclusive forensic testimony, the jury relied entirely on multiple eyewitnesses who had picked Willis out of a lineup, including the rape victim. On February 13, 1992, a jury found Willis guilty, and he was sentenced to 45 years in prison.

Both of the victims of the sexual assaults identified Willis in photographic lineups as their attacker, as did most of the other witnesses from the salons. A total of 11 eyewitnesses identified Willis as the perpetrator.

While Willis was being held without bond awaiting trial, the string of rapes and robberies continued in Chatham, all following the same unusual pattern.

In April 1992, Chicago Police arrested Dennis McGruder for a string of five rapes and robberies that occurred between November 11, 1991 and March 21, 1992. McGruder pleaded guilty to five crimes that followed the identical pattern of the crimes for which Willis was arrested, including the rape for which he was convicted. One occurred in a beauty salon and four others in taverns.

In November 1993, Willis went to trial for the second rape, after McGruder was jailed for the latter five crimes. A jury again convicted Willis on the basis of identification testimony of the rape victim and other eyewitnesses, along with evidence of the previous rape conviction. Though McGruder had been charged with a string of remarkably similar crimes in the same neighborhood since Willis' arrest, Willis' jury never heard about McGruder.

In an effort to bolster the defense of mistaken identity, Willis' lawyers tried to introduce McGruder's photo into evidence (Willis and McGruder bear a substantial resemblance in their facial features, though Willis is several inches taller than McGruder and noticeably heavier). The prosecution successfully argued to the judge that the McGruder crimes were irrelevant to the case at hand.

At one point during this second trial, Willis became so upset that he tried to blurt out to the jury that the police had someone else in custody for these crimes, waiving a newspaper clipping about the McGruder case in the air. The judge quickly silenced him.

At his sentencing hearing, eyewitnesses from the remaining three crimes with which Willis was charged testified against him. After he was sentenced to an additional 100 years, prosecutors dropped the remaining cases.

In 1997, Cook County Public Defender Greg O'Reilly, the office's leading forensic expert, was brought onto the case to help pursue DNA testing under a new post-conviction DNA statute. When Willis petitioned the court for testing, Assistant State's Attorney Earl Grinbarg, who prosecuted the Willis cases, declared, "John Willis absolutely, positively is the rapist." Nonetheless, Judge Thomas Fitzgerald ordered DNA testing. When O'Reilly sought access to the evidence, he was told that it was all unaccounted for.

An investigation established that Grinbarg had checked the evidence out of the Chicago police evidence room and had not returned the evidence that was not presented as an exhibit at trial, including the biological evidence. The missing evidence—some twenty pieces from three different locations—included swabs taken from the rape victims and a semen-stained toilet paper wrapper, any of which could have been tested for DNA.

Frustrated by the disappearance of the key physical evidence that would allow DNA testing, O'Reilly sought Fish's lab notes. He had been skeptical of her court testimony about inconclusive results and wondered why further testing had not been conducted.

Fish's notes contained evidence of Willis' innocence: they indicated that the blood type of the semen donor of the crime scene evidence was type A, different from Willis' type B. Willis could not have been the source of the crime scene semen.

THE EXONERATION

In September 1998, Willis' lawyers were preparing to appeal based on suppression of the blood-type exclusion and official misconduct. For 6 months, no biological evidence could be located. Nonetheless, a microscopic slide was eventually discovered in the prosecutor's manila folder among the Willis case files. The slide contained a tiny amount of semen from the first rape for which Willis was convicted.

DNA testing excluded John Willis—and identified Dennis McGruder as the true perpetrator. McGruder was by that time serving a 40 year sentence for the five armed robberies and sexual assaults that occurred after Willis' arrest.

Willis was released on February 24, 1999. He had lost eight and a half years in prison.

At a March 15, 1999 hearing, prosecutors formally dropped all charges against Willis. Thomas Fitzgerald, presiding judge of the criminal division of the Cook County Circuit Court, told Willis, "I wish to God it hadn't happened to you. I hope you can get back on track. And I hope you can live a life that gives you some personal satisfaction and happiness."

The City of Chicago and Cook County settled Willis' civil suit out of court for $2.5 million. He also received $100,000 from the State of Illinois.

Larry Fuller's Story

Larry Fuller spent over 18 years in prison, after being wrongfully convicted of aggravated rape as the result of an erroneous identification—despite the fact that he had a full beard at the time of the identification, which stood in stark contrast to the witness' memory of the perpetrator. Fuller was excluded as the rapist though advanced DNA testing methods, and Governor Rick Perry granted him a full pardon in January 2007.

On the morning of April 26, 1981, a 37-year-old woman was attacked in her apartment in Dallas, Texas by a black man wielding a knife. He cut her several times, raped her, and then ran away. The victim was taken to the hospital, and a rape kit was collected. The attack occurred 45 minutes before sunrise, and the victim testified that it was dark in the room, although she was able to ascertain that the attacker was a black male "somewhere in his twenties" and that she had never seen him before. She also reported that she did not remember any facial hair on the attacker.

THE INVESTIGATION AND EYEWITNESS

At the time of the April rape, Fuller was a decorated Vietnam War veteran raising two young children with his girlfriend while pursuing an education. While he had served three years for robbery after his return from Vietnam, Fuller had no record of sex crimes.

Nonetheless, investigators had obtained Fuller's photograph while investigating an incident that occurred three months earlier. In this previous incident, on the morning of January 19, 1981, another woman had been similarly raped, just a few buildings down from the victim of the April rape.

Fuller was stopped by police after the earlier attack because he matched the victim's description, but when his photograph was placed in a photo array, the victim positively stated that the photo array did not contain her attacker. Another man, Larry James Johnson, later confessed to the January crime and was arrested and prosecuted.

Two days after the April attack, police included Larry Fuller's picture in a photo array presented to the victim of the April attack. The victim failed to conclusively identify Fuller as her attacker, however, telling investigators Fuller "looks a lot like the guy" but she could not identify him. The investigating officer then issued a report recommending that the investigation be suspended because the victim "was unsure of the suspect at this time."

Five days after the first photo lineup, on May 3, 1981, police showed the victim a second photo array, this time with a more recent picture of Fuller, taken the same day. Fuller's was the only photograph included in both photo arrays.

This time, the victim positively identified Fuller, though she was confused by the fact that Fuller had a heavy and distinct beard. She had stated previously that she did not remember any facial hair on the attacker.

The victim later stated, "I looked at it, and I knew that was the face; but I couldn't figure out why there was facial hair because I didn't remember the facial hair I looked at the picture again and I put my finger over the part, the hair, and then I could identify him."

THE TRIAL

At trial, the prosecution relied on the eyewitness identification, stating that the victim "never wavered" in her identification, and the victim testified that she was certain Fuller was her attacker.

In addition, the prosecution introduced complex expert testimony on serological testing of semen from the rape kit collected from the victim. Though technology at the time did not allow for advanced DNA testing, the Southwestern Institute of Forensic Sciences did perform more basic tests on the semen evidence. A forensic serologist testified that Fuller could have been the source of the semen based on this testing, but it was inconclusive. The prosecution incorrectly argued that the semen evidence was consistent with Fuller's to the exclusion of 80% of the population—a major exaggeration of the evidentiary value of the testing.

The defense called Fuller's girlfriend, who testified Fuller was at their house at the time of the attack. Despite his alibi, on August 25, 1981, Fuller was convicted of aggravated rape after only 35 minutes of jury deliberation. He received a sentence of 50 years in prison on September 10, 1981.

THE EXONERATION

Fuller wrote the Innocence Project in the mid 1990s, and they agreed to help him pursue more advanced DNA testing of the physical evidence. Meanwhile, in 1999, after having served 18 years of his sentence, Fuller was released on parole, but was sent back to prison in 2005 for a parole violation.

In November 2000, the Innocence Project located the biological evidence at Southwestern Institute of Forensic Sciences and requested that the Dallas County District Attorney's Office consent to post-conviction DNA testing. In March 2001, the Office refused, noting that the Texas legislature was considering a new DNA statute, and they wanted to wait for the statutory criteria.

In August 2001, the Innocence Project again requested testing under Texas' new post-conviction DNA statute, but the state opposed testing. However, after a hearing in judicial court, the judge ordered that DNA testing be conducted by the Department of Public Safety (DPS).

Unfortunately, DPS was unable to obtain the profile of the male DNA on the vaginal slide, and in November 2004, the Innocence Project renewed its request to the District Attorney's Office for more-developed DNA testing using another method. On April 14, 2006, the District Attorney's Office agreed, and the Court ordered Y-STR testing at Orchid Cellmark, a private laboratory.

Having waited a quarter of a century, Fuller received unassailable proof of his innocence—Y-STR testing conclusively excluded him as the source of the semen.

At a hearing on October 31, 2006 in the 203rd Judicial District Court in Dallas, Judge Lana McDaniel released Fuller. Although not involved in the original case, the judge said she felt sick to her stomach over the time he spent in prison for a crime he did not commit.

On January 25, 2007, Fuller received a full pardon from Texas Governor Rick Perry. He was the tenth person from Dallas County to be exonerated by DNA evidence in the last five years.

SNAPSHOTS OF SUCCESS

If it works in these states and jurisdictions, why not the rest of the country?

NEW JERSEY

The first state in the nation to officially adopt the National Institute of Justice recommendations issued in 1999 (*Eyewitness Evidence: A Guide for Law Enforcement*), New Jersey provides an example of the successful implementation of reform protocols and their pragmatic effectiveness. While most law enforcement agencies or departments are controlled locally, the Attorney General of New Jersey was able to mandate changes in procedure across the entire state due to the unique supervisory authority of the Attorney General in that state. Since April 2001, New Jersey has conducted double-blind, sequential lineups. In addition, police officers issue cautionary instructions, ensure that lineups are constructed effectively with an adequate number of appropriate fillers, and document the identification procedures, including the witness' statement of certainty.

On July 31, 2006, the New Jersey Supreme Court, noting the importance of a complete record of an identification procedure in ensuring the reliability of eyewitness evidence presented to a jury, made complete documentation of the identification procedure a condition of admissibility of out-of-court identifications.[33] According to the opinion, "[G] iven the importance of ensuring the accuracy and integrity of out-of-court identifications, we will exercise our rulemaking authority to require that the police record, to the extent feasible, the dialogue between witnesses and police during an identification procedure." The decision was unanimous.

NORTH CAROLINA

In November 2002, Justice I. Beverly Lake created the North Carolina Actual Innocence Commission to study and recommend potential strategies for lessening the incidence of wrongful convictions. The Commission issued recommendations for eyewitness identification in October 2003 and endorsed changes in procedures such as the delivery of cautionary instructions, documentation of a witness' confidence in the identification without any feedback given by the administrator, effective use of fillers (a minimum of eight photos in photo identification procedures and a minimum of six individuals in live identification procedures), and sequential double-blind presentation.[34]

While the Commission has no official authority over law enforcement agencies in the state, the Commission members include the North Carolina attorney general, district attorneys, police chiefs, Supreme Court Justices, and others. A number of North Carolina's law enforcement agencies are increasingly implementing the Commission's eyewitness recommendations to date.

WISCONSIN

After studying the problem of mistaken identifications, the Training and Standards Bureau of the Wisconsin Department of Justice, working with the University of Wisconsin Law School's Frank J. Remington Center, developed a comprehensive set of eyewitness identification guidelines for law enforcement, which were adopted and distributed to law enforcement throughout the state in March 2005.[35] The guidelines—which include cautionary instructions to eyewitnesses, assessments of confidence immediately after identifications, proper selection of fillers, and double-blind, sequential presentation of lineups—represent a model for implementation of the "best practices" in eyewitness identification.

Legislation passed in November 2005 requires each law enforcement agency in the state to adopt policies or guidelines on eyewitness identification procedures. Though the model policy developed by the Attorney General is not mandatory, the Wisconsin Department of Justice has developed a training program to educate law enforcement across the state on the need for changes in procedure to lessen the risk of misidentification. Some departments have adopted the model policy, and more are likely to follow. To date, the program has trained over 800 investigators on the new procedures. Training on these procedures has also been incorporated into the curriculum for new investigators.[36]

MINNESOTA

Beginning in 2003, Hennepin County Attorney Amy Klobuchar spearheaded an effort to implement a sequential, double-blind pilot program in four police departments in the state, including Minneapolis. A follow-up study analyzing the pilot found that the pilot project was relatively easy to implement, with projects up and running in the smaller counties in two weeks, and in the larger counties in under a month. The reforms incurred minimal costs, no perceived drop in suspect identifications, and a reduction in filler identifications.[37] The study showed increased protections against misidentification, practical benefits for investigators, and a higher quality of eyewitness evidence. As a result of the pilot, the Hennepin County Attorney urged adoption of the reform protocol county-wide.

OTHER STATES

In 2003, the Illinois legislature passed legislation mandating cautionary instructions, as well as documentation and lineup composition requirements. In addition, a number of individual jurisdictions throughout the country have adopted reforms at the local level, though no action has been taken on the state level. These jurisdictions include the Boston Police Department and other departments in Suffolk County (in coordination with the Suffolk County District Attorney), Northampton, Massachusetts, Virginia Beach, Virginia and Santa Clara, California, among others.[38]

VOICES OF SUPPORT

"I did see many flaws in witnesses who felt like they were trying to be people pleasers, felt they had to select someone. Now people are actually comparing the one photo in front of them to what's in their mind, not going through process of elimination."[39]

Joy Rikala
Chief of Police
Minnetonka Police Department
Governing Magazine, May 2006

"It is axiomatic that eyewitness identification evidence is often crucial in identifying perpetrators and exonerating the innocent. However, recent cases, in which DNA evidence has been utilized to exonerate individuals convicted almost exclusively on the basis of eyewitness identifications, demonstrate that this evidence is not fool-proof. … While it is clear that current eyewitness identification procedures fully comport with federal and state constitutional requirements, the adoption of these Guidelines will enhance the accuracy and reliability of eyewitness identifications and will strengthen prosecutions in cases that rely heavily, or solely, on eyewitness evidence."[41]

John J. Farmer, Jr.
New Jersey Attorney General
Memorandum, April 18, 2001

"Every time you see something coming along that makes your job a little harder, you kind of cringe a little. It's going to take extra time and personnel, but if it's going to make a case a little more solid or if it's going to eliminate a bad identification or a situation where an officer may try to influence an identification, then it's beneficial."[42]

John E. Miliano
Chief of Police, Linden, New Jersey
New York Times, July 21, 2001

"If you don't do this, you risk having good convictions and good identifications thrown out."[47]

David Angel
Deputy District Attorney
Santa Clara County, California
Pittsburgh Post-Gazette, May 9, 2005

"We hadn't changed the way we do eyewitness procedures in decades DNA [exonerations] obviously have shown us that we have to change."[46]

Ken Patenaude
Detective Lieutenant
Northampton, MA Police Department
Pittsburgh Post-Gazette, May 9, 2005

"The psychology behind these procedures is to have witnesses focus on their actual memory of the incident and the suspect. We want to eliminate any kind of extraneous influence or bias in the identification process."[44]

Robert Olson
Chief of Police, Minneapolis, Minnesota
November 3, 2003

"I will never forget the day I learned about the DNA results. I was standing in my kitchen when the detective and the district attorney visited. They were good and decent people who were trying to do their jobs—as I had done mine, as anyone would try to do the right thing. They told me: "Ronald Cotton didn't rape you. It was Bobby Poole." The man I was so sure I had never seen in my life was the man who was inches from my throat, who raped me, who hurt me, who took my spirit away, who robbed me of my soul. And the man I had identified so emphatically on so many occasions was absolutely innocent. ... If anything good can come out of what Ronald Cotton suffered because of my limitations as a human being, let it be an awareness of the fact that eyewitnesses can and do make mistakes."[40]

Jennifer Thompson
Victim/Activist for Eyewitness Identification Reform
New York Times, June 18, 2000

"God forbid that we would put an innocent person in jail because of a less than confident eyewitness. And then we would be allowing a guilty person to go out and commit more crimes."[45]

William Mullen
Chief Deputy Sheriff of Allegheny County and
Former Assistant Chief of Police, Pittsburgh, PA
Associated Press, May 9, 2005

QUESTIONS & ANSWERS

Why change our existing protocol, which has worked for years?

Given the firm scientific basis for recommending the protocol, it is worth comparing these justifications with the current standard protocol. The standard way of conducting lineups today is not rooted in careful science. Rather, it was developed as an ad hoc procedure created and embraced in the law enforcement community because of its intuitive plausibility. Nothing more recommends or justifies it than tradition.

Nonetheless, eyewitness memory science has established that many factors related to eyewitness memory that seem intuitive and obvious are not necessarily true. For example, a witness' confidence in an identification is not a reliable predictor of accuracy. This is counter-intuitive, but the lack of a close correlation has been very well documented. Traditional methods need to be updated and procedures modernized to catch up with our modern understanding of eyewitness memory issues.

While no one can deny that many guilty people have been convicted based on evidence obtained with the traditional protocol, we have witnessed far too many innocent people convicted based on incorrect eyewitness testimony and later exonerated by DNA testing. The result—investigations led off course and prematurely ended, allowing predators to go uninvestigated and unpunished. It is incumbent upon us to live up to our commitment to public safety and base our procedures on the best science, not tradition.

Why haven't we heard of the research or improved procedures before?

It is not surprising that many people in law enforcement are unfamiliar with this scientific research. Police officers typically do not read technical peer reviewed academic journals (who could blame them?) or attend conferences about experimental psychology. Increasingly, however, opportunities have been created to foster a dialog, and many law enforcement agencies have modernized procedures based on the science. Only in recent years, upon the dawning of the age of DNA, have people begun to appreciate the problem of mistaken eyewitness identification, leading people in all aspects of the criminal justice system to look more carefully at ways of enhancing accuracy and putting higher quality evidence into the courtroom.

Isn't the blind administration component an insult to the integrity and professionalism of detectives?

Requiring a neutral administrator is NOT about challenging the integrity or professionalism of law enforcement personnel. Structuring procedures to generate the best quality of evidence is what professionalism demands. The issues addressed here have nothing to do with suggestions of misconduct. Rather, they address certain realities about normal human psychology and the possibility of the inadvertent cuing of a witness. All manner of verbal and nonverbal human behaviors may have the unintended effect of influencing a witness. Using a neutral administrator eliminates this possibility and ensures the best quality of evidence.

Just as in double-blind clinical drug trials, we are not assuming doctors and medical researchers are nefarious and dishonest; requiring neutral administrators is simply good practice—especially with such important matters as liberty and public safety on the line.

The courts don't seem to have any problems with the standard procedures, so why change?

The courts have increasingly begun to recognize that many of our traditional assumptions about eyewitness memory are wrong (such as the link between certainty and accuracy). Exonerations have made clear the need for change (and the terrible human costs of persisting with traditional practices), and developments in eyewitness memory science have identified ways of enhancing accuracy through more carefully designed procedures. Because the state of the science is now very solid, courts have often been more willing to allow challenges to existing protocols. Rather than picking apart in-court identifications that follow from flawed procedures, it is in the best interest of all parties to implement best practices that guarantee the best quality of evidence at the outset, on the front end of the process. Some courts have already ordered new procedures on that basis.

Why should we care about experiments with "staged crimes" and "mock witnesses"?

Experimental psychologists carefully design their experiments to isolate certain phenomena so that they may be better observed and understood in ways that 'real world' observation does not allow. These methods are the only way to fully control the different variables and track their changes under different conditions. In actual cases, for example, we cannot otherwise be completely certain whether an identified suspect is, in fact, the perpetrator the way we can in experiments. While the experiments have created a solid basis for the various elements of the protocol, we know from real world applications (statewide in New Jersey, as well as in many other individual jurisdictions) that the system is practical and pragmatically workable. There is already a track record of real world success.

Is the protocol practically feasible, especially for some smaller departments?

Experience in other jurisdictions across the country shows that the protocol is practical and workable. The protocol is sensitive to the potential problem of finding a neutral administrator, and provides for alternatives that accomplish the same goals.

STATISTICS

The Innocence Project found that mistaken eyewitness identifications were the leading cause of the first 130 DNA exonerations, accounting for 101 of the total. A subsequent study by the Innocence Project found that over 75 percent of the now nearly 200 post-conviction DNA exonerations in the U.S. involve mistaken eyewitness identification testimony, making it the leading cause of these wrongful convictions.

In addition, the Center on Wrongful Convictions at Northwestern University School of Law also studied the cases of 86 defendants who had been sentenced to death but legally exonerated based on strong claims of actual innocence, finding that eyewitness testimony played a role in the convictions of 54 percent of the death-sentenced defendants. Eyewitness testimony was the only evidence used against 38 percent of the defendants.

The Innocence Project also found that photo lineups were the most oft-used identification method in the first 82 DNA exonerations. Investigators used a photo lineup in 45 percent of the cases.

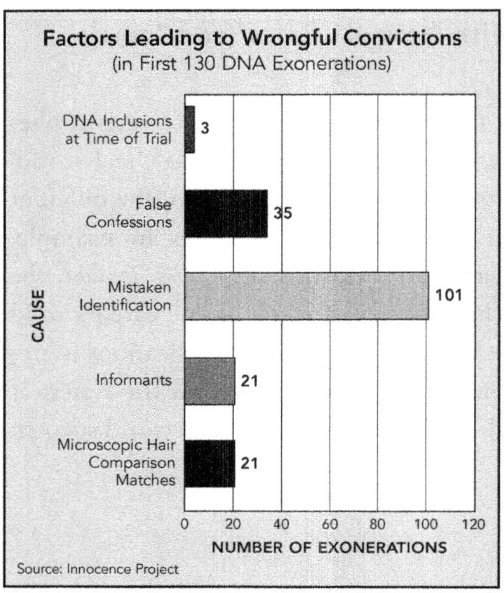

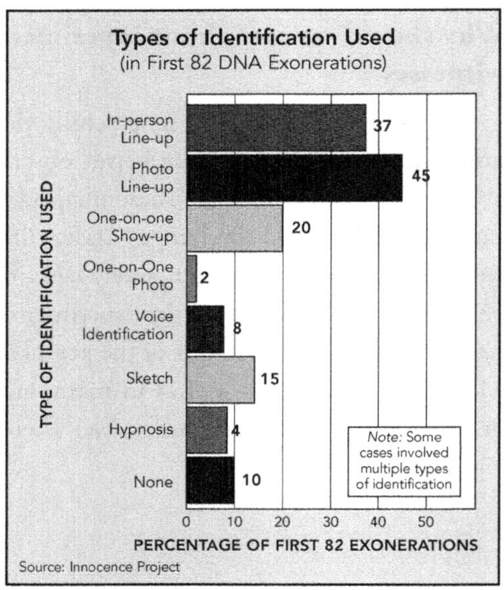

A MODEL POLICY

AN ACT CONCERNING EYEWITNESS IDENTIFICATION PROCEDURES

WHEREAS the goal of a police investigation is to accurately identify and apprehend the true perpetrators of crimes; and
WHEREAS eyewitness error is the leading cause of mistaken convictions; and
WHEREAS cases of mistaken conviction in [insert jurisdiction] owing to eyewitness misidentification have resulted in the actual perpetrators remaining free to commit more crimes; and
WHEREAS scientific studies of eyewitness memory have demonstrated that eyewitness evidence is, like trace physical evidence, susceptible to contamination if not handled properly; and
WHEREAS well-intentioned witnesses and authorities acting in good faith may sometimes inadvertently undermine the accuracy of an identification procedure unless appropriate safeguards are in place; and
WHEREAS extensive scientific research has shown that modified methods of conducting identification procedures greatly enhance accuracy;
We hereby enact the following

EYEWITNESS ACCURACY ENHANCEMENT ACT

Section 1: Definitions. For purposes of this section the following definitions apply:

1. Photo Lineup: a selected group of photographs of persons presented to an eyewitness to a crime, containing a single suspect and several fillers, for the purpose of determining whether the eyewitness is able to identify the suspect as the perpetrator.
2. Live Lineup: A selected group of persons presented to an eyewitness to a crime containing a suspect and several fillers for the purpose of determining whether the eyewitness is able to identify the suspect as the perpetrator.
3. Suspect: A person under investigation for participation in a crime.
4. Filler: A person, not a suspect in the crime under investigation, not known to the witness, who is made part of a live lineup; or a photograph of a person, not a suspect in the crime under investigation, not known to the witness, made part of a photo lineup and presented to a witness.
5. Neutral Blind Administrator: A person who conducts photo or live lineup procedures while unaware of which person in the lineup is the suspect and which are fillers.

Section 2: Development and Dissemination of Eyewitness Identification Protocol. Prior to [insert date] the [insert jurisdiction] Attorney General shall consult with law enforcement and scientific experts in eyewitness memory to develop, adopt, and disseminate to all law enforcement jurisdictions in the state comprehensive, written policies and procedures and associated training materials for [insert jurisdiction] law enforcement agencies regarding photo and live lineup eyewitness identification procedures that implement the requirements set forth in section 3 of this act.

Section 3: Requirements for Photo and Live Line-up Identification Procedures.

For any offense alleged to have been committed on or after [insert date], all photo and live lineup identification procedures conducted by law enforcement officers shall be administered pursuant to the procedures developed by the Attorney General described in section 2 of this act and consistent with the requirements in this section.

A. Witness Instructions. Prior to presenting a live lineup or photo array identification procedure, the lineup administrator shall instruct the witness that:

1. The procedure is intended to identify guilty parties as well as to clear innocent suspects from suspicion;
2. The witness should not guess or conclude that the perpetrator is among the persons in the lineup;
3. The witness should not feel compelled to make an identification because the perpetrator may or may not be among those shown;
4. The person administering the lineup may not be aware of which person in the lineup is the suspect;
5. Individuals depicted in lineup photos may not appear exactly as they did on the date of the incident because features such as head and facial hair are subject to change;
6. The police will continue to investigate the incident whether or not the witness identifies someone.

B. Documentation of Identification Procedures.

1. All photo and live lineup identification procedures conducted in connection with a criminal investigation shall be documented, regardless of whether an identification is made, made a part of the case record, and provided to the prosecuting authority in the event any prosecution related to the crime being investigated occurs. The documentation shall include:
   a. The time, date, location and identities of all persons present;
   b. A form listing the instructions enumerated in section A. of this act signed by the witness to confirm understanding of the instructions prior to administration of the identification procedure;
   c. A photograph of any live lineup as presented to a witness; or all photographs used in any photo lineup preserved in their original condition;
   d. The order of presentation of photographs or individuals.

2. All comments and exchanges during an identification procedure shall be electronically recorded with audio or audio/video recording equipment whenever possible. When it is not feasible to electronically record the identification procedure, comments and exchanges among persons present during an identification procedure shall be documented in writing, and an explanation of why electronic recording was not feasible shall be included in the record. The documentation, whether electronic or written, shall include all witness comments, using the witness' own words, regarding the persons or photos in the lineup and all questions and commentary by the lineup administrator and any other persons present during the identification procedure.
3. If the witness makes an identification as a result of a photo or live lineup, the lineup administrator shall immediately ask the witness to state in his or her own words how confident he or she is that the person identified is the perpetrator, and make the witness' words part of the record prior to any commentary or feedback from the lineup administrator or any other persons present.
4. If no electronic recording of the identification procedure is made, the witness shall review and sign the written record of the identification procedure, including all comments regarding the persons or photos presented, and any statements regarding an identification and degree of certainty, prior to any feedback or communication of information from the administrator or others involved in the investigation regarding the identification procedure.

C. General requirements for composition and conduct of lineup identification procedures.

1. During the identification procedure, the administrator shall refrain from any commentary or feedback to the witness regarding particular persons or photographs in a lineup until after the procedure is concluded and the witness certifies the record of the procedure.
2. At least five fillers shall be included in a photo lineup, in addition to the suspect, and at least four fillers shall be included in a live lineup, in addition to the suspect.
3. Only one member of a photo or live lineup shall be a suspect, and the remainder shall be fillers who are not suspects.
4. Fillers shall be selected who generally fit the witness' description of the perpetrator. When there is a limited or inadequate description of the perpetrator provided by the witness, or when the description of the perpetrator differs significantly from the appearance of the suspect, fillers should resemble the suspect in significant features.
5. Lineup administrators shall create a consistent appearance between the suspect and fillers with respect to any unique or unusual feature such as scars or tattoos used to describe the perpetrator by artificially adding or concealing that feature in filler photographs.

6. In photo line-ups, the suspect's photo should resemble his or her appearance at the time of the offense and not unduly stand out.
7. If the eyewitness has previously viewed a photo lineup or live lineup in connection with the investigation of another person suspected of involvement in the offense, the fillers in the lineup in which the suspected perpetrator participates shall be different from the fillers used in any prior lineups.
8. Law enforcement shall seek identification of any particular suspect through photo or live lineup only once from any given witness.
9. In a photo lineup, no writings or information concerning any previous arrest, indictment, or conviction of the suspected perpetrator shall be visible or made known to the eyewitness.
10. The position of the suspect in a photo or live lineup should be changed for each new witness to view the photo lineup.
11. In a live lineup, any identifying actions, such as speech, gestures, or other movements, shall be performed by all lineup participants.
12. In a live lineup, witnesses shall not be exposed to the members of the lineup before the procedure begins.

D. Neutral Blind Administration of Photo and Live Line-ups.

1. Whenever possible, the administrator of photo or live lineup identification procedures shall be someone who is not aware of which member of the lineup is the suspect in the case and which are fillers, and no person familiar with the identity of the suspect shall be present during the identification procedure.
2. When it is not feasible to have the procedure administered by someone unaware of which person is the suspect, that reason shall be documented, and a photo lineup procedure may be conducted using an alternative method specified and approved by the Attorney General. Any alternative procedure shall be structured to achieve neutral blind administration and prevent the administrator from viewing the lineup simultaneously with the witness or knowing the order of photographs as presented to the witness during the identification procedure. Alternative methods may include the following:
   i. automated computer programs approved by the Attorney General for such use that can automatically administer the line-up identification procedure directly to a witness, and during which the administrator cannot see which photo the witness is viewing until after the procedure is completed; or, alternatively,
   ii. a procedure approved by the Attorney General in which photographs are placed in folders, randomly numbered and shuffled, and then presented to a witness such that the administrator cannot see or determine the order

of photograph being presented to the witness until after the procedure is completed; or, alternatively,

iii. other such procedures as specified by the Attorney General which achieve neutral blind administration.

Note: Due to a lack of comprehensive data from pilot studies, the above model does not include a provision regarding sequential procedure. Nonetheless, researchers are currently pairing with other jurisdictions to add to the credible literature on the topic. While some questions have been raised about the value of sequential presentation, on balance most experts believe that it has proven to be superior in both experimental research and in the field. Thus, jurisdictions may also want to consider the addition of the sequential procedure, if and only if, neutral-blind administration is employed. In that event, the following provision may be inserted in the above model:

E. Sequential Procedure.

1. Live line-up and photo array identification procedures shall be presented to witnesses using a sequential method, in which a witness is shown photographs or live lineup participants one at a time, and not simultaneously. The witness shall be asked to state for each person whether the individual shown is the perpetrator, prior to viewing the next lineup participant.
2. The administrator shall not offer any comment or feedback to the witness regarding the witness' responses.
3. If there are multiple eyewitnesses, witnesses shall be presented with the identification procedure separately, and the suspect shall be placed in a different position in the lineup for each eyewitness.
4. Under no circumstances shall a sequential presentation be used unless the procedure complies fully with neutral blind administration specified in section D.

LITERATURE

SUGGESTED READINGS

The following materials are essential reading for individuals interested in improving eyewitness identification procedures.

Klobuchar, A., N.K.M. Steblay, and H.L. Caligiuri. "Improving Eyewitness Identifications: Hennepin County's Blind Sequential Lineup Pilot Project." Cardozo Public Law, Policy & Ethics Journal 4 (2006): 381–413. http://web.augsburg.edu/~steblay/ImprovingEyewitnessIdentifications.pdf

Wells, G.L., M. Small, S.D. Penrod, R.S. Malpass, S.M. Fulero, and C.A.E. Brimacombe. "Eyewitness Identification Procedures: Recommendations for Lineups and Photospreads," Law and Human Behavior 22 (1998): 603–647. http://www.psychology.iastate.edu/FACULTY/gwells/Wellsarticlespdf/whitepaperpdf.pdf

Wisconsin Office of the Attorney General. Training and Standards Bureau. Model Policy and Procedures for Eyewitness Identification (2005). http://www.doj.state.wi.us/dles/tns/eyewitness.asp

SELECTED BIBLIOGRAPHY

The following listing includes some of the key source material used in developing the content of this policy review. While by no means an exhaustive list of the sources consulted, it is intended as a convenience for those wishing to engage in further study of the topic of improved eyewitness identification procedures. Many of the entries contain hyperlinks for ease in locating an article, report or document on the web.

1. Journals and Law Reviews

Bradfield, A.L., G.L. Wells, and E.A. Olson. "The Damaging Effect of Confirming Feedback on the Relation between Eyewitness Certainty and Identification Accuracy." Journal of Applied Psychology 87 (2002): 112–120.

Gross, S.R., K. Jacoby, D.J. Matheson, N. Montgomery, and S. Patil. "Exonerations in the United States, 1989 Through 2003." The Journal of Criminal Law & Criminology 95 (2005): 523–560. http://www.thejusticeproject.org/press/reports/pdfs/17220.pdf

Malpass, R.S. "A Policy Evaluation of Simultaneous and Sequential Lineups." Psychology, Public Policy and Law 12, no. 4 (2006): 394–418. http://eyewitness.utep.edu/Documents/Malpass06PolicyEvaluationOfSimultaneousAndSequentialLineups-PPPL.pdf

Penrod, S.D., and B.L. Cutler. "Witness confidence and witness accuracy: Accessing their forensic relation." Public Policy, Psychology & Law 1 (1995): 817–845.

Semmler, C., N. Brewer, and G.L. Wells. "Effects of Postidentification Feedback on Eyewitness Identification and Nonidentification." Journal of Applied Psychology 89, no. 2 (2004): 334–346. http://www.psychology.iastate.edu/faculty/gwells/Wellsarticlespdf/JEPASemmleretal.pdf

Steblay, N.M. "Social Influence in Eyewitness Recall: A Meta-Analytic Review of Lineup Instruction Effects." Law and Human Behavior 21, no. 3 (1997): 283–297. http://web.augsburg.edu/%7Esteblay/LineupInstructionAnalysis.pdf

Steblay, N., J. Dysart, S. Fulero, and R.C.L. Lindsay. "Eyewitness Accuracy Rates in Sequential and Simultaneous Lineup Presentations: A Meta-Analytic Comparison." Law and Human Behavior 25, no. 5 (2001): 459–473. http://web.augsburg.edu/%7Esteblay/EyewitnessAccuracy.pdf

Turtle, J., R.C.L. Lindsay, and G.L. Wells. "Best Practice Recommendations for Eyewitness Evidence Procedures: New Ideas for the Oldest Way to Solve a Case." The Canadian Journal of Police & Security Services 1 (2003): 5–18. http://www.ryerson.ca/~jturtle/cjpss.html

Wells, G.L. "Applied Eyewitness-Testimony Research: System Variables and Estimator Variables." Journal of Personality and Social Psychology 26, no. 12 (1978): 1546–1557.
Wells, G.L. Eyewitness Identification: Systemic Reforms, Wisconsin Law Review 2006, no. 2 (2006): 615–643. http://www.psychology.iastate.edu/FACULTY/gwells/WisconsinLawarticle.pdf
Wells, G.L., and A.L. Bradfield. "'Good, You Identified the Suspect': Feedback to Eyewitnesses Distorts their Reports of the Witnessing Experience." Journal of Applied Psychology 83 (1998): 360–376.
Wells, G.L., M. Small, S.D. Penrod, R.S. Malpass, S.M. Fulero, and C.A.E. Brimacombe. "Eyewitness Identification Procedures: Recommendations for Lineups and Photospreads," Law and Human Behavior 22, no. 6 (1998): 603–647. http://www.psychology.iastate.edu/FACULTY/gwells/Wellsarticlespdf/whitepaperpdf.pdf

2. Commission and Association Reports & Policies

American Bar Association. "Achieving Justice: Freeing the Innocent, Convicting the Guilty." Report of the ABA Criminal Justice Sections Ad Hoc Innocence Committee to Ensure the Integrity of the Criminal Process (2006).
American Bar Association. Criminal Justice Section. Report to the House of Delegates: Resolution Adopting the American Bar Association Statement of Best Practices for Promoting the Accuracy of Eyewitness Identification Procedures dated August 2004. http://www.abanet.org/leadership/2004/annual/111c.doc
California Commission on the Fair Administration of Justice. Report and Recommendations Regarding Eyewitness Identification Procedures (April 13, 2006). http://www.ccfaj.org/documents/reports/eyewitness/official/eyewitnessidrep.pdf
Illinois Governor's Commission on Capital Punishment Report (April 15, 2002). http://www.idoc.state.il.us/ccp/ccp/reports/commissionreport/index.html
National Institute of Justice. Convicted by Juries, Exonerated by Science: Case Studies in the Use of DNA Evidence to Establish Innocence After Trial 15 (June 1996). http://www.ojp.usdoj.gov/nij/pubs-sum/161258.htm
National Institute of Justice, Eyewitness Evidence: A Guide for Law Enforcement iii (1999). http://www.ojp.usdoj.gov/nij/pubs-sum/178240.htm
New Jersey Department of Law and Public Safety. Office of the Attorney General. Memorandum Re: Attorney General Guidelines for Preparing and Conducting Photo and Live Lineup Identification Procedures to all County Prosecutors, Police Chiefs, and Law Enforcement Chief Executives (April 18, 2001). http://www.state. nj.us/lps/dcj/agguide/photoid.pdf
North Carolina Actual Innocence Commission. Recommendations for Eyewitness Identification (October 2003). http://www.ncids.org/News% 2 0& % 2 0Updates/Eyewitness %2 0ID.pdf

Northampton Police Department. "Eyewitness Identification Procedure." Administration & Operations Manual O-408: 1–9. http://www.innocenceproject.org/docs/NorthamptonMAID Protocols.pdf

Santa Clara County Police Chiefs' Association. Santa Clara County Line-up Protocol. http://www.innocenceproject.org/docs/SantaClaraeyewitness.pdf

Virginia State Crime Commission. "Mistaken Eyewitness Identification." Report to the Governor and the General Assembly of Virginia, House Document No. 40 (2005). http://leg2.state.va.us/dls/h&sdocs.nsf/By+Year/HD402005/$file/HD40.pdf

Wisconsin Office of the Attorney General. Training and Standards Bureau. Model Policy and Procedures for Eyewitness Identification (2005). http://www.doj.state.wi.us/dles/tns/eyewitness.asp

3. Field Studies

Klobuchar, A., and H.L. Caligiuri. "Protecting the Innocent/Convicting the Guilty: Hennepin County's Pilot Project in Blind Sequential Eyewitness Identification." William Mitchell Law Review 32 (2005): 1–26.

Klobuchar, A., N.K.M. Steblay, and H.L. Caligiuri. "Improving Eyewitness Identifications: Hennepin County's Blind Sequential Lineup Pilot Project." Cardozo Public Law, Policy & Ethics Journal 4 (2006): 381–413. http://web.augsburg.edu/~steblay/ImprovingEyewitnessIdentifications.pdf

Malpass, R.S. "Notes on the Illinois Pilot Program on Sequential Double-Blind Identification Procedures." Public Interest Law Reporter 11, no. 2 (2006): 5–47. http://eyewitness.utep.edu/Documents/Malpass06NotesOnTheIllinoisPilotProgram.pdf

Mecklenburg, S.H. Report to the Legislature of the State of Illinois: The Illinois Pilot Program on Sequential Double-Blind Identification Procedures (March 2006). http://www.chicagopolice.org/IL%20Pilot%20on%20Eyewitness%20ID.pdf

Steblay, N. "Observations on the Illinois Lineup Data" (May 3, 2006), http://web.augsburg.edu/~steblay/ObservationsOnTheIllinoisData.pdf.

Wells, G.L. "Gary L. Wells' comments on the Mecklenburg Report" (Updated May 2006), http://www.psychology.iastate.edu/FACULTY/gwells/IllinoisProjectWellscomments.pdf.

NOTES

1. See Edward Connors et al., Nat'l Inst. of Justice, U.S. Dep't of Justice, Convicted by Juries, Exonerated by Science: Case Studies in the Use of DNA Evidence to Establish Innocence After Trial 2, 15 (1996); Gary L. Wells et al., Eyewitness Identification Procedures: Recommendations for Lineups and Photospreads, 22 Law & Hum. Behav. 603, 605 (1998); Samuel R. Gross et al., Exonerations in the United States, 1989 Through 2003, 95 J. Crim. L. & Criminology 523, 542 (2005).

2. See current DNA exoneration statistics and case profiles at The Innocence Project at the Benjamin N. Cardozo School of Law, http://www.innocenceproject.org.
3. Gary L. Wells, Eyewitness Identification: Systemic Reforms, 2006 Wis. L. Rev. 615, 632 (2006).
4. Technical Working Group for Eyewitness Evidence, Nat'l Inst. of Justice, U.S. Dep't of Justice, Eyewitness Evidence: A Guide for Law Enforcement (1999), http://www.ojp.usdoj.gov/nij/pubs-sum/178240.htm.
5. Wells, supra note 3, at 635.
6. Id. at 623.
7. Gary L. Wells et al., Eyewitness Identification Procedures: Recommendations for Lineups and Photospreads, 22 Law & Hum. Behav. 603, 618 (1998).
8. Id. at 614.
9. Id.
10. Id. at 624.
11. Id.
12. James M. Doyle, True Witness: Cops, Courts, Science, and the Battle Against Misidentification 17 (2005).
13. Id.
14. Gary L. Wells, Applied Eyewitness-Testimony Research: System Variables and Estimator Variables, 36J. Personality & Soc. Psych. 1546, 1548 (1978).
15. Wells, supra note 3, at 625.
16. Id. See also Nancy M. Steblay, Social Influence in Eyewitness Recall: A Meta-Analytic Review of Lineup Instruction Effects, 21 Law & Hum. Behav. 283, 284–85 (1997).
17. Wells et al., supra note 7, at 632.
18. Id. at 633.
19. Wells, supra note 3, at 624.
20. Wells et al., supra note 7, at 635.
21. Wells, supra note 3, at 629.
22. Nancy Steblay et al., Eyewitness Accuracy Rates in Sequential and Simultaneous Lineup Presentations: A Meta-Analytic Comparison, 25 Law & Hum. Behav. 459, 464 (2001).
23. Id. at 469.
24. Wells, supra note 3, at 627.
25. Amy Klobuchar, Nancy M. Steblay & Hilary Lindell Caligiuri, Improving Eyewitness Identifications: Hennepin County's Blind Sequential Lineup Pilot Project, 4 Cardozo Pub. L. Pol'y & Ethics J. 381, 410 (2006).
26. Sheri H. Mecklenburg, Report to the Legislature of the State of Illinois: The Illinois Pilot Program on Sequential Double-Blind Identification Procedures (March 2006), http://www.chicagopolice.org/IL%20Pilot%20on%20Eyewitness%20ID.pdf.
27. See, e.g., Gary L. Wells, Comments on the (Mecklenburg Report Updated May 2006), http://www.psychology.ias-tate.edu/FACULTY/gwells/IllinoisProjectWellscomments.

pdf; Nancy Steblay, Observations on the Illinois Lineup Data, (May 3, 2006), http://web.augsburg.edu/~ste-blay/ObservationsOnTheIllinoisData.pdf.

28. See Bernice Yeung, Innocence Arrested, SF Weekly, October29, 2003.
29. "Yes, I'm sure-That's The One!" Memory Loss & the Brain, The Newsletter of the Memory Disorders Project at Rutgers University, Summer 2003, http://www.memory-lossonline.com/eyewitness.htm.
30. See, e.g., State of Wisconsin, Office of the Attorney General, Model Policy and Procedure for Eyewitness Identification (2005) [hereinafter Wisconsin Model Policy], http://www.doj.state.wi.us/dles/tns/EyewitnessPublic.pdf.
31. State v. Delgado, 188 N.J. 48, 902 A.2d 888 (2006).
32. North Carolina Actual Innocence Commission, Recommendations for Eyewitness Identification (October 2003), http://www.ncids.org/News%20&%20Updates/Eyewitness%20ID.pdf.
33. See Wisconsin Model Policy, supra note 30.
34. Telephone interview with Ken Hammond, WI Dept. of Justice Training and Standards Bureau (Jan. 26, 2007).
35. Klobuchar, Steblay & Caligiuri, supra note 25, at 411.
36. Wells, supra note 3, at 642.
37. See Anya Sostek, Blind Sighted: Eyewitness Identification Doesn't Always Mesh with DNA Evidence, and That's Leading Police Departments To Rethink Their Lineup Procedures, Governing Magazine, May 2006.
38. See Jennifer Thompson, 'I Was Certain, but I Was Wrong,' New York Times, June 18, 2000.
39. See John J. Farmer, Jr., Office of the Attorney General, Attorney General Guidelines for Preparing and Conducting Photo and Live Lineup Identification Procedures (April 18, 2001), http://www.state. nj.us/lps/dcj/agguide/photoid.pdf.
40. See Gina Kolata and Iver Peterson, New Jersey Is Trying New Way For Witnesses to Say, 'It's Him,' New York Times, July 21, 2001.
41. See Police and Prosecutors Team Up for Better Eyewitness IDs, November 3, 2003, http://www.psychology.iastate.edu/FACULTY/gwells/Minnesota new procedures.html.
42. Id.
43. See Local Police Unaware of Federal Eyewitness Guidelines, Associated Press, May 9, 2005.
44. See Bill Moushey and Nathan Crabbe, Questionable Identifications Sent 2 to Jail, Pittsburgh Post-Gazette, May 9, 2005.
45. Id.
46. See Amy Klobuchar & Hillary Lindell Caligiuri, Protecting the Innocent/Convicting the Guilty: Hennepin County's Pilot Project in Blind Sequential Eyewitness Identification, 32 Wm. Mitchell L. Rev. 1, 25 (2005).

47. State v. Delgado, 188 N.J. 48, 902 A.2d 888 (2006).

The Justice Project is a nonpartisan organization dedicated to fighting injustice and to creating a more humane and just world. The Justice Project, which lobbies for criminal justice reform, and The Justice Project Education Fund, which increases public awareness and reaffirms America's core commitment to fairness and accuracy, work together to design and implement national and state-based campaigns to advance reforms that address significant flaws in the American criminal justice system, with particular focus on the capital punishment system.

This report is made possible primarily through the support of The Pew Charitable Trusts. For additional information, questions and comments, please contact our offices at (202) 638–5855, or email info@thejusticeproject.org.

Model Policy and Procedure for Eyewitness Identification

Wisconsin Department of Justice,
Office of the Attorney General

INTRODUCTION

In order to implement the most reliable method for the collection of eyewitness evidence, this model policy and procedure recommends that law enforcement officials conduct double-blind, sequential photo arrays and lineups with non-suspect fillers chosen to minimize suggestiveness, non-biased instructions to eyewitnesses, and assessments of confidence immediately after identifications.

This policy is designed to ensure that the highest quality evidence possible is obtained from eyewitnesses. For some of the policy objectives, there is no one right method for implementing the principles. Some methods will require more resources and effort than others. Recognizing that not all law enforcement agencies have the same resources or face the same local challenges, these guidelines, where appropriate, provide alternative procedures designed to allow individual agencies to adapt procedures that best meet local circumstances.

This model and its associated recommendations were written to provide information regarding legal requirements and best practices surrounding collection and preservation of eyewitness evidence. No one document can address all the circumstances and/or exigencies that are encountered in the field. This model and guidelines are not intended to be a comprehensive treatment of all of the factors involved in criminal investigation. Rather, it is a general policy and procedural guide outlining methods for collecting and preserving evidence. Readers should keep in mind that the information and procedures presented here are intended to be used as guidelines when encountering circumstances and factors not specifically covered. These recommendations are not intended to create, do not create, and may not be relied on to create, any rights, substantive or procedural, enforceable at law by any party in any matter civil or criminal.

EYEWITNESS IDENTIFICATION POLICY

Eyewitness[1] identification has always been a powerful tool for investigating and prosecuting criminal cases. Eyewitness evidence can be the most important and convincing evidence in a case. Research and nationwide experience have demonstrated that eyewitness evidence can be a particularly fragile type of evidence, and that eyewitnesses can be mistaken. Eyewitnesses can make significant identification errors, but those errors can be difficult to detect, because the witnesses are sincere and have no motive to lie. When wrong, they usually are not being deceitful, but just simply mistaken.

Recent studies of eyewitnesses and human memory have suggested that eyewitness evidence is much like trace evidence left at a crime scene.[2] Like trace evidence, eyewitness memory is an imprint left in the mind of the witness. But also like trace evidence, it is susceptible to contamination if not handled properly. The result can be failure to identify the true perpetrator or erroneous identification of an innocent person.

Recently, scientific research has uncovered psychological factors that can cause well-meaning eyewitnesses to make mistakes, and has shown that new methods of conducting eyewitness procedures can address these factors and reduce error.[3] These new methods represent the best techniques for accurately capturing and preserving eyewitness memories thereby enhancing the reliability of criminal investigations and prosecutions.

Eyewitness errors have been linked to two psychological factors: 1) unintentional suggestion to witnesses,[4] and 2) the 'relative judgment process',[5] which refers to the tendency when viewing a simultaneous presentation (viewing an entire photo array or lineup at once) for eyewitnesses to identify the person who looks the most like the real perpetrator relative to the other people. When the real perpetrator is not in the array, the relative judgment process can lead to misidentification.

> Note: 2005 Wisconsin Act 60 created § 175.50 Eyewitness Identification Procedures. Section 175.50(2) reads in part "Each law enforcement agency shall adopt written policies for using an eyewitness to identify a suspect upon viewing

1 In this document, the term 'eyewitness' is often synonymous with 'victim.'

2 Wells, G.L., et. al. "Eyewitness Identification Procedures: Recommendations for Lineups and Photospreads," Law and Human Behavior, Vol. 22, No. 6, p. 14, 1998.

3 Wells, G.L. and Olson, E.A. "Eyewitness Testimony." Annual Review of Psychology, Vol. 54, p. 286–289, 2003.

4 See footnote 3 at 289.

5 See footnote 3 at 286.

the suspect in person or upon viewing a representation of the suspect. The policies shall be designed to reduce the potential for erroneous identifications by eyewitnesses in criminal cases."[6]

The following model procedures address these causes of eyewitness error in a number of ways, but most prominently by recommending the following:

1. Utilize non-suspect fillers chosen to minimize any suggestiveness that might point toward the suspect;
2. Utilize a 'double blind' procedure, in which the administrator is not in a position to unintentionally influence the witness's selection;
3. Give eyewitnesses an instruction that the real perpetrator may or may not be present and that the administrator does not know which person is the suspect;
4. Present the suspect and the fillers sequentially (one at a time) rather than simultaneously (all at once). This discourages relative judgment and encourages absolute judgments of each person presented, because eyewitnesses are unable to see the subjects all at once and are unable to know when they have seen the last subject;
5. Assess eyewitness confidence immediately after identification;
6. Avoid multiple identification procedures in which the same witness views the same suspect more than once.

Scientific Rationale for Major Recommendations

1) Photo arrays and lineups should be constructed with non-suspect fillers chosen to minimize any suggestiveness that might point toward the suspect.

Unintentional suggestion can lead an eyewitness to identify a particular individual in a photo array or lineup. This can occur if one individual stands out from the others due to the composition of the array or lineup.[7] For instance, if one of the individuals in the array or lineup has unique facial hair or is photographed with a different background, that person may stand out from the others and may be identified or excluded due to that distinguishing characteristic.

Additionally, suggestion can occur if the suspect is the only person in the array or lineup who resembles the witness's description of the perpetrator.[8] Therefore, non-suspect fillers should generally be chosen to match the witness's description of the perpetrator. If a person who has never seen the perpetrator would be able to guess which person in the array or

6 http://nxt.legis.state.wi.us/nxt/gateway.dll?f=templates&fn=default.htm&d=stats&jd=175.50(2)

7 See Footnote 2 at 23–27.

8 See Footnote 2 at 24–27.

lineup is the suspect based on knowing only the eyewitness's description of the perpetrator, then the non-suspect fillers may not sufficiently match the description of the perpetrator.[9]

2) Photo arrays and lineups should use a 'double blind' procedure, in which the administrator is not in a position to unintentionally influence the witness's selection. Individual agencies are free to devise methods for meeting this recommendation consistent with their own staffing and resource constraints.

Research has demonstrated that human beings, when conducting experiments in any context in which they know the desired or correct outcome, often unwittingly cue the subject of the experiment or misinterpret the results of the experiment based on their knowledge of the desired or correct outcome—even despite their best efforts not to do so.[10] For this reason, it is a fixture of scientific and medical research that the person conducting the experiment must be 'blind' to the desired or correct outcome. For example, in a study of a given drug's effectiveness, no researcher administering the drug to a subject is allowed to know whether the subject is being given the real drug or a placebo, because administrators' expectations can affect both how the subject responds to the substance he/she is given and how the administrator interprets the subject's response. Researchers have learned that the same principle applies to photo array and lineup procedures.[11] Simply stated, if the administrator of a photo array or lineup does not know the identity of the suspect, he/she cannot provide any cues to the eyewitness. This recommendation does not presume any deliberate impropriety by law enforcement officers. It merely recognizes the potential for unintentional suggestion.

3) Witnesses viewing photo arrays and lineups should be instructed that the real perpetrator may or may not be present and that the administrator does not know which person is the suspect.

At first glance, it might seem that informing an eyewitness that the perpetrator may or may not be present in an array or lineup would be stating the obvious. However, eyewitnesses may feel pressure to identify someone from a lineup or array because they believe the police would not be presenting the individuals if all were innocent. When the true perpetrator is not present, this tendency may influence eyewitnesses to identify an innocent person. Studies show that telling the witness that the perpetrator may or may not be present counteracts the tendency to identify the person who looks the most like the perpetrator

---

9 See Footnote 2 at 24–27.

10 See Footnote 2 at 21–22.

11 See footnote 3 at 289 and footnote 2 at 21–22.

and reduces mistaken identification rates by as much as 41.6%.[12] Telling witnesses that the administrator does not know who the suspect is will also help prevent witnesses from mistakenly looking to the administrator for cues about which person is the perpetrator.

4) Witnesses viewing photo arrays and lineups should view the suspect and fillers one at a time (sequentially) rather than all at once (simultaneously).

When witnesses are given a simultaneous presentation of multiple photographs or lineup subjects, they tend to make relative judgments, comparing one person to the next and identifying the person who looks the most like the actual perpetrator.[13] Obviously, this tendency does not pose a problem if the perpetrator is present in the array—because if the perpetrator is present, selecting the person who looks the most like the perpetrator will lead to selecting the correct person. However, when the perpetrator is absent from the array, witnesses still tend to make identifications of the person in the array who looks the most like the suspect. If the perpetrator is absent from the array, that person will be a filler or an innocent suspect. To overcome this tendency, researchers have learned that presenting subjects one at a time—sequentially—helps witnesses to make absolute judgments rather than comparative ones. Studies show that witnesses given a simultaneous presentation make approximately twice as many identifications of innocent people as witnesses shown a sequential presentation.[14] There is some indication that the number of accurate identifications of actual perpetrators diminishes slightly with a sequential presentation, but much of this is largely the effect of pure guessing inherent in the relative judgment process. Therefore, research suggests that the value of identifications made under sequential presentations is significantly greater than those made under simultaneous presentations.

5) Eyewitnesses' confidence should be assessed immediately after identification.

An eyewitness's statement of confidence in identification can be very important evidence at trial. However, confidence is particularly susceptible to influence by information provided to the witness after the identification process. Research shows that information provided to a witness after an identification suggesting that the witness selected the right person can dramatically, yet artificially, increase the witness's confidence in the identification.[15] Even worse, this effect is greater for eyewitnesses who receive positive feedback after

12 See footnote 3 at 286–7.

13 See footnote 3 at 288.

14 See footnote 3 at 288.

15 Wells, G.L. and Bradfield, A.L. "'Good, You Identified the Suspect': Feedback to Eyewitnesses Distorts their Reports of the Witnessing Experience." Journal of Applied Psychology, Vol. 83, p. 360–76, 1998.

misidentifications than for eyewitnesses who receive positive feedback after accurate identifications.[16] To protect against artificially inflated confidence levels, it is imperative that the witness's confidence in identification be recorded immediately after an identification procedure to prevent influence from information learned after the procedure.

6) Avoid multiple identification procedures in which the same witness views the same suspect more than once.

The practice of conducting multiple identification procedures with the same witness and the same suspect should ordinarily be avoided because of the potential for suggestiveness and the potential to contaminate a witness's memory.[17] An eyewitness viewing a second procedure with the same suspect may believe that the suspect's presence in both procedures suggests that authorities believe the suspect is the perpetrator. Or, an eyewitness may become confused and identify the suspect based on recognizing him/her from the prior procedure rather than from remembering the suspect's presence at the crime. In either case, the suggestiveness of the second procedure may taint the eyewitness. Therefore, eyewitness identification procedures should be approached with the understanding that officers have one opportunity to conduct an eyewitness procedure. Except in unusual cases, conduct only one identification procedure—the most reliable procedure available under the circumstances—in which the same suspect views the same witness once.

PREPARATION

Generally, investigators should possess some credible & verifiable indication that a person is the actual perpetrator before implementing eyewitness identification procedures such as photo arrays or line-ups.

Every lineup has the potential of jeopardy for innocent suspects. So, investigators must ask when a person should be placed in a line-up procedure. There should be some credible and/or verifiable indication that the suspect is actually the perpetrator before placement in an identification procedure. This concept precludes using line-up procedures for a "fishing expedition." Rather, consider the consequences of presenting a lineup to a witness if there is a strong possibility that the culprit is not in it—it is not a risk free practice. Before you begin

---

16 Bradfield, A.L., Wells, G.L., Olson, E.A. "The Damaging Effect of Confirming Feedback on the Relation between Eyewitness Certainty and Identification Accuracy." Journal of Applied Psychology, Vol. 87, p. 112–20, 2002.

17 See Hinz, T. & Pezdek, K. "The Effect of Exposure to Multiple Lineups on Face Identification Accuracy." Law and Human Behavior, Vol. 25, p. 185–198, 2001; Gorenstein, G.W. & Ellsworth, P.C. "Effect of Choosing an Incorrect Photograph on a Later Identification by an Eyewitness." Journal of Applied Psychology. Vol. 65, No. 5, p. 616, 1980.

consider carefully "why is this suspect being placed into the lineup to begin with?" Remember that a misidentification is harmful not only because it can lead to a wrongful conviction, but also because it can irreparably taint an eyewitness's memory, making that eyewitness less useful for future identification procedures that might contain the true perpetrator.

Some agencies do not arrest based solely on eyewitness identification. In the early stages of investigation it is risky to utilize eyewitnesses prematurely. It is incumbent upon investigators to at least check alibis before conducting a procedure. Alibi verification may not be the only thing that needs to happen before a photo array: follow-up, tips, and perhaps additional testing should be considered. But a cautious approach should also consider how time affects memory. More time investigating results in a longer delay leading up to the procedure. While caution should be the watchword, long time delays risk less accuracy or effectiveness for the victim and eyewitness.

When possible, investigators should approach a case with an understanding that obtaining an eyewitness identification ought to be one of the later, not one of the first, steps in an investigation. Other kinds of evidence, such as physical evidence or evidence of alibi, can lead investigators to rule out any given suspect before ever having to conduct an identification procedure. To promote investigative integrity, every procedure should be grounded in a viable suspect. Investigations necessarily should have an emphasis on corroborating evidence—such as physical evidence, an alibi, phone records, and the like—before making an arrest.

PROCEDURE FOR PHOTO ARRAYS

Consistent with the policy described previously, a double-blind, sequential presentation is recommended for all photo arrays. However, if a simultaneous presentation is used, it is still important to follow a double-blind procedure, select non-suggestive fillers, and properly instruct the witness. The double-blind requirement may be met in different ways, and individual departments are encouraged to devise appropriate methods that accommodate staffing and resource considerations. These procedures outline two ways to meet the requirement—with an independent administrator or with a folder system.

METHOD #1: The photo array is conducted by an independent administrator, someone who does not know the suspect's identity.

1. Gather Photographs. This step should be conducted by the investigating officer. In total, gather one suspect's photo, a minimum of five filler (non-suspect) photos, and at least two blank photos.

    a. Suspect's Photo.

i. Multiple Suspects. If there are multiple suspects, include only one suspect's photo in the array.

ii. Multiple Photos of the Suspect. If multiple photos of the suspect are available, choose the photo that most resembles the suspect's appearance at the time of the crime. If you do not know what the suspect looked like at the time of the crime, choose the photo that most resembles the description of the perpetrator.

b. Filler Photos.

i. Number of Fillers. Whenever possible, include a minimum of five fillers in each array. Since increasing the number of fillers tends to increase the reliability of the procedure, include as many above the minimum as desired.

ii. Resemblance of Fillers to Suspect. In general, fillers should resemble the witness's description of the perpetrator in significant features (such as face, profile, height, weight, age, build, posture, hair and facial hair, specific articles of clothing, etc., to the extent applicable to the photos being used) or, in cases where a composite was used, fillers should resemble the composite. If a person who has never seen the perpetrator would be able to pick out the suspect from the array based on knowing only the description of the perpetrator given by the eyewitness, then the fillers may not sufficiently resemble the description of the perpetrator.

A. For instance, if the perpetrator was described as having an unusual identifying mark, all fillers should have similar markings or all photos should include similar coverings over the described area.

B. When there is an inadequate description of the perpetrator, or when there is a suspect whose appearance differs from the description of the perpetrator, fillers should resemble the suspect in significant features.

iii. Set Aside Lead Filler. Set aside one filler, so that the administrator will know to place it in the lead position.

Explanation: Research suggests witnesses are reluctant to identify someone in the first position and, if that person is the perpetrator, he/she may go free and a misidentification may result.

c. Blank Photos. Set aside two blank photos, so that the administrator will know to place them at the end of the array.

Explanation: Research suggests witnesses should not know when they are viewing the last photo. Witnesses who believe they are viewing the last photo may feel a heightened need to make an identification. Blanks after the last photo will prevent the witnesses from knowing when they are looking at the last photo.

d. Assess the Array. Make sure that no person stands out from the rest.

2. Put Photographs in Order.

Key Principle: Bring in an independent administrator—someone who does not know who the suspect is—to conduct the procedure.

a. Arrange the Photos. Give the administrator the suspect's photo and the remaining filler photos. Do not tell the administrator which photo is the suspect's. Have the administrator mix these photos and place them after the lead filler photo and before the two blank photos. Then have the administrator number all the photos in the series.

3. Conduct the Array.

a. Record the Identification Procedure. If practical, record to videotape, audiotape, CD or DVD the entire photo identification procedure. Videotaping is preferable. For information on video and audio recording procedures, see the Wisconsin Department of Justice's Physical Evidence Handbook 8th Edition, p. 39–44.

b. Restrict Availability of Other Results to Witness. Ensure that no writings or information concerning previous identification results are visible to the witness.

c. Presence of Persons Aware of Suspect's Identity. No one should be present during the photo array procedure who knows the suspect's identity.

d. Witness's Awareness of Number of Photos. The witness should not know how many photos will be shown.

e. Instruct the Witness. The photo array administrator should give the witness a written copy of the following instruction and should read the instruction aloud at the beginning of each identification procedure:

> **In a moment, I am going to show you a series of photos. The person who committed the crime may or may not be included. I do not know whether the person being investigated is included. Even if you identify someone during this procedure, I will continue to show you all photos in the series.**
>
> **Keep in mind that things like hair styles, beards, and mustaches can be easily changed and that complexion colors may look slightly different in photographs.**
>
> **You should not feel you have to make an identification. It is as important to exclude innocent persons as it is to identify the perpetrator.**
>
> **The photos will be shown to you one at a time and are not in any particular order. Take as much time as you need to look at each one. After each photo, I will ask you "Is this the person you saw [insert description of act here]?" Take your time answering the question. If you answer "Yes," I will then ask you, "In your own words, can you describe how certain you are?"**
>
> **Because you are involved in an ongoing investigation, in order to prevent damaging the investigation, you should avoid discussing this identification procedure or its results.**
>
> **Do you understand the way the photo array procedure will be conducted and the other instructions I have given you?**

Witnesses should then be asked to read the following additional paragraph and sign and date below. (Some witnesses may decline to sign. When a witness declines to sign, it is sufficient for the investigating officer to document that the witness was appropriately instructed.)

> **I have read these instructions, or they have been read to me, and I understand the instructions. I am prepared to review the photographs that will be presented to me, and I will follow the instructions provided on this form.**

f. Present the Photos. Present each photo to the witness separately, in order. When the witness is done viewing the photo, have the witness hand the photo back.

g. Question the Witness. After the witness has looked at a photo and handed it back to you, ask: "Is this the person you saw [insert description of act here]?" If the witness answers "Yes," ask the witness, "In your own words, can you describe how certain you are?"

h. Document the Witness's Responses. As stated previously, recording to videotape, audiotape, CD or DVD the entire identification procedure is recommended. Whether or not this is possible, document the witness's response using the witness's own words when possible.

1. After identification, a follow-up interview should assess any relevant factors that support the identification, such as: special facial features, hair, marks, etc.

i. Show All Photos to the Witness. Even if the witness makes an identification, show the witness the next photo until you have gone through all the photographs. If a witness asks why he/she must view the rest of the photos despite already making an identification, simply tell the witness that the procedure requires the officer to show the rest of the photos.

Explanation: Showing all photos in the series ensures that the photo array procedure will reveal as much information as possible. For instance, a witness may make an identification of an early photo, but then change his/her mind after viewing a later photo. This change supplies important information about both the suspect and the witness.

j. Commenting on Selection and Outcome. Do not give the witness any feedback regarding the individual selected or comment on the outcome of the identification procedure in any way. Be aware that witnesses may perceive such things as unintentional voice inflection or prolonged eye contact, in addition to off-handed words or phrases, as messages regarding their selection. Avoid casual comments such as "very good." Be polite but purposeful when you speak.

k. Request for Additional Viewing. Only upon request of the witness, the witness may view one or more of the photos again after the first photo procedure has been completed. If this occurs, it must be thoroughly documented. The administrator should never suggest an additional viewing to the witness.

Explanation: Allowing a witness to view an array a second time converts the procedure from a sequential to a quasi-simultaneous array, thereby risking the benefits of the sequential procedure. In the interest of facilitating an identification, a witness who asks to see the array a second time may be permitted to do so, but because this can diminish the reliability of the identification it should not be offered without request.

l. Alteration of Materials by Witness. Ensure that if the witness writes on, marks, or in any way alters identification materials, those items are not used in subsequent procedures.

4. Document Procedures and Results.

a. Have the Witness Sign and Date the Results. Once the procedure is completed, show the witness the written record of the results, and ask the witness to sign and date that record.

b. Preserve the Photos. Preserve the photos and the order in which they were presented to the witness.

c. Document the Procedure. The administrator should document:

-the administrator's name
-the procedure employed
-date, time, and location of the procedure
-the total number of filler photos and blank photos
-names of persons present during the array
-if additional viewing occurred

5. Procedures for Multiple Suspects or Multiple Witnesses.

a. No Communication between Witnesses. To the extent possible, prevent witnesses from conferring with each other before, during, and after the photo array procedure.

b. Separate Instructions. Each witness should be instructed outside the presence of the other witnesses.

c. Showing the Same Suspect to a New Witness. If you need to show the same suspect to a new witness, have the administrator remix all but the lead filler and the two blank photos and renumber them accordingly.

Explanation: Placement in this way reduces any possibility that a subsequent witness identifies someone based on the position number communicated to them by a previous witness.

d. Showing a Different Suspect to the Same Witness. When showing a different suspect to the same witness, do not reuse the same fillers from a previous array shown to that witness.

e. Multiple Arrays with Same Suspect and Same Witness. Avoid multiple identification procedures in which the same witness views the same suspect more than once. Should you decide to do more than one identification procedure you are likely to be called upon to clarify and/or justify the action.

Explanation: Showing a witness the same suspect in more than one photo array can be highly suggestive and can influence the witness to pick out that suspect based on remembering the suspect from the first identification procedure, rather than from the crime.

METHOD #2: The photo array is conducted by the investigating officer, but with safeguards to ensure that the investigating officer is not in a position to unintentionally influence the witness's selection.

In some situations, it may be difficult to have an independent administrator conduct the array. In those situations, the investigating officer may conduct the array, but only with safeguards to ensure that he/she is not in a position to unintentionally influence the witness's selection. Departments are encouraged to come up with their own methods for meeting this recommendation. One option is to use a computer to randomly present the photos to the witness out of view of the investigator. A simpler and less expensive alternative is the folder system, described below.

1. Gather Photographs. Follow the procedures described in Method #1 for gathering one photo of the suspect, at least five filler photos, and at least two blank photos. Since increasing the number of fillers tends to increase the reliability of the procedure, include as many above the minimum as desired.

2. Prepare the Folders.

a. Gather Folders. Gather folders, each large enough to hold and fully conceal one photograph.

b. Set Aside Lead Filler. Place a filler's photograph in one folder and set that folder aside.

c. Set Aside Two Empty Folders. Take two of the empty folders and set them aside, separate from the filler folder that you have set aside.

d. Place the Other Photos in Folders. Randomly place the other photos (of the suspect and remaining fillers) into the remaining empty folders, one photograph per folder.

e. Shuffle the Folders. Shuffle the folders you are holding, so that you no longer know which folder contains the suspect's photo.

> *Explanation*: This ensures that you will not be in a position to unintentionally influence the witness's selection.

f. Lead with Filler Photo. Place the single photo containing a filler—the one you set aside earlier—on the top of your pile.

> *Explanation*: Witnesses are reluctant to identify someone in the first position and, if that person is the suspect, a failure to identify the perpetrator or a misidentification may result.

g. End with Empty Folders. Place the empty folders—the ones you set aside earlier—at the bottom of your pile.

> *Explanation*: You do not want the witness to know when he/she is viewing the last photo. Witnesses who believe they are viewing the last photo may feel a heightened need to make an identification.

h. Number the Folders.

3. Conduct the Array.

a. Record the Identification Procedure. If practical, record to videotape, audiotape, CD or DVD the entire photo identification procedure. Videotaping is preferable.

For information on video and audio recording procedures, see the Wisconsin Department of Justice's Physical Evidence Handbook 8th Edition, p. 39–44.

b. Restrict Availability of Other Results to Witness. Ensure that no writings or information concerning previous identification results are visible to the witness.

c. Bring in the Witness. Seat the witness at a desk or table or otherwise provide a comfortable environment.

d. Position Yourself. Position yourself close enough to the witness to verbally communicate with him/her but in a place where the witness will be able to open a folder and look at the photo without your being able to see the photo.

> *Explanation*: This will make it impossible for you to unintentionally communicate information to the witness about which folder contains the suspect's photo.

e. Instruct the Witness. Give the witness a written copy of the following instruction sheet and read the instruction aloud:

The folders in front of you contain photos. In a moment, I am going to ask you to look at the photos. The person who committed the crime may or may not be included in the photos. Although I placed the photos into the folders, I have shuffled the folders so that right now I do not know which folder contains a particular photo.

Even if you identify someone during this procedure, I will continue to show you all photos in the series.

Keep in mind that things like hair styles, beards, and mustaches can be easily changed and that complexion colors may look slightly different in photographs.

You should not feel you have to make an identification. It is as important to exclude innocent persons as it is to identify the perpetrator.

You will look at the photos one at a time and, since I have shuffled them, they are not in any particular order. When you open a folder, please open it in a manner that does not allow me to see the photo inside the folder. Take as much time as you need to look at each one. When you have finished looking at a photo, close the folder and hand it to me. I will then ask you, "Is this the person you saw [insert description of act here]?" Take your time answering the question. If you answer "Yes," I will then ask you, "In your own words, can you describe how certain you are?"

Because you are involved in an ongoing investigation, in order to prevent compromising the investigation, you should avoid discussing this identification procedure or its results.

Do you understand the way the photo array procedure will be conducted and the other instructions I have given you?

Witnesses should then be asked to read the following additional paragraph and sign and date below. (Some witnesses may decline to sign. When a witness declines to sign, it is sufficient for the investigating officer to document that the witness was appropriately instructed.)

I have read these instructions, or they have been read to me, and I understand the instructions. I am prepared to review the photographs, and I will follow the instructions provided on this form.

f. Give the Witness the Folders. Hand the witness the folders one at a time.

g. Question the Witness. After a witness has looked at a photo and handed the folder back to you, ask: "Is this the person you saw [insert description of act here]?" If the witness answers "Yes," ask the witness, "In your own words, can you describe how certain you are?"

h. Document the Witness's Responses. As previously stated, recording to videotape, audiotape, CD or DVD the entire identification procedure is recommended. Whether or not this is possible, document the witness's response using the witness's own words when possible.

1. After identification, a follow-up interview should assess any relevant factors that support the identification, such as: special facial features, hair, marks, etc.

i. Show Every Folder. Even if the witness makes an identification, hand the witness the next folder until you have gone through all the folders containing photographs. If a witness asks why he/she must view the rest of the photos despite already making an identification; tell the witness the procedure requires the officer to show the rest of the photos.

Explanation: Showing all photos in the series ensures that the photo array procedure will reveal as much information as possible. For instance, a witness may make an identification of an early photo, but then change his/her mind after viewing a later photo. This change supplies important information about both the suspect and the witness.

j. Commenting on Selection and Outcome. Do not give the witness any feedback regarding the individual selected or comment on the outcome of the identification procedure in any way. Be aware that witnesses may perceive such things as unintentional voice inflection or prolonged eye contact, in addition to off-handed words or phrases, as messages regarding their selection. Avoid casual conversation comments such as "very good." Be polite but purposeful when you speak.

k. Request for Additional Viewing. Only upon request of the witness, the witness may view one or more of the photos again after the first photo procedure has been completed. If this occurs, it must be thoroughly documented. The administrator should never suggest an additional viewing to the witness.

Explanation: Allowing a witness to view an array a second time converts the procedure from a sequential to a quasi-simultaneous array, thereby risking the benefits of the sequential procedure. In the interest of facilitating an identification, a witness who asks to see the array a second time may be permitted to do so, but because this may diminish the value of the identification it should not be offered without request.

l. Alteration of Materials by Witness. Ensure that if the witness writes on, marks, or in any way alters identification materials, those items are not used in subsequent procedures.

4. Document Procedures and Results.

a. Have the Witness Sign and Date the Results. Once the procedure is completed, show the witness the written record of the results, and ask the witness to sign and date that record.

b. Preserve the Photos. Preserve the photos and the order in which they were presented to the witness.

c. Document the Procedure. The administrator should document:

-the administrator's name
-the procedure employed
-date, time, and location of the procedure

-the total number of filler photos and blank photos
-names of persons present during the array
-if additional viewing occurred

5. Procedures for Multiple Suspects or Multiple Witnesses

a. No Communication between Witnesses. To the extent possible, prevent witnesses from conferring with each other before, during, and after the photo array procedure.

b. Separate Instructions. Each witness should be instructed outside the presence of the other witnesses.

c. Showing the Same Suspect to a New Witness. If you need to show the same suspect to a new witness, re-shuffle all but the lead filler and the two blank photos and renumber them accordingly.

> *Explanation*: Placement in this way reduces any possibility that a subsequent witness identifies someone based on the position number communicated to them by a previous witness.

d. Showing a Different Suspect to the Same Witness. When showing a different suspect to the same witness, do not reuse the same fillers from a previous array shown to that witness.

e. Multiple Arrays with Same Suspect and Same Witness. Avoid multiple identification procedures in which the same witness views the same suspect more than once. Should you decide to do more than one identification procedure you are likely to be called upon to clarify and/or justify the action.

> *Explanation*: Showing a witness the same suspect in more than one photo array can be highly suggestive and can influence the witness to pick out that suspect based on remembering the suspect from the first identification procedure, rather than from the crime. Also, two identification procedures (showup, followed by a live lineup or photo array) are not better than just one. A witness viewing a second procedure with the same suspect may believe that presence in both procedures suggests that authorities believe the suspect is the actual perpetrator.

PROCEDURE FOR LIVE LINEUPS

The principles described in the model policy apply equally to photo arrays and live lineups. Just as witnesses viewing photo arrays can be vulnerable to unintentional suggestion, so can witnesses viewing live lineups; just as witnesses viewing photo arrays tend to identify the person in the array who looks most like the perpetrator, so do witnesses viewing live lineups.

Unfortunately, while photo arrays can be conducted using the folder system, which allows the investigating officer to conduct the array; live lineups cannot be conducted in that way. Live lineups should be conducted by an independent administrator—someone who does not know which person in the lineup is the suspect.

This may impose a logistical burden because it will mean bringing in an additional person from outside the investigation to conduct the lineup. However, in those rare situations in which a live lineup is necessary, investigators should find another agency or officer or departmental employee who can briefly break away from his/her duties to assist with an investigation. If a lineup is absolutely necessary, and no independent administrator can be found, the investigating officer must take great care to avoid any unintentional cues to the witness.

1. Compose the Lineup.

a. Number of Suspects. Include only one suspect at a time in each lineup.

b. Number of Fillers. Whenever possible, include a minimum of four fillers (non-suspects) per lineup. Since increasing the number of fillers tends to increase the reliability of the procedure, include as many above the minimum as desired.

i. Resemblance of Fillers to Suspect. In general, fillers should resemble the witness's description of the perpetrator in significant features (such as face, profile, height, weight, age, build, posture, hair and facial hair, specific articles of clothing, etc., to the extent applicable to the photos being used) or, in cases where a composite was used, fillers should resemble the composite. If a person who has never seen the perpetrator would be able to pick out the suspect from the lineup based on knowing only the description given by the eyewitness, then the fillers may not sufficiently resemble the description of the perpetrator.

A. For instance, if the perpetrator was described as having an unusual identifying mark, all fillers should have similar markings or similar coverings over the described area.

B. When there is an inadequate description of the perpetrator, or when there is a suspect whose appearance differs from the description of the perpetrator, fillers should resemble the suspect in significant features.

c. Assess the Lineup. Make sure that no person stands out from the rest.

d. Filler as Lead Subject. Always lead lineups with a filler.

Explanation: Research suggests witnesses are reluctant to identify someone in the first position and, if that person is the suspect, a misidentification may result.

e. Limit Contact between Witnesses and Fillers. Take precautions to ensure that witnesses do not encounter suspects or fillers at any time before or after the identification procedure.

2. Conduct the Lineup.

a. Record the Identification Procedure. If practical, record to videotape, audiotape, CD or DVD the entire photo identification procedure. Videotaping is preferable. For information on video and audio recording procedures, see the Wisconsin Department of Justice's Physical Evidence Handbook, p. 39–44.

b. Availability of Other Results to Witness. Ensure that no writings or information concerning previous identification results are visible to the witness.

c. No Persons Present Who Know the Suspect's Identity. To the extent possible, ensure that no one who knows the suspect's identity is present during the lineup procedure except defense counsel (if present).

d. Witness's Knowledge of Number of Suspects. The witness should not know how many individuals will be shown.

e. Instruct the Witness. The lineup administrator should give the witness a written copy of the following instruction and should read the instruction aloud at the beginning of each identification procedure:

In a moment, I am going to show you a series of individuals. The person who committed the crime may or may not be included. I do not know whether the person being investigated is included. Even if you identify someone during this procedure, I will continue to show you all individuals in the series.

Keep in mind that things like hair styles, beards, and mustaches can be easily changed.

You should not feel you have to make an identification. It is as important to exclude innocent persons as it is to identify the perpetrator.

The individuals will be shown to you one at a time and are not in any particular order. Take as much time as you need to look at each one. After each individual, I will ask you "Is this the person you saw [insert description of act]?" Take your time answering the question. If you answer "Yes," I will then ask you, "Can you describe how certain you are?"

Because you are involved in an ongoing investigation, in order to prevent compromising the investigation, you should avoid discussing this identification procedure or its results.

Do you understand the way the lineup procedure will be conducted and the other instructions I have given you?

Witnesses should then be asked to read the following additional paragraph and sign and date below. (Some witnesses may decline to sign. When a witness declines to sign, it is sufficient for the investigating officer to document that the witness was appropriately instructed.)

I have read these instructions, or they have been read to me, and I understand the instructions. I am prepared to review the individuals who will be presented to me, and I will follow the instructions provided on this form.

f. Present Subjects One at a Time. Begin with all lineup participants out of the view of the witness. Present each individual to the witness separately, in a previously determined order, removing those previously shown from the field of view.

g. Question the Witness. After each individual is shown, ask the witness: "Is this the person you saw [insert description of act]?" If the witness answers "Yes," ask the witness, "In your own words, can you describe how certain you are?" Whether or not this is possible, document the witness's response using the witness's own words when possible.

i. After identification, a follow-up interview should assess any relevant factors that support the identification, such as: special facial features, hair, marks, etc.

h. Show Every Subject. Even if the witness makes an identification, show the witness the next subject until all subjects have been shown. If a witness asks why he/she must view the rest of the subjects despite already making an identification; simply tell the witness that the procedure requires the officer to show all the subjects.

Explanation: Showing all subjects in the series ensures that the lineup will reveal as much information as possible. For instance, a witness may make an identification of an early subject, but then change his/her mind after viewing a later subject. This change supplies important information about both the suspect and the witness.

i. Actions of Lineup Members. Ensure that any identification actions (e.g., speaking, moving, etc.) are performed by all members of the lineup.

j. Commenting on Selection and Outcome. Do not give the witness any feedback regarding the individual selected or comment on the outcome of the identification procedure in any way. Be aware that witnesses may perceive such things as unintentional voice inflection or prolonged eye contact, in addition to off-handed words or phrases, as messages regarding their selection. Avoid casual comments such as "very good." Be polite but purposeful when you speak.

k. Request for Additional Viewing. Only upon request of the witness, the witness may view one or more of the subjects again after the lineup has been completed. If this occurs, it must be thoroughly documented. The lineup administrator should never suggest additional viewing.

Explanation: Allowing a witness to view a lineup a second time converts the procedure from a sequential to a quasi-simultaneous lineup, thereby risking the benefits of the sequential procedure. In the interest of facilitating an identification, a witness who asks to see the lineup a second time may be permitted to do so, but because this diminishes the value of the identification it should not be offered without request.

3. Document Procedures and Results.

a. Have the Witness Sign and Date the Results. Once the procedure is completed, show the witness the written record of the results, and ask the witness to sign and date that record.

b. Photograph the Lineup Subjects. As stated above, video or audio recording the entire identification procedure is recommended. Whether or not this is possible, photo documentation of the suspect and fillers should be taken. Photo documentation can be of either the group or each individual, but should preserve the appearances of the suspect and fillers and the order of the lineup.

c. Document the Procedure. The administrator should document:

-the administrator's name
-the procedure employed
-date, time, and location of the procedure
-the number of fillers
-names of persons present during the lineup
-if additional viewing occurred

4. Procedures for Multiple Suspects or Multiple Witnesses.

a. No Communication between Witnesses. To the extent possible, prevent witnesses from conferring with each other before, during, and after the lineup procedure.

b. Separate Instructions. Each witness should be instructed outside the presence of the other witnesses.

c. Showing the Same Suspect to a New Witness. Place the suspect in different positions in each lineup. Position all other members of the lineup randomly.

Explanation: Placement in this way reduces the possibility that a second or third witness will identify someone based on the position number communicated to them by the first witness.

d. Multiple Lineups with Same Suspect and Same Witness. Avoid multiple identification procedures in which the same witness views the same suspect more than once. Should you decide to do more than one identification procedure you are likely to be called upon to clarify and/or justify the action.

Explanation: Showing a witness the same suspect in more than one identification procedure can be highly suggestive and can influence the witness to pick out that suspect based on remembering the suspect from the first identification procedure, rather than from the crime.

e. Showing a Different Suspect to the Same Witness. When showing a different suspect to the same witness, do not reuse the same fillers from a previous lineup shown to that witness.

PROCEDURE FOR SHOW-UPS[18]

A show-up occurs when law enforcement officials show one suspect to one witness for the purpose of eyewitness identification. Although courts have recognized that showup procedures can be suggestive,[19] showups have benefits for both public safety and innocent suspects. First, in situations in which police lack probable cause to arrest but have temporarily detained a suspect who matches a general eyewitness description, show-ups allow police to conduct an eyewitness identification procedure rather than simply releasing a potentially guilty perpetrator. Second, show-ups benefit innocent suspects because they have the potential to immediately clear an innocent person from suspicion without suffering the indignity of arrest or further investigation.

Despite these benefits, show-ups have risks, as well. First, show-ups can be suggestive, in the sense that they are likely to convey the impression to witnesses that the police think they have caught the perpetrator and want confirmation. In addition, research shows that show-ups produce a greater risk for innocent suspects than properly conducted photo arrays and lineups.[20] However, the reason for this risk is somewhat surprising. Eyewitnesses make identifications at an equal or lesser rate for show-ups than for photo arrays.[21] Show-ups are riskier for innocent suspects because some eyewitness errors made during photo arrays are harmless identifications of fillers known to be innocent, while all false identifications during show-ups result in false evidence against innocent suspects.

Researchers have pointed out another advantage lineups and photo arrays have over show-ups: they provide a test of a given eyewitness's reliability. If an eyewitness viewing a photo array identifies an innocent filler, the police can conclude that the witness is not

18 The Wisconsin Supreme Court has recently ruled in *State v. Dubose*, regarding the admissibility of show-up identification evidence.

19 *State v. Marshall*, 92 Wis. 2d 101, 119 (1979).

20 Wells, G.L. "Police Lineups: Data, Theory, and Policy." *Psychology, Public Policy, and the Law*. Vol. 7, No. 4, p. 795, 2001.

21 See footnote 19.

useful for future identification procedures. However, if an eyewitness viewing a show-up incorrectly states that the suspect is not the perpetrator, the police are likely to continue to rely upon that eyewitness for other identification procedures despite the witness's unreliability. This can have negative consequences if the unreliable witness is later shown a photo array or lineup and identifies an innocent person.

The Wisconsin Supreme Court weighed these risks and benefits and implemented a rule for the admissibility of evidence obtained using show-ups. According to State v. Dubose, show-up identification evidence will be inadmissible unless, based on the totality of the circumstances, the show-up was necessary.[22] A show-up will not be deemed necessary unless the police lacked probable cause to make an arrest or, as a result of other exigent circumstances, could not have conducted a lineup or photo array. Furthermore, the admissibility of show-up identification evidence will turn on whether police conducting a show-up utilized appropriate safeguards to minimize the suggestiveness of the procedure.[23] Specifically, factors such as whether the show-up was conducted in a squad car and whether the witness was given a non-biased instruction before the show-up will be relevant to whether show-up identification evidence is admissible.[24]

Given the risks and benefits of show-ups and WI Supreme Court's Legal ruling regarding admissibility, the use of show-ups should strike a delicate balance. Before conducting a show-up, officers should consider the fact that properly conducted photo arrays and lineups are more reliable than show-ups and decide whether a show-up, instead of a photo array or lineup, is necessary and appropriate under the circumstances. It is not possible to list all the factors that figure in to this decision, nor is it possible to devise a precise formula for when show-ups are appropriate. However, certain factors are clearly relevant. For instance, law enforcement officers should consider the proximity—both geographic and temporal—of the suspect to the crime. Show-ups should generally be avoided if they cannot be conducted close in time and place to the crime. In any case, if officers plan to make an arrest with or without a show-up, they should consider conducting a photo array or lineup after the arrest instead of a show-up. Finally, officers should consider exigent circumstances such as the future availability of witnesses. If a witness will be unavailable in the future, a show-up may be necessary. Otherwise a proper lineup or photo array will ordinarily be more appropriate as it avoids the inherent suggestiveness of the show-up.

The use of a show up can provide investigative information at an early stage, but the inherent suggestiveness of a show up requires careful use of procedural safeguards. The following procedures are designed to address those risks and outline the proper use of show-ups. The procedures apply regardless of whether other practices would be legally permissible. For instance, even if a given suspect consents to a show-up, a show-up still

---

22 Dubose, 2005 WI 126, ¶ 2.

23 Id. at ¶ 35–37.

24 *Id.*

should not be conducted unless the investigating officer decides that the exigencies of the situation outweigh any possible risk of misidentification presented by conducting a show-up. Consent may legally authorize police to detain a suspect for a show-up, but it does nothing to remove the suggestiveness of the procedure.

1. Prepare for the Show-up.

   a. Document the Witness's Description. Before the show-up is conducted, it is important the witness be asked to give a detailed description of the perpetrator, and this description should be carefully documented.

   b. Location of Suspect. Whenever practical, transport the witness to the location of the detained suspect (as opposed to transporting the suspect to the witness) to limit the potential legal impact of the suspect's detention and to minimize the influence on the witness of seeing the suspect transported under custody.

      i. Show-ups should not be conducted at a police station or other law enforcement building.

   c. Record the Identification Procedure. If practical, record to videotape, audiotape, CD or DVD the entire photo identification procedure. Videotaping is preferable. For information on video and audio recording procedures, see the Wisconsin Department of Justice's Physical Evidence Handbook, p. 39–44.

2. Conduct the Show-up.

   a. Instruct the Witness. Witnesses should be given a written copy of the following instruction and the instruction should be read aloud:

> **In a moment, I am going to show you an individual. That person may or may not be the true perpetrator. I do not know if the person is the true perpetrator.**
>
> **You should not feel you have to make an identification. It is as important to exclude innocent persons as it is to identify the perpetrator.**
>
> **After you have observed the individual, I will ask you "Is this the person you saw [insert description of act]?" Take your time answering the question. If you answer "Yes," I will then ask you, "In your own words, can you describe how certain you are?"**

Because you are involved in an ongoing investigation, in order to prevent compromising the investigation, you should avoid discussing this identification procedure or its results.

Do you understand the way this procedure will be conducted and the other instructions I have given you?

Witnesses should then be asked to read the following additional paragraph and sign and date below. (Some witnesses may decline to sign. When a witness declines to sign, it is sufficient for the investigating officer to document that the witness was appropriately instructed.)

I have read these instructions, or they have been read to me, and I understand the instructions. I am prepared to observe the individual who will be presented to me, and I will follow the instructions provided on this form.

b. Present the Suspect. If possible and safe, have the witness view the suspect while the suspect is not restrained by handcuffs or by the officer, and while the suspect is not seated in a squad car. When circumstances dictate that the suspect must be controlled and/or separated from the witness then take practical steps to minimize the suggestiveness of the procedure.

c. Avoid Suggestive Words or Conduct. Words or conduct of any type that may suggest to the witness that the individual is or may be the perpetrator must be carefully avoided.

d. Question the Witness. After the witness views the suspect, ask the witness, "Is this the person you saw [insert description of act]?" If the witness answers "Yes," ask the witness, "In your own words, can you describe how certain you are?"

e. Document the Witness's Responses. Record the witness's responses to each question. Whether or not video or audio recording is possible, document the witness's response using the witness's own words when possible.

i. After identification, a follow-up interview should assess any relevant factors that support the identification, such as; special facial features, hair, marks, etc.

3. Document Procedures and Results.

a. Have the Witness Sign and Date the Results. Once the procedure is completed, show the witness the written record of the results, and ask the witness to sign and date that record.

b. Photograph the Suspect. Whenever possible, photograph the suspect at the time of the show-up.

c. Document the Procedure. The administrator should document:

-the administrator's name
-the procedure employed
-date, time, and location of the procedure
-names of persons present during the show-up

d. Multiple Witnesses. Show-ups should not be conducted with more than one witness present at a time. If there are multiple witnesses and one witness makes an identification during a show-up, that identification should provide probable cause for an arrest, and the remaining witnesses should ordinarily be shown a photo array or lineup rather than a show-up.

e. Multiple Show-ups with Same Suspect and Same Witness. Avoid multiple identification procedures in which the same witness views the same suspect more than once. Should you decide to do more than one identification procedure you are likely to be called upon to clarify and/or justify the action.

4. Multiple Suspects. If there are two suspects, the witness should view two separate show-ups, each conducted in accordance with these procedures. Two or more suspects should not be shown to the witness at the same time.

PROCEDURE FOR FACIAL COMPOSITES

In some investigations, law enforcement authorities have an eyewitness description but have either 1) no specific suspect or 2) no visual likeness of a known suspect. The use of composite images can yield investigative leads in cases in which no suspect has been determined. In these situations, some law enforcement authorities may try to produce a facial composite of the perpetrator based on the eyewitness's description. Various methods exist for carrying out this goal, including manual sketches, mechanical systems such as Identikit, and, more recently, computer-based systems such as E-fit. Composites produced with these methods have been used to gather suspects who resemble the composite or to confirm that an unavailable suspect's appearance matches the description given by an eyewitness.

Because of concerns about the reliability of composites and their potential to taint eyewitnesses' memories, law enforcement authorities should use them cautiously. Research tends to show that none of the existing methods can reliably produce recognizable composites in real-world settings.[25] In the experiments, subjects look at a target photo, the photo is taken away, and the subjects are then asked to produce a composite using one of the methods mentioned above. Despite the best efforts of the subjects making the composites, people who know the person in the target photo are generally not able to recognize the person depicted in the composite.

The unreliability of composites raises concern about the possibility that an inaccurate composite might taint an eyewitness's memory and lead to a misidentification. For instance, if authorities produce a composite and then arrest a person who resembles the composite but who unknown to them is innocent, the eyewitness may then identify the innocent suspect because of the suspect's resemblance to the composite. In this way, an inaccurate composite, and the innocent suspect who resembles it, can contaminate an eyewitness's actual memory of the perpetrator.

New research also suggests that the process of making a composite can damage an eyewitness's ability to identify the true perpetrator in a later lineup.[26] In an experiment, eyewitnesses were first directed to build a composite of a perpetrator using a computer-based system. Later, the same eyewitnesses were asked to try to pick the same perpetrator out of a lineup. Compared to eyewitnesses who did not build composites, the eyewitnesses who built composites were less able to identify the perpetrator in a lineup.

In addition to the concerns discussed above, inaccurate information from outside an eyewitness's memory can taint a composite. As with photo arrays, lineups, and show-ups, composites can be compromised if the witness's description relies on information learned from external sources after the crime or if the person administering the procedure either unintentionally supplies the witness with information or unintentionally incorporates outside knowledge of the case into the production of the composite. For this reason, in the rare situation in which a composite must be used, these guidelines recommend a double-blind composite procedure, in which both the witness and the person making the composite are unaware of external information about the case. It may not be feasible in some circumstances to conduct a completely double-blind procedure because it may not be possible to prevent both the witness and the administrator from learning about the case. In such situations, witnesses should be told to rely on their independent recollection of the event—not information learned from other sources—and administrators should be

25 Davies, G., van der Willik, P., and Morrison, L.J. "Facial Composite Production: A Comparison of Mechanical and Computer-Driven Systems." Journal of Applied Psychology, Vol. 84, Issue 1, February 1, 2000.

26 See Manuscript of Wells, G.L., et al, "Building Face Composites Can Harm Lineup Identification Performance," at http://www.psychology.iastate.edu/faculty/gwells/Composite_damage_manuscript.pdf.

mindful of the natural tendency to incorporate prior knowledge into the interaction with the witness and into the production of the composite itself.

Procedure: Preparing the composite:

1. Assess the ability of the witness to provide a description of the perpetrator.
2. Select the procedure to be used from those available (e.g., identikit-type templates, artist, or computer-generated images).
3. Unless part of the procedure, avoid showing the witness any photos immediately prior to development of the composite.
4. Select an environment for conducting the procedure that minimizes distractions.
5. Conduct the procedure with each witness separately.
6. Determine with the witness whether the composite is a reasonable representation of the perpetrator. (These recommendations are consistent with two recent publications of the United States Department of Justice.[27])

A NOTE ON "MUG BOOKS"

PHOTO COLLECTION DISPLAY

"Mug books" (i.e., collections of photos/images of previously arrested persons) may be useful in cases in which a suspect has not yet been determined and other reliable sources have been exhausted. This technique may provide investigative leads, but results should be evaluated with caution. Avoid individual photos/images that are suggestive or cause any one to stand out unnecessarily.

Mug books must be objectively compiled to yield investigative leads that will be admissible in court. Individuals should be selected who are uniform with regard to physical characteristics such as race, age, gender, etc.

In the tradition of the Wisconsin Idea, these model policies and procedures spring from a partnership of the Attorney General and the Frank J. Remington Center at the University of Wisconsin Law School. Just as other products of this partnership have improved the state's criminal justice system, these policies and procedures are designed to bring to bear the best techniques for the collection of eyewitness evidence.

---

27 The two publications are: Eyewitness Evidence: A Guide for Law Enforcement (October 1999), and Eyewitness Evidence: A Trainer's Manual for Law Enforcement (September, 2003). These publications are included in the Jan. '04 instructor manual/CD in the Investigations Unit for basic law enforcement training.

DISCUSSION QUESTIONS

1. Given the unreliability of eyewitness identification, should lineup identification be given less evidentiary weight? If so how?
2. What makes eyewitness identification so difficult and ultimately so unreliable?
3. Do you believe identifications by victims are more reliable than by witnesses? Less reliable? No difference?
4. Should every jurisdiction develop eyewitness identification guidelines? If so, at minimum what should be included?

FORENSICS ISSUES REGARDING THE DEATH PENALTY

Introduction

Wrongful Convictions and Forensic Science: The Need to Regulate Crime Labs
By Paul C. Giannelli

Science and the Death Penalty: DNA, Innocence, and the Debate over Capital Punishment in the United States
By Jay D. Aronson and Simon A. Cole

This chapter presents two readings on forensics pertaining to capital cases. The first, by Paul Giannelli, presents strong evidence regarding miscarriages of justice amounting to "scientific fraud or junk science" on the part of forensic laboratories in the U.S., followed by an urge to strenuously monitor and regulate crime laboratories and their employees. According to Giannelli a paradox exists because, while DNA analysis (which accounts for less than five percent of forensic analysis work) is extensively regulated, most other forensic techniques (microscopic hair analysis, bullet lead analysis, and fingerprint analysis, to mention a few) are not. This explains why there is such a long list of forensic mistakes in capital (and other) cases, and a correlation between death row exonerations and faulty forensic science (Gianelli 2007).

Aronson and Cole call our attention to another paradox—the heavy reliance on forensic science (the belief in "epistemic certainty" in forensic science) when, in fact, forensic science is fraught with error, subjectivity, and other inconsistencies, as most philosophers of science understand. This paradox between the belief in scientific certainty and the actual uncertainty that pervades all science might actually be counterproductive (a "double-edged sword") for the death penalty abolitionists who have "embraced the innocence argument," an argument that relies heavily on the utilization of DNA forensic analysis (Aronson and Cole 2009). Aronson and Cole present a systematic challenge to the belief in the certainty of forensic science, offering numerous, documented, examples of errors and uncertainty in DNA forensic analysis, that should leave the reader wondering why Paul Giannelli argues so passionately for crime laboratory regulation on the basis of extensive regulation of DNA analysis.

Wrongful Convictions and Forensic Science

The Need to Regulate Crime Labs

Paul C. Giannelli*

DNA testing has exonerated over 200 convicts, some of whom were on death row. Studies show that a substantial number of these miscarriages of justice involved scientific fraud or junk science. This Article documents the failures of crime labs and some forensic techniques, such as microscopic hair comparison and bullet lead analysis. Some cases involved incompetence and sloppy procedures, while others entailed deceit, but the extent of the derelictions—the number of episodes and the duration of some of the abuses, covering decades in several instances—demonstrates that the problems are systemic.

Paradoxically, the most scientifically sound procedure—DNA analysis—is the most extensively regulated, while many forensic techniques with questionable scientific pedigrees go completely unregulated. The regulation of DNA profiling, which has developed gradually over the last twenty years, can serve as a model for other laboratory units. The accreditation of crime laboratories, the certification of examiners, and the standardization and promulgation of written protocols for each technique would go a long way in professionalizing forensic science. In addition, quality assurance programs, including proficiency testing and external audits, should be mandated. Finally, forensic science commissions should be established in every jurisdiction to implement these and other reforms.

* Albert J. Weatherhead III & Richard W. Weatherhead Professor, Case Western Reserve University. I would like to thank Brandon Garrett for his helpful comments on an earlier draft of this article.

† Footnote irregularities appear in the original source article.

"At present, forensic science is virtually unregulated—with the paradoxical result that clinical laboratories must meet higher standards to be allowed to diagnose strep throat than forensic labs must meet to put a defendant on death row."

—Eric S. Lander, molecular biologist, 1989[1]

INTRODUCTION

In the fall of 2004, the Chief of the Houston Police Department called for a moratorium on executions of convicts from Harris County until after his crime laboratory had completed a review of numerous old case files.[2] This breathtaking development in the county where the most death penalty cases originate[3] is not an isolated incident of laboratory failure. Earlier, the Governor of Illinois had imposed a moratorium on executions in that state due in part to faulty scientific evidence.[4]

The extent of forensic science's role in convicting the innocent is difficult to gauge, although it is clearly substantial. In Actual Innocence, Barry Scheck and his colleagues examined sixty-two of the first sixty-seven DNA exonerations secured in North America through Cardozo Law School's Innocence Project, concluding that a third of these cases involved "tainted or fraudulent science."[5] A subsequent review identified forensic science testing errors in 63% of the wrongful convictions and false or misleading testimony by

---

1 Eric S. Lander, DNA Fingerprinting On Trial, 339 NATURE 501, 505 (1989).

2 See Maurice Possley et al., Scandal Touches Even Elite Labs: Flawed Work, Resistance to Scrutiny Seen Across U.S., CHI. TRIB., Oct. 21, 2004, § 1, at 1 ("Gov. Rick Perry has rejected a plea from Houston's police chief to halt executions of inmates convicted in Harris County until the scope of problems at the police crime lab can be determined."). According to state senator Rodney Ellis, "the validity of almost any case that has relied upon evidence produced by the lab is questionable." Rodney Ellis, Editorial, Want Tough on Crime? Start by Fixing HPD Lab, HOUSTON CHRON., Sept. 5, 2004, at D1.

3 See Adam Liptak & Ralph Blumenthal, New Doubt Cast on Crime Testing in Houston Cases, N.Y. TIMES, Aug. 5, 2004, at A19 ("Since the death penalty was reinstated in 1976, Texas has executed 323 people, 73 for crimes in Harris County.").

4 See generally REPORT OF THE GOVERNOR'S COMMISSION ON CAPITAL PUNISHMENT (State of Ill. 2002), available at http://www.state.il.us/defender/ccpr.html (recommending independent crime labs). Governor George Ryan imposed a moratorium on January 31, 2000 and appointed the Commission on March 9, 2000. Id. at i.

5 BARRY SCHECK ET AL., ACTUAL INNOCENCE: FIVE DAYS TO EXECUTION AND OTHER DISPATCHES FROM THE WRONGLY CONVICTED 246 (2000). There have been 208 DNA exonerations. Brandon L. Garrett, Judging Innocence, 108 COLUM. L. REV. (forthcoming 2008) (manuscript at 2, on file with the North Carolina Law Review).

forensic experts in 27%.[6] A 2004 Chicago Tribune series on crime laboratories reported that an examination of "the 200 DNA and Death Row exoneration cases since 1986 ... found that more than a quarter involved faulty crime lab work or testimony."[7] A 2005 study identified twenty-four prosecutions in which forensic scientists committed perjury.[8]

The most recent study of 200 DNA exonerations found that forensic evidence (present in 57% of the cases) was the second leading type of evidence (after eyewitness identifications at 79%) used in wrongful conviction cases.[9] Pre-DNA serology of blood and semen evidence was the most commonly used forensic technique (79 cases).[10] Next came "hair evidence (43 cases), soil comparison (5 cases), DNA tests (3 cases), bite mark evidence (3 cases), fingerprint evidence (2 cases), dog scent identification (2 cases), spectrographic voice evidence (1 case), shoe prints (1 case), and fiber comparison (1 case)."[11] This does not mean, however, that the forensic evidence was improperly used. For example, serological testing at the time of many of these convictions was simply not as discriminating as DNA profiling.[12] Yet, some evidence was clearly misused.[13]

---

6 Michael J. Saks & Jonathan J. Koehler, Review, The Coming Paradigm Shift in Forensic Identification Science, 309 SCIENCE 892, 892 fig. 1 (2005) (reviewing eighty-six DNA exoneration cases).

7 Possley et al., supra note 2.

8 Samuel R. Gross et al., Exonerations in the United States: 1989 Through 2003, 95 J. CRIM. L. & CRIMINOLOGY 523, 543 (2005). This study identified 340 exonerations, 196 of which did not involve DNA evidence. Id. at 524.

9 Garrett, supra note 5 (manuscript at 24 tbl. 2).

10 Id. (manuscript at 31).

11 Id.

12 This type of evidence involved ABO typing and enzyme/protein analysis. See 1 PAUL C. GIANNELLI & EDWARD J. IMWINKELRIED, SCIENTIFIC EVIDENCE § 17.09[c], at 977 (4th ed. 2007) (discussing red cell enzymes and serum proteins).

13 The DNA cases

> involved experts who offered misleading testimony and mischaracterized their own laboratory reports. Two cases involved improper analysis and testimony that resulted in false inclusions. In one case, that of Gilbert Alejandro, the criminalist claimed a DNA match even though neither he nor anyone else had conducted the DNA testing.

Garrett, supra note 5 (manuscript at 34). The expert was Fred Zain. For a discussion of Zain, see infra notes 52–58 and accompanying text.

In addition to Houston,[14] lab problems have surfaced in Baltimore,[15] Chicago,[16] Cleveland,[17] Los Angeles,[18] Fort Worth,[19] Montana,[20] Oklahoma City,[21] San Antonio,[22]

---

14 See infra notes 165–207 and accompanying text.

15 See Possley et al., supra note 2 ("In Baltimore County, for instance, officials pledged a review of analyst Concepcion Bacasnot's cases after DNA Tests in 2003 exonerated an inmate whom her work helped convict of rape. In another case, she said she did not understand the science involved in her work.").

16 See Barry Scheck & Peter Neufeld, Editorial, Junk Science, Junk Evidence, N.Y. TIMES, May 11, 2001, at A31 ("In Chicago, a police lab analyst, Pamela Fish, left out exculpatory serological results in testimony at a 1992 rape trial, contributing to a wrongful conviction. In 1999, the defendant was exonerated by DNA tests. Questions have now been raised about Ms. Fish's conduct in a 1986 murder case."); infra notes 150–64 and accompanying text.

17 See Connie Schultz, City to Pay $1.6 Million for Man's Prison Time, CLEV. PLAIN DEALER, June 8, 2004, at A1 (reporting that City of Cleveland agreed to pay Michael Green $1.6 million for the thirteen years he spent in prison for a rape he did not commit, and an independent master was appointed to review a lab examiner's prior cases).

18 See Anna Gorman, LAPD Narcotics Analyst Erred: Botched Evidence Raises Question on Credibility. Public Defender's Office Demands an Accounting, L.A. TIMES, Sept. 2, 2004, at B1 (noting that Jeff Lowe, who analyzed drugs for the LAPD since May 2003, failed to weigh drugs separately from the containers in which they were seized "in forty-seven cases, leading to a review of 972 that he handled").

19 See Deanna Boyd, Crime Lab Subject of Criminal Inquiry, FORT WORTH STAR TELEGRAM, April 13, 2003, at 1 ("[A DNA] proficiency test revealed that a senior forensic scientist did not follow proper procedures and protocol. The review will involve almost 100 cases.").

20 See Adam Liptak, DNA Will Let a Montana Man Put Prison Behind Him, but Questions Linger, N.Y. TIMES, Oct. 1, 2002, at A22; infra notes 125–47 and accompanying text.

21 See Lois Romano, Police Chemist's Missteps Cause Okla. Scandal, WASH. POST, Nov. 26, 2001, at A1 (citing what is "arguably the biggest law enforcement scandal in Oklahoma history"); infra notes 68–124 and accompanying text.

22 See Laurie P. Cohen, 'Scared of Science': Crime Labs' Work Is Rarely Challenged by Defense Lawyers, WALL ST. J., July 22, 1997, at A1 (discussing the case of Sonia Cacy). Cacy received a ninety-nine year sentence for murder by arson based on an inaccurate chemical test. See Dateline: Body of Evidence (NBC television broadcast Apr. 21, 1999) (analyzing the Cacy case). Cacy was paroled after serving only six months. See John MacCormack, Woman is Paroled Despite Big Sentence, SAN ANTONIO EXPRESS-NEWS, Nov. 24, 1998, at 1A.

Seattle,[23] Virginia,[24] and West Virginia,[25] as well as other locations.[26]

Moreover, a series of embarrassing incidents has plagued the FBI Laboratory, this country's premier forensic facility, leading to the issuance of Inspector General reports that

---

23 See Ruth Teichroeb, Rare Look Inside State Crime Labs Reveals Recurring DNA Test Problems, SEATTLE POST-INTELLIGENCER, July 22, 2004, at A1 [hereinafter Teichroeb, Rare Look]; Ruth Teichroeb, Oversight of Crime-Lab Staff Has Often Been Lax, SEATTLE POST-INTELLIGENCER, July 23, 2004, at A1 [hereinafter Teichroeb, Oversight of Crime-Lab Staff]; Ruth Teichroeb, Crime Labs Too Beholden to Prosecutors, Critics Say, SEATTLE POST-INTELLIGENCER, July 23, 2004, at A13 [hereinafter Teichroeb, Crime Labs Too Beholden].

24 See infra notes 208–35 and accompanying text.

25 See Lawrence Messina, State Police Lab Review Leaves Agency With Another Shiner, CHARLESTON GAZETTE (Charleston, W. Va.), Mar. 13, 2002, at 1A ("The trooper who discovered one of the more recent scandals at the State Police crime lab was placed on leave Tuesday pending an investigation of his own work there."); infra notes 52–67 and accompanying text.

26 See, e.g., Laura Cadiz, Maryland-Based DNA Lab Fires Analyst Over Falsified Tests, BALT. SUN, Nov. 18, 2004, at 1A (reporting that, on November 18, 2004, Orchid Cellmark—the world's largest private DNA testing firm—announced that it fired analyst Sarah Blair for falsifying test data); Terry Horne, Crime Lab Boss Placed on Leave, INDIANAPOLIS STAR, Jan. 25, 2004, at 1A ("Mayor Bart Peterson relieved Forensic Services Agency Director James E. Hamby of his duties … amid growing concern that the crime lab chief had covered up problems in his agency."); Keith Matheny, Supervisor Accused of Passing Off DNA Test, TRAVERSE CITY RECORD-EAGLE (Traverse City, Mich.), Dec. 19, 2004, at 1A ("A former supervisor in the Michigan State Police Crime Lab's DNA analysis unit had a subordinate take a required proficiency test for him last year, an internal investigation found."); James Randerson & Andy Coghlan, Forensic Evidence Stands Accused, NEW SCIENTIST, Jan. 31, 2004, at 6 ("The UK has been troubled this past week by revelations that flawed scientific advice given to courts may have led to the wrongful conviction of hundreds of men and women accused of harming their children."); Vic Ryckaert, Crime Lab to Retest DNA in 64 Cases, INDIANAPOLIS STAR, July 18, 2003, at 1A ("The Marion County crime lab is reviewing 64 criminal cases—mostly rapes and killings—because of fears that one of its lab technicians cut corners on DNA testing."); Robert Tanner, Standards, Autonomy Sought for Crime Labs; Mishandling of Evidence, Mismanagement Cited, SEATTLE TIMES, July 7, 2003, at A1 ("In Orlando, Fla., an analyst with the Florida Department of Law Enforcement admitted falsifying results of a test designed to check his work and his lab's ability to analyze DNA. The state said that his transgression did not affect any criminal cases and that it would pay for retests where he was lead analyst.").

were critical of the explosives unit in 1997[27] and a DNA unit in 2004.[28] Further, an FBI metallurgist pleaded guilty for giving false testimony concerning comparative analysis of bullet lead in 2003,[29] and a scathing internal report on the Bureau's misidentification of fingerprints in the Madrid train bombing was issued in 2004.[30]

Some of the crime lab failures involved incompetence and sloppy procedures, while others entailed fraud, but the extent of the derelictions—the number of episodes and the duration of some of the abuses, covering decades in several instances[31]—precludes dismissal of the controversy as the errant work of only a "few bad apples."[32] Forged fingerprints,[33]

---

27 OFFICE OF THE INSPECTOR GENERAL, U.S. DEPARTMENT OF JUSTICE, THE FBI LABORATORY: AN INVESTIGATION INTO LABORATORY PRACTICES AND ALLEGED MISCONDUCT IN EXPLOSIVES-RELATED AND OTHER CASES (1997) [hereinafter 1997 I.G. REPORT]; see infra notes 236–41 and accompanying text.

28 OFFICE OF THE INSPECTOR GENERAL, U.S. DEPARTMENT OF JUSTICE, THE FBI DNA LABORATORY: A REVIEW OF PROTOCOL AND PRACTICE VULNERABILITIES (2004) [hereinafter 2004 I.G. REPORT]; see infra notes 242–53 and accompanying text.

29 See Steve Bailey, Prosecutor Challenged in Ragland Murder Case, CINCINNATI POST, Sept. 6, 2002, at 13A ("Attorneys for both sides were in court for a hearing in which FBI ballistics expert Kathleen Lundy was scheduled to testify about lying during a preliminary hearing in Shane Ragland's murder case."); infra text accompanying notes 254–65.

30 See Robert B. Stacey, A Report on the Erroneous Fingerprint Individualization in the Madrid Train Bombing Case, 54 J. FORENSIC IDENTIFICATION 707 (2004); infra notes 290–309 and accompanying text.

31 Fred Zain was at the West Virginia lab for ten years. See infra notes 52–58 and accompanying text. Joyce Gilchrist was at the Oklahoma City lab for twenty years. See infra notes 68–124 and accompanying text.

32 This is a claim that some forensic scientists have made. See, e.g., Tanner, supra note 26 ("'There are always bad actors in any profession,' said Paul Ferrara, director of the Virginia Division of Forensic Science. 'The difference is that our mistakes do not get buried.'"). But see Janine Arvizu, Forensic Laboratories: Shattering the Myth, 24 THE CHAMPION, May 2000, at 18, 20 ("The problems in these high-profile cases are a clear reflection of the forensic community's widespread failure to develop and implement effective quality assurance programs."). Ferrara's Virginia State Lab would later have its own problems. See infra notes 208–35 and accompanying text.

33 See Boris Geller et al., A Chronological Review of Fingerprint Forgery, 44 J. FORENSIC SCI. 963, 964–67 (1999) (discussing history of fingerprint forgeries); Mark Hansen, Troopers' Wrongdoing Taints Cases, A.B.A. J., Mar. 1994, at 22, 22 (discussing New York police officers' fabrication of fingerprint evidence in numerous cases).

faked autopsies,[34] false laboratory reports,[35] and perjured testimony,[36] including the falsification of credentials,[37] have all been documented. Indeed, the Florida Supreme Court felt compelled to cite the "rising nationwide criticism of forensic evidence" in denying the admissibility of expert evidence in one case.[38]

Paradoxically, these scandals are occurring as the power of DNA evidence to identify the guilty[39] and exonerate the innocent[40] is being reported weekly, if not daily, and

---

34 See Richard L. Fricker, Pathologist's Plea Adds to Turmoil: Discovery of Possibly Hundreds of Faked Autopsies Helps Defense Challenges, A.B.A. J., Mar. 1993, at 24, 24 ("If the prosecution theory was that death was caused by a Martian death ray, then that was what [pathologist] Dr. Erdmann reported.") (internal quotes omitted); Chip Brown, Pathologist Accused of Falsifying Autopsies, Botching Trial Evidence, L.A. TIMES, Apr. 12, 1992, at A24 ("[F]ormer Dallas County assistant medical examiner Linda Norton was quoted as saying [Dr.] Erdmann routinely performs 'made-to-order autopsies that support a police version of a story.'"); Roy Bragg, New Clues May be Dug from Grave; Furor Touches on Autopsies, Brains, HOUSTON CHRON., Mar. 28, 1992, at A1 ("[C]all him 'McErdmann. ... He's like McDonald's—billions served.'") (quoting Dallam County District Attorney Barry Blackwell).

35 See United States v. Gault, 141 F.3d 1399, 1403 (10th Cir. 1998) ("Defendant sought to question Goldston about a former DEA colleague's submission of falsified reports. The DEA agent, Ann Castillo, had admitted to failing to perform the controlled substance tests upon which her reports were based."); State v. Ruybal, 408 A.2d 1284, 1285 (Me. 1979) (FBI analyst "reported results of lab tests that he did not in fact conduct"); State v. DeFronzo, 394 N.E.2d 1027, 1031 (Ohio Ct. Com. Pl. 1978) (expert represented that certain lab tests were conducted when "no such tests were ever conducted").

36 See supra note 29; see also Logerquist v. McVey, 1 P.3d 113, 120 (Ariz. 2000) (en banc) ("It turned out that the witness presenting the dog-scent evidence in Roscoe was a charlatan.").

37 See United States v. Gale, 314 F.3d 1, 1 (D.C. Cir. 2003) (observing that a government expert, who had testified for years in narcotics cases, "pleaded guilty to having committed perjury about his educational background"); Drake v. Portuondo, 321 F.3d 338, 342 (2d Cir. 2003) ("It is now apparent that Walter's testimony concerning his qualifications was perjurious."); Doepel v. United States, 434 A.2d 449, 460 (D.C. 1981) (a FBI serologist testified that he had a master's degree in science, "whereas in fact he never attained a graduate degree"); Commonwealth v. Mount, 257 A.2d 578, 579 (Pa. 1969) (prosecution expert "had never fulfilled the educational requirements for a laboratory technician"). See generally James E. Starrs, Mountebanks Among Forensic Scientists, in 2 FORENSIC SCIENCE HANDBOOK 1, 7, 20–29 (Richard Saferstein ed., 1988) (discussing false credential cases).

38 Ramirez v. State, 810 So. 2d 836, 853 (Fla. 2001) (excluding expert testimony comparing a knife with impression in cartilage).

39 See David Lazer, Introduction to DNA AND THE CRIMINAL JUSTICE SYSTEM 7 (David Lazer ed., 2004) ("[T]hrough March 2004, 16,100 crime investigations in the United States had been aided through convict DNA databases.").

40 See Barbara Novovitch, Free After 17 Years for a Rape That He Did Not Commit, N.Y. TIMES, Dec. 22, 2004, at A18 (discussing the case of Brandon Moon, who was released from prison after seventeen years for a rape that he did not commit; he was the 154th person exonerated by DNA analysis).

while the Supreme Court is ratcheting up the standards for the admissibility of scientific evidence in its Daubert trilogy.[41] The scandals have prompted Texas[42] and Oklahoma[43] to require their crime laboratories to be accredited, joining New York, which has mandated accreditation since 1994.[44] Moreover, in 2004, Congress required states receiving federal funds to designate an agency to investigate laboratory fraud and misfeasance.[45] In 2005, the Virginia legislature made the Division of Forensic Science a separate agency under the Secretary of Public Safety[46] and created a Forensic Science Board and Scientific Advisory Committee[47]—another byproduct of a lab controversy.[48] While these reforms reflect

41 The Supreme Court revolutionized the standards for admitting expert testimony in Daubert v. Merrell Dow Pharm., Inc., 509 U.S. 579 (1993), which was followed by Gen. Elec. Co. v. Joiner, 522 U.S. 136 (1997), and Kumho Tire Co. v. Carmichael, 526 U.S. 137 (1999). Daubert has been transformed over time, so that in Weisgram v. Marley Co., 528 U.S. 440 (2000), the Supreme Court referred to Daubert as imposing "exacting standards of reliability." Id. at 455.

42 TEX. CODE CRIM. PROC. ANN. art. 38.35 (Vernon 2005) (requiring accreditation by the Department of Public Safety). Texas also created a Forensic Science Commission. TEX. CODE CRIM. PROC. ANN. art. 38.01 (Vernon 2005).

43 OKLA. STAT. ANN. tit. 74, § 150.37 (West 2004) (requiring accreditation by the American Society of Crime Laboratory Directors/Laboratory Accreditation Board ("ASCLD/LAB") or the American Board of Forensic Toxicology).

44 N.Y. EXEC. LAW § 995b (McKinney 2003) (requiring accreditation by the state Forensic Science Commission); see also CAL. PENAL CODE § 297 (West 2004) (requiring accreditation of DNA units by ASCLD/LAB or any certifying body approved by ASCLD/LAB); MINN. STAT. ANN. § 299C.156(2)(4) (West 2007) (specifying that Forensic Laboratory Advisory Board should encourage accreditation by ASCLD/LAB or other accrediting body).

Indiana does not require accreditation but does require "[a] laboratory conducting forensic DNA analysis" to "implement and follow nationally recognized standards for DNA quality assurance and proficiency testing, such as those approved by" ASCLD/LAB. See IND. CODE ANN. § 10-13-6-14 (LexisNexis 2003).

45 In 2004, as part of the "Justice for All Act," the Omnibus Crime Control and Safe Streets Act of 1968 was amended to require

> a certification that a government entity exists and an appropriate process is in place to conduct independent external investigations into allegations of serious negligence or misconduct substantially affecting the integrity of the forensic results committed by employees or contractors of any forensic laboratory system, medical examiner's office, coroner's office, law enforcement storage facility, or medical facility in the State that will receive a portion of the grant amount.

42 U.S.C.A. § 3797k(4) (West Supp. 2007).

46 VA. CODE ANN. § 9.1–1100 (2005) (changing Division of Forensic Science into the Department of Forensic Science). Previously, the Division was under the Department of Criminal Justice Services. Id.

47 VA. CODE ANN. §§ 9.1–1109 to 9.1–1113 (2005).

48 See infra notes 208–35 and accompanying text.

improvement, they are also long overdue[49] and, more importantly, inadequate. All crime laboratories should be regulated in a comprehensive manner.

Part I of this Article examines a number of laboratory failures. These examples involve both municipal and state facilities, as well as the FBI Laboratory, and they cover a wide variety of techniques, including hair comparisons, serological examinations, drug analyses, fingerprint identifications, and even DNA profiling, the current gold standard in forensic science. In some of these cases, it is difficult to distinguish between malfeasance and misfeasance because the lack of quality assurance protocols creates an environment in which both can flourish undetected for long periods of time. Moreover, some abuses can be traced to the lack of empirical validation of a technique—e.g., microscopic hair comparisons and comparative analysis of bullet lead. These examples demonstrate the need for regulating crime labs.

Part II discusses the regulation of DNA profiling, which has developed gradually over the last twenty years, and can serve as a model for other laboratory units. The complexity of DNA profiling forced the FBI to establish a technical working group on DNA analysis in 1988 in order to promulgate testing standards.[50] In 1994, Congress enacted the DNA Identification Act,[51] which authorized a national DNA database. Significantly, this legislation also created a DNA Advisory Board to promulgate quality assurance standards and required proficiency testing of examiners and external audits. This landmark Act was the first federal legislation regulating a forensic science. Other requirements for an effective regulatory scheme include the accreditation of crime laboratories, the certification of examiners, and the standardization and promulgation of written protocols for each technique. Moreover, forensic science commissions should be established in each jurisdiction to implement these and other reforms.

---

49 Professor Jonakait wrote about the issue sixteen years ago. See Randolph N. Jonakait, Forensic Science: The Need for Regulation, 4 HARV. J.L. & TECH. 109, 191 (1991) ("Current regulation of clinical labs indicates that a regulatory system can improve crime laboratories."). Professor Bernstein and I wrote about forensic abuses a decade ago. See David Bernstein, Junk Science in the United States and the Commonwealth, 21 YALE J. INT'L L. 123 (1996) (discussing cases in Canada, Australia, New Zealand, and England); Paul C. Giannelli, The Abuse of Scientific Evidence in Criminal Cases: The Need for Independent Crime Laboratories, 4 VA. J. SOC. POL'Y & L. 439 (1997) (discussing cases involving expert misconduct).

50 See infra note 329 and accompanying text.

51 Pub. L. No. 103–322, 108 Stat. 2065 (codified as amended at 42 U.S.C.A. §§ 1413114134 (West 2005)).

I. CRIME LAB FAILURES

A. West Virginia

One of the most notorious cases of crime lab failure involved Fred Zain, the Chief Serologist in the West Virginia State Police Crime Laboratory, who falsified test results in as many as 134 cases from 1979 to 1989.[52] In reviewing a judicial report on Zain's decade of misconduct, the Supreme Court of Appeals of West Virginia spoke of "shocking and ... egregious violations" and the "corruption of our legal system."[53] The judicial inquiry concluded that "as a matter of law, any testimonial or documentary evidence offered by Zain at any time in any criminal prosecution should be deemed invalid, unreliable, and inadmissible."[54] The report commented:

> The acts of misconduct on the part of Zain included (1) overstating the strength of results; (2) overstating the frequency of genetic matches on individual pieces of evidence; (3) misreporting the frequency of genetic matches on multiple pieces of evidence; (4) reporting that multiple items had been tested, when only a single item had been tested; (5) reporting inconclusive results as conclusive; (6) repeatedly altering laboratory records; (7) grouping results to create the erroneous impression that genetic markers had been obtained from all samples tested; (8) failing to report conflicting results; (9) failing to conduct or to report conducting additional testing to resolve conflicting results; (10) implying a match with a suspect when testing supported only a match with the victim; and (11) reporting scientifically impossible or improbable results.[55]

Numerous defendants were imprisoned based on Zain's testimony.[56] In fact, Zain was such a treasured prosecution witness that even after he left the state to accept a position in a

52 See In re Investigation of the W. Va. State Police Crime Lab., Serology Div., 438 S.E.2d 501, 511 (W. Va. 1993); George Castelle, Lab Fraud: Lessons Learned from the Fred Zain Affair, THE CHAMPION, May 1999, at 12, 13. A number of TV shows documented his abuses. See 60 Minutes: Right on, Fred Zain (CBS television broadcast Apr. 24, 1994); Dateline: Body of Evidence, supra note 22.

53 In re Investigation of the W. Va. State Police Crime Lab., 438 S.E.2d at 508.

54 Id. at 520. As part of the judicial inquiry, the Chairman of the Laboratory Accreditation Board of the American Society of Crime Laboratory Directors selected two experts to conduct an analysis of the policies, procedures, and records of the Serology Division during Zain's tenure. Id. at 503, 510-11.

55 Id. at 503; see also In re Investigation of W. Va. State Police Crime Lab., 445 S.E.2d 165, 167 (W. Va. 1994) ("Trooper Zain's misconduct was insidious and extensive.").

56 See Giannelli, supra note 49, at 442–49 (examining Zain's conduct in detail); SCHECK ET AL., supra note 5, at 107–17 (discussing Woodall, Davis, and Harris exonerations).

San Antonio crime lab, West Virginia prosecutors sent evidence to him for retesting.[57] The prosecutors relied on him because the remaining West Virginia serologists were incapable, in their view, of reaching the "right" results.[58]

In response to the Zain affair, the West Virginia State Police revamped its crime lab.[59] Astonishingly, despite this effort, the lab continued to fall victim to misconduct. On September 7, 2000, as a result of an established quality control procedure, Sergeant Timothy White discovered certain inconsistencies in a lab report prepared by chemist Todd Owen McDaniel.[60] When White reported the inconsistencies, the State Police contacted the FBI and placed five members of the lab on administrative leave.[61] When confronted, McDaniel admitted to skipping required tests on suspected marijuana and cocaine evidence and subsequently pleaded guilty to fraud.[62] Drug Enforcement Administration ("DEA") chemists had to take over the drug unit.[63]

The FBI investigation found that McDaniel was not the only employee who ignored procedures. The report mentioned that White had also violated lab policy,[64] but he apparently failed to learn from this lesson. In June of 2001, less than a year later, a discrepancy was detected in one of his reports.[65] Adding to the problem, Captain Rick Theis, director

---

57 See In re Investigation, 438 S.E.2d at 512 (noting that a West Virginia serologist sent evidence to Texas for Zain to test). Zain's work in Texas also proved troublesome: "In the case of Gilbert Alejandro, the expert, Fred Zain, claimed a DNA match when in fact Zain had never conducted any testing beyond initial inconclusive testing and the DNA excluded Alejandro." Garrett, supra note 5 (manuscript at 35 n.109).

58 According to Zain's subordinate, "several prosecutors expressed dissatisfaction with the reports they were receiving from serology and specifically requested that the evidence be analyzed by Zain." In re Investigation, 438 S.E.2d at 512 n.16.

[Serologist] Myers also testified that after he had been unable to find blood on a murder suspect's jacket, it was sent to Texas, where Zain found a bloodstain which tested consistent with the blood of the victim. ... [Serologist] Bowles also testified that at least twice after Zain left the lab, evidence on which Bowles had been unable to obtain genetic markers was subsequently sent to Texas for testing by Zain, who again was able to identify genetic markers.

Id. at 512.

59 See Messina, supra note 25.

60 Id. ("The trooper who discovered one of the more recent scandals at the State Police crime lab was placed on leave Tuesday pending an investigation of his own work there.").

61 Press Release, W. Va. State Police, New Employees Staff Drug Lab (Oct. 2, 2000), www.wvstatepolice.com/news/druglab1.htm.

62 See Messina, supra note 25.

63 See New Employees Staff Drug Lab, supra note 61.

64 Id. A second civilian chemist, Mills Dillard, who was one of the lab members on administrative leave, resigned during the investigation. Id.

65 See Messina, supra note 25.

of the lab, neglected to notify the State Police Superintendent, as required.[66] Both White and Theis were placed on leave.[67]

B. Oklahoma City

Joyce Gilchrist, who began working as a forensic chemist in the Oklahoma City Police Department crime laboratory in 1980, is another prominent illustration of misconduct continuing unchecked for many years.[68] She was also a prosecution superstar.[69]

1. Curtis McCarty Prosecution

In 1982, Gilchrist initially excluded Curtis McCarty as a suspect in a rape-murder investigation based on microscopic hair comparison.[70] After another suspect identified McCarty as the killer, Gilchrist reviewed a second set of hair samples from McCarty, which she then matched to the crime scene exemplars.[71]

Two months before trial, the defense requested discovery of all scientific reports as well as access to hair, fiber, and serological samples for an independent evaluation.[72] John Wilson, a Kansas City Police Crime Lab examiner, analyzed the evidence after being hired as a defense consultant.[73] Gilchrist sent the samples so that Wilson received them on March 17, 1986, the day McCarty's trial began.[74] Gilchrist then used her tardiness against the defense by testifying that Wilson could not have conducted a competent examination in the length of time he had the hair slides.[75] Further, after Wilson testified that, according

---

66 Id.

67 Id.

68 See MARK FUHRMAN, DEATH AND JUSTICE: AN EXPOSÉ OF OKLAHOMA'S DEATH ROW MACHINE 232 (2003) (concluding that Gilchrist "appears to have used her lab tests to confirm the detectives' hunches rather than seek independent scientific results. … She treated discovery requests with contempt and kept evidence from the defense. She systematically destroyed evidence at the very time when she knew that much of that evidence might be retested").

69 See id. at 70 (noting that after "the successful prosecution of Malcolm Rent Johnson, Joyce Gilchrist's star began to rise"); see also Bennett L. Gershman, Misuse of Scientific Evidence By Prosecutors, 28 OKLA. CITY U. L. REV. 17, 23 (2003) (using Gilchrist's conduct as example of abuse of scientific evidence).

70 See FUHRMAN, supra note 68, at 90.

71 Id.

72 McCarty v. State, 765 P.2d 1215, 1217 (Okla. Crim. App. 1988).

73 Id.

74 Id.

75 Id. at 1217–18.

to Gilchrist's report, none of the pubic hairs found on the victim matched McCarty's, Gilchrist testified that she had simply failed to include in her report that a pubic hair found on the victim was consistent with McCarty's hair.[76] Additionally, Gilchrist testified that, based on her examination, McCarty was present at the time of the crime; there was no basis—scientific or otherwise—for this statement.[77] McCarty was sentenced to death.[78]

The Oklahoma Court of Criminal Appeals reversed McCarty's conviction, finding that Gilchrist had improperly delayed sending her report, as well as the sample, to the defense expert.[79] The court also criticized Gilchrist for omitting critical information from the report, labeling her conduct "trial by ambush."[80] Finally, the court found that Gilchrist had testified beyond the state of the art.[81]

This was not the only trial at which Wilson and Gilchrist would clash. Wilson testified against Gilchrist in another case.[82] After examining hair evidence that, according to Gilchrist's testimony, matched the defendant, Wilson reached the opposite conclusion. After the trial, he registered a complaint against Gilchrist with the Southwestern Association of Forensic Scientists ("SWAFS"), which conducted an investigation and concluded that Gilchrist should distinguish between her personal and scientific opinions.[83] Despite this

76 Id. at 1218.

77 Id.

78 Id. at 1217.

79 Id. ("Ms. Gilchrist's delay and neglect in not completing her forensic examination and report ... was inexcusable, since she began her forensic examination in December of 1982.").

80 Id. at 1218 ("[T]he forensic report was at best incomplete, and at worst inaccurate and misleading. ... Gilchrist admitted at trial, however, that she failed to include her conclusion ... in the forensic report given to Mr. Wilson. This significant omission, whether intentional or inadvertent, resulted in a trial by ambush. ...") (citations omitted).

81 Id. ("We find it inconceivable why Ms. Gilchrist would give such an improper opinion, which she admitted she was not qualified to give."). McCarty was later convicted at a retrial. McCarty v. State, 904 P.2d 110 (Okla. Crim. App. 1995). However, his conviction was once again vacated during post-conviction proceedings due to Gilchrist's misconduct. McCarty v. State, 114 P.3d 1089, 1092 n.12 (Okla. Crim. App. 2005) (noting that a departmental "Review Board found the circumstantial evidence indicated Ms. Gilchrist had destroyed the evidence in order to prevent DNA testing"). A third trial was subsequently aborted. See Cheryl Camp, Convicted Murderer Is Freed In Wake of Tainted Evidence, N.Y. TIMES, May 22, 2007, at A16 (reporting that trial judge released McCarty because the "evidence in the case against him had been tainted or destroyed by the actions of a former police chemist, Joyce Gilchrist, who lawyers say switched out samples to get a match").

82 FUHRMAN, supra note 68, at 95 (discussing the Alvin King Parker case).

83 See McCarty, 765 P.2d at 1219 ("[O]n December 14, 1987, Max Courtney, President of the Southwestern Association of Forensic Scientists, Inc., issued a prepared statement of the Board of Directors concerning allegations of professional misconduct lodged against Ms. Gilchrist. A certified copy of this statement, which was filed with this Court on January 4, 1988, concluded that Ms. Gilchrist

admonishment, Gilchrist was not otherwise disciplined. In the end, Wilson was the one punished: the Oklahoma City Police Department called Wilson's supervisor at the Kansas City Police Department, complaining that he had testified against its expert.[84] Kansas City subsequently forbade him from working on private cases.[85]

2. Jeffrey Pierce Prosecution

In 1985, Sandra Burton was raped in her apartment.[86] When the police brought Jeffrey Pierce, a landscaper at her apartment complex, to Burton, she said that he was not the rapist.[87] In addition, two witnesses corroborated Pierce's alibi.[88] Eight months later, however, Pierce was arrested, and minutes after he voluntarily agreed to provide head and pubic hair exemplars, Gilchrist determined that Pierce's hairs "matched" the crime scene hairs.[89] Pierce was subsequently convicted and sentenced to sixty-five years in prison.[90]

The Oklahoma Court of Criminal Appeals upheld the conviction, despite several troubling aspects of the case. First, Gilchrist had violated a court order by failing to turn over evidence to the defense.[91] Second, her report was incomplete.[92] While the court

---

had violated the ethical code, but interestingly she was not disciplined. That statement reads in relevant part: 'Our Professional Conduct Committee thoroughly investigated the allegations against Ms. Joyce Gilchrist and ... communicated with [her] that she should distinguish personal opinion from opinions based upon facts derived from scientific evaluation. ... We further conclude that, in our system of jurisprudence, undue pressure can be placed upon the forensic scientist to offer personal opinions beyond the scope of scientific capabilities.' (citation omitted)).

84 FUHRMAN, supra note 68, at 98.

85 Id.

86 Pierce v. State, 786 P.2d 1255, 1258 (Okla. Crim. App. 1990); see also FUHRMAN, supra note 68, at 191–210.

87 Pierce v. Gilchrist, 359 F.3d 1279, 1282 (10th Cir. 2004).

88 Id.

89 Pierce, 786 P.2d at 1258 ("Joyce Gilchrist testified that twenty-eight scalp hairs and three pubic hairs recovered from either S.B., her clothing or her apartment, were microscopically consistent with the characteristics found in Appellant's hair.").

90 Id.

91 Id. at 1261 ("Instead of following either the letter of the Order or taking steps to have the Order changed or clarified by the court, she took it upon herself to determine the portions of the Order with which she wished to comply. This was not her decision to make.").

92 Id. at 1263 n.8 ("Appellant claims that it was error for Gilchrist not to set out in the report, her opinion that the attacker was a non-secretor."). At trial, Gilchrist testified that Pierce was a non-secretor, a person whose blood type cannot be determined through other body fluids, including semen. FUHRMAN, supra note 68, at 203. Between twenty and twenty-five percent of the population falls into this category. 1 GIANNELLI & IMWINKELRIED, supra note 12, § 17.09, at 959.

acknowledged these deficiencies, it nevertheless concluded that Pierce's constitutional rights had not been violated.[93]

A later FBI investigation of Gilchrist's analyses in eight cases determined that she had misidentified hairs in six instances and fibers in another.[94] One of the cases was Pierce's; the FBI found that none of the hairs taken from Pierce exhibited the same microscopic characteristics as those found at the crime scene.[95] As a result, the Oklahoma City Police Department had the evidence retested by a private DNA laboratory.[96] That testing exonerated Pierce, who is now suing Gilchrist for violating his constitutional rights.[97]

3. Alfred Mitchell Prosecution

In Mitchell v. State?[98] a rape-murder case tried in 1992, Gilchrist testified that Mitchell's sperm had been detected on anal and vaginal swabs taken from the victim.[99] She made this statement despite two key facts: (1) pretrial DNA testing performed by the FBI (at Gilchrist's request) established the absence of sperm on the swabs; and (2) sperm found on the victim's panties matched the DNA of her boyfriend.[100] Gilchrist did not turn over the

---

93 Pierce, 786 P.2d at 1263–64. Gilchrist misstated her qualifications. Id. at 1264 ("During the trial, Gilchrist testified that she was a member of the American Academy of Forensic Sciences. Appellant has provided this Court with several letters which reveal that at the time of trial, Gilchrist had been suspended from the organization for nonpayment of dues.").

94 See SPECIAL AGENT DOUGLAS DEEDRICK, SUMMARY OF CASE REVIEWS OF FORENSIC CHEMIST, JOYCE GILCHRIST, OKLAHOMA CITY POLICE DEPARTMENT CRIME LABORATORY 1 (2001) (concluding that lab notes "were often incomplete or inadequate to support the conclusions reached by the examiner" and finding a lack of documentation "to identify textile fibers" in one of the cases and no indication of "a confirmation or review by another qualified examiner" in hair cases) (on file with the North Carolina Law Review).

95 Id. at 3 ("[T]hese [pubic] hairs do not exhibit the same microscopic characteristics as the suspect's known pubic hairs.").

96 DNA testing was not available at the time of Pierce's trial in 1986.

97 See Pierce v. Gilchrist, 359 F.3d 1279, 1300 (10th Cir. 2004) (finding that Gilchrist does not have immunity).

98 884 P.2d 1186 (Okla. Crim. App. 1994).

99 Id. at 1199 ("Gilchrist's findings indicated the presence of sperm in the vaginal and anal canals (the latter consistent with Mitchell). Sperm consistent with Mitchell was also found on the medical examiner's transport sheet in the area where [the victim's] genitals lay during transport."); see also FUHRMAN, supra note 68, at 126 (noting Gilchrist's testimony that the FBI's DNA test "had been 'inconclusive'").

100 Mitchell v. Gibson, 262 F.3d 1036, 1063 (10th Cir. 2001). The appellate court further noted: [H]and-written notes taken by Ms. Gilchrist during telephone conversations with Agent Vick indicat[ed] that the agent had conducted two DNA probes on the samples. These probes showed that the semen on

FBI report to the defense, although, as the Tenth Circuit subsequently noted, "[t]he results thus completely undermined Ms. Gilchrist's testimony.'"[101] The court went on to observe:

> *Ms. Gilchrist thus provided the jury with evidence implicating Mr. Mitchell in the sexual assault of the victim which she knew was rendered false and misleading by evidence withheld from the defense. Compounding this improper conduct was that of the prosecutor, whom the district court found had "labored extensively at trial to obscure the true DNA test results and to highlight Gilchrist's test results," and whose characterization of the FBI report in his closing argument was "entirely unsupported by evidence and … misleading."*[102]

4. Malcolm Rent Johnson Prosecution

In the trial of Malcolm Rent Johnson, another rape-murder prosecution, Gilchrist testified that semen recovered from the victim's bed was consistent with Johnson's blood type and that hairs found on the bed matched hair taken from Johnson's arm.[103] Johnson's request for a defense expert to counter Gilchrist's testimony was denied,[104] and he was convicted and then executed on January 6, 2000.[105] When the Gilchrist scandal later erupted,

---

the panties matched that of Mr. Taylor only, that no DNA was present on the rectal swab, and that the only DNA on the vaginal swab was consistent with the victim.

Id.

101 Id. at 1064 ("An expert testified at the evidentiary hearing that the DNA testing … unquestionably eliminated Mr. Mitchell … [and Gilchrist's testimony was] based on the use of test methods Ms. Gilchrist knew were less precise than the DNA tests which eliminated Mr. Mitchell. Moreover, he pointed out that one of the tests she performed in fact excluded Mr. Mitchell.").

102 Id.; see also Gilchrist v. Bd. Rev. Okla. Employment Sec. Comm'n, 94 P.3d 72, 75 (Okla. 2004) ("Gilchrist's conduct in Mitchell, that is knowingly giving false and misleading testimony in a criminal case, constituted 'misconduct' sufficient to support the denial of unemployment benefits. …").

103 Johnson v. State, 731 P.2d 993, 1007 (Okla. Crim. App. 1987); FUHRMAN, supra note 68, at 61; see also Johnson v. State, 823 P.2d 370 (Okla. Crim. App. 1991) (denying state habeas relief).

104 Johnson, 731 P.2d at 1007 ("The techniques used and manner of investigation were discussed on direct and on cross examination. The test results were available for discovery prior to trial. The experts called were forthright concerning their findings and the limitations inherent in the tests and investigation."). See generally Paul C. Giannelli, Ake v. Oklahoma: The Right to Expert Assistance in a Post-Daubert, Post-DNA World, 89 CORNELL L. REV. 1305 (2004) [hereinafter Giannelli, The Right to Expert Assistance] (discussing the need to bolster the right to defense experts).

105 FUHRMAN, supra note 68, at 253. During the appeals process, Skip Palenik, a forensic scientist, criticized Gilchrist's trial testimony, stating that she had testified beyond the bounds of accepted science

Johnson's attorneys asked for the evidence to be reexamined.[106] Four police chemists later concluded that there was no sperm present on the slides taken from the victim's bed.[107] Yet, for her work on the Johnson case, Gilchrist had received a certificate of achievement.[108] Questions about the execution linger.[109]

---

when she claimed to have matched arm hair to the defendant. Id. at 64. According to Palenik, arm hairs are not individual enough for such comparisons. Id.

106 Id. at 65–66. The District Attorney's office informed them that the evidence no longer existed. Id. at 66. When the defense attorney searched the evidence archives, however, he found the smear slides right where they were supposed to be. Id.

107 Id. at 66–67 (noting that Laura Schile, an OCPD crime lab scientist, "wrote a memo stating that 'spermatozoa is not present' on six slides that Gilchrist had said contained semen matching Johnson's blood type and secretor status. Schile's conclusions were supported by three other police chemists. ..."); see also Lois Romano, Police Chemist's Missteps Cause Okla. Scandal, WASH. POST, Nov. 26, 2001, at A1 ("But last July, in a startling development, the police lab stated in a memo ... that it had recently reexamined the original slides purportedly containing the sperm and found no sperm there—contrary to Gilchrist's claims 19 years ago.").

108 FUHRMAN, supra note 68, at 70.

109 Id. at 68 ("Even David Prater [an assistant D.A.] admits that the 'Malcolm Rent Johnson case is the one case, out of the ones who have been executed, that is questionable.'"); Jim Yardley, Oklahoma Police Lab Scientist Probed; Future Executions Put on Hold, CHI. TRIB., May 2, 2001, at 9 ("State Atty. Gen. Drew Edmondson, whose office began reviewing the capital cases last week ... said he still wants to review the case of Malcolm Rent Johnson, who was executed in January 2000 for murdering a woman. He did not offer a reason to believe Johnson was wrongly executed but said he wants to more thoroughly examine the case.").

5. Additional Cases

These cases were not the only ones in which Gilchrist's work was criticized.[110] In Fox v. State,[111] a death penalty case, the appellate court questioned her testimony concerning hair analysis: "The lack of scientific weight of such a conclusion is apparent on reflection by those dealing with similar evidence on a regular basis. But to a lay jury, usually ill-equipped to assimilate hair analysis findings on their own, such an opinion may appear too substantial."[112] In Miller v. State,[113] the court reversed a rape conviction, noting that once again Gilchrist turned over hair evidence to the defense in an untimely manner[114] and omitted crucial conclusions from her report.[115] Mitochondrial DNA analysis later exonerated Miller.[116] Another suspect, Ronnie Lott, whom Gilchrist had cleared, was subsequently convicted of the crime.[117]

---

110 See, e.g., Cannon v. Gibson, 259 F.3d 1253, 1275 n.22 (10th Cir. 2001) (denying habeas relief, the court wrote: "This court recognizes that recently information has come to light casting serious doubt on the veracity of Gilchrist's testimony in a large number of criminal prosecutions. ... In fact, there is serious reason to doubt the veracity of Gilchrist's testimony in this particular case."); LaFevers v. Gibson, 238 F.3d 1263, 1266 (10th Cir. 2001). Denying habeas relief in LeFevers, the court wrote:

When habeas counsel ultimately succeeded in having Exhibit 83 submitted for DNA testing, the testing revealed that the blood on the pants actually belonged to Cannon, not the victim. ... LaFevers asserted that ... (1) [Gilchrist] lied when she asserted that the blood splatters on the pants were not sufficiently large to conduct electrophoresis testing; and (2) she lied when she testified that she had not conducted electrophoresis testing on the pants.

Id.

111 779 P.2d 562 (Okla. Crim. App. 1989) (upholding a murder conviction and death penalty sentence).

112 Id. at 571. The court also noted that "Ms. Gilchrist admitted that an individual could not be positively identified by hair evidence. However, she went on to testify that, '[in] her opinion ... Mark Fowler and Bill Fox were in contact with John Barrier prior to death.'" Id. at 571 (alteration in original).

113 809 P.2d 1317 (Okla. Crim. App. 1991).

114 Id. at 1319–20 ("[I]t was approximately two weeks after the deadline ordered by Judge Owens that Ms. Gilchrist mailed the hair evidence to the appellant's expert. Thus, appellant's expert received the evidence six and one-half days before trial began.").

115 Id. at 1320 ("What is even more disturbing ... is the fact that Ms. Gilchrist's pretrial forensic report made absolutely no mention of her finding of a 'unique characteristic' concerning appellant's pubic hairs. However, in his opening argument, the prosecutor alerted the jury to the State's expert's finding of the 'unique characteristic.'").

116 SCHECK ET AL., supra note 5, at 87.

117 Lott v. State, 98 P.3d 318 (Okla. Crim. App. 2004).

6. Other Problems

A January 2001 report by the chief of the laboratory documented additional problems concerning Gilchrist's job performance, including: (1) missing evidence in numerous cases; (2) contamination issues due to evidence being "stacked all over the chemist's area"; (3) systematic destruction of rape evidence after two years, well before the statute of limitations expired; (4) lack of peer review in many cases; and (5) the absence of proficiency testing, although such testing had been paid for.[118] This review came ten years after Professor Starrs had criticized Gilchrist's work in a forensic science journal.[119] He wrote: "[I]n her missionary zeal to promote the cause of the prosecution she had put blinders on her professional conscience so that the truth of science took a back seat to her acting the role of an advocate."[120]

Although her conduct had been questioned for over fifteen years, Gilchrist's supervisors were either unaware of the courtroom controversies or they did not care as long as her testimony resulted in convictions.[121] When interviewed by Dan Rather in 2001, Wilson, the expert who had filed the ethics complaint against Gilchrist, succinctly captured the problem: "The whole criminal justice system has failed."[122] He then elaborated: "You have to look at the prosecutor's office. They must have understood what was going on with all those flags being waved. The judges are no different."[123] Of the twenty-three death penalty

---

118 Memorandum from Captain Byron Boshell, Lab. Servs. to Major Garold Spencer, Investigations Bureau 16–17 (Jan. 16, 2001) (on file with the North Carolina Law Review).

119 See James E. Starrs, The Forensic Scientist and the Open Mind, 31 J. FORENSIC SCI. SOC'Y 111 (1991).

120 Id. at 132–33.

121 Memorandum from Captain Byron Boshell, Lab Servs. to Major Garold Spencer, Investigations Bureau, supra note 118, at 10 ("I knew from previous articles published over the years that she had been the subject of scrutiny by the courts, but I assumed they had been addressed by the department and resolved. I later found no indication in her personnel file that they had ever been investigated or addressed administratively."). On September 25, 2001, Gilchrist was discharged. Gilchrist v. Bd. Rev. Okla. Employment Sec. Comm'n, 94 P.3d 72, 74 (Okla. 2004).

122 60 Minutes: Black Magic: Under the Microscope (CBS television broadcast May 8, 2001).

123 Id.; see also FUHRMAN, supra note 68, at 71 (noting that Detective Bemo claimed that Gilchrist began giving the detectives test results that were so good "that he didn't believe [she] was doing proper lab work, because her results were 'too good.' Bemo says that now, but it didn't stop him and his partner Bill Cook from using Gilchrist's lab results in many of their cases."). Fuhrman further notes:

Cook had given Gilchrist the nickname "Black Magic" because she was able to get results that no other chemist could. When Cook and other homicide detectives gave Gilchrist a hair sample from a suspect, they would often let her know that this was the person that they wanted to arrest.

Id. at 91.

cases in which Gilchrist testified, twelve defendants have been executed. Oklahoma now requires its laboratories to be accredited.[124]

C. Montana

The problems in Montana surfaced when Jimmy Ray Bromgard, convicted of rape in 1987,[125] was exonerated by DNA testing sponsored by the Cardozo Law School Innocence Project—after serving fifteen years in prison.[126] Arnold Melnikoff, the founder and one-time director of the Montana State Police Crime Laboratory, testified about hair analysis at Bromgard's trial.[127] Melnikoff used a statistical analysis that he had apparently invented.[128] According to Melnikoff, "the odds were one in one hundred that two people would have head hair or pubic hair so similar that they could not be distinguished by microscopic comparison and the odds of both head and pubic hair from two people being indistinguishable would be about one in ten thousand."[129] There was no scientific basis for these statements.

An independent panel of five trace evidence experts concluded that Melnikoff's testimony contained "egregious misstatements" and demonstrated a "fundamental lack of understanding" of hair comparisons.[130] The Innocence Project then sought out other cases in which Melnikoff had testified.[131] As a result, DNA analysis also exonerated Chester

124 See OKLA. STAT. ANN. tit. 74, § 150.37 (West 2004) (requiring accreditation by the American Society of Crime Laboratory Directors/Laboratory Accreditation Board or the American Board of Forensic Toxicology).

125 State v. Bromgard, 862 P.2d 1140 (Mont. 1993); see also CNN Presents:
Reasonable Doubt: Can We Trust Crime Labs? (CNN television broadcast Jan. 9, 2005) (examining the Bromgard case).

126 See Liptak, supra note 20.

127 See Adam Liptak, 2 States to Review Lab Work of Expert Who Erred on ID, N.Y. TIMES, Dec. 19, 2002, at A24.

128 Id. ("'The 1-in-100 estimate was without any scientific basis. …'") (quoting Professor Walter Rowe, George Washington University).

129 Bromgard, 862 P.2d. at 1141.

130 INNOCENCE PROJECT, PEER REVIEW REPORT: MONTANA V. JIMMY RAY BROMGARD 2 ("[T]here is not—and never was—a well established probability theory for hair comparison. … If this witness has evaluated hair in over 700 cases as he claims in his testimony, then it is reasonable to assume that he has made many other misattributions.") (on file with the North Carolina Law Review); see also Liptak, supra note 127 ("An F.B.I. report issued yesterday concluded that the scientist had misidentified the hair samples that were the central evidence in the case.")..

131 Peter J. Neufeld, The (Near) Irrelevance of Daubert to Criminal Justice and Some Suggestions for Reform, 95 AM. J. PUB. HEALTH (SUPP. I) 107, 107 (2005) ("A Lexis search identified two other

Bauer, convicted of rape in 1983, and Paul Kordonowy, convicted of rape in 1990.[132] In these two cases, Melnikoff had also used bogus statistical analysis in his testimony.[133] When the state Attorney General refused to investigate past cases, the Innocence Project, along with five former Montana Supreme Court justices, sought review of the more than 200 cases in which Melnikoff had been involved.[134] The Montana Supreme Court, however, used jurisdiction grounds to dismiss a petition that sought an independent audit and retesting of evidence.[135]

Melnikoff had moved on to the Washington State Patrol Crime Lab in 1989.[136] An investigation there revealed additional problems. An internal audit found flaws in thirty out of 100 drug-analysis cases assigned to Melnikoff.[137]

Gilchrist and Melnikoff were not the only experts abusing hair comparison evidence; many of the wrongful conviction cases involved this type of evidence.[138] In *Williamson*

---

cases in which the Montana Supreme Court viewed Melnikoff's hair evidence favorably and affirmed convictions. In both cases, postconviction DNA testing on the original semen samples excluded the convicted offenders, and the men were exonerated.").

132 See http://www.innocenceproject.org/Content/52.php (Chester Bauer); http://www.innocenceproject.org/Content/194.php (Paul Kordonowy).

133 See State v. Bauer, 683 P.2d 946, 951 (Mont. 1984) ("Melnikoff estimated that the chances of another person having the same type of pubic and head hair were one in ten thousand."); State v. Kordonowy, 823 P.2d 854, 856 (Mont. 1991) ("Arnold Melnikoff ... testified that with caucasian head and pubic hair, he could microscopically distinguish an individual's respective head and pubic hair from another individual's respective head and pubic hair in ninety-nine out of 100 cases.").

134 See Jennifer McKee, High Court Won't Rule on Crime Lab Decision, BILLINGS GAZETTE, Sept. 2, 2004, at 1C.

135 In re Investigation in the Trace Evidence and Serology Section of the Montana Forensic Lab, No. 04–582, at 3–4 (Mont. 2004) ("We express no view on the serious matters asserted in the petition or on the extent to which the petitioners may have other remedies. We conclude, however, that this Court has no authority or jurisdiction to take the actions requested by the petitioners via an original proceeding."); see also McKee, supra note 134 (reporting four-to-three decision in which court held that it lacked authority to order an investigation); Possley et al., supra note 2.

136 McKee, supra note 134.

137 See Teichroeb, Oversight of Crime-Lab Staff, supra note 23 ("Washington State Patrol officials will notify prosecutors in seven counties that drug evidence handled by one of their employees—a crime lab forensic scientist facing termination—has been called into question.").

138 See, e.g., FRED KAUFMAN, ONTARIO MINISTRY OF THE ATTORNEY GENERAL, 1 REPORT OF THE KAUFMAN COMMISSION ON PROCEEDINGS INVOLVING GUY PAUL MORIN 83 (1998) (finding that Morin was erroneously convicted based, in part, on "valueless" hair evidence). Recommendation 2 noted: "Trial judges should undertake a more critical analysis of the admissibility of hair comparison evidence as circumstantial evidence of guilt." Id. at 311.

v. Reynolds,[139] a federal district court correctly noted that microscopic hair analysis lacks scientific support.[140] Williamson was later exonerated by DNA profiling, and the hair evidence was shown to be "patently unreliable."[141] Still another expert testified at Edward Honaker's trial that the crime scene hair sample "'was unlikely to match anyone'" else.[142] Actually, hundreds or even hundreds of thousands of hair exemplars could have "matched." Honaker was also freed by DNA profiling.[143] Despite this record, courts (including in McCarty[144] in Oklahoma) continued to admit this suspect evidence.[145] Indeed, one court judicially noticed the reliability of hair evidence,[146] implicitly finding this evidence indisputable,[147] and yet there is an embarrassing lack of basic research on this "well-accepted" technique.[148]

---

139 904 F. Supp. 1529 (E.D. Okla. 1995).

140 Id. at 1556. The district court had "been unsuccessful in its attempts to locate any indication that expert hair comparison testimony meets any of the requirements of Daubert." Id. at 1558. The court further observed: "Although the hair expert may have followed procedures accepted in the community of hair experts, the human hair comparison results in this case were, nonetheless, scientifically unreliable." Id. Nevertheless, the Tenth Circuit reversed on this issue. Williamson v. Ward, 110 F.3d 1508, 1523 (10th Cir. 1997) (holding that due process (fundamental fairness), not the more stringent Daubert, standard applies in habeas proceedings).

141 SCHECK ET AL., supra note 5, at 146. See generally JOHN GRISHAM, THE INNOCENT MAN (2006) (examining the Williamson case).

142 See EDWARD CONNORS ET AL., CONVICTED BY JURIES, EXONERATED BY SCIENCE: CASE STUDIES IN THE USE OF DNA EVIDENCE TO ESTABLISH INNOCENCE AFTER TRIAL 58 (1996), available at http://www.ncjrs.gov/pdffiles/dnaevid.pdf.

143 See id. at 59.

144 McCarty v. State, 904 P.2d 110, 125 (Okla. Crim. App. 1995) (admitting hair evidence); see also supra notes 70–85 and accompanying text.

145 See, e.g., State v. Fukusaku, 946 P.2d 32, 44 (Haw. 1997) ("Because the scientific principles and procedures underlying hair and fiber evidence are well-established and of proven reliability, the evidence in the present case can be treated as 'technical knowledge.' Thus, an independent reliability determination was unnecessary."); McGrew v. State, 682 N.E.2d 1289, 1292 (Ind. 1997) (concluding that hair comparison is "more a 'matter of the observations of persons with specialized knowledge' than 'a matter of scientific principles'" (internal quotation marks omitted) (quoting Jervis v. State, 679 N.E.2d 875, 881 (Ind. 1997)).

146 See Johnson v. Commonwealth, 12 S.W.3d 258, 262–63 (Ky. 1999).

147 See FED. R. EVID. 201(b) (limiting judicial notice to facts that are not subject to reasonable dispute); Daubert v. Merrell Dow Pharm., Inc., 509 U.S. 579, 592 n.11 (1993) ("[T]heories that are so firmly established as to have attained the status of scientific law, such as the laws of thermodynamics, properly are subject to judicial notice under Federal Rule of Evidence 201.").

148 See Paul C. Giannelli & Emmie West, Hair Comparison Evidence, 37 CRIM. L. BULL. 514 (2001) (discussing the DNA exoneration cases in which hair evidence was used to convict the innocent);

In an FBI study comparing microscopic and mitochondrial DNA analysis of hair, the former was wrong approximately twelve percent of the time—even though, in all cases reviewed, the conclusion had been limited to an "association" ("consistent with" testimony).[149] In the hair cases, the lack of a scientific basis and lab protocols—limiting the conclusions that may be derived from the evidence—camouflaged the misconduct.

D. Chicago

John Willis was convicted of rape in 1992, despite his protests of innocence.[150] Dr. Pam Fish, a serologist in the Chicago crime lab, testified that her tests were "inconclusive"—i.e., that they neither included nor excluded Willis as the source of semen.[151] Willis, dubbed the "beauty shop rapist," was convicted and sentenced to 100 years of imprisonment.[152] Seven years later, DNA testing exonerated him.[153] At that time, Fish's lab notes surfaced, indicating that Willis's blood type (type B) excluded him as the source of the semen (type A).[154] Fish failed to acknowledge this finding in her testimony.[155] After reviewing the file, a respected forensic scientist concluded that "labeling the typing of the semen stains as 'inconclusive' misrepresents the laboratory findings."[156] Willis sued, and the city, county,

---

Clive A. Stafford Smith & Patrick A. Goodman, Forensic Hair Comparison Analysis: Nineteenth Century Science or Twentieth Century Snake Oil?, 27 COLUM. HUM. RTS. L. REV. 227, 231 (1995–1996) ("If the purveyors of this dubious science cannot do a better job of validating hair analysis than they have done so far, forensic hair comparison analysis should be excluded altogether from criminal trials.").

149 Max M. Houck & Bruce Budowle, Correlation of Microscopic and Mitochondrial DNA Hair Comparisons, 47 J. FORENSIC SCI. 964, 966 (2002) ("Of the eighty hairs that were microscopically associated, nine comparisons were excluded by mtDNA analysis.").

150 See Maurice Possley & Jeremy Manier, Police Crime Lab on the Hot Seat, CHI. TRIB., Oct. 9, 1998, § 1, at 1.

151 Id.

152 Id.

153 See Steve Mills et al., When Labs Falter, Defendants Pay: Bias Toward Prosecution Cited in Illinois Cases, CHI. TRIB., Oct. 20, 2004, § 1, at 1.

154 Id. ("[Willis] had blood type B and was a secretor—that is, his blood type could be determined from his bodily fluids, such as semen or saliva. The semen taken from the toilet tissue wrapper came from someone with blood type A.").

155 See SCHECK ET AL., supra note 5, at 125 ("Fish's misleading testimony in the Willis case, which led to the conviction of an innocent man and allowed a predator to continue roaming the streets, shows why the state should have turned over all of Fish's laboratory notes and data, rather than merely presenting her final report.").

156 Letter from George F. Sensabaugh, Professor, University of California at Berkeley, to Locke E. Bowman, Legal Director, The MacArthur Justice Center, University of Chicago Law School (Oct. 16, 2003) [hereinafter Letter from Sensabaugh] (emphasis omitted) (on file with the North Carolina Law

and state settled for over $2.5 million, without admitting wrongdoing.[157] The Chicago Tribune reported: "By her own account, Fish could have redone the tests in the Willis case to clarify the results, and even her bosses still say she should have."[158] Fish was also involved in other wrongful convictions.[159]

The problems at the Chicago lab were not limited to Fish. Dr. Howard Harris, the former head of the New York City police crime lab from 1974 to 1985 and a former president of the American Society of Crime Lab Directors, was asked to examine the Chicago police crime laboratory in connection with a civil suit. In his findings, Harris described the lab as "disorganized, poorly supervised, almost completely lacking in written procedures and performance standards, and staffed by inadequately trained workers."[160] He noted that "records management 'was relegated to the lowest ranking employees in the laboratory, who were provided with minimal training and seemingly an almost complete lack of written procedures and standards of performance.'"[161] Further, "[t]here was no system to ensure that all relevant materials were sent in response to a subpoena, and 'laboratory

---

Review). Sensabaugh reached two more conclusions: first, "[g]iven that Dr. Fish had reservations about the reliability of blood group test results and apparently did no retesting, she had an obligation to specify her reservations in the lab report"; and second,

> Overall, the documentation of the lab work as described in the three pages of lab notes is inadequate and incomplete. Moreover, the formal lab reports describe results of testing for which there is no record in the lab notes. In short, the documentation in this case falls short of accepted scientific standards.

Id. (emphasis omitted).

157 See Mills et al., supra note 153.

158 Id.

159 See Margaret Cronin Fisk, Lawyer Frees Chicago Trio After Retesting of Lab Sample, NAT'L L.J., Dec. 17, 2001, at A6 (discussing DNA exonerations of Omar Saunders and Larry Ollins after thirteen years in prison; at trial, Fish had testified there were no stains from a rape kit which included a vaginal swab, but the evidence reportedly showed that the killer was an O-secretor and that none of the defendants were).

Donald Reynolds and Billy Wardell, other rape defendants, were also exonerated by DNA. Wardell v. City of Chicago, No. 98 C 8002, 2001 WL 1345960, at *1 (N.D. Ill. Oct. 31, 2001). Reynolds alleged that Fish had falsely testified about the results of blood tests. Id. A federal court dismissed Wardell and Reynolds' lawsuit because plaintiffs failed to show that a municipal policy was involved. Id. at *6. Thus, Fish's culpability was not determined.

160 Maurice Possley & Steve Mills, Crime Lab Disorganized, Report Says: Consultant Alleges Meager Supervision, Inadequate Training, CHI. TRIB., Jan. 15, 2001, § 2, at 1.

161 Id.

senior supervisory personnel did not seem to know if there were any records of what was actually sent.'"[162]

In 1996, the Illinois State Police took over the city crime lab, and Fish was named head of the state lab's biochemistry section.[163] When the Willis controversy erupted, the State went back and reviewed the cases in which she was involved as a state examiner. In contrast, the city cases were never audited.[164]

E. Houston

The Houston Police Department Crime Lab is the paradigmatic example of a failed forensic agency. According to a state senator, "the validity of almost any case that has relied upon evidence produced by the lab is questionable."[165]

---

162 Id. The Chicago lab had other problems. Gary Dotson was convicted of the rape of Cathleen Webb. CONNORS ET AL., supra note 142, at 51. Six years later she recanted, stating that she had fabricated the charge. Id. at 52. Subsequent DNA tests excluded Dotson as the source of the crime-scene semen. Id. At Dotson's 1979 trial, Timothy Dixon testified that seminal material found in Webb's panties matched Dotson's blood type. Blake Fleetwood, From the People Who Brought You the Twinkie Defense; The Rise of the Expert Witness Industry, WASH. MONTHLY, June 1987, at 33, 37. He failed to disclose, however, that Webb's own vaginal discharges, not necessarily semen, could have caused the stains. Id. Years later when a Washington Post reporter asked Dixon why he had not spoken up. He replied: "I guess I wasn't asked." Id. A DNA scientist later remarked that "Dixon's trial testimony was 'exceedingly misleading and, in my judgment, dishonest.'" Mark Thompson, DNA's Troubled Debut, CAL. LAW., June 1988, at 43 (quoting Edward Blake, Forensic Sciences Associates); see also Jones v. Chicago, 856 F.2d 985, 991 (7th Cir. 1988) ("[P]olice laboratory technician Mary Furlong ... discovered that George Jones had different semen and blood types from the types found in Sheila Pointer's vagina. Furlong failed to include this information in the lab report that she was preparing for the prosecution of Jones.").

163 Possley & Mills, supra note 160.

164 Mills et al., supra note 153 ("But her former boss, Kearney, acknowledged that a review of all her cases might have been warranted. 'Maybe we should have gone back and looked at them,' he said in a recent interview. 'But it didn't happen.'").

165 Rodney Ellis, supra note 2. Similarly, the chair of the legislative committee investigating the lab has stated: "It's a comedy of errors, except it's not funny." Adam Liptak, Houston DNA Review Clears Convicted Rapist, and Ripples in Texas Could Be Vast, N.Y. TIMES, Mar. 11, 2003, at A14 (quoting State Representative Kevin Bailey).

The story began with a television station's investigation,[166] which led in turn to a state audit of the lab in December 2002.[167] The audit revealed a dysfunctional organization with serious contamination issues and an untrained staff using shoddy science.[168] As described by a later investigation, the DNA unit was in shambles … operating for years without a line supervisor, overseen by a technical leader who had no personal experience performing DNA analysis and who was lacking the qualifications required under the FBI standards, staffed by underpaid and undertrained analysts, and generating mistake-ridden and poorly documented casework.[169]

As a result of these findings, the crime lab was not allowed to perform DNA testing for several years.[170]

Some defendants who were convicted based on evidence provided by the lab have been exonerated. For example, Josiah Sutton[171] was convicted of rape in 1999 based on flawed

---

166 See MICHAEL R. BROMWICH, THIRD REPORT OF THE INDEPENDENT INVESTIGATOR FOR THE HOUSTON POLICE DEPARTMENT CRIME LABORATORY AND PROPERTY ROOM 1 (2005) [hereinafter THIRD HOUSTON REPORT], available at http://www.hpdlabinvestigation.org.

167 TEXAS DPS CRIME LAB HEADQUARTERS & TARRANT COUNTY ME CRIME LAB, QUALITY ASSURANCE AUDIT FOR FORENSIC DNA AND CONVICTED OFFENDER DNA DATABASING LABORATORIES: HOUSTON POLICE DEPARTMENT CRIME LABORATORY—DNA/SEROLOGY SECTION (2002) (on file with the North Carolina Law Review).

168 Id.; see also Nick Madigan, Houston's Troubled DNA Crime Lab Faces Growing Scrutiny, N.Y. TIMES, Feb. 9, 2003, § 1, at 20 (reporting that operations were suspended in December after an audit found numerous problems, "including poor calibration and maintenance of equipment, improper record keeping, and a lack of safeguards against contamination of samples. Among other problems, a leak in the roof was found to be a potential contaminant of samples on tables below.").

169 THIRD HOUSTON REPORT, supra note 166, at 5.

170 MICHAEL R. BROMWICH, FINAL REPORT OF THE INDEPENDENT INVESTIGATOR FOR THE HOUSTON POLICE DEPARTMENT CRIME LABORATORY AND PROPERTY ROOM, Executive Summary at 2 (2007) [hereinafter FINAL HOUSTON REPORT], available at http://www.hpdlabinvestigation.org/reports/070613report.pdf.

171 Sutton v. State, No. 14-99-00951-CR, 2001 WL 40349 (Tex. App. Jan. 18, 2001) (denying appeal in which appellant asserted ineffective assistance of trial counsel for failing to retest DNA).

DNA evidence.[172] Retesting freed him.[173] In 2004, six independent experts determined that a second man, George Rodriguez,[174] had been convicted on serological testimony that was "false and scientifically unsound."[175] Rodriguez had an alibi and the police had evidence pointing to another person, whose DNA was later matched to the crime.[176] A panel of experts suggested that similar problems in other cases should be expected.[177]

Other revelations concerned the toxicology[178] and ballistics[179] units of the lab. Moreover, these problems were compounded by the district attorney's failure to recuse himself from

---

172 See Adam Liptak & Ralph Blumenthal, New Doubt Cast on Testing in Houston Police Crime Lab, N.Y. TIMES, Aug. 5, 2004, at A19 ("[P]rosecutors in Mr. Sutton's case had used [DNA] to convict him, submitting false scientific evidence asserting that there was a solid match between Mr. Sutton's DNA and that found at the crime scene. In fact, one of every eight black people, including Mr. Sutton, shared the relevant DNA profile. More refined retesting cleared him."); see also Roma Khanna & Steve McVicker, Police Chief Shakes Up Crime Lab: 2 Officials Quit, Others Disciplined, HOUSTON CHRON., June 13, 2003, at 1A ("Christi Kim is a DNA analyst who tested the DNA used to convict Josiah Sutton. … Police investigators cited her for incorrectly documenting the results of DNA profiles, failing to report the full set of DNA results in an unnamed case and making an incorrect data entry in an unnamed capital murder case.").

173 See Liptak & Blumenthal, supra note 172.

174 Rodriguez v. State, 766 S.W.2d 358 (Tex. Ct. App. 1989).

175 EDWARD T. BLAKE ET AL., PEER REVIEW REPORT TEXAS V. GEORGE RODRIGUEZ 6 (2004) (on file with the North Carolina Law Review); see also Liptak & Blumenthal, supra note 172 (reporting that the panel of experts wrote "that a crime laboratory official—because he either lacked basic knowledge of blood typing or gave false testimony—helped convict an innocent man of rape in 1987").

176 See Litpak & Blumenthal, supra note 172.

177 See Sylvia Moreno, Police Lab's Troubles Grow: Problems in Houston Lead to Moratorium on Executions, WASH. POST, Oct. 2, 2004, at A3 ("[T]his week, the district attorney's office announced that a new, independent analysis of chemical testing used to convict Rodriguez found the testing was inaccurate.").

178 See Ralph Blumenthal, Double Blow, One Fatal, Strikes Police in Houston, N.Y. TIMES, Oct. 30, 2003, at A25 ("The acting police chief announced on Wednesday that he had shut down the Police Department's toxicology section after its manager failed a competency test. …").

179 Problems in the firearms identification section have also been reported. Nanon Williams was convicted of a 1992 drug-related murder, and a lab expert testified that the victim was shot with a .25 caliber bullet. Six years later, reviewing the case, the same expert determined the bullet was a .22 caliber from a co-defendant's gun. He admitted that he had never tested that weapon. Possley et al., supra note 2. The Houston Chronicle further noted:

> [T]he attorneys handling his appeal discovered that before Rousseau's trial, HPD's ballistics lab had matched the bullet that killed [the victim] to bullets from another killing. … [A]bout one month after Rousseau was sentenced the police crime lab matched bullets from both shootings to a gun found on Juan Guerrero, who was convicted of the other murder. Prosecutors never

the case, as twenty-two judges had requested.[180] Two grand juries looking into the role of the prosecutors in the lab cases rejected the assistance usually provided by the D.A.'s office and called their own witnesses, thus becoming that rare phenomenon: a "runaway" grand jury.[181]

Texas now requires its labs to be accredited,[182] and Houston commissioned an independent investigation of its laboratory.[183] In the first three months, that investigation found myriad deficiencies. First, four instances of "dry labbing" (reporting results without doing tests) in the drug section were disclosed.[184] These incidents were apparently well known within the lab.[185] One of the two examiners involved was still employed by the laboratory, having been reinstated by the police chief after being removed from his position by the lab.[186] This examiner filed a harassment complaint against one of his superiors who had discovered the malfeasance. They both received the same disciplinary sanction.[187]

Second, the technical leader in the DNA unit had been removed and never replaced, leaving a six-year vacancy in an important supervisory position.[188] Matters were further exacerbated when the lab reassigned him to head the quality assurance program, a critical

---

> turned over the crucial findings that would have supported Rousseau's innocence as required, his attorneys said.

Roma Khanna & Steve McVicker, Fingers Pointed at HPD Crime Lab in Death Row Case, HOUSTON CHRON., April 24, 2003, at 1A.

180 Roma Khanna & Steve McVicker, DA Office Kept in Dark on Lab, Rosenthal Says, HOUSTON CHRON., July 11, 2003, at 27A ("Rosenthal also adamantly refused to recuse himself from investigations of the lab's problems, allowing for the appointment of a special prosecutor, despite the urging of 22 state district judges and others.").

181 Adam Liptak, Prosecutions Are a Focus in Houston DNA Inquiry: Grand Juries Seen as Widening Investigation, N.Y. TIMES, June 9, 2003, at A20.

182 See TEX. CODE CRIM. PROC. ANN. art. 38.35 (Vernon 2005) (requiring accreditation by the Department of Public Safety to admit "[p]hysical evidence subjected to forensic analysis, and testimony regarding the evidence" in a criminal proceeding).

183 See THIRD HOUSTON REPORT, supra note 166.

184 SEE MICHAEL R. BROMWICH, SECOND REPORT OF THE INDEPENDENT INVESTIGATOR FOR THE HOUSTON POLICE DEPARTMENT CRIME LABORATORY AND PROPERTY ROOM 12 (2005), available at http://www.hpdlabinvestigation.org/reports/050531report.pdf.

185 Id. at 12 n.9 (noting that discussions with witnesses "plainly established" the facts).

186 Id. at 12.

187 Id. at 13.

188 THIRD HOUSTON REPORT, supra note 166, at 21.

job that he did—by his own admission—in a lackluster fashion.[189] In short, having failed in one job, he was "booted upstairs."[190]

Third, serious backlog problems with the processing of rape kits remained unaddressed. In March 2002, a lab supervisor "estimated that there were 19,500 sexual assault kits received by HPD that had never been processed, some dating as far back as 1980."[191] The lab was analyzing only "known suspect" cases—i.e., persons already arrested.[192] Thus, the lab was not entering the profiles from "cold cases" into the national DNA database, the Combined DNA Index System ("CODIS"),[193] where they might have generated a cold hit. Consequently, rapes occurred that probably could have been prevented. Even with arrestees, the lab was incredibly slow. For example, when Lynn Jones was charged with the sexual assault of a child, he remained in jail for nine months before the DNA tests that would eventually exonerate him were performed.[194]

Fourth, in 2001, Tropical Storm Allison badly damaged thirty-four homicide and sexual assault case files due to a leaking roof.[195] According to the investigation's report, in 2003, "several Crime Lab employees told internal affairs investigators that this biological evidence had become so saturated with water that they observed bloody water dripping out of the boxes containing the evidence and pooling on the floor."[196]

Fifth, the laboratory "stopped performing lab-wide quality control audits in 1997,"[197] and audits performed in the DNA unit (as required by federal standards) were superficial at best.[198] The report noted that, although the DNA unit had successfully passed its internal reviews in 2000 and 2001, the 2002 external audit (using the same quality assurance standards) painted "a very different picture."[199] Indeed, the section was shut down after this audit.[200]

---

189 See id. at 30 ("By Dr. Shama's own admission, he did approximately a year's worth of work in the four-plus years he remained in the position; a more exacting assessment, would put the volume of work performed by Dr. Sharma at much less than that."). Sharma was reassigned due, in part, to conflicts with superiors. Id.

190 Id. at 29–30.

191 Id. at 47–48.

192 Id. at 47.

193 See id. at 48 (noting that "'cold case' rape kits must be outsourced to other laboratories").

194 Id. at 22.

195 Id. at 45.

196 Id. at 45.

197 Id., Executive Summary, at 5.

198 Id.

199 Id.

200 Id. at 51.

Sixth, the laboratory director was oblivious to these problems.[201] The investigation also identified poor proficiency testing results[202] and the failure of staff to meet educational requirements.[203]

The final report concluded that forty-three of the 135 DNA cases reviewed had "major issues," four of which involved death row inmates.[204] The report recommended that a special master be appointed to review these cases, as well as 180 suspect blood cases from the 1980s and early 1990s, for which convicts are still serving time.[205] These 180 cases represented twenty-one percent of those reviewed—"an extraordinarily high and extremely disturbing proportion of cases in which to find problems of this magnitude."[206] Local officials, however, rejected this recommendation, arguing that the prosecutor and courts could handle these cases.[207]

F. Virginia

In 1984, Earl Washington, Jr., a mentally retarded farmhand with an IQ of sixty-nine, was convicted of the rape-murder of Rebecca Williams and sentenced to death.[208] Although Washington "confessed" to the crime, he also confessed to several other offenses

---

201 "On December 13, 2002, the audit team briefed Mr. Krueger on its findings. Mr. Krueger recalls that the audit team told him the DNA Section was in shambles. He told us that he was completely surprised by this report. ..." Id. at 50–51.

202 Id. at 61 ("We found numerous errors in the typing results in the serology proficiency tests.").

203 Id. at 65. The report noted:

Mr. Bolding, who had served as the technical lead [sic] of the DNA/Serology Section [since 1996], lacked sufficient training and education in statistics. Our preliminary reviews suggest that in several cases involving mixtures, the DNA analysts performed the statistical calculations incorrectly. We also already have encountered deficiencies in the documentation contained in analysts' case files.

Id.

204 FINAL HOUSTON REPORT, supra note 170, Executive Summary, at 4.

205 Id., Executive Summary, at 12.

206 Id., Executive Summary, at 11.

207 See Joe Stinebaker, Houston Rejects Crime Lab Recommendation, ASSOCIATED PRESS, Jun. 14, 2007, available at http://abcnews.go.com/US/wirestory?id=3278325 (quoting District Attorney Rosenthal) ("We have special masters. ... They're called judges in our building.").

208 Washington v. Commonwealth, 323 S.E.2d 577, 581–84 (Va. 1984). See generally MARGARET EDDS, AN EXPENDABLE MAN: THE NEAR-EXECUTION OF EARL WASHINGTON JR. (2003) (examining the Washington case); Eric M. Freedman, Earl Washington's Ordeal, 29 HOFSTRA L. REV. 1089 (2001) (using Washington's case to highlight systemic flaws in the criminal justice system).

that the police soon determined he could not have committed.[209] In addition, his blood type (type O) did not match the type developed from a semen stain (type A), a fact that his trial attorney overlooked.[210]

In 1993, Governor Douglas Wilder ordered DNA testing, which was conducted by Jeff Ban, a state analyst.[211] On January 14, 1994, nine days before Washington's scheduled execution, Wilder commuted his sentence to life imprisonment.[212] The Governor's office, however, refused to give the DNA report to the defense attorneys, leaving them to wonder what type of results could have led to a commutation but not a pardon.[213] In a bizarre turn of events, the lab director, Paul Ferrara, gave the DNA report to a documentary filmmaker in 1999.[214] The previously-withheld report excluded Washington as a suspect.[215] Ban had eliminated Washington as the source of semen on a blanket but found a vaginal swab

---

209 Washington's incriminatory statements mainly consisted of affirmative responses to detectives' statements. Freedman, supra note 208, at 1092–93. The detectives claimed these statements revealed knowledge that only the perpetrator could have known. Washington v. Wilmore, 407 F.3d 274, 276 (4th Cir. 1995). In a later civil action against the detectives, a document surfaced that supported Washington's claim that his statements had been misrepresented at his criminal trial: "[Detective] Wilmore said that he felt like either he or Hart must have mentioned the shirt to Washington before Washington said he left the shirt at the scene, and that his testimony in the record did not accurately reflect that the shirt had been first mentioned by the police." Id. at 277 (citation omitted). The district court denied summary judgment because "Washington had proffered evidence from which a reasonable juror could conclude that Wilmore possessed nonpublic information about the crime and falsely represented that Washington had volunteered that information during interrogation." Id. at 278. The Fourth Circuit affirmed. Id. at 284. Washington later won a $2.25 million lawsuit against Wilmore's estate. See Jerry Markon, Wrongfully Jailed Man Wins Suit: va. Officer Falsified Confession, Jury Rules, WASH. POST, May 6, 2006, at B1.

210 The victim's husband was also type O. Washington v. Murray, 4 F.3d 1285, 1286 (4th Cir. 1993) (finding no violation of Sixth Amendment right of effective assistance of counsel).

211 See Possley et al., supra note 2.

212 Id.

213 EDDS, supra note 208, at 161.

214 Frontline: The Case for Innocence (PBS television broadcast Jan. 11, 2000), transcript available at http://www.pbs.org/wgbh/pages/frontline/shows/cases/etc/script.html (discussing Washington's case along with those of other exonerated convicts). Henry Erlich, who had developed the DNA test that Ban used, later concluded that Ban had misinterpreted the results. EDDS, supra note 208, at 150 (noting Erlich's conclusion "that these test results cast very significant doubt about Mr. Washington's contribution to the sample").

215 EDDS, supra note 208, at 170–71.

less clear.[216] This interpretation was incorrect,[217] a mistake that extended Washington's incarceration by six years.

By this time, newspapers began to clamor for more information, leading another governor, James Gilmore, to order further testing, this time with a more sophisticated technique, Short Tandem Repeats ("STRs").[218] Surprisingly, Ban was once again chosen to conduct the tests.[219] An unknown profile was detected on the blanket and matched the profile of Kenneth Tinsley, a twice-convicted rapist.[220] Gilmore then pardoned Washington, who had spent seventeen years in prison.[221] The pardon, however, was not based on a finding of actual innocence, but rather on reasonable doubt.[222]

Still, the matter would not rest. Ban's STR interpretation next came under attack. The defense hired Edward Blake, a prominent DNA scientist, who tested duplicate slides from the Medical Examiner's Office and excluded Washington as a possible match.[223] He found that Ban's report was "logically incoherent" and "fundamentally flawed."[224] The Innocence Project called for an audit, but the laboratory director balked, rejecting the criticism as "unfounded" and labeling Blake a "hired gun."[225] Other experts, however, disagreed, one arguing that the incident should have been reported as a quality breach under the lab's accreditation standards.[226]

---

216 Id. at 170.

217 Although Ban found a genetic trait on the blanket that did not belong to Washington, the victim, or the victim's husband, he believed Washington could not be eliminated. Id. This test involved the PCR DQ-alpha test, which is no longer used. The victim's and her husband's genetic alleles were 4 and 4. DIV. OF FORENSIC SCI. CENT. LAB., COMMONWEALTH OF VA., ASCLD/LAB LIMITED SCOPE INTERIM INSPECTION REPORT 4–5 (2005) [hereinafter ASCLD VA. REPORT]. Washington's was 1.2 and 4. Id. Ban found a mixture of 1.1, 1.2, and 4. Later reviews, however, concluded that the 1.2 should not have been reported. Id. app., at 19. Without the 1.2 allele finding, Washington would have been excluded. The ASCLD/LAB review found that "reporting of the 1.2 allele in the mixture ... [was] questionable. ... [The] profiles ... represented a 1.1 and 4 pattern." Id.

218 See EDDS, supra note 208, at 171–76.

219 See Possley et al., supra note 2.

220 Id.

221 Id.

222 See EDDS, supra note 208, at 185.

223 See Possley et al., supra note 2.

224 Letter from Edward Blake, Forensic Sci. Assocs., Richmond, Cal., to Peter J. Neufeld (Apr. 1, 2004) (on file with the North Carolina Law Review).

225 Possley et al., supra note 2.

226 State DNA Lab Needs Oversight, THE VIRGINIAN-PILOT (HAMPTON ROADS, VA.), June 24, 2004, at B10.

On September 30, 2004, Governor Mark Warner ordered an audit of the Washington case by the American Society of Crime Laboratory Directors/Laboratory Accreditation Board ("ASCLD/LAB"), which made several findings, including that Ban had erroneously interpreted the DNA tests.[227] In addition, "[p]ressures from outside the laboratory and excessive managerial influence from within the laboratory during the STR analyses phase had a detrimental affect on the analyst's decisions, examinations and reports in this case."[228] This pressure led to deviations from normal protocols.[229] (The pressure was to obtain a result, not to reach a particular result.)

The governor also ordered the lab to review old case files in which serological, but not DNA, analysis had been conducted.[230] This review was the first random-sample case audit, albeit limited, in the country.[231] As a result, five convicts have been exonerated,[232] and a more sweeping review is now underway.[233] Meanwhile, the Virginia legislature made the Division of Forensic Science a separate agency under the Secretary of Public Safety[234] and created a Forensic Science Board and a Scientific Advisory Committee.[235]

---

227 ASCLD VA. REPORT, supra note 217, at 16 ("The analyst's reported conclusions in the September 8, 2000 Certificate of Analysis with regard to the sperm fraction of Item 58 vaginal smear are incorrect."). ASCLD also disagreed with the lab's internal audit: "It should be noted that the internal DFS auditors agreed with the reported results in the September 8, 2000, Certificate of Analysis as they pertained to the exclusion of listed suspects, saying the results were scientifically supported by the data in the case file. ASCLD/LAB disagrees." Id. at 13.

228 Id. at 17.

229 Id. at 13. The erroneous conclusion resulted in part on "deviations from the standard protocol." Id.

230 Michael D. Shear & Jamie Stockwell, DNA Tests Exonerate 2 Former Prisoners: Va. Governor Orders Broad Case Review, WASH. POST, Dec. 15, 2005, at A1. Evidence in the old cases existed only because a lab analyst, Mary Jane Burton, meticulously retained evidence samples from 1973 to 1988, even though she was not required to. Id.

231 Press Release, Gov. Mark Warner, Gov. Warner Releases Audit of DNA Testing and Rape and Murder of Rebecca Williams (May 6, 2005) (on file with the North Carolina Law Review).

232 Editorial, A Light on Justice Denied, N.Y. TIMES, Dec. 31, 2005, at A14.

233 Shear & Stockwell, supra note 230. This review, however, has not progressed as quickly as it should have. See Candace Rondeaux, virginia DNA Review Hobbled: As Crime Lab Chief Steps Down, Slow Pace Is Criticized, WASH. POST, Dec. 27, 2006, at B1. ("We could see as many as 30 possible exonerations when this is all over with." (quoting lab director Paul Ferrara)).

234 VA. CODE ANN. § 9.1–1100 (2005) (changing Division of Forensic Science into the Department of Forensic Science). Previously, it was under the Department of Criminal Justice Services. Id.

235 Id. §§ 9.1–1111 to -1112.

G. FBI Laboratory

Although the FBI crime laboratory is widely regarded as the premier forensic facility in the country,[236] it too has had its problems.

1. EXPLOSIVES UNIT

The Department of Justice's 1997 report on the FBI laboratory, issued by the Inspector General ("I.G."), documented numerous deficiencies,[237] including inaccurate testimony, testimony beyond the competence of examiners, improperly prepared laboratory reports, insufficient documentation of test results, inadequate record management and retention, and failure to resolve serious and credible allegations of incompetence.[238] For example, in the Oklahoma City bombing case, the report found that an examiner's conclusion about the identity of the explosive charge was speculation and "tilted in such a way as to incriminate the defendants."[239] This presented federal prosecutors with a significant

---

236 Scott Bales, Turning the Microscope Back on Forensic Scientists, LITIGATION, Winter 2000, at 51, 53 (noting that "many people regarded [it] as the foremost crime lab in the world"). See generally DAVID FISHER, HARD EVIDENCE: HOW DETECTIVES INSIDE THE FBI'S SCI-CRIME LAB HAVE HELPED SOLVE AMERICA'S TOUGHEST CASES (1996) (discussing the FBI Lab's successes); Modern Marvels: FBI's Crime Lab (A&E Home Video 2006) (documentary).

237 See generally 1997 I.G. REPORT, supra note 27, Executive Summary, pt. IA; see also JOHN F. KELLY & PHILLIP K. WEARNE, TAINTING EVIDENCE 2 (1998) (concluding that FBI examiners "had given scientifically flawed, inaccurate, and overstated testimony under oath in court; had altered the lab reports of examiners to give them a pro-prosecutorial slant; and had failed to document tests and examinations from which they drew incriminating conclusions, thus ensuring that their work could never be properly checked"); Bales, supra note 236, at 53 ("[T]he report did contain deeply disturbing findings of inadequate procedures, insufficient supervision, and improper conduct.").

238 1997 I.G. REPORT, supra note 27, Executive Summary, pt. IA.

239 Id., Executive Summary, pt. IIIG. Scott Bales noted:

> [T]he report concluded that an examiner from the lab's explosives unit had erred by purporting to identify the particular explosives used in the [1993] World Trade Center and Oklahoma City bombings. The error stemmed from the examiner's reliance on information that was tied to suspects but not relevant to his scientific analysis.

Bales, supra note 236, at 52. The New York Times further explained:

> Two laboratory workers said [the chief laboratory examiner] had changed their dictated reports, in violation of F.B.I. policy. They said he made slight alterations in the wording of reports to eliminate uncertainties in the explosives evidence and making it easier for prosecutors to present the evidence as unequivocally consistent with the Government's theory of the case.

David Johnston, F.B.I. Lab Practices Faulted in Oklahoma Bomb Inquiry, N.Y. TIMES, Jan. 31, 1997, at A1.

dilemma,[240] which they solved by going outside the country to obtain a bomb expert from the Ministry of Defence in the United Kingdom.[241]

The report's recommendations are riveting in their simplicity. They include: (1) seeking ASCLD/LAB accreditation; (2) requiring examiners in the Explosives Unit to have scientific backgrounds in chemistry, metallurgy, or engineering; (3) mandating that each examiner who performs work prepare and sign a separate report instead of a composite report "without attribution to individual examiners"; (4) establishing report review procedures by unit chiefs; (5) preparing adequate case files to support reports; (6) monitoring court testimony in order to preclude examiners from testifying to matters beyond their expertise or in ways that are unprofessional; and (7) developing written protocols for scientific procedures.[242]

2. DNA UNIT

A second I.G. Report (2004) focused on Jacqueline Blake, who was hired by the FBI in 1988 as a serologist.[243] From March 2000 to June 2002, she worked with DNA-Polymerase Chain Reaction ("PCR").[244] For two years, while performing analyses on crime scene evidence in more than 100 cases, she failed to complete negative control tests, a required part of the lab protocol designed to identify whether contamination has been introduced

---

240 See United States v. Nichols, 169 F.3d 1255 (10th Cir. 1999) (upholding Nichols's conviction despite a defense challenge to refusing a witness's testimony that would have criticized the FBI's handling of the case); United States v. McVeigh, 153 F.3d 1166 (10th Cir. 1998) (upholding McVeigh's conviction despite challenges to evidentiary rulings).

241 Nichols, 169 F.3d at 1261–62 ("Mr. Nichols next contends the district court erred when it permitted Linda Jones, a forensic explosives expert from the Ministry of Defense in England, to give opinions about the type and size of the bomb that destroyed the Murrah building.").

242 See generally 1997 I.G. REPORT, supra note 27, Executive Summary, pt. VII (summarizing these recommendations). With respect to the fourth recommendation, the report commented: "Our central point is that peer review by qualified personnel is an essential aspect of a high-performing forensic science laboratory. The Rudolph matter, certain conclusions in the Oklahoma City report, and other cases demonstrate the importance of vigorous, substantive peer review." Id. Addressing the fifth recommendation, it elaborated:

> The Rudolph files and some of Martz's work underscore the importance of case files containing all of the documentation necessary for another appropriately qualified examiner to be able to understand and replicate the examiner's data and analysis. We encountered the problem of incomplete or missing documentation in many case files.

Id.

243 2004 I.G. REPORT, supra note 28, at 8.

244 Id. at i.

into the process.[245] This omission "rendered her work scientifically invalid and unusable in court."[246] In addition, she falsified lab documents to conceal her misdeeds.[247] In May 2004, she pleaded guilty to a misdemeanor charge of providing false information in her lab reports.[248]

Several aspects of this affair warrant further attention. First, although the FBI was an accredited laboratory by this time and thus subject to audits, Blake's malfeasance was not revealed through established safeguards, but rather by accident.[249] As the I.G. Report observed, "weaknesses in DNA [Unit I] procedures and protocols allowed a technician routinely to disregard required steps in the analysis of DNA, even while the Unit received clean audit reports from both internal and external auditors and while the Unit was accredited by ASCLD/LAB."[250]

Second, in reviewing the laboratory's protocols, the I.G. Report identified several significant problems:

> [I]n approximately 20 percent of the protocol sections we reviewed we identified one or more of the following deficiencies: 1) the protocol lacks sufficient detail; 2) the protocol fails to inform the exercise of staff discretion; 3) the protocol fails to ensure the precision of manual notetaking; and 4) the protocol is outdated.[251]

Third, the FBI's response to this incident proved insufficient in some important respects. The agency's audit covered only the two years when Blake worked as a PCR Biologist but should have extended to the prior twelve years, when she was a serologist

---

245 Id.

246 Id. Blake was a technician, not an examiner, and therefore did not testify.

> By itself, however, the failure to process the negative controls does not change the test results or lead to a particular testing outcome (e.g., creating a match between a known and unknown evidence sample). The retesting of evidence in Blake's cases to date indicates that, while she did not properly conduct the contamination testing, the DNA profiles that she generated were accurate.

Id. In some cases, however, her testing consumed all the available DNA in the case. Id. at ii.

247 Id. at i.

248 Id. at ii.

249 Id. ("In April 2002, a colleague of Blake was working late one evening after Blake had left the Laboratory for the day, and noticed that the testing results displayed on Blake's computer were inconsistent with the proper processing of the control samples.").

250 Id. at 21. Blake also failed to run the negative controls in her qualifying and proficiency tests, but this was not detected at the time. Id. at 40–41.

251 Id. at 130.

and then a Restriction Fragment Length Polymorphism ("RFLP") analyst.[252] In addition, the Office of General Counsel failed to appreciate the seriousness of the problem when informed of it.[253]

3. COMPARATIVE BULLET LEAD ANALYSIS

a. The Examiner

As part of her job responsibilities, Kathleen Lundy, an FBI examiner, performed comparative bullet lead analysis ("CBLA"), a process that compares trace chemicals found in bullets at crime scenes with ammunition found in the possession of a suspect.[254] For over thirty years, FBI experts had testified about bullet lead composition, a technique that was first used in the investigation into President Kennedy's assassination.[255] The technique was not seriously challenged until a retired FBI examiner, William Tobin, began questioning the procedure in scientific and legal journals,[256] as well as in-court testimony.[257]

---

252 Id. at 67.

253 Id. at 65 ("[T]he Laboratory did not receive the quality of legal services that one would expect from FBI OGC, and Laboratory management was not sufficiently assertive when soliciting legal advice.").

254 NAT'L RESEARCH COUNCIL, FORENSIC ANALYSIS: WEIGHING BULLET LEAD EVIDENCE 1-2 (2004). The Council is the research arm of the National Academies, formerly the National Academy of Sciences. Various analytical techniques (e.g., neutron activation analysis, inductively coupled plasma-atomic emission spectrometry) have been used to determine the concentrations of seven elements—"arsenic (As), antimony (Sb), tin (Sn), copper (Cu), bismuth (Bi), silver (Ag), and cadmium (Cd)—in the bullet lead alloy of both the crime-scene and suspect's bullets." Id. at 2. Statistical tests are then used to compare the elements in each bullet: "If any of the fragments and suspect's bullets are determined statistically to be analytically indistinguishable for each of the elemental concentration means, they probably came from the same 'source.'" Id.

255 See generally Erik Randich & Patrick M. Grant, Proper Assessment of the JFK Assassination Bullet Lead Evidence from Metallurgical and Statistical Perspectives, 51 J. FORENSIC SCI. 717 (2006) (discussing the original analysis of the bullet fragments).

256 See, e.g., Edward J. Imwinkelried & William A. Tobin, Comparative Bullet Lead Analysis (CBLA) Evidence: Valid Inference or Ipse Dixit?, 28 OKLA. CITY U. L. REV. 43 (2003); Erik Randich et al., A Metallurgical Review of the Interpretation of Bullet Lead Compositional Analysis, 127 FORENSIC SCI. INT'L 174 (2002) (Tobin was a coauthor); William A. Tobin & Wayne Duerfeldt, How Probative is Comparative Bullet Lead Analysis?, CRIM. JUSTICE, Fall 2002, at 26.

257 See Ragland v. Commonwealth, 191 S.W.3d 569, 577 (Ky. 2006); Clemons v. State, 896 A.2d 1059, 1068 (Md. 2006); State v. Behn, 868 A.2d 329, 339–40 (N.J. Super. Ct. App. Div. 2005) (Tobin's affidavit submitted). Although a metallurgist, Tobin worked in a different section of the lab; he was not a CBLA examiner.

In Ragland v. Commonwealth,[258] a Kentucky murder case, Lundy got herself in trouble while testifying at a pretrial admissibility hearing.[259] She stated that the elemental composition of a .243 caliber bullet fragment removed from the victim's body was "analytically indistinguishable" from bullets found at the home of the defendant's parents.[260] Lundy further testified that the Winchester Company purchased its bullet lead in block form prior to 1996 and then remelted it at its manufacturing plant.[261] During cross-examination at trial, however, Lundy admitted that she knew prior to the hearing that Winchester had purchased its lead in billet form in 1994.[262] This was not a minor point. Millions more bullets could have the same "source" if they were last melted by a secondary smelter instead of by Winchester.[263] Lundy subsequently admitted to her superiors that she had lied,[264] and on June 17, 2003, she pleaded guilty to testifying falsely and was sentenced to a suspended ninety-day jail sentence and a $250 fine.[265]

---

258 191 S.W.3d 569 (Ky. 2006).

259 Id. at 580; see Dan Eggen, FBI Laboratory Moves to New Home, WASH. POST, Apr. 25, 2003, at A21 (discussing Lundy's erroneous testimony and her subsequent indictment); Joseph Gerth, Judge Rules Attorney's Office Can Remain on Ragland Case, LOUISVILLE COURIER-J., Oct. 19, 2002, at B4 (addressing the aftermath of Lundy's false testimony); John Solomon, FBI Lab Still Plagued by Problems, CINCINNATI POST (Ohio), Apr. 16, 2003, at 20 ("Weeks after testifying at a court hearing in a Kentucky murder, FBI scientist Kathleen Lundy told her superiors a secret. She knowingly gave false testimony about her specialty of lead bullet analysis.").

260 Ragland, 191 S.W.3d at 574.

261 Id. at 580.

262 Id. ("Lundy admitted that her testimony at the Daubert hearing was false and that she knew prior to the Daubert hearing that Winchester purchased its bullet lead in billets in 1994.").

263 The court noted this point in Ragland:

> The significance of the difference is that Winchester's furnace has only a 15,000-pound capacity whereas some secondary smelters melt lead in crucibles having up to 200,000-pound capacities. Lundy testified that approximately one million bullets can be manufactured from a 15,000 pound melt. If so, approximately thirteen million bullets can be manufactured from a 200,000 pound melt, significantly increasing the number of bullets that would be analytically indistinguishable. …

Id. at 576.

264 See Charles Piller & Robin Mejia, Science Casts Doubt on FBI's Bullet Evidence, L.A. TIMES, Feb. 3, 2003, at A1 (reporting that, in a sworn affidavit, Lundy "admitted that her trial testimony was untruthful" and that she "blamed her conduct partly on a sense of crisis in her work, fed by 'new and repeated challenges to the validity of the science associated with bullet lead comparison analysis'").

265 Mark Pitsch, Ex-FBI Scientist Pleads Guilty, LOUISVILLE COURIER-J., June 18, 2003, at B1; see also Maurice Possley, Study Shoots Holes in Bullet Analysis by FBI, CHI. TRIB., Feb. 11, 2004, § 1, at 14 (noting Lundy's conviction and fine as an example of why bullet lead analysis has fallen under intense scrutiny in recent years); Prosecutors Challenged in Ragland Murder Case, CINCINNATI

b. The Technique

The underlying problems with CBLA went beyond Lundy's prevarication. Although CBLA evidence had been used in trials for over three decades, few studies had been published on the technique.[266] Nevertheless, until recently, the courts admitted this evidence. The published cases reveal a wide variety of interpretive conclusions. In some cases, experts testified only that two exhibits were "analytically indistinguishable."[267] In other cases, experts concluded that samples could have come from the same source or "batch"[268]; in still others, experts stated that the samples came from the same source.[269] The testimony in a number of cases went further and referred to a "box" of ammunition (usually fifty loaded cartridges, sometimes twenty). For example, two specimens:

- could have come from the same box[270];
- could have come from the same box or a box manufactured on the same day[271];
- were consistent with their having come from the same box of ammunition[272];
- probably came from the same box[273];
- must have come from the same box or from another box that would have been made by the same company on the same day.[274]

POST (Ky.), Sept. 6, 2002, at 13A ("Attorneys for both sides were in court for a hearing in which FBI ballistics expert Kathleen Lundy was scheduled to testify about lying during a preliminary hearing in Shane Ragland's murder case.").

266 The overwhelming majority of cases were homicide prosecutions, some of which were capital cases. Because there are few federal homicide prosecutions, CBLA evidence was most commonly used in state prosecutions. See infra notes 267–75 and accompanying text.

267 See Wilkerson v. State, 776 A.2d 685, 689 (Md. Ct. Spec. App. 2001).

268 See State v. Krummacher, 523 P.2d 1009, 1012–13 (Or. 1974) (en banc).

269 See United States v. Davis, 103 F.3d 660, 673–74 (8th Cir. 1996); People v. Lane, 628 N.E.2d 682, 689–90 (Ill. App. Ct. 1993) ("He testified that the two bullets were analytically indistinguishable. Special Agent Riley opined that the two bullets came from the same source and that the match was as good as he had ever seen in his twenty years with the FBI.") (emphasis added).

270 See State v. Strain, 885 P.2d 810, 817 (Utah Ct. App. 1994); State v. Jones, 425 N.E.2d 128, 131 (Ind. 1981).

271 See State v. Grube, 883 P.2d 1069, 1078 (Idaho 1994); People v. Johnson, 499 N.E.2d 1355, 1366 (Ill. 1986); Earhart v. State, 823 S.W.2d 607, 614 (Tex. Crim. App. 1991) (en banc) ("He later modified that statement to acknowledge that analytically indistinguishable bullets which do not come from the same box most likely would have been manufactured at the same place on or about the same day; that is, in the same batch."), vacated, 509 U.S. 917 (1993).

272 See State v. Reynolds, 307 N.C. 184, 187, 297 S.E.2d 532, 534 (1982).

273 See Bryan v. State, 935 P.2d 338, 360 (Okla. Crim. App. 1997).

274 See United States v. Davis, 103 F.3d 660, 666 (8th Cir. 1996) ("An expert testified that such a finding is rare and that the bullets must have come from the same box or from another box that would

Several other (and different) statements appear in the opinions. An early case reported that the specimens "had come from the same batch of ammunition: they had been made by the same manufacturer on the same day and at the *same hour*."[275] One case reports the expert's conclusion with a statistic.[276] In another case, the court discussed the expert's testimony using the expressions "such a finding is rare"[277] and "a very rare finding."[278] In still another case, the expert "opined that the same company produced the bullets at the same time, using the same lead source. Based upon Department of Justice records, she opined that an overseas company called PMC produced the bullets around 1982."[279] Thus, FBI experts ignored the limitations of the technique in many cases. Further, as these cases demonstrate, the testimony was not consistent among the Bureau's own experts, suggesting that the FBI was not monitoring the trial testimony.

In 2004, a National Research Council report undercut much of the FBI expert testimony: "The available data do not support any statement that a crime bullet came from a particular box of ammunition. In particular, references to 'boxes' of ammunition in any form should be avoided as misleading under Federal Rule of Evidence 403."[280] The most

---

have been made by the same company on the same day."); Commonwealth v. Daye, 587 N.E.2d 194, 207 (Mass. 1992) ("Special agent John Riley at the Federal Bureau of Investigation testified that two bullet fragments found in [the victim's] body came from the same box of ammunition or from different boxes that were manufactured at the same place on or about the same date as a bullet retrieved from [the defendant's basement]."); State v. King, 353 N.C. 457, 465, 546 S.E.2d 575, 584 (2001) ("[Kathleen Lundy] opined that, based on her lead analysis, the bullets she examined either came from the same box of cartridges or came from different boxes of the same caliber, manufactured at the same time.").

275 Brown v. State, 601 P.2d 221, 224 (Alaska 1979) (emphasis added).

276 Earhart, 823 S.W.2d at 614.

277 Davis, 103 F.3d at 666.

278 Id. at 667.

279 People v. Villarta, No. H021354, 2002 Cal. App. Unpub. LEXIS 4776, at *15 (Cal. Ct. App. Jan. 17, 2002). In recent years, the testimony became more limited. A 2002 FBI publication states the conclusion as follows: "Therefore, they likely originated from the same manufacturer's source (melt) of lead." Charles A. Peters, The Basis for Compositional Bullet Lead Comparisons, FORENSIC SCI. COMM., July 2002, http://www.fbi.gov/hq/lab/fsc/backissu/july2002/peters.htm (emphasis added). Testimony to the same effect has also been proffered. Transcript of Record at 6, Commonwealth v. Wilcox, No. 0CR2727 (Ky. Cir. Ct. Jefferson County Feb. 28, 2002) (trial testimony of Charles Peters, FBI examiner) ("Well, bullets that are analytically indistinguishable likely come from the same molten sources of lead, uh, as opposed to bullets that have different compositions come from different, uh, melts of lead.").

280 NAT'L RESEARCH COUNCIL, supra note 254, at 7.

disturbing case is Earhart v. State,[281] a capital murder case in which the CBLA evidence apparently played a significant role.[282] The transcript contains the following expert testimony: "We can—from my 21 years experience of doing bullet lead analysis and doing research on boxes of ammunition down though the years I can determine if bullets came from the same box of ammunition. …"[283] The amount of bullets that can be produced from a melt, however, "can range from the equivalent of as few as 12,000 to as many as 35 million 40-grain, .22 caliber longrifle bullets."[284] Earhart was subsequently executed.[285]

In 2003, a federal district court excluded CBLA testimony under the Daubert standard,[286] and in 2005, a New Jersey appellate court reversed a conviction involving CBLA evidence, finding it was "based on erroneous scientific foundations."[287] The FBI

---

281 823 S.W.2d 607 (Tex. Crim. App. 1991). The court summarized the flawed testimony:

> He concluded that the likelihood that two .22 caliber bullets came from the same batch, based on all the .22 bullets made in one year, is approximately .000025 percent, 'give or take a zero.' He subsequently acknowledged, however, that the numbers which he used to reach the .000025 percent statistic failed to take into account that there are different types of .22 caliber bullets made each year. …

Id. at 614 (emphasis added).

282 See Earhart v. Johnson, 132 F.3d 1062, 1068 (5th Cir. 1998) (denying habeas relief, the court noted: "Given the significant role the bullet evidence played in the prosecution's case, we shall therefore assume Earhart could have made a sufficient threshold showing that he was entitled to a defense expert under Texas law.").

283 Transcript of Record at 5248–49, State v. Earhart, No. 4064, Dist. Ct. Lee County, 21st Judicial Dist., Texas (testimony of John Riley). Riley testified:

Well, bullets that are … analytically indistinguishable compositions … typically are found within the same box of ammunition and that is the case that we have here. Now, bullets that are the same composition can also be found in other boxes of ammunition, but it's most likely those boxes would have been manufactured at the same place on or about the same date.

Id. at 5258. But see Transcript of Record, supra note 279, at 1-2 (Daubert testimony of Charles Peters). In a Daubert hearing, Peters noted:

We have never testified, to my knowledge, that that bullet came from that box. We'd never say that. All we are testifying is that that bullet, or that victim fragment or something, the bullet, either came from that box or the many boxes that were produced at the same time.

Id. (emphasis added).

284 NAT'L RESEARCH COUNCIL, supra note 254, at 6.

285 See Death Penalty Information Center, Searchable Database of Executions, http://www.deathpenaltyinfo.org/executions.php (search for "Earhart" under "Find Person" search box) (last visited Oct. 10, 2007).

286 United States v. Mikos, No. 02 CR 137, 2003 WL 22922197 (N.D. Ill. Dec. 9, 2003).

287 State v. Behn, 868 A.2d 329, 331 (N.J. Super. Ct. App. Div. 2005).

discontinued CBLA testing in 2005, although the Bureau maintained that the test was reliable.[288] Other courts rejected this type of evidence the following year.[289]

4. FINGERPRINT UNIT

a. The Mayfield Affair

Like many other forensic sciences, fingerprint comparisons gained judicial acceptance long before the demanding Daubert standard became operative.[290] Numerous attacks, albeit unsuccessful, have been launched against fingerprint evidence in recent years.[291] In many of these cases, FBI examiners testified that there is a "zero error" rate in fingerprint

288 Eric Lichtblau, F.B.I. Abandons Disputed Test for Bullets from Crime Scene, N.Y. TIMES, Sept. 2, 2005, at A2; see also John Solomon, FBI's Forensic Test Full of Holes, WASH. POST, Nov. 18, 2007, at A1 (reporting that the FBI had failed to take adequate steps to notify affected defendants and courts of the NRC report's negative conclusions).

289 See Ragland v. Commonwealth, 191 S.W.3d 569, 580 (Ky. 2006) (noting that "[i]f the FBI Laboratory that produced the CBLA evidence now considers such evidence to be of insufficient reliability to justify continuing to produce it, a finding by the trial court that the evidence is both scientifically reliable and relevant would be clearly erroneous"); Clemons v. State, 896 A.2d 1059, 1070 (Md. 2006) ("CBLA is not admissible under the Frye-Reed standard because it is not generally accepted within the scientific community as valid and reliable."); id. at 1078 ("Based on the criticism of the processes and assumptions underlying CBLA, we determine that the trial court erred in admitting expert testimony based on CBLA because of the lack of general acceptance of the process in the scientific community."). Other defendants have not been as fortunate. See Commonwealth v. Fisher, 870 A.2d 864, 871 (Pa. 2005) ("The CBLA evidence, at best, established a possible connection between Appellant and the bullets recovered from the victim's body."); see also United States v. Davis, 406 F.3d 505, 509 (8th Cir. 2005) ("Davis's trial counsel cannot be said to be ineffective for failing to challenge the FBI's methodology on a basis that was not advanced by the scientific community at the time of trial.").

290 The first reported case was People v. Jennings, 96 N.E. 1077 (Ill. 1911).

291 See generally Simon A. Cole, Grandfathering Evidence: Fingerprint Admissibility Rulings from Jennings to Llera Plaza and Back Again, 41 AM. CRIM. L. REV. 1189 (2004) (discussing the post-Daubert fingerprint challenges); Jennifer Mnookin, Fingerprint Evidence in an Age of DNA Profiling, 67 BROOK. L. REV. 13, 43 (2001) ("[W]hat is striking, even astonishing, is that no serious effort to challenge either the weight or admissibility of fingerprint evidence ever emerged—until 1999."); Sandy L. Zabell, Fingerprint Evidence, 13 J.L. & POL'Y 143, 170 (2005) ("The argument that no latent print has ever been found to match the rolled print from a different person is … misleading because no systematic search for such pairs on the entire databank of millions of fingerprints has ever been performed.").

examinations.[292] Although courts have accepted this astounding statement, the investigation of the terrorist train bombing in Madrid on March 11, 2004, which killed 191 and injured 2,000, undermined this claim.[293] The FBI got it wrong, misidentifying Brandon Mayfield, a Portland lawyer, as the source of the crime scene prints.[294]

To its credit, the FBI initiated an investigation using outside experts. The resulting report[295] raised a number of disquieting issues. First, the "dissimilarities [between prints] ... were easily observed when a detailed analysis of the latent print was conducted."[296] In short, it was not a difficult fingerprint to interpret. Second, the mistake was attributed in part to "confirmation bias"[297]—a well-established phenomenon that is frequently ignored in forensic work.[298] In other words, once the examiner made up his mind, he saw what he expected to see during reexaminations. Third, a review by another examiner was not conducted blind—i.e., the reviewer knew that a positive identification had already been made[299]—and thus was also subject to the influence of confirmation bias. Fourth, the culture at the laboratory was poorly suited to detecting mistakes. As the report noted, "[t]o disagree was not an expected response."[300] Fifth, proficiency testing was apparently not sufficiently rigorous.[301] Surprisingly, the report repeatedly alluded to the need to be cautious due to the "inherent pressure of a high-profile case,"[302] leaving one to wonder about the routine case.

---

292 See, e.g., United States v. Havvard, 117 F. Supp. 2d 848, 854 (S.D. Ind. 2000) ("The government claims the error rate for the method is zero."), aff'd, 260 F.3d 597 (7th Cir. 2001).

293 See Sarah Kershaw & Eric Lichtblau, Spain Had Doubts Before U.S. Held Lawyer in Blast, N.Y. TIMES, May 26, 2004, at A1.

294 See Sara Kershaw, Spain and U.S. at Odds on Mistaken Terror Arrest, N.Y. TIMES, June 5, 2004, at A1 (reporting that Spanish authorities cleared Brandon Mayfield and matched the fingerprints to an Algerian national); Flynn McRoberts & Maurice Possley, Report Blasts FBI Lab: Peer Pressure Led to False ID of Madrid Fingerprint, CHI. TRIB., Nov. 14, 2004, § 1, at 1.

295 Stacey, supra note 30.

296 Id. at 714.

297 Id. at 713.

298 See infra notes 399–413 and accompanying text (discussing cognitive bias).

299 Stacey, supra note 30, at 715. Indeed, a third expert, from outside the FBI, also confirmed the identification. Id. at 709.

300 Id. at 713.

301 Id. at 716 ("Verifiers should be given challenging exclusions during blind proficiency tests to ensure that they are independently applying ACE-V methodology correctly. ...").

302 Id. at 713, 716.

The I.G. also reviewed the Mayfield case.[303] Among other things,[304] the I.G. Report concluded that "the misidentification could have been prevented through a more rigorous application of several principles of latent fingerprint identification."[305] In addition, a significant cause of the misidentification was "reasoning 'backward' from features that were visible in the known prints of Mayfield."[306] As the Report explained: "Having found as many as 10 points of unusual similarity, the FBI examiners began to 'find' additional features in [the print] that were not really there, but rather were suggested to the examiners by features in the Mayfield prints."[307] After noting the controversy among examiners about Level 3 details, the Report concluded that the examiners "apparently misinterpreted distortions in [the print] as real features corresponding to Level 3 details seen in Mayfield's known fingerprints."[308] Furthermore, the FBI Lab ignored the possibility that it had erred: "FBI examiners did not attempt to determine the basis of the [Spanish National Police's] doubts before reiterating that they were 'absolutely confident' in the identification on April 15, a full week before the FBI Laboratory met with the SNP."[309]

---

303 See OFFICE OF THE INSPECTOR GENERAL, U.S. DEPARTMENT OF JUSTICE, A REVIEW OF THE FBI'S HANDLING OF THE BRANDON MAYFIELD CASE, UNCLASSIFIED EXECUTIVE SUMMARY 9 (2006) [hereinafter 2006 I.G. REPORT].

304 The I.G. Report also highlighted the lack of blind verification: "[U]nder procedures in place at the time of the Mayfield identification, the verifier was aware that an identification had already been made by a prior FBI examiner at the time he was requested to conduct the verification." Id. at 10–11.

305 Id. at 6.

306 Id. at 7.

307 Id.

308 Id. at 8 ("Because Level 3 details are so small, the appearance of such details in fingerprints is highly variable, even between different fingerprints made by the same finger. As a result, the reliability of Level 3 details is the subject of some controversy within the latent fingerprint community."). Level 1 details are general ridge patterns—whorls, loops, and arches. Level 2 features involve ridge characteristics, such as ridge endings, bifurcations, islands, and dots. Level 3 features are "even smaller details of the number and shape of the [sweat] pores on the ridges." GIANNELLI & IMWINKELRIED, supra note 12, § 16.07[a], at 897.

309 2006 I.G. REPORT, supra note, 303, at 10. The I.G. made several recommendations that went beyond the Bureau's internal report:

> These include recommendations that the Laboratory [1] develop criteria for the use of Level 3 details to support identifications, [2] clarify the "one discrepancy rule" to assure that it is applied in a manner consistent with the level of certainty claimed for latent fingerprint identifications, [3] require documentation of features observed in the latent fingerprint before the comparison phase to help prevent circular reasoning, [4] adopt alternate procedures for blind verifications, [5] review prior cases in which the identification of a criminal suspect was made on the basis of only one latent fingerprint searched through IAFIS [Integrated Automated Fingerprint Identification

b. Other Mistakes

The Mayfield imbroglio was not the only fingerprint mishap recently reported.[310] Stephan Cowans was released after serving six years in a Massachusetts prison for the nonfatal shooting of a police officer.[311] His was the first conviction overturned on DNA evidence in which fingerprint evidence had been crucial in securing the wrongful conviction.[312] Commenting on the case, Professor Mnookin wrote: "[T]he fingerprint community has little motivation to investigate how often they make mistakes. Fingerprint examiners regularly assert in court that the technique is error-free and that fingerprint matches are a sure thing. ... [F]ingerprints cannot possibly be as perfect a technique as the experts presently claim."[313]

Riky Jackson's prints were similarly misidentified. He was convicted of murder in 1997 based on bloody fingerprints discovered on a window fan.[314] The police expert, Anthony Paparo, matched eleven friction points to Jackson's prints.[315] At trial, Paparo and two other prosecution experts testified to a match. In contrast, two defense experts, both retired FBI examiners, testified that there was no match.[316] Nevertheless, Jackson was convicted

---

> System], and [6] require more meaningful and independent documentation of the causes of errors as part of the Laboratory's corrective action procedures.

Id. at 14.

310 See Simon A. Cole, More Than Zero: Accounting for Error in Latent Fingerprint Identification, 95 J. CRIM. L. & CRIMINOLOGY 985, 1001–16 (2005) (collecting twenty-two cases involving mistakes). Other problematic fingerprint cases include Imbler v. Craven, 298 F. Supp. 795 (C.D. Cal. 1969) (expert failed to observe an exculpatory fingerprint in a murder case, in which the death penalty was imposed), aff'd, 424 F.2d 631 (9th Cir. 1970) and State v. Caldwell, 322 N.W.2d 574, 586 (Minn. 1982) ("The fingerprint expert's testimony was damning—and it was false."). See also Michael Specter, Do Fingerprints Lie?, NEW YORKER, May 27, 2002, at 96 (discussing a holding by a Philadelphia judge that limited the use of fingerprint evidence due to scientific fallibility); James E. Starrs, A Miscue in Fingerprint Identification: Causes and Concerns, 12 J. POLICE SCI. & ADMIN. 287 (1984) (discussing the misidentification of fingerprints in State v. Caldwell).

311 Commonwealth v. Cowans, 756 N.E.2d 622, 625 (Mass. App. Ct. 2001) ("A fingerprint left on the glass mug was matched to the defendant.").

312 See Elizabeth F. Loftus & Simon A. Cole, Letter, Contaminated Evidence, 304 SCIENCE 959, 959 (2004) ("[F]orensic scientists remain stubbornly unwilling to confront and control the problem of bias, insisting that it can be overcome through sheer force of will and good intentions.").

313 Jennifer L. Mnookin, Editorial, A Blow to the Credibility of Fingerprint Evidence, BOSTON GLOBE, Feb. 2, 2004, at A15.

314 Flynn McRoberts et al., Forensics Under the Microscope: Unproven Techniques Sway Courts, Erode Justice, CHI. TRIB., Oct. 17, 2004, § 1, at 1.

315 Id.

316 See CNN Presents: Reasonable Doubt: Can We Trust Crime Labs? (CNN television broadcast Jan. 9, 2005).

and sentenced to life imprisonment.[317] Frustrated, the defense experts filed a complaint with the International Association of Identification concerning the prosecution experts' testimony.[318] This triggered an FBI review, which concluded that the government experts had erred.[319] Jackson was released from prison.[320]

c. Lack of Research

Another distressing revelation surfaced in United States v. Mitchell,[321] the first post-Daubert attack on fingerprint evidence. In March 2000, the National Institute of Justice ("NIJ"), the research arm of the Department of Justice, released a solicitation for fingerprint research. The "Introduction" to the solicitation stated that Daubert "require[d] scientists to address the reliability and validity of the methods used in their analysis. Therefore, the purpose of this solicitation is to … provide greater scientific foundation for forensic friction ridge (fingerprint) identification."[322] After the Mitchell trial, the defense attorney learned that the solicitation had been postponed, arguably so it could not be used in Mitchell to support the defense challenge.[323] The Third Circuit commented on the testimony of Dr. Richard Rau, the NIJ official who coordinated the drafting of the solicitation for the Department of Justice:

We are deeply discomforted by Mitchell's contention—supported by Dr. Rau's account of events, though contradicted by other witnesses—that a conspiracy within the Department of Justice intentionally delayed the release of the solicitation until after Mitchell's jury reached a verdict. Dr. Rau's story, if true, would be a damning indictment of the ethics of those involved.[324]

---

317 Id.

318 Id.

319 See 60 Minutes: The Fallibility of Fingerprints As Evidence (CBS television broadcast Jan. 5, 2003).

320 Id.

321 365 F.3d 215 (3d Cir. 2004).

322 NAT'L INST. OF JUSTICE, SOLICITATION: FORENSIC FRICTION RIDGE (FINGERPRINT) EXAMINATION VALIDATION STUDIES 3 (2000).

323 See Robert Epstein, Fingerprints Meet Daubert: The Myth of Fingerprint "Science" Is Revealed, 75 S. CAL. L. REV. 605, 628 n.122 (2002) ("Internal documents of the NIJ presently on file with the author … reveal that the Institute was ready to publish the Solicitation in September of 1999, but that at the FBI's request, publication was delayed until after Mitchell's trial."). Epstein was the defense counsel in Mitchell.

324 Mitchell, 365 F.3d at 255. The court also noted:

> [Mitchell's] most damaging evidence came from Dr. Richard Rau of the NIJ, who coordinated the drafting of the solicitation. Rau testified to conversations at a September 1999 meeting among

Moreover, a subsequent attempt to establish an empirical basis for fingerprints was thwarted. An editorial in the prestigious scientific journal Science, entitled "Forensic Science: Oxymoron?" and written by the editor in chief, discussed the cancellation of a National Academies project designed to examine various forensic science techniques, including fingerprinting, because the Departments of Justice and Defense insisted on a right of review that the Academies had refused to other grant sponsors.[325] In sum, not only is there a lack of empirical support for fingerprints,[326] but the proponents of the technique are undercutting efforts to establish such a basis.[327]

II. REGULATING CRIME LABORATORIES

A. The DNA Model

As the above cases demonstrate, the problems with crime labs are systemic. Regulation is the answer, but there is no need to start from scratch. DNA labs are presently regulated and can serve as a model for all crime laboratory units.[328]

> himself, Donald Kerr (the Assistant Director of the FBI in charge of the FBI crime laboratory), David Boyd (the Deputy Director of the NIJ), and others. Rau claimed that at that meeting Kerr and Boyd agreed to withhold release of the solicitation until the end of Mitchell's trial. In response to Dr. Rau's testimony, the government called Kerr, Boyd, and the other individuals at the meeting to testify that Dr. Rau's account of the delay in releasing the solicitation was incorrect and that the delay was caused by budgetary issues.

Id. at 232.

325 Donald Kennedy, Editorial, Forensic Science: Oxymoron?, 302 SCIENCE 1625, 1625 (2003).

326 See Donald Kennedy & Richard A. Merrill, Assessing Forensic Science, ISSUES SCI. & TECH., Fall 2003, at 33, 34. The authors note:

> The increased use of DNA analysis, which has undergone extensive validation, has thrown into relief the less firmly credentialed status of other forensic science identification techniques (fingerprints, fiber analysis, hair analysis, ballistics, bite marks, and tool marks). These have not undergone the type of extensive testing and verification that is the hallmark of science elsewhere.

Id.

327 Congress appropriated $1,500,000 to the National Academies to create an independent Forensic Science Committee to study forensic science and issue a report. See H.R. REP. NO. 109–272, at 121 (2005) (Conf. Rep.); S. REP. NO. 109–088, at 46 (2005). A committee has recently been appointed.

328 See Paul C. Giannelli, Regulating Crime Laboratories: The Impact of DNA Evidence, 13 J. L. & POL'Y 59 (2006) (discussing the history of crime labs in this country and the affect DNA profiling has had on them).

[Mitchell's] most damaging evidence came from Dr. Richard Rau of the NIJ, who coordinated the drafting of the solicitation. Rau testified to conversations at a September 1999 meeting among himself, Donald Kerr (the Assistant Director of the FBI in charge of the FBI crime laboratory), David Boyd (the Deputy Director of the NIJ), and others. Rau claimed that at that meeting Kerr and Boyd agreed to withhold release of the solicitation until the end of Mitchell's trial. In response to Dr. Rau's testimony, the government called Kerr, Boyd, and the other individuals at the meeting to testify that Dr. Rau's account of the delay in releasing the solicitation was incorrect and that the delay was caused by budgetary issues.

In 1988, the FBI established the Technical Working Group on DNA Analysis Methods ("TWGDAM") to develop quality control standards for DNA labs.[329] Moreover, the National Academies issued two reports on the subject, noting the importance of certain practices: "No laboratory should let its results with a new DNA typing method be used in court, unless it has undergone ... proficiency testing via blind trials."[330] Perhaps the most important development was the passage of the DNA Identification Act of 1994.[331] It authorized the creation of a national database for the DNA profiles of convicted offenders as well as one for crime scene profiles: the Combined DNA Index System ("CODIS"). Bringing CODIS online was a monumental endeavor, and its successful operation required an effective quality assurance program.[332] To effectuate this goal, the statute created a DNA Advisory Board ("DAB") to assist in promulgating quality assurance standards.[333] The Act also required proficiency testing for analysts in the FBI as well as those in labs participating

329 TWGDAM would later function under the statutorily-created DNA Advisory Board ("DAB"). It was renamed Scientific Working Group on DNA Analysis Methods ("SWGDAM") in 1999 and replaced the DAB when the latter expired. See infra notes 457–65 and accompanying text (discussing the Board's composition).

330 NAT'L RESEARCH COUNCIL, DNA TECHNOLOGY IN FORENSIC SCIENCE 55 (1992) [hereinafter NRC I REPORT]; see also NAT'L RESEARCH COUNCIL, THE EVALUATION OF FORENSIC DNA EVIDENCE 73 (1996) [hereinafter NRC II REPORT]. The Council is the Academies' research arm. The FBI requested and funded both reports.

331 Pub. L. No. 103–322, 108 Stat. 2065 (codified as amended at 42 U.S.C.A. §§ 1413114134) (West 2005).

332 OFFICE OF INSPECTOR GEN., U.S. DEP'T OF JUSTICE, AUDIT REPORT, THE COMBINED DNA INDEX SYSTEM ii (2001) [hereinafter 2001 I.G. REPORT] ("[T]he integrity of the data contained in CODIS is extremely important since the DNA matches provided by CODIS are frequently a key piece of evidence linking a suspect to a crime.").

333 42 U.S.C.A § 14131(a) (West 2005). The legislation contained a sunset provision: DAB would expire after five years unless extended by the Director of the FBI. The Board was extended through the sixth year to complete tasks and the Scientific Working Group on DNA Analysis Methods ("SWGDAM") again took over responsibility. NORAH RUDIN & KEITH INMAN, AN INTRODUCTION TO FORENSIC DNA ANALYSIS 176, 180 (2d ed. 2002).

in the national database or receiving federal funding.[334] DAB Standard 13 implements these requirements.[335]

DAB also promulgated standards governing (1) analytical protocols, (2) equipment calibration and maintenance procedures, and (3) administrative and technical reviews of test results.[336] Among other requirements, labs must (a) review their procedures "annually or whenever substantial changes are made to protocol(s)," and (b) compare their results with available National Institute of Standards and Technology ("NIST") reference materials or "standards traceable to NIST standards."[337] The DNA Act, however, suffered from one significant drawback: it failed to require the accreditation of DNA labs,[338] an omission rectified by the enactment of the "Justice for All Act of 2004."[339]

---

334 42 U.S.C.A § 14132(b)(2) (West 2005) (requiring external proficiency testing for CODIS participation); id. § 1433(a)(1)(A) (requiring external proficiency testing for FBI examiners). The statute was subsequently amended to require accreditation, which in turn mandates proficiency testing.

335 DNA Advisory Board, Quality Assurance Standards for Forensic DNA Testing Laboratories, Standard 13 (1998), available at http://www.fbi.gov/hq/lab/fsc/backissu/july2000/codis2b.htm ("Examiners and other personnel designated by the technical manager or leader who are actively engaged in DNA analysis shall undergo, at regular intervals of not to exceed 180 days, external proficiency testing in accordance with these proficiency standards. Such external testing shall be an open proficiency testing program."). An open test is a non-blind test. See RUDIN & INMAN, supra note 333, at 180 ("The power of the DAB has been substantial, primarily because any agency requesting federal development funds for forensic DNA testing or DNA databasing must demonstrate compliance with the standards set by this group.").

336 DNA Advisory Board, supra note 335, Standard 9 (analytical procedures), Standard 10 (equipment calibration and maintenance), and Standard 12 (administrative and technical review of all case files).

337 Id., Standard 9.5.

338 In an attempt to address this deficiency, the preface to the DAB Standards recommended that "forensic laboratories performing DNA analysis seek such accreditation with all deliberate speed." Id., Preface. Some states require accreditation of DNA labs. See, e.g., CAL. PENAL CODE § 297 (West Supp. 2007) (requiring accreditation by ASCLD/LAB or any certifying body approved by ASCLD/LAB); see also supra note 44 (discussing Indiana's accreditation requirement).

339 Pub. L. No. 108–405, § 1(a), 118 Stat. 2260 (codified as amended in scattered sections of 18 U.S.C. & 42 U.S.C.). The DNA Identification Act of 1994 was amended to require accreditation "by a nonprofit professional association of persons actively involved in forensic science that is nationally recognized within the forensic science community" within two years and to "undergo external audits, not less than once every 2 years, that demonstrate compliance with standards established by the Director of the Federal Bureau of Investigation." Pub. L. No. 103–322, 118 Stat. 2065 (codified as amended at 42 U.S.C.A. § 14132(b)(2) (West 2005)).

DNA cases, however, make up only a small portion of crime lab work—under four percent[340]—and only a few jurisdictions require accreditation of labs conducting other forensic examinations.[341] Thus, the paradox: the most scientifically sound procedure—DNA analysis—is the most extensively regulated, while many forensic techniques with questionable scientific pedigrees are completely unregulated.

As a discipline, forensic science has been moving toward the accreditation of laboratories, the certification of examiners, and the standardization of procedures.[342] These requirements should be mandatory, not permissive. Self-regulation is a lofty ideal but not nearly enough to ensure the integrity of a crime laboratory's work product.[343] An effective quality assurance program requires written procedures and a designated professional who is specifically responsible for the implementation of the program, as the DAB standards mandate for DNA analysis.[344] An enforcement mechanism, such as accreditation, also needs to be in place.

B. Accreditation of Crime Laboratories

Citing clinical laboratories, which are regulated under the Clinical Laboratory Improvements Act of 1988,[345] commentators have argued that crime laboratories should also be regulated.[346] Currently, ASCLD/LAB operates an accreditation program for

340 See Jan S. Bashinski & Joseph L. Peterson, Forensic Sciences, in LOCAL GOVERNMENT: POLICE MANAGEMENT 559, 562 (William Geller & Darrel Stephens eds. 4th ed. 2003) ("[R]equests for serology/DNA, arson, trace evidence, and questioned document cases represent only a small fraction (3.4 percent) of the cases. ...").

341 See infra notes 353–56 and accompanying text.

342 See Bashinski & Peterson, supra note 340, at 577–78.

343 See Stacey, supra note 30, at 717 ("Many agencies are slow to [report erroneous identifications] or refuse to admit that errors have occurred.").

344 See generally DNA Advisory Board, supra note 335, Standard 3 (1998) (requiring a quality assurance program).

345 Pub. L. No. 100-578, 102 Stat. 2903 (codified as amended in 42 U.S.C. § 263a (2004)).

346 See, e.g., Randolph N. Jonakait, Forensic Science: The Need for Regulation, 4 HARV. J. L. & TECH. 109, 191 (1991) ("Current regulation of clinical labs indicates that a regulatory system can improve crime laboratories."); Lander, supra note 1, 505 ("At present, forensic science is virtually unregulated—with the paradoxical result that clinical laboratories must meet higher standards to be allowed to diagnose strep throat than forensic labs must meet to put a defendant on death row."); Jack B. Weinstein, Science, and the Challenges of Expert Testimony in the Courtroom, 77 OR. L. REV. 1005, 1011 (1998) ("Accreditation of laboratories presenting research in courts should provide a minimum standard for gauging the credibility of the research and testimony offered."); see also Scheck & Neufeld, supra note 16 ("There is a model for improvement. The 1988 Clinical Laboratory Improvement Act

public and private crime laboratories.[347] Requirements include ensuring the integrity of evidence, adhering to valid and generally accepted procedures, employing qualified examiners, and operating quality assurance programs—i.e., proficiency testing, technical reviews, audits, and corrective action procedures.[348] Over 240 laboratories have been accredited, and judicial opinions are approvingly citing these accreditation standards in their admissibility decisions.[349] Only ten percent of the laboratories that apply satisfy these standards on the first inspection.[350] In addition, Forensic Quality Services accredits laboratories, including those conducting DNA profiling, according to standards defined by the International Organization for Standardization ("ISO").[351] The National Association of Medical Examiners ("NAME") runs an accreditation program for Coroners and Medical

---

provided accountability for laboratories that perform medical tests. A mistake in health tests can have dire results—not only for the patient, but also for the lab, which risks losing accreditation.").

347 Established in 1981, ASCLD/LAB accredits labs for a five-year period. See AM. SOC'Y OF CRIME LAB. DIRS., LAB. ACCREDITATION BD., PROFICIENCY REVIEW PROGRAM 2 (2006), http://www.ascld-lab.org/legacy/pdf/alpd1002.pdf. ASCLAD/LAB has been criticized for being too close to the labs it accredits. See Arvizu, supra note 32, at 20–21 ("The ASCLD/LAB is essentially a trade organization of crime laboratory directors. The membership of the ASCLD/LAB delegate assembly consists solely of the laboratory directors of ASCLD accredited laboratories."); Possley et al., supra note 2 (quoting former Cook County prosecutor and Republican state representative James Durkin) ("'I believe they are more of a fraternal organization than an authoritative scientific body.'"). This criticism is overblown. ASCLD/LAB has been one of the most effective reform mechanisms in forensic science over the last decade by operating a voluntary accreditation program, by investigating the Zain fiasco in West Virginia, and by issuing a critical report in the Earl Washington case in Virginia. See supra notes 54 (Zain inquiry) and 217 (Washington case).

348 Bashinski & Peterson, supra note 340, at 578.

349 See, e.g., Smith v. State, 702 N.E.2d 668, 673 (Ind. 1998) ("[T]he [DNA] lab was accredited by the American Society of Crime Lab Directors in 1990. Furthermore, the lab runs its tests under controlled conditions, follows specific protocols, and conducts quality testing on the kits and the analysts.").

350 See Kenneth E. Melson, Crime Laboratory Accreditation: The Assurance of Quality in the Forensic Sciences, in A.B.A. CRIMINAL JUSTICE SECTION, THE STATE OF CRIMINAL JUSTICE 6–7 (2003) ("[L]ess than ten percent of applicant laboratories achieve accreditation following the initial inspection.").

351 See Forensic Quality Services, http://www.forquality.org/(last visited Nov. 29, 2007) (explaining accreditation procedures). Forensic Quality Services is also one of six accreditation bodies recognized by the National Cooperation for Laboratory Accreditation. National Cooperation for Laboratory Accreditation, Accreditation Bodies Recognized by NACLA, http://nacla. net/recognized.htm (last visited Nov. 29, 2007).

Examiner Offices, and the American Board of Forensic Toxicology accredits toxicology laboratories.[352]

These programs are all voluntary, however, and many laboratories remain unaccredited. Currently, only New York,[353] Oklahoma,[354] and Texas[355] require all their crime labs to be accredited; the California statute covers only DNA labs.[356] In 2002, the President of the American Academy of Forensic Sciences observed:

> Unfortunately, while the ASCLD/LAB program has been successful in accrediting over 200 laboratories, a large number of forensic laboratories in the U.S. remain unaccredited by any agency. ... The same dichotomy exists in certification programs for the practicing forensic scientist, even though forensic certification boards for all the major disciplines have been in existence for over a decade. Why have forensic laboratories and individuals been so reluctant to become accredited or certified?[357]

As the National Academies 1992 DNA Report commented, "[v]oluntary accreditation programs are not enough. Because professional organizations, such as ASCLD-LAB, lack regulatory authority, forensic laboratories could avoid accreditation and still offer DNA typing evidence in criminal proceedings."[358] As noted above, the Justice for All Act of 2004 now mandates accreditation for DNA labs participating in the national database.[359] An accreditation requirement should apply to the entire crime laboratory, not only to DNA units.

---

352 See National Association of Medical Examiners, http://www.thename.org/(follow "About NAME" hyperlink; then follow "General Information" hyperlink) (last visited Oct. 7, 2007); American Board of Forensic Toxicology, http://www.abft.org (last visited Oct. 29, 2007).

353 N.Y. EXEC. LAW § 995b (McKinney Supp. 2007) (requiring accreditation by state Forensic Science Commission).

354 OKLA. STAT. ANN. tit. 74, § 150.37 (West Supp. 2007) (generally requiring accreditation by the American Society of Crime Laboratory Directors/Laboratory Accreditation Board or the American Board of Forensic Toxicology).

355 TEX. CODE CRIM. PROC. ANN. art. 38.35 (Vernon Supp. 2006–2007) (requiring accreditation by the Department of Public Safety).

356 CAL. PENAL CODE § 297 (West Supp. 2007) (requiring accreditation by ASCLD/LAB or any certifying body approved by ASCLD/LAB).

357 Graham R. Jones, President's Editorial—The Changing Practice of Forensic Science, 47 J. FORENSIC SCI. 437, 438 (2002).

358 NRC I REPORT, supra note 330, at 106.

359 See supra note 339.

C. Quality Assurance

The key to laboratory performance is quality assurance. Yet, "[s]omewhat surprisingly, crime labs are not generally subject to mandatory quality-assurance standards imposed by federal or state law."[360] Quality assurance consists of several activities: proficiency testing, laboratory audits, technical reviews, and corrective action procedures.

1. Proficiency Testing

Proficiency testing in the forensic sciences dates back thirty years. In 1978, the Laboratory Proficiency Testing Program, sponsored by the Law Enforcement Assistance Administration ("LEAA"), reported the results of the first proficiency tests.[361] Over 200 crime laboratories participated in this program, which involved such common forensic examinations as firearms, blood, drug, and trace evidence analyses.[362] Seventy-one percent of the crime laboratories tested provided unacceptable results in a blood test, 51.4% made errors in matching paint samples, 35.5% erred in a soil examination, and 28.2% made mistakes in firearms identifications.[363] The report concluded: "A wide range of proficiency levels among the nation's laboratories exists, with several evidence types posing serious difficulties for the laboratories …"[364] Thus, although some laboratories performed exceptionally well, the performances of others were disturbing: "65 percent of the laboratories had 80 percent or more of their results fall into the acceptable category. At the other end of the spectrum, 3 percent of laboratories had less than 50 percent of their responses considered acceptable."[365] Similarly, certain types of examinations caused few problems, whereas others produced very high rates of "unacceptable proficiency."[366] Unacceptable proficiency was most often attributed to: (1) misinterpretation of test results due to carelessness or inexperience; (2) failure to employ adequate or appropriate methodology;

---

360 Bales, supra note 236, at 54; see also Joseph L. Peterson, The Crime Lab, in THINKING ABOUT POLICE 184, 196 (Carl B. Klockars ed., 1983) ("Crime laboratories are unique among publicly supported scientific operations in that few participate in external quality assurance programs.")

361 See JOSEPH L. PETERSON ET AL., CRIME LABORATORY PROFICIENCY TESTING RESEARCH PROGRAM (1978).

362 Id. at 251.

363 Id. at 251 tbl. 89. One blood test had only 3.8% unacceptable results. Id.

364 Id. at 3.

365 Peterson, supra note 360, at 195.

366 See id. at 188–91. The number of laboratories responding ranged from a low of 65 to a high of 205. Id. at 194. An unacceptable response did not necessarily mean an incorrect one. Id. at 191. Other reasons for an unacceptable designation included a correct response for the wrong reason, an unsupported, inclusive response, multiple responses, and incomplete responses. Id.

(3) mislabeling or contamination of primary standards; and (4) inadequate databases or standard spectra.[367]

Given these results, one would have expected the implementation of fairly extensive reforms. However, "[t]he startling conclusions from that research led to some efforts to improve conditions in the laboratories, but these encounter[ed] institutional inertia against reform."[368] In sum, widespread reform failed to materialize.

The Forensic Science Foundation was the next organization to conduct proficiency testing—from 1978 to 1991.[369] The results of these tests confirmed the findings of the LEAA study—that forensic labs show unacceptably high error rates in certain fields. Several types of examinations caused concern: fiber, paint, glass, and body fluid comparisons resulted in incorrect results in more than ten percent of the cases.[370] A review of five handwriting comparison proficiency tests in 1987 showed that, at best, "[d]ocument examiners were correct 57% of the time and incorrect 43% of the time."[371] This program has continued: "By 2000, more than 400 laboratories worldwide were participating in the program. Although the majority of laboratories have been found to produce correct results, the program has revealed errors stemming from inadequate standard reference

---

367 PETERSON ET AL., supra note 361, at 258. Professor Peterson, one of the report's authors, later commented: "In spite of being a firm advocate of forensic science, I must acknowledge that a disturbingly high percentage of laboratories are not performing routine tests competently, as shown by our proficiency testing." Symposium on Science and the Rules of Legal Procedure, 101 F.R.D. 599, 645 (1983).

368 Symposium, supra note 367, at 645 (remarks of Professor Joseph L. Peterson). For a more detailed discussion of proficiency testing, see Michael J. Saks, Prevalence and Impact of Ethical Problems in Forensic Science, 34 J. Forensic Sci. 772, 775–78 (1989) (reviewing proficiency testing results and stating, "[p]erhaps the major lessons to be drawn from this are that errors are indeed made and that there is a wide range of interlaboratory variation").

369 See generally Joseph L. Peterson & Penelope N. Markham, Crime Laboratory Proficiency Testing Results, 1978–1991. I: Identification and Classification of Physical Evidence, 40 J. Forensic Sci. 994 (1995) [hereinafter Peterson & Markham, Crime Labs I] (finding that labs had a high degree of success in identifying drugs and typing bloodstains; had moderate success in identifying flammables, explosives, and fibers; and had trouble with animal hair identifications and human hair body location); Joseph L. Peterson & Penelope N. Markham, Crime Laboratory Proficiency Testing Results, 19781991. II: Resolving Questions of Common Origin, 40 J. Forensic Sci. 1009 (1995) [hereinafter Peterson & Markham, Crime Labs II] (finding that labs performed best in determining the origin of finger and palm prints, firearms identifications, and footwear; had moderate success in determining the source of bloodstains, questioned documents, tool marks, and hair; and the least success in identifying paint, glass, fibers, and body fluid mixtures).

370 Peterson & Markham, Crime Labs II, supra note 369, at 1028.

371 D. Michael Risinger et al., Exorcism of Ignorance as a Proxy For Rational Knowledge: The Lessons of Handwriting Identification "Expertise," 137 U. Pa. L. Rev. 731, 748 (1989).

materials, inexperienced examiners, inappropriate tests, or misinterpretation of otherwise good data."[372]

The DNA Identification Act of 1994 required proficiency testing for DNA examiners in the FBI Laboratory and for those in laboratories participating in the national DNA database or receiving federal funding.[373] In addition, a laboratory voluntarily accredited by ASCLD/LAB must engage in a documented program of proficiency testing that measures the capability of its examiners and the reliability of its analytical results.[374] All forensic disciplines should be legislatively obliged to participate in meaningful proficiency testing.[375]

There are several types of proficiency testing: internal or external, and blind or non-blind. External blind testing is by far the best. The DNA Act authorized a study of the feasibility of blind proficiency testing; that study raised questions about the cost and practicability of this type of examination, as well as its effectiveness when compared to other methods of quality assurance, such as accreditation and more stringent external case audits.[376]

---

372 Bashinski & Peterson, supra note 340, at 579.

373 42 U.S.C.A § 14132(b)(2) (West 2005) (mandating external proficiency testing for CODIS participation); id. § 14133(a)(1)(A) (mandating the same for FBI DNA analysts) (2004). As noted earlier, DAB Standard 13 implements this requirement. See supra note 335 and accompanying text. The 1996 National Academies DNA report also recommended proficiency testing. NRC II Report, supra note 330, at 88 ("Recommendation 3.2: Laboratories should participate regularly in proficiency tests, and the results should be available for court proceedings.").

374 Melson, supra note 350, at 8–9. The proficiency tests must be conducted by external providers, where available. Id. at 9. Laboratories are also encouraged to conduct proficiency testing using blind tests prepared internally or externally and submitted as normal casework evidence or by re-examination by another examiner on completed casework. Id. at 9–10.

375 See Bashinski & Peterson, supra note 340, at 579 ("Laboratory proficiency cannot be assumed. It must be positively demonstrated."); see also Third Houston Report, supra note 166, at 37–38 (reporting that the examiner "failed her competency test after, among other things, she indicated the presence of PCP in both blood samples where it was not present, did not detect the morphine presence in the first blood sample, and did not detect either substances in the second blood sample").

376 Joseph L. Peterson et al., The Feasibility of External Blind DNA Proficiency Testing. I. Background and Findings, 48 J. Forensic Sci. 21 (2003). That study concluded:

1. The accreditation system and associated quality assurance guidelines of the DNA Advisory Board need to be given the opportunity to take hold.
2. It is recommended that the DNA Advisory Board generate guidelines for more stringent external case audits for use by ASCLD-LAB, or another relevant accrediting body, as part of the accreditation process. The external case audits should be conducted regularly and serve as a measure of how well accreditation and its associated requirements are working in a quality assurance context.
3. In the extreme, blind proficiency testing is possible, but fraught with problems (including costs), and it is recommended that a blind proficiency testing program be deferred

In addition, the rigor of some voluntary proficiency tests is suspect.[377] For example, a fingerprint examiner from New Scotland Yard testified in one case that the FBI proficiency tests were deficient: "It's not testing their ability. It doesn't test their expertise. I mean I've set these tests to trainees and advanced technicians. And if I gave my experts these tests, they'd fall about laughing."[378] The district court agreed, noting that "the FBI examiners got very high proficiency grades, but the tests they took did not … [O]n the present record I conclude that the proficiency tests are less demanding than they should be."[379] The FBI's own report acknowledged this shortcoming.[380] Similarly, in a trial involving handwriting comparisons, the court wrote:

There were aspects of Mr. Cawley's testimony that undermined his credibility. Mr. Cawley testified that he achieved a 100% passage rate on the proficiency tests that he took and that all of his peers always passed their proficiency tests. Mr. Cawley said that his peers always agreed with each others' results and always got it right. Peer review in such a "Lake Woebegone" environment is not meaningful.[381]

If proficiency programs are not rigorous, they provide only an illusion of reliability. Indeed, by bestowing an undeserved imprimatur, they are affirmatively misleading.

2. Laboratory Audits

Inspections or audits are another significant quality assurance mechanism. They "may range from internal peer review (review of one laboratory section by another or review of

---

> for now until it is more clear how well implementation of the first two recommendations are serving the same purposes as blind proficiency testing.

Id. at 30.

377 See, e.g., United States v. Yee, 134 F.R.D. 161, 208 (N.D. Ohio 1991) ("[T]he F.B.I. program of [DNA] proficiency testing has serious deficiencies, even without consideration of the troubling hint in the record of an impulse at one point to destroy some of the small amount of test data that had been accumulated earlier."), affd sub nom. United States v. Bonds, 12 F.3d 540 (6th Cir. 1993).

378 United States v. Llera Plaza, 188 F. Supp. 2d 549, 558 (E.D. Pa. 2002).

379 Id. at 565; see also United States v. Crisp, 324 F.3d 261, 274 (4th Cir. 2003) (Michael, J., dissenting) ("Proficiency testing is typically based on a study of prints that are far superior to those usually retrieved from a crime scene."); Mnookin, supra note 313 ("There are no systematic proficiency tests to evaluate examiners' skill. Those tests that exist are not routinely used and are substandard.").

380 See supra note 301 and accompanying text.

381 United States v. Lewis, 220 F. Supp. 2d 548, 554 (S.D.W. Va. 2002); see also Crisp, 324 F.3d at 279 (Michael, J., dissenting) ("[A]lthough the government's expert here testified to his success on proficiency tests, the government provides no reason for us to believe that these tests are realistic assessments of an examiner's ability. … See J.A. 342 (testimony of the government's handwriting expert that he has always achieved a perfect score on proficiency tests). …").

the laboratory unit by the audit unit of the department) to a full-scale inspection by a team of external scientists such as the ASCLD/LAB accreditation inspectors."[382]

DAB standards mandate annual internal audits and biannual external audits for DNA labs.[383] Yet, a 2001 I.G. Report found that the audit procedures for CODIS were defective. A review of eight state and local laboratories "disclosed that four laboratories did not fully comply with the FBI's quality assurance standards and national index requirements."[384] In addition, labs had entered unallowable or incomplete profiles into CODIS. The problem stemmed from the fact that the audit did not review the actual DNA profiles, and labs could certify their own compliance instead of reporting audit results directly to the FBI. Here, again, the experience with regulating DNA analysis provides a template. The new federal legislation dictates that "external audits, not less than once every 2 years ... [must] demonstrate compliance with standards established by the Director of the Federal Bureau of Investigation."[385]

As the Houston fiasco demonstrated, internal audits are often not rigorous. That lab passed its internal audits with flying colors, only to be shut down following an external audit.[386]

3. Corrective Action Procedures

DAB standards also require corrective action procedures "whenever proficiency-testing discrepancies and/or casework errors are detected."[387] The value of such a program is illustrated by a series of news articles on the Washington state DNA program. Over a four-year period, the lab documented "contamination or errors in twenty-three of more than 5,000 DNA cases."[388] Because PCR-DNA is extremely sensitive,

382 Bashinski & Peterson, supra note 340, at 587; see also Arvizu, supra note 32, at 25 ("[O]nly an on-site laboratory audit can provide a complete picture of a laboratory. It is one thing to have acceptable written procedures for a laboratory's activities. It is quite another to comply with the procedures on a daily basis.").

383 DNA Advisory Board, supra note 335, Standard 15.1 ("The laboratory shall conduct audits annually in accordance with the standards outlined herein."); id. Standard 15.2 ("Once every two years, a second agency shall participate in the annual audit.").

384 2001 I.G. REPORT, supra note 332, at iii.

385 42 U.S.C.A § 14132(b)(2)(B) (West 2005).

386 See supra notes 199–200 and accompanying text.

387 DNA Advisory Board, supra note 335, Standard 14.1.

388 See Barry K. Logan, Crime Lab Committed to Improvements, SEATTLE POST-INTELLIGENCER, July 30, 2004, at B7. Logan was the lab director.

cross-contamination is always a concern.[389] The reported deficiencies are troublesome,[390] but the lack of any corrective action file would be far more worrisome. In other words, this information may show that the system is working—mistakes are being reported, the first step toward remediation.

D. Standardization of Technical Procedures

Valid procedures, of course, are critical to ensure the accuracy of test results. The 1997 I.G. Report recommended the development of written protocols for scientific procedures.[391] According to the first National Academies Report, "[e]ach DNA typing procedure must be completely described in a detailed, written laboratory protocol."[392] Current DAB standards require DNA analytical protocols, equipment calibration and maintenance procedures, and administrative and technical reviews of test results.[393] They also prescribe developmental and internal validation.[394] Further, all ASCLD/LAB-accredited laboratories must maintain written copies of appropriate technical procedures. These protocols include descriptions of sample preparation methods, controls, standards,

---

389 See John E. Smialek et al., The Microscopic Slide: A Potential DNA Reservoir, FBI LAW ENFORCEMENT BULL., Nov. 2000, at 18, 19. Smialek notes:

> Contamination occurs when the evidence comes in contact with another individual's body fluids through actions, such as sneezing, coughing, or touching. … But, the PCR process cannot distinguish between DNA from a suspect and another source. Therefore, any substantial contamination to the DNA material will result in a confusing result.

Id.

390 See Teichroeb, Rare Look, supra note 23 (reporting that examiners "tainted tests with their own DNA in eight of the 23 cases" and that cross-contamination between cases occurred in three incidents and other mistakes included "throwing out evidence swabs to misreading results, fingering the wrong rape suspect"; the source of contamination in five other tests was unknown).

391 See 1997 I.G. REPORT, supra note 27, Executive Summary, at pt. VII; see also supra note 242 and accompanying text.

392 NRC I REPORT, supra note 330, at 8. The second report stated that "[laboratories should adhere to high quality standards. …" NRC II REPORT, supra note 330, at 88 (citing TWGDAM and DAB standards as examples in Recommendation 3.1).

393 DNA Advisory Board, supra note 335, Standards 9, 10 & 12.

394 Id. Standard 2(ff): ("Validation is a process by which a procedure is evaluated to determine its efficacy and reliability. … Developmental validation is the acquisition of test data and the determination of conditions and limitations of a new or novel DNA methodology …; (2) Internal validation is the accumulation of test data within the laboratory to demonstrate that established methods and procedures perform as expected in the laboratory."). SWGDAM promulgated revised validation guidelines in 2003. See Revised Validation Guidelines, FORENSIC SCI. COMM., July 2004, http://www.fbi.gov/hq/lab/fsc/backissu/july2004/standards/2004_03_standards02.htm.

and calibration procedures, as well as a discussion of precautions, sources of possible error, and literature references.[395]

Based on the DNA experience with TWGDAM, established by the FBI in 1988, comparable groups were set up in fingerprints, controlled substances, trace evidence or materials analysis, questioned documents, fire and explosives, imaging technology, digital evidence, and firearms examination.[396] Moreover, the American Society for Testing and Materials ("ASTM") has promulgated standards in some forensic areas.[397]

In Daubert, the Supreme Court cited the "existence and maintenance of standards controlling the technique's operation" as a relevant factor in assessing the reliability of expert testimony.[398] The adoption and public promulgation of written laboratory protocols would seem to be required by this factor. In fact, any laboratory without such protocols cannot be called a "scientific" laboratory.

E. Problem Issues

Several vexing issues concerning lab procedures surface on a recurring basis. This section addresses four of those issues.

1. Cognitive Bias

Commentators have identified both motivational and cognitive bias as a concern in the forensic setting.[399] As one commentator noted: "To the extent that we are aware of

---

395 Melson, supra note 350, at 8. During accreditation audits, a representative number of laboratory reports are subjected to review to ensure that the conclusions of examiners are reasonable and within the constraints of scientific knowledge. Id. at 9. This technical review assures that laboratory protocols are being utilized. Id. at 8. All new technical procedures must be scientifically validated before being used in casework. Id. See generally AM. SOC'Y OF CRIME LAB. DIRS., supra note 347 (explaining accreditation program).

396 See Bashinski & Peterson, supra note 340, at 580.

397 See generally John J. Lentini, ASTM Standards for Forensic Sciences, 40 J. FORENSIC SCI. 146 (1995) (explaining the work of Committee E30 on Forensic Sciences); Eric Stauffer & John J. Lentini, ASTM Standards for Fire Debris Analysis: A Review, 132 FORENSIC SCI. INT'L 63 (2003), available at http://www.atslab.com/fire/PDF/ASTMStandardsForFireDebrisAnalysis.pdf (discussing updated standards for arson investigations).

398 Daubert v. Merrell Dow Pharm., Inc., 509 U.S. 579, 594 (1993).

399 See infra notes 449–53 and accompanying text (discussing motivational bias); see also Elizabeth F. Loftus & Simon A. Cole, Letter, Contaminated Evidence, 304 SCIENCE 959, 959 (2004) ("[F]orensic scientists remain stubbornly unwilling to confront and control the problem of bias, insisting that it can be overcome through sheer force of will and good intentions.").

our vulnerability to bias, we may be able to control it. In fact, a feature of good scientific practice is the institution of processes—such as blind testing, the use of precise measurements, standardized procedures, statistical analysis—that control for bias."[400] Similarly, the 1996 National Academies DNA Report notes, "[l]aboratory procedures should be designed with safeguards to detect bias and to identify cases of true ambiguity. Potential ambiguities should be documented."[401]

External information provided to lab analysts will often taint their conclusions. For example, "[Professor] Peter DeForest has described investigators who responded to inconclusive results by saying to forensic examiners: 'Would it help if I told you we know he's the guy who did it?'"[402] Joyce Gilchrist often received detectives' views on suspects before she conducted her examinations.[403] Confirmation bias also arose in the misidentification of fingerprints of Brian Mayfield in the Madrid train bombing investigation[404] and other FBI investigations.[405]

As a result of the Mayfield case, several British researchers devised an experiment to test whether external influences can affect the identification process.[406] In particular, they were concerned with confirmation bias similar to that which occurred in the Mayfield misidentification. Fingerprint examiners who were unfamiliar with the Mayfield prints were asked by colleagues to compare a crime scene and suspect print: "They were told that the pair of prints was the one that was erroneously matched by the FBI as the Madrid

---

400 MIKE REDMAYNE, EXPERT EVIDENCE AND CRIMINAL JUSTICE 16 (2001).

401 NRC II REPORT, supra note 330, at 85. The Report adds: "Bias in forensic science usually leads to sins of omission rather than commission. Possibly exculpating evidence might be ignored or rejected." Id. at 84–85.

402 D. Michael Risinger et al., The Daubert/Kumho Implications of Observer Effects in Forensic Science: Hidden Problems of Expectation and Suggestion, 90 CAL. L. REV. 1, 39 (2002) (quoting Peter DeForest, Address at 2d International Conference on Forensic Document Examination (June 14–18, 1999) (notes of Michael Saks, who was present)).

403 See FUHRMAN, supra note 68, at 91 ("When Cook and other homicide detectives gave Gilchrist hair samples from a suspect, they would often let her know that this was the person they wanted to arrest.").

404 See supra notes 297–99 and accompanying text.

405 See Bales, supra note 236, at 52 ("[The 1997 I.G. Report] concluded that an examiner from the lab's explosives unit had erred by purporting to identify the particular explosives used in the [1993] World Trade Center and Oklahoma City bombings. The error stemmed from the examiner's reliance on information that was tied to suspects but not relevant to his scientific analysis.").

406 Itiel E. Dror et el., Contextual Information Renders Experts Vulnerable to Making Erroneous Identifications, 156 FORENSIC SCI. INT'L 74, 75–76 (2006) (explaining the experiment's methodology).

bomber, thus creating an extraneous context that the prints were a non-match."[407] The participants were then instructed to ignore this information.[408] The prints, in fact, were from cases that each of the participants had previously matched.[409] Of the five examiners, only one still judged the print to be a match.[410] The other four changed their opinions; three directly contradicted their prior identifications, and the fourth concluded that there was insufficient data to reach a definite conclusion.[411] "This is striking given that all five experts had seen the identical fingerprints previously and all had decided that the prints were a sound and definite match."[412]

In sum, information from an investigation should not be given to the analyst interpreting the results—i.e., the examiner should generally be "blind" to the case's circumstances and other evidence.[413]

2. Contemporaneous Recordation

The lack of bench notes is often cited in the lab scandals. The West Virginia,[414] Chicago,[415] Houston,[416] and FBI explosive unit[417] investigations all found inadequate

---

407 Id. at 76.

408 Id.

409 Id. at 75.

410 Id.

411 Id.

412 Id. The authors of the study concluded:

> Our study shows that it is possible to alter identification decisions on the same fingerprint, solely by presenting it in a different context. This does not imply that fingerprint and other forensic identifications are not a science, but it does highlight problems of subjectivity, interpretation, and other psychological and cognitive elements that interact and may distort any scientific inquiries.

Id. at 77.

413 One crime lab examiner, "who has worked in the crime lab system since 1998, said she tried not to be swayed by detectives' belief that they had a strong suspect. 'We're all human,' she said. 'I tried not to let it influence me. But I can't say it never does.'" Teichroeb, Rare Look, supra note 23.

414 See supra note 55 and accompanying text.

415 Letter from Sensabaugh, supra note 156 ("Overall, the documentation of the lab work as described in the three pages of lab notes is inadequate and incomplete. Moreover, the formal lab reports describe results of testing for which there is no record in the lab notes. In short, the documentation in this case falls short of accepted scientific standards.").

416 THIRD HOUSTON REPORT, supra note 166, at 28 ("Among other problems it identified, the 2002 DPS audit found that no such written procedures [for case notes and lab reports] existed and identified numerous deficiencies in the documentation contained in the lab reports.").

417 See 1997 I.G. REPORT, supra note 27 (recommending the preparation of adequate case files to support reports); Bales, supra note 236, at 57 (noting that one FBI examiner "testified that he had

documentation in forensic case files.[418] Moreover, in one Supreme Court case, Delaware v. Fensterer,[419] an FBI analyst testified that he could not remember which of three methods he had used to determine that hair found at a murder scene had been forcibly removed.[420] He apparently neglected to record this critical information.

DAB Standards require laboratories to adopt and follow written procedures for taking and maintaining case notes to support the conclusions drawn in laboratory reports: in particular, a case record containing all documentation generated by examiners relating to case analysis is standard practice.[421] Unfortunately, the standards do not specify that the notes be recorded contemporaneously with the examination, a deficiency noted in the 2004 I.G. Report.[422]

3. Laboratory Reports

Most pretrial discovery statutes provide for the disclosure of scientific reports.[423] For example, Federal Rule of Criminal Procedure 16 makes the "results or reports of any physical or mental examination and of any scientific test or experiment" discoverable.[424]

---

performed certain tests that were not described in his notes").

418 See Law v. State, 307 S.E.2d 904, 908 (Ga. 1983) (Smith, J., dissenting) ("It is an insult to intelligent people to say that a scientific test was conducted from which absolutely no notes or records survive. … A basic principle of scientific testing is that careful records of test procedure and results are to be scrupulously maintained. A scientific test without an accompanying report of the testing environment, number of trials, raw results and analyzed data is in reality no test at all.").

419 474 U.S. 15 (1985).

420 Id. at 17. Nevertheless, the Supreme Court declined to find a confrontation violation in this situation. Id. at 20. On remand, however, the Delaware Supreme Court held the opinion inadmissible, but on evidentiary, rather than constitutional, grounds. Fensterer v. State, 509 A.2d 1106, 1109 (Del. 1986). According to court: "While a witness's mere lack of memory as to a particular fact may go only to the weight of that evidence, an expert witness's inability to establish a sufficient basis for his opinion clearly renders the opinion inadmissible under D.R.E. 705." Id. at 1109–10.

421 DNA Advisory Board, supra note 335, Standard 11.1.

422 2004 I.G. Report, supra note 28, at 107. The report commented: "[C]ontemporaneous documentation is important to ensure that the case file accurately reflects the work performed on each evidence item that is tested. … [S]taff members may be unduly influenced by protocol requirements when relying on memory, and document what they know should have occurred when their recollection is vague." Id.

423 See Unif. R. Crim. P. 421(a) (Approved Draft 1974) (specifying that "expert reports" are discoverable); ABA Standards for Criminal Justice: Discovery and Trial by Jury, Standard 11-2.1(a)(iv) (3d ed. 1996).

424 Fed. R. Crim. P. 16(a)(1)(F).

Yet, these rules contain no requirement regarding the content of a laboratory report.[425] The Journal of Forensic Sciences, the official publication of the American Academy of Forensic Sciences, published a symposium on the ethical responsibilities of forensic scientists in 1989.[426] One article discussed a number of laboratory reporting practices, including (1) "preparation of reports containing minimal information in order not to give the 'other side' ammunition for cross-examination," (2) "reporting of findings without an interpretation on the assumption that if an interpretation is required it can be provided from the witness box," and (3) "[o]mitting some significant point from a report to trap an unsuspecting cross-examiner."[427] Fred Zain,[428] Joyce Gilchrist,[429] and Pam Fish,[430] among others, omitted critical information from their reports. These practices could be curbed, if not eliminated, by requiring comprehensive laboratory reports.

Comprehensive lab reports are simply good science.[431] Both DAB[432] and ASCLD/LAB[433] have standards governing laboratory reports. By ensuring that the examiner has

---

425 As a result, the reports are often cryptic or confusing. See Bales, supra note 236, at 56 ("Reports of forensic examinations are sometimes terse to the point of being indecipherable."); Final Houston Report, supra note 170, at 21 ("The awkwardly-stated conclusions appearing in many of the Crime Lab's DNA reports are difficult to understand.").

426 Joseph L. Peterson, Symposium: Ethical Conflicts in the Forensic Sciences, 34 J. Forensic Sci. 717–93 (1989).

427 Douglas M. Lucas, The Ethical Responsibilities of the Forensic Scientist: Exploring the Limits, 34 J. Forensic Sci. 719, 724 (1989). Lucas was the Director of the Centre of Forensic Sciences, Ministry of the Solicitor General, Toronto, Ontario.

428 See supra note 55 and accompanying text.

429 See supra notes 70–117 and accompanying text.

430 See supra notes 150–59 and accompanying text.

431 One scientist has observed that a crime lab report at a minimum should include:

> (a) a description of the analytical techniques used in the test requested by the government or other party, (b) the quantitative or qualitative results with any appropriate qualifications concerning the degree of certainty surrounding them, and (c) an explanation of any necessary presumptions or inferences that were needed to reach the conclusions.

Professor Anna Harrison, Mount Holyoke College, Symposium on Science, supra note 367, at 632.

432 See DNA Advisory Board, supra note 335, Standard 11.1.2 (requiring reports to include (1) a case identifier, (2) a "description of evidence examined," (3) "[a] description of the methodology," (4) the locus tested, (5) the "[r]esults and/or conclusions," (6) "[a]n interpretative statement (either quantitative or qualitative)," (7) the "[d]ate issued," (8) the "[d]isposition of evidence," and (9) "[a] signature and title, or equivalent identification, of the person(s) accepting responsibility of the content of the report").

433 See ASCLD Guidelines for Forensic Laboratory Management Practices, 14 Crime Laboratory Dig. 39, 43 (1987) ("The documentation should be such that a knowledgeable analyst or supervisor, in the absence of the primary analyst, would be able to evaluate and interpret the data." Competent laboratory reports must include (1) an "accurate summary of significant material contained in the case notes,"

followed the prescribed procedure and by permitting external review, lab reports can function as a quality control mechanism. In particular, the report should contain an express statement of the limitations of the technique.[434]

Comprehensive reports also promote good legal policy.[435] Because they are discoverable, they assist attorneys in preparing for trial and in rendering effective representation. Further, determining whether defense counsel should seek the appointment of a defense expert often requires a preliminary assessment by an expert. An expert might be willing to review a report but not want to become further involved in a case without compensation. Unless the report is comprehensive, such a review may be worthless.

4. Testifying Beyond the Report

Experts should generally not testify beyond the scope of the report without issuing a supplemental report. Troedel v. Wainwright,[436] a capital murder case, illustrates the problem. In that case, a report of a gunshot residue test based on neutron activation analysis concluded that swabs "from the hands of Troedel and Hawkins contained antimony and barium [primer residues] in amounts typically found on the hands of a person who has discharged a firearm or has had his hands in close proximity to a discharging firearm."[437] An FBI expert testified in accordance with this report at Hawkins' trial but enhanced his testimony at Troedel's trial, when he testified that "Troedel had fired the murder weapon."[438] In contrast, during federal habeas proceedings, the same expert testified in a deposition that "he could not, from the results of his tests, determine or say to a scientific certainty who had fired the murder weapon" and that "the differences in the amount of

(2) "interpretive information as well as examination results wherever possible," and (3) identification of "the analyst(s) and, if appropriate, the testing methodology.").

434 See NAT'L RESEARCH COUNCIL, supra note 254, at 110 ("The conclusions in laboratory reports should be expanded to include the limitations of compositional analysis of bullet lead evidence. Moreover, a section of the laboratory report translating the technical conclusions into language that a jury could understand would greatly facilitate the proper use of this evidence in the criminal justice system.").

435 The Canadian investigation into the wrongful conviction of Guy Paul Morin made the following recommendation: "The Centre of Forensic Science should establish a written policy on the form and content of reports issued by its analysts. ... In addition to other essential components, these reports must contain the conclusions drawn from the forensic testing and the limitations to be placed upon those conclusions." 1 KAUFMAN, supra note 138, Recommendation 7, at 331.

436 667 F. Supp. 1456 (S.D. Fla. 1986), affd, 828 F.2d 670 (11th Cir. 1987).

437 Id. at 1458.

438 Id.

barium and antimony on the hands of Troedel and Hawkins were basically insignificant."[439] The district court found the trial testimony, "at the very least," misleading.[440] In granting habeas relief, the court wrote:

[T]he Court concludes that the opinion Troedel had fired the weapon was known by the prosecution not to be based on the results of the neutron activation analysis tests, or on any scientific certainty or even probability. Thus, the subject testimony was not only misleading, but also was used by the State knowing it to be misleading.[441]

In addition to other functions, comprehensive reports afford substantial protection to experts from overreaching by attorneys. In Troedel, the expert claimed that the prosecutor had "pushed" him to enhance his testimony, a claim the prosecutor substantiated.[442] The issue also surfaced in Joyce Gilchrist's cases.[443] Experts are often pressured by attorneys to "push the envelope"—not a surprising occurrence in an adversarial system.[444] ABA Criminal Justice Standards state that a

> prosecutor who engages an expert for an opinion should respect the independence of the expert and should not seek to dictate the formation of the expert's opinion on the subject. ... [T]he prosecutor should explain to the expert his or her role in the trial as an impartial expert. ...[445]

---

439 Id. at 1459.

440 Id.

441 Id. at 1459–60.

442 They may lose their objectivity."); Ellis, supra note 2 ("[C]rime Labs should operate as a separate and independent third party force in the criminal justice system. When crime labs are operating within a police department, examiner bias can undermine the integrity of scientific results.").

443 See McCarty v. State, 765 P.2d 1215, 1219 (Okla. Crim. App. 1988) ("[W]e are greatly disturbed by the implications that the Oklahoma County District Attorney's Office may have placed undue pressure upon Ms. Gilchrist to give a so-called expert opinion, which was beyond scientific capabilities."); id. at 1219 (quoting a prepared statement from the Board of Directors of the Southwestern Association of Forensic Scientists, Inc., that "in our system of jurisprudence, undue pressure can be placed upon the forensic scientist to offer personal opinions beyond the scope of scientific capabilities' ") (citation omitted); see also Bank of Nova Scotia v. United States, 487 U.S. 250, 258 (1988) ("District Court further concluded that one of the prosecutors improperly argued with an expert witness during a recess of the grand jury after the witness gave testimony adverse to the Government.").

444 See SCHECK ET AL., supra note 5, at 31 (quoting Dr. Robert Shaler, former head of N.Y.C. Medical Examiner's DNA unit) ("Most attorneys like to let you know what their opinions of the facts of the case are—irrespective of the scientific conclusions.").

445 ABA STANDARDS FOR CRIMINAL JUSTICE: PROSECUTION FUNCTION AND DEFENSE FUNCTION, Standard 3-3.3(a) (3d ed. 1993). A comparable standard applies to defense counsel. See id., Standard 404.4(a).

The commentary to this standard elaborates:

> Statements made by physicians, psychiatrists, and other experts about their experiences as witnesses in criminal cases indicate the need for circumspection on the part of prosecutors who engage experts. Nothing should be done by a prosecutor to cast suspicion on the process of justice by suggesting that the expert color an opinion to favor the interests of the prosecutor.[446]

F. Certification of Examiners

A number of organizations offer examiner certification programs.[447] Some certifying organizations, however, appear to lack stringent requirements. Instead, they issue what are reported to be "checkbook credentials."[448] Rigorous certification standards should be instituted for examiners in order to ensure competence. Demanding written examinations, proficiency testing, continuing education, recertification procedures, an ethical code, and effective disciplinary procedures should form the basis of such a program.

G. Forensic Science Commissions

Commentators have argued for the establishment of crime laboratories that are independent of the police in order to minimize police pressure that may bias lab results.[449] In

---

446 Id. at 59.

447 For example, the American Board of Criminalistics has had such a program since 1993. It is a two-step process. The first tier requires an examination on general knowledge, and the second involves specialty areas, which include molecular biology, drug analysis, fire debris, and trace evidence. Bashinski & Peterson, supra note 340, at 577. To maintain certification, ongoing proficiency testing is required. Id. The International Association of Identification established a program for latent print examiners in 1977. Id. The Association of Firearms and Tool Mark Examiners established one in 2001. Id. The American Academy of Forensic Sciences has set up a number of national boards in the field of pathology, toxicology, anthropology, odontology, and questioned documents. See id.; RUDIN & INMAN, supra note 333, at 175. Of course, these programs are valuable only to the extent they apply exacting standards.

448 See Mark Hansen, Expertise to Go, A.B.A. J., Feb. 2000, at 44, 45; Elizabeth MacDonald, The Making of an Expert Witness: It's in the Credentials, WALL ST. J., Feb. 8, 1999, at B1.

449 See, e.g., Giannelli, supra note 49, at 469–73; Andre A. Moenssens, Novel Scientific Evidence in Criminal Cases: Some Words of Caution, 84 J. CRIM. L. & CRIMINOLOGY 1, 5 (1993) ("[Crime labs] may be so imbued with a pro-police bias that they are willing to circumvent true scientific investigation methods for the sake of 'making their point.' "); Symposium on Science, supra note 367, at 642 (statement of Joseph L. Peterson) ("[T]he police agency controls the formal and informal system of

2002, the Illinois Governor's Commission on Capital Punishment proposed the creation of an independent state laboratory as a way to provide access to forensic services.[450] The problem of improper police and/or prosecutorial influence on lab results weaves throughout the reported scandals.[451] Independent crime labs are a solution, but whether they are politically viable seems doubtful,[452] and they would present some disadvantages.[453] A

rewards and sanctions for the laboratory examiners. Many of these laboratories make their services available only to law enforcement agencies. All of these factors raise a legitimate issue regarding the objectivity of laboratory personnel."); James E. Starrs, The Seamy Side of Forensic Science: The Mephitic Stain of Fred Salem Zain, SCI. SLEUTHING REV., Winter 1993, at 1, 8 ("The inbred bias of crime laboratories affiliated with law enforcement agencies must be breached."); see also Regina v. Ward, 96 Crim. App. 1, 51 (A.C. 1993) (appeal taken from England) (U.K.) ("Forensic scientists may become partisan. The very fact that the police seek their assistance may create a relationship between the police and the forensic scientists. ... Forensic scientists employed by the government may come to see their function as helping the police. They may lose their objectivity."); Ellis, supra note 2 ("[C]rime Labs should operate as a separate and independent third party force in the criminal justice system. When crime labs are operating within a police department, examiner bias can undermine the integrity of scientific results.").

450 See, e.g., REPORT OF THE GOVERNOR'S COMMISSION ON CAPITAL PUNISHMENT, supra note 4, at 52 (noting in Recommendation 20 that "[an] independent state forensic laboratory should be created, operated by civilian personnel, with its own budget, separate from any police agency or supervision."); see also Craig M. Cooley, Reforming the Forensic Science Community to Avert the Ultimate Injustice, 15 STAN. L. & POL'Y REV. 381, 422–23 (2004) (highlighting Illinois and Houston public officials' support for an independent lab system).

451 See FUHRMAN, supra note 68, at 223 ("If [Gilchrist] were simply incompetent, her mistakes would have been all over the map. Instead, her mistakes benefited the prosecution."); Mills et al., supra note 153 ("Many forensic scientists at the state police labs, [former lab director] Plautz said, saw their role as members of the state's attorney's team. 'They thought they were prosecution witnesses,' he said. 'They didn't understand they were just scientists.'"); Teichroeb, Crime Labs Too Beholden, supra note 23 (quoting co-founder of New York-based Innocence Project Barry Scheck) ("Forensic science has to be an independent third force in the justice system, not beholden to prosecutors and police.").

452 The British have experimented with a "market system" provided by nongovernment experts: "The [Forensic Science Service] predicts that, in the medium term, 20 per cent of the market will go to non-FSS sources." REDMAYNE, supra note 400, at 27.

453 For example:

> Increasing the laboratory's geographical or organizational remoteness, however, can limit the effectiveness of the laboratory's participation in the investigative phases of a case, when its scientific input may have the greatest chance of contributing to justice. Remoteness also makes the police department less able to direct the efforts of the laboratory toward the cases that the department considers most important. ...

Bashinski & Peterson, supra note 340, at 581.

forensic commission with outside membership, on the other hand, could provide some insulation from impermissible external pressure.

A New York statute established a Commission on Forensic Science,[454] which is authorized to (1) develop minimum standards and a program of accreditation for all state laboratories, (2) establish minimum qualifications for laboratory directors and other personnel, and (3) approve forensic laboratories for the performance of specific forensic methodologies.[455] This approach has advantages over the Oklahoma approach, which only requires ASCLD/LAB (a nonpublic organization) accreditation.[456] A forensic commission could employ an established accreditation program, such as ASCLD/LAB, but it should do much more than monitor lab procedures. These commissions should also ensure adequate funding, investigate misconduct, and compile a registry of independent experts whom the defense could consult.

Before addressing these issues, however, the commission's membership should be discussed.

1. Composition of Commission

Representatives from the police, prosecution, judiciary, and forensic sciences are obvious candidates for membership. It is critical, however, that research scientists[457] and the defense bar also be represented, as is the case in New York.[458] The 1992 National

---

454 N.Y. EXEC. LAW § 995-a (McKinney 1996).

455 See generally Michael J. Saks et al., Model Prevention and Remedy of Erroneous Convictions Act, 33 ARIZ. ST. L.J. 665, 698–703 (2001) (proposing a Commission on Forensic Science Services).

456 See OKLA. STAT. ANN. tit. 74, § 150.37 (West Supp. 2006–2007) (requiring accreditation by ASCLD/LAB or the American Board of Forensic Toxicology).

457 n the early 1990s, a British Royal Commission recommended the establishment of a Forensic Science Advisory Council that would, among other things, review the performance and standards of crime laboratories:

> [W]e are ... concerned at the lack of external oversight. ... We therefore see great attraction in the proposal put to us by the Royal Society for Chemistry that a Forensic Science Advisory Council should be set up which would report to the Home Secretary on the performance, achievements and efficiency of the forensic science laboratories.

ROYAL COMM'N ON CRIMINAL JUSTICE, REPORT, 1993, Cm. 2263, at 150–51. Unfortunately, it was not adopted. REDMAYNE, supra note 400, at 27 (explaining that when the government hesitated in adopting RCCJ's recommendations, forensic experts made their own, different suggestions); see also David E. Bernstein, Junk Science in the United States and the Commonwealth, 21 YALE J. INT'L L. 123, 170–73 (1996) (discussing this proposal).

458 See N.Y. EXEC. LAW § 995-a (McKinney 1996); see also 1 KAUFMAN, supra note 138, at 363 (noting in Recommendation 19 that "[a]n advisory board to the Centre of Forensic Sciences should

Academies report recommended the establishment of a National Committee on Forensic DNA Typing, commenting that accreditation should be a responsibility of the Department of Health and Human Services (DHHS), in consultation with the Department of Justice (DOJ). DHHS is the appropriate agency, because it has extensive experience in the regulation of clinical laboratories through programs under the Clinical Laboratory Improvement Act and has extensive expertise in molecular genetics through the National Institutes of Health.[459]

The DNA Identification Act of 1994, however, located the authority to appoint DAB members in the FBI, despite the NRC report's conclusion that a law enforcement agency would be unsuitable for this purpose.[460] The Act, at least, did require the Director of the FBI to select members from "among nominations proposed by the head of the National Academy of Sciences and professional societies of crime laboratory officials" and to "include as members scientists from State, local, and private forensic laboratories, molecular geneticists and population geneticists not affiliated with a forensic laboratory, and a representative from the National Institute of Standards and Technology."[461] This requirement expired when the DAB ceased to exist after five years.[462]

Congress subsequently established a National Forensic Science Commission to improve forensic science.[463] This legislation constitutes an important step in the right direction, but

---

be established consisting of Crown and defence counsel, police, judiciary, scientists and laypersons. It should be created by statute.").

459 NRC I REPORT, supra note 330, at 107. The 1996 report mentioned only an "appropriate organization." NRC II REPORT, supra note 330, at 87 ("We recognize the need for guidelines and standards and for accreditation by appropriate organizations.").

460 NRC I REPORT, supra note 330, at 107; see also William C. Thompson, Accepting Lower Standards: The National Research Council's Second Report on Forensic DNA Evidence, 37 JURIMETRICS J. 405, 409 (1997) ("Due in part to the political clout of the FBI on Capitol Hill, an independent national committee was never created. Instead, we have the DNA Advisory Board, which is appointed by the FBI Director.").

461 42 U.S.C. § 14131(a)(1)(A)-(B) (2000) (emphasis added).

462 The statutory requirements governing DAB do not apply to SWGDAM, the group that replaced DAB at its expiration.

463 Its responsibilities include:

(1) assess[ing] present and future resource needs of the forensic science community;

(2) mak[ing] recommendations to the Attorney General [("A.G.")] for maximizing the use of forensic technologies and techniques to solve crimes and protect the public;

(3) identify[ing] potential scientific advances that may assist law enforcement in using forensic technologies and techniques to protect the public;

(4) mak[ing] recommendations to the [A.G.] for programs that will increase the number of qualified forensic scientists available to work in public crime laboratories;

the statute does not specifically require the membership of outside scientists or members of the defense bar—persons who would bring different perspectives to the commission's tasks.[464] Instead, the Attorney General appoints members from "persons experienced in criminal justice issues, including persons from the forensic science and criminal justice communities."[465]

2. Investigations

A Forensic Science Commission should be assigned the task of investigating all cases of alleged misconduct or incompetence. The lack of a government agency specifically designated with investigative responsibility leaves a conspicuous regulatory void. The I.G. satisfies this need on the federal level,[466] but the states are another matter. In West Virginia, the state supreme court, at the behest of a prosecutor, appointed a judge to conduct an

---

(5) disseminat[ing], through the National Institute of Justice, best practices concerning the collection and analyses of forensic evidence to help ensure quality and consistency in the use of forensic technologies and techniques to solve crimes and protect the public;

(6) examin[ing] additional issues pertaining to forensic science as requested by the [A.G.];

(7) examin[ing] Federal, State, and local privacy protection statutes, regulations, and practices relating to access to, or use of, stored DNA samples or DNA analyses, to determine whether such protections are sufficient;

(8) mak[ing] specific recommendations to the [A.G.], as necessary, to enhance the protections described in [point] (7) to ensure—

(A) the appropriate use and dissemination of DNA information;

(B) the accuracy, security, and confidentiality of DNA information;

(C) the timely removal and destruction of obsolete, expunged, or inaccurate DNA information; and

(D) that any other necessary measures are taken to protect privacy; and

(9) provid[ing] a forum for the exchange and dissemination of ideas and information in furtherance of the objectives described in paragraphs (1) through (8).

42 U.S.C.A § 14136c(b) (West 2005).

464 Some states have adopted a more inclusive approach. See, e.g., MINN. STAT. ANN. § 299C.156(1) (West Supp. 2006–2007) (requiring public defender, defense attorney, and university professor as members of Forensic Science Advisory Board); TEX. CODE CRIM. PROC. ANN. art. 38.01 (Vernon Supp. 2006) (requiring defense attorney and university faculty or staff as members of Forensic Science Commission).

465 42 U.S.C.A § 14136c(a) (West 2005).

466 See 1997 I.G. REPORT, supra note 27, at pt. I (explaining the I.G.'s role in investigating the explosives unit); 2004 I.G. REPORT, supra note 28, at iii (explaining the I.G.'s role in policing the matter of Jacqueline Blake).

inquiry into Fred Zain's misconduct.[467] That judge, in turn, requested that ASCLD appoint a team to review the allegations.[468] In contrast, the Montana Supreme Court ruled that it lacked authority to make this type of appointment.[469] In Houston, the District Attorney provoked controversy because he refused to refuse himself from a grand jury investigation when his office's use of the suspect evidence was one of the issues that needed to be examined.[470] Internal investigations have repeatedly failed to discover or report the nature and extent of lab failures.[471]

The primary responsibility for detecting, investigating, and correcting instances of misconduct and gross negligence rests with the laboratory and its personnel.[472] However, external and independent review is also critical and is now mandated by recent federal

---

467 In re Investigation of the W. Va. State Police Crime Lab., Serology Div., 438 S.E.2d 501, 502–03 (W. Va. 1993).

468 See id. at 504 (stating that "Judge Holliday notes that there was evidence that Trooper Zain's supervisors may have ignored or concealed complaints of his misconduct" where such complaints were based on the team's review of the allegations).

469 See supra note 135 and accompanying text.

470 See Adam Liptak, Prosecutions Are a Focus In Houston DNA Inquiry: Grand Juries Seen as Widening Investigation, N.Y. TIMES, June 9, 2003, at A20 ("In April, the county's 22 criminal district court judges asked Mr. Rosenthal to recuse himself from the investigation."); see also Nick Madigan, Houston's Troubled DNA Crime Lab Faces Growing Scrutiny, N.Y. TIMES, Feb. 9, 2003, at A20 (reporting that operations in the Houston lab were suspended in December after an audit found numerous problems).

471 The investigations concerning the Earl Washington case, the FBI explosive unit, and Fred Zain are all examples.

472 Cf. NRC I REPORT, supra note 330, at 148 ("Laboratories and experts have a particular responsibility to ensure that they are open and candid with the courts. Any reservations about inadequacies or errors should be promptly revealed, and failure to do that should be dealt with seriously.").

legislation.[473] A forensic science commission would have the expertise to conduct such an investigation or to appoint an independent committee to do so.[474]

3. Adequate Funding

A commission should also ensure that labs are adequately funded. Crime labs have become chronically underfunded in the last half century. In 1967, President Johnson's crime commission noted that "the great majority of police department laboratories have only minimal equipment and lack highly skilled personnel able to use the modern equipment now being developed."[475] In 1974, President Nixon's crime commission commented: "Too many police crime laboratories have been set up on budgets that preclude the recruitment of qualified, professional personnel."[476]

Twenty years later, a report on Washington state crime labs revealed that a "staggering backlog of cases hinders investigations of murder, rape, arson, and other major crimes."[477] At any time, "thousands of pieces of evidence collected from crime scenes sit unanalyzed and ignored on shelves in laboratories and police stations across the state."[478] A USA Today survey of 215 laboratories reached the same conclusion: "Evidence that could imprison

473 The Omnibus Crime Control and Safe Streets Act of 1968 was amended by requiring a "certification that a government entity exists . . . to conduct independent external investigations into allegations of serious negligence or misconduct substantially affecting the integrity of the forensic results committed by employees or contractors of any forensic laboratory system, medical examiner's office, coroner's office, law enforcement storage facility, or medical facility" in any state receiving a grant. Pub. L. No. 90-351, 82 Stat. 197 (codified as amended at 42 U.S.C.A. § 3797k(4) (West Supp. 2007)). Unfortunately, this requirement has not been rigorously implemented. See OFFICE OF THE INSPECTOR GENERAL, U.S. DEPARTMENT OF JUSTICE, REVIEW OF THE OFFICE OF JUSTICE PROGRAMS' FORENSIC SCIENCE IMPROVEMENT GRANT PROGRAM i (2005), available at http://www.usdoj.gov/oig/reports/OJP/e0602/final.pdf (concluding that the National Institute of Justice "did not enforce the external investigation certification requirement imposed by the Justice for All Act of 2004").

474 A few states have set up investigatory agencies. See, e.g., MINN. STAT. ANN. § 299C.156(2) (West Supp. 2006–2007); TEX. CODE CRIM. PROC. ANN. art. 38.01(4)(a) (Vernon Supp. 2006). Early results, however, have not been encouraging. See States' Efforts to Probe Crime Labs Stall at Start, AUGUSTA CHRON. (Ga.), Mar. 24, 2007, at A13 ("But not one of the new boards has yet reopened a case—either because they have refused to do so or because they haven't been funded.").

475 PRESIDENT'S COMM'N ON LAW ENFORCEMENT AND ADMIN. OF JUSTICE, THE CHALLENGE OF CRIME IN A FREE SOCIETY 255 (1967).

476 NAT'L ADVISORY COMM'N ON CRIMINAL JUSTICE STANDARDS AND GOALS, REPORT ON POLICE 304 (1974).

477 Tomas Guillen & Eric Nalder, Overwhelming Evidence: Crime Labs in Crisis, SEATTLE TIMES, Jun. 19, 1994, at A14.

478 Id.

the guilty or free the innocent is languishing on shelves and piling up in refrigerators of the USA's overwhelmed and underfunded crime labs."[479] While budgets increased by ten percent in five years, caseloads increased by almost twenty-five percent.[480] In one case, a suspected serial rapist was released because DNA analysis would have taken months to perform.[481] "Weeks later, [the suspect] raped victim No. 4 as she slept in her home. When the DNA tests finally came back—18 months after samples first went to the lab—a jury convicted [the suspect] of all four rapes."[482]

Congress recognized the need for federal funding for public crime laboratories and medical examiner offices by enacting the Paul Coverdell National Forensic Science Improvement Act in 2000.[483] Appropriations, however, have fallen well below authorized limits.[484] The validity of forensic evidence depends on funding for facilities, equipment, and personnel, as well as for accreditation, certification, and standardization. The Houston experience is not uncommon: "It is clear that, over the 15 years preceding the DNA/Serology Section's closure in December 2002, HPD and the City failed to provide the Crime Lab with adequate resources to meet growing demands."[485]

---

479 Becky Beaupre & Peter Eisler, Crime Lab Crisis, USA TODAY, Aug. 20, 1996, at 1A.

480 Id.

481 Id.

482 Id.

483 Pub. L. No. 106–561, 114 Stat. 2787 (codified as amended at 42 U.S.C.A. § 3797j-o (West 2003)).

484 See Beth Lavach, Legislative Corner, ACAD. NEWS, Sept. 2007, at 3 ("For well over a decade, the Congress has given off-again-on-again support to the forensic sciences."). In contrast, DNA technology has been funded. On March 11, 2003, the Attorney General of the United States announced the President's DNA initiative, entitled "Advancing Justice Through DNA Technology." This initiative proposes over $1 billion in funding for fiscal year 2004 through fiscal year 2008 to reduce casework and database backlogs in DNA laboratories, to improve the DNA analysis capacity of public laboratories, to support training, and to assist research and development. U.S. DEP'T OF JUSTICE, ADVANCING JUSTICE THROUGH DNA TECHNOLOGY, Executive Summary (2003), available at http://www.usdoj.gov/ag/dnapolicybook_exsum.htm.

485 THIRD HOUSTON REPORT, supra note 166, at 62.

4. Register of Defense Experts

Finding qualified experts to testify for the defense is difficult.[486] The British have had some success in registering experts.[487] A forensic science commission could be tasked with this responsibility. Retired FBI experts have often played a positive role in this context.[488] Moreover, prosecution experts in one jurisdiction should be encouraged to consult with the defense in other jurisdictions. Currently, such contacts are frequently discouraged as John Wilson learned when he testified as a defense expert against Joyce Gilchrist.[489]

CONCLUSION

Scientific proof is often critical in criminal prosecutions.[490] Moreover, it is frequently better than other types of evidence commonly used in criminal trials (i.e., eyewitness identifications, confessions, and informant testimony[491]), a point that the Supreme Court has made on several occasions.[492] DNA profiling, for example, has repeatedly demonstrated

---

486 See Weinstein, supra note 346, at 1008 ("Courts, as gatekeepers, must be aware of how difficult it can be for some parties—particularly indigent criminal defendants—to obtain an expert to testify. The fact that one side may lack adequate resources with which to fully develop its case is a constant problem."). See generally Giannelli, The Right to Expert Assistance, supra note 104 (discussing the right to defense experts).

487 See R. Bramley, Quality in the Laboratory, 43 SCI. & JUST. 104, 106 (2003) (discussing the Council for the Registration of Forensic Practitioners, which requires a "formal assessment by independent peer practitioners of ... proof of competence"); see also REDMAYNE, supra note 400, at 218 (noting the existence of the British program to register experts).

488 Retired FBI fingerprint examiners testified in the Riky Jackson case. See supra notes 314–20 and accompanying text.

489 See supra notes 84–85 and accompanying text.

490 See Joseph L. Peterson et al., The Uses and Effects of Forensic Science in the Adjudication of Felony Cases, 32 J. FORENSIC SCI. 1730, 1748 (1987) (reporting the results of a survey which revealed that "[a]bout one quarter of the citizens who had served on juries which were presented with scientific evidence believed that had such evidence been absent, they would have changed their verdicts—from guilty to not guilty"); see also Bales, supra note 236, at 51 (commenting that "prosecutors, defense attorneys and judges agree that scientific evidence can powerfully affect—and often determine—the outcome in criminal cases").

491 See generally REPORT OF THE ABA CRIMINAL JUSTICE SECTION'S AD HOC INNOCENCE COMM. TO ENSURE THE INTEGRITY OF THE CRIMINAL PROCESS, ACHIEVING JUSTICE: FREEING THE INNOCENT, CONVICTING THE GUILTY (Paul C. Giannelli & Myrna Raeder eds., 2006) (discussing misidentifications, false confessions and jailhouse snitches).

492 For example, in Escobedo v. Illinois, 378 U.S. 478 (1964), the Court observed that history has taught that "a system of criminal law enforcement which comes to depend on the 'confession' will, in the

the importance of scientific evidence in the criminal justice system—both to exonerate the innocent and convict the guilty.

Paradoxically, the most scientifically sound procedure—DNA analysis—is the most extensively regulated, while many forensic techniques with questionable scientific pedigrees go completely unregulated. As the 1992 National Academies report commented: "Because the application of DNA typing in forensic science is to be used in the service of justice, it is especially important for society to establish mechanisms for accountability and to ensure appropriate public scrutiny."[493] The same should apply to the entire laboratory. The regulation of DNA profiling, which developed gradually over the last twenty years, can serve as a paradigm for other laboratory units. The accreditation of crime laboratories, the certification of examiners, and the standardization and promulgation of written protocols for each technique would go a long way in professionalizing crime labs. In addition, quality assurance programs, including proficiency testing and external audits, should be mandated. Finally, forensic science commissions should be created in each jurisdiction to implement these reforms.

---

long run, be less reliable and more subject to abuses than a system which depends on extrinsic evidence independently secured through skillful
investigation." Id. at 488–89; see also Davis v. Mississippi, 394 U.S. 721, 727 (1969) (noting that "fingerprinting is an inherently more reliable and effective crime-solving tool than eyewitness identifications or confessions and is not subject to such abuses as the improper line-up and the 'third degree'").
493 NRC I REPORT, supra note 330, at 162.

Science and the Death Penalty

DNA, Innocence, and the Debate over Capital Punishment in the United States

Jay D. Aronson and Simon A. Cole

The death penalty debate in the United States has recently undergone a fundamental shift. The possibility of executing the innocent has emerged as some abolitionists' most salient argument, displacing debates over such issues as fairness, deterrence, and cost. Innocence has managed to move to the fore of the debate in part because of the epistemological certainty attached to one particular kind of postconviction exoneration, one vouched for by the authority of DNA evidence. We suggest that such rhetorical moves draw upon the epistemic authority of science as a lever with which to challenge law's claims to truth-making authority. A few abolitionists and other scholars have expressed misgivings about the abolitionist embrace of the innocence argument. We push this concern further, suggesting that both abolitionists and death penalty reformers, who seek to promote a "scientific" death penalty centered on DNA evidence, draw upon a mythologized notion of "science" as a producer of epistemic certainty. Paradoxically, this association of science with certainty is inconsistent with contemporary notions of science as characterized by efforts to measure, manage, but always acknowledge, uncertainty.

Jay D. Aronson is an Assistant Professor of Science, Technology, and Society in the History Department at Carnegie Mellon University (aronson@andrew.cmu.edu).
Simon A. Cole is Associate Professor of Criminology, Law, and Society at the University of California, Irvine (scole@uci.edu).

The authors wish to thank Austin Sarat, Franklin Zimring, and five anonymous referees for their constructive comments.

This material is partially based upon work supported by the National Science Foundation under Grant Nos. SES-0115305 and IIS-0527729, and the National Institutes of Health under Grant No. HG-03302. Any opinions, findings, and conclusions or recommendations expressed in this material are those of the authors and do not necessarily reflect the views of the National Science Foundation or the National Institutes of Health.

> Eighty-four years ago, Judge Learned Hand observed that "[o]ur procedure has been always haunted by the ghost of the innocent man convicted," but posited, optimistically, that "[i]t is an unreal dream" (United States v. Garsson, 291 F. 646, 649 (S.D. n.Y. 1923). Today, with the advance of forensic DNA technology, our desire to join Learned Hand's optimism has given way to the reality of wrongful convictions—a reality which challenges us to reaffirm our commitment to the principle that the innocent should be freed.
>
> Judge Calabresi (McKithen v. Brown 2007, 2–3)

INTRODUCTION

This article focuses on the recent "turn to innocence" in American death penalty discourse. Although death penalty discourse has always been, and remains, multifaceted—encompassing morality, religion, cost, deterrence, theories of punishment, fairness, race, class, and human rights—we suggest that over the past decade innocence has emerged as perhaps the dominant issue in death penalty discourse with "an unprecedented effect on the debate about capital punishment" (Bandes 2008, 5; Baumgartner, De Boef, and Boydstun 2008, 157). This phenomenon has been referred to by such labels as the "age of innocence" (Rosen 2006, 237) or even an "innocence revolution" (Marshall 2004, 573; Steiker and Steiker 2005, 613). The abolitionist movement has embraced innocence as a new rhetorical asset in the death penalty debate, one with the potential to decisively shift the weight of public opinion in abolition's favor (Radelet and Borg 2000; Bedau 2004a; Acker in press). "Unlike other challenges to the fairness of capital proceedings, which have failed to stimulate widespread public outrage," Marshall (2004) argues, "evidence of the system's propensity to factual error has the power to open closed minds and trigger reexamination of the costs and benefits of capital punishment" (579). Banner (2002) notes, "the prospect of killing an innocent person seemed to be the one thing that could cause people to rethink their support for capital punishment" (304). He goes on to suggest that "if any development had the potential to change" the popularity of the death penalty, "this was the one" (305). Thus, one scholar claims, "it is no exaggeration to say that wrongful convictions spurred … the most successful death penalty reform movement in our lifetime" (Bandes 2008, 4).

Already, scholars claim that innocence "has produced a massive shift in the terms of the national death-penalty debate" (Hoffman 2005, 562), a shift "away from moral and procedural considerations, and toward the more substantive question of guilt and innocence" (Hall 2005, 373). Even the strongest supporters of the death penalty acknowledge this trend. Joshua Marquis, vice president of the National District Attorneys Association, stated, "We're seeing fewer executions. We're seeing fewer people sentenced to death. People really do question capital punishment. The whole idea of exoneration has really penetrated popular culture" (quoted in Liptak 2007, A1).

Innocence has become a powerful argument in death penalty discourse over the past decade because abolitionists have been able to point to the near-execution of inmates whose innocence is supported by postconviction DNA tests. In contrast to earlier debates about the potential execution of innocent people, the cultural authority afforded to DNA evidence as a "truth machine" (Kreimer 2005, 655) that generates "scientific answers to the question of guilt or innocence" (Rosen 2003, 68) has effectively ended debates about whether or not particular exonerated condemned inmates were factually innocent. "The advent of DNA testing," Bandes (2008) notes, "offers the promise of innocence as an entity with clearly delineated boundaries, discoverable by scientific means" (9). In effect, some abolitionists have used the cultural authority of science, in the form of postconviction DNA testing, to win broad social acceptance of the notion that the state has nearly executed factually innocent people, may well have executed some factually innocent people, and stands at risk to eventually execute a factually innocent person if capital punishment continues. As one leading abolitionist scholar puts it, "the innocence revolution is born of science and fact, as opposed to choice among a competing set of controversial values" (Marshall 2004, 574).

The issue of innocence played a central role in the New York State legislature's failure to reinstate the death penalty after it was overturned on a constitutional violation (Purnick 2004; Duggan 2005; Healy 2005; Lentol, Weinstein, and Aubry 2005). On March 18, 2009, Governor Bill Richardson signed a law repealing the death penalty in New Mexico. Once again, innocence was given pride of place as the single most important reason for Governor Bill Richardson's decision, although given recent economic turmoil, cost was also noted as a significant factor in the decision. Innocence was one of two principal reasons behind the American Bar Association's landmark call for a moratorium on capital punishment in 1997 (American Bar Association 1997). The issue of wrongful conviction (highlighted by several prominent DNA exonerations in the state) was given pride of place in Governor George Ryan's rationale for his historic clearing of Illinois' death row in 2003 (Sarat 2006, 276).[1] Actual innocence, Sarat notes, was "the issue that drew his [Ryan's] most intense attention" and provided him with an entrée into other crucial issues, such as fairness (275).

Perhaps the most powerful impact of the innocence argument was felt in the case *United States v. Quinones* (2002b), in which federal district Judge Jed Rakoff ruled that the evidence concerning the near-execution of factually innocent people rendered capital punishment unconstitutional. Although the decision was subsequently overturned by the Second Circuit Court of Appeals in 2002, the *Quinones* (2002b) opinion disseminated the notion that the risk of executing the innocent might render capital punishment

---

1 As Sarat and Hussain (2004) point out, imputing a coherent rationale to Ryan's actions is difficult because of his tendency, in his public statements, to invoke all possible rationales, including some philosophically inconsistent with one another. Most notable in this regard was Ryan's invocation of the retributivist reasoning to commute all Illinois death sentences was that life in prison was a punishment worse than death.

unconstitutional. Rakoff's reasoning was subsequently adopted by four dissenting US Supreme Court justices, who called judicial awareness of DNA exonerations "a new body of fact" that "must be accounted for in deciding what, in practical terms, the Eighth Amendment guarantees should tolerate" for capital punishment (*Kansas v. Marsh* 2006, 2544). The "repeated exonerations of convicts under death sentences, in numbers never imagined before the development of DNA tests," the dissenters argued, have ushered in "a period of new empirical argument about how 'death is different'" (2544–45, Souter, J., dissenting).

Some scholars have expressed reservations about the turn to innocence or about "the new abolitionism" more generally (Steiker and Steiker 2003). These scholars have noted that the focus on actual innocence may distract from other important problems with capital punishment and with the American criminal justice system more generally, such as overpunishment, fairness, and race (Raymond 2001; Davis 2003; Steiker and Steiker 2005; Berman 2006; Sarat 2006). In this article, we want to focus on a different, less explored (but see Bandes 2008), issue: the use of the cultural authority of science in the turn to innocence.

Scholars have worried that, as Liebman (2002) puts it, "What DNA giveth the death penalty reform impulse ... DNA reform can taketh away" (549). Indeed, little more than a year after *Quinones* (2002b), the cultural authority of DNA evidence was turned against abolition. In 2003, in a proposal often dubbed "the guilty project" (an ironic counterpart to the Innocence Project), Massachusetts Governor (and later presidential candidate) Mitt Romney drew on the cultural authority of DNA evidence to support reforming and rejuvenating capital punishment rather than abolishing it. Just as some abolitionists argued that exculpatory DNA evidence provided epistemological certainty that states had at least come close to executing factually innocent persons, Romney argued the incriminating DNA evidence could provide epistemological certainty of the guilt of candidates for execution.

This article is a study of the rhetorical invocation of science and innocence (particularly exonerations involving DNA evidence) in the American capital punishment debate. We argue that associating a particular factual or normative claim with DNA evidence is a way of seeking to have that claim treated as "scientific" and therefore indisputably and unassailably "true." Such rhetorical invocations draw on caricatures of DNA profiling as a purportedly infallible "truth machine," which perpetuates a notion of "science" as a category of knowledge characterized by epistemological certainty that somehow justifies taking what would otherwise be viewed as risky legal actions (i.e., the freeing of a convicted murderer or the execution of an accused murderer). Although this notion does not reflect most academic and philosophical views of science (which tend to emphasize the provisional and probabilistic nature of scientific knowledge), it is representative of the rhetorical use of "science" in law more broadly. Law's tendency to attribute epistemological certainty to many forms of science, we suggest, is an indication of law's uneasiness with its own role in making life and death decisions under conditions of uncertainty (Golan 2004).

The use of the rhetorical authority of science to advance abolitionist arguments is perhaps necessary, but it also carries risks for the abolitionist. The first is that DNA evidence is a double-edged sword: the epistemic certainty that defense advocates claim when using it to exonerate the wrongfully convicted can easily be turned against the abolitionist project by increasing the public's perception that those being executed on the basis of DNA evidence are, without a doubt, worthy of execution. Second, such arguments perpetuate and strengthen the myth of epistemic certainty surrounding the technique.

To be sure, DNA profiling is different in many ways than previous forensic techniques. Because it emerged out of academic science rather than the police laboratory, there was a large pool of academically credentialed witnesses who were able to testify on behalf of the prosecution or defense in court (Aronson 2007; Mnookin 2001). In contrast to, say, fingerprinting, frequency data is available from which it is possible to generate estimates of the probability of a random match between two profiles. However, even though the stated practice of forensic laboratories is based on settled understandings of DNA identification techniques, the actual production of DNA evidence is, like all other human activities (including basic scientific research), subject to error (e.g., sample contamination or mix-up), bias, unspoken practices, and even corruption.

Our findings are based on an analysis of voluminous contemporary discourse on the death penalty—including judicial opinions, scholarly work, media reports, and public statements by government officials. Our approach to this material is grounded in Science & Technology Studies (STS). Methodologically, this means that we do not seek to define what counts as "science" ourselves or arbitrate which knowledge claims or knowledge-producing activities are or are not properly called "science" or are better than others. While we recognize that not all knowledge claims that purport to be science are equal,[2] it is not our mission in this article to evaluate which forms are better or worse than others or to demarcate "science" from "pseudo-science." Rather, we are interested in the use of the terms "science" and "scientific" as rhetorical assets in discourse over the death penalty.

THE AGE OF INNOCENCE

Opposition to capital punishment in Anglo-American law began as early as the seventeenth century among English radicals and Quakers (Banner 2002) and as early as the eighteenth century on the continent (Zimring 2003). American abolitionists did use the innocence argument during the nineteenth century, but, for the most part, the morality

2 For the record, we do think that certain forensic techniques are more accurate and reliable than others but that none are infallible. Unfortunately, there is a dearth of data that would allow an external observer to know the relative accuracy of various techniques (Giannelli 2007).

of capital punishment took center stage (Banner 2002; Warden 2005). During the 1960s, the National Association for the Advancement of Colored People (NAACP) legal defense fund, placing hope in the Warren Court, treated capital punishment as a constitutional issue. Innocence was mentioned in only one (Justice Marshall's) of the nine opinions in Furman v. Georgia, which invalidated American death penalty statutes in 1972. Even in Marshall's opinion, however, innocence was mentioned "only as the last of numerous considerations that might turn informed public opinion against the death penalty" (Steiker and Steiker 2005, 593). After the reinstatement of the death penalty (Gregg v. Georgia 1976), fairness became perhaps the most salient issue, at least until the Court turned a deaf ear on the argument that capital punishment was inherently unfair because it was meted out in a racially discriminatory manner (McCleskey v. Kemp 1987).

During the mid-1980s and early 1990s, abolitionists embraced cost as an argument to convince even those Americans who did not share their moral compass to turn against the death penalty (Dieter 1994). Although cost is still an issue (see Liebman 2002), it has not strongly swayed public opinion in any particular direction. During the 1970s (and continuing today in academic literature), a battle has been waged about the deterrent effect of the death penalty (Forst 2004). But it appears unlikely that social scientific evidence concerning deterrence, even if it were not as equivocal as it is, would change many minds because of the moral nature of the death penalty debate (Gross and Ellsworth 2003). As Weisberg (2005) suggests, the "human reality" of innocence "may prove to be more important than masses of social science evidence on deterrence and other issues in determining support for the death penalty in the long run" (168).

Although many of these issues remain actively contested and new, previously unforeseen issues have gained traction (e.g., the current attention to methods of execution), empirical evidence suggests that innocence has emerged as "the most powerful new set of arguments ever to enter" the death penalty debate (Baumgartner, De Boef, and Boydstun 2008, 135). But why has the death penalty debate not always been about the possibility of executing innocent people? Cases of executed innocents have long been known; they arguably played a role in prompting abolition in some jurisdictions, such as Michigan in 1846 (Clarke, Lambert, and Whitt 2000–2001), and abolitionists have long tracked cases of the execution of allegedly innocent people.[3]

The answer, we would suggest, is that with a few exceptions (Warden 2005), cases of innocence have always been contestable. This can be most clearly demonstrated by the controversy over the Bedau and Radelet's massive study (1987) of 350 known wrongful convictions in "potentially capital cases" (i.e., cases for which the death penalty could have

3 Anti-death penalty activists and organizations have been keeping track of death row exonerations since at least 1932, when Yale University law professor Edwin Borchard profiled sixty-five cases of known wrongful conviction in Convicting the Innocent (1942 [1932]).

conceivably been handed down even if it ultimately was not) from 1900–1985.[4] They conducted this study both to put the study of wrongful conviction on firm empirical grounding and to make it impossible for death penalty proponents to claim that there was little or no risk of executing innocent individuals. Ultimately, they found that 139 factually innocent people were sentenced to death, 23 of them were eventually executed, and 22 had close calls (i.e., coming within days or hours of execution).

While Bedau and Radelet's study greatly advanced wrongful conviction scholarship, it remained vulnerable to several epistemological critiques, most notably (1) subjectivity in the choice and description of cases (Markman and Cassell 1988); (2) the irony that innocence claims depended on the same kind of evidence that was often cited as a primary cause of wrongful convictions—another person's confession, the implication of another person, a state official's declaration, and "subsequent scholarly judgment" (i.e., expertise) (Markman and Cassell 1988); and (3) the lack of evidence to prove factual innocence (that the convicted individual was not the perpetrator of the crime) as opposed to legal innocence (that the convicted individual may or may not have been the perpetrator of the crime, but he is not legally convictable for the offense because of a constitutional or procedural error).

Anticipating such criticisms, Bedau and Radelet (1987) made clear the difficulty in definitively establishing innocence in the postconviction context. They wrote that the "most one can hope to obtain is a consensus of investigators after the case reaches its final disposition" (47). They went on to state that their criterion for inclusion in their catalogue was a belief that "a majority of neutral observers, given the evidence at our disposal, would judge the defendant in question to be innocent" (47). Generous death penalty proponents concede that since there is essentially no legal proceeding capable of producing a finding of "innocence," it is not surprising that ironclad evidence of innocence is difficult to come by (Latzer 2003).

Death penalty proponents could, therefore, neutralize innocence arguments by claiming to be unconvinced of the actual innocence of one, or most, or all of the claimed instances of execution of innocents. They could further use the tactic of casting doubt on the weakest of the claimed innocence cases and thus undermine the remainder by insinuation (Risinger 2007). Some abolitionists have suggested that they erred by allowing death penalty proponents to define "innocence" in a manner so epistemologically exacting as to be impossible to satisfy (Warden quoted in Lutton; Radelet 2001).

4 When they revised and expanded their initial Stanford Law Review article into book form in 1992, their database increased to 416 (Radelet, Bedau, and Putnam 1992).

A NEW KIND OF EXONERATION

In 1989, however, a new kind of exoneration occurred, one that was much less vulnerable to skepticism than those that came before it. On August 14 of that year, Gary Dotson, who had been convicted of rape in 1979, became the first American prisoner to be cleared by postconviction DNA testing. Although the supposed victim had a crisis of conscience when she became a born-again Christian and recanted her story in 1985 on national television (Serrill 1985), Dotson was not formally declared innocent for nearly four years. Instead, he was merely paroled early without the conviction being formally expunged from his record. Subsequent investigation into his case revealed that he had been convicted based on questionable forensic evidence (both hair analysis and blood typing), false testimony of the victim, and unsubstantiated claims about the character of the victim and the defendant made by the prosecutor.[5]

By 1996, sixty-five people had been exonerated on the basis of DNA evidence. These cases were detailed in a National Institute of Justice report titled Convicted by Juries, Exonerated by Science (Connors et al. 1996). The title presaged the invocation of the authority of "science" that has become so commonly associated with postconviction DNA exoneration. The phrase "exonerated by science" set up an opposition between law and science, and a presumption of epistemic privilege for science that would set the tone for the discourse in the years to come. In 2000, Barry Scheck and Peter Neufeld (who founded the Innocence Project at Cardozo School of Law in 1992), along with journalist Jim Dwyer, published Actual Innocence, which also used DNA exonerations as a fulcrum with which to explore the failings of the American criminal justice system. To be sure, most of the cases profiled in the book—more than two hundred postconviction DNA exonerations to date—were not capital cases. Moreover, most of the post-Gregg death row exonerations were generated by means other than postconviction DNA testing. And yet, we suggest, the DNA-driven death row exonerations, though few in number, lend credibility to all the death row exonerations, even those generated by means other than DNA, by definitively shattering the air of inconceivability that previously had shrouded the idea of a post-Gregg wrongful capital conviction. Indeed, the salience of DNA exoneration for the issue of capital punishment was nicely indicated by the subtitle of the first edition of Actual Innocence: Five Days to Execution and Other Dispatches from the Wrongly Convicted.[6]

---

5 Described by the prosecutor as a "16-year-old virgin" at trial, the "victim" admitted many years after Dotson was freed that she had fabricated the crime because she feared that her boyfriend had made her pregnant through unprotected sex (Warden 2006).

6 The subtitle of the latest edition (2001) is "When Justice Goes Wrong and How to Make It Right," which shifts the focus from the perspective of condemnation of the system to one of remedying its shortcomings (Scheck, Neufeld, and Dwyer 2000, 2001).

DNA PROFILING

For those legal actors frustrated with the increasingly apparent failures of law as a truth-making enterprise, the idea that DNA profiling is inherently superior to other forms of evidence understandably has a lot of appeal. It allows commentators to say things like

> we now have nearly irrefutable factual evidence that our past reliance on existing procedures to protect the innocent was misplaced. ...One reason for this certainty that we convict innocents is DNA ... that can, in some cases, be used by scientists to provide us with scientific answers to the question of guilt or innocence. (Rosen 2003, 68)

Or they can say that "newly probative DNA evidence offers the possibility of defendants who can demonstrate with scientific certainty that they are factually innocent of a crime to which they pleaded guilty" (Kreimer 2005, 660, emphasis added). "Science," Zimring (2003) notes, could "provide critics of capital punishment with an opportunity to contradict official versions of capital crimes with more persuasive data than alibi witnesses or the reported confessions of others" (170). But from the perspective of STS, it is clear that such discourse reflects an idealized (or rather carefully fashioned) image of DNA profiling more than its actual practice.[7] A brief review of how DNA evidence is produced helps to make this point much more clear.

We should note that in making this assertion, it is not necessary for us to arbitrate among the many competing philosophical views of the nature of scientific knowledge-making. (And, indeed, we do not necessarily share precisely the same view.) To say that the discourse described in this article represents an idealized notion of science" is broadly compatible with virtually any contemporary view of science.

DNA profiling is based on the fundamental premise that, with the exception of identical twins, no two human beings have exactly the same genetic make-up.[8] There are various forms of difference—polymorphism—within the human genome. For example, any two individuals will have different nucleotides at about one in one thousand sites as a result of random mutation. There are also regions of the genome called tandem repeats, where short sequences of DNA are repeated one after the other. The number of repetitive sequences at certain locations in the genome can be highly variable from person to person. The DNA profiling method most commonly used today focuses on very short tandem repeats that are two to six nucleotides long and is called short tandem repeat (STR) analysis. STR

---

7 To understand science this way would be akin to the understanding of law before the law and society movement, that is, to take law's expressed ideals at face value without inquiring into to what extent they are realized in practice.

8 Butler (2005) provides an excellent introduction to the science of DNA profiling for those who are unfamiliar with the technology.

analysis was developed in the early 1990s and largely replaced the slower, more laborious, and less sensitive restriction fragment length polymorphism (RFLP) analysis by the late 1990s (Aronson 2007).

The first step of the DNA profiling procedure is to extract DNA from the biological material, whether it is a semen stain from a rape case or a blood sample from a criminal suspect. Once isolated, the DNA is subjected to the polymerase chain reaction (PCR), which is an enzymatic process that replicates a specific region of the genome over and over and over. The process entails heating and cooling DNA at precise temperatures through about thirty cycles in the presence of various chemicals, enzymes, and molecules (see Butler 2005). It should be noted that although PCR has become standardized and routinized within the forensic context, subjective decisions must still be made about how to optimize the run conditions for the condition of evidence left at the crime scene (Jordan and Lynch 1998). Further, because of the extreme sensitivity of the technique, even a small amount of contamination has the potential to lead to false results (Butler 2005).

At the end of the reiterative PCR cycle, several hundred million copies of the regions of interest are produced from only a few original DNA molecules. The next step in the process is to analyze the results by measuring the size of the fragments produced from biological samples. Based on this information, which is recorded as a series of peaks on an electropherogram (which looks a bit like a Technicolor heart-rate monitor), a specialized computer program interprets this data. This computer program must distinguish between the numerous alleles of more than a dozen STR loci from data that is not always perfect. Numerous technical problems can lead to interpretation mishaps and occasional miscalls, most of which involve interpreting whether small peaks are true peaks or are spurious (Butler 2005). While these ambiguous peaks are relatively easy to resolve in single DNA contributor samples, they are much more troublesome in mixtures, which frequently occur in rape cases. In addition to these problems, there are a range of other issues that require human intervention in the interpretation process (Butler 2005; Thompson et al. 2003).

Because of the complexity of the operation, and despite significant automation, human intervention and judgment is sometimes necessary. This is especially true in cases of mixture—when there is more than one contributor to a particular crime scene sample—and degraded DNA. At present, however, there are no generally accepted or nationally recognized standards for declaring a match between two profiles. As in other realms of DNA profiling and forensic science, there are only guidelines and recommendations.

Thus, DNA analysts at two different labs might make different decisions about whether a peak is a valid allele or a technical artifact or whether an allelic dropout (i.e., loss of a peak) is caused by degraded DNA or represents nonmatching DNA profiles. Further, there is no strict standard for how many alleles can be missing from one profile for it to match another. This can distort the reported probative value of the evidence (because many different profiles might have been capable of "matching" the crime scene profile) (Thompson 2008). Moreover, it can lead to bias if the analyst uses the suspect profile as a guide to interpreting the ambiguous data found in the crime scene profile (Risinger et al. 2002; Krane et al. 2008).

The Authority of "Science"

Despite these contingencies, DNA profiling is deployed in the innocence discourse as a rhetorical foil to legal decision-making processes that are flawed, imperfect, error-prone, subjective, and so on. Much of Scheck and Neufeld's public writing and speaking have drawn on the trope of using DNA to pose a validity test not just for other forms of evidence, but also for the criminal justice system itself. By treating DNA evidence as ground truth, past attempts by the criminal justice system to get at truth may be tested. The criminal justice system, Scheck and Neufeld argue, fails the test. And now, claims Scheck, DNA testing provides a "magic black box" that can be used to go back and look at cases of wrongful conviction to determine what went wrong (Frontline 1997). He states,

> When you saw a case, depending whether you're a judge, a prosecutor, a defense lawyer, anyone in the system, you see a case where somebody is convicted and they drag that individual out of the courtroom and he is screaming, "I'm innocent, I'm innocent," and you walk away sometimes saying, "I don't know, there's some doubt." Now we can go back to those cases 15, 20 years later and we can find out. (Frontline 1997)

Or, as Neufeld put it, "the reason we have had success where other efforts have failed is that DNA is a kind of gold standard of innocence, so people cannot dispute these cases" (quoted in Nowak 2003). Neufeld's reference to the gold standard invokes the classic idea of validity testing in which the value of something (in the case the routine accuracy of American criminal justice) is calibrated against some known and well-accepted standard (in this case DNA).

Liebman's (2002) effort to characterize the "reason why DNA exonerations have such a hold of the popular imagination" (543) draws on yet another trope, religion, to convey the way in which DNA functions as an irrefutable arbiter of truth and thus as a test of the law's version of truth.[9] DNA exonerations, he writes, "involve something like divine intervention—the inscrutable and unpredictable intercession by grace of a power to see an otherwise unknowable and undiscoverable truth, that truth being the inherent fallibility and corruption of humans and their institutions" (543). Liebman further points out that DNA exonerations play a particularly important role in undermining the law's epistemic authority because, unlike non-DNA exonerations, which are typically exposed

---

9 Of course, science and religion are not nearly as unrelated as the contemporary popular imagination would have them (Fuller 2006).

by some aspect of "the [legal or criminal justice] system," one must conclude that most DNA exonerations would never have come to light were it not for the fortuitous development of technology at that particular historical moment (not to mention the fortuitous preservation of the biological evidence in that particular case). Similarly, Garrett (2008) has shown that, for almost all of the postconviction DNA exonerations, innocence arguments were rejected, or not even put forward, before the appearance of the DNA evidence. Without DNA, innocence was indiscernible. This is an important finding because it demonstrates that normal legal mechanisms were incapable of detecting innocence in these (now indisputable) innocence cases. Thus, for DNA exonerations, it is more difficult to argue that "the system worked," and, in capital cases, it is more difficult to argue that the system would have stopped the execution had DNA evidence not been developed (Liebman 2002, 545–47). "It is this sense of insecurity in the face of an only infrequently and arbitrarily—but, when it occurs, infallibly—revealed truth about ... our institutions' weaknesses that DNA most forcibly instills, and that, in turn, most powerfully motivates our national doubts about the current application of the death penalty" (547).[10]

Law, like science, is a truth-producing social institution, but it does not carry the same epistemic authority as science within Anglo-American society (Loevinger 1967; Huber 1991; Goldberg 1994; Jasanoff 1995; Angell 1996; Bourdieu 1998). Society relies on law to determine truth about many important matters, but our reliance is based on a belief that law has the pragmatic ability to resolve questions (reasonably) efficiently and, above all, fairly in circumstances of messy contingency (Jasanoff 1995). The preference for law is in part methodological: usually, the circumstances in which law serves as arbiter of truth are circumstances in which the methods of science, however epistemically privileged, would be unusable.

As a system, designed in part around the need for efficient and expeditious resolution of disputes, rather than a search for "ultimate truth," law has developed a variety of principles designed to bring the process of inquiry to an end even in the face of uncertainty. These principles are generally summed up under the rubric of "finality" (Berger 2000, 2). Finality essentially means that at various points in the process of inquiry (verdict, resolution of direct appeal, etc.), law becomes increasingly (and, from an epistemological point of view, unreasonably) attached to the version of the truth to which it has committed itself. Indeed, our criminal justice system does not possess a method for reviewing factual

---

10 Rosen (2003) sees a plausible legal argument in the evidence of innocence amassed by exonerations: he argues that Gregg approved the constitutionality of the death penalty only "in the absence of more convincing evidence" and that "now such evidence exists—powerful evidence of innocents on death row" (106). With the overturning of Quinones (2002b) and the current makeup of the courts, such legal arguments are probably academic.

mistakes unless there is a procedural error that accompanies it. Legally speaking, "truth" is largely irrelevant in postconviction litigation (Rosen 2003, 75).[11]

The use of the authority of science in the death penalty debate has the potential to cause society to question law's epistemic claims as truth-generating institution. Moreover, the law's historic opposition to even consider its own accuracy may come under sustained pressure from the injection of DNA evidence into the death penalty debate. Innocence activists frequently make invidious comparisons between the response to errors in, say, transportation or medicine and the response in law (Scheck and Neufeld 2002). Law, they point out, has no mechanisms to undertake investigations of its own errors or assessments of its own accuracy. Indeed, legal principles such as finality render such undertakings suspect. Innocence activists have managed to use this attitude to portray the law as a defiantly premodern institution.

Such arguments invoke the language of system failure against the criminal justice system. The Innocence Project has always sought to do more than merely exonerate individuals; it has tried valiantly to use exonerations as "windows" into the workings and failings of the criminal justice system.[12] It has consistently tried to resist the media's inexorable tendency to turn exonerations into heartwarming individual stories of tragedy and triumph. Instead, it relentlessly focuses attention on the systemic failings revealed by exonerations and to the inevitable conclusion that each known exoneration must represent many more wrongly convicted whose innocence simply cannot be demonstrated. To shift media, public, or even political attention in this way is far from an easy task, and how successful the Innocence Project has been is open to debate. For our purposes here, it is sufficient to note that, again, the epistemic authority of science is crucial to the task. Only with the tendency to quibble over the factual innocence of the exonerated neutralized is it possible to proceed to discussion of systemic reform.

Perhaps one of the most powerful such invocations is that of former Illinois Governor George Ryan who drew on his own occupational identity as a practitioner of that most quotidian of sciences, pharmacy. Notably, even if pharmacists are not "high" scientists, they are quite concerned with quality control and sensitive to the problem of undiscovered

---

11 Indeed, criminal law places extraordinary limits on the ability of facts to dislodge the established version of truth. This is true even in the case of DNA evidence; a great deal of the work of postconviction DNA exoneration consists of overcoming procedural obstacles to having the evidence tested or testing results considered by a court. In most cases, innocence claimants have little or no legal right to have DNA evidence tested or testing results considered by a court; typically, they must rely on discretionary decisions by judges to allow testing and hearing of evidence to go forward (Kreimer and Rudovsky 2002). That innocence claimants usually eventually succeed in these efforts (Dewan 2004) is itself testament to the persuasive authority of DNA evidence.

12 For more on the Innocence Project, see http://www.innocenceproject.org/about (accessed February 5, 2009).

errors concealed within routine practice. Thus, Ryan declared himself perplexed by the law's seeming indifference to catastrophic errors, something that would be met with aggressive remedial measures if it had occurred within pharmaceutical practice. The system failure argument also plays into another abolitionist argument. It is one thing to tolerate a certain level of routine errors in exchange for the benefits of transportation or the delivery of medicines that alleviate suffering. But why tolerate errors in a system that, abolitionists claim, we can do without (Zimring 2005, 122)?

Another way in which the epistemic authority of science is invoked is by pointing to DNA evidence's purported ability to overturn "commonsensical" intuitions and stereotypes. In an interview with New Scientist magazine, Neufeld stated,

> In about 50 per cent of all the cases we take to the laboratory, the DNA exonerates them. In about 50 per cent of the cases the DNA confirms guilt. We had two guys a few years ago who went to the laboratory the same week. One fellow was the most pleasant, lovely, supportive, young man. Sent Mother's Day cards to the students, talked about how he couldn't wait to get back to his ailing grandmother, could not have been nicer. And the other fella was a real nasty son of a bitch, cursed out the students, was furious with everybody, talked about crimes he would commit if he could only get out. The students were convinced that the first person would be excluded by the DNA and the second person implicated. Just the opposite occurred. The beauty of the science is that it topples the common intuitions that we rely on to make important decisions. (quoted in Nowak 2003)

Epistemological Closure

DNA evidence appears to be able to provide what we might call epistemological closure of disputed postconviction exonerations.[13] Importantly for our purposes, "closure" does not entail complete proof of any particular position. Rather, it refers to the point at which almost all of the relevant stakeholders agree not to debate the point any longer. Unlike the alleged wrongful convictions debated by Bedau and Radelet (1987) and Markman and Cassell (1988), the Dotson case was successfully brought to the point of epistemological closure. In other words, in the Dotson case, the relevant stakeholders, which in legal discourse Edmond (2002b) has called the "law set," agreed on the version of truth provided by DNA evidence. It is not that the DNA evidence could not be disputed. Unlikely but possible theories of the crime that accommodate the DNA evidence could

13 This framing draws on Collins's (1981) notion of "closure" in scientific controversies.

be devised (e.g., the notorious "unindicted co-ejaculator" theory[14]), the implication of laboratory contamination or sample mix-up could be raised, or the "black box" of DNA evidence itself could be opened up and contested (Halfon 1998; Jordan and Lynch 1998). But, in an environment of scarce epistemological resources, the costs of disbelieving DNA evidence are too high. As Zimring (2003) observes, "DNA exonerations end the debate about whether a reversal or nonprosecution is really an exoneration. A broad public opinion accepts DNA findings as definitive, so there is no tactical advantage to prosecutors denying definitive DNA results as establishing innocence" (159).

The decreasing tenability of arguments against DNA exonerations is well illustrated by the press reports of the Bruce Godschalk case in Montgomery County, Pennsylvania, in 2002.[15] Even after the court ordered Godschalk released, District Attorney Bruce Castor declared the "DNA testing is flawed" and that Godschalk was guilty. The slender cultural plausibility of such a statement is aptly conveyed by the ironic tone of the New York Times's report of the statement: "Asked what scientific basis he had for concluding the testing was flawed, Mr. Castor said in an interview today: 'I have no scientific basis. I know because I trust my detective and my tape-recorded confession. Therefore, the results must be flawed until someone proves to me otherwise'" (Rimer 2002). In addition to the New York Times's implicit criticism, Castor's view was explicitly mocked in editorials around the country (Tucker 2002). These characterizations illustrate the cultural implausibility of Castor's radically skeptical assertion that "DNA testing is flawed" because it contradicts the conclusions of a detective and a confession.

Such prosecutorial and judicial expressions of skepticism about DNA evidence are becoming increasingly rare. Even if doubt is expressed about some individual DNA exonerations, with over two hundred postconviction DNA exonerations recorded, innocence activists can invoke numbers. At the time of this writing, the vast majority of criminal justice system actors appear to have conceded the broader point: DNA exonerations are largely factual innocence cases. In short, DNA exonerations appear to be armed with a resistance to the sort of radically skeptical moves that for so long neutralized exonerations from having any power to undermine faith in capital punishment (or criminal justice more generally).

A DOUBLE-EDGED SWORD

As scholars who specialize in the social study of science, we will admit to some discomfort with the rhetorical employment of science in the discourse reported above. Before

---

14 In this scenario, prosecutors argue that convict was involved in the crime with another unknown assailant, and that only the unknown assailant's biological material was recovered from the crime scene.

15 For a review of Godschalk's case, see http://www.innocenceproject.org/Content/154.php (accessed February 5, 2009).

turning to our own analysis however, we will first discuss some of the misgivings that the actors themselves have expressed about their own deployment of DNA profiling in the death penalty debate. Even amidst the heady euphoria of having hit upon an issue that provides some hope of breaking the long deadlocked capital punishment debate, some abolitionists perceive moral and strategic hazards posed by embrace of the innocence argument.

Many abolitionists, for instance, worry that an overemphasis on innocence can distract attention from other good reasons to oppose capital punishment, as well as other important problems with our criminal justice system (such as over punishment and racism) (Davis 2003; Berman 2006). Similarly, the tactical call for moratoria based on revelations of innocence may potentially backfire by allowing death penalty proponents to claim that the system has been "repaired" (Bedau 2004b, 26). Zimring (2003) has also noted that in the courts, greater attention to innocence has coexisted with strenuous—and contradictory—efforts, such as the Anti-Terrorism and Effective Death Penalty Act of 1996, "to remove the obstacles to executions by strict enforcement of procedural defaults" (174). Sarat (2003) perhaps summed it up best when he characterized some abolitionists' embrace of innocence as at once morally indefensible and morally necessary.

Further, it would be difficult to dispute that in some ways the innocence movement has provided useful cover and an image of political neutrality for the increasing use of DNA technology in forensic investigations. It has allowed the insertion of the humane phrase "and protect the innocent" to the resonant tough-on-crime phrase "convict the guilty" in justifications for the expansion of DNA testing, thus creating an unbeatable rhetorical justification for the expansion of DNA technology. Moreover, DNA exonerations did not merely facilitate the expanded use of investigative DNA technology, they also strengthened its epistemic authority. Indeed, this is surely one reason that DNA exonerations achieve the epistemological closure described above. It might be imagined that even those criminal justice system actors who were least pleased to see exonerations—prosecutors and judges—saw the concession of even two hundred exonerations as a small price to pay for solidifying the mantle of truth and certainty around the inculpatory uses of DNA evidence—especially if Scheck and Neufeld's more general critique of the criminal justice system could be neutralized. Inculpatory uses of DNA evidence are indeed becoming increasingly difficult to challenge, and courts are coming under increasing pressure to essentially anoint all DNA evidence as truthful and discourage inquiries into potential problems with the evidence (Aronson 2007; Lynch et al. 2008).

In the death penalty discourse as well, DNA has been turned on its head. The authority and credibility of DNA have been used not just to undermine faith in the criminal justice, but also to bolster it. As Senator Orrin Hatch stated in a 2001 congressional hearing on postconviction testing, "It is indisputable that advanced DNA testing lends support and credibility to the accuracy and integrity of capital verdicts. In short, we are in a better position than ever before to ensure that only the guilty are executed" (Hatch 2000). Similarly,

Justice Scalia, in response to Justice Souter's treatment of DNA exonerations as evidence of the unreliability of capital punishment, not only treats exonerations as "a vindication of [the capital justice system's] effectiveness," but also touts DNA as a "scientific means of establishing guilt" (Kansas v. Marsh 2006, 2534–36, Scalia, J., concurring). Similarly, in recent hearings held by the Maryland Commission on Capital Punishment, Scheck was forced to rebut claims that "advances in DNA testing in recent years significantly diminish the chance of wrongful conviction in capital cases" and that "with today's forensic science, it is unlikely that an innocent man could be executed" (quoted in Bykowicz 2008).

Such a turn of events was in a sense a predictable outcome of the ways in which DNA-based claims of innocence have been deployed in the death penalty debate. Indeed, in retrospect, it is possible to discern the seeds of this development even in the innocence argument's finest hour, Judge Rakoff's decision in Quinones (2002b). In one breath, Rakoff argued that exonerations vouched for with the authority of DNA provided the proof that was lacking in Herrera v. Collins (1993) that innocent people can be convicted of capital crimes, and possibly executed. "We now know," Rakoff wrote, "in a way almost unthinkable even a decade ago, that our system of criminal justice, for all its protections, is sufficiently fallible that innocent people are convicted of capital crimes with some frequency" (United States v. Quinones 2002b, 420). Postconviction DNA exonerations tell us that errors occur in our death penalty system, thus rendering it, for Rakoff, unconstitutional. But in the next breath, Rakoff anticipates the invoking of the authority of DNA in favor of the argument that the "broken system" (Liebman, Fagan, and West 2000) is now fixed. "Fortunately, as DNA testing illustrates, scientific developments and other innovative measures (including some not yet even known) may enable us not only to prevent future mistakes but also to rectify past ones by releasing wrongfully-convicted persons—but only if such persons are still alive to be released" (United States v. Quinones 2002b, 420, emphasis added).

Rakoff's argument focused not merely on the epistemic certainty of the exonerees' innocence claims, but also on their temporal nature: "that ... convincing proof of their innocence often does not emerge until long after their convictions," thus inviting risk of wrongful execution (United States v. Quinones 2002a, 257). The question is whether Rakoff's view of the danger of wrongful execution can survive the period in which preconviction DNA typing becomes routine. We might still infer from the era of postconviction DNA testing that we probably execute the innocent, but we would no longer have any proof that we do, lacking a "truth machine" to overturn settled convictions with the finality of DNA evidence. Thus, the reliance on DNA as the authority that vouches for the claim that we execute the innocent renders some abolitionists vulnerable to the argument—whatever its merits—that DNA fixes capital punishment. As Mandery (2004) puts it, abolitionists "succumbed to the lure of innocence. ... But now they've been called on it" (519).

Mandery was referring to the so-called guilty project. On September 23, 2003, Governor Mitt Romney's office issued a press release announcing his plans to reinstate the death penalty in Massachusetts, one of only twelve states at the time without capital punishment. Titled "Romney Takes Scientific Approach to Death Penalty," the press release stated that Romney hoped to rely on "the latest advances in forensic science" to ensure that the death penalty would be "narrowly applied and used in accordance with the highest standard of proof (Massachusetts Governor's Office 2003).

The reason he turned to science was clear to friend and foe alike. As James P. Rooney, a Massachusetts anti-death penalty advocate explained:

> The nagging question of innocence also brought a new moral calculus to the old death penalty debate, one expressed in Massachusetts by recently retired House Speaker Thomas Finneran. A one-time death penalty supporter, this conservative Democrat now believes that, in taking the life of a wrongfully convicted person, society would be killing a person as innocent as the murder victim whose death had occasioned society's revenge. This philosophy can brook no error. The only human construct that offers the hope of such certainty is science (at least in the opinion of non-scientists), so it is to science that Governor Romney turned. (Rooney, emphasis added)

In order to achieve the goal of what the press quickly labeled as a "foolproof death penalty, Romney commissioned a panel of leading scientific and legal experts to come up with a plan that would ensure that only the guilty were executed and only for a very narrow set of crimes. Their charge was two-fold: first, to create a narrowly defined subset of first degree murders that would trigger the death penalty, so as to ensure that only the "worst of the worst" were executed, and, second, to place a "strong emphasis on the use of scientific evidence to help establish the defendant's guilt, which will ensure—as much as humanly possible—that no innocent person will ever wrongly be condemned to death" (Governor's Council Final Report 2004, 4). In a sense, Massachusetts sought to achieve through science the Furman-dictated goals of reliability and narrow tailoring that other states had sought to achieve through legal procedures.

As one member noted shortly after the panel issued its final report, the debate about the death penalty over the past several years had been dominated by two polar opposite approaches: the path of the status quo versus complete abolition (Hoffman 2005). He argued that Romney and the council had decided to embark down a different, reformist path: "pursuit of the Holy Grail of a death penalty that can meet society's standards for accuracy and fairness" (565).[16]

In their final report, the Governor's Council on Capital Punishment offered a series of ten proposals (including statutory, procedural, legal, and technical recommendations)

---

16 It might be argued that New York State took this third path in its reinstatement of capital punishment during the 1990s.

that "if adopted in their entirety, can allow creation of a fair capital punishment statute for Massachusetts that is as narrowly tailored, and as infallible, as humanly possible" (Governor's Council Final Report 2004, 3). Throughout the report, the council made it clear that the recommendations would only be effective if they were adopted as a whole, and that the best way to ensure accuracy was through multiple layers of review, including a rigorous review of scientific evidence in capital cases (4).

The sixth proposal—the need for "conclusive scientific evidence (i.e., physical or other associative evidence), reaching a high level of scientific certainty, that connects the defendant to either the location of the crime scene, the murder weapon, or the victim's body, and that strongly corroborates the defendant's guilt of capital murder" (20) in order for a death sentence to be imposed—is particularly interesting in this context. The council stated that while the current benchmark for the kind of "physical or other associative evidence" that can satisfy this recommendation is a full single-source DNA profile, other categories of "physical or other associative evidence" may be capable of providing conclusive associations of suspects, victims, crime scenes, and/or the implements of crime. These include photographs, video-and audiotapes, fingerprints, and certain impression evidence (e.g., some footwear impressions, tire impressions, tool marks, firearms-related impressions, and other physical pattern matches). (20)

Perhaps the most obvious flaw in this proposal is the ironic fact that, if considered as a broad, undifferentiated category of evidence, "science" itself (in the form of forensic techniques that, according to some critics, have never been subjected to validation studies and have high rates of error) is the second leading cause of wrongful conviction among postconviction DNA exonerations (Saks and Koehler 2005; Garrett 2008). In other words, purportedly unassailable science (DNA) today tells us that one of the chief causes of wrongful convictions was scientific evidence that was touted as unassailable at the time of the conviction. This alone would seem to suggest that the lesson to take from the learning opportunity afforded by postconviction DNA testing is not so much a need for better technology, but a need for continuous skepticism concerning whatever technology is currently touted as the "latest." Indeed, despite claims of infallibility of the technique, DNA profiling errors have been discovered with surprising regularity over the past decade (Thompson 2006; Aronson 2007).

Moreover, the Massachusetts proposal uses "science" as a monolithic category to describe a wide range of forms of evidence. The proposal is conspicuously vague in its description of science, and, as it stands, the proposal would count as "science" everything ranging from DNA profiling to handwriting identification to microscopic hair analysis to footwear comparison. Indeed, the proposal's notion of science is so unspecified that it is not clear whether it would actually narrow the set of cases subject to the death penalty very much, if at all.[17]

An obvious problem with this notion of "science" is that the urge behind the sixth proposal (the requirement of "scientific evidence to corroborate the defendant's guilt"), which clearly was the urge to have a DNA-based death penalty, has ended up, through this vague wording, dragging in all sorts of other forms of evidence calling themselves "science" that may be of questionable reliability. The accuracy of most of the techniques that would fall into the proposal's broad category of science is simply unknown. An example is fingerprint evidence, which certainly would qualify under the Massachusetts guidelines (Pokorak 2005; Cole 2006). Other techniques, such as handwriting identification, microscopic hair comparison, and bite mark analysis are known to have high rates of inaccuracy.

It is true that the report notes that "not all 'physical or associative evidence' will be capable of satisfying this requirement of conclusive evidence reaching the level of scientific certainty that adequately connects the defendant to the crime" (Governor's Council Final Report 2004, 20). But the main thrust of the critiques of many types of associative evidence is precisely that practitioners routinely overclaim the scientific certainty of their own conclusions (Friedman 2003; Cole 2007). Moreover, the Massachusetts proposal would increase the incentive for such overclaiming. Rather than acknowledging scientific evidence as inherently uncertain and pushing it toward its strength, which is its potential ability to quantify and transparently convey uncertainty, the Massachusetts proposal pushes forensic witnesses toward greater claims of certainty.

The council's recommendation, however, went well beyond the mere existence of sound scientific evidence of guilt. They also argued that it was crucial to review that evidence to ensure that it was collected, handled, preserved, analyzed, stored, and interpreted according to the "highest standards of the medical and scientific community" (Governor's Council Final Report 2004, 24). In order to fulfill this function, the council recommended the creation of an Independent Scientific Review (ISR) Panel. In addition to reviewing the actual evidence in the particular capital case, the ISR Panel would also be charged with ensuring that all crime laboratories and other forensic science providers in the case were properly accredited by an appropriate accrediting organization (24). This measure, they hoped, would "provide strong incentives for systematic reforms across the forensic science community" (25). Although the council did not state explicitly what would happen if such a review turned up major problems, it seems that they would bar this evidence from being used during the sentencing phase of the trial.

---

17 On the other hand, it has been suggested that other aspects of the Massachusetts proposal might narrow the set of cases to null. It has also been noted that the proposal might raise arbitrariness issues, in that the death penalty might be applied, not according to the ratio of aggravation to mitigation as currently required by the Supreme Court, but according to availability of evidence (Pokorak 2005).

On April 28, 2005, Mitt Romney filed his death penalty bill in the Massachusetts House, which was based almost entirely on the final report of the Governor's Council. In announcing the bill in his press release, titled "Relying on Science, Romney Files Death Penalty Bill," Governor Romney was quoted as saying that previous efforts to reintroduce the death penalty in the state failed because "of concerns that it would be too broadly applied or that evidentiary standards weren't high enough or proper safeguards weren't in place" (Massachusetts Governor's Office 2005).

In editorials lambasting the governor and the council's final report, however, abolitionists found numerous reasons to reject capital punishment, only some of which had to do with accuracy. In an editorial in the Bergen County Record, University of Houston Law Professor David R. Dow (2003) called Romney's plan "stunningly naive." He argued that creating an infallible death penalty system was like trying to develop risk-free space travel, perfect mail delivery, or a national highway system with zero fatalities. At a deeper level, though, Dow saw the execution of innocents as only one part of the problem with the death penalty. Issues such as racial inequities in sentencing are just as pernicious and were not going to be addressed at all by the council. This meant that any death penalty statute that came out of its deliberations would still be fundamentally unjust.

In an editorial in the Boston Globe titled "Foolproof or Foolish?", James Alan Fox (2003), a professor of criminal justice at Northeastern University, noted that Romney hoped to exploit the power of DNA evidence and other forms of science to produce an infallible death penalty that could serve as a model for the rest of the nation. Despite the great power of DNA that citizens read about in the newspaper and see on CSI, however, Fox noted that the human beings who perform the test do indeed make mistakes (see below).

Romney's proposal was resoundingly voted down by a margin of 100–53 in November 2005 (Helman 2005). Skepticism that a "system that relies on scientific evidence" would operate "flawlessly" was among the reasons for the bill's defeat (Jasanoff 2006, 332). The significance of this vote is put into perspective when one realizes that preliminary versions of a bill to reinstate the death penalty passed both the Massachusetts House and Senate and lost by just one vote in the final House vote in 1997 (Walker and Wong 1997).

Although the Massachusetts proposal is the clearest example, there are other instances of the ways in which some abolitionists' deployment of innocence may be seen to have had "bite back" effects (Tenner 1996). Following Massachusetts, another abolitionist state, Wisconsin, recently introduced a nonbinding ballot measure asking whether the death penalty should be reinstated "if the conviction is supported by DNA evidence." The sponsor of the initiative said that he included the DNA clause "to defang opponents. 'It was my hope that this would dispel some of the fence-sitters from saying that the sky is falling and that someone is going to be wrongly convicted'" (Erickson 2006). So, just as some abolitionists hoped that ironclad innocence, vouched for by DNA, would sway the "center" in the death penalty debate, proponents of capital punishment are now hoping that ironclad guilt will sway the center the other way.

DEATH IS DIFFERENT, BUT IS DNA?

The tendency, discussed above, to characterize DNA as a "truth machine," fueled in part by the use of DNA to undermine trust in the death penalty itself, obscures the fact that DNA evidence is evidence, too, and therefore subject to error, misinterpretation, and uncertainty. Recent problems in DNA laboratories around the country suggest that we should not be so fast to assume the sanctity of DNA evidence. While some mistakes have been the result of simple clerical errors, others have revealed overt fraud and inexcusable incompetence on a grand scale. The most well-known of these cases is the Houston Police Department's (HPD) Crime Laboratory, which was closed down in 2002 after it was discovered that employees regularly fabricated DNA and other forensic evidence in their labs and lied in court about the results of their test. An ongoing investigation of the HPD casework has revealed forty-three DNA cases "in which there are significant doubts about reliability of the work performed, the validity of the Crime Lab's analytical results, or the correctness of the analysts reported conclusions" (Office of the Independent Investigator for the Houston Police Department Crime Laboratory and Property Room 2006).

While the Houston story is no doubt the most dramatic, other laboratories have not been immune from embarrassment, including the FBI, where an analyst had been faking the quality control portion of her work for more than two years (US Department of Justice 2004). Related problems have been discovered in Seattle's crime laboratory, where DNA contamination and other errors were found in at least twenty-three cases (Seattle Post-Intelligencer 2004). In North Carolina, the state Bureau of Investigations DNA unit has recently come under fire in an exposé by the Winston-Salem Journal (Zerwick 2005). Although an audit by the American Society of Laboratory Directors/Laboratory Accreditation Board (ASCLD/LAB) cleared the laboratory of wrong-doing in the particular case in question, the organization urged the state to improve the way it collected, handled, and stored biological evidence (Zerwick 2005). Cross-contamination and sample mislabeling problems have also been documented in Pennsylvania, Nevada, California (Thompson 2006), and elsewhere (Ruethling 2005; Cadiz 2004; McGlone 2006).

Postconviction testing has not been immune from similar mistakes. In a highly publicized Virginia case, investigations associated with the postconviction exoneration of death-row inmate Earl Washington, Jr., led to the discovery that the State Division of Forensic Sciences Central Laboratory in Richmond, which long held a reputation as one of the nation's finest, had made numerous mistakes in the course of their 2000 review of Washington's 1983 conviction for rape and murder. According to an ASCLD/LAB audit, the Virginia state laboratory had not followed accepted procedures when conducting PCR-based DNA profiling; misinterpreted the results of the test, leading to erroneous exclusion of the victim from the vaginal smear taken from her dead body; and made numerous conclusions that were unsupported by available data (ASCLD/LAB 2005). The report also concluded that the laboratory's own mechanisms for catching errors failed in this case since the technical reviewer did not observe the errors in the processes and the reported results (17).

It is, of course, hardly surprising that fraud and incompetence would occur in forensic DNA testing, as would be expected for any technical practice. However, even competently and honestly performed DNA analyses may not always function as the archetypal "truth machine." DNA "matches" may represent many things in addition to evidence that the matched individual committed the crime in question. The match may be "coincidental"—the suspect may share the same alleles as the true perpetrator at some number of loci. The possibility of a coincidental match is, of course, significantly higher for a "partial" (fewer than thirteen loci) match, and several such coincidental matches for partial profiles have occurred (Mnookin 2001; Murphy 2007). However, even at the thirteen loci used by the FBI's CODIS[18] system, some coincidental matches are likely in populations the size of countries like the United States and United Kingdom, though none have yet been found (Weir 2007; Thompson 2008). The likelihood of coincidental match is greater if a close blood relative is the true perpetrator.

In addition, the DNA match may have been left innocently at a time other than the occurrence of the crime or through third-party transfer. Or the DNA may have been maliciously planted, something that is becoming increasingly possible (Dent 2006; Thompson 2008). Even setting those possibilities aside, in many cases, DNA evidence can be subject to conflicting interpretations. Cases involving partial profiles, mixtures of several different DNA profiles, or low copy number DNA (profiles produced from very small amounts of DNA) are particularly vulnerable to what sociologists of science call "interpretive flexibility" (Pinch and Bijker 1984), in which the evidence may be consistent with more than one version of "the facts." In cases involving mixtures, for example, the "truth" told by DNA evidence can depend on assumptions about how many contributors there are to a mixture and who they are. In such cases, far from functioning as a "truth machine," DNA analysis requires making judgment calls about whether ambiguous results should be treated as true representations of genetic material or as artifacts (Thompson et al. 2003; Lynch et al. 2008).

The tendency among defenders of forensic science is to attribute such problems to pathologies—either pathological individuals or pathological practices—while preserving a zone of purity for the technique itself. This allows such defenders to claim that "the significance of forensic evidence, when performed properly and interpreted reasonably, is beyond dispute" (Bieber 2005, 71). Such pronouncements benefit from hindsight that is unavailable to the finders of fact in capital—or criminal—trials. Often the conclusion that

18 CODIS is the acronym for Combined DNA Index System.

a forensic assay was "performed properly and interpreted reasonably" is based on nothing more than whether one agrees with the results. For example, latent print misidentifications that were presumed to have been performed properly and interpreted reasonably at the time of trial, when exposed as misidentifications, are then deemed to have been performed incompetently (Cole 2005).[19] Whether the forensic tests were performed and interpreted properly or improperly is precisely what is unknown to the fact finder, and this is precisely what makes the jury verdict an exercise in decision making under conditions of uncertainty.

CONCLUSION

In contemporary death penalty discourse, some abolitionists have used DNA evidence as an epistemological lever with which to undermine trust in the American criminal justice system. This rhetorical strategy invited death penalty reformers to similarly portray science as a truth-producer with epistemic authority sufficient to enable the American public to accept the deliberate taking of the lives of fellow citizens without worry. Such arguments have tended to treat science as an epistemic system fundamentally different from—and superior to—law. In such treatments, abolitionists and reformers alike seem to share a notion that DNA offers an escape from the fundamental uncertainties that necessarily undergird any system of criminal justice or state killing. The claim that science is certain and law is uncertain is a common one in both law and the popular imagination. Many existing legal practices stem from this idea. For example, the "beyond a reasonable doubt" standard derives from the seventeenth-century argument that law could generate "moral certainty" (i.e., a level of certainty that would allow the fair conduct of human affairs), but not the higher level of "mathematical certainty" achievable of science (Shapiro 1991, 7–8).

This notion, however, relies on an idealized image of science as certain, objective, and epistemically indisputable that is not shared among most practicing philosophers of science or even scientists themselves. The nature of science is now described in terms of probability (see Gigerenzer et al. 1989; Kruger, Daston, and Heidelberger 1990). In other words, the strength of science is now thought to lie in its ability to grasp, control, and, in some cases, quantify uncertainty, and to continuously strive to reduce it through systematic investigations into nature. The ability to deal with uncertainty, albeit without the opportunity to regularly revisit decisions, is what law does as well. Although the legal fact finder (either the judge or the jury) can never know for sure that they have the story (and the verdict) correct, they must get as close to the right decision as possible.

DNA does not and cannot answer questions of guilt or innocence with epistemological certainty. As Edmond (2002a) has demonstrated, the notion that science produces

19 If competent performance is intended to serve as an indicator of accuracy of result, then there must be a measure of competence that is independent of the result.

epistemically certain facts about criminal cases can only be sustained by evaluating the quality of scientific evidence based on one's a priori conclusions about guilt or innocence. The widespread agreement that a particular conviction was "wrongful" or "just" is, in fact, a product of social consensus, not something dictated by the scientific evidence. In the case of the DNA exonerations, they are "ironclad" because the cultural authority of DNA renders the costs of doubting them too high, not because they are, in any fundamental sense, epistemically unchallengeable. Scientific evidence is, at bottom evidence, like any other. It is and should be, as Jasanoff (2006) puts it in a double entendre, "just evidence."

Arguments that rely on purportedly ironclad science elide the fundamentally probabilistic nature of scientific knowledge. The value of DNA evidence lies not in the fact that it escapes probability, but in the fact that, in contrast to much evidence, it makes possible calculations of probability based on actual data (however imperfect it may be). Interestingly, probabilistic thinking has been gaining ground in legal thinking recently, though there are still many areas of legal discourse, like the death penalty, that are still almost completely avoid probabilistic thinking. Indeed, in its effort to avoid such probabilistic approaches, law turns to ostensibly certain science. But there will be no escape from uncertainty, in science or in capital punishment. DNA profiling offers no easy escape from the epistemological ties that bind capital punishment.

REFERENCES

Acker, James R. in press. Actual Innocence: Is Death Different? Behavioral Sciences and the Law.

American Bar Association. 1997. Recommendation No. 107. Chicago: American Bar Association.

Angell, Marcia. 1996. Science on Trial: The Clash of Medical Evidence and the Law in the Breast Implant Case. New York: Norton.

Aronson, Jay D. 2007. Genetic Witness: Science, Law, and Controversy in the Making of DNA Profiling. New Brunswick, NJ: Rutgers University Press.

ASCLAD/LAB. 2005. ASCLAD/LAB Limited Scope Interim Inspection Report: Commonwealth of Virginia Division of Forensic Science Central Laboratory. April 9. http://www.dfs.virginia.gov/services/forensicBiology/externalReviewAuditReport.pdf (accessed February 5, 2009).

Bandes, Susan A. 2008. After Innocence: Framing Wrongful Convictions. Utah Law Review, 5. http://ssrn.com/abstract=1034472 (accessed February 20, 2009). Banner, Stuart. 2002. The Death Penalty. Cambridge, MA: Harvard University Press.

Baumgartner, Frank R., Suzanna L. De Boef, and Amber E. Boydstun. 2008. The Decline of the Death Penalty and the Discovery of Innocence. Cambridge: Cambridge University Press.

Bedau, Hugo Adam. 2004a. Abolishing the Death Penalty in the United States: An Analysis of Institutional Obstacles and Future Prospects. In Capital Punishment: Strategies for Abolition, eds. Peter Hodgkinson and William A. Schabas, 186–207. Cambridge: Cambridge University Press.

______. 2004b. An Abolitionist's Survey of the Death Penalty in America Today. In Debating the Death Penalty: Should America Have Capital Punishment? The Experts from Both Sides Make

Their Case, ed. Hugo Adam Bedau and Paul G. Cassell, 15–50. Oxford: Oxford University Press.

Bedau, Hugo, and Michael Radelet. 1987. Miscarriages of Justice in Potentially Capital Cases. Stanford Law Review 40: 21–173.

Berger, Margaret A. 2000. Expert Testimony: The Supreme Court's Rules. Issues in Science and Technology 16 (4): 57–63.

Berman, Douglas A. 2006. Of Innocence and Over-Punishment. In Sentencing Law and Policy. http://sentencing.typepad.com/sentencing_law_and_policy/2006/01/of_innocence_an.html (accessed March 6, 2009).

Bieber, Frederick. 2005. Ethics, Science and the Law of Capital Punishment. Indiana Law Journal 80:69–72.

Borchard, Edwin. 1942 [1932]. Convicting the Innocent: Errors of Criminal Justice. Hamden, CT: Archon.

Bourdieu, Pierre. 1998. The Specificity of the Scientific Field and the Social Conditions of the Progress of Reason. In The Science Studies Reader, ed. Mario Biagioli, 31–50. New York: Routledge.

Butler, John M. 2005. Forensic DNA Typing: Biology, Technology, and Genetics of STR Markers, 2nd ed. New York: Elsevier Academic Press. Bykowicz, Julie. 2008. Sizing Up Wrongful Execution Risk. Baltimore Sun, September 6.

Cadiz, Laura. 2004. MD-based DNA Lab Fires Analyst over Falsified Tests. Baltimore Sun, November 18.

Clarke, Alan W., Eric Lambert, and Laurie Anne Whitt. 2000–2001. Executing the Innocent: The Next Step in the Marshall Hypotheses. New York University Review of Law and Social Change 26:309–44.

Cole, Simon A. 2005. More than Zero: Accounting for Error in Latent Fingerprint Identification. Journal of Criminal Law and Criminology 95:985–1078.

______. 2006. Is Fingerprint Identification Valid? Rhetorics of Reliability in Fingerprint Proponents' Discourse. Law and Policy 28 (1): 109–35.

______. 2007. Where the Rubber Meets the Road: Thinking about Expert Evidence as Expert Testimony. Villanova Law Review 52:803–42.

Collins, H. M. 1981. Introduction: Stages in the Empirical Programme of Relativism. Special Issue: Knowledge and Controversy: Studies of Modern Natural Science. Social Studies of Science 11 (1): 3–10.

Connors, Edward, Thomas Lundregan, Neal Miller, and Tom McEwen. 1996. Convicted by Juries, Exonerated by Science: Case Studies in the Use of DNA Evidence to Establish Innocence After Trial. Washington, DC: National Institute of Justice.

Davis, Angela Y. 2003. Are Prisons Obsolete? New York: Seven Stories Press.

Dent, Rebecca. 2006. The Detection and Characterization of Forensic DNA Profiles Manipulated by the Addition of PCR Amplicon. MA thesis, Centre for Forensic Science, University of Western Australia.

Dewan, Shalia K. 2004. In Georgia Case, the Reach of DNA Appeals Is Tested. New York Times, July 19.
Dieter, Richard C. 1994. Millions Misspent: What Politicians Don't Say About the High Costs of the Death Penalty. Death Penalty Information Center, http://www.deathpenaltyinfo.org/node/599 (accessed March 6, 2009).
Dow, David. 2003. Can There Be a Foolproof Death-penalty System? Bergen County Record, October 13.
Duggan, Erin. 2005. Death Penalty Foes Have Their Say. Albany Times Union, January 26.
Edmond, Gary. 2002a. Constructing Miscarriages of Justice: Misunderstanding Scientific Evidence in High Profile Criminal Appeals. Oxford Journal of Legal Studies 22 (1): 53–89.
______. 2002b. The Law-Set: The Legal-Scientific Production of Medical Propriety. Science, Technology, and Human Values 26 (2): 191–226.
Erickson, Doug. 2006. Tying DNA to the Needle, Oct. 21. http://www.madison.com/archives/read.php?ref=/wsj/2006/10/22/0610210525.php (accessed October 17, 2008).
Forst, Brian. 2004. Errors of Justice: Nature, Sources and Remedies. Cambridge: Cambridge University Press.
Fox, James Alan. 2003. Foolproof or Foolish? Boston Globe, September 28, H11.
Friedman, Richard D. 2003. Squeezing Daubert Out of the Picture. Seton Hall Law Review 33:1047–70.
Frontline. 1997. "What Jennifer Saw: Barry Scheck." Frontline. http://www.pbs.org/wgbh/pages/frontline/shows/dna/interviews/scheck.html (accessed February 5, 2009).
Fuller, Steve. 2006. A Step toward the Legalization of Science Studies. Social Studies of Science 36 (6): 827–34.
Garrett, Brandon L. 2008. Judging Innocence. Columbia Law Review 108 (1): 55–142.
Gigerenzer, Gerd, Zeno Swijtink, Theodore Porter, Lorraine Daston, John Beatty, and Lorenz Kruger. 1989. The Empire of Chance: How Probability Changed Science and Everyday Life. Cambridge: Cambridge University Press.
Golan, Tal. 2004. Laws of Men and Laws of Nature. Cambridge, MA: Harvard University Press.
Goldberg, Steven. 1994. Culture Clash: Law and Science in America. New York: New York University Press.
Governor's Council Final Report. 2004. Massachusetts Governor's Council on Capital Punishment. http://www.lawlib.state.ma.us/docs/5-3-04Governorsreportcapitalpunishment.pdf (accessed March 6, 2009).
Gross, Samuel R., and Phoebe C. Ellsworth. 2003. Second Thoughts: Americans' Views on the Death Penalty at the Turn of the Century. In Beyond Repair? America's Death Penalty, ed. Stephen P. Garvey, 7–57. Durham, NC: Duke University Press.
Halfon, Saul. 1998. Collecting, Testing and Convincing: Forensic DNA Experts in the Courts. Social Studies of Science 28 (5–6): 801–28.
Hall, Bradley R. 2005. From William Henry Furman to Anthony Porter: The Changing Face of the Death Penalty Debate. Journal of Criminal Law and Criminology 95 (2): 371–80.

Hatch, Orrin. 2000. Statement from Hearing on Post-Conviction DNA Testing: When Is Justice Served? United States Senate Committee on the Judiciary, June 13.

Healy, Patrick D. 2005. Death Penalty Is Blocked by Democrats. New York Times, April 13, B1-B6.

Helman, Scott. 2005. Death Penalty Bill Fails in House, Romney Initiative Roundly Defeated. Boston Globe, November 16.

Hoffman, Joseph L. 2005. Protecting the Innocent: The Massachusetts Governor's Council Report. Journal of Criminal Law and Criminology 95:561–85.

Huber, Peter W. 1991. Galileo's Revenge: Junk Science in the Courtroom. New York: Basic.

Jasanoff, Sheila. 1995. Science at the Bar: Law, Science, and Technology in America, Twentieth Century Fund. Cambridge, MA: Harvard University Press.

______. 2006. Just Evidence: The Limits of Science in the Legal Process. Journal of Law, Medicine and Ethics 34 (2): 328–41.

Jordan, Kathleen, and Michael Lynch. 1998. The Dissemination, Standardization and Routinization of a Molecular Biological Technique. Social Studies of Science 28 (5–6): 773–800.

Krane, Dan E., Simon Ford, Jason R. Gilder, Keith Inman, Allan Jamieson, Roger Koppl, Irving L. Kornfield, D. Michael Risinger, Norah Rudin, Mark Scott Taylor, and William C. Thompson. 2008. Sequential Unmasking: A Means of Minimizing Observer Effects in Forensic DNA Interpretation. Journal of Forensic Sciences 53 (4): 1006–07.

Kreimer, Seth F. 2005. Truth Machines and Consequences: The Light and Dark Sides of "Accuracy" in Criminal Justice. New York University Annual Survey of American Law 60:655–74.

Kreimer, Seth F., and David Rudovsky. 2002. Double Helix, Double Bind: Factual Innocence and Postconviction DNA Testing. University of Pennsylvania Law Review 151:547–617.

Kruger, Lorenz, Lorraine Daston, and Michael Heidelberger. 1990. The Probabilistic Revolution, vol. 1. Cambridge, MA: MIT Press.

Latzer. 2003. Reflections on Innocence. Criminal Law Bulletin 39 (2): 133–49.

Lentol, Joseph, Helene Weinstein, and Jeffrion Aubry. 2005. The Death Penalty in New York. New York: New York State Assembly.

Liebman, James S. 2002. The New Death Penalty Debate: What's DNA Got to Do with It? Columbia Human Rights Law Review 33:527–54.

Liebman, James S., Jeffrey Fagan, and Valerie West. 2000. A Broken System: Error Rates in Capital Cases, 1973–1995. New York: Columbia University http://www.2law.columbia.edu/instructionalservices/liebman/liebman2.pdf (accessed March 6, 2009).

Liptak, Adam. 2007. At 60% of Total, Texas Is Bucking Execution Trend. New York Times, December 26, A1.

Loevinger, Lee. 1967. Law and Science as Rival Systems. University of Florida Law Review 19:530–51.

Lutton, Linda. 2000. The End of Executions? In These Times, October.

Lynch, Michael, Simon A. Cole, Ruth McNally, and Kathleen Jordan. 2008. Truth Machine: The Contentious History of DNA Fingerprinting. Chicago: University of Chicago Press.

Mandery, Evan J. 2004. Massachusetts and the Changing Debate on the Death Penalty. Criminal Law Bulletin 40 (5): 518–22.

Markman, Stephen, and Paul Cassell. 1988. Protecting the Innocent: A Response to the Bedau-Radelet Study. Stanford Law Review 41:121–60.

Marshall, Lawrence C. 2004. The Innocence Revolution and the Death Penalty. Ohio State Journal of Criminal Law 1:573–84.

Massachusetts Governor's Office. 2003. Romney Takes Scientific Approach to Death Penalty. Press release.

Massachusetts Governor's Office. 2005. Relying on Science, Romney Files Death Penalty Bill. Press release.

McGlone, Tim. 2006. Nearly 500 Military DNA Cases Under Investigation. Virginian-Pilot, May 17.

Mnookin, Jennifer L. 2001. Fingerprint Evidence in an Age of DNA Profiling. Brooklyn Law Review 67 (1): 13–70.

Murphy, Erin. 2007. The New Forensics: Criminal Justice, False Certainty, and the Second Generation of Scientific Evidence. California Law Review 95:721–97.

Nowak, Rachel. 2003. Rough Justice. New Scientist. http://www.newscientist.com/article/mg17823985.300-rough-justice.html?full=true (accessed February 5, 2009).

Office of the Independent Investigator for the Houston Police Department Crime Laboratory and Property Room. 2006. Independent Investigator Issues Fifth Report on Houston Police Department Crime Lab. May 11. http://www.hpdlabinvestigation. org/pressrelease/060511pressrelease.pdf (accessed November 7, 2008).

Pinch, Trevor, and Wiebe E. Bijker. 1984. The Social Construction of Facts and Artifacts: Or How the Sociology of Science and the Sociology of Technology Might Benefit Each Other. Social Studies of Science 14:399–441.

Pokorak, Jeffrey J. 2005. Unintended Consequences of the Scientific Evidence Requirement. Indiana Law Journal 80:75–80.

Purnick, Joyce. 2004. Temperature Seems to Cool on Death Law. New York Times, December 20, B1.

Radelet, Michael. 2001. The Death Penalty and the Conviction of the Innocent. Paper presented at the Wrongful Convictions: Causes and Remedies conference, Cardozo Law School, March 22, New York, NY.

Radelet, Michael L., Hugo Adam Bedau, and Constance L. Putnam. 1992. In Spite of Innocence: Erroneous Convictions in Capital Cases. Boston, MA: Northeastern University Press.

Radelet, Michael L., and Marian J. Borg. 2000. The Changing Nature of Death Penalty Debates. Annual Review of Sociology 26:43–61.

Raymond, Margaret. 2001. The Problem with Innocence. Cleveland State Law Review 49:449–63.

Rimer, Sara. 2002. Convict's DNA Sways Labs, Not a Determined Prosecutor. New York Times, February 6, A14.

Risinger, D. Michael. 2007. Innocents Convicted: An Empirically Justified Factual Wrongful Conviction Rate. Journal of Criminal Law and Criminology 97 (3): 761806.

Risinger, D. Michael, Michael J. Saks, William C. Thompson, and Robert Rosenthal. 2002. The Daubert/Kumho Implications of Observer Effects in Forensic Science: Hidden Problems of Expectation and Suggestion. California Law Review 90 (1): 1–56.

Rooney, James P. The Demise of the Scientific Death Penalty. Massachusetts Citizens against the Death Penalty. http://mcadp.org/EndSciDP.html (accessed February 5, 2009).

Rosen, Richard A. 2003. Innocence and Death. North Carolina Law Review 82:61–113.

Ruethling, Gretchen. 2005. Illinois State Police Cancels Forensic Lab's Contract, Citing Errors. New York Times, August 20, A8.

Saks, Michael J., and Jonathan J. Koehler. 2005. The Coming Paradigm Shift in Forensic Identification Science. Science 309:892–95.

Sarat, Austin. 2003. The Future of the Death Penalty. Paper presented at Executing Justice: America and the Death Penalty, April 26, University of California, Santa Barbara.

______. 2006. The Rhetoric of Race in the "New Abolitionism." In From Lynch Mobs to the Killing State: Race and the Death Penalty in America, ed. Charles J. Ogletree, Jr. and Austin Sarat, 260–84. New York: New York University Press.

Sarat, Austin, and Nasser Hussain. 2004. On Lawful Lawlessness: George Ryan, Executive Clemency, and the Rhetoric of Sparing Life. Stanford Law Review 56 (5): 1307–44.

Scheck, Barry, and Peter Neufeld. 2002. Toward the Formation of "Innocence Commissions" in America. Judicature 86:98–105.

Scheck, Barry, Peter Neufeld, and Jim Dwyer. 2000. Actual Innocence: Five Days to Execution and Other Dispatches from the Wrongly Convicted. New York: Penguin Putnam, Inc.

______. 2001. Actual Innocence: When Justice Goes Wrong and How to Make it Right. New York: Penguin Putnam, Inc.

Seattle Post-Intelligencer. 2004. Errors in Evidence. Seattle Post-Intelligencer, March 9. Serrill, Michael. 1985. Cathy and Gary in Medialand. Time, May 27, 66.

Shapiro, Barbara J. 1991. Beyond Reasonable Doubt and Probably Cause: Historical Perspectives on the Anglo-American Law of Evidence. Berkeley: University of California Press.

Steiker, Carol S., and Jordan M. Steiker. 2003. Abolition in Our Times. Ohio State Journal of Criminal Law 1:323–43.

______. 2005. The Seduction of Innocence: The Attraction and Limitations of the Focus on Innocence in Capital Punishment Law and Advocacy. Journal of Criminal Law and Criminology 95:587–624.

Tenner, Edward. 1996. Why Things Bite Back: Technology and the Revenge of Unintended Consequences. New York: Knopf.

Thompson, William C. 2006. Tarnish on the "Gold Standard": Recent Problems in Forensic DNA Testing. The Champion, January/February, 10–16.

_____. 2008. The Potential for Error in Forensic DNA Testing (and How that Complicates the Use of DNA Databases for Criminal Identification). GeneWatch. http://www.gene-watch.org/genewatch/fullpaper_Bill_Thompson.pdf (accessed February 4, 2009).

Thompson, William C., Simon Ford, Travis Doom, Michael Raymer, and Dan E. Krane. 2003. Evaluating Forensic DNA Evidence: Essential Elements of a Competent Defense Review. Part 1. The Champion, April, 16–25.

Tucker, Cynthia. 2002. Promote Use of DNA Tests for All Suspects. Atlanta Journal-Constitution, February 10, E10.

US Department of Justice. 2004. The FBI DNA Laboratory, A Review of Protocol and Practice Vulnerabilities. Washington, DC: Office of the Inspector General.

Walker, Adrian, and Doris Sue Wong. 1997. No Death Penalty, By One Vote. Boston Globe, November 7.

Warden, Rob. 2005. Wilkie Collins's The Dead Alive: The Novel, the Case, and Wrongful Convictions. Evanston, IL: Northwestern University Press.

_____. 2006. The Rape that Wasn't: The First DNA Exoneration in Illinois. http://www.law. northwestern.edu/wrongfulconvictions/exonerations/ilDotsonSummary.html (accessed February 19, 2009).

Weir, Bruce S. 2007. The Rarity of DNA Profiles. Annals of Applied Statistics 1 (2): 358–70.

Weisberg, Robert. 2005. The Death Penalty Meets Social Science: Deterrence and Jury Behavior Under New Scrutiny. Annual Review of Law and Social Science 1:151–70.

Zimring, Franklin E. 2003. The Contradictions of American Capital Punishment. Oxford: Oxford University Press.

_____. 2005. Symbol and Substance in the Massachusetts Commission Report. Indiana Law Journal 80:115–29.

CASES CITED

Furman v. Georgia, 1 408 U.S. 238 (1972.).

Gregg v. Georgia, 429 U.S. 153 (1976).

Herrera v. Collins, 1506 U.S. 390 (1993).

Kansas v. Marsh, 126 S. Ct. 2516 (2006).

McCleskey v. Kemp, 481 U.S. 279 (1987).

United States v. Quinones [2002a], 205 F. Supp. 2d 256 (S.D. n.Y. 2002).

United States v. Quinones [2002b], 196 F. Supp. 2d 416 (S.D. n.Y. 2002).

STATUTES CITED

Anti-Terrorism and Effective Death Penalty Act of 1996, Public Law No. 104–132, 110 Stat. 1214—(April 24, 1996).

DISCUSSION QUESTIONS

1. Are Gianelli and Aronson and Cole really at odds, based on these two articles? Think about the reasons that they wrote their respective articles, and the purposes they hope to achieve. Might they be more compatible than appears at first?
2. Giannelli makes a number of specific recommendations regarding improvements in the monitoring and regulation of crime laboratories and their analysts. He refers to, or at least hints at, some possible difficulties in attaining such rigorous and systematic regulation (to meet the evidentiary demands of the legal process), but certainly there must be more difficulties and obstacles to a statewide, or national, system of rigorous control of crime laboratories. Develop a list of the difficulties and obstacles that must be accounted for to at least make improvements in the forensic laboratory situation that Giannelli describes, as well as some ways to overcome them, or render them less problematical. Then, make the same argument without spending any extra taxpayer money!
3. Aronson and Cole explain that both the legal system and science pursue "truth." Explain what this means, making specific references to contexts, stakes for the concerned parties, standards of evidence or proof in the different arenas, and the societal benefit from the "truth" that each system produces. Is there "truth" in justice? If so, where does it come from? If not, what does all the legal and scientific work amount to?
4. If science is fallible, as Aronson and Cole convincingly argue (and we must argue that law and justice are fallible too), this means that there will always be mistakes. Under what conditions, then, might we accept the death penalty (or any penalty) based on scientific evidence, or on the legal process?

CAPITAL PUNISHMENT AND RELIGION

Introduction

Christian Fundamentalism and Support for Capital Punishment
By James D. Unnever and Francis T. Cullen

Religious Groups' Official Positions on Capital Punishment
By The Pew Forum on Religion and Public Life

This chapter examines the thorny question of whether fundamentalist Christian beliefs are properly aligned with views on capital punishment, and if so, does being for or against capital punishment reflect core fundamentalist Christian beliefs? Specifically, the question this chapter attempts to address is whether holding core fundamentalist Christian beliefs is an indicator of which side of the death penalty argument one would land, as well as looking at the overarching question: Is there room for capital punishment in core fundamentalist Christianity?

James D. Unnever and Francis T. Cullen[1] in "Christian Fundamentalism and Support for Capital Punishment"[2] tackle these and other questions. The scope of their article covers four fundamental areas of inquiry. First, the article explores whether Christian fundamentalists are more likely to support capital punishment than other more moderate and/or liberal denominations. Next, the article investigates the relationship between being a

1 James D. Unnever, Mississippi State University and Francis T. Cullen, University of Cincinnati.

2 Christian Fundamentalism and Support for Capital Punishment: Journal of Research in Crime and Delinquency, Volume 43, Number 2, May 2006 SAGE Publications....etc

Christian fundamentalist and a number of beliefs (i.e. literal interpretation of the Bible and having a harsh hierarchical image of God with regard to compassion and forgiveness).

The article also considers the relationship between belonging to a Christian fundamentalist denomination, religious beliefs, and the importance that individuals attach to religion when the question of support for, or opposition to, capital punishment is raised.

Finally, the article examines whether there is a measurable relationship between support for the death penalty, religious salience, religious beliefs, and whether the individual belonged to a Christian fundamentalist denomination.

The article reveals that there is a vast range of views within religious denominations on both sides of this issue. Traditionalists would assume, and probably correctly, that core fiundamentalist Christian beliefs endorse the use of capital punishment as a remission of sin underwritten by Old Testament edicts such as "an eye for and eye."[3] However, the authors suggest that "a new image of Christian fundamentalism is emerging that counters the narrow portrayal of fundamentalists as Bible thumping, 'Hell and brimstone' social conservatives who oppose all liberal programs with one voice."[4]

Consider, for example, that the authors arrived at the conclusion, when addressing the issue of whether Christian fundamentalists are more likely to support capital punishment than other more moderate liberal denominations, that some research has shown that Christian fundamentalism does not predict greater support for capital punishment regardless of the variables used to measure Christian fundamentalism.

Further consider that even when Christian fundamentalist support for the death penalty is isolated within the ranks of core Christian fundamentalists, the evidence demonstrated that the prediction of greater support among southerners splintered along racial lines. The results revealed that southern whites were more supportive of capital punishment than southern minorities.

The authors conclude with this striking result: the holding of Christian fundamentalist beliefs as a predictor of greater support for the death penalty generates "mixed" results at best. Perhaps even more striking, the authors posit that the relationship between Christian fundamentalism and support for capital punishment "is of little substantive importance"! (Emphasis added).

We included this article for its candor and quantitative approach to the four fundamental questions presented at the outset. It is instructive to note that the article shakes the preconception that Christian fundamentalists are a monolithic group when it comes to the

---

3 Exodus Chapter 21: verse 24 The Holy Bible, King James Version "an eye for and eye, a hand for a hand, a tooth for a tooth and a foot for a foot." This verse has been extrapolated to justify that punishment for the taking of a life and the subsequent execution of the murderer is "ordained" by the Old Testament.

4 Unnever and Cullen Christian Fundalism and Support of Capital Punishment, Journal of Research in Crime and delinquency, Vol 43, Number 2, May 2006 p. 170, Sage Publications.

question of support of, or opposition to, the death penalty and as such, the inquiry into the continued viability of the sanction should continue to be examined.

It is informative to review the official position of various religious organizations on the issue of capital punishment. The following is a synopsis, from the Pew Forum on Religion and Public Life:

American Baptist Churches in the USA: Since 1982, the American Baptists have opposed capital punishment.

Buddhism: There is no common position among Buddhists on capital punishment, but many emphasize nonviolence and appreciation for life. As a result, in countries with large Buddhist populations, such as Thailand, capital punishment is rare.

Catholicism: although the Catechism of the Catholic Church sanctions the use of the death penalty as a last recourse, the U.S. Conference of Catholic Bishops has repeatedly called for the abolition of capital punishment in the United States in all circumstances.

Church of Jesus Christ of Latter-day Saints: This Church has no official position on the issue and considers the death penalty to be a matter of the state and civil law.

Episcopal Church: since the 1958 General Convention, U.S. Episcopal bishops have maintained a position against the death penalty.

Evangelical Lutheran Church in America: although the Church-wide Assembly added the death penalty to the church's social agenda in 1989, the Evangelical Lutheran Church in America has yet to establish an official stance on the issue.

Hinduism: There is no official position on capital punishment among Hindus, and Hindu theologians fall on both sides of the issue.

Islam: In the U.S., where Islamic law—shariah—is not legally enforced, there is no official Muslim position on the issue of the death penalty. In Islamic countries, however, capital punishment is sanctioned in only two instances: cases involving intentional murder or physical harm; and intentional harm or threat against the state, including the spread of terror.

Judaism: All of the major Jewish movements have called for at least a temporary moratorium on its use. The Conservative, Reform and Reconstructionist movements oppose the penalty in all instances. In 2001, Orthodox Jewish leaders called for a moratorium in light of perceived problems in the nation's criminal justice system, and urged the creation of a commission to review death penalty procedures.

Lutheran Church-Missouri Synod: In 1976, the Lutheran Church-Missouri Synod asserted, "that capital punishment is in accord with the Holy Scriptures and the Lutheran Confessions."

National Association of Evangelicals: Since its 1972 and 1973 resolutions on the issue, they have continued to support the use of capital punishment in cases involving premeditated murder as well as crimes such as hijacking and kidnapping where people are physically harmed.

National Council of Churches: has advocated the abolition of the death penalty since 1968.

Presbyterian Church: since its first official statement on the issue in 1959, the Presbyterian Church has opposed the death penalty.

Southern Baptist Convention: supports the fair and equitable use of the death penalty.

United Methodist Church: In 2000 the united Methodist Church declared its opposition and encouraged its membership to advocate for the abolition of capital punishment.

Christian Fundamentalism and Support for Capital Punishment

James D. Unnever and Francis T. Cullen

Keywords: death penalty; Christian fundamentalism; punitiveness

Few public policy issues have inflamed passions as consistently and as strongly as the debate over capital punishment. Religious denominations have been deeply involved on both sides of the issue, drawing both on teachings and traditions of justice and on those that emphasize the dignity of human life. Scholarly researchers have investigated the role that religious beliefs play in shaping sentiments toward crime control policies, with a particular focus on the relationship between belonging to a Christian fundamentalist denomination and support for the death penalty. Researchers have reasoned that Christian fundamentalists should be more likely to support capital punishment than other more moderate denominations because they hold conservative religious beliefs that justify the use of the death penalty. Using 1998 data from the General Social Survey, the authors initially show that contrary to common views, Christian fundamentalist affiliation is unrelated to support for capital punishment. Subsequent analyses reveal, however, that this null relationship is not straightforward but complex: fundamentalists embrace certain religious beliefs and involvement that both increase and decrease punitiveness. The study thus suggests that understanding the impact of religion on crime control attitudes potentially requires disentangling countervailing effects of different features of religiosity.
(Pew Forum on Religion and Life 2003). Despite this deep involvement, the role that religious beliefs have in defining the level of support for capital punishment has not been clearly identified. Most of the research has investigated whether the relatively high level of support for capital punishment within the United States is related to the religious beliefs expressed by individuals who endorse Christian fundamentalism. Researchers

have reasoned that Christian fundamentalists should be more likely to support the death penalty than members of more moderate denominations because they have a unique set of religious beliefs that justify punitive correctional policies (Grasmick, Bursik, and Blackwell 1993; Grasmick, Cochran, et al. 1993; Grasmick and McGill 1994).

However, a new image of Christian fundamentalism is emerging that counters the narrow portrayal of fundamentalists being Bible thumping, "hell and brimstone," social conservatives who oppose all liberal programs with one voice (Gallagher 2004). For example, a recent issue of U.S. News & World Report had "New" evangelicals on its cover, and the magazine's special report was titled, "Evangelicals defy easy labels. Here's why—and why their numbers are growing The New Old-Time Religion" (Tolson 2003). In addition, a recent edition of the American Prospect featured an article on Christian fundamentalists with the title, "Reaching to the Choir: Think all evangelicals are right-wingers? Don't believe everything you read. Just as many are politically moderate. Can democrats win their votes? God only knows, it's worth a try" (McGarvey 2003). These new portrayals question the academic rendering of Christian fundamentalism as the foundation of support for conservative national policies such as the death penalty. In this context, it is possible that many fundamentalists' views toward capital punishment mirror those held by members of more mainstream denominations that are rooted in a more progressive theological tradition.

In this article, we investigate a number of interrelated questions that taken together, have the potential to unravel the complex relationships between being a Christian fundamentalist, religious beliefs, religious salience, and attitudes toward the death penalty. First, we explore whether Christian fundamentalists are more likely to support capital punishment than other more moderate and liberal denominations while controlling for relevant factors. Second, we investigate the relationship between being a Christian fundamentalist and a number of religious beliefs, including interpreting the Bible literally, having a harsh hierarchal image of God, compassion, and forgiveness. Third, we consider the relationship between belonging to a Christian fundamentalist denomination, religious beliefs, and the importance that individuals attach to religion. Finally, we examine the relationships between support for the death penalty, religious salience, religious beliefs, and whether the individual belonged to a Christian fundamentalist denomination.

ARE CHRISTIAN FUNDAMENTALISTS MORE LIKELY TO SUPPORT CAPITAL PUNISHMENT?

Scholars have suggested that Christian fundamentalists have unique religious beliefs that should cause them to be more supportive of the death penalty than members of more moderate or liberal denominations. Greeley (1995) argues that Christian fundamentalists tend to have religious stories—that is, images of God—that produce a rigid, harsh, and moralistic religious orientation. He attributes this religious orientation to "Reformation skepticism" about God imagery. Greeley (1995:253) further suggests that Christian fundamentalists, particularly Southern Baptists, have not only kept alive the theology of the Reformation, but they have also sustained the moral rigidity, the self-righteous religious style, and the harsh religious imagery that marked some of the Reformers.

The fundamentalist hierarchal image of God is consistent with their belief that the Bible should be interpreted as the literal word of God. A literal interpretation of the Bible assumes that the Bible is unitary and inerrant, and that scripture contains necessary and sufficient information to guide the conduct of all human affairs (Ellison and Musick 1993; Ellison and Sherkat 1993a; Ellison and Sherkat 1993b). Christian fundamentalists also recognize the authority of religious leaders and are willing to accept their interpretation of biblical passages (Ellison and Musick 1993; Grasmick, Cochran, et al. 1993). Ellison and Sherkat (1993a) argue that the willingness of Christian fundamentalists to accept the authority of religious leaders mirrors their acceptance of authority in human institutions.

Christian fundamentalists also believe in the doctrine of original sin and further equate criminal behavior with sinful behavior (Curry 1996). The belief that criminal behavior is sinful behavior allows Christian fundamentalists to endorse the view that crime results from the offender's character and not from unfortunate or unjust conditions (Grasmick and McGill 1994). Therefore, Christian fundamentalists have little doubt as to what should happen to criminals: Biblical passages mandate that sinful behavior should be swiftly and decisively punished (Ellison and Shekrat 1993a; Grasmick and McGill 1994).

In sum, a belief in a hierarchal punitive God who has mandated that sinful behavior should be decisively punished provides Christian fundamentalists with religious justifications for believing that convicted murderers should be put to death. The belief that individuals choose to engage in crime and therefore deserve to be punished further justifies supporting capital punishment. Finally, the Christian fundamentalists' acceptance of authority allows them to believe that state-sanctioned capital punishment is a legitimate use of force.

Researchers have found that members of Christian fundamentalist denominations are more likely to support the death penalty. Most recently, two studies found that belonging to a Christian fundamentalist denomination, as defined by Smith's (1990) classification scheme, positively predicted support for capital punishment. Stack (2003) analyzed data from the General Social Survey (GSS) for the years 1985 and 1990 and discovered that respondents who belonged to a Christian fundamentalist denomination were more likely to support the death penalty, while controlling for other covariates. Young (2000) assessed three years of the GSS—1985, 1990, and 1996—and reported that belonging to a Christian fundamentalist denomination was significantly correlated with support for the death penalty at the bivariate level. Other scholars have found a direct relationship between Christian fundamentalism and support for capital punishment (see, e.g., Grasmick, Bursik, et al. 1993; Grasmick and McGill 1994; Young 1992).

Other scholars, however, have failed to uncover a positive relationship between support for the death penalty and Christian fundamentalism. Sandys and McGarrell (1997) analyzed data from Indiana that included two indicators of Christian fundamentalism—belonging to a Christian fundamentalist denomination and believing that the Bible is the literal word of God—and found that neither predicted greater support for capital punishment. In addition, Soss, Langbein, and Metelko (2003) examined data collected in 1992 by the National Election Study (NES), which included a self-report measure of being a Christian fundamentalist, and found that it was insignificantly related to support for capital punishment, while controlling for other covariates. Also, Baumer, Messner, and Rosenfeld (2003) found a null relationship between belonging to a Christian fundamentalist denomination and support for capital punishment after pooling the GSS for the years 1974 to 1998. It is also instructive that researchers report that the effect of a religious belief associated with Christian fundamentalism, encouraging people to accept Jesus Christ as their savior, varies across race, with African American "evangelicals" significantly more likely to oppose capital punishment (see, e.g., Young 1992; Young and Thompson 1995).

In sum, we draw the following conclusions from the extant research on Christian fundamentalism and public support for the death penalty. Note that our conclusions parallel those suggested by Unnever, Cullen, and Applegate (2005). First, some studies show that Christian fundamentalism does not predict greater support for capital punishment regardless of the variables used to measure Christian fundamentalism (e.g., belonging to a Christian fundamentalist denomination, biblical literalism, self-report being a fundamentalist). Second, the research that has investigated whether the association between Christian fundamentalism and support for the death penalty varies across specific populations has generated inconsistent results. For example, Borg (1997) reports that Christian fundamentalism predicted greater support for the death penalty among Whites who resided in the South. By contrast, Young and Thompson (1995) report that among African Americans, belonging to a Christian fundamentalist denomination predicts opposition to capital punishment. Third, the previous research investigating whether Christian fundamentalist beliefs positively predict greater support for the death penalty has also generated mixed results. For example, some research shows that literalism positively predicts and evangelicalism negatively predicts support for capital punishment. Finally, even when a study shows a direct relationship, the magnitude of the fundamentalism coefficient and its statistical significance are marginal—that is, the relationship between Christian fundamentalism and support for capital punishment is of little substantive importance.

In this article, we further investigate whether Christian fundamentalists are more likely to support capital punishment than members of more moderate and liberal denominations. We also, at the end of the article, discuss possible reasons for why the research on the relationship between support for the death penalty and Christian fundamentalism has generated mixed results.

CHRISTIAN FUNDAMENTALISTS, COMPASSION AND FORGIVENESS, AND SUPPORT FOR CAPITAL PUNISHMENT

Most of the existing research has narrowly focused on elucidating the relationship between being a Christian fundamentalist and support for "get tough" crime-control policies. Thus, researchers have focused on establishing the relationships among being a Christian fundamentalist, conservative religious beliefs such as biblical literalism, having a harsh hierarchal image of God, and support for capital punishment. However, Applegate et al. (2000) and Unnever et al. (2005) have argued that this relatively narrow focus has been at the expense of identifying the more compassionate aspects of religion and whether they predict opposition to the death penalty.

These scholars have identified two religious beliefs that predict opposition to the death penalty, forgiveness and compassion (Applegate et al. 2000; Unnever et al. 2005). Forgiveness is overcoming the "negative affect and judgment toward the offender, not by denying ourselves the right to such affect and judgment, but by endeavoring to view the offender with compassion, benevolence, and love while recognizing that he or she has abandoned the right to harm them" (Enright, Gassin, and Wu 1992:101). Unnever et al. (2005) define compassion as "the empathetic understanding of the suffering of others facilitated by an awareness of one's own suffering."

Applegate et al. (2000) administered a single-state survey that included a scale measuring forgiveness (we should "hate the sin" but "love the sinner," forgiveness is required, and forgiveness is limitless as long as the offender repents) and found that it negatively predicted support for the death penalty while controlling for other covariates, including measures of Christian fundamentalism. Unnever et al. (2005) add to the research by Applegate et al. (2000) by arguing that a secular belief, with strong ties to most religious beliefs, compassion may also negatively predict support for the death penalty. They report, using the 1998 GSS, that both forgiveness and compassion were negatively associated with support for capital punishment. They concluded that religion has divergent effects; it produces beliefs (e.g., having a harsh hierarchal image of God) that shape punitive crime-control policies and it generates beliefs (e.g., compassion) that are supportive of more progressive views toward crime and its control.

Applegate et al. (2000) and Unnever et al. (2005) present rather convincing evidence that models explaining public opinion about the death penalty may be misspecified if they do not include measures of forgiveness and compassion. However, the extant research, to our knowledge, has failed to investigate whether members of Christian fundamentalist denominations are more likely to express these beliefs than members of other religious denominations.

It could be argued that Christian fundamentalists are compelled to express compassionate and forgiving beliefs because these sentiments are found throughout the Bible. It is also possible that forgiveness and compassion, although central to Christianity, are not core beliefs held by Christian fundamentalists. Using the 1998 GSS data, we test whether compassion and forgiveness are positively related to belonging to a Christian fundamentalist denomination. We also examine whether these religious beliefs are related to religious salience and support for the death penalty.

CHRISTIAN FUNDAMENTALISTS, RELIGIOUS SALIENCE, AND SUPPORT FOR CAPITAL PUNISHMENT

Scholars have argued that models examining the relationship between belonging to a Christian fundamentalist denomination and support for the death penalty are misspecified if they do not include measures of religious salience. Applegate et al. (2000) propose that such models would be misspecified because Christian fundamentalists attach a greater importance to religion in guiding their daily lives than do nonfundamentalists and, in turn, the degree to which religion is salient in a person's life should influence their support of capital punishment. Thus, for two reasons, the current research includes a measure of how strongly individuals identify with and practice their religion. First, we include religious salience as a control variable because it could confound the relationship between Christian fundamentalism and support for the death penalty. Second, we explore whether the relationship between religious salience and support for capital punishment could, in part, explain why the research on Christian fundamentalism and support for the death penalty has generated inconsistent conclusions.

The most consistent finding generated by the research on religion and support for the death penalty is that the more individuals identify with and practice their religion, the less likely they are to support "get tough" crime-control policies (Applegate et al. 2000; Grasmick, Bursik, et al. 1993; Grasmick, Cochran, et al. 1993; Young 1992). However, while researchers consistently report that there is a negative relationship between religious salience and support for the death penalty, they have not put forth an account for why this negative relationship exists; nor have they fully explored the relationships among being a Christian fundamentalist having a strong religious practice and support for the death penalty.

In summary, we present a series of sequential models that attempt to clarify the relationships among being a Christian fundamentalist, conservative and compassionate religious beliefs, religious salience, and support for capital punishment. Our first model regresses support for capital punishment on membership in a Christian fundamentalist denomination and the control variables. The second model regresses four divergent religious beliefs, biblical literalism, having a hierarchal image of God, compassion, and forgiveness on whether the individual belonged to a Christian fundamentalist denomination. The third model regresses the strength of the individual's religious practice on the four religious beliefs and membership in a Christian fundamentalist denomination. Our full regression equation regresses support for the death penalty on strength of the individual's religious practice, compassion, forgiveness, biblical literalism, whether the individual belonged to a Christian fundamentalist denomination, and having a harsh hierarchal image of God.

In the end, our analyses generate a complex picture that addresses whether Christian fundamentalists are, indeed, more likely to support the death penalty.

METHOD

Data

The data we analyzed are from the 1998 GSS, which is conducted by the National Opinion Research Center. The GSS is a replicated cross-sectional survey that is based on a representative sample of adults residing within the United States. We purposively selected the 1998 GSS because it is the only year that includes a broad range of variables that measure different aspects of religion and spirituality, which we highlight in this research. For example, the 1998 GSS contains measures regularly included in the GSS such as whether respondents belong to a Christian fundamentalist denomination and whether they interpret the Bible literally. However, it also includes two modules focusing on different aspects of religious beliefs and practices. Accordingly, the 1998 GSS presents the opportunity to assess the relationship between belonging to a Christian fundamentalist denomination, compassion, forgiveness, and public support for the death penalty while controlling for other religious beliefs and practices as well as other correlates of support for capital punishment.

Variables

Support for the death penalty. The GSS contains one measure that assesses support for capital punishment. Respondents were asked whether they favor or oppose the death penalty for persons convicted of murder. The response categories included "favor," "oppose," and "don't know." A binary measure, Death Penalty (1 = favor, 0 = other), was constructed and 73 percent of the respondents reported that they favor the use of the death penalty for persons convicted of murder.[1] The extant research has often used the GSS and its binary measure on public support for the death penalty (see, e.g., Baumeretal. 2003; Borg 1997,1998; Stack 2000, 2003; Young 2000). Notably, Unnever and Cullen (2005) found that variables, which often predict support for a yes–no death penalty question, also predicted respondents' choosing the death penalty over the alternative of life imprisonment without the possibility of parole.

Christian fundamentalists. We used the classification scheme developed by Smith (1990), denoting whether respondents belonged to a Christian fundamentalist denomination to construct, Fundamentalist Church. Those belonging to a Christian fundamentalist denomination were coded 1, and those belonging to moderate or liberal denominations were coded 0.

Conservative religious beliefs. We include two measures to assess whether the respondents held conservative Protestant beliefs usually identified with Christian fundamentalism.

Our first measure is a dummy variable, Literalist, and it identifies persons who endorsed biblical literalism. Briefly, GSS respondents were presented with three possible interpretive positions concerning the Bible, and they were asked to choose the view closest to their own. Individuals who agreed "the Bible is the actual word of God and is to be taken literally, word for word" are coded as literalists (1 = literalist, 0 = other). Our second measure, Harsh God, is whether individuals had a harsh hierarchal image of God. To create this measure, we first reproduced Greeley's (1993, 1995) "grace scale" by summing across the responses to a set of four semantic differential items in the GSS (see Unnever et al. 2005). Respondents were shown a card with sets of contrasting images, and they were asked to place their image of God between the two images on a scale of 1 to 7. The relevant sets of images were as follows: (a) mother versus father, (b) master versus spouse, (c) judge versus lover, and (d) king versus friend. We reverse coded Greeley's grace scale to assess whether the individual had a harsh hierarchal image of God. Thus, individuals who score high on the Harsh God scale tend to have an image of God as being a father, master, judge, and king. The alpha coefficient for our Harsh God scale is .61. A factor analysis of the four semantic differential items generated a single factor.

Forgiveness. Our scale measuring forgiveness was constructed by summing across responses to three items that were included in the 1998 GSS. Respondents were queried as to how often their religious or spiritual beliefs have led them: (a) to forgive themselves for things they have done wrong, (b) to forgive others who hurt them, and (c) to know that God forgives them. For each item, responses range from (1) never to (5) always or almost always. Higher scores on Forgiveness indicate that respondents were more forgiving. The alpha coefficient for Forgiveness was .65. A factor analysis of the three forgiveness items generated a single factor. As mentioned earlier, Applegate et al. (2000) and Unnever et al. (2005) found that people who were more forgiving were less likely to support capital punishment.

Compassion. We used a single-item as our measure of compassion: "I feel a deep sense of responsibility for reducing pain and suffering in the world." Responses were recoded to range from (1) strongly disagree to (4) strongly agree. We recognize that compassion can be both a secular and religious belief. For example, we consider the use of compassion in the phrase "compassionate conservative" as more of a secular than a religious use of the term (Wang 1999). Compassion has been found to negatively predict support for the death penalty (Unnever et al. 2005).

Religious Salience. Our measure of religious salience, Salience, is a scale composed of the following six questions: (a) "To what extent do you consider yourself a religious person?" (b) "To what extent do you consider yourself a spiritual person?" (c) "I try hard to carry my religious beliefs over into all my other dealings in life." (d) "How often do you pray privately in places other than at church or synagogue?" (e) "About how often do you pray?" (f) "Within your religious or spiritual tradition, how often do you meditate?" The responses on the scale ranged from 6 to 34 with higher values indicating greater religious salience. The alpha coefficient for Salience was .86. A factor analysis of the salience items generated a single factor.

Political measures. We investigated three variables related to respondents' attitudes toward salient political issues other than the death penalty. Our first measure, School Prayer, is a binary variable constructed from the following question: "The United States Supreme Court has ruled that no state or local government may require the reading of the Lord's Prayer or Bible verses in public schools. What are your views on this—do you approve or disapprove of the court ruling?" School Prayer was recoded so that 1 = disapproved and 0 = approved. We also included a binary variable, Abortion, based on the following question: "Please tell me whether or not you think it should be possible for a pregnant woman to obtain a legal abortion if the woman wants it for any reason?" Abortion was recoded so that 1 = disapproved and 0 = approved. Our last variable is a scale, Civil Liberties, that measures the degree to which individuals supported the civil liberties of gays and lesbians. The following three questions were used to construct the scale, (a) "And what about a man who admits that he is a homosexual? Suppose this admitted homosexual wanted to make a speech in your community. Should he be allowed to speak, or not?" (b) "Should such a person be allowed to teach in a college or university, or not?" (c) "If some people in your community suggested that a book he wrote in favor of homosexuality should be taken out of your public library, would you favor removing this book, or not?" The responses to these questions were recoded so that higher values indicate that respondents opposed the civil liberties of gays and lesbians. The scale, Civil Liberties, ranged from 0 to 3 and its alpha coefficient was .78. A factor analysis of the three items indicated that one factor should be retained.

Controls

As controls, we included variables that research has identified as significant predictors of support for the death penalty. We include these measures because they could confound the relationship between the two variables of concern here, support for the death penalty and belonging to a Christian fundamentalist denomination.

The previous research indicates that one of the most consistent predictors of support for the death penalty is race, with African Americans significantly less likely to support capital punishment (see, e.g., Bobo and Johnson 2004). We included a measure of race, African American (1 = African American, 0 = other). Research has also reported regional differences with southern White fundamentalists expressing higher levels of support for the death penalty (e.g., Borg 1997). We created a measure, Southerner, that assesses whether respondents resided in the south when they were 16 years old and were living in the south when the interview was conducted (1 = southerner, 0 = all others). Other researchers have used similar measures to predict punitiveness (Borg 1997; Ellison and Sherkat 1993a, 1993b; Stack 2003). We also controlled for gender (Gender, 1 = male, 0 = female) because past studies have reported that males are more likely to support the death penalty (see, e.g., Evans and Adams 2003).

In addition, we controlled for the respondent's level of education, Education (years completed). Research has reported that higher education negatively predicts support for the death penalty (Soss et al. 2003; Stack 2003). Moreover, we control for the respondent's subjective class identification, Social Class (scale ranging from 1 = lower class to 4 = upper class). Scholars suggest that measures of class should negatively predict support for the death penalty because low-income people may perceive that they have a greater probability of encountering the costs of more punitive sentences (Soss et al. 2003). However, researchers mainly report a null or weak relationship between measures of class and support for capital punishment (Applegate et al. 2000; Evans and Adams 2003; Stack 2003; Young and Thompson 1995).

An additional consistent predictor of greater support for the death penalty is political conservatism (see, e.g., Unnever and Cullen 2005). Our measure of the political orientation of the respondents, Political Conservative, was based on the following question: "We hear a lot of talk these days about liberals and conservatives. I'm going to show you a seven-point scale on which the political views that people might hold are arranged from extremely liberal—point 1—to extremely conservative—point 7. Where would you place yourself on this scale?" The responses ranged from 1 to 7, with higher values indicating greater conservatism. Last, we control for Age (measured in years) because it has been shown to be negatively related to punitiveness (Evans and Adams 2003), and we include Foreigner (1 =not born in U.S., 0 = born in U.S.), indicating whether respondents were born outside the United States. Unnever et al. (2005) report that being foreign born, a growing percentage of the U.S. population, negatively predicts support for the death penalty.

Analytical Strategy

We used binary logistic regression if our dependent variables were dichotomous (Death Penalty, Literal, School Prayer, and Abortion), ordinal regression if the dependent variable had four categories (Compassion and Civil Liberties), and ordinary least squares when we analyzed scales (Salience, 29 values, Forgiveness, 10 values, and Harsh God, 24 values). Odds ratios and their confidence limits are reported for the binary logistic regression analyses, parameter estimates and their standard errors are reported for the ordinal-regression analyses, and standardized regression coefficients and their standard errors are reported for the ordinary least squares analyses. Using LISREL 8.50 for Windows and the EM algorithm (Schafer 1997), we substituted values for missing cases. The EM algorithm generated values based on a data set that included the variables used in the present analysis. All analyses were run with and without missing cases; the results did not differ substantively. After imputing values for the missing cases, the sample included 1,445 respondents.

Results

We begin our analysis by presenting a cross-tabulation of the percentage of GSS respondents who supported capital punishment by year and by denomination. Based on the classification system developed by Smith (1990), three denominations are included: fundamentalist, moderate, and liberal. Table 1 shows a clear and consistent pattern; Christian fundamentalists were not more supportive of the death penalty when compared to members affiliated with more moderate and liberal denominations. It is also instructive that the zero-order correlation between support for the death penalty and belonging to a Christian fundamentalist denomination is nonsignificant (-.019, $p = .46$) when examining the 1998 GSS.

The regression equation in Table 2 investigates whether Christian fundamentalists were more likely to support capital punishment than members of other more moderate or liberal denominations while controlling for other factors. The results show that individuals who belonged to a Christian fundamentalist denomination were not more likely to support the death penalty than nonfundamentalists. The results also show that African Americans and individuals born outside the United States were significantly less likely to support capital punishment, whereas males, native southerners, and political conservatives were significantly more likely to support the death penalty.

Table 3 assesses whether Christian fundamentalists hold divergent religious beliefs. Model 1 of Table 3 investigates whether Christian fundamentalists were more likely to interpret the Bible literally and Model 2 examines whether Christian fundamentalists were more likely to have a harsher hierarchal image of God than members of more moderate

Table 1
Analysis of the General Social Survey: Support for Capital Punishment by Religious Affiliation by Year

Year	Fundamentalist	Moderate	Liberal
1974	62.0	72.4	57.6
1975	56.5	70.1	61.6
1976	64.7	72.4	65.2
1977	67.5	75.8	66.8
1978	66.1	73.5	70.0
1980	68.7	74.5	70.3
1982	63.1	77.9	78.0
1983	74.9	77.2	78.8
1984	71.9	76.5	75.8
1985	80.7	78.6	80.2
1986	73.4	76.2	76.6
1987	62.7	72.4	77.2
1988	74.2	78.3	77.8
1989	78.3	77.8	79.1
1990	78.7	81.4	79.1
1991	76.2	78.1	74.4
1993	79.7	75.5	77.2
1994	80.0	79.5	79.8
1996	77.8	75.4	78.3
1998	72.5	74.7	73.4
2000	69.0	71.7	67.5
All cases	71.8	75.6	74.3

Table 2
A Binary Logistic Regression Analysis of the Relationship between Support for Capital Punishment and Fundamentalist Denomination Affiliation (odds ratios and confidence limits in parentheses)

Variable	Result	
Age	1.00	(.99-1.01)
African American	.24***	(.17-.35)
Gender (male = 1)	1.35*	(1.04-1.73)
Born outside United States	.61**	(.41-.90)
Education	.96	(.92-1.01)
Social class	1.04	(.85-1.27)
Political conservative	1.18***	(1.07-1.29)
Native southerner	1.44**	(1.07-1.96)
Fundamentalist	1.02	(.75-1.38)
Model chi-square	107.01***	
Correctly classified	66.6	

* $p < .05$. ** $p < .01$. *** $p < .001$.

denominations. Model 3 of Table 3 considers whether Christian fundamentalists expressed more forgiving attitudes, and Model 4 explores whether Christian fundamentalists held more compassionate beliefs than members of more moderate or liberal denominations.

Model 1 of Table 3 indicates that Christian fundamentalists were substantially more likely to interpret the Bible literally. The predicted odds of a Christian fundamentalist being a biblical literalist were over four times the predicted odds of nonfundamentalists. The results also show that African Americans, individuals born outside the United States, political conservatives, and native southerners were more likely to interpret the Bible literally. Males and the more educated were less likely to be biblical literalists. The results from Model 2 of Table 3 show that Christian fundamentalists were significantly more likely to have a harsher hierarchal image of God than non-fundamentalists. Similar to the results regarding biblical literalists, individuals who had a harsh hierarchal image of God tended to be African American, politically conservative, and native southerners. In addition, age positively predicted having a harsher hierarchal image of God.

The results from Models 1 and 2 of Table 3 indicate that Christian fundamentalists hold more religiously conservative beliefs than nonfundamentalists. The results presented in Models 3 and 4 of Table 3 address whether Christian fundamentalists not only hold conservative religious beliefs but also express beliefs more closely identified with the compassionate and loving aspects of religion. Model 3 presents an ordinary least squares regression analysis of whether forgiving individuals were more likely to belong to Christian fundamentalist denominations, and Model 4 presents an ordinal regression analysis of whether compassionate individuals were more likely to affiliate with a Christian fundamentalist denomination. Forgiveness and compassion were coded so that higher values indicate that respondents expressed more forgiving or more compassionate beliefs.

The results from Model 3 of Table 3 show that Christian fundamentalists were significantly more likely to express forgiving beliefs than nonfundamentalists. The results also indicate that forgiving individuals tended to be older, African American, female, politically conservative, and native southerners. Model 4 of Table 3 shows that Christian

Table 3
Regression Analyses of the Relationship between Fundamentalist Denomination Affiliation and Biblical Literalism, Harsh Hierarchal Image of God, Forgiveness, and Compassion

Variable	Model 1 Biblical Literalism		Model 2 Harsh Image of God		Model 3 Forgiveness		Model 4 Compassion	
Age	1.00	(.99-1.01)	.05*	(.00)	.08***	(.00)	.00***	(–.00-.01)
African American	1.45*	(1.02-2.07)	.05*	(.38)	.07**	(.14)	–.10	(–.40-.18)
Gender (male = 1)	.75*	(.58-.97)	–.00	(.25)	–.12***	(.09)	–.28**	(–.47 - –.08)
Born outside the United States	1.88**	(1.22-2.90)	–.00	(.43)	.01	(.16)	–.02	(–.37-.32)
Education	.83***	(.79-.88)	–.01	(.04)	.02	(.01)	.05***	(.02-.09)
Social class	.92	(.75-1.13)	–.02	(.20)	.05	(.07)	.07	(–.08-.23)
Political conservative	1.20***	(1.09-1.33)	.18***	(.09)	.07**	(.03)	–.01	(–.08-.05)
Native southerner	1.38*	(1.04-1.82)	.07**	(.29)	.07**	(.11)	–.00	(–.22-.22)
Fundamentalist	4.33***	(3.29-5.69)	.13**	(.29)	.14***	(.11)	.35**	(.12-.58)
Model chi-square	303.81***						32.31***	
Correctly classified	77.6							
F value			15.06***		14.01***			
R^2			.08		.08		.02	

Note: Model 1 is a binary logistic regression equation with odds ratios and confidence limits in parentheses. Models 2 and 3 are ordinary least squares regression equations with standardized estimates and standard errors in parentheses. Model 4 is an ordinal regression with estimates and confidence limits in parentheses. The Nagelkerke R^2 is presented for the ordinal regression equation.
* $p < .05$. ** $p < .01$. *** $p < .001$.

Table 4
Ordinary Least Squares Regression Analysis of the Relationship between Religious Salience and Fundamentalist Denomination Affiliation (standardized estimates and standard errors in parentheses)

Variable	Result	
Age	.15***	(.00)
African American	.12***	(.47)
Gender (male = 1)	−.11***	(.31)
Born outside United States	.03	(.53)
Education	.07***	(.05)
Social class	−.01	(.24)
Political conservative	.05**	(.11)
Native southerner	.05**	(.35)
Biblical literalist	.18***	(.37)
Harsh image of God	−.01	(.03)
Forgiveness	.32***	(.08)
Compassion	.22***	(.19)
Fundamentalist	.07**	(.38)
F value	72.64***	
R^2	.39	

* $p < .05$. ** $p < .01$. *** $p < .001$.

fundamentalists were not only more likely to express forgiving beliefs but they also were more likely to hold compassionate beliefs. The results from Model 4 further indicate that compassionate individuals tended to be older, tended to be female, and had higher levels of education.

Table 4 assesses whether Christian fundamentalists had a more rigorous religious practice than members of more moderate denominations. It also investigates the relationships between religious beliefs and religious salience. The results of the ordinary least squares analysis show that Christian fundamentalists were significantly more likely to have stronger religious practices than members of more moderate or liberal denominations. Notably, the results also show that biblical literalism, forgiveness, and compassion significantly predicted religious salience, with forgiveness, compassion, and biblical literalism having the strongest relationship, respectively. Thus, individuals with a more rigorous religious practice were more likely to express forgiving beliefs, be more compassionate, and interpret the Bible literally. In addition, the results show that individuals who had a strong religious practice tended to be older, African American, female, more educated, born outside the United States, politically conservative, and native southerners.

Table 5 presents our full binary logistic regression equation. It assesses whether Christian fundamentalists were more likely to support capital punishment, whether individuals who support the death penalty held divergent religious beliefs, and the relationship between religious salience and support for capital punishment. The results from Table 5 show that Christian fundamentalists were not more likely to support the death penalty than members of more moderate denominations while controlling for the other variables

Table 5
Binary Logistic Regression Analysis of the Relationship between Support for Capital Punishment and Fundamentalist Denomination Affiliation (odds ratios and confidence limits in parentheses)

Variable	Result	
Age	1.00	(.99-1.01)
African American	.25***	(.17-.36)
Gender (male = 1)	1.16	(.89-1.51)
Born outside United States	.63*	(.41-.95)
Education	.98	(.94-1.03)
Social class	1.08	(.88-1.32)
Political conservative	1.16**	(1.05-1.28)
Native southerner	1.55**	(1.13-2.12)
Biblical literalist	1.06	(.77-1.45)
Harsh image of God	1.06***	(1.03-1.09)
Forgiveness	.94	(.86-1.02)
Compassion	.76**	(.64-.91)
Religious salience	.95***	(.93-.98)
Fundamentalist	1.07	(.80-1.53)
Chi-square	181.08***	
Correctly classified	72.3	

* $p < .05$. ** $p < .01$. *** $p < .001$.

in the equation.[2] Table 5 also indicates that two religious beliefs significantly predicted support for capital punishment: having a harsh image of God and compassion. However, the relationships were in opposite directions; individuals who had a harsh hierarchal image of God were more likely and those who were compassionate were less likely to support the death penalty. The results further show that the stronger an individual's religious practice, the less likely they were to support capital punishment.[3] In addition, Table 5 indicates that individuals who opposed the death penalty were more likely to be African American and born outside the United States and that those who supported capital punishment tended to be politically conservative and native southerners.[4]

The following section explores the possibility of whether the association between belonging to Christian fundamentalist denomination and support for capital punishment differs across race and region. We first discuss whether the association between Christian fundamentalism and support for the death penalty varies across race; subsequently, we explore whether the association between Christian fundamentalism and capital punishment varies across regions.

Of the 1,445 respondents, 198 (13.7 percent) were African Americans. African Americans were significantly more likely to belong to a Christian fundamentalist denomination. Of the African Americans, 61.6 percent belonged to a Christian fundamentalist denomination in comparison to 24.8 percent for Whites and others. Research indicates that the positive effect of conservative religious beliefs and support for the death penalty may be restricted to Whites (Grasmick and McGill 1994). Research additionally shows that African Americans are significantly less likely to support capital punishment than are Whites (Barkan and Cohn 1994; Borg 1997; Britt 1998; Grasmick and McGill 1994; Soss et al. 2003; Unnever and Cullen 2004).

We investigated whether the effect of belonging to a Christian fundamentalist denomination on support for the death penalty was significant among Whites but insignificant among African Americans. We divided our sample into two groups, African Americans and others (n = 1, 247) and reproduced the analysis presented in Table 5 for each group. The effect of belonging to a fundamentalist denomination on support for capital punishment was insignificant regardless of which group we analyzed. We also included the interaction term Christian Fundamentalist × African American in the full-regression equation presented in Table 5 and it was insignificant.

We also separately tested whether the influence of belonging to a Christian fundamentalist denomination on support for the death penalty varied across whether the respondent was a native southerner. We included the interaction term Christian Fundamentalist × Native Southerner in the full binary logistic regression equation presented in Table 5 and it was significant (p = .051). We generated a set of cross-tabulations to investigate why the influence of belonging to a Christian fundamentalist denomination on support for capital punishment significantly varied across whether the respondent was a native southerner. These cross-tabulations showed that members of Christian fundamentalist denominations who were not native southerners were less likely to support the death penalty, 66 percent, than nonnative southerners of other denominations, 75 percent (Chi-square = 6.03, p = .01). Another cross-tabulation showed that fundamentalists who were native southerners were not significantly more likely to support capital punishment, 80 percent, than native southerners who were not fundamentalists, 76 percent (Chi-square = 1.12, p = .28). The cross-tabulations also showed that native southern fundamentalists were more likely to support capital punishment, 80 percent, than fundamentalists who resided in other regions, 66 percent. However, fundamentalists who were native southerners were not significantly more likely to support the death penalty, 80 percent, than native southerners of other denominations 76 percent. Thus, these data suggest that it is not belonging to a fundamentalist denomination that escalates support for capital punishment but rather being raised in the South. In fact, fundamentalists who were nonnative southerners were significantly less likely to support the death penalty than nonnative southerners belonging to other denominations.

Finally, we present an analysis that places the Christian fundamentalists' support for capital punishment in a relative context. We investigated the degree to which belonging to a Christian fundamentalist denomination predicted four politically salient issues: capital punishment, abortion, prayer in school, and support for the civil liberties of gays and lesbians. Model 1 of Table 6 shows the binary logistic regression results for capital punishment, Model 2 of Table 6 presents the binary logistic regression results for disapproval of abortion, Model 3 of Table 6 shows the binary logistic regression results for school

Table 6
Regression Analyses of the Relationship between Support for Capital Punishment, Support for Abortion, Support for School Prayer, Support for the Civil Liberties of Gays and Lesbians, and Fundamentalist Denomination Affiliation

Variable	Model 1 Support for Capital Punishment (*n* = 1,445)		Model 2 Support for Abortion (*n* = 790)		Model 3 Support for School Prayer (*n* = 806)		Model 4 Support for the Civil Liberties of Gays and Lesbians (*n* = 780)	
Age	1.00	(.99-1.01)	.99	(.99-1.00)	1.02***	(1.01-1.03)	.02***	(.00)
African American	.24***	(.17-.35)	.72	(.44-1.17)	1.58	(.96-2.59)	.28	(.22)
Gender (male = 1)	1.35*	(1.04-1.73)	1.05	(.77-1.44)	.80	(.59-1.08)	.18	(.15)
Born outside of United States	.61**	(.41-.90)	2.09*	(1.11-3.92)	1.18	(.67-2.09)	.95***	(.28)
Education	.96	(.92-1.01)	.89***	(.83-.94)	.90***	(.85-.95)	−.17***	(.02)
Social class	1.04	(.85-1.27)	.77	(.59-1.00)	.83	(.64-1.07)	.04	(.12)
Political conservative	1.18***	(1.07-1.29)	1.52***	(1.35-1.71)	1.41***	(1.25-1.58)	.20***	(.05)
Native southerner	1.44**	(1.07-1.96)	1.19	(.83-1.72)	1.67**	(1.17-2.39)	.47**	(.17)
Fundamentalist	1.02	(.75-1.38)	2.67***	(1.80-3.97)	1.46*	(1.02-2.10)	.79***	(.17)
Model chi-square	107.01***		126.03***		127.37***		148.50***	
Correctly classified	66.672.2		72.0					
Nagelkerke R^2	.25							

Note: Models 1 through 3 are binary logistic regression equations with odds ratios and confidence limits in parentheses. Model 4 is an ordinal regression equation with estimates and standard errors in parentheses.

* $p < .05$. ** $p < .01$. *** $p < .001$.

prayer, and Model 4 presents the ordinal regression results for the civil liberties of gays and lesbians.

The results from Table 6 reproduce the results presented earlier that indicated a null relationship between support for capital punishment and belonging to a Christian fundamentalist denomination. However, Model 2 of Table 6 shows that members of Christian fundamentalist denominations were significantly more likely than members of other denominations to disapprove of abortions if the woman wants it for any reason. The predicted odds of a member of a Christian fundamentalist denomination disapproving of abortion were nearly two and a half times larger than the predicted odds of non-fundamentalists. Model 3 of Table 6 indicates that members of Christian fundamentalist denominations were significantly more likely than members of other denominations to disagree with the U.S. Supreme Court ruling regarding school prayer. Model 4 of Table 6 shows that members of Christian fundamentalist denominations were significantly more likely to oppose the civil liberties of gays and lesbians. Note that the results show that Christian fundamentalists were opposed to abortion, the civil liberties of gays and lesbians, and school prayer; however, capital punishment was not a salient issue.[5]

Discussion

Religious beliefs are a potentially salient force in shaping political issues and predicting the public's sentiments concerning crime control policies. Perhaps the most contentious crime control policy is capital punishment. The importance of this topic takes on a global significance, because the United States is one of the few countries in the world that carries out the death penalty. Within the United States, the debate that encompasses capital punishment ignites deeply held convictions that individuals tend to morally justify. Quite often, individuals quote biblical scriptures justifying their position on capital punishment (Murphy 2003). Accordingly, an understanding of why the death penalty has such a wide base of support involves illuminating the linkages between religious beliefs and support for capital punishment for convicted murderers.

Scholars have taken on the task of discovering the pathways between religious beliefs and support for capital punishment. This effort has focused on establishing the relationship between conservative religious beliefs and support for the death penalty. Particularly since the 1980s, there is one religious group that has become prominently identified with having conservative religious beliefs: members of Christian fundamentalist denominations. Researchers have reasoned that because members of Christian fundamentalist denominations have more conservative religious beliefs than members of more moderate or liberal denominations, they should be more likely to support capital punishment—just as they are more likely to embrace a number of politically conservative policy positions.

This reasoning has been so widely accepted that researchers universally include measures of Christian fundamentalism in their models of public support for capital punishment (see, e.g., Baumer et al. 2003). Although, this assumption has substantial face validity, the research based on this supposition has not generated a convincing body of supporting evidence; indeed, the extant research is divided. A number of widely cited studies implicate that Christian fundamentalists are more likely to support the death penalty (Borg 1998; Grasmick, Bursik, et al. 1993; Grasmick, Cochran, et al. 1993; Grasmick and McGill 1994), but more recent research has concluded that Christian fundamentalists are not more likely to support capital punishment than members of other denominations (Applegate et al. 2000; Baumer et al. 2003; Soss et al. 2003; Unnever et al. 2005).

In this current project, we found convincing evidence that members of Christian fundamentalist denominations were more religiously conservative than members of other religious denominations. Our results showed that Christian fundamentalists were more likely to interpret the Bible literally and were more likely to have a harsh image of God. However, we found that Christian fundamentalists were not more likely to support capital punishment than members of more moderate or liberal denominations.

It is our position that religious beliefs can justify support and opposition to capital punishment. We found that members of Christian fundamentalist denominations were more likely to have a harsher image of God than members of more moderate denominations, and that individuals who had a harsher image of God were more likely to support capital punishment. However, we also found that Christian fundamentalists were more forgiving and compassionate than members of other, more moderate denominations and that individuals who more strongly believed in compassion were less likely to support the death penalty. Thus, we discovered that members of Christian-fundamentalist denominations had conflicting religious beliefs. These beliefs justified supporting the death penalty but also diminished their level of support.

We also found an additional reason why support for capital punishment was not greater among Christian fundamentalists than members of other denominations. Our results showed that Christian fundamentalists were significantly more likely to rigorously practice their religion than members of other denominations. However, it could be argued that support for the death penalty should be more pronounced among Christian fundamentalists who rigorously practice their religion: more rigorous practice should intensify their conservative religious beliefs, thus increasing their level of support for the death penalty. Our results do not support this argument.

Our analyses indicate that rather than inculcating conservative religious beliefs, an intense religious practice tends to instill religious and secular beliefs that moderate an individual's support for the death penalty. More specifically, we found that forgiveness and compassion were positively associated with religious salience, which, in turn negatively predicted support for capital punishment. Thus, an additional reason why Christian fundamentalists were not more likely to support the death penalty than members of more moderate denominations was because their intense religious practice infused them with beliefs that lessened their overall level of support.[6]

We are not unmindful that public support for capital punishment is high; in most years, more than 70 percent of Americans support the death penalty. It is possible that the relative lack of variation in capital punishment attitudes reduced the social space in which religion might operate to differentiate those who support or do not support capital punishment.[7] Two considerations remain, however. First, Christian fundamentalism often is portrayed as a force that binds its adherents to especially right-wing social positions. Indeed, we found that Christian fundamentalists were more likely to support prayer in school and to oppose abortion and the civil liberties of gays and lesbians. But in regards to the death penalty, we found that their support did not hinge on their religious allegiance. Second, more subtlety, fundamentalism exerts complex influences whose effects should not be easily stereotyped.

Our finding that Christian fundamentalists are a diverse group who should not be easily stereotyped parallels the conclusions drawn from the research on Christian fundamentalism and punitive parenting beliefs. Initially, research reported that Christian fundamentalists were more likely than parents of other denominations to value child obedience and approve of corporal punishment. In addition, researchers argued that these punitive parenting beliefs were a product of the theological and cultural conservatism associated with Christian fundamentalism (Ellison and Sherkat 1993a, 1993b). However, recent analyses question the portrait painted by past researchers. Wilcox (1998) found that although it is true that Christian fundamentalists were more likely to rely on corporal punishment, it would be wrong to characterize their parenting style as punitive or authoritarian. Rather, Wilcox (1998:807) reports that Christian fundamentalists harness theological psychological values "that dictate a warm, expressive style of parenting for most parent–child interaction." The findings by Bartkowski and Wilcox (2000) further challenge the image of Christian fundamentalist parents as being punitive. They found that Christian fundamentalists were significantly less likely to report yelling at their preschoolers and school-age children than their nonconservative counterparts. These findings, tangentially related to our own, show a complexity among Christian fundamentalists that is inaccurately portrayed by characterizations that they are a monolithic group with a punitive orientation.

We end by making some methodological observations. Grasmick and his colleagues have presented the strongest case for arguing that Christian fundamentalists are more likely to support the death penalty than members of other more theologically liberal traditions (Grasmick, Bursik, et al. 1993; Grasmick, Cochran, et al. 1993; Grasmick and McGill 1994). Clearly, our analysis questions such a conclusion. The differences in our samples could be a possible reason why our results differ from those generated by Grasmick and his colleagues. We used the 1998 GSS, which is a national probability sample, whereas Grasmick's single-city survey collected data from residents of Oklahoma City. Grasmick found that Christian fundamentalists in Oklahoma City were more supportive of capital punishment than Oklahoma City residents of other denominations.

Unnever et al. (2005) argue that there may be contextual effects that affect the likelihood of finding a relationship between Christian fundamentalism and public opinion about the death penalty. Soss et al. (2003) demonstrate an example of a contextual effect when they show that White opinion about capital punishment depends on African American residential proximity. They report that as the African American percentage of county residents increases, so also does the impact of racial animus on White support for the death penalty (Soss et al. 2003). Therefore, Unnever et al. (2005) suggest that the discrepancies found in the literature examining the association between Christian fundamentalism and support for the death penalty could arise, in part, from whether the study analyzed a nationally representative sample or was conducted in areas with high concentrations of Christian fundamentalists, such as in Oklahoma City.

Regnerus (2003) and Baier and Wright (2001) argue that individuals' behavior may be influenced if they are living in areas that are relatively homogenous in religious beliefs. Thus, Unnever et al. (2005) suggest that it is possible that fundamentalists residing in Oklahoma City may have constructed "moral communities" that have resulted in individual fundamentalists more stridently supporting the death penalty than if they were living in areas that were more religiously diverse. They further suggest that this could explain why the studies conducted by Grasmick (Grasmick, Bursik, et al. 1993; Grasmick, Cochran, et al. 1993; Grasmick and McGill 1994) found significant relationships between fundamentalism and support for the death penalty in Oklahoma City, whereas others using national probability samples have failed to find a relationship.

We also note that studies using national probability samples have generated inconsistent findings. For example, studies using the GSS—such as Stack (2003)—report that belonging to a Christian fundamentalist denomination positively predicts greater support for the death penalty, whereas the current project and others report a null relationship (e.g., Baumer et al. 2003; Soss et al. 2003). It is our position that these discrepancies result from the inherent weakness of the relationship between Christian fundamentalism and support for the death penalty (e.g., review Table 1). Moreover, it is instructive that even when such studies show a direct relationship, the magnitude of the fundamentalism coefficient and its statistical significance are marginal. In short, it is reasonable to conclude that because of conflicted religious beliefs, Christian fundamentalism is neither a robust nor consistent predictor of greater support for the death penalty; it explains an insignificant amount of the variance in public opinion about capital punishment.

In sum, our results clearly indicate that Christian fundamentalists were not more likely to support the death penalty for convicted murderers than members of more moderate and liberal denominations. We offer two reasons for this finding. First, their religious beliefs generated a conflicted level of ambiguity, in effect weakening their overall level of support for the death penalty. As noted above, Christian fundamentalists hold beliefs that positively predict support for capital punishment (e.g., a harsh image of God) but also express beliefs that negatively predict support for the death penalty (e.g., compassion). Second, our data show that Christian fundamentalists were more likely than nonfundamentalists to have a rigorous religious practice. Our results further indicate having a rigorous religious practice was positively related to being more compassionate and forgiving. Thus, the more Christian fundamentalists rigorously practiced their religion, the more they were infused with compassionate and forgiving beliefs, which in turn further moderated their overall level of support for the death penalty.

Our analysis supports recent media accounts that question the portrayal of Christian fundamentalists as staunch conservatives who oppose liberal issues with one voice. Our analysis suggests that Christian fundamentalists have varied secular opinions that are infused with diverse theological beliefs (Gallagher 2004). These theological beliefs may allow Christian fundamentalists to fervently support conservative social policies such as abortion but at the same time have mainstream attitudes toward the death penalty. They also may allow Christian fundamentalists to passionately oppose gay rights but be infused with compassion and forgiveness for those who have "failed." Notably, Feldman and Steenbergen (2001) argue that humanitarian prosocial beliefs are and always have been part of the American landscape. Indeed, they contend that the marriage between capitalism and humanitarianism is perhaps as old as this country. Thus, it is reasonable to suppose that Christian fundamentalists can be socially conservative on some issues such as abortion but at the same time support humanistic-oriented social programs.

Recent developments within the Christian fundamentalist movement support our last conclusion. In 2004, the National Association of Evangelicals unanimously adopted an historic document on public engagement that calls "evangelicals to a biblically balanced concern that reflects the full range of God's concerns for the well-being of marriage, the family, the sanctity of human life, justice for the poor, care for creation, peace, freedom and racial justice" (National Association of Evangelicals 2004). It is instructive that this document, while endorsing pro-life and family issues, omits the issue of the death penalty. Thus, we suggest that politicians may find it easier to mobilize Christian fundamentalists to oppose abortion and gay marriages than to galvanize their support for capital punishment.

Finally, our results do not rule out the possibility that there may be factions within Christian fundamentalism that might be more or less supportive of the death penalty. Although we found no evidence that White and African American Christian fundamentalists significantly differed in their support for capital punishment, research indicates that the interplay between religion and politics may vary across race (Calhoun-Brown 1998). A recent poll by the Pew organization documents that although African American and White evangelical Christians are remarkably similar in their views about the role of religion in politics (e.g., both oppose abortion and gay marriages), they come to sharply different partisan conclusions (e.g., African American evangelical Christians leaned strongly against President Bush and Republicans, whereas White evangelicals leaned strongly toward President Bush and the Republican party; Pew Forum on Religion and Life 2003b). Thus, future research may want to further explore whether African American Christian fundamentalists are less supportive of the death penalty than White Christian fundamentalists. In addition, future research may wish to explore whether native southerners who are Christian fundamentalists are more likely to support the death penalty than other Christian fundamentalists. Moreover, researchers may want to investigate whether evangelists are less supportive of capital punishment than other Christian fundamentalists (Calhoun-Brown 1998). However, we argue that if researchers factionalize "Christian fundamentalism" into assemblies that have divergent attitudes, they are implicitly acknowledging that it is an ineffectual concept for understanding why the United States is one of the few countries in the world that carries out the death penalty.

NOTES

1. A total of 8 percent of the respondents, when asked, "Do you favor or oppose the death penalty for persons convicted of murder?" reported that they "don't know."
2. It could be argued that our inability to find a significant relationship between fundamentalism and support for the death penalty resulted from our use of Smith's (1990) classification of denominations. It also could be argued that if we had used a more rigorous measure of fundamentalism, we would have found that they were more likely to support the death penalty. It could be further argued that a more rigorous measure of fundamentalism should include whether the respondent belonged to a fundamentalist denomination and whether they were biblical literalists. We tested for this possibility by constructing an interaction term Fundamentalist × Literal and included it in the full binary logistic regression equation presented in Table 5. Its effect on support for the death penalty was insignificant.
3. We investigated whether the influence of belonging to a Christian fundamentalist denomination on support for capital punishment varied across levels of religious salience. We included the interaction term Christian Fundamentalist × Salience in the full binary logistic regression equation presented in Table 5 and it was insignificant.
4. We also substituted family income (summary scale ranging from 1 to 23, where the minimum category denotes an income of "under $ 1K" and the maximum category denotes "$ 11 0K or over") in the binary logistic regression equation presented in Table 5 for the self-reported variable, Social Class. The results with family income in the equation were substantively identical to those reported in Table 5.
5. These results must be seen as suggestive. Although we take into account major demographic variables, it is possible that controls for other factors might diminish the impact of fundamentalism on these three other dependent variables. It is beyond the scope of the current study, however, to review diverse sets of literature and to expand the analysis and to incorporate a range of alternative independent variables. Even so, the results provide a tentative basis for proposing that the impact of fundamentalism on views

toward capital punishment likely differs from its impact on sentiments toward other social or moral policy issues.

6. It could be argued that compassionate and forgiving individuals are more likely to rigorously practice their religion rather than a rigorous religious practice infuses individuals with more forgiving and compassionate beliefs. We cannot disentangle the causal ordering between a rigorous religious practice and forgiving and compassionate beliefs. The data we analyzed, the General Social Survey (GSS), are cross-sectional. Future researchers may wish to address this causal ordering question using longitudinal data.
7. It is instructive that previous studies have shown that even though the mean level of support for the death penalty is high (76 percent), belonging to a Christian fundamentalist denomination positively predicted support for the death penalty (Young 1992). Indeed, it is reasonable to argue that the overall mean level of support for the death penalty (grouping Christian fundamentalists with nonfundamentalists) is skewed to the right because the mean level of support among Christian fundamentalists is significantly higher. Thus, it is unlikely that our finding of a null relationship between belonging to a Christian fundamentalist denomination and support for capital punishment can be attributed to the mean level of support being high—73 percent of the respondents in our sample supported the death penalty. We cross-tabulated our data and found that 73 percent of Christian fundamentalists in comparison to 75 percent of nonfundamentalists supported the death penalty.

References

Applegate, Brandon, Francis T. Cullen, Bonnie Fisher, and Thomas Vander Ven. 2000. "Forgiveness and Fundamentalism: Reconsidering the Relationship between Correctional Attitudes and Religion." Criminology 38:719–54.

Baier, Colin J. and Bradley R. E. Wright. 2001. "If You Love Me, Keep My Commandments: A Meta-analysis of the Effect of Religion on Crime." Journal of Research on Crime and Delinquency 38:3–21.

Barkan, Steven A. and Steven F. Cohn. 1994. "Racial Prejudice and Support for the Death Penalty by Whites." Journal of Research in Crime and Delinquency 31:202–9.

Bartkowski, John P. and W. Bradford Wilcox. 2000. "Conservative Protestant Child Discipline: The Case of Parental Yelling." Social Forces 79:265–90.

Baumer, Eric P., Steven F. Messner, and Richard Rosenfeld. 2003. "Explaining Spatial Variation in Support for Capital Punishment: A Multilevel Analysis." American Journal of Sociology 108:844–75.

Bobo, Lawrence and Devon Johnson. 2004. "A Taste for Punishment Black and White Americans' Views on the Death Penalty and the War on Drugs." Du Bois Review 1:151–80.

Borg, Marian J. 1997. "The Southern Subculture of Punitiveness? Regional Variation in Support for Capital Punishment." Journal of Research in Crime and Delinquency 34:25–46.

____. 1998 "Vicarious Homicide Victimization and Support for Capital Punishment: A Test of Black's Theory of Law." Criminology 36:537–67.

Britt, Chester. L. 1998. "Race, Religion, and Support for the Death Penalty: A Research Note." Justice Quarterly 15:175–91.

Calhoun-Brown, Allison. 1998. "The Politics of Black Evangelicals: What Hinders Diversity in the Christian Right?" American Politics Quarterly 26:81–110.

Curry, Theodore R. 1996. "Conservative Protestantism and the Perceived Wrongfulness of Crimes: A Research Note." Criminology 34:453–64.

Ellison, Christopher G. and Marc A. Musick. 1993. "Southern Intolerance: A Fundamentalist Effect?" Social Forces 72:379–99.

Ellison, Christopher G. and Darren E. Sherkrat. 1993a. "Conservative Protestantism and Support for Corporal Punishment." American Sociological Review 58:131–44.

____. 1993b. "Obedience and Autonomy: Religion and Parental Values Reconsidered." Journal for the Scientific Study of Religion 32:313–29.

Enright, Robert D., Elizabeth A. Gassin, and Ching-Ru Wu. 1992. "Forgiveness: A Developmental View." Journal of Moral Education 21:99–114.

Evans, David T. and Mike Adams. 2003. "Salvation or Damnation? Religion and Correctional Ideology." American Journal of Criminal Justice 28:15–35.

Feldman, Stanley and Marco R. Steenbergen. 2001. "The Humanitarian Foundation of Public Support for Social Welfare." American Journal of Political Science 45:658–77.

Gallagher, Sally K. 2004. "Where Are the Antifeminist Evangelicals? Evangelical Identity, Subcultural Location, and Attitudes Toward Feminism." Gender and Society 18:12–28.

Grasmick, Harold G., Robert J. Bursik, Jr., and Brenda S. Blackwell. 1993. "Religious Beliefs and Public Support for the Death Penalty for Juveniles and Adults." Journal of Crime and Justice 16:59–86.

Grasmick, Harold G., John K. Cochran, Robert J. Bursik Jr., and M'Lou Kimpel. 1993. "Religion, Punitive Justice, and Support for the Death Penalty." Justice Quarterly 10:289–313.

Grasmick, Harold G. and Anne L. McGill. 1994. "Religion, Attributional Style, and Punitiveness toward Juvenile Offenders." Criminology 32:23–46.

Greeley, Andrew M. 1993. "Religion and Attitudes toward the Environment." Journal for the Scientific Study of Religion 32:19–28.

____. 1995. Religion as Poetry. New Brunswick, NJ: Transaction.

McGarvey, Ayelish. 2003. "Preaching to the Choir." American Prospect 15:41–4.

Murphy, Jeffrie G. 2003. "Christianity and Criminal Punishment." Punishment & Society 5:261–77.

National Association of Evangelicals. 2004. "Evangelical Leaders Adopt Landmark Document Urging Greater Civic Engagement." Retrieved December 6, 2004 from http://www.nae. net/index.cfm?FUSEACTION=editor.page&pageID=127&idCategory=5

Pew Forum on Religion and Life. 2003a. "Death Penalty." Retrieved August 20, 2003 from http://pewforum.org/issues/display.php?IssueID=2

_____. 2003b. Religion and Politics: Contention and Consensus. Washington, DC: The Pew Research Center.

Regnerus, Mark D. 2003. "Moral Communities and Adolescent Delinquency: Religious Contexts and Community Social Control." Sociological Quarterly 44:523–44.

Sandys, Marla and Edmund F. McGarrell. 1997. "Beyond the Bible Belt: The Influence (or Lack Thereof) of Religion on Attitudes toward the Death Penalty." Journal of Crime and Justice 20:179–90.

Schafer, Joseph L. 1997. Analysis of Incomplete Multivariate Data. Monographs on Statistics and Applied Probability, 72. London: Chapman and Hall.

Smith, Tom W. 1990. "Classifying Protestant Denominations." Review of Religious Research 31:225–45.

Soss, Joe, Laura Langbein, and Alan R. Metelko. 2003. "Why Do White Americans Support the Death Penalty?" Journal of Politics 65:397–421.

Stack, Steven. 2000. "Support for the Death Penalty: A Gender-Specific Model." Sex Roles: A Journal of Research 43:163–79.

_____. 2003. "Authoritarianism and Support for the Death Penalty: A Multivariate Analysis." Sociological Focus 36:333–52.

Tolson, Jay. 2003. "The New Old Time Religion." U.S. News & World Report 135:36–44.

Unnever, James D. and Francis. T. Cullen. 2004, November 18. "Reassessing the Racial Divide in Support for Capital Punishment: The Continuing Significance of Race." Paper presented at the annual meeting of the American Society of Criminology, Nashville, TN.

_____. 2005. "Executing the Innocent and Support for Capital Punishment: Implications for Public Policy." Criminology and Public Policy 4:3–37.

Unnever, James D., Francis T. Cullen, and Brandon Applegate. 2005. "Turning the Other Cheek: Reassessing the Impact of Religion on Punitive Ideology." Justice Quarterly 22:304–339.

Wang, Alice. 1999. "Bridging the Gap. (Republican Party Launches the 'Compassionate Conservative' Movement)." The Washington Quarterly 22:215.

Wilcox, Bradford W. 1998. "Conservative Protestant Childrearing: Authoritarian or Authoritative?" American Sociological Review 63:796–809.

Young, Robert L. 1992. "Religious Orientation, Race and Support for the Death Penalty." Journal for the Scientific Study of Religion 31:76–87.

_____. 2000. "Symposium: Religion's Role in the Administration of the Death Penalty: Punishment at All Costs: On Religion, Convicting the Innocent, and Supporting the Death Penalty." William & Mary Bill of Rights Journal 9:237–45.

Young, Robert L. and Carol Y. Thompson. 1995. "Religious Fundamentalism, Punitiveness, and Firearm Ownership." Journal of Crime and Justice 18:81–98.

James D. Unnever is a professor of sociology at Mississippi State University. His most recent research focuses on whether egalitarianism and racial resentment predict support for crime reduction policies, the racial divide in support for capital punishment, and the relationship between victimization and political beliefs.

Francis T. Cullen is Distinguished Research Professor of Criminal Justice and Sociology at the University of Cincinnati. His most recent works include Combating Corporate Crime: Local Prosecutors at Work, Criminological Theory: Context and Consequences, and Criminological Theory: Past to Present—Essential Readings.

Authors' Note: We thank Tom Smith and Christopher G. Ellison for their insights on an earlier draft of this article. Address correspondence to James D. Unnever, Department of Sociology, Mississippi State University, Mississippi State, MS, 39762; e-mail: junnever@msstate.edu.

Religious Groups' Official Positions on Capital Punishment

The Pew Forum on Religion and Public Life

American Baptist Churches in the U.S.A.

Since 1982, the American Baptist Churches in the U.S.A. has opposed capital punishment in the United States.

- http://www.abc-usa.org/resources/resol/cappun.htm, American Baptist Churches in the U.S.A., Resolution on Capital Punishment

Buddhism

There is no common position among Buddhists on capital punishment, but many emphasize nonviolence and appreciation for life. As a result, in countries with large Buddhist populations, such as Thailand, capital punishment is rare.

- http://www.bbc.co.uk/religion/religions/buddhism/buddhistethics/capitalpunishment.shtml, Religion & Ethics—Buddhism and Capital Punishment
- http://www.buddhanet.net/e-learning/dharmadata/fdd20.htm, Buddha Dharma Education Association & BuddhaNet, Dharma Data: Capital Punishment

Catholicism

Although the Catechism of the Catholic Church sanctions the use of the death penalty as a last recourse, the U.S. Conference of Catholic Bishops has repeatedly called for the abolition of capital punishment in the United States in all circumstances.

- http://www.vatican.va/archive/catechism/p3s2c2a5.htm, The Vatican, Catechism of the Catholic Church

- http://www.usccb.org/sdwp/national/deathpenalty/deathpenaltybrochure.pdf, United States Conference of Catholic Bishops, Catholic Campaign to End the Use of the Death Penalty
- http://www.americancatholic.org/News/DeathPenalty, American Catholic, The Death Penalty and the Catholic Church

Church of Jesus Christ of Latter-day Saints

The Church of Jesus Christ of Latter-day Saints has no official position on the issue and considers the death penalty to be a matter of the state and civil law.

- http://www.lds.org/ldsnewsroom/v/index.jsp?vgnextoid=a620b63c092c1110VgnVCM100000176f620aRCRD&vgnextchannel=726511154963d010VgnVCM1000004e94610aRCRD&vgnextfmt=tab1, The Church of Jesus Christ of Latter-day Saints, Newsroom, Public Issues: Capital Punishment

Episcopal Church

Since the 1958 General Convention, U.S. Episcopal bishops have maintained a position against the death penalty.

- http://www.episcopalarchives.org/cgi-bin/acts/acts_resolution.pl?resolution=1991–D056, Religious Organizing Against the Death Penalty, Statement of the 1979 General Conference
- http://www.episcopalarchives.org/cgi-bin/acts/acts_resolution.pl?resolution=1991–D056, The Archives of the Episcopal Church, The Acts of the Convention 1976–2006, Reaffirm Opposition to Capital Punishment

Evangelical Lutheran Church in America

Although the Churchwide Assembly added the death penalty to the church's social agenda in 1989, the Evangelical Lutheran Church in America has yet to establish an official stance on the issue.

- http://www.elca.org/socialstatements/deathpenalty/, Evangelical Lutheran Church in America, Social Statement on the Death Penalty

Hinduism

There is no official position on capital punishment among Hindus, and Hindu theologians fall on both sides of the issue.

- http://www.hinduismtoday.com/archives/2006/10-12/58-63_punishment.shtml, HinduismToday.com, October/November/December 2006, Capital Punishment: Time to Abandon It?

Islam

In the United States, where Islamic law—Shariah—is not legally enforced, there is no official Muslim position on the issue of the death penalty. In Islamic countries, however, capital punishment is sanctioned in only two instances: cases involving intentional murder or physical harm of another; and intentional harm or threat against the state, including the spread of terror.

- http://www.understanding-islam.com/related/text.asp?type=question&qid=392, Understanding Islam: An Affiliate of Al-Mawrid Institute of Islamic Sciences, Regarding the Death Penalty
- http://www.bbc.co.uk/religion/religions/islam/islamethics/capitalpunishment.shtml, Religion & Ethics—Islam and Capital Punishment
- http://www.islamicsupremecouncil.org, Islamic Supreme Council of America, Mateen Siddiqui, Vice President

Judaism

All of the major Jewish movements in the United States either advocate for the abolition of the death penalty or have called for at least a temporary moratorium on its use. The Conservative, Reform and Reconstructionist movements in the United States oppose the death penalty in all instances. In 2001, Orthodox Jewish leaders called for a moratorium in light of perceived problems in the nation's criminal justice system, and urged the creation of a commission to review death penalty procedures.

- http://rac.org/Articles/index.cfm?id=1665&pge_prg_id=8089&pge_id=2396, Religious Action Center of Reform Judaism, The Death Penalty and Jewish Value
- http://www.ouradio.org/images/uploads/Summary.pdf, Union of Orthodox Jewish Congregations, A Summary of Standing Policy Positions of the Orthodox Union
- http://www.pjalliance.org/UserFiles/movement%20bulletin.doc, Conservative Judaism, Rabbinical Assembly, 1960: Proceedings of the Committee on Jewish Law and Standards 1927–1970 Volume III, p. 1537–1538. Rabbi Ben Zion Bokser (provided by the Progressive Jewish Alliance)
- http://www.pjalliance.org/UserFiles/movement%20bulletin.doc, Reconstructionist Judaism, April 2003, Reconstructionist Rabbinical Association (provided by the Progressive Jewish Alliance)

Lutheran Church-Missouri Synod

In 1976, the Lutheran Church-Missouri Synod asserted "that capital punishment is in accord with the Holy Scriptures and the Lutheran Confessions."

- http://www.lcms.org/pages/internal.asp?NavID=2112, The Lutheran Church-Missouri Synod, The Death Penalty

National Association of Evangelicals

Since its 1972 and 1973 resolutions on the issue, the National Association of Evangelicals has continued to support the use of capital punishment in cases involving premeditated murder as well as crimes such as hijacking and kidnapping where people are physically harmed.

- http://www.nae.net/index.cfm?FUSEACTION=editor.page&pageID=172&IDCategory=9,NationalAssociationofEvangelicals,CapitalPunishment1973

National Council of Churches

The National Council of Churches, which represents 35 mainstream Protestant and Orthodox churches, has advocated for the abolition of the death penalty since 1968.

- http://www.ncccusa.org/news/00news74.html, National Council of Churches, NCC Supports Moratorium on Death Penalty: A Statement by the Rev. Dr. Robert W. Edgar, General Secretary

Presbyterian Church (U.S.A.)

Since its first official statement on the issue in 1959, reaffirmed again in 1977 and 1978, the Presbyterian Church (U.S.A.) has opposed the death penalty.

- http://www.pcusa.org/101/101-capital.htm, Presbyterian Church (U.S.A.), Presbyterian 101: Capital Punishment
- http://www.deathpenaltyreligious.org/education/statements/presbyterian.html, Religious Organizing Against the Death Penalty, Presbyterian Church (USA): Continuing Opposition to Capital Punishment

Southern Baptist Convention

In 2000, the Southern Baptist Convention issued a resolution in support of the fair and equitable use of capital punishment.

- http://www.sbc.net/resolutions/amResolution.asp?ID=299, Southern Baptist Convention, Resolutions, On Capital Punishment

Unitarian Universalist Association of Congregations

The Unitarian Universalist Association of Congregations has called for a moratorium on executions since 1961.

- http://www.25.uua.org/uuawo/new/article.php?id=47, Unitarian Universalist Association of Congregations, Washington Office for Advocacy, Summary of Resolutions on Capital Punishment

United Methodist Church

In 2000, the United Methodist Church declared its opposition to the death penalty and encouraged its membership to advocate for the abolition of capital punishment.

- http://archives.umc.org/interior.asp?ptid=4&mid=1071, United Methodist Church, Book of Resolutions, In Opposition to Capital Punishment

The Pew Forum on Religion & Public Life

1615 L Street, NW Suite 700 Washington, DC 20036–5610 T: 202.419.4550 F: 202.419.4559

The Pew Forum on Religion & Public Life is a project of the Pew Research Center, a subsidiary of The Pew Charitable Trusts.

DISCUSSION QUESTIONS

1. Do fundamentalist Christian beliefs allow the possibility of individual choice on the issue of support for capital punishment while still adhering to core Christian fundamentalist values?
2. If a literal interpretation of such Biblical principles as "an eye for and eye" is employed, does core fundamentalist Christian views provide any room for compassion? Forgiveness? Rehabilitation?
3. Given the statements contained in both the Old and New Testaments of the Bible, can support for either position be accurately relied upon when using the Bible as a source of justification?
4. Given the ambiguity of Biblical support for the death penalty, should a thoughtful introspective religious person support the death penalty in good conscience?

Acknowledgments

Stephen B. Bright, "Will the Death Penalty Remain Alive in the Twenty-First Century?: International Norms, Discrimination, Arbitrariness, and the Risk of Executing the Innocent," from *Wisconsin Law Review*, Vol. 2001, No. 1. Copyright © 2001 by The Board of Regents of the University of Wisconsin System. Permission to reprint granted by the Wisconsin Law Review.

Rita K. Lomio, "Working Against the Past: The Function of American History of Race Relations and Capital Punishment in Supreme Court Opinions," from the *Journal of Law in Society*, Vol. 9, No. 1. Copyright © 2008 by Wayne State University Law School. Permission to reprint granted by the rightsholder.

Glenn L. Pierce and Michael L. Radelet, "Race, Region, and Death Sentencing in Illinois, 1988–1997." Copyright © 2002 by Glen L. Pierce and Michael L. Radelet. Permission to reprint granted by the rightsholders.

Scott Phillips, "Racial Disparities in the Capital of Capital Punishment," from the Houston *Law Review*, Vol. 45, No. 3. Copyright © 2008 by Houston Law Review. Permission to reprint granted by the publisher.

Isaac Ehrlich, "Capital Punishment and Deterrence: Some Further Thoughts and Additional Evidence," from the *Journal of Political Economy*, Vol. 45, No. 4. Copyright © 1977 by the University of Chicago Press. Permission to reprint granted by the publisher.

Jeffrey Fagan, "Death and Deterrence Redux: Science, Law and Causal Reasoning on Capital Punishment," from the *Ohio State Journal of Criminal Law*, Vol. 4, pp. 254–320. Copyright © 2006 by the Ohio State University College of Law. Permission to reprint granted by the rightsholder.

James W. Douglas and Helen King Stockstill, "Starving the Death Penalty: Do Financial Constraints Limit Its Use?" from *The Justice System Journal*, Vol. 29, No. 3, pp. 326–337. Copyright © 2008 by the National Center for State Courts. Permission to reprint granted by the rightsholder.

Philip J. Cook, "Potential Savings from Abolition of the Death Penalty in North Carolina," from *American Law and Economics Review*, Vol. 11, No. 2. Copyright © 2009 by Oxford University Press. Permission to reprint granted by the publisher.

The Justice Project, "Eyewitness Identification: A Policy Review." Copyright © The Justice Project. Permission to reprint granted by the rightsholder.

The Wisconsin Department of Justice, Office of the Attorney General, "Model Policy and Procedure for Eyewitness Identification." Copyright © The Wisconsin Department of Justice, Office of the Attorney General. Permission to reprint granted by the rightsholder.

Paul C. Giannelli, "Wrongful Convictions and Forensic Science: The Need to Regulate Crime Labs," from *Case Research Paper Series in Legal Studies*, pp. 163–236. Copyright © 2007 by the Case Western Reserve University School of Law. Permission to reprint granted by the rightsholder.

Jay D. Aronson and Simon A. Cole, "Science and the Death Penalty: DNA, Innocence, and the Debate over Capital Punishment in the United States," from *Law and Social Inquiry*, Vol. 34, Issue 3, pp. 603–633. Copyright © 2009 by John Wiley & Sons. Permission to reprint granted by the rightsholder.

James D. Unnever and Francis T. Cullen, "Christian Fundamentalism and Support for Capital Punishment," from the *Journal of Research in Crime and Delinquency*, Vol. 43, No. 2, pp. 169–197. Copyright © 2006 by Sage Publications. Permission to reprint granted by the rightsholder.

Religious Groups' Official Positions on Capital Punishment," from The Pew Forum on Religion & Public Life, pp. 1–3. Copyright © 2009 by Pew Research Center. http://pewforum.org/. Permission to reprint granted by the publisher.